Entrepreneurial Strategy
Text and Cases

ENTREPRENEURIAL STRATEGY
TEXT AND CASES

Donald F. Kuratko
Ball State University

Harold P. Welsch
DePaul University

THE DRYDEN PRESS
Harcourt Brace College Publishers
Fort Worth   Philadelphia   San Diego   New York   Orlando   Austin   San Antonio
Toronto   Montreal   London   Sydney   Tokyo

Publisher:	Elizabeth Widdicombe
Acquisitions Editor:	Ruth Rominger
Project Management:	Elm Street Publishing Services, Inc.
Compositor:	Monotype Composition Company, Inc.
Text Type:	10.5/12 Garamond
Cover Images:	Background Photo: Greg Pease/© Tony Stone Worldwide; Inset Photo: Marc Vaughn/Sharp Shooters

Address for Editorial Correspondence
The Dryden Press, 301 Commerce Street, Suite 3700,
Fort Worth, TX 76102

Address for Orders
The Dryden Press, 6277 Sea Harbor Drive, Orlando, FL 32887
1-800-782-4479, or 1-800-433-0001 (in Florida)

ISBN: 0-03-097579-4

Library of Congress Catalogue Number: 93-37082

Printed in the United States of America

3 4 5 6 7 8 9 0 1 2 090 9 8 7 6 5 4 3 2 1

The Dryden Press
Harcourt Brace College Publishers

To my wife and counsel, Deborah A. Kuratko—D.F.K
To my wife and colleague, Gemma M. Welsch—H.P.W.

The Dryden Series in Entrepreneurship
Advisory Editor for Entrepreneurship—Donald F. Kuratko

Eckert, Ryan, and Ray
Small Business: An Entrepreneur's Plan
Third Edition

Foegen
Business Planning Guide
Revised Edition

Hodgetts and Kuratko
Effective Small Business Management
Fourth Edition

Kuehl and Lambing
Small Business: Planning and Management
Third Edition

Kuratko and Hodgetts
Entrepreneurship: A Contemporary Approach
Second Edition

Kuratko and Welsch
Entrepreneurial Strategy: Text and Cases

The Dryden Press Series in Management

Anthony, Perrewe, and Kacmar
Strategic Human Resource Management

Bartlett
Cases in Strategic Management for Business

Bedeian
Management
Third Edition

Bedeian and Zammuto
Organizations: Theory and Design

Bereman and Lengnick-Hall
Compensation Decision Making: A Computer-Based Approach

Boone and Kurtz
Contemporary Business
Seventh Edition

Bowman and Branchaw
Business Report Writing
Second Edition

Bracker, Montanari, and Morgan
Cases in Strategic Management

Calvasina and Barton
Chopstick Company: A Business Simulation

Costin
Readings in Total Quality Management

Czinkota, Ronkainen, and Moffett
International Business
Third Edition

Daft
Management
Third Edition

Eckert, Ryan, and Ray
Small Business: An Entrepreneur's Plan
Third Edition

Etienne-Hamilton
Operations Strategies for Competitive Advantage: Text and Cases

Foegen
Business Planning Guide
Revised Edition

Gaither
Production and Operations Management
Sixth Edition

Gatewood and Feild
Human Resource Selection
Third Edition

Gold
Exploring Organizational Behavior: Readings, Cases, Experiences

Greenhaus
Career Management
Second Edition

Harris and DeSimone
Human Resource Development

Higgins and Vincze
Strategic Management: Text and Cases
Fifth Edition

Hills, Bergmann, and Scarpello
Compensation Decision Making
Second Edition

Hodgetts
Management: Theory, Process, and Practice

Hodgetts
Modern Human Relations at Work
Fifth Edition

Hodgetts and Kroeck
Personnel and Human Resource Management

Hodgetts and Kuratko
Effective Small Business Management
Fourth Edition

Hodgetts and Kuratko
Management
Third Edition

Holley and Jennings
The Labor Relations Process
Fifth Edition

Huseman, Lahiff, and Penrose
Business Communication: Strategies and Skills
Fourth Edition

Jauch and Coltrin
The Managerial Experience: Cases and Exercises
Sixth Edition

Kemper
Experiencing Strategic Management

Kuehl and Lambing
Small Business: Planning and Management
Third Edition

Kuratko and Hodgetts
Entrepreneurship: A Contemporary Approach
Second Edition

Kuratko and Welsch
Entrepreneurial Strategy: Text and Cases

Lewis
Io Enterprises Simulation

Luthans and Hodgetts
Business
Second Edition

McMullen and Long
Developing New Ventures: The Entrepreneurial Option

Matsuura
International Business: A New Era

Mauser
American Business: An Introduction
Sixth Edition

Montanari, Morgan, and Bracker
Strategic Management: A Choice Approach

Northcraft and Neale
Organizational Behavior: A Management Challenge
Second Edition

Penderghast
Entrepreneurial Simulation Program

Sandburg
Career Design Software

Sawyer
Business Policy and Strategic Management: Planning, Strategy, and Action

Schoderbek
Management
Second Edition

Schwartz
Introduction to Management: Principles, Practices, and Processes
Second Edition

Varner
Contemporary Business Report Writing
Second Edition

Vecchio
Organizational Behavior
Second Edition

Walton
Corporate Encounters: Law, Ethics, and the Business Environment

Wolford and Vanneman
Business Communication

Wolters and Holley
Labor Relations: An Experiential and Case Approach

Zikmund
Business Research Methods
Fourth Edition

The Harcourt Brace College Outline Series

Pentico
Management Science

Pierson
Introduction to Business Information Systems

Sigband
Business Communication

PREFACE

Entrepreneurship has evolved into one of the most popular and, arguably, one of the most important fields of study in contemporary schools of business. This academic emergence has coincided with the economic emergence of entrepreneurs throughout the past two decades. During the last ten years, the annual number of new incorporations has averaged 600,000 while most of the employment growth, innovation, and overall vitality of the U.S. economy has been sparked by the entrepreneurial sector.

This remarkable entrepreneurial growth, both economic and academic, has ignited contemporary researchers to examine all of the particular facets of entrepreneurship. For example, within major Fortune 500 corporations there has been a recognition and new respect for the entrepreneurial perspective within individuals. Thus, "corporate entrepreneurship" or "intrapreneurship" has been adopted by many firms as a strategy for innovation and growth. This strategy attempts to capitalize upon the entrepreneurial abilities of individuals *within* the corporate framework.

Additional facets of entrepreneurship include Family Business, International Entrepreneurship, Women Entrepreneurs, Entrepreneurial Growth, and Entrepreneurial Careers. While this list may not be exhaustive, it does provide a clear example of the particular areas of research within entrepreneurship that are emerging.

Organization

This book is designed to be a contemporary view of several important dimensions of entrepreneurship. As this field matures into major differentiated segments, the latest innovations and writings must be communicated to a growing audience of entrepreneurship students. *Entrepreneurial Strategy: Text and Cases* was developed as a graduate-level book that invites the exploration of some of these particular facets of entrepreneurship. While there are ten selected topics of text material provided, the major focus of this book is for analysis of the comprehensive cases that illustrate various strategies within entrepreneurial firms. As professors and students examine, discuss, and develop the critical issues of these cases, there will emerge a greater understanding of and insight into the entrepreneurial process.

The first part of the text (Part 1) is designed with five chapters that examine the critical issues in new venture initiation, business planning, growth, development, and succession. The second part contains five chapters covering some key emerging issues within the entrepreneurship domain. Corporate entrepreneurship, women entrepreneurs, careers in entrepreneurship, family business, and international entrepreneurship were selected for research and discussion. Since the field of entrepreneurship is dynamic and evolving, professors are encouraged to add other topics for their students. However, it is our hope that this book provides a solid foundation for examining the emerging issues of entrepreneurship. Through this contemporary examination, students will become more fully aware of today's entrepreneurial process and more fully prepared to accept their challenge for tomorrow's business environment.

Acknowledgments

Many individuals played an important role in helping us write, develop, and refine our text, and they deserve special recognition. Our families, from whom we took so much time, deserve our deepest love and appreciation, especially our wives Deborah A. Kuratko and Gemma M. Welsch. We would also like to express our appreciation to the staff at The Dryden Press who worked closely with us on this project, in particular, Ruth E. Rominger, Acquisitions Editor, who was a major supporter for our book. We would also like to recognize the professionals at Elm Street Publishing Services who provided the editorial work for this book including Nancy Shanahan, Barb Bahnsen, and Cate Rzasa.

We would like to acknowledge the authors of our comprehensive entrepreneurial cases. These professors and case researchers developed the excellent comprehensive cases that provide the focus of this text. Without their contributions, a book such as this could not be developed.

Case Authors	*Affiliations*
Allen C. Amason	University of South Carolina
Claire J. Anderson	Old Dominion University
Candida G. Brush	Boston University
Barbara B. Buchholz	Family Industry Resource Management
Michael E. Busing	Clemson University
James W. Camerius	Northern Michigan University
James J. Chrisman	University of Calgary
Ronald L. Christy	Wichita State University
Margaret Crane	Family Industry Resource Management
Kendra Earley	Kent State University
Frank J. Fish III	Panasonic Communications Systems Company
Darin M. Floyd	Ball State University
Fred L. Fry	Bradley University
Ken Gardner	University of South Carolina
Brian C. Gnauck	Northern Michigan University
Keith R. Hausman	Iowa State University
Marilyn M. Helms	University of Tennessee-Chattanooga
Jack B. Hess, III	Ball State University
Charles W. Hofer	University of Georgia
Sandra Honig-Haftel	Wichita State University

Wu-Ming Hou	Iowa State University
J. David Hunger	Iowa State University
Cynthia Iannarelli	Seton Hill College
Beth Jack	University of Tennessee-Chattanooga
John Leslie	University of South Carolina
David Molian	David Molian Associates and INSEAD
John W. Newman	Babson College
G. R. Patton	Seton Hill College
Vernon A. Quarstein	Old Dominion University
Julie Schmidt	Babson College
Jerry Sheppard	Simon Fraser University
Charles B. Shrader	Iowa State University
Frederick T. Stein	Kent State University
Thomas A. Teal	Harvard Business Review
Michael Ullman	INSEAD
Harold Valentine	University of South Carolina
Thomas L. Wheelen	University of South Florida
Geraldine E. Willigan	Harvard Business Review
Ann Walsh	Iowa State University
John K. Wong	Iowa State University
Irvin Zaenglein	Northern Michigan University

Finally, we would like to express our appreciation to our colleagues at Ball State University and DePaul University. In particular Jatinder N.D. Gupta, Chairman of the Management Department, Ball State University, and Neil A. Palomba, Dean of the College of Business, Ball State University, for their enthusiastic support. Also thanks to The Coleman Foundation, Ilya Meiertal, administrative assistant, DePaul University; Kenneth Thompson, former Chairman of the Management Department, DePaul University; Raymond W. Coye, Chairman of the Management Department, DePaul University; Ronald J. Patten, Dean of the Kellstadt Graduate School of Business, DePaul University, for their assistance and support.

Donald F. Kuratko
Ball State University

Harold P. Welsch
DePaul University

November 1993

About the Authors

Donald F. Kuratko, D.B.A., is The Stoops Distinguished Professor in Business and Director of the Entrepreneurship Program, College of Business, at Ball State University. He is the first professor to be named a Distinguished Professor for the College of Business at Ball State University. He has published more than 90 articles on aspects of entrepreneurship, new venture development, and corporate intrapreneurship. Dr. Kuratko is the Advisory Editor on Entrepreneurship for The Dryden Press/Harcourt Brace, Inc. as well as a Consulting Editor for *Entrepreneurship Theory & Practice Journal.* He has also been a consultant on corporate intrapreneurship to major corporations such as Blue Cross/Blue Shield, AT&T, Union Carbide Corp., Ameritech, and United Technologies. Professor Kuratko's work has been published in such journals as *Strategic Management Journal, Journal of Small Business Management, Entrepreneurship Theory & Practice, Training and Development Journal, Entrepreneurship Development Review, Advanced Management Journal,* and *The Small Business Forum.* Professor Kuratko has written seven books, including *Effective Small Business Management* (Dryden Press/Harcourt Brace, Inc., 1992); *Entrepreneurship: A Contemporary Approach* (Dryden Press/Harcourt Brace, Inc., 1992); and *Entrepreneurial Development Within Organizations* (Quorum Books, 1994).

The academic program in entrepreneurship that Dr. Kuratko developed at Ball State University has received national acclaim with such honors as the George Washington Medal of Honor (1987); the Leavey Foundation Award for Excellence in Private Enterprise (1988); the National Model Entrepreneurship Program Award (1990); and The NFIB Excellence Award (1993).

Dr. Kuratko was named Professor of the Year for five consecutive years at the College of Business, Ball State University; Outstanding Young Faculty for Ball State University in 1987; and was recipient of Ball State University's Outstanding Teaching Award in 1990. Dr. Kuratko was also honored as the 1990 Entrepreneur of the Year for the State of Indiana (sponsored by Ernst & Young, *Inc.* magazine, and Merrill Lynch), inducted into the Institute of American Entrepreneurs Hall of Fame in 1990, and named the nation's Outstanding Entrepreneurship Educator in 1993.

Harold P. Welsch, Ph.D., who holds the Coleman Foundation Endowed Chair in Entrepreneurship at DePaul University, has been active in entrepreneurship development since early in his career.

Dr. Welsch is well known for his research in the area of privatization of centrally planned economies, entrepreneurship career paths, formal and informal strategic planning, information seeking and decision behavior, ethnic entrepreneurship, economic development, and small business problems. Dr. Welsch's work has appeared in several publications including *Entrepreneurship: Theory and Practice, International Small Business Journal, Journal of Small Business Management, Frontiers of Entrepreneurship Research, Revue Internationale PME, Research in Entrepreneurship, Group and Organization Studies, Internationales Gewerbe Archiv and Human Relations.* He was co-editor of *Research at the Marketing/Entrepreneurship Interface* and recently published *International Entrepreneurship and Small Business Bibliography* containing more than 8000 reference items.

He currently serves as Chairman of the Academy of Management Entrepreneurship Division. In addition to his role as founder/director of the Entrepreneurship Program at DePaul University, Dr. Welsch has served as president of the International Council for Small Business (ICSB) and president of the U.S. Association for Small Business and Entrepreneurship (USASBE). He serves as consulting Editor of the *International Journal of Small Business* and is on the editorial review board of *Entrepreneurship Theory and Practice, Journal of Small Business Management, Entrepreneurship, Innovation and Change, Family Business Review,* and is a board member of the Council of Entrepreneurship Awareness Education. He serves on various boards of directors and consults for both large and small firms.

Dr. Welsch was awarded the Harold Washington Community Service Award for his economic development efforts in Chicago neighborhoods and serves as Director of the Small Business Institute and on the Executive Committee of the MIT Enterprise Forum. He has served as national judge for several prestigious entrepreneurial awards including The Blue Chip Enterprise Initiative's Entrepreneur of the Year Award sponsored by the U.S. Chamber of Commerce and Connecticut Mutual Insurance Company, and Peat-Marwick's Hi-Tech Entrepreneur of the Year Award. He was instrumental in establishing Small Business Development Centers in Poland and served in a pilot program in establishing an MBA program in Prague, Czechoslovakia. His current research carries him throughout the world in his efforts to promote entrepreneurship development and education internationally.

Dr. Welsch has received grants from the Coleman Foundation, the Booz-Allen-Hamilton Foundation, National Aeronautics and Space Administration (NASA), Commonwealth Edison, Department of Transportation, United States Information Agency (USIA) and Argonne National Laboratories.

Dr. Welsch received his Ph.D. degree from Northwestern University's Kellogg Graduate School of Management.

Contents in Brief

Contents

Alphabetical Listing of Comprehensive Entrepreneurial Cases

THE ENTREPRENEURIAL PROCESS

1

Entrepreneurial Strategy
A Multistaged Approach

Key Topics

- Entrepreneurial Process Approaches
- Assessment and Multidimensional Models
- Entrepreneurial Strategy: A Multistaged Approach
- The Nature of Contingency Strategic Planning for Emerging Firms

Comprehensive Entrepreneurial Cases

- Hickory Ridge Golf Club—Revised
- The Kitchen King Company

Introduction

Entrepreneurs today are considered to be the heroes of free enterprise. Innovation and creativity have helped many of them build multimillion-dollar enterprises from fledgling businesses, some in less than a decade! These individuals have created new products and services and have assumed the risks associated with these ventures. Many people now regard entrepreneurship as "pioneership" on the business frontier.

> Entrepreneurship is the ability to create and build a vision from practically nothing: fundamentally it is a human, creative act. It is the application of energy to initiating and building an enterprise or organization, rather than just watching or analyzing. This vision requires a willingness to take calculated risks—both personal and financial—and then to do everything possible to reduce the chances of failure. Entrepreneurship also includes the ability to build an entrepreneurial or venture team to complement your own skills and talents. It is the knack for sensing an opportunity where others see chaos, contradiction, and confusion. It is possessing the know-how to find, marshal, and control resources (often owned by others).[1]

In order to understand this venture-building activity, it is important to view entrepreneurship's innovative elements as a systematic discipline.[2] One recurring concept emerges in the study of contemporary entrepreneurship: It is an interdisci-

---

[1]Jeffry A. Timmons, Leonard E. Smollen, and Alexander M. Dingee, *New Venture Creation* (Homewood, IL: Irwin, 1985), 1.

[2]Peter F. Drucker, "The Discipline of Innovation," *Harvard Business Review* (May–June 1985): 67–72.

plinary concept, and, as such, it contains various approaches that must be learned in order to understand the field.[3]

Entrepreneurial Process Approaches

One way to examine entrepreneurial activities is with a process approach. Unique to the process approach is its major focus on the start-up of a venture. Process-approach models developed by various researchers are interdisciplinary because entrepreneurship includes factors from numerous disciplines. However, as you will see in the illustrations that appear in this chapter, these process approaches attempt to be integrative while focusing on individual elements that harmoniously fit together. Although there are many methods and models that try to structure the entrepreneurial process[4] and its various factors, we shall examine only three key integrative approaches here.

Entrepreneurial Assessment Approach

One model, the **assessment approach,** developed by Robert C. Ronstadt, stresses assessments that must be made qualitatively, quantitatively, strategically, and ethically in regard to the entrepreneur, the venture, and the environment.[5] (Figure 1.1 depicts this model.) The results of these assessments must be compared with the stages of the entrepreneurial career—early, mid-career, or late. Ronstadt called this process "the entrepreneurial perspective," and viewed its strategic formulation as a leveraging of unique elements;[6] that is, unique markets, unique people, unique products, or unique resources are identified, used, or constructed into effective venture formations. The interdisciplinary aspects of strategic adaptation become apparent in the following characteristic elements.

- *Unique markets:* Mountain versus **mountain gap strategies,** which refer to major market segments as well as intersticed (in-between) markets that arise from larger markets.
- *Unique people:* **Great chef strategies,** which refer to the skills or special talents of one or more individuals around whom the venture is built.
- *Unique products:* **Better widget strategies,** which refer to innovations that encompass new or existing markets.
- *Unique resources:* **Water well strategies,** which refer to the ability to gather or harness special resources (land, labor, capital, raw materials) over the long term.

---

[3]William B. Gartner, "What Are We Talking About When We Talk About Entrepreneurship?" *Journal of Business Venturing* (January 1990): 15–28. *See also* Lanny Herron, Harry J. Sapienza, and Deborah Smith-Cook, "Entrepreneurship Theory From An Interdisciplinary Perspective: Volume II," *Entrepreneurship Theory and Practice* (Spring 1992): 5–12.

[4]William D. Bygrave, "Theory Building in the Entrepreneurship Paradigm," *Journal of Business Venturing* (May 1993): 255–280.

[5]Robert C. Ronstadt, *Entrepreneurship* (Dover, MA: Lord Publishing Co., 1984).

[6]Robert C. Ronstadt, *Entrepreneurship* (Dover, MA: Lord Publishing Co., 1984), 112–115.

Figure 1.1   **Entrepreneurial Assessment Approach**

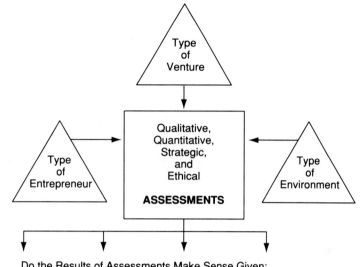

Source: Robert C. Ronstadt, *Entrepreneurship* (Dover, MA: Lord Publishing Co., 1984), 39.

Without question, strategic formulation encompasses a breadth of managerial capability that requires an interdisciplinary approach.

Multidimensional Approach

A more detailed process approach to entrepreneurship is the **multidimensional approach.**[7] From this viewpoint, entrepreneurship is a complex, multidimensional framework that emphasizes the individual, the environment, the organization, and the venture process. Specific factors that relate to each of these dimensions are as follows:

The individual
  1. Need for achievement
  2. Locus of control
  3. Risk-taking propensity
  4. Job satisfaction

---

[7]Bradley R. Johnson, "Toward a Multidimensional Model of Entrepreneurship: The Case of Achievement Motivation and the Entrepreneur," *Entrepreneurship: Theory and Practice* (Spring 1990): 39–54.

  5. Previous work experience
  6. Entrepreneurial parents
  7. Age
  8. Education

The environment
  1. Venture capital availability
  2. Presence of experienced entrepreneurs
  3. Technically skilled labor force
  4. Accessibility of suppliers
  5. Accessibility of customers or new markets
  6. Governmental influences
  7. Proximity of universities
  8. Availability of land or facilities
  9. Accessibility of transportation
  10. Attitude of the area population
  11. Availability of supporting services
  12. Living conditions

The organization
  1. Type of firm
  2. Entrepreneurial environment
  3. Partners
  4. Strategic variables
       Cost
       Differentiation
       Focus
  5. Competitive entry wedges

The process
  1. The entrepreneur locates a business opportunity
  2. The entrepreneur accumulates resources
  3. The entrepreneur markets products and services
  4. The entrepreneur produces the product
  5. The entrepreneur builds an organization
  6. The entrepreneur responds to government and society[8]

Figure 1.2 depicts the interaction of the four major dimensions of this entrepreneurial, or new-venture, process. It is this type of process that moves entrepreneurship from a segmented school of thought to a dynamic, interactive process approach.[9]

---

[8]William B. Gartner, "A Conceptual Framework for Describing the Phenomenon of New Venture Creation," *Academy of Management Review* (October 1985): 702.

[9]Gartner, 702.

Figure 1.2   Multidimensional Approach

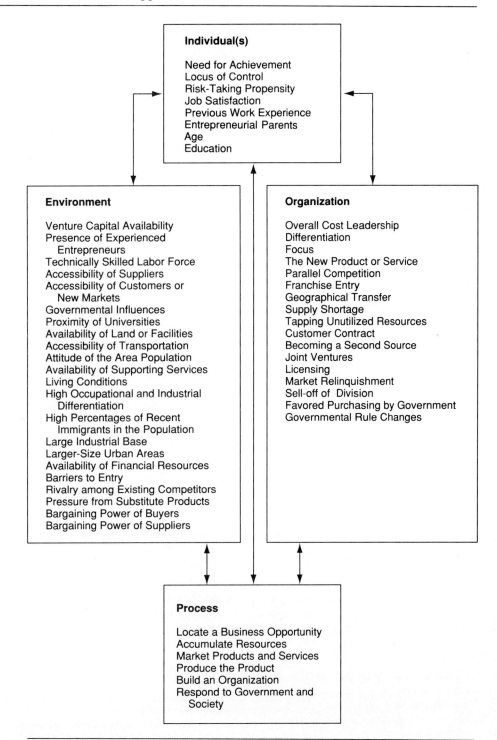

Individual(s)

Need for Achievement
Locus of Control
Risk-Taking Propensity
Job Satisfaction
Previous Work Experience
Entrepreneurial Parents
Age
Education

Environment

Venture Capital Availability
Presence of Experienced
    Entrepreneurs
Technically Skilled Labor Force
Accessibility of Suppliers
Accessibility of Customers or
    New Markets
Governmental Influences
Proximity of Universities
Availability of Land or Facilities
Accessibility of Transportation
Attitude of the Area Population
Availability of Supporting Services
Living Conditions
High Occupational and Industrial
    Differentiation
High Percentages of Recent
    Immigrants in the Population
Large Industrial Base
Larger-Size Urban Areas
Availability of Financial Resources
Barriers to Entry
Rivalry among Existing Competitors
Pressure from Substitute Products
Bargaining Power of Buyers
Bargaining Power of Suppliers

Organization

Overall Cost Leadership
Differentiation
Focus
The New Product or Service
Parallel Competition
Franchise Entry
Geographical Transfer
Supply Shortage
Tapping Unutilized Resources
Customer Contract
Becoming a Second Source
Joint Ventures
Licensing
Market Relinquishment
Sell-off of Division
Favored Purchasing by Government
Governmental Rule Changes

Process

Locate a Business Opportunity
Accumulate Resources
Market Products and Services
Produce the Product
Build an Organization
Respond to Government and
    Society

Source: William B. Gartner, "A Conceptual Framework for Describing the Phenomenon of New Venture Creation," *Academy of Management Review* (October 1985): 702. Reprinted with permission.

Venture Initiation Approach

Attempting to integrate the interdisciplinary yet behavioral nature of entrepreneurship, Lanny Herron and Harry J. Sapienza developed a process model that focuses on entrepreneurs' aspirations, skills, and satisfaction levels. Thus, the model depicted in Figure 1.3 emphasizes not only the centrality of the individual to the entrepreneurial process, but also the importance of the relationship between behavior and context. This approach is limited to the activities of venture creation that lead up to the actual initiation of the project. Therefore, it concentrates on the "flow" of elements from the entrepreneur's perspective that influence the search, discovery, and launch of a new venture.[10]

Contingency Entrepreneurial Strategy: A Multistaged Approach

After reviewing the process approaches to studying entrepreneurship, it becomes apparent that three distinct variables are critical to any strategic analysis: the individual, the venture, and the environment. However, the stages of any venture (idea, pre-venture, start-up, early growth, harvest) are also critical to strategic analysis. In addition, a career perspective should be considered, which means that the entrepreneur's career stage (early, middle, or late) can be a decisive factor in differentiating the variables within the venture development stages. Thus, it may be necessary to visualize entrepreneurial strategies as contingencies. In other words, all of the evolving and emerging conditions involved with any entrepreneurial pursuit cause a constant dynamism. If newly emerging entrepreneurial issues such as global expansion, the growth in numbers of women entrepreneurs, and corporate entrepreneurship are also introduced, then a model of entrepreneurial strategy would be multidimensional, multistaged, and contingency-based. Figure 1.4 attempts to capture all of these factors into a three-dimensional model that emphasizes the need for contingency strategies based upon the evaluation and assessment of the various elements.

While all of these variables must be examined from a strategic perspective, the traditional strategic management process may provide assistance. This perspective is summarized in the acronym SWOT, which stands for strengths, weaknesses, opportunities, and threats.[11] Thus, Figure 1.4 shows an entrepreneurial contingency strategy model that assesses critical entrepreneurial variables in light of emerging issues for the purpose of entrepreneurial development and, eventually, entrepreneurial continuation. This multilayered model can serve as the basis for analyzing and assessing cases contained in the following chapters. Each case expands on a particular

---

[10]Lanny Herron and Harry J. Sapienza, "The Entrepreneur and the Initiation of New Venture Launch Activities," *Entrepreneurship Theory and Practice* (Fall 1992): 49–55.

[11]Thomas L. Wheelen and J. David Hunger, *Strategic Management and Business Policy,* 4th ed. (Reading, MA: Addison-Wesley Publishing Co., 1992): 47. *See also* William R. Sandberg, "Strategic Management's Potential Contribution To a Theory of Entrepreneurship," *Entrepreneurship Theory and Practice* (Spring 1992): 73–90.

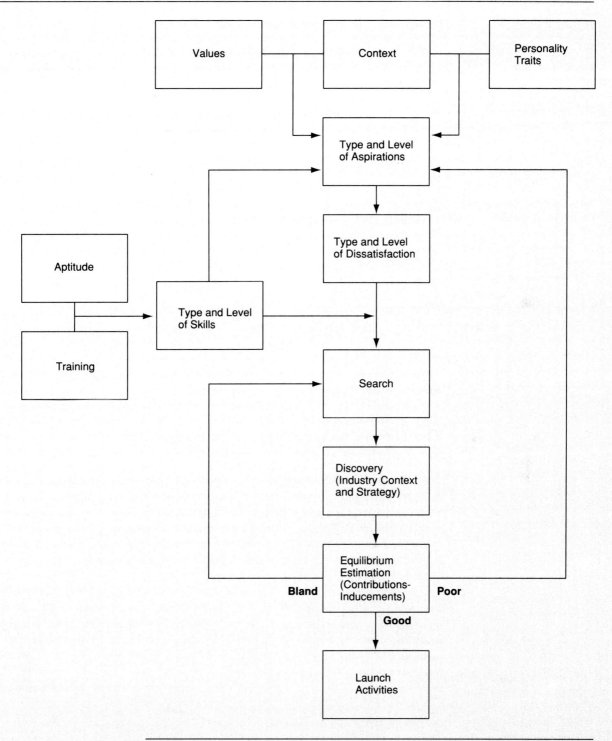

Source: Lanny Herron and Harry J. Sapienza, "The Entrepreneur and the Initiation of New Venture Launch Activities," *Entrepreneurship Theory and Practice* (Fall 1992): 51.

Figure 1.4		**Entrepreneurial Strategy: A Multistaged Approach**	

Strategic Entrepreneurial Assessment	**New Venture Initiation**	**Entrepreneurial Development and Continuation**	**Emerging Entrepreneurial Issues**

Opportunity Evaluation

Entrepreneurial Growth and
Development:
New Venture Initiation   Understanding the   Corporate Entrepreneurship
Creativity: Entrepreneurial
Assessment Evaluation   Company   International:
SWOT Analysis   Feasibility Criteria   Managing Paradox and   The Global Expansion
Contradiction
(Strengths/Weaknesses   Acquisition of a Venture   Women Entrepreneurs
Opportunities/Threats)   The Business Plan Process
Definition   Family Business
Benefits
Business Plan   Valuation and Succession of   Entrepreneurial Careers
Development   Entrepreneurial Ventures:
Methods of Valuation
Succession Strategy

dynamic facet of entrepreneurship to better illustrate the strategic development of
new and emerging ventures.

The Nature of Contingency Strategic Planning for Emerging Firms

Although most entrepreneurs plan for their new ventures, the planning often tends
to be informal and unsystematic.[12] The actual need for systematic planning varies
with the nature, size, and structure of the business. In other words, a small two-
person operation could successfully plan informally because there is little complexity
involved. But an emerging venture that is rapidly expanding with constantly
increasing personnel size and market operations needs to formalize its planning
because there is a great deal of complexity.

An entrepreneur's planning needs to shift from an informal to a formal systematic style for other reasons. First, there is uncertainty about whether the venture
will become established and grow. When higher levels of uncertainty exist, entrepreneurs have a stronger need to deal with the challenges facing their venture, and a
more formal planning effort can help them to do this. Second, the stronger the
competition (in both numbers and quality of competitors) for a new venture, the
more important it becomes to have a more systematic planning in order to more

---

[12]Douglas W. Naffziger and Donald F. Kuratko "An Investigation into the Prevalence of Planning in
Small Business," *Journal of Business and Entrepreneurship* (October 1991): 99–110.

closely monitor operations and objectives.[13] Finally, the entrepreneur's amount and type of experience may be a factor in deciding the extent of formal planning. A lack of adequate experience, either technological or business, may constrain the entrepreneur's understanding, causing a need for formal planning that will help determine future paths for the organization.

In recent years, researchers have found that planning among small firms is increasing. In a study of 732 U.S. firms, Ackelsburg and Arlow found that most small businesses planned and that these planning firms engaged in more goal-setting activities, forecasting, and planning procedures than did nonplanners.[14] Shuman, Shaw, and Sussman surveyed planning practices of the *Inc.* 500 and found that a majority of these entrepreneurs did not have a business plan when they started their firms but, as the firms grew, their planning processes became more prevalent and formalized.[15] CEO's attitudes toward the impact of planning influenced the strategic planning activities of this group. Seventy-two percent of the *Inc.* 500 CEOs surveyed perceived that planning leads to better decisions which, in turn, lead to increased profitability. The CEOs also believed that planning leads to increased time efficiency, company growth, and better knowledge of the market.

A number of other studies have focused on the impact of planning on small firms, and these studies support the contention that strategic planning is of value to a venture.[16] Most of the studies imply, if they do not directly state, that planning influences a venture's survival. As noted in Robinson and Pearce's study, a number of researchers found planning to be an important criterion for differentiating successful from unsuccessful firms.[17] More recently, a study of 9,000 firms established lack of planning as a major cause of failure,[18] and another investigation demonstrated that those firms that engaged in strategic planning outperformed those that did not.[19]

More specifically, a study conducted by Jeffrey S. Bracker and John N. Pearson categorized planning levels of small firms into structured strategic plans (SSP), structured operational plans (SOP), intuitive plans (IP), and unstructured plans (UP).[20] The research concentrated on a sample of homogeneous, small, mature firms in the dry cleaning industry and revealed that firms using structured strategic planning financially outperformed firms using other types of plans. In a more recent application of the same planning categories to a sample of growth-oriented firms

[13]Radha Chaganti, Rajeswararo Chaganti, and Vijay Mahajan, "Profitable Small Business Strategies under Different Types of Competition," *Entrepreneurship: Theory and Practice* (Spring 1989): 21–36.

[14]Robert Ackelsburg and Peter Arlow, "Small Businesses Do Plan and It Pays Off," *Long Range Planning* (October 1985): 61–67.

[15]Jeffrey C. Shuman, John J. Shaw, and Gerald Sussman, "Strategic Planning in Smaller Rapid Growth Companies," *Long Range Planning* (December 1985): 48–53.

[16]Richard B. Robinson, Jr., and John A. Pearce, II, "Research Thrusts in Small Firm Strategic Planning," *Academy of Management Review* (January 1984): 132–133.

[17]Ibid.

[18]R. Ryatt, "The Business Failure Record," *Dun & Bradstreet,* 1987.

[19]Richard B. Robinson, "The Importance of Outsiders in Small Firm Strategic Planning," *Academy of Management Journal* (March 1982): 80–93.

[20]Jeffrey S. Bracker and John N. Pearson, "Planning and Financial Performances in Small Mature Firms," *Strategic Management Journal* 7 (1986): 503–522.

in the electronics industry, the results supported the previous research by showing that firms with structured strategic plans outperformed all others.[21]

In further recent research of 188 small firms it was found that firms with formal plans emphasized more aspects of the strategic choice process, adapted a wider range of competitive and cooperative strategies, and grew more rapidly than did nonformal planners.[22]

In summary, much of the recent research indicates that firms that engage in strategic planning can better prepare for the future stages through which the venture will progress. Most important, the studies emphasize the importance of the planning process, rather than merely the plans, as a key to successful future performance. In other words, the quality of the business owner's input to the planning process, even if it is informal (i.e., not a structured, written document), becomes the critical factor for entrepreneurs' planning.

Contingency strategic planning may be the primary step in determining the business's future direction. The "best" strategic plan will be influenced by many factors, including the entrepreneur's abilities, the complexity of the venture, and the nature of the industry, as well as the other variables depicted in Figure 1.4. Yet whatever the specific situation, five basic steps must be followed in strategic planning: (1) understand the venture, (2) establish long-range and short-range objectives, (3) outline alternative courses of action, (4) implement a plan of action, and (5) analyze the results and take follow-up action. Focusing on these basic steps, this text examines the variables that impact emerging ventures.

Entrepreneurial Strategy: The Flow of the Book

While the major thrust of this book is to provide comprehensive cases that illustrate different aspects of the entrepreneurship process, we believe some framework or structure should also be presented. Thus, based upon the introductory models presented in this chapter, the book is organized to flow from some of the critical entrepreneurial variables for new-venture initiation and growth to the major elements needed for growth and development and finally to an examination of some emerging entrepreneurial issues. Figure 1.5 provides an illustration of this flow of our text.

No contemporary book relating to entrepreneurship will be able to address all of the relevant variables that comprise an entrepreneurial strategy. Therefore, we have isolated some of the key areas, with the hope that the chapters and the comprehensive entrepreneurial cases will serve as a basis for discussion, research, and debate. It is with this approach that today's contingency entrepreneurial strategies can be better understood.

---

[21]Jeffrey S. Bracker, Barbara W. Keats, and John N. Pearson, "Planning and Financial Performance among Small Firms in a Growth Industry," *Strategic Management Journal* 9 (1988): 591–603.

[22]Marjorie Lyles, Inga S. Baird, J. Burdeane Orris, and Donald F. Kuratko, "Formalized Planning in Small Business: Increasing Strategic Choices," *Journal of Small Business Management* (April 1993): 38–50.

Figure 1.5   Contingency Entrepreneurial Strategy

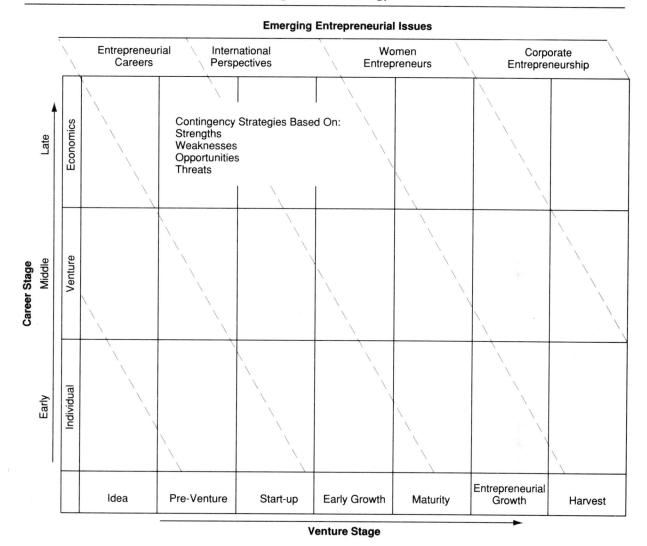

CASE • *Hickory Ridge Golf Club (Revised)*

James J. Chrisman, University of Calgary
Harold Valentine, University of South Carolina
Allen C. Amason, University of South Carolina

Greg Hamilton, owner and manager of Hickory Ridge Golf Club (HRGC), a modest nine-hole golf course in Columbia, South Carolina, nursed his first cup of coffee of the day lost in thought. Normally, Hamilton would have been bustling around the course, preparing for the day's business. Play was generally brisk in the mornings of warm, June days, and the morning of June 1, 1989, promised to be no exception. In spite of this, Hamilton knew he had to make several decisions that could have an important short- and long-term impact on the profitability, and perhaps even the survival, of his business.

In 1988, its first year of business, Hickory Ridge generated revenues in excess of $116,000. However, the firm lost $17,000. Exhibit 1 provides the 1988 Profit and Loss Statement for HRGC. Exhibit 2 provides HRGC's common size Balance Sheet for 1988. As seen in Exhibit 3, greens fees accounted for the largest single portion of the revenues, followed by cart rentals.

Exhibit 1
Hickory Ridge Golf Club: Profit and Loss
Statement, 1988
(from IRS Schedule C)

Sales	$116,270	
Cost of goods sold	− 21,079	
Gross profit	95,191	
Salaries and administrative		
expenses	− 112,801	
Wages and salaries		36,327
Repairs		7,532
Supplies		13,885
Utilities and telephone		7,549
Advertising		900
Car and truck expenses		2,353
Insurance		6,411
Dues and publications		693
Rent on business property		1,338
Taxes		4,905
Interest expense		13,459
Depreciation		13,590
Other		3,859
Net profit	− $ 17,610	

The facilities at Hickory Ridge also needed improvement. The course needed restoration, the clubhouse needed extensive work, and much of the equipment was inadequate. In addition, the club's fleet of nine electric carts had not been sufficient to meet 1988 demand, much less the increase in cart usage expected for the remainder of 1989. The current fleet of carts was old and required frequent repair; this further aggravated the profit situation. Hamilton knew a decision was needed on whether or not to purchase or lease new carts, and if so, from whom. He was also aware that to supply the money for all the improvements to the facilities, revenues would have to increase substantially.

Unfortunately, several unanswered questions complicated the decision-making process. How much revenue had previously been lost due to the inadequate cart fleet? How much could be gained by improving the course or the clubhouse? More importantly, Hamilton wondered how any decision, on the carts or other matters, would affect revenues in 1989. To further complicate the situation, Hamilton was unsure whether his course was positioned to attract the influx of new golfers and the large base of experienced golf enthusiasts in the area. To formulate a strategy, Hamilton knew he would have to rely on his own knowledge and experience as well as the advice of the course architect and mechanic, Harold Valentine. As

Exhibit 2
Hickory Ridge Golf Club: Common Size Balance Sheet Compared to Industry Averages

	Hickory Ridge	Industry*
Assets		
Current assets	10.0	18.9
Cash and equivalents	4.0%	7.4%
Inventory	2.2%	10.9%
Other current	3.8%	0.6%
Fixed assets	78.0%	73.3%
Intangibles and other noncurrent assets	12.0%	7.8%
Total Assets	100.0%	100.0%
Liabilities		
Short-term payables	4.8%	9.1%
Other payables	10.0%	15.9%
Long-term debt	80.0%	44.5%
Equity	5.2%	30.5%
Total Liabilities and Equity	100.0%	100.0%

*SIC #7992, Public golf courses with sales of less than $500,000.

Industry Source: Robert Morris Associates, '90 *Annual Statement Studies,* 1990.

Exhibit 3
Hickory Ridge Golf Club Revenues, 1988–1989

	Greens Fees	Golf Carts	Pull Carts	Snack Bar, Pro Shop	Beer	Total Revenues
1988						
January	$ 1,069	$ 290	$ 38	$ 280	$ 800	$ 2,476
February	2,906	833	92	360	1,920	6,110
March	4,601	1,728	127	997	2,400	9,852
April	7,713	2,773	271	2,337	1,380	14,474
May	6,463	2,236	252	1,443	1,960	12,354
June	5,193	1,866	210	1,116	1,880	10,264
July	5,665	2,436	204	1,691	2,000	11,996
August	5,811	2,657	188	1,242	1,900	11,798
September	5,616	2,382	204	465	1,800	10,467
October	5,024	1,943	201	864	1,100	9,132
November	4,969	1,762	190	883	1,000	8,804
December	4,925	1,664	210	748	996	8,543
Total	$59,954	$22,569	$2,186	$12,426	$19,136	$116,270
1989						
January	$ 5,497	$ 1,803	$ 206	$ 665	$ 1,680	$ 9,851
February	3,700	1,023	163	853	800	6,539
March	7,472	2,404	338	1,347	2,040	13,601
April	10,531	3,297	509	2,511	2,080	18,928
May	11,056	4,209	566	2,404	2,000	20,235
Total	$38,256	$12,736	$1,782	$ 7,780	$ 8,600	$ 69,154

he finished his coffee, Hamilton vowed to bring up the subject with Valentine that afternoon.

Hamilton's Background

For Hamilton, the purchase of Hickory Ridge was an important step in fulfilling a lifelong dream—to own and run a public golf course. Born on May 18, 1950, and raised in Columbus, Ohio, Hamilton was introduced to golf by Arnold Adams, owner of Possum Run Golf and Swim Club. Adams, who gave Hamilton his first job, was far more than just an employer. He passed on to Hamilton his love of golf, and his conviction that golf should be a game easily accessible to the general public. For several years Hamilton spent nearly every spare moment of his time on the course with Adams.

Marriage at age 21 brought many changes to Hamilton's life, including three children, but his dream to own a golf course remained unchanged. His wife, Dr. Cynthia Hamilton, supported Hamilton emotionally and financially through her psychiatry practice. In 1978, the couple moved to Columbia, South Carolina, where Hamilton took the position of assistant pro at a local golf club, Linrick Golf Course. While there, Hamilton earned his PGA assistant's license and hoped to eventually earn his PGA professional's license.

Background of Hickory Ridge Golf Club

HRGC opened in 1957 as an 18-hole, par-71 golf course. It was built on a modest budget by the Williams family who owned the land. The Williams family operated the course for less than a decade before selling it in 1964. Following several ownership changes over the next 15 years, the McAllister family bought the course in 1978. Almost immediately, the McAllisters, who were in the construction business, cut the golf course to nine holes and built a housing development on what had been the "back nine." The McAllisters invested minimal amounts of money in maintaining the course and gradually it fell into the dilapidated state in which Hamilton found it in 1988.

Conditions at Purchase

At the time of Hamilton's purchase, there was little reason to believe that HRGC had ever been a pleasant, well-kept golf course. The clubhouse and the equipment shed had accumulated an abundance of garbage over the years. What little equipment remained was virtually unusable. One old tractor was the only piece of heavy equipment available and it had to be jump-started before being used. The gang and greens mowers were almost beyond repair and were unable to perform the functions for which they had been designed. There was no mechanical sand trap rake, necessitating hand-raking of all the bunkers. There was an ancient fairway aerator and a fleet of 14, 1976, E-Z-GO carts. Of these, only six carts worked at all, and they were extremely dangerous to use; some did not have brakes or a reverse gear.

The condition of the course was not much better. The grounds were overgrown, and the encroaching bushes, weeds, and trees gave the course an air of abandonment. There was a significant amount of grass in the sand traps, and sand that had escaped discouraged grass from growing where it was needed. The greens were receding from lack of care and were being eaten away by fungus and weeds. The tees were eroding noticeably due to improper cart path management and design. Inadequate aeration produced ground that was hard, making it difficult for the grass to infiltrate the topsoil and grow properly. Finally, the pond on the course was an eyesore. The pond was overgrown and full of garbage, with less than three feet of water at its deepest point, making it unsuitable for irrigation.

Improvements and Changes

Needless to say, Hamilton's refurbishing encompassed the course's buildings, equipment, and grounds. Hoping to keep the transition of ownership smooth, Hamilton sought to retain the employees who had worked at the course under the McAllisters. Poor communication and personal conflicts, however, led to frequent disagreements between these workers and Hamilton in the early months of HRGC's development. By July 1988, the course superintendent had been fired and most of the other personnel problems were resolved. Johnny Clayton was hired as greenskeeper and Harold Valentine as architect/mechanic.

Because the clubhouse and shop areas were nearly inaccessible, the trash that had accumulated was removed, clearing the way for several improvements. Hamilton's original office was a 50-foot-square closet which he unwillingly shared with the pesticides and herbicides. To solve this problem, Hamilton had a larger office built on the back of the clubhouse. He installed a pro shop and, from scratch, built up its inventory to be able to provide golfers with some basic supplies and accessories. He also improved the snack bar, buying some new tables and chairs, a refrigerator, and a hot dog machine.

In addition, there were improvements to the equipment. Hamilton was able to repair the gang mower but the other pieces of equipment, including the greens mower and the tractor, had to be replaced. In May 1988, in an effort to bolster the pathetic cart fleet, HRGC purchased 12, 1984 model Club Car electric carts. Two of the older carts were then junked, giving HRGC a total of 16 usable carts.

Another major capital expenditure was the purchase of a new irrigation system, an absolute necessity in maintaining a quality golf course. The irrigation system was installed on all greens and tees, and on five of the nine fairways. A submersible pump in a newly dug quartz aquifer kept the reservoir pond well filled. A new 30-horsepower pump was installed to provide pressure for the system. To help reduce algae and aquatic weed growth, the pond was stocked with fish.

The holes in the course required a great deal of attention. Eroded areas were filled and the turf grass and greens revamped. Fairways were aerated and brush was cut away from the roughs to widen the holes. New tee markers and flags were purchased and areas that might be damaged by the carts were roped off. Additionally, cables were installed along the road to prevent damage from vandals who had previously driven cars on the fairways and greens.

Hamilton also took action to ensure that the course met the needs and preferences of its customers. Based on a marketing research project completed in April 1989, Hamilton decided to change the price structure of the course and restrict alcohol use to that which was purchased at the course.

Industry Environment

By 1988, golf had become a booming business that was expected to grow rapidly in the 1990s. Nearly every authority agreed that the number of players and the volume of revenues they brought in were steadily increasing. According to *Golf Market Today* (1989), there were approximately 11.2 million golfers in the United States in 1970. At the beginning of 1989, that figure had nearly doubled to 21.7 million. Also important was that the rate of growth had accelerated over each of the past four years. Researchers from the National Golf Foundation estimated that over 30 million people would be golfing in the United States by the year 2000.

This explosive growth was largely attributed to increased interest among women, the elderly, and the "baby boomers" (*PGA Magazine,* 1989). Of particular importance was the impact women were likely to have on the future of the game. In 1989, women represented around 25 percent of all golfers yet accounted for 40 percent of all new players. Like their male counterparts, many had careers and found golf an excellent way to relax and conduct business (*Savvy,* 1989).

The growth of golf also caught the attention of the business world. *Business Week* (1989) called golf "a global phenomenon" and a "$20 billion industry with a growth rate that is nothing short of phenomenal." The golf boom had been felt in the stock market too, with many corporations—such as Emhart Industries, a maker of club shafts, and American Brands, a maker of golf shoes—seeing significant changes in their stock prices (Research Recommendations, 1989). This growth had also led to increased corporate sponsorship on the PGA tour, as well as higher purses at PGA events (*Golf Digest,* 1989).

The possibilities for growth seemed limitless, and it appeared unlikely that supply could keep up with demand, even though both the number of courses opened and under construction rose from 1987 to 1988 (*Golf Market Today,* 1989; *Golf Digest,* 1989). In 1987, there were 145 new courses opened and 513 under construction or in the planning stage; in 1988, 211 courses opened and 662 were being constructed or planned. Nevertheless, overcrowded courses were becoming more common and the situation in some areas was becoming serious (*Business Week,* 1989). Even planning for 50 percent growth over the next decade—some believed this growth would be closer to 100 percent (*Golf Digest,* 1989)—the golf industry estimated that 4,000 new facilities, or an average in excess of one course opening per day, would be necessary over the next ten years (*Golf Market Today,* 1989).

The Golf Course Superintendents Association singled out the lack of public golf courses as the major contributor to the overall facility shortage (*Golf Course Management,* 1989). Over 80 percent of all golfers used public courses, and this figure was expected to increase. For this reason *Golf Market Today* estimated that at least 60 percent of all new courses needed to be public.

Keys to Success

Despite the rapid growth, the keys to running a successful course had not changed much; for example, it was important to have a clean, well-maintained course and polite, well-trained employees. However, by 1989 golf was becoming more and more a common man's game. It had become increasingly important for golf course owners to understand the needs and habits of a changing and diverse group of customers. For instance, some courses in Florida sought to lure in the seniors with special senior citizens discount packages, failing to consider the fact that most of their golfers were already seniors. Many of these courses were driven out of business because they did not understand their customers.

Diversity was a watchword within the industry. Experienced golfers were fascinated with gadgets: the newer, the more innovative, the more original, the better. Therefore, pro shops were stocking more golf-related novelty items and gadgets. Moreover, golfers desired courses with a variety of views and shots; a course layout that lacked variety bored the average golfer.

Local Environment

HRGC was located in Columbia, South Carolina, a city with a population of approximately 465,000. Between 1980 and 1988, the city had grown by about 13.5 percent. With an unemployment rate of only 3.9 percent, the area was generally considered to be prosperous. The average per capita income of the area was $13,795 in 1987. Exhibit 4 provides selected demographic data on the area.

Exhibit 4
Demographic Characteristics of the Columbia, South Carolina, SMA

	Population Estimates (in 000s)		Estimated Average Household Effective Buying Income		Estimated Retail Sales per Household	
	1988	1993	1988	1993	1988	1993
Lexington County	180.5	203.6	$31,251	$44,888	$12,532	$17,729
Columbia SMA	465.8	498.3	$32,602	$46,758	$17,026	$24,153
South Carolina	3,511.0	3,712.0	$27,058	$38,954	$15,932	$22,761
South Atlantic Region	42,921.5	46,127.2	$31,915	$45,074	$18,252	$25,918
United States	247,920.3	259,268.5	$33,198	$46,997	$17,745	$24,989

Source: "Survey of Buying Power: Part II," *Sales & Marketing Management*, November 13, 1989, 81, 102.

Population Breakdowns by Age, Sex, and Race

	Total	< 5 Years	5–17 Years	18–64 Years	≥ 65 Years	Median	Percent Male	Percent White
Columbia SMA								
1980 actual	410,088	28,510	86,026	265,429	30,123	27.3	49.2%	69.9%
1990 projected	472,800	34,570	82,820	312,570	42,890	31.0	NA	NA
South Carolina								
1980 actual	3,121,820	238,516	703,450	1,892,526	287,328	28.0	48.6%	68.8%
1990 projected	3,622,000	272,600	619,200	2,248,700	409,500	32.0	NA	NA

Source: *South Carolina Statistical Abstract 1989*, South Carolina Budget and Control Board, 288–289, 297.

The majority of the existing population was distributed in the areas north, west, and east of downtown, extending in each direction about 15 miles. New retail and residential developments were concentrated primarily in the northeast and northwest quadrants of the city, as a large portion of the area's future growth was expected to be centered in these two regions.

Furthermore, in 1987 there were approximately 34,000 students enrolled in the nine colleges and universities in the area. A single state university, located in the middle of downtown, represented the majority of the student population. Exhibit 5 provides information on college and university enrollments in the Columbia area.

Exhibit 5   **College and University Enrollments in Columbia, South Carolina**

	1987	1988	1989	1990	1992 (est)
University of South Carolina	23,946	26,435	25,692	25,613	26,625
Other area colleges	10,540	10,986	11,654	12,768	13,604
Total enrollments	34,486	37,421	37,346	38,381	40,229

Local Golf Industry

The local golf scene was changing and growing with the community. The southeastern by-pass was expected to be completed by late 1990. This by-pass would complete the interstate's encirclement of the metropolitan area, making most public golf courses in the region accessible to local golfers (within a 30-minute drive). There also was the possibility of new competition in the local industry. Four syndicates, two from Florida and one each from Texas and California, were analyzing the potential profitability of constructing major 27–36-hole golf complexes in the area. Other local groups had received approval to build additional holes, the local government was seeking to obtain grants to build an 18- or 27-hole course southeast of town, and a country club on the west side of town was considering the construction of nine additional holes to complement the nine holes it had recently completed. If it did so, this club would be able to offer its customers a total of 27 holes of golf. Generally, there was a regional trend toward clubs offering a combination of memberships and pay-for-play options. Golf was also becoming more accessible to the public because prices were rising slower than the cost of living.

A 1989 marketing study, conducted for Hickory Ridge Golf Club, helped explain local conditions. This study targeted 210 golfers, both familiar and unfamiliar with HRGC, and had a margin of error of plus or minus 2 percent (see Exhibit 6). The following summarizes the findings of the study:

Exhibit 6	**The Columbia Public Golfer: Market Survey Results, 1989**

The survey summarized below was based on the responses of 210 individuals in the Columbia, South Carolina, SMA.

1. Sixty-eight percent of the respondents were from 20 to 40 years old.
2. Fifty-six percent of the respondents drove between 5 and 15 miles to play golf.
3. Thirty-eight percent of the respondents' income was below $10,000; 28 percent of the respondents' income was between $20,000 and $30,000.
4. Eighty-three percent of the respondents located new golf courses through word of mouth.
5. Fifty-one percent of the respondents would play more golf if lower greens fees were available.
6. Sixty-five percent of the respondents play golf more than 15 times per year.
7. Sixty-two percent of the respondents that were pro shop customers said that their most frequent purchase was golf balls.
8. Fifty-seven percent of the respondents said that they would prefer food items such as hot dogs and hot sandwiches offered in the clubhouse.
9. Seventy-two percent of the respondents prefer to play 18 holes of golf per outing.
10. Eighty-seven percent of the respondents prefer to ride in a cart or walk with a pull cart while golfing.
11. Sixty-two percent of the respondents said that the primary determinant in the selection of a golf course is the condition of the fairways and greens.
12. Sixty percent of the respondents said that they expect to pay between $4 and $6 per round.
13. Ninety-seven percent of the respondents prefer to play with a friend or a foursome.
14. Twenty-seven percent of the respondents prefer to play on Saturdays.
15. Eighty percent of the respondents were male.
16. Thirty-four percent of the respondents were college students; 49 percent were in the work force.

Source: Postich, Miller, & Valentine, 1989.

Hickory Ridge Golf Club, as well as other area public golf courses, have a clientele that consists mainly of twenty- to forty-year-old males who prefer to play eighteen holes of golf per day. These individuals play more than fifteen times per year. Of these players almost 43 percent are college students. We believe that the level of college play can be increased by sponsoring a student/professor day early during each semester. It is our finding that lower green fees coupled with good greens and fairways are the most important factors to the public golfer. Financial records revealed that weekdays hold the greatest opportunity for increased profitability. This may be accomplished by increasing league play. It should be noted that in order to avoid simply shifting weekend play to weekday play, courses should refrain from lowering weekday rates.

Our study has determined that the public golfer seeks a greater selection of golf balls and hot food. While riding carts are most preferred, a ratio of seven pull carts to ten riding carts should be maintained in future purchases. Word of mouth is by far the most prevalent manner in which golfers learn about new courses. Therefore road signs should be used for directional purposes only, keeping all forms of advertising within a fifteen-mile radius. By following these recommendations, Hickory Ridge Golf Club should continue to have a substantial increase in play.

Competitors

In 1989 HRGC had 21 competitors in the area. Of these, 11 were public and 10 were private (see Exhibit 7). Only one course, Sedgewood Golf Course, was located within five miles of HRGC. Exhibits 8 through 10 provide information on the characteristics of each golf course in the area.

Sedgewood Golf Course

Sedgewood Golf Course, HRGC's only local competitor, was very different in significant ways. Sedgewood as an 18-hole, 6,810-yard, par-72 public course with restricted tee times on weekends and holidays. Besides the fact that Sedgewood was a regulation, 18-hole course, the most noticeable difference was in the price structure. A round of nine holes costs $7 to $11, depending on the day it was played, and a round of 18 holes costs $11 to $13. A riding cart cost an additional $9 per person for nine holes and $18 per person for 18 holes. In comparison, on weekdays HRGC charged $4.50 for nine holes, $7 for 18, and $8 for the entire day; its rates were $1.50 higher on weekends and holidays. Furthermore, at HRGC it cost only $6.50 per nine holes per cart regardless of the time of week. One notable similarity between the two courses, however, was a lack of adequate course maintenance.

Other Facilities

Also noteworthy were the facilities of other competitors. All area courses had pro shops on the premises, and there were a total of 29 pro shops in the area. These ranged from broad-based, discount shops, such as Nevada Bob's, to extremely exclusive shops at some of the finer country clubs, most of which were run by sales representatives. The majority of shop revenues tended to come from club repair

---

Exhibit 7   **Columbia Area Golf Courses, May 1989**

	Location and Distance from Downtown	
Private		
1. Coldstream Country Club Inc., Irmo, SC	Northwest	16 miles
2. Columbia Country Club, Columbia, SC	Northeast	20 miles
3. Crickentree Golf Club, Columbia, SC	Northeast	25 miles
4. Forest Lake Country Club, Columbia, SC	Northeast	5 miles
5. Golden Hills Golf & Country Club, Lexington, SC	West	20 miles
6. Mid Carolina Club Inc., Prosperity, SC	Northwest	30 miles
7. Timberlake Plantation, Chapin, SC	Northwest	35 miles
8. Wild Wood Country Club, Columbia, SC	Northeast	15 miles
9. The Windermere Club, Blythwood, SC	Northeast	20 miles
10. Woodlands Country Club, Columbia, SC	Northeast	17 miles
Public		
11. Charwood Country Club, West Columbia, SC	Southwest	12 miles
12. Coopers Creek Golf Club, Pelion, SC	Southwest	20 miles
13. Hickory Ridge Golf Club, Columbia, SC	Southeast	10 miles
14. Hidden Valley Country Club, West Columbia, SC	South	15 miles
15. Lake Marion Golf Club, Santee, SC	South	40 miles
16. Linrick Golf Course, Columbia, SC	North	15 miles
17. Paw Paw Country Club, Bamberg, SC	Southwest	40 miles
18. Persimmon Hill Golf Club, Johnston, SC	Southwest	30 miles
19. Pineland Plantation Golf Club, Sumter, SC	East	30 miles
20. Sedgewood Country Club, Hopkins, SC	Southeast	15 miles
21. White Pines Country Club, Camden, SC	East	40 miles

---

and the sale of clubs, golf balls, tees, and golf gloves. The average shop was likely to stock around 30 sets of clubs, although in extreme cases local shops were known to stock in excess of 100 sets. In addition, most shops stocked golf clothing such as socks, shoes, and hats, and many also carried shirts and pants. Certain pro shops, particularly those in country clubs, stocked extremely large inventories of clothing items. Often, the inventory of the pro shop was related to the exclusivity of the club and the wealth of the club's clientele. It was difficult for the pro shops to compete with the discount stores when the customers were price sensitive.

Only three courses offered full restaurants and all of them were private courses. The remaining private courses had limited dining facilities. Most clubs operated snack bars. Generally, the operators of public courses felt the profit potential of a restaurant was limited. Only two had grills. These offered hot sandwiches, hamburgers, etc., as well as drinks and snacks, and were open during lunch and dinner hours. Almost all of the public courses had simple snack bar facilities, however, offering hot dogs, cold drinks, chips, and candy.

Another thing many public courses lacked were locker areas and shower facilities. These were potentially appealing to the blue-collar workers, who would often golf on the way to or from work. Although eight of the ten private courses offered locker areas, only two of the eleven public courses did so.

Exhibit 8   Characteristics of Columbia Area Golf Courses: Dues, Greens Fees, and Hours

---

Private Courses

Number	Dues/Fees	Open Hours	Closed	Tee Time
1.	$77/month, $210 initiation	7:30am–6:00pm	Thanksgiving and Xmas	8am
2.	Not Available (NA)	Not Available	Not Available	NA
3.	$9,500 equity	8:30am–Dark	Mondays	NA
4.	$2,500 equity	8:00am–6:30pm		9am
5.	$75/month, $2,187 initiation	8:00am–6:30pm	Monday, Thanksgiving, Xmas, and New Years	8am
6.	$30/month, $750 initiation	8:00am–8:00pm	Xmas	8am
7.	$90/month, $2,500 initiation**	8:00am–7:00pm	Xmas	9am
8.	$100/month, $7,500 initiation	7:30am–8:00pm	Xmas and New Years	8am
9.	$100/month, $2,500 initiation	8:00am–8:00pm	Monday, Thursday, Friday, Thanksgiving, Xmas, and New Years	10am
10.	$105/month, $2,000 initiation	8:00am–7:00pm		8am

Public Courses

Number	Dues/Fees Weekdays, Weekends (9/18)		Open Hours	Closed	Tee Time
11.	$6.00/10.00,	$8.00/12.00	7:30am–9:30pm		8am
12.	$9.00/11.00,	$9.00/11.00	7:00am–Dark		10am
13.*	$4.50/7.00,	$6.00/8.50	8:00am–Dark		Open
14.	$6.00/8.00,	$12.00/12.00	8:00am–Dark		8am
15.	$15.00/25.00,	$15.00/25.00	Daylight–Dark		7am
16.	$5.50/8.50,	$6.50/10.50	7:30am–Dark	Xmas	8am
17.	$10.50/16.80,	$13.65/21.00	8:00am–Dark	Xmas	10am
18.	$5.50/11.00,	$8.00/16.00	8:00am–7:00pm	Xmas	8am
19.	$5.00/10.00,	$8.00/12.00	7:00am–Dark	Xmas	8am
20.	$7.00/11.00,	$11.00/13.00	7:30am–Dark	Xmas	10am
21.	$8.00/8.00,	$10.00/10.00	7:30am–Dark		Open

*Nine-hole course.

**Property ownership required.

Current Operations

In practical terms, Hamilton believed that HRGC was without any direct competition because of its distinctive characteristics. It was the only nine-hole golf course in the area. It was unusually level and short (2,807 yards, compared to the local average of 3,313 yards for nine holes) for a par-35, nine-hole course, making it especially suitable for elderly and young players. Its length, the absence of hills, and the lack of water, which came directly into play on only one hole, made HRGC a good course for the beginning golfer or the experienced golfer who wanted to walk the course or wanted a safe course on which to practice (see Exhibit 11 for course layout). Besides Hickory Ridge, only six of the other area courses were open 365 days per year, and only one of them had entirely unrestricted tee times. Overall,

Exhibit 9	Characteristics of Columbia Area Golf Courses: Amenities and Special Rates

Private Courses

Number	Pro Shop	Senior Rate (9/18)	Student Rate (9/18)	Restaurant	Snack Bar	Lockers
1.	Yes	No	No	Yes	No	No
2.	NA	NA	NA	NA	NA	NA
3.	Yes	No	No	Grill	Yes	Yes
4.	Yes	No	No	Yes	Yes	Yes
5.	Yes	No	No	Yes	Yes	Yes
6.	Yes	No	No	Yes	Yes	Yes
7.	Yes	No	No	Grill	No	Yes
8.	Yes	No	No	Grill	No	Yes
9.	Yes	No	No	Yes	Yes	Yes
10.	Yes	No	No	Yes	Yes	Yes

Public Courses

Number	Pro Shop	Senior Rate (9/18)	Student Rate (9/18)	Restaurant	Snack Bar	Lockers
11.	Yes	$5.00/6.00	$5.00/6.00	No	Yes	No
12.	Yes	No	No	No	Yes	Yes
13.*	Yes	$4.50 weekday	$4.50 weekday	No	Yes	Yes
14.	Yes	$6.00	$6.00	No	Yes	No
15.	Yes	No	No	No	Yes	No
16.	Yes	$4.50/6.00	$4.50/6.00	No	Yes	No
17.	Yes	No	No	No	Yes	No
18.	Yes	No	No	Yes	No	No
19.	Yes	Varies	No	No	Yes	No
20.	Yes	$1 off	$1 off	No	Yes	No
21.	Yes	Varies	No	Yes	Yes	Yes

*Nine-hole course.

these factors attracted many beginners, senior citizens, students, women, and blue-collar customers to HRGC.

As noted earlier, these customers represented a rapidly growing segment of the golfing public. Golf had traditionally been a sport of middle-aged males. However, the growing popularity of golf was being driven by groups of people who had not been especially interested in the game in the past. Hamilton believed that the other courses in the area were not designed to serve these newer, more diverse customer groups. He believed that Hickory Ridge could exploit a great opportunity by focusing its facility and efforts on the needs of the new golfer. Hamilton knew, however, that it would be unwise to alienate traditional golfers.

Sales

Sales were broken down into five areas: greens fees, cart rentals, snack bar and pro shop sales, beer sales, and pull cart rentals (see Exhibit 3). During the first five

Exhibit 10
Characteristics of Columbia Area Golf Courses: Course and Cart Information

Number	Yardage	Par	Cart Fees (9/18)
Private Courses			
1.	6,155	71	$4.75/8.40 per person
2.	NA	NA	Not Available
3.	6,471	72	$8.00/16.00 per cart
4.	6,450	72	$2.50/5.00 per person
5.	6,461	71	$5.00/8.00 per person
6.	6,600	72	$3.50/7.00 per person
7.	6,703	72	$4.75/8.50 per person
8.	6,726	72	$9.05 + tax per person for 18 holes
9.	6,900	72	$5.25/10.50 per person
10.	6,786	72	$4.00/8.00 per person
Public Courses			
11.	6,100	72	$4.00/8.00 per person
12.	6,550	72	$4.00/8.00 per person
13.*	2,807	35	$6.50 per cart
14.	6,700	72	$4.00/8.00 per person
15.	6,615	72	Included in greens fee
16.	7,080	73	$6.00/12.00 per cart
17.	6,700	72	Included in greens fee
18.	7,050	72	$4.50/9.00 per person
19.	7,084	72	$4.00/8.00 per person
20.	6,810	72	$9.00/18.00 per cart
21.	6,400	72	$4.00/8.00 per person

*Nine-hole course.

Exhibit 11
Hickory Ridge Golf Club: Course Layout

Hole	Length	Par	Features
1	324 yards	4	Straight, narrow, next to road
2	328 yards	4	Straight, next to road, bordered by water
3	313 yards	4	Straight, next to road, water barrier
4	360 yards	4	Dog leg right, wooded obstruction
5	214 yards	3	Straight, narrow, close trees
6	282 yards	4	Straight, narrow, close trees
7	166 yards	3	Straight, open
8	382 yards	4	Straight, open
9	438 yards	5	Straight, open

months of 1989, course revenues from greens fees, golf carts, and pull carts amounted to $52,774.

In addition to course revenues, HRGC sold golf balls, a moderate selection of golf clubs (as well as some rentals), golf gloves, and other complementary items such as socks. The shop did not carry golf shoes or clothes. HRGC kept approximately six sets of golf clubs in stock, at a value of approximately $2,000. After a round of golf, players could also relax with a chili dog and a cold drink at the snack bar and watch the PGA tour or a ballgame on television before making the trip back home. Through May, snack bar, beer, and pro shop sales contributed $16,380 to revenues in 1989.

Fees and Tee Times

The marketing survey Hamilton commissioned provided the impetus for changes in pricing and advertising. For weekdays, greens fees were raised by 50 cents across the board to $4.50 for nine holes, $7.00 for 18 holes, and $8.00 for the entire day. Weekend and holiday rates were increased by $1.00 to $6.00 for nine holes, $8.50

for 18 holes, and $9.50 for the entire day. The cart rates were raised from $6.00 to $6.50 per nine holes and senior citizens and student discount fees were restricted to weekdays.

The new fee structure was designed with two purposes in mind. It was intended to underprice the competition while still allowing an acceptable profit margin (between 2.5 and 4 percent). It was also intended to make golf accessible to as many residents of the area as possible, many of whom were new to the sport and were very conscious of price.

Hamilton made no change in tee times, however, keeping them open and making the course available on a first-come-first-served basis 365 days a year. His reason for this was to allow the greatest number of people to tee off in the shortest amount of time possible, while providing the maximum number of tee-off hours; he did not want any unnecessary restrictions on the golfers.

Advertising

The market survey had also recommended targeting certain groups that might find HRGC appealing, such as elderly and student golfers. As a result, Hamilton formulated an advertising strategy designed to entice a greater number of college students to HRGC. In hopes of catching the eye of new students, Hamilton concentrated his advertising efforts at the beginning of each semester, reducing his efforts as final exams neared. He advertised in the local paper, and planned to advertise in the university paper. The local paper, a statewide publication, charged $85.50 for a one-weekend advertisement. The university newspaper, which was published during the spring and fall semesters, charged $25.00 per week for advertisements. Billboards were also employed along the main roads to provide directions as well as to bring in golfers who might not have otherwise known about HRGC. In addition, because the survey indicated that the vast majority of golfers (more than four-fifths) try out new courses as a result of word of mouth, Hamilton concentrated on promoting a friendly atmosphere at HRGC and rejected both radio and television advertising, which he had previously been considering.

Maintenance and Facilities

To make the course more appealing and playable, Hamilton continued his efforts to clean up the course and the clubhouse and the existing facilities had taken on a markedly different and improved appearance as a consequence. Despite the improvements, HRGC still suffered from problems with erosion at the tee areas and inconsistent conditions on the greens. Conditions were steadily improving though because the newer equipment led to more efficient and productive course maintenance. Nevertheless, HRGC's facilities had not changed much since Hamilton bought the course. The only addition were the office built in the clubhouse and the pumphouse constructed near the pond.

Employees

Hamilton continued to employ Jim Alsing and Pete Peterson to operate the counter. Their work consisted of collecting greens and cart fees, controlling cart usage, managing the snack bar and pro shop, keeping the area clean, and some miscellaneous administrative duties.

Hamilton had hired Johnny Clayton to be the course greenskeeper and Harold Valentine as course architect and mechanic. The bulk of the maintenance work fell upon these two individuals. Clayton's primary duties were to maintain the greens, fairways, and roughs, along with a host of other special projects. His devotion to the golf business was largely due to his father who had previously been an employee at the course. Valentine, along with being the course agronomist and chemical specialist, worked as part-time mechanic. He had ten years of experience as a mechanic with the Navy, as well as years of agricultural experience growing up on his father's farm in Tennessee. Valentine also worked on a variety of miscellaneous projects as schedules required.

Strategic Issues

Hamilton owned a 15-acre, pie-shaped plot of ground adjacent to the golf course. He was considering adding a nine-hole, par-27 course there. However, construction costs would be $75,000 at the minimum, money which would have to be borrowed. Hamilton also wondered whether the lot would be sufficient to support a quality nine-hole course.

Another potential use for the land would be to add a driving range. A driving range could be completed at a significantly lower cost and might appeal to Hickory Ridge's customers. Hamilton estimated that a driving range could be built for $30,000. However, there was a new driving range currently being developed less than two miles away. The new range was not, however, connected to any area golf course.

Operating Issues

Besides his long-range concerns, Hamilton had many pressing operating issues that had to be resolved before his goals for HRGC could be attained.

Course Equipment

Improvement of the course was a top priority. Unfortunately, Hickory Ridge's equipment was barely sufficient for maintenance, much less improvement. With no mower for the rough, Hamilton was trying to use the fairway mower. This, however, did not work well on the higher, thicker rough grass. A new mower would cost $1,150.

A new rotivator would allow HRGC to use more efficient aeration techniques. A rotivator cuts thin slices in the ground and can be used year-round. Unfortunately, the old aerator made large holes in the turf and was only used once a year to minimize interference with play. Rotivators cost $3,000.

In addition, the sand traps had to be raked by hand, a slow and tedious job that was not done as often as it should have been. A mechanical trap rake would allow for daily maintenance of the bunkers but would cost around $1,200.

The irrigation system reached all tees and greens, but only five of the nine fairways. Although quality irrigation was a necessity on any golf course, it was especially important in the South where long, hot, dry summers could destroy good turf. Unfortunately, expanding the irrigation system would involve digging on the affected fairways. In spite of the interruption in play that this would cause, Hamilton wanted to add the irrigation to the other four fairways. Expanding the irrigation system would cost approximately $6,000.

Clubhouse and Snack Bar Improvements

The clubhouse was in need of significant renovation; the ceiling leaked and the paneling was generally unattractive. Hamilton's desire to renovate became more earnest as the ratio of revenues from clubhouse activities (pro shop and snack bar) to revenues from the golf course increased. Renovation costs were expected to be approximately $8,000.

In addition to the clubhouse, new equipment was also needed for the snack bar. The most immediate concern was the cooler. When Hamilton bought HRGC, the only cooler in the snack bar was a whiskey barrel filled with ice. Although adequate, it was inefficient. Each time a drink was ordered the attendant had to reach down into the ice and find the desired brand. The attendant also had to keep track of how much of each brand was on ice to be sure that he did not run out of any one drink. The cost of replacing the cooler was estimated at $1,585.

Cart Fleet Replacement

Hamilton's cart fleet was sorely depleted. Out of the original 14 E-Z-GO carts, only two were still running. The brakes on one of those were irreparably damaged and unlikely to last much longer. Nine of the 12 recently acquired Club Car carts were also usable. The other three had been rendered completely useless by cracks in the transaxles and main drive gears. The nine which were still in use suffered from various mechanical problems, however. The fusible links on two of the carts, parts which normally last for years, were burning out about every two weeks. On a third cart the rear support bracket for one of the shock absorbers had broken. Because the frame to which the bracket was attached was constructed of aluminum, it required a special type of welding not available at a reasonable cost.

There were other problems which pointed to the general deterioration of the fleet. Hamilton was beginning to recognize that extensive body damage could occur to fiberglass carts on a heavily wooded course such as HRGC, and that fiberglass repairs were extremely expensive. On several carts, the batteries were no longer holding their charges all day, and tires were beginning to lose air overnight. Both of these problems were becoming progressively worse. Furthermore, 3 of the 12 battery chargers had suffered failures in the power supply units, rendering them completely useless. Since none of the replacement parts ordered from Club Car had arrived, it was necessary to cannibalize parts from the three useless carts to keep the fleet operational.

These mechanical problems were causing trouble for Hamilton. For one thing, he had contracted to supply 15 carts for a golf league of 30 people. On any given day he could be certain of only six to nine working carts. Even more significant was the fact that the proportion of golfers at HRGC who desired to use riding carts (the cart rental ratio) had increased from 26 to 31 percent. Likewise, while the level of play had increased by 36 percent over the previous year, the number of cart rentals had increased by 42 percent over the same period. More than ever, Hamilton's customers wanted to use carts but fewer and fewer were available. New carts would cost between $2,580 and $3,500 each.

Workshop Addition

A temperature-controlled workshop was also needed adjacent to the clubhouse. Because of extremely high temperatures in the metal cart shed in the summer, repair work there was almost impossible. If a new fleet of carts was bought or rented, or if the old fleet was repaired, this workshop improvement would be mandatory. A workshop would cost at least $1,000.

Hamilton's Decision

All of these issues weighed upon Hamilton's mind. He knew that he would need to spend money in order to turn Hickory Ridge into the kind of facility he wanted it to be. However, his limited budget meant that he had to prioritize his efforts; he realized he could not possibly do everything at once since there were so many areas that needed attention.

Because of their ability to contribute revenue directly and to enhance the perception of the course, Hamilton believed that before he did anything else he would have to replace his aging cart fleet. The expanded cart fleet could provide a vehicle to increased revenue, which could then be invested in new equipment for the course.

The problem was that Hamilton was not sure how he should proceed in solving the cart dilemma. If he repaired the current fleet, he might risk continued problems. On the other hand, leasing and purchasing both involved long-term commitments and large amounts of money. He could not, however, ignore the problem. Every day he waited meant lost revenues and lost golfers. A frustrated golfer who decided to go somewhere else to play might never come back. Hamilton and Valentine had investigated various options available to alleviate the cart crisis. There were several options, each with its own set of questions to consider.

Alternatives

The first alternative considered was to repair the current fleet with borrowed funds. Following this plan meant that the cost of repairs and the remaining life of the used carts would be important. Valentine believed that repairing the current fleet would provide no more than four years of extended operation and would provide a minimum amount of visible improvement in the overall situation.

A second alternative was to purchase an entirely different fleet or a fleet of used carts, as they had in 1988. Either option would require borrowed funds. With the prime rate at 11.5 percent, HRGC's ability to obtain and repay such a loan was open to debate.

A third alternative was to lease a fleet, which would require no additional borrowing. If this alternative was selected, Hamilton would need to decide whether or not to purchase a maintenance agreement along with the leased fleet. Under a lease agreement, Hamilton would control the number of carts to be maintained by the course, but not how they could be used. For example, some leases prohibit the use of carts to do maintenance work.

There were several other factors which Hamilton and Valentine needed to consider. First, they had to consider what types of options would be necessary to meet the expectations of the customers. Do customers want sun roofs, full cart enclosures for winter golf, and sweater baskets? Second, they needed to decide if they wanted to use three-wheel or four-wheel carts. Although more expensive, four-wheelers caused less turf damage and had a lower insurance cost because of their greater riding stability. They also had to decide if they wanted gas or electric carts. Gas-powered carts required the purchase of fuel and oil, and needed more daily maintenance. They were also noisier, gave off fumes, and did not ride smoothly. Electric-powered carts were heavier, caused greater soil compaction and grass deterioration, but provided a smoother ride. Because they ran on electricity, they required the purchase of battery packs, which had to be replaced every three years. Finally, they had to determine how many carts would be needed.

To help make the correct decision, four regional cart companies were investigated: Melex, Yamaha, Club Car, and E-Z-GO. Each of these companies was well established and provided carts for lease or purchase. Valentine visited each of these firms, seeking information on purchase prices and on four-year lease agreements without a maintenance contract. Exhibit 12 provides the specific information Valentine obtained from each vendor.

Exhibit 12   **Golf Cart Vendor Comparisons**

	Melex	Yamaha	Club Car	E-Z-GO
Purchase Price				
Gas	$2,800	$3,500	$3,250	$2,900
Electric	$2,580	$3,200	$2,800	$2,680
Lease Price				
Monthly	$ 59	$ 72	$ 71	$ 59
Residual value	$ 675	$1,400	$ 450	$ 675
Location				
Service	Raleigh, NC	Newnan, GA	Augusta, GA	Augusta, GA
Manufacturing plant	Yugoslavia	Japan	USA	USA
Industry Experience				
In USA	10 years	8 years	30 years	35 years
Company Products and Services				
Cart quality	Good	Average	Average	Excellent
Appearance	Good	Average	Good	Good
Service	Good	Below average	Good	Good
Parts availability	Average	Average	Below average	Good
Cart body	Metal	Fiberglass	Fiberglass	Metal

Source: Harold Valentine's perceptions and factual data collected from visits to each company.

Conclusion

Certainly, the cart situation was one of many critical issues and Hamilton's decision on its resolution would affect business at the club for a long time. However, Hamilton could not help but wonder what impact addressing the cart fleet first would have on the rest of his plans. Clearly, he could not do everything at once. He had to be patient and develop the course at a rate he could afford. However, he still wondered what his next step should be. He knew that he had to rejuvenate the course's cart fleet, but wondered if he might be better-off concentrating his resources on the new equipment for the course or trying to improve the clubhouse and pro shop facilities before tackling the carts. If the carts were to be addressed first, however, he still needed to decide whether to lease or buy, and from whom.

In addition, Hamilton had to decide how he might further increase his business with traditional and nontraditional golfers. He wondered whether it would be possible to meet the needs of both groups. If their needs were significantly different, targeting one group might alienate the other. If this turned out to be the case, Hamilton knew he had to make sure that the course and facilities were tailored to meet the needs of the group that would most likely generate the greatest revenues and profits for the business. Related to this, in the longer term he knew he would have to grapple with the expansion issue. Would it be better to expand the course to 18 holes or build a driving range on the adjacent land?

These were the issues that Hamilton was considering. The market was expanding but so was the competition. He knew that he had to quickly formulate and implement a strategy that could adequately address these matters and place Hickory Ridge in a position that would lead to a long-term competitive advantage with respect to its customers and competitors.

References

"Course Development on the Upswing in the U.S." *Golf Market Today* 28, No. 3 (May/June 1989), 3–5.

"Golf: Business Challenges and Opportunities." *Business Week*, March 27, 1989.

Golf Course Management, 1989.

Postich, Miller, and Valentine, "Hickory Ridge Golf Club." University of South Carolina, 1989.

Research Recommendations, Feb. 20, 1989.

"Taking a Swing At Success." *Savvy*, April 1989.

"The Explosive Future of Golf." *Golf Digest*, March/April 1989.

"Wanted: More Golf Courses." *PGA Magazine*, March 1989.

C A S E • *The Kitchen King Company*

Marilyn M. Helms, University of Tennessee at Chattanooga

Introduction

In November 1985, Billy Sanders, vice president of the Kitchen King Company, asked a team of consultants to examine his company's inventory and delivery problems. Mr. Sanders was somewhat concerned about the company's lack of ability to forecast inventory needs and to deliver merchandise accurately and promptly.

History

Kitchen King was started by Tom King in 1949. The company is a wholesaler for the major lines of built-in appliances and cabinets for kitchen and baths. The company maintains a modern showroom floor with its different cabinet styles and sizes as well as various combinations of built-in refrigerators, compactors, ice makers, dishwashers, food processing centers, sinks, barsinks, microwave ovens, warming drawers, built-in or drop-in ovens, cooktops, and hoods arranged in attractive kitchen and bath displays.

The company is divided into two main divisions, as shown in Exhibit 1. The Dealer Sales Division, with its five sales representatives (all men), sells to retail cabinet and appliance dealers in Tennessee, Arkansas, Mississippi, and Kentucky. The salesmen help set up displays in the stores and keep them stocked with literature and current price sheets. The retail stores call in orders or send them by the salesmen. Orders are delivered by Kitchen King free of charge for large-volume orders. Small shipments and rush orders are sent by local truck lines or UPS and normally the dealer pays the freight cost. Orders are delivered by Kitchen King in two weeks. The company waits until it has enough orders to fill a truck before delivering.

The other division, Builder Sales, has four salesmen who sell to local home builders and contractors within the west Tennessee area. Each salesman has assigned customers. The salesmen visit builders at new home sites and either draw up plans for kitchens and baths or use the builder's blueprints. They write up the order and the cabinets and appliances are delivered to the job site by Kitchen King. The cabinets and appliances are installed by one of the two Kitchen King installers, by subcontractors, or by the builder's own staff.

Environment

Because the Builder Division only sells to contractors building new homes and offices (no remodeling jobs), its demand for cabinets and appliances depends on the local economy, interest rates, weather conditions, and the percentage of new housing starts in the area. The new-home growth in the Memphis and west Tennessee areas have been particularly strong with a more stable economy and a large number of residents moving to the outlying suburbs of Memphis and Germantown, Tennessee. Local businesses, including Federal Express, International Paper Corporation,

Exhibit 1   **Kitchen King Organizational Chart**

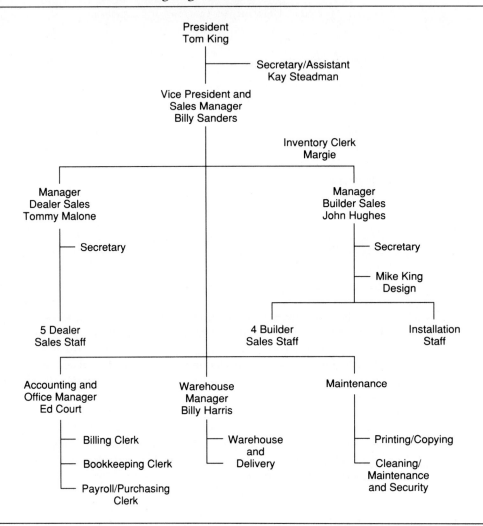

and Holiday Corporation are expanding and many executives are relocating to the Memphis area.

With the increasing emphasis on gourmet cooking and relaxation innovations in bath fixtures, Kitchen King customers are demanding more of the luxury products. The typical Kitchen King kitchen costs about $10,000. The average sales price of the homes with these products ranges from $125,000 to $500,000.

The Dealer Sales Division sells to retail stores whose customers are homeowners or small remodeling contractors. Demand also depends on interest rates for home improvement loans and advertising. The appliance manufacturers (Kitchen Aid, Thermador, Sub Zero, and Elkay) and the cabinet manufacturer (Merillat) advertise in home improvement and building magazines to stimulate primary demand for the products. The retail stores run ads in local newspapers and radio stations on an individual basis. Kitchen King pays a portion of the retail stores' advertising expenses on a cooperative basis depending on the stores' purchases.

All the items sold by Kitchen King are high-quality, top-of-the-line goods and consequently the profit per unit is high. Customers seek out homes with these products, so builders and retail customers are willing to pay the premium costs to obtain such high-quality appliances and cabinets.

Sales have been increasing steadily since the 1980–1982 recession. Exhibit 2 shows gross sales for Kitchen King since 1978.

Kitchen King, once the only wholesaler for cabinets in the Memphis and surrounding area, was joined by a major competitor in 1988. It is still the exclusive distributor for all its appliance and cabinet lines, but other lines are advertising and competing in the area. For its Dealer Sales Division (customer kitchens), it has little competition in the high-end market. Its Builder Sales Division also has competition from local cabinetmakers and other appliance distributors. Frequently builders want to save costs and will purchase only cabinets from Kitchen King and buy less expensive appliances from other distributors.

Interview with the President

To gain insight into the inventory problems at Kitchen King, the consultants first talked to the president, Tom King.

Tom King was a thin, gray-haired man in his early 60s. He began the company as a small distributorship and through the years watched it grow and prosper. His primary duties are to answer correspondence, sign payroll checks, and order all inventory. The remainder of his time is spent traveling or on the golf course. Frequently he comes in to fix a major problem or just to let the workers know he is "the boss."

Mr. King described his company to the consultants: "We have over 200 cabinet sizes and types which we use as well as various types of moldings, trims, fillers, and specialty wood parts. We presently stock three styles of cabinets. The Americana line is our most economical line. The doors are laminated and the body of the

---

Exhibit 2
Gross Sales (in Million Dollars)

1978	$4.34
1979	4.87
1980	4.68
1981	4.77
1982	4.42
1983	6.15
1984	6.77
1985	6.91
1986	7.20
1987	7.78

cabinet is oak. The Homestead Oak line is the same body as Horizon only with solid oak doors. The Omni line is again the same body with almond-colored doors with oak trim. We can also special-order cherry or walnut lines.

It's so expensive to carry an entire line of cabinets in inventory plus we must stock the appliances as well. I try to keep costs down to a bare minimum by ordering just what I think we need. I look at our incoming orders each week and just order this amount or just a little extra. We frequently have many back orders for items not in stock. It usually takes three weeks to a month to fill the back orders and a week to two weeks to get our regular shipments from the factory. I try to order a full truckload of cabinets each time so I can pay lower shipping costs. The biggest problem is that we never know what we will need."

Work Flow Patterns

Next the consultants observed the work flow patterns at Kitchen King for a week. They hoped that by examining these patterns they could locate some of the inventory and ordering problems. The following is a summary of their findings. A diagram of the workstation arrangement can be seen in Exhibit 3.

Order Processing   A customer, be it a builder or a dealer, calls Kitchen King with an order. The customer's first contact is with the receptionist who is often too busy chewing gum or talking with her friends to connect the caller with the proper department. She sees the customer as an interruption of her day.

The customer finally reaches the proper sales office and the secretary fills out the order form by hand. She puts the customer on hold while she checks inventory to see if the goods are in stock. With the customer on hold, the inventory clerk checks stock, which is recorded in pencil on cards filed in a large tub-shaped bin. There is a card for each item Kitchen King carries. After she has checked stock and told the secretary, the secretary then tells the customer the order's status and terminates the call.

The order is hand-written by the secretary and carried to the order clerk. She files the top copy and then updates her inventory cards as she checks off the items on the order. She writes separate back orders for items not in stock and files these back orders.

The order/inventory clerk then sends the order by pneumatic tube to the credit manager. He checks the customer's account status and then sends the order to the warehouse manager. In the warehouse, the order is pulled from inventory and either scheduled for delivery or shipped out. After the order is delivered or shipped (this may be as much as two weeks later) the warehouse then sends the order form back through the tubes to the inventory clerk. She makes sure all items were sent. (Frequently her cards and the warehouse inventory do not agree and she must make changes on her cards.) She adjusts back orders if needed and then gives the order to the proper secretary (either Builder Sales or Dealer Sales) for pricing. The secretaries hand-price and total the orders from price sheets. They then give the priced order forms to the president's secretary, Kay Steadman. Kay rechecks the prices and totals. Once Kay approves them, she gives them to the billing clerk. (Kay frequently takes three to four days to check the prices since she must do this

Exhibit 3 **Workstation Arrangement**

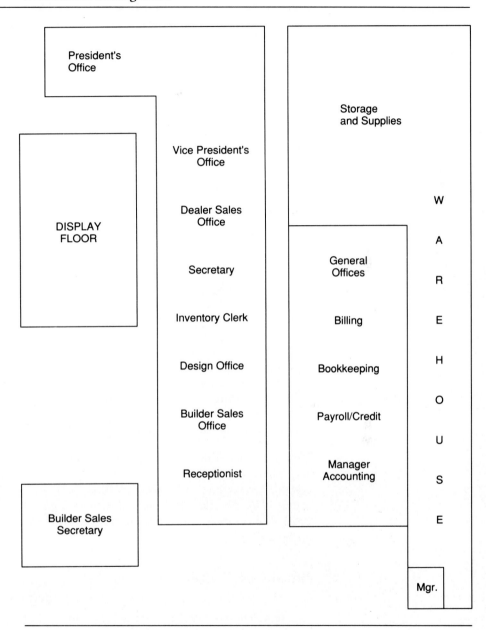

in addition to her other work that includes typing correspondence for the company and preparing new price sheets.)

When the billing clerk in the general office receives the checked orders, she then types an invoice from these orders. The invoice contains the same information as the original order, only it is now in typewritten form. The billing clerk frequently has to remove the order from the typewriter and correct all the carbon copies with liquid paper if she makes a mistake in her typing.

After she has typed up the invoices, she gives them to the office manager, Ed Court, to verify. He checks the totals and returns them to the billing clerk.

The billing clerk now separates the invoices. She mails the top copy to the customer for payment. She sends a green copy to the sales department. This copy is given to the salesman for his records. One copy is stapled to the hand-written order and is filed, and the final copy is sent by Mr. Court to a computer company that processes the information. Kitchen King receives printouts by product lines and customers by the second week of the following month.

The file copy of the invoice is kept by the billing clerk. If the order contains any appliance purchases, she must sign out the appliances by serial number in one of her five product line books. She finds the book for the particular appliance and then finds the correct model number and writes the customer's name by the correct serial number. After this time-consuming process is completed, she then files the invoices.

Receiving Reports   Incoming goods are also handled in the same jumbled way. Mr. King checks the inventory clerk's cards every Thursday and places an order. The clerk pencils this tentative order in on her cards. When the goods arrive in the warehouse, they are recorded on a receiving form. Appliances with their serial numbers go on one form and cabinets and goods with no serial numbers go on another receiving report. The receiving forms are sent to Margie, the inventory clerk, who records the items on the same cards. This process usually takes from one to two days, so an item might be in inventory, but her cards will not reflect this until some time later. Next Margie sends the receiving reports to the billing clerk. The billing clerk writes the new products and their serial numbers in her books and then sends the invoices to the office manager who approves them for payment (to the manufacturer).

Payroll   Each Friday all employees give their time sheets to Mr. King's secretary, Kay. She approves the time sheets and carries them to the payroll clerk. She hand-computes taxes and insurance and then hand-writes the checks. The checks are approved by the office manager and then are signed by Mr. King and Mr. Sanders. Paychecks are then distributed by the payroll clerk to all the employees by noon on Friday.

Employee Profile

After a review of the work arrangement, the consultants asked Mr. Sanders, the vice president, to describe the employees in his firm. He replied: "Ed Court is a good office manager. He has been with the company for over 15 years. He is our only employee with a college degree, and he's been trying to pass the CPA exam too. He keeps the girls in the office straight. He does the best he can with our outdated equipment. He would like to see us get a computer and automate our inventory and billing. But, Mr. King keeps telling him that we can't afford it and besides computers are changing daily so we must just wait until they are perfected.

"Billy Harris is our fourth warehouse manager. He is in his late 50s and he's been sick and the warehouse has not been properly supervised lately. But, he's trying to get things back in order. Many of the cabinets are in the wrong place or out of their boxes. We frequently take doors off cabinets to 'make' the style we are out of, so the cabinets are scattered everywhere. Harris has a hard time keeping the seven warehouse workers in line. They often come to work late and get orders messed up. We don't really need that many people, why one or two people could do that job, but since all the workers don't show up or have problems, Harris just keeps that many to be sure.

"Tommy Malone is a good dealer sales manager. He helps me out with some of the management functions and he has good ideas. I think that he would like to have more responsibility, but Mr. King is the *BOSS*. So Malone just does his job and that's all.

"John Hughes is the manager of the Builder Sales Division. He has an overconfident attitude. For example, he often goes out to design a kitchen and never makes any notes or measurements. He says he can remember them but in his office he forgets. Because of this he sends the wrong cabinets to the job site. He has his favorite salesman and neglects the others. He doesn't give them any training or supervision. He gives a new salesman a catalog and price lists and says 'go and sell. I know you will because you're paid on a commission.' Turnover in his division is high because he is hard to work with. But Mr. King especially likes him because he has sold more than any other sales manager in the company's history. He's top notch in King's book.

"Mike King is Mr. King's nephew and he has no official job or job title—he just works where he is needed, which is mostly in Builder Sales. He designs some kitchen plans and helps with promotions and displays. He has no management responsibility so I wonder if he'll ever be able to prove himself worthy to take over Kitchen King someday."

When asked to describe himself, Mr. Sanders said, "Well, I mostly design displays and plan company-sponsored parties and trips. We have promotions to enhance sales and I plan the incentive trips and prizes. I don't have a business background so I leave matters to Mr. King. I own a portion of the company, but I'm in my early 50s and I don't know what will happen to Kitchen King after Mr. King and I are no longer around."

Interviews

Next the consultants interviewed many people at different levels in the organization to try to define the problem at Kitchen King. The interviews were fairly unstructured, but in general the following topics were discussed: their feelings, the on-the-job experiences of these individuals, and what they see as problem areas in the company.

Mr. King's Secretary—Kay Steadman   "I've been with this company 18 years. I came to Kitchen King straight out of high school. I stay very busy checking prices and typing new price lists. I wish we had a better way to verify prices, but

Mr. King won't trust anyone else to do it. He's out frequently so I handle all his business and approve time sheets and sign checks. I'm so busy that I have to take work home with me.

"Most of our help comes to us from high school. We get them trained and they get married or quit. I like my job but I'm so tired all the time. I don't know if I'll be able to keep up with the job's demands."

Inventory Clerk—Margie Boyer   "Oh, Mr. King thinks that I'm the only one who can keep these inventory cards straight. He hates it when I take a vacation because he worries the cards won't be right. I've kept inventory this way forever both here and at my old job. I have it down to a system. My only problem is that I have to make so many trips back to the warehouse to check on items or see why we're out of something my cards show that we should have. We straighten out the cards every year at inventory time though.

"I see our problem as lack of organization in the warehouse. We often are out of, say, an Omni cabinet so they send a Homestead Oak cabinet with no doors and back order the doors, or they frequently change doors on the styles to make what we need. All these change-outs are what gets my cards all confused. But we just have to make do with what we have on hand.

"Some of our contractors and dealers just can't wait for cabinets, so we send out whatever we have and correct it later—when we receive the needed cabinets or doors. It's hard to know what we'll need. Some styles and sizes we use more than others but we are always out of something. The salesmen should use more standard sizes in their designs or not wait till the last minute to check on inventory. They should try to work with their clients and order what they need ahead of time."

Secretary—Dealer Sales   "We add so many new dealers and lose others that I spend most of my time typing up new phone and address lists of the dealers for the salesmen. I also have to spend time pricing orders. Each customer gets a different price and it's hard to know which one to use. If only we had a better system for all of this. I'm glad Kay (Mr. King's secretary) double-checks them. I'm new so I don't know about problems too well. We just have hectic days, with one crisis after another."

Secretary—Builder Sales   "My biggest problem is handling builders who call demanding their orders. They have completion deadlines to meet and need their entire orders on time, but we're often out of something or substituting something else. Part of the problem is that we never know in advance how many kitchens a builder has in progress or what they'll need. You just can't predict it. Always it's up and down.

"I have to handle complaints from the homeowners too. When they move in they want us to come and fix things. Often it is work that our subcontractors do. We shouldn't have to fix it, but we usually do. Our own installation men stay so busy making service calls or going back to a home to install an item that came in late. I wish we could stay on schedule and keep the builders happy."

Dealer Salesmen's Comments   "Our best customer in Jonesboro, Arkansas, always complains to me that he never gets what he ordered. The warehouse ships the wrong things or fails to load trucks with his complete order. He then has to wait two weeks or more to get the remainder of his order. This hurts his business and makes him mad at us. I wish the warehouse would shape up.

"The appliances my customers get are often scratched or bent. The warehouse loads them wrong and they get damaged in shipping. The warehouse men don't know how to drive the tow-motors or how to properly arrange and stack appliances.

"The billing process is so slow that orders don't get posted to my credit. I'm paid on a commission. They need a computer to speed up billing. Also, all those back orders cost me a delayed commission."

Builder Salesmen's Comments   "My boss, John Hughes, is difficult to work for. He's so moody. One day you're his best friend, the next day, you're his worst enemy. He always says that when he takes over Kitchen King, things will be run differently. He plays favorites among the sales staff and his customer assignments aren't fair.

"Our builders are always complaining about their orders. They would buy from someone else if we weren't the only one. I don't blame them for being mad. Someone should ask them what they are working on so we could order what they need in advance. Back orders are more expensive than carrying proper inventory. I know we lose sales and customer goodwill. John Hughes also treats the customers badly. They seem to all hate him after they've had to work with him, but they need our cabinets and still buy from us. With new companies around though, this may change."

Warehouse Manager—Billy Harris   "I just can't get my workers to do their jobs. I find them hiding behind boxes and goofing off. Why, just yesterday they made a ball out of wrapping paper and strapping tape and were throwing it around. We frequently have accidents because of their horseplay. The workers just won't act the way they should. They damage things with the forklift. I bet I have to yell at them ten times a day. 'Just one more time and you're out,' I tell them constantly. Last year I tried to fire a dock worker, but Mr. King gave him his job back. He said not to fire him because they really needed him on the company basketball team. You just can't keep decent help. Of course, we only pay them $4.00 an hour. King says we have to keep costs down.

"The boys never load an order right. I caution the delivery men when they deliver an order to check it and double-check it again. I'm going to have to do something about this."

Warehouse Workers' Comments   "Mr. Harris treat us like children. He punishes us in front of Mr. King, but when King leaves, he goes in his office and drinks coffee and we do nothing."

"Really, there is nothing to do. We load trucks in the morning and try to look busy in the afternoon."

"Even Mr. Harris has fun when King's gone. Last week he was cleaning his pocket knife and accidently cut another employee in the leg. The worker came up behind him and he said it was an accident."

"Harris doesn't know how to run a warehouse. The place is messed up and unorganized. No one thinks he is effective."

"We don't feel we have to do much for what we make. No one stays for long. You can't support a family, much less yourself, on $140 a week. We do as little as possible. Some even take a few items home to make up for their low salary. The warehouse and inventory is so messed up, they'll never miss a few things."

Delivery Drivers' Comments   "We have to rush to get the stops delivered. We do nothing for a week and then have to speed to get the truck unloaded."

"No one ever has a chauffeur's license at the warehouse, but Harris never asked. I hope we don't get caught."

"One driver doesn't even have a regular driver's license. He'll tell you if you ask. He just laughs about it."

Installers' and Subcontractors' Comments   "I deal with the builders. They are pretty upset about the way John Hughes runs the department. They always have been. They never get their orders on time."

"We spend all our time correcting doors. If only they would order and send the right thing in the first place."

"Often when we arrive at the job site, the salesman forgets to leave the plans and we don't know how to set the kitchen."

"John Hughes also uses us to help him fix up his own house. I've had to fix his closets, install shelves, and even build his kids a tree house on company time. I'm not sure what my duties are. Anything he says, I guess."

"The salesmen do not work with us on designs. They draw islands and counters that are impossible to install. They should use more standard designs and sizes. They try to get too creative and fancy."

"No one ever checks our work. We may get a pat on the back from a builder, but Mr. Hughes only talks to us when we've done something wrong."

Office Manager—Ed Court   "Mr. King wants his monthly runs from the computer service center sooner than we can get them back, but he won't buy a company computer. He doesn't understand how it can help us. He looked at one once but the costs scared him off. He only looks at bottom-line profit. A computer could really help us in payroll; with just a few terminals and some packaged programs we could eliminate much of our paper problems. We could do ordering and billing and pricing with only one invoice and our time could be cut in half. But, we don't have the personnel to run it anyway. King would want to pay a computer person only $3.35 an hour too.

"I worry about the future of the company when King is gone. The company will be gone too. I spend all my time training new billing clerks. They find out how tedious the job is and stay about six months. A computerized system would change all this, but no one will listen. King has all the money he'll ever need. He will never agree to any changes or improvements that cost him money. I believe you consultants are just wasting your time. King will never agree to anything."

The Consultants' Report

After these interviews and other data had been collected, the consultants prepared a brief outline of the survey findings. A meeting with Mr. King and Mr. Sanders was scheduled. They listened to these findings and asked, "What do we do to correct these things?" and "How will this program and changes affect our costs and expenses?"

Survey Results

Problematic Aspects—A Summary

- Lack of forecasting or planning inventory needs.
- No clear goals or objectives for the company, just make more money and keep costs low.
- Unwillingness on the part of top management to modernize and automate outdated procedures and machines.
- Failure to attract quality, knowledgeable workers and managers because of the low salary structure. (The president's secretary, with 18 years' service, makes only $5.50 per hour.)
- No management training or development. Managers treat workers according to Theory X rules
- Workers experience confusion and dissatisfaction with their work, which leads to turnover.
- Work load for employees is frantic. Always had to deal with problems and "put out fires."
- Customer relations are a problem. Builders and dealers are angry at the company's delivery mistakes and holdups.
- Failure of Mr. King to see these problems due to the fact that the company continually makes money despite all the apparent problems.

2

New Venture Initiation

Key Topics

- The Role of Creativity
- Critical Factors for Assessment
- The Evaluation Process
- Feasibility Criteria Approach

Comprehensive Entrepreneurial Cases

- Splatterball Adventure Games, Inc.
- The Science Education Company
- Kitchen Made Pies—Revised

The Role of Creativity

It is important to recognize the role of creativity in the innovative process because **creativity,** the generation of ideas, results in the improved efficiency and effectiveness of a system.[1] Although the origin of an idea is important, it is the role of creative thinking that is critical to its development.[2] In other words, there is a major difference between speculating about an idea and initiating one that is the product of extended thinking, research, experience, and work. More important, a prospective entrepreneur must have the desire to take a good idea through the various development stages. Thus, innovation is a marriage of the vision to create a good idea and the perseverance and dedication to remain with the concept through its implementation.

Successful entrepreneurs are able to blend imaginative, creative thinking with systematic, logical processing abilities; this combination is the key to success. In addition, potential entrepreneurs should always look for unique opportunities to fill needs or wants. If they are able to sense economic potential in business problems by continually asking "What if . . . ?" or "Why not . . . ?" they will develop an ability to see, recognize, and develop opportunity where others find only problems.

---

[1]Lloyd W. Fernald, Jr. "The Underlying Relationship between Creativity, Innovation, and Entrepreneurship," *Journal of Creative Behavior* 22, No. 3 (1988): 196–202.

[2]Timothy A. Matherly and Ronald E. Goldsmith, "The Two Faces of Creativity," *Business Horizons* (September–October 1985): 8. See also Bruce G. Whiting, "Creativity and Entrepreneurship: How Do They Relate?" *Journal of Creative Behavior* 22, No. 3 (1988): 178–183.

The Nature of the Creative Process

Thinking creatively is a process that can be developed and improved.[3] Everyone is creative to some degree; however, as is the case with many abilities and talents (e.g., athletic, artistic), some individuals have greater aptitudes for creativity than do others. Also, some people have been raised and educated in environments that encourage them to think and act creatively. For others the process is more difficult because their creativity has not been positively reinforced and, if they are to become creative, they must learn how to implement the creative process.

Creativity is not some mysterious and rare talent reserved for a select few. It is a distinct, sometimes illogical, way of looking at the world. The creative process depends on seeing relationships between things that others cannot see (e.g., modems or using telephones to transfer data between computers).[4]

There are four commonly agreed upon phases or steps in the creative process. Most experts agree on the general nature and relationship between these phases, although they refer to them by a variety of names.[5] Experts also agree that these phases do not always occur in the same order for every creative activity. For creativity to occur, there first needs to be chaos, but it should be a chaos that is structured and focused. We shall examine this four-step process using the most typical structural development.

Phase 1: Background or Knowledge Accumulation   Successful creations are generally preceded by investigation and information gathering, which usually involves extensive reading, conversations with others working in the field, attendance at professional meetings and workshops, and a general absorption of information relative to the problem or issue under study. Additional investigation in both related and unrelated fields is sometimes involved. This exploration gives the individual a variety of perspectives on the problem, and it is of particular importance to the entrepreneur, who needs a basic understanding of all aspects of the development of a new product, service, or business venture.

Some of the more useful ways to practice the creative search for background knowledge include: (1) read informational material from a variety of fields; (2) join professional groups and associations; (3) attend professional meetings and seminars; (4) travel to new places; (5) talk to anyone and everyone about your subject; (6) scan magazines, newspapers, and journals for articles related to your subject; (7) develop a subject library for future reference; (8) carry a small notebook and record useful information; and (9) devote time to pursue your natural curiosities.[6]

---

[3]See Edward deBono, *Teaching Thinking* (New York: New Market Press, 1986).

[4]See Dale Dauten, *Taking Chances: Lessons in Putting Passion and Creativity in Your Work Life* (New York: New Market Press, 1986).

[5]Edward deBono, *Six Thinking Hats* (Boston: Little, Brown, 1986); and *Lateral Thinking: Creativity Step by Step* (New York: Harper & Row, 1970).

[6]For a discussion on the development of creativity, see Eugene Raudsepp, *How Creative Are You?* (New York: Perigee Books, 1981); and Arthur B. Van Gundy, *108 Ways to Get a Bright Idea and Increase Your Creative Potential* (Englewood Cliffs, NJ: Prentice-Hall, 1983).

Phase 2: The Incubation Process   Creative individuals allow their subconscious thoughts to mull over the tremendous amounts of information they gather during the preparation phase. This incubation process often occurs while they are engaged in activities totally unrelated to the subject or problem. It happens even when they are sleeping, which accounts for the advice frequently given to a person who is frustrated by what appears to be an unsolvable problem: "Why don't you sleep on it?"[7] Getting away from a problem and letting the subconscious mind work on it often allows creativity to spring forth. Some of the most helpful steps to induce incubation include: (1) engaging in routine, mindless activities (cutting the grass, painting the house); (2) exercising regularly; (3) playing (sports, board games, puzzles); (4) thinking about the project or problem before falling asleep; (5) meditating and/or practicing self-hypnosis; and (6) sitting back and relaxing on a regular basis.[8]

Phase 3: The Idea Experience   This phase of the creative process is often the most exciting because it is at this time that the idea or solution the individual is seeking is discovered. Ironically, the average person incorrectly perceives this phase to be the only component of creativity.

As with the incubation process, new and innovative ideas often emerge while the person is doing something unrelated to the enterprise, venture, or investigation (e.g., taking a shower, driving on an interstate highway, leafing through a newspaper). Sometimes the idea appears as a bolt out of the blue, but usually the answer comes to the individual incrementally—slowly but surely the person begins to formulate the solution. Because it is often difficult to determine when the incubation process ends and the idea experience phase begins, many people are unaware of when they move from Phase 2 to Phase 3.

In any event, there are ways to speed up the idea experience: (1) daydream and fantasize about your project; (2) practice your hobbies; (3) work in a leisurely environment (e.g., at home instead of the office); (4) put the problem on the back burner; (5) keep a notebook at bedside to record late-night or early-morning ideas; and (6) take breaks while working.[9]

Phase 4: Evaluation and Implementation   This is the most difficult step of a creative endeavor and requires a great deal of courage, self-discipline, and perseverance. Successful entrepreneurs are able to identify those ideas that are workable and that they have the skills to implement. More important, they do not give up when they run into temporary obstacles.[10] Often they will fail several times before they

---

[7]T. A. Nosanchuk, J. A. Ogrodnik, and Tom Henigan, "A Preliminary Investigation of Incubation in Short Story Writing," *Journal of Creative Behavior* 22, No. 4 (1988): 279–280. This study reported that an eight-day incubation period was associated with significantly elevated story writing creativity.

[8]W. W. Harman and H. Rheingold, *Higher Creativity: Liberating the Unconscious for Breakthrough Insights* (Los Angeles: Tarcher, 1984).

[9]For more on idea development, see A. F. Osborn, *Applied Imagination,* 3d ed. (New York: Scribners, 1963); and William J. Gordon, *Synetics* (New York: Harper & Row, 1961).

[10]Martin F. Rosenman, "Serendipity and Scientific Discovery," *Journal of Creative Behavior* 22, No. 2 (1988): 132–138.

successfully develop their best ideas, and in some cases entrepreneurs will take the idea in an entirely different direction or discover a new and more workable ideal while struggling to implement the original idea. Another important part of this phase is to rework ideas to get them into final form. Because an idea frequently emerges from Phase 3 in rough form, it needs to be modified or tested in order to put it in final shape. Some of the most useful suggestions for carrying out this phase are to increase your energy level with proper exercise, diet, and rest; educate yourself in the business planning process and all facets of business; test your ideas with knowledgeable people; take notice of your intuitive hunches and feelings; educate yourself about the selling process; learn about organizational policies and practices; seek advice from others; and view the problems that you encounter while implementing your ideas as challenges.[11]

New Venture Assessment: Critical Factors

A number of critical factors are important in new venture assessment. One way to identify and evaluate them is with the help of a checklist (see Table 2.1). In most cases, however, such a questionnaire approach is too general; the assessment must be tailor-made for the specific venture.

A new venture progresses through three specific phases: prestart-up, start-up, and poststart-up. The prestart-up phase begins with an idea for the venture and ends when the doors are opened for business; the start-up phase commences with initiation of sales activity and delivery of products and/or services and ends when the business is firmly established and beyond short-term threats to survival; and the poststart-up phase lasts until the venture is terminated or the surviving organizational entity is no longer controlled by an entrepreneur.

This chapter focuses on the prestart-up and start-up phases, since these are critical segments for entrepreneurs. Five critical factors can determine the venture's success or failure during these two phases: (1) the relative **uniqueness** of the venture, (2) the relative **investment** size at start-up, (3) the **expected growth** of sales and/or profits as the venture moves through its start-up phase, (4) the **availability of products,** and (5) the **availability of customers.**

Uniqueness

A new venture's range of uniqueness can be considerable, extending from fairly routine to highly nonroutine. The amount of innovation required during prestart-up separates the routine from the nonroutine, and this distinction is based on the need for new-process technology to produce services or products and/or on the need to service new-market segments. Venture uniqueness is further characterized by the length of time a nonroutine venture remains nonroutine. For instance, will new products, new technology, and new markets be required on a continuing basis? Or

---

[11]For more on implementation, see John M. Keil, *The Creative Mystique: How to Manage It, Nurture It, and Make It Pay* (New York: Wiley, 1985). See also James F. Brandowski, *Corporate Imagination Plus: Five Steps to Translating Innovative Strategies into Action* (New York: The Free Press, 1990).

Table 2.1   **A New-Venture Idea Checklist**

Basic Feasibility of the Venture

1. Can the product or service work?
2. Is it legal?

Competitive Advantages of the Venture

1. What specific competitive advantages will the product or service offer?
2. What are the competitive advantages of the companies already in business?
3. How are the competitors likely to respond?
4. How will the initial competitive advantage be maintained?

Buyer Decisions in the Venture

1. Who are the customers likely to be?
2. How much will each customer buy and how many customers are there?
3. Where are these customers located and how will they be serviced?   ˎ

Marketing of the Goods and Services

1. How much will be spent on advertising and selling?
2. What share of market will the company capture? By when?
3. Who will perform the selling functions?
4. How will prices be set? How will they compare with the competition's prices?
5. How important is location, and how will it be determined?
6. What distribution channels will be used—wholesale, retail, agents, direct mail?
7. What are the sales targets? By when should they be met?
8. Can any orders be obtained before starting the business? How many? For what total amount?

Production of the Goods and Services

1. Will the company make or buy what it sells? Or will it be a combination of these two strategies?
2. Are there sources of supply available at reasonable prices?
3. How long will delivery take?
4. Have adequate lease arrangements for premises been made?

will the venture be able to "settle down" after the start-up period and use existing products, technologies, and markets?

Investment

The capital investment required to start a new venture can vary considerably. In some industries less than $50,000 may be required, whereas in other industries millions of dollars are necessary. Moreover, in some industries only large-scale start-ups are feasible. For example, in the retail industry one can start a small venture with a small capital investment that can remain small or grow into a larger venture. By contrast, an entrepreneur attempting to break into the airline industry needs a considerable up-front investment.

Another critical finance-related issue is the extending and timing of funds needed to move through the venture process. To determine the amount of investment needed, questions such as these must be answered: Will industry growth be sufficient to maintain break-even sales to cover a high fixed-cost structure during the start-up period? Do the principal entrepreneurs have access to substantial financial reserves to protect a large initial investment? Do the entrepreneurs have the appropriate contacts to take advantage of various environmental opportunities? Do the entrepre-

Table 2.1   *continued*

5. Can the needed equipment be available on time?
6. Are there any special problems with plant setup, clearances, or insurance? How will they be resolved?
7. How will quality be controlled?
8. How will returns and servicing be handled?
9. How will pilferage, waste, spoilage, and scrap be controlled?

Staffing Decisions in the Venture

1. How will competence in each area of the business be ensured?
2. Who will have to be hired? By when? How will they be found and recruited?
3. Will a banker, lawyer, accountant, or other advisers be needed?
4. How will replacements be obtained if key people leave?
5. Will special benefit plans have to be arranged?

Control of the Venture

1. What records will be needed? When?
2. Will any special controls be required? What are they? Who will be responsible for them?

Financing the Venture

1. How much will be needed for development of the product or service?
2. How much will be needed for setting up operations?
3. How much will be needed for working capital?
4. Where will the money come from? What if more is needed?
5. Which assumptions in the financial forecasts are most uncertain?
6. What will be the return on equity, or sales, and how does it compare with the industry?
7. When and how will investors get their money back?
8. What will be needed from the bank, and what is the bank's response?

Source: Karl H. Vesper, *New Venture Strategies,* © 1990, p. 172. Adapted by permission of Prentice-Hall, Inc., Englewood Cliffs, New Jersey.

neurs have both industry and entrepreneurial track records that justify the financial risk of a large-scale start-up?[12]

Sales Growth

Sales growth in the start-up phase is another critical factor. Key questions to ask include: What is the anticipated growth pattern for new-venture sales and profits? Are sales and profits expected to grow slowly or level off shortly after start-up? Are large profits expected at some point with only small or moderate sales growth? Or are both high-sales growth and high-profit growth likely? Or will there be limited initial profits with eventual high-profit growth over a multiyear period? In answering these questions, it is important to remember that most ventures fit into one of the three following classifications.

The primary driving forces of **lifestyle ventures** are independence, autonomy, and control. Neither large sales nor profits are important beyond providing an adequate, comfortable living for the entrepreneur.

[12]Robert C. Ronstadt, *Entrepreneurship* (Dover, MA: Lord Publishing, 1984), 74.

In **smaller profitable ventures,** financial considerations play a major role. Autonomy and control are also important in the sense that the entrepreneur does not want venture sales (and employment) to become so large that he or she must relinquish equity or ownership position, thus giving up control over cash flow and profits, which, it is hoped, will be substantial.

In **high-growth ventures,** significant sales and profit growth are expected to the extent that it may be possible to attract venture capital money and/or funds raised through public or private placements.[13]

Product Availability

Product availability and the availability of a salable good or service are essential to the success of any venture at the time the venture opens its doors. Some ventures have problems in this regard because the product or service is still in development and needs further modification or testing. Other ventures find that they bring their products to market too soon so they must be recalled for additional work. A typical example is a software firm that rushes the development of its product and is then besieged by customers who find bugs in the program. Lack of product availability in finished form can affect the company's image and its bottom line.

Customer Availability

If a product is available before the venture is started, the odds are greater that the venture will be successful. Similarly, venture risk is affected by customer availability at start-up. At one end of the risk continuum is a venture that has customers who are willing to pay cash for products or services before delivery. At the other end of the continuum is the enterprise that gets started without knowing exactly who will buy its product. A critical consideration is how long it will take to determine who the customers are and what they buying habits are. As Ronstadt notes:

> The decision to ignore the market is an extremely risky one. There are, after all, two fundamental criteria for entrepreneurial success. The first is having a customer who is willing to pay you a profitable price for a product or a service. The second is that you must actually produce and deliver the product or service. The farther a venture removes itself from certainty about these two rules, the greater the risk and the greater the time required to offset this risk as the venture moves through the prestart-up and start-up periods.[14]

The Environment for New Ventures

There are many ways to make an environmental assessment for a new venture, but, generally, these approaches are neither highly sophisticated nor heavily quantitative.[15] Being neither an economist nor a quantitative analyst, the average new-

---

[13]Adapted from Ronstadt, *Entrepreneurship,* 75.

[14]Ibid., 79.

[15]Andrew H. Van de Ven, "The Development of an Infrastructure for Entrepreneurship," *Journal of Business Venturing* (May 1993): 211–230.

venture entrepreneur will stay within the confines of what he or she understands and can use to conduct an assessment. This often entails evaluating the general environment and compiling a detailed evaluation of the industry with primary consideration given to such areas as common industry characteristics, barriers to entry, and competitive analysis.

Evaluation of the industry environment is a critical step in the overall economic assessment of a new venture. Many major elements of industry structure exist and an assessment of the entire industry structure can be detailed and comprehensive.[16] For our purposes here, however, we shall examine only those segments of which entrepreneurs need to be aware.

Common Industry Characteristics

Although industries vary in size and development, certain characteristics are common to new and emerging industries. The most important of these characteristics are discussed next.

Technological Uncertainty   There is usually a great deal of uncertainty about the technology of an emerging industry: What product configuration will ultimately prove to be the best? Which production technology will prove to be the most efficient? How difficult will it be to develop this technology? How difficult will it be to copy technological breakthroughs in the industry?

Strategic Uncertainty   Related to technological uncertainty is a wide variety of strategic approaches often tried by industry participants. Since no "right" strategy has been clearly identified, industry participants formulate different approaches to product positioning, advertising, pricing, and the like, as well as to different product configurations or production technologies.

First-Time Buyers   Buyers of an emerging industry's products or services are first-time buyers. The marketing task is thus one of substitution, or getting the buyer to make the initial purchase of the new product or service.

Short-Time Horizons   The pressure to develop customers or produce products to meet demand is so great in many emerging industries that bottlenecks and problems are dealt with expediently rather than on the basis of an analysis of future conditions.[17] Short-run results are often given major attention, while long-run results are given too little consideration.

---

[16]See, for example, Michael E. Porter, *Competitive Strategy* (New York: Free Press, 1980); Michael E. Porter, *Competitive Advantage* (New York: Free Press, 1985); and Michael E. Porter, "From Competitive Advantage to Corporate Strategy," *Harvard Business Review* (May–June 1987): 43–59.

[17]For a detailed discussion of this topic, see Porter, *Competitive Strategy;* and Michael E. Porter and Victor E. Millar, "How Information Gives You Competitive Advantage," *Harvard Business Review* (July–August 1985): 149–160.

Barriers to Entry   In addition to the structural hurdles an emerging industry faces, there are also barriers to entry. These barriers may include proprietary technology (expensive to access), access to distribution channels (limited or closed to newcomers), access to raw materials and other inputs (e.g., skilled labor), cost disadvantages due to lack of experience (magnified by technological and competitive uncertainties), or risk (which raises the effective opportunity cost of capital).

Some of these barriers decline or disappear as the industry develops; however, it is still important for entrepreneurs to be aware of them.

Competitive Analysis   Analyzing the competition in the industry involves consideration of the number of competitors as well as the strength of each. Both the quality and quantity of the competition must be carefully scrutinized.

When assessing the competition, it is important to keep in mind that various elements affect the profile. Figure 2.1 illustrates the components of a competitive analysis from the standpoint of (1) what drives the competition and (2) what the competition can do. The competition's current strategy and future goals help dictate its response. So too will the assumptions that each competitor has about itself as well as its perceived strengths and weaknesses.

Figure 2.1   **Components of a Competitive Analysis**

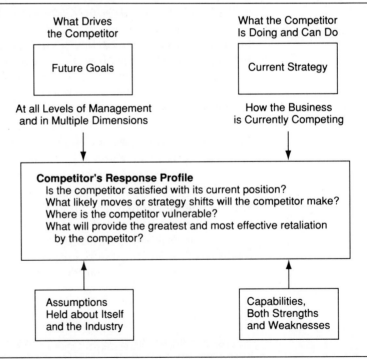

Source: Adapted with permission of The Free Press, a division of Macmillan, Inc., from *Competitive Strategy: Techniques for Analyzing Industries and Competitors* by Michael E. Porter, p. 49. Copyright © 1980 by The Free Press.

This figure provides a framework that allows an entrepreneur to better assess the competition. A good competitive analysis is vital to the ultimate success of any new venture.

The Right Steps for Industry Analysis

There are a number of useful steps that can assist an entrepreneur in examining an industry. Following are five of the most helpful:

1. *Clearly define the industry for the new venture.* The key here is to develop a relevant definition that describes the focus of the new venture. Definitions will vary, of course, depending on the venture and its specific target market. The more clearly the entrepreneur can define the industry for the new venture, the better the chance that the venture will get off to a sound start.

2. *Analyze the competition.* An analysis of the number, relative size, traditions, and cost structures of direct competitors in the industry can help establish the nature of the competition. Will competition become more or less intense as the number and characteristics of competitors change over time? This question can also be answered through detailed analysis. For instance, what will happen to the degree of competition if (a) market growth increases rapidly, (b) direct competitors equalize in size, (c) one or two direct competitors become substantially larger in size, or (d) product/service differentiation slows down?

3. *Determine the strength and characteristics of suppliers.* The important factor here is to establish the stance of the venture in relation to suppliers. How will the new firm be treated compared to other, more established firms? Is there a choice of many suppliers offering diverse services or must the new venture be prepared to accept limited services from a few?

4. *Establish the "value added" measure of the new venture.* The concept of *value added* is a basic form of contribution analysis in which sales minus raw material costs equal the value added. The purpose behind this measure is to determine how much value is being added to the product or service by the entrepreneur. This introduces the concept of integration, backward or forward. Backward integration is a buyer's movement to acquire supplier services. Forward integration is a supplier's movement to absorb the duties of a buyer. The likelihood of integration taking place is substantially determined by the degree to which value added is essential to the final processing and consumption by the user.

5. *Project the market size for the particular industry.* Markets are dynamic and prone to change over time. Therefore, it is important to examine the historical progression of the market, establish its present size, and extrapolate the data to project the likely potential of market growth. This can be done by studying the industry life cycle, consumers (numbers and trends), product/service developments, and competitive analysis.

These five key points are not all-inclusive; however, they do represent an initial analysis of the industry environment faced by a new venture. This type of macro analysis is needed to establish the framework within which a venture will start, grow, and, it is hoped, prosper.

The Evaluation Process

A critical task in starting a new-business enterprise is to determine the feasibility of the product or service idea getting off the ground by solid analysis and evaluation. Entrepreneurs must put their ideas through this analysis to discover if they contain any fatal flaws.

Ask the Right Questions

Many important evaluation-related questions should be asked. Ten sets of preliminary questions that can be used to screen an idea are presented here.

1. Is it a new product or service idea? Is it proprietary? Can it be patented or copyrighted? Is it unique enough to get a significant head start on the competition? Or can it be easily copied?
2. Has a prototype been tested by independent testers who try to blow the system or rip the product to shreds? What are its weak points? Will it stand up? What level of research and development should it receive over the next five years? If it is a service, has it been tested on customers? Will customers pay their hard-earned money for it?
3. Has it been taken to trade shows? If so, what reactions did it receive? Were any sales made? Has it been taken to distributors? Have they placed any orders?
4. Is the product or service easily understood by customers, bankers, venture capitalists, accountants, lawyers, and insurance agents?
5. What is the overall market? What are the market segments? Can the product penetrate these segments? Are there special niches that can be exploited?
6. Has market research been conducted? Who else comprises the market? How big is the market? How fast is it growing? What are the trends? What is the projected life cycle of the product or service? What degree of penetration can be achieved? Are there any testimonials from customers and purchasing agents? What type of advertising and promotion plans will be used?
7. What distribution and sales methods will be used—jobbers, independent sales representatives, company sales force, direct mail, door-to-door sales, supermarkets, service stations, company-owned stores? How will the product be transported: company-owned trucks, common carriers, postal service, or air freight?
8. How will the product be made? How much will it cost? For example, will it be produced in-house or by others? Will production be by job shop or continuous process? What is the present capacity of company facilities? What is the break-even point?
9. Will the business concept be developed and licensed to others, or developed and sold away?
10. Can the company get, or has it already lined up, the necessary skills to operate the business venture? Who are the workers? Are they dependable and competent? How much capital will be needed now? How much more in the future? Have major stages in financing been developed.[18]

---

[18]John G. Burch, *Entrepreneurship* (New York: Wiley, 1986), 68–69.

Feasibility Criteria Approach

A single strategic variable seldom shapes the ultimate success or failure of a new venture. In most situations a combination of variables influences the outcome. Thus, it is important that these variables be identified and investigated before the new idea is put into practice. The results of a feasibility criteria approach enables the entrepreneur to judge the business's potential.

The feasibility criteria approach, developed as a criteria selection list from which entrepreneurs can gain insights into the viability of their venture, is based on the following questions.

Is It Proprietary? The product does not have to be patented, but it should be sufficiently proprietary to permit a long head start against competitors and a period of extraordinary profits early in the venture to offset start-up costs.

Are the Initial Production Costs Realistic? Most estimates are too low. A careful, detailed analysis should be made so that there are no large unexpected expenses.

Are the Initial Marketing Costs Realistic? This answer requires the entrepreneur to identify target markets, market channels, and promotion strategy.

Does the Product Have Potential for Very High Margins? This is almost a necessity for a fledgling company. The financial community understands gross margins, and without high margins, funding can be difficult.

Is the Time Required to Get to Market and to Reach Break Even Realistic? In most cases faster is better. In all cases the venture plan is tied to this answer, and an error here can spell trouble later on.

Is the Potential Market Large? In determining the potential market, one must look three to five years into the future because some markets take this long to emerge. The cellular telephone, for example, had an annual demand of approximately 400,000 units in 1982. However, by 1992 this market had grown by 700,000 units annually.

Is the Product the First of a Growing Family? If it is, the venture is more attractive to investors because if a large return is not made on the first product, it might be made on the second, third, or fourth product.

Is There an Initial Customer? Financial backers are impressed when a venture can list its first ten customers by name. This pent-up demand also means that the first quarter's results are likely to be good and the focus of attention can be directed to later quarters.

Are Development Costs and Calendar Times Realistic? Preferably, they are zero. A ready-to-go product give the venture a big advantage over competitors. If there are costs, they should be complete and detailed and tied to a month-by-month schedule.

Is This a Growing Industry?   This is not absolutely essential if profits and company growth are evident, but there is less room for mistakes. In a growing industry, good companies do even better.

Is the Product and the Need for It Understood by the Financial Community?   If financiers can grasp the concept and its value, chances for funding will increase. For example, a portable heart-monitoring system for postcoronary patient monitoring is a product that many will understand. Undoubtedly, some of those hearing the presentation for the product will have already had coronaries or heart problems of some sort.[19]

This criteria selection approach provides a means of analyzing the internal strengths and weaknesses that exist in a new venture by focusing on the marketing and industry potential that is critical to assessment. If the new venture meets fewer than six of these criteria, it typically lacks feasibility for funding. If the new venture meets seven or more of the criteria, it may stand a good chance of being funded.

Comprehensive Feasibility Approach

A more comprehensive and systematic feasibility analysis, a comprehensive feasibility approach, incorporates external factors in addition to those outlined in the questions above. Figure 2.2 presents a breakdown of the factors involved in a critical feasibility study of a new venture: technical, market, financial, organizational, and competitive. A more detailed feasibility analysis guide is provided in Table 2.2, which identifies the specific activities involved in each feasibility area. Although all five of the areas presented in Figure 2.2 are important, two merit special attention: technical and market.

Technical Feasibility

An entrepreneur should evaluate a new-venture idea by first identifying the technical requirements—the technical feasibility—for producing a product or service that

Figure 2.2   **Key Areas in Assessing the Feasibility of a New Venture**

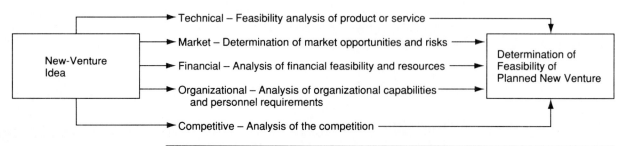

[19]Gordon B. Baty, *Entrepreneurship: Playing to Win* (Reston, VA: Reston Publishing, 1974), 33–34.

Table 2.2
Specific Activities of Feasibility Analyses

Technical Feasibility Analysis	Market Feasibility Analysis	Financial Feasibility Analysis	Analysis of Organizational Capabilities	Competitive Analysis
Crucial Technical Specifications	*Market Potential*	*Required Financial Resources for*	*Personnel Requirements*	*Existing Competitors*
Design	Identification of potential customers and their dominant characteristics (e.g., age, income level, buying habits)	Fixed assets	Required skills levels and other personal characteristics of potential employees	Size, financial resources, market entrenchment
Durability		Current assets		
Reliability		Necessary working capital	Managerial requirements	Potential reaction of competitors to newcomer by means of price cutting, aggressive advertising, introduction of new products, etc.
Product safety	Potential market share (as affected by competitive situation)	*Available Financial Resources*	Determination of individual responsibilities	
Standardization				
Engineering Requirements		Required borrowing	Determination of required organizational relationships	
Machines	Potential sales volume	Potential sources for funds		Potential new competitors
Tools	Sales price projections		Potential organizational development	
Instruments	*Market Testing*	Cost of borrowing		
Work flow	Selection of test	Repayment conditions	Competitive analysis	
Product Development	Actual market test	Operation cost analysis		
Blueprints	Analysis of market	Fixed costs		
Models	*Marketing Planning Issues*	Variable costs		
Prototypes	Preferred channels of distribution, impact of promotional efforts, required distribution points (warehouses), packaging considerations, price differentiation	Projected cash flow		
Product Testing		Projected profitability		
Lab testing				
Field testing				
Plant Location				
Desirable characteristics of plant size (proximity to suppliers, customers), environmental regulations				

Source: Hans Schollhammer and Arthur H. Kuriloff, *Entrepreneurship and Small Business Management* (New York: Wiley, 1979), 56.

will satisfy the expectations of potential customers. The most important of these are:

- Functional design of the product and attractiveness in appearance.
- Flexibility, permitting ready modification of the external features of the product to meet customer demands or technological and competitive changes.
- Durability of the materials from which the product is made.
- Reliability, ensuring performance as expected under normal operating conditions.

- Product safety, posing no potential dangers under normal operating conditions.
- Reasonable utility, an acceptable rate of obsolescence.
- Ease and low cost of maintenance.
- Standardization through elimination of unnecessary variety among potentially interchangeable parts.
- Ease of processing or manufacture.
- Ease in handling and use.[20]

The results of this investigation provide a basis for deciding whether a new venture is feasible from a technical point of view.

Marketability

Assembling and analyzing relevant information about the marketability of a new venture is vital in judging its potential success. Three major areas in this type of analysis include (1) investigating the full market potential and identifying customers (or users) for the goods or service, (2) analyzing the extent to which the enterprise might exploit this potential market, and (3) using market analysis to determine the opportunities and risks associated with the venture. To address these areas, a variety of information sources must be found and used. General sources for a market feasibility analysis would include:

- *General economic* trends—various economic indicators such as new orders, housing starts, inventories, and consumer spending.
- *Market data*—customers, customer demand patterns (e.g., seasonal variations in demand, governmental regulations affecting demand).
- *Pricing data*—range of prices for the same, complementary, and substitute products, base prices, and discount structures.
- *Competitive data*—major competitors and their competitive strength.

It is important to note the value of marketing research in the overall assessment and evaluation of a new venture.[21]

Thus, as demonstrated by Table 2.2, the comprehensive feasibility analysis approach is closely related to the preparation of a thorough business plan (covered in detail in Chapter 3). The approach clearly illustrates the need to evaluate each segment of the venture before initiating the business or presenting it to capital sources.

---

[20]Hans Schollhammer and Arthur H. Kuriloff, *Entrepreneurship and Small Business Management* (New York: Wiley, 1979), 58.

[21]Gerald E. Hills, "Marketing Analysis in the Business Plan: Venture Capitalists' Perceptions," *Journal of Small Business Management* (January 1985): 38–46. *See also* Gerald E. Hills and Raymond W. LaForge, "Research at the Marketing Interface To Advance Entrepreneurship Theory," *Entrepreneurship Theory and Practice* (Spring 1992): 33–60.

CASE • *Splatterball Adventure Games, Inc.*

Beth Jack and Marilyn M. Helms, The University of Tennessee at Chattanooga

Splatterball Adventure Games, Inc. conducts paintball games in the Chattanooga, Tennessee, area. The company also maintains a store located in East Ridge, Tennessee, approximately five miles outside of the Chattanooga city limits. The playing field location for the game is in Apison, Tennessee, approximately 20 miles form Chattanooga.

As of 1992, Splatterball has one principal, Mr. Doug Gray, who runs all aspects of the business including monitoring the games, conducting sales, bookkeeping, and gun repair.

What Is Paintball?

Paintball became popular nationally in the early 1980s and includes both amateur and professional players in the sport. The development of the professional player occurred in the late 1980s. Like other sports, professional status is obtained when players earn money for playing paintball. In the case of paintball, money is earned by winning tournaments. Some of these tournaments have first place prizes as high as $30,000 for a ten-member team. For a team to be designated as a professional team, three-fifths of the members must be professional players.

Paintball is played mainly in the United States. Mr. Gray estimates there are approximately 300 fields across the United States. There are some fields located around the world. It is difficult to know exactly how many fields do exist outside the United States because many are located in countries that consider the guns used in paintball illegal.

The development of the sport has also led to the development of standard governing. Although several different governing organizations do exist, the most prevalent is the International Paintball Player's Association (IPPA). This organization was set up to create tournament and field guidelines. It also monitors any pending legislation that may be harmful to the industry and attempts to bring together the participants in paintball to prevent any adverse actions.

There are several variations in the way paintball is played. These variations depend on the location of the field, the type of field, and the field operator. However, because tournaments usually follow the IPPA rules, these are the guidelines most commonly followed in field operations.

There is some standard equipment for all players. Comfortable clothing and shoes for running through the obstacles are required. Many people choose to wear camouflage although it is not necessary. All players must wear protective eye goggles whenever on the field. Also required are the guns, carbon dioxide tanks, and paintballs. All of the equipment, with the exception of the clothing, can be bought or rented from the field operator.

Additional equipment used by regular players includes semiautomatic guns, gun cleaners, replacement parts for guns, vests, and speedloaders. This equipment is allowed in tournament play and is used to increase the playing ability of the players. It can be ordered from vendors across the country or purchased from paintball specialty stores.

Games are usually played in densely wooded areas. This gives players obstacles to hide behind and adds to the difficulty of the game. The games can be played in backyards; however there are usually not enough obstacles for effective play. Paintball is not played in parks unless prior approval is received from park managers. The paint used in the paintball is water-based, but it still leaves marks on trees and other obstacles until there is enough rain to wash the paint away. The paint used is environmentally safe. Also, the plastic casing around the paintball will be left behind.

The object of paintball is to capture the opponent's flag and return it to your own flag station. The flags remain at the flag stations until a member of the opposing team captures it. These flag stations are simply a small area from which a flag is hung from a tree or some type of pole placed in the clearing. The area around the flag station varies from field to field. In some cases there will be natural barrier from which a player can defend the station. In other cases it is wide and open and must be defended from its perimeter. If the person who has captured the flag is shot while carrying the flag, the flag is considered "dead." That individual must return the flag to its original station and it then must be recaptured by another team member. It cannot simply be transferred to another teammate.

There are two main differences between tournament play and casual play. In casual play the team returning the captured flag to its own station wins the game. However, in tournament play teams advance through round-robin brackets in a point system. Points are awarded for the number of opposing players shot, first flag pulled, and returning the flag to one's own flag station. There are point penalties for safety violations, foul or abusive language, and physical contact during a game. The maximum number of points awarded is 100.

Each member of the team carries a carbon dioxide-based gun that shoots the paintball. The original guns were pressed plastic with few moving parts. The carbon dioxide came in small metal tubes that were pierced when inserted into the gun and would shoot approximately 20 to 30 rounds of paintballs. The guns now used have become more complicated with more moving parts. These guns are made of metal and often more closely resemble real guns. Manufacturers have begun the introduction of new types of guns such as semiautomatics. The carbon dioxide used in the guns can be obtained in refillable tanks and can be used for an entire game.

The paintballs are about the size of a marble. They were originally made of oil-based paint enclosed in a thin plastic shell. This quickly changed because once this paint dried onto clothing, it was extremely difficult to get out. The paintballs are now water-based so the paint can easily be washed out. They come in a wide variety of colors. However, most fields avoid using red so injuries are not mistaken for paint. The manufacturing process for the paintball is constantly being improved so that a more uniform ball can be made for better accuracy.

Professional teams have developed from 15-member teams to 10- and 5-member teams. This development has occurred so that games could be played under a 45-minute time limit.

Amateur games, usually played on weekends, are not as strict about time limits and the number of members on a team. Usually the field operator will split individuals up to form two to four teams, depending on the number of people at the field. They try not to allow more than 25 players on a team, if possible. Games are usually limited to one hour, although amateur games tend to end within 30 minutes.

The typical paintball player is male. There are some females who play as amateurs and a few on professional teams. The average professional player is 22–35 years old. The average casual player is 18–30. Players come from a wide variety of backgrounds including professional managers, physicians, blue-collar workers, and students.

Tournaments are sponsored year round in the United States. A tournament circuit holds games in San Francisco, Chicago, and two in Nashville. The most prestigious tournament takes place every October in Nashville, Tennessee. This tournament, the International Masters Tournament, is the biggest of its kind with a 64-team field and a $30,000 first prize. This tournament lasts five days and includes both five-member and ten-member team competitions. This tournament usually includes at least two British teams every year. The top eight finishers of this tournament are able to get sponsorship from manufacturers of paintball equipment. This tournament is also a chance for vendors to display their new products and innovations to the players.

History of Splatterball Adventure Games, Inc.

Splatterball Adventure Games, Inc. is located in Chattanooga, Tennessee, and runs local paintball games. Also, it has a store that sells some paintball supplies and repairs guns. It is through this store that many of the games are scheduled.

The owner of Splatterball, Doug Gray, began his involvement with the sport of paintball in 1981. He was a member of a small team based out of Chattanooga. Shortly after joining, the team moved to Nashville when the field they were using was sold and was no longer available for their use. Many of the players lived in Nashville at that time, so they decided to open a field in Nashville rather than look for a new field in Chattanooga. The team in Nashville became known as the Nashville Ridgerunners. Mr. Gray is still an active member of the Nashville Ridgerunners Professional Paintball Team.

Because there was no longer a field in Chattanooga, Mr. Gray drove two hours to Nashville almost every weekend to play the sport. It was during these trips that he decided to open a field of his own in Chattanooga so he could practice closer to home.

Mr. Gray began to get his friends and acquaintances to go to Nashville with him in order to generate interest. Eventually, he was able to get enough people interested in paintball to support his field in Chattanooga.

Mr. Gray leased a parcel of land approximately 20 miles southeast of Chattanooga. According to Mr. Gray, "Since this was more of a hobby than business, I decided to run the operations from my home." He bought some of the plastic guns to use for rentals so he could continue to bring in new players to his field.

During this time the field in Nashville became very successful at organizing paintball tournaments. Many tournaments were organized to bring in teams from the southeast region. Mr. Gray worked closely with the Nashville field in setting up his own field. His close ties enabled him to obtain many of his supplies at volume discount prices, as well as gain other advantages that would otherwise have been denied to him as an independent.

Mr. Gray's business continued to grow as paintball began to receive more attention nationally. Businesses and groups began to schedule games for their members only. As his business expanded, Mr. Gray began to carry more rental equipment and supplies for the part-time player.

Eventually the business grew so large it became difficult to manage from his home. The rental equipment took up so much room that he decided it was time to establish a center of operations. However, in order to make this feasible, Mr. Gray needed an infusion of capital for the store lease, furniture lease, and the addition of even more equipment. He figured the total cost would run approximately $7,500. It was at this time that he took in one partner and the business incorporated with each partner owning 500 shares of stock.

Unfortunately, the partnership was not successful. Both partners had differing ideas on how the income should be distributed. Mr. Gray wanted most of the money reinvested into the business for further growth. However, his partner decided he wanted his capital infusion paid back immediately. After one year the partnership was dissolved through Mr. Gray's purchase of his partner's 500 shares of stock for $11,000. The original investment was $10,000 and his partner had received approximately $1,200 in capital withdrawals when the repurchase was made.

The Situation in 1992

As of 1992, Mr. Gray is the sole stockholder of Splatterball and he has decided to reevaluate what he is trying to accomplish. What is the future of Splatterball? Where is he trying to go with the business? How does he get there?

The business itself is quickly becoming a full-time operation. The hours of operation of the store are currently 11:00 a.m. to 3:00 p.m. Monday through Friday. It is only open on weekends if no games are being played at the field. Mr. Gray would like to increase the hours of operation but currently is not in the position to do so. Mr. Gray has a full-time job as a computer programmer and he works 4:00 p.m. to 12:15 a.m. Monday through Friday. Eventually he would like to leave this position and have the business as his main source of income.

The store does bring some walk-in business, often from people who play the game on their own land. Mr Gray offers a gun repair service on the premises. He is able to sell guns, supplies, and trade magazines at the store. Most of Splatterball's income is derived from the games. The field is available all year but games are scheduled in advance, especially during the winter months. With scheduling, the proper amount of supplies can be ordered and the appropriate number of field judges can be obtained. Splatterball only keeps 100 rental guns in stock, so if extremely large groups play, Mr. Gray has to borrow guns from another field. He has worked out an agreement with a field in Atlanta in which each field makes guns available to the other at no charge.

Splatterball has its own professional and amateur teams that play regularly at the Splatterball field and in national tournaments. These teams were started in

1990 and have no sponsorship. There is no fee to become a member as each member is responsible for all tournament entry fees and supplies. Mr. Gray relies heavily on his professional team members to give their support in running the store and in officiating games when they are not playing. Their compensation is in the form of discounts on supplies and gun repairs. New members are recruited from individuals playing the game with a group who have decided that they would like to play on a regular basis. These individuals will generally play with the team for six months before becoming a team member.

Currently, almost all of the games are scheduled on Saturday and Sunday mornings and afternoons. Groups schedule the field for an entire day. It is also possible for Mr. Gray to run the games during the week before 2:00. Splatterball continues to run walk-on games on weekends, enabling individuals to try paintball without having to find other players to make up two teams. In addition to the typical player, Mr. Gray has some school groups that regularly rent the field for an entire day.

As previously mentioned, Mr. Gray has been involved with paintball since 1981. His business background includes several years of college courses and his own trial-and-error experience when he first started Splatterball. He has taken a small-business management course at a local junior college, but feels that he learned the most about management from starting the business. When asked about his management style, Mr. Gray says, "Currently I am a doer out of necessity, but I am a delegator by nature. I am great at long-range planning and I need to be careful not to forget the small daily details that keep me in business."

The Competition

Splatterball's competition is primarily from the amusement industry and other paintball fields. Movies, music, and sport hunting are just three examples of the competition. Also, because of the great deal of physical activity involved, Mr. Gray feels he competes for the physical fitness dollar as well.

Competition between the paintball fields is actually very friendly. The closest fields to Chattanooga are in Atlanta, Knoxville, and Nashville. Each of these fields is approximately a two-hour drive from Chattanooga. Because there are no fields close by, he does not compete directly with them for local players. Instead he has worked out arrangements with many of them that enable each of them to host all of the participating regional teams in a league play. This league has ten teams from Chattanooga, Nashville, Atlanta, and Birmingham. Ten times a year, all the teams meet at different fields to play each other. This was set up to give each of the teams a chance to play different types of fields with a higher level of competition. Although a trophy is awarded to the team accumulating the most points at the end of a calendar year, the main purpose of this league is to provide a higher level of practice for the major tournaments. Most of the fields in this league are about the same size as Mr. Gray's, with the exception of the Nashville field. The Nashville field is able to handle approximately three to four times the size of the Splatterball field. Also, the Nashville field has an agreement with a local campground to use the campgrounds for major tournaments in the spring and the fall. As it is privately held, the exact earnings are unknown, but it is estimated to be around $1 million annually, including field operations, store operations, and tournaments.

In competing with the physical fitness activity, Splatterball has actually been able to work in cooperation with different programs. The game has been included as an activity in an intensive six-week fitness program in Chattanooga. This program is used to build self-confidence as well as physical fitness.

Splatterball also competes with the hobby/entertainment industry in general. Often it can be heard around the field that someone played that weekend instead of hunting or buying some personal item.

Costs

The cost of playing Splatterball depends on the experience of the player. Novice players will generally have lower costs, because they rent their equipment. Mr. Gray typically charges a $22.52 flat field fee which includes the $12 gun rental, 40 rounds of paint, and one small tank of carbon dioxide. Novice players generally shoot less than more experienced players and often do not have to purchase extra paint. The typical charge is $1.08 for one tube of paint (eight rounds).

The experienced player tends to incur much higher costs as most will purchase their own guns, which will start at about $150. Also, there is the purchase of camouflage and other extra equipment to maintain the performance of their equipment. It is not uncommon for an experienced player to shoot up to 30 tubes of paint per game. Since most play a minimum of three 45-minute games, this will add up quickly.

The players that are part of a team will often have expenses on top of those incurred by the experienced player. Many own several guns in case of gun failure. These failures are usually due to wear on parts and do not occur regularly, but if a gun fails during a tournament, then the team is short a player. Also, there is the high entrance fees for tournaments which can be as much as $200 per member.

Financial Situation

Splatterball Adventure Games, Inc. actually has a very "loose" accounting system. However, Mr. Gray has recently had an offer of free accounting services for 100 shares of stock. (Mr. Gray owns 1,000 shares of the 1,500 shares; 500 shares are retained by the business.)

Exhibit 1 shows the current financial statements for the firm. The largest debt is Mr. Gray's repayment of the $11,000 loan used to repurchase the stock from his former partner. Other expenses, such as supplies, can usually be directly matched to the sales since most supplies are received within two days of use. This helps eliminate spoilage of the supplies. The paintballs have a shelf life of several months, but they do tend to become soft. The sooner they are used, the better they perform.

Mr. Gray has also had on offer from two of the members of his team to work for 150 shares of stock each in the business. These players have helped Mr. Gray run Splatterball for two years. Neither would invest any money at this time but instead would reinvest their share of the profits plus provide free services. They would be able to assist in running the games and working in the store to increase its hours of operations. Both are experienced in gun repair and would be able to assist in this aspect of the business, as well. One is a computer programmer with a college degree in this field and the other assists in the management of his family's convenience store. The other individual is an accountant who will contribute free accounting and tax services to Splatterball. Both individuals would be able to work

Exhibit 1

Splatterball Adventure Games, Inc.
Income Statement
For the Quarter Ending
December 31, 1991

INCOME	
Sales	7,107.00
Net Sales	7,107.00
COST OF GOODS SOLD	
Total Cost of Goods Sold	0.00
Gross Profit	7,107.00
EXPENSES	
Advertising	2,195.00
Auto Expense	15.22
Bank Service Charges	22.50
Bank Wire Transfer Fees	18.00
Casual Labor	175.00
Dues & Subscriptions	58.00
Entertainment	173.28
Entry Fees	278.00
Miscellaneous Expense	190.10
Office Expense	377.69
Paint & CO_2 Supplies	6,280.71
Postage	10.24
Rent	100.00
Field Supplies	1,204.97
Telephone	111.88
Uniforms	128.56
Total Expenses	11,339.15
Net Operating Income	(4,232.15)
OTHER INCOME	
Interest Income	13.00
Total Other Income	13.00
OTHER EXPENSES	
Total Other Expenses	0.00
Income Before Taxes	(4,219.15)
Net Income	(4,219.15)

(continued)

Exhibit 1	*Continued*

Splatterball Adventure Games, Inc.
Balance Sheet
December 31, 1991

ASSETS

CURRENT ASSETS		
Cash	(1,777.58)	
Inventory	260.99	
Total Current Assets		(1,516.59)
FIXED ASSETS		
Office Equipment	189.95	
Paint Guns	8,539.10	
Field Equipment	2,592.25	
Total Fixed Assets		11,321.30
OTHER ASSETS		
Total Other Assets		0.00
Total Assets		9,804.71

LIABILITIES & EQUITY

CURRENT LIABILITIES		
Accounts Payable	1,145.00	
Notes Payable	11,363.26	
Sales Tax Payable	515.60	
Total Current Liabilities		13,023.86
LONG-TERM LIABILITIES		
Total Long-Term Liabilities		0.00
Total Liabilities		13,023.86
STOCKHOLDERS' EQUITY		
Common Stock	1,000.00	
Current Earnings	(4,219.15)	
Total Equity		(3,219.15)
Total Liabilities & Equity		9,804.71

during the hours Mr. Gray is at his full-time job. This is currently under consideration with the attorneys in regards to fair value and distribution of future income through dividends or through salaries.

Legal Environment

The current legal environment is of great concern to Splatterball. Although every player signs a waiver form (see Exhibit 2) each time he or she plays, these waivers have not been tested through a lawsuit. Mr. Gray has had several attorneys review his form and has always received approval.

Injuries are one of the main concerns for Mr. Gray. Last year a new player was hit in the eye with a paintball and lost his vision. This player had taken his goggles

Exhibit 2

SPLATTERBALL ADVENTURE GAMES, INC.

APPLICATION TO PLAY
WAIVER OF LIABILITY AND ASSUMPTION OF RISK

1. I, the undersigned wish to play the Splatterball Adventure game. I recognize and understand that playing the game involves running certain risks. Those risks include, but are not limited to, the risk of injury relating from the impact of the paint pellets used in the Game. Injuries resulting from possible malfunction of equipment used in the Game and injuries resulting from tripping or falling over obstacles in the Game playing field. In addition, I recognize that the exertion of playing the game could result in injury or death.

2. Despite these and other risks, and fully understanding such risks, I wish to play the Game and hereby assume the risks of playing the Game. I also hereby hold harmless Splatterball Adventure Game, Inc., hereafter called the Sponsors, and John Felts (landowner) and indemnify them against any and all claims, actions, suits, procedures, costs, expenses (including attorney's fees and expenses), damages and liabilities arising out of, connected with, or resulting from my playing the Game, including without limitation, those resulting from the manufacture, selection, delivery, possession, use or operation of such equipment. I hereby release the sponsors from any and all such liability, and I understand that this release shall be binding upon my estate, my heirs, my representatives and assigns. I hereby certify to the Sponsors that I am in good health and do not suffer from a heart condition or other ailment which could be exacerbated by the exertion involved in playing the Game.

3. I hereby promise to play the Game only in accordance with the rules of the Game as set forth by the Sponsors. In particular, I agree:

   a. to wear safety goggles at all times when I am on the playing field or at the target area, even after I have been marked with paint or the game is over and to keep the goggles snug by pulling the straps tight; I understand that serious eye injury, including loss of eyesight, could occur if the safety goggles are not on when marking pistols may be discharged anywhere near me. Should my safety goggles fog up or for any reason be such that I cannot see through them properly, I will ask someone near me, on the playing field or in the target area, to lead me out of the area I am into to one where all marking pistols are on "SAFETY". Only then will I remove my safety goggles to clean them. I understand that any "safety goggle" is subject to fogging up or getting dirty and that if I am anywhere near a marking pistol as it discharges, and my "safety goggles" are not properly on, I may get seriously and permanently injured;

   b. to avoid any physical contact or fighting with other players;

   c. to stay within the boundaries of the playing field and not to chase or run after anyone over ledges or mountainous terrain; and

   d. to keep the marking pistol I am using on "safety" (the no-shoot position) in the staging area at all times, in the target area while not shooting and on the playing field before and after each game, to aim or point the pistol at another person ONLY during an active game and never to wave or brandish the pistol about in the staging area or the target area.

   e. to avoid pointing at or shooting at the head of any player at any time.

4. For safety reasons I agree to use only equipment and/or supplies provided to me by the Sponsors while playing the game or in the target area. Written permission of the Sponsors is necessary should I elect to use other equipment or supplies. If I have chosen not to use the goggles or marking pistol available from the Sponsors, I hereby certify that the goggles or

(continued)

Exhibit 2   *Continued*

---

marking pistol, which I have chosen to use, are at least as safe as the Sponsor's form claims arising out of any additional risk resulting from my use of goggles or marking pistol other than those available from the Sponsors.

5. I agree to ask the Sponsor for clarification of any rule or safety procedure, for further instruction as regard anything that I don't understand about the equipment and supplies as regards anything else that may affect the safety of or playing of the Game.

6. I have read this waiver of liability and assumption of risk carefully, and understand that by signing below, I am agreeing, on behalf of myself, my estate, my heirs, representatives and assigns not to sue the Splatterball Adventure Games, Inc. or to hold them or their insurors liable for any injury including death, resulting from my playing the Game, I intend to be fully bound by this Agreement.

By virtue of my signature, I acknowledge and agree to all terms and conditions set forth on this form.

XSignature _____

Date Signed _____

Is this your first visit to our field? YES ( )   NO ( )

---

off even though he had been instructed not to and had signed the waiver stating he would wear the goggles at all times. In this particular instance, Splatterball was very lucky as a spectator had just taken a picture of the injured player not wearing the required safety goggles. This picture prevented a lawsuit for negligence. However, the potential legal problems were brought to the forefront by this incident.

The entire paintball industry has worked very hard to promote safe usage practices both on and off the fields. *Paintball Sports Magazine* has published several articles regarding the usage of guns off the field. Tournaments impose penalties against teams whenever a player is found not to be wearing goggles. Off the field, barrels are required to have plugs in them so that if they accidentally are shot, the paintball breaks in the gun. Field operators also monitor how hard the guns are shooting the paintball. They chronograph the guns to ensure the guns do not shoot so hard as to injure a player who is shot. Even though the guns are carefully monitored, being hit by a paintball will hurt. If shot from a very close range it will leave a bruise and occasionally a small welt. This welt, although painful, usually disappears within 1 to 2 days with no special attention required.

Most fields, including Splatterball, and all tournaments discourage shooting other players in the head. They have simply ruled head shots do not count as "kills" or points. If a player is hit in the head, he or she may call a judge over to help him/her wipe off the paint. The judge will declare the player neutral until the paint is wiped off and then puts the player back into the game.

Whenever new players come out to the field, they are given instructions before the game begins. The field operator will walk over the field with the new player(s) to point out the boundaries and the flag stations. The field operator also points out any areas that players may want to avoid because of potential injury.

The entire industry has also worked together in regards to concerns about their equipment. There have been attempts in several states, most notably California where there are several major fields, to ban the sale of toys that closely resemble guns. This is due to the very publicized shooting of children because someone thought they had real guns. Because the newer guns do closely resemble real guns, the industry is notably concerned.

Teams, field operators, and suppliers have worked together to keep paintball games as safe as possible. Because of the nature of the sport, there are sometimes injuries, but the people involved know that when care and caution are used, most of these injuries can be avoided. These same people have also worked very hard to keep the sport legal in all states through letter-writing campaigns and lobbying.

The Future

Mr. Gray would eventually like to turn Splatterball into his full-time job. Currently he works evenings to supplement his income. He states, "If I could create a larger demand in the off-season, I could depend on Splatterball as my sole source of income."

Because of his expansion, the addition of shareholders to ease the financial burden is another consideration of Mr. Gray's. It would enable Splatterball to run more games, especially during the week.

There is no real marketing strategy in place for Splatterball and Mr. Gray feels it is needed. Although Mr. Gray had some informational brochures printed for distribution, the main source of new business comes from word-of-mouth advertising. Mr. Gray would like to implement a strategy that will not deplete too much of his personal financial resources yet will enable him to work full time in his hobby.

CASE • *The Science Education Company*

Marilyn M. Helms, The University of Tennessee at Chattanooga

Robert Krampf and his wife, Lisa, were visiting with their friend, Michelle Riley, a college professor and business consultant. Michelle had known Robert since childhood and was anxious to help him with his current business hurdle.

"I just don't know where to go next with my business," Robert explained. "Should I hire someone to help me run the day-to-day operations of my company so I can concentrate on my shows, or should I attempt to franchise my business? What do you think?"

After a lengthy discussion with Robert, Michelle began to summarize his business operations in order to put his company into perspective. Robert seemed to have a well-developed idea but was having difficulty in moving the Science Education Company (SEC) into its next stage of operations. At 32, Robert was a thin man with a lively personality and bright expressive eyes hidden behind large glasses. Robert had always been fascinated by science, and as a child was either reading about science, performing experiments, or assembling rocks and fossils for yet another collection. Robert agreed that his lifelong science interest began with dinosaurs. Dinosaurs led to fossils, then to rocks, minerals, chemistry, biology, and physics. His other current interests include science fiction, computers, cooking, traveling, spelunking, and almost anything new or adventurous.

He excelled in high school, graduating at the top of his class. In college, however, Robert was frustrated by all the required classes he had to complete to obtain an undergraduate degree. He wanted to take science courses exclusively. He completed 129 credit hours toward a bachelor's degree at The University of Tennessee at Martin. He quit school with just two semesters to go and moved to Memphis and took a job as a curator at the Pink Palace Museum. Lisa had mentioned that Robert's dislike of details was one of the reasons he never made the effort to finish his degree. He simply felt his time was too valuable to waste on school. Robert began working part time at the museum as a collections geologist, responsible for cataloging and displaying fossils and other rocks. He taught a few fill-in classes on fossils and discovered he liked teaching as much as he liked rocks, and he began teaching geology in the Education Department of the museum. He took students on weekend trips and longer summer "field schools" for the museum. These trips were rewarding to Robert because they got him away from work and let him teach.

He attempted to finish his degree at Memphis State University and he took 47 semester hours at night but he took only science courses he was most interested in. He neglected to take business classes or education classes as well as other required courses needed to complete a degree. He dropped out of college again and began to work full time at the museum where he branched out into teaching biology, archaeology, chemistry, and physics. The many classes ranged from kindergarten to adult groups and were a mixture of lab and field programs. The physics classes led to his development of a high-voltage electric show, which he presented to groups at the museum. He was given more and more teaching duties and responsibilities, but because he lacked a college degree, promotion and advancement opportunities were limited.

At various times during his 13 years at the museum, Robert considered beginning his own business. Finally he reached the point where there was absolutely no room for advancement at the museum, even though his boss had delegated most of his duties and responsibilities to Robert. Resentful of the recognition Robert was receiving, the boss subsequently pulled Robert out of many of the very successful museum programs and away from the shows and public appearances. (A copy of Robert's resume is provided in Appendix 1.)

On a whale-watching trip for the museum in Mexico, Robert developed the idea to form a company to perform a high-voltage electricity show (a presentation detailing the birth of electricity and the properties and uses of electricity). Robert had listed the characteristics of the museum job which he liked and those which he disliked. (Robert's list is shown below.)

Likes	Dislikes
Teaching (worthwhile work)	Red tape (city job)
The spotlight (I'm a ham)	Advancement limitations
Travel	Office politics
Science-oriented work	Paperwork
Flexibility	Routine tasks
Working with children	Bureaucracy
Teaching workshops	

Robert liked his teaching and performing in front of groups, and he enjoyed traveling and taking groups on science study trips. He disliked the bureaucracy of the museum job and its limitations on his freedom and creativity. The more Robert looked at the "t-account" of his interests, the more he liked the idea of starting his own company. With his own company he could keep the benefits and circumvent most of the problems he disliked. He outlined a business plan and his idea for the electricity show and asked his father-in-law to review it. Lisa's dad liked the show and the idea so well he agreed to loan Robert $10,000 to begin his business.

Phase I   During the first stage of developing his company, Robert rewrote his museum electric show and added revised material and new demonstrations for a traveling show. Because the equipment is either handmade or is a rare, special-order item, Robert initially had to work full time building and ordering the needed equipment for the show. He first marketed the traveling electricity show to schools and museums. His alternative plans, or fall-back options, had included smaller classroom presentations and electric birthday parties. He also mentioned that he could fall back on computer consulting, a field that he is very talented in, but one he found to be too confining. However, computer consulting had provided him the free time needed to complete his mail-outs and scheduling of shows.

The Electricity Show

The Product

Robert's show is an introduction to electricity. As described in his brochure (see Exhibit 1), each demonstration is dramatic, exciting, visible to a large audience, safe, easily transported and set up and, most important, educational.

The equipment setup takes about 30 minutes. This involves moving the equipment into the area (gymnasium, cafeteria, or multipurpose spaces at most schools), setting up the equipment, and testing both the equipment and the sound system. Robert does not allow anyone, including Lisa, to help him with the setup. Most of the information on the proper equipment organization is in his head or is from his own intuition, and this does not allow anyone else to assemble the materials the way he wants. The show presentation lasts approximately 40 minutes, depending on the number of questions following the show and the length of the class period.

Exhibit 1

The Science Education Company
Teaching science from the ground up

WHO IS THIS MAN AND WHY ISN'T HE LOCKED UP?

Robert Krampf is Director of The Science Education Company.   A lifelong fascination with science combined with an uncontrollable urge to teach has led him on adventures such as excavating dinosaur bones in South Dakota, petting whales off the coast of Mexico and exploring the caves of Tennessee and Arkansas.

While majoring in geology at the University of Tennessee at Martin, Mr. Krampf worked part time as a collections geologist and instructor at the Memphis Pink Palace Museum.   This later developed into a full time position, first as a laboratory and field instructor and later as Science Services Coordinator for the Education Department.   During his thirteen years at the Memphis Museum, he wrote and taught classes in geology, biology, chemistry, archaeology and physics.   It was during this time that he became interested in electricity.

For three years, he presented The Great Electricity Show, a high voltage Theater of Science program at the Memphis Museum.   This show was so popular, that at the end of its three year run, Mr. Krampf decided to take it on the road.   After rewriting the show and custom tailoring his own equipment, he formed The Science Education Company.   With "Watt is Electricity", the million volt electrical show, he has played at museums, universities, fairs, and schools across the Eastern United States.   This spring will lead him westward, with bookings in New Mexico, Utah, Wyoming and Idaho.

His recent appearance on **Late Night with David Letterman** was so well received that he was invited to come back in the near future and stimulated inquiries from the staff of the **Tonight Show**.

In addition to high voltage shows, The Science Education Company also presents teacher inservice workshops and classroom presentations in a variety of topics in geology, biology, archaeology, chemistry and physics.   Beginning this summer, extended field programs will be offered as well.

In his spare time, Robert enjoys spelunking, rock hounding, Chinese cooking, computer graphics design and reading.   At thirty two, he has been married for seven years.   His wife, Lisa, often travels with him, participates in the show and holds his life insurance policy, just in case...

4508 Leatherwood, P.O. Box 17521, Memphis, TN 38117   (901) 763-4348

Exhibit 1   *continued*

THEATER OF SCIENCE PRESENTATIONS: By setting up in your auditorium, meeting room or planetarium, we can serve a large number of people in a short time. By performing up to eight shows per day, even a one hundred seat auditorium can serve tremendous crowds. The lighting, backdrop and sound capabilities of these settings enhance the dramatic aspects of the presentation.

LOBBY SHOWS: If you plan to include the show in the regular admission price, we can set up in your exhibit area or lobby and handle even larger crowds. This can be a great addition to exhibit openings or special events, such as Halloween or Energy Day.

IN-SCHOOL SHOWS: If you don't have the room for large crowds at your facility, we can take the show to individual schools, performing in auditoriums, cafeterias, gymnasiums, etc. The same is true for libraries and community centers. This is an excellent way to reach large numbers of students.

FAIR EXHIBITS: Let us be your exhibit at the local fair. Cosponsored by the local power system, radio station, etc., it can be a great way to get media attention, stimulate interest and increase membership. As the Memphis Light, Gas & Water exhibit for the 1987 MidSouth fair, we had an attendance of over eight thousand and won an award for outstanding educational exhibit.

BETWEEN SHOW DEMOS: We can make arrangements to set up demos of equipment such as the Van de Graff between presentations. These make great show teasers and give people a chance to ask questions and see the equipment in a more personal setting.

ASSOCIATED PROGRAMMING: In conjunction with high voltage electricity shows, we can present teacher workshops and classroom demonstrations in electricity. These programs are packed with hands-on experiments, using materials found around the house. They can be taught as a general overview, or we can concentrate on static charges, electromagnetism, current electricity or the Tesla coil.

PHYSICAL REQUIREMENTS: Although our electric show is flexible enough to be presented almost anywhere, it works best in a location with subdued lighting. We will need an area at least 10' X 15' for our equipment and a standard 110 outlet.

CHARGES: Cost per show is based on the number of performances, time span, audience and travel. We will gladly work out a package which fits your needs and your budget. If you decide to charge admission, you can easily cover program cost and generate revenue, while getting all the media attention and crowds associated with a high voltage show. If co-sponsors work better for you, we will do everything we can to plug their product and make them happy. Even including the show in your admission price, the increased attendance will more than pay for the presentations.

For more information, contact: **Robert Krampf** at P.O. box 17521, Memphis, TN 38117 or by phone at (901) 763-4348.

Starting with static charges and a 400,000 volt Van de Graaff generator, the show progresses to a discussion of current electricity topics and demonstrations of generators, voltage and amperage (using a Jacob's ladder), electromagnetism, and high-frequency current (using the 1 million-volt tesla coil). As few people are familiar with the concepts covered, there are very few script changes required to shift the show from young audiences to adult groups. His finale is shooting five sparks off his hands and head as a human electrode. This demonstration does give a mild sensation that others fear, but Robert doesn't mind the spectacular performance. The presentation ends with a question-and-answer period.

Robert has performed a version of his electricity show at local fairs. This is a seasonal event and he wears a costume for this act. Traditionally he just wears a suit and tie for his performance. His show is professional and he tries to present to students that science is real and not tricks and magic.

Tearing down the equipment takes another 30 minutes and Robert talks to his new "fans" for at least 15 minutes following the show and before teardown begins. Both the setups and teardowns are extremely hard on the equipment. With this time structure, a maximum of two schools per day can be scheduled, depending on their locations. Many schools schedule two shows, so he has the potential to conduct a maximum of four shows per day.

The preshow setup and preparation are often more complex because many of the locations lack a stage. Therefore, Robert is typically on the same floor level as his audience and the people in the rear often have trouble seeing the demonstrations. Acoustics are often a problem and Robert does not have good sound equipment. He also has not found a way to keep the show's high voltage from "frying" the sound system. The rooms he uses are frequently too bright and he needs a dark backdrop to use in these locations. Other concerns are Robert's lack of backup equipment, which forces him to search for parts in various locations. He does not have much spare equipment at home and it could take weeks or more to get some of the needed parts, so he sometimes has to improvise.

Marketing

Robert obtained names and addresses of schools in the United States from a selection of phone books at the library. In late 1988 he discovered a company which supplied preprinted labels for U.S. schools. By purchasing the complete list, he could arrange the schools by zip code, state, city, type of school (public, private, etc.), age of students, and the size of school. This organization would allow him to concentrate his efforts in a particular geographic area and not just travel from one end of the country to another chasing new business. By purchasing this service, he boosted his mailings by 400 percent in quantity and lowered the number of incorrect addresses from 6 percent to less than 1 percent.

Lisa, although recently diagnosed with Lupus disease (a potentially serious muscle disorder), can control her condition with medication and enjoys traveling with Robert. In addition, Lisa sometimes helps with the show's clerical duties. Robert has an answering machine at his Memphis home to take his messages. He does all the show scheduling because he feels it is too hard for someone else to do the complex routing. Others, he believes, do not know how to allow for setup time;

plus he can capitalize on scale economies by scheduling more than one show per location.

Robert's biggest break happened in September of 1988 when he and his electric show appeared on the "Late Night with David Letterman" show. Most of the benefit from this exciting appearance came in the form of extensive, local news coverage and the credit of having made the appearance on this popular talk show, with Letterman actually participating in the demonstration. The only cost for this publicity was his travel expense in driving to Philadelphia. The Letterman show provided lodging expenses. Robert has capitalized on this appearance in his mailouts. See Exhibit 2.

Lisa had mentioned that Robert wrote to the David Letterman Show only after she pointed out that they would be performing an electricity show in the Philadelphia area. Michelle recalled Lisa's comments, "Robert is hesitant to sell himself to the public so he doesn't take advantage of all his opportunities. He just wants to do his shows and not the other support work that goes with it. Robert is big on ideas but he is lacking on his follow-through."

The Competition

Robert's primary competition has been from "Dr. Zap," a small electric show based out of the Chicago area. This is a small show and resembles a magic show more than a true science presentation. Other traveling shows include Tom Noddy, "The Bubble Man," and a 3-D show in the New York area. Robert has been approached by several persons about franchising his electricity show. Selling the idea, equipment, and know-how to run the business would probably bring in $15,000, depending on the amount of instruction the new owner would require. The show has yet to make a profit, so Robert would be selling only his ideas, his program script, and his equipment (worth $6,000). Robert estimated the cost of a franchise for his show to be $6,000 plus an additional $6,000 for the equipment. Franchising would give Robert free time to develop even more show ideas.

Phase II—The Future During the next phase of his scheduling (perhaps in one more year), Robert would like to add museums and power companies to his contact list. These additions would minimize his work (i.e., scheduling, setup, teardown, and advertising) and expenses. Museums, fairs, and even colleges request up to ten shows per day and this would allow him to maximize the number of shows he could conduct in one location.

As for the future, Robert has a vast reserve of additional ideas he would like to pursue. Some of the topics he would like to explore are outlined below:

• Robert would like to work under contract for the education departments of museums. He could provide a network of presentations, including the electric shows, docent (museum guides and volunteer) training, traveling exhibits, and other associated programs. He feels this would be ideal for the budget-rich, staff-poor, small- to mid-range museums. To capitalize on this idea Robert would need an additional one to three electric show teams to continue his mainline business. This could begin slowly right away and increase each year as profits permit.

Exhibit 2   **Example of a Mailout**

WATT IS ELECTRICITY
The Million Volt Electric Show

Most museums have at one time or another looked into setting up a high voltage electricity show. Imagine combining the thrill of million volt sparks with the fun of a "hair-raising" static generator. Think about an entertaining, educational show which can be performed in your museum or at outreach sites such as schools and fairs. But after looking into equipment costs, staff requirements, and all of the other aspects, the idea is usually filed away as far too expensive. Now there is a way you can offer your patrons spectacular, high voltage electricity shows at a price that will fit any budget.

The Science Education Company has a polished presentation which has been performed in museums, schools and fairs from New York to Key West, as well as making a recent appearance on the David Letterman Show. By contracting our show, you can concentrate your Theater of science or in-school electric shows into a few weeks of media-intensive, high volume programming. You reach the same number of people as you would by booking shows intermittently throughout the year, and you have no dead time with expensive equipment and staff sitting around for days or weeks waiting for someone to book a show.

If you would like to eventually have your own electric show, this is a great way to test the waters in your market. We can even set you up with all the equipment, script and staff training, if you find that your market will support a year round electric show.

WATT IS ELECTRICITY
$$$ A GREAT FUND RAISER $$$

More and more schools are using "Watt is electricity" as a fund raiser. This is a perfect way for your science club, student council, etc. to generate money. Your student body gets an exciting, entertaining presentation, your sponsoring organization raises a lot of money, and we do all the work.

By charging $1.00–$1.50 per student, most schools generate at least $500.00 above the cost of the show, while many break $1000.00 for a single show. The highly visible demonstrations in our show make it perfect for large audiences.

- He would like to investigate markets for educational materials, museum consulting, and science tours. This would include slides for science teachers and perhaps videos on science subjects. Slides, workshops, and tours could be designed to train museum instructors to guide nature tours, whale-watching expeditions, and rock digs. (During his summer expeditions, he takes many photographs that could be structured into slide presentations of rock hunting, archaeology, etc.) He would also like to conduct teacher workshops during the summer. These programs could help to generate fall business for the traveling show as well as utilize his down time during the summer off-season. This could begin immediately with little expense except mail-outs.
- Another idea is to prepare rock and mineral kits to sell to science classes. His hobby is rock collecting and he has a reserve of rocks and fossils. He would need a kit or case to organize the specimens and a way to market them to schools. He would also need to hire a photographer to assist with the accompanying slide presentations.

Exhibit 2	*Continued*

If your auditorium won't hold a thousand people, you can still make money. Additional shows on the same site/same day are half price. Some schools have even invited science classes from other schools to attend. This works especially well with private schools.

A GREAT PROGRAM!

"Watt is Electricity" has received rave reviews at museums, colleges and schools across the eastern U.S. Our recent appearance on Late Night with David Letterman went so well that we got an invitation to come back. Here are some of the unsolicited comments we have received.

"I co-sponsor the science club. . . The members were so caught up with the show that they want their project to be the building of a Van de Graaff generator!"

> Ms. Linda Silnas
> Glasgow School, Falls Church VA

"What you can't 'see, hear or smell' offers a real challenge for explanation; you surpass that challenge for making electricity become alive with new meaning."

> Mr. Jerry Campbell
> Executive Director,
> Tennessee Valley Public Power Association

"What can I say? You were a smash hit!"

> Ms. Mary O'Mella
> Events Management, Inc., Maplewood New Jersey

"Response at the college was so strong that I heard back all the way from the President's office about the quality and the excitement of the performances."

> Dr. Ed Slout
> Physical Sciences Dept. Head, Pensacola Junior College

- His ideas for other traveling shows and their limitations are:
  —Flame and combustion (must be safe and not a fire hazard)
  —Cold cryogenics (this one has probably been done too much)
  —Light (needs a darkened room for presentation)
  —Sound (bad acoustics in many locations)
  —Chemistry (expensive and generates toxic waste)
  Each of these demonstrations has possibilities and, with research, Robert feels he could produce usable demos for each idea.
- Robert also has writing and publishing interests. He feels a pamphlet or monograph on the use of electrical equipment for schools would be profitable. Most schools have the needed equipment in their science labs but many do not use it because they don't know how. He also feels a children's science workbook to supplement his electricity show would be profitable. (A sample of experiments Robert has designed and written is shown in Exhibit 3.) From his rock expeditions he would like to prepare a possible rock book or road log

Exhibit 3

Detecting Static Charges:

Not everything is light enough to stick to the wall. One of the easiest ways to detect static charges is with a device known as a versorium. You can easily construct a versorium with a plastic, drinking straw, a thin nail and a piece of cardboard. In the center of the straw, make a hole through one side, large enough for the nail point to enter. Push the nail through the center of a three inch square of cardboard. Now balance the straw on the point of the nail. Your versorium is now complete.

How it works: Charge your balloon and bring it close to one end of the straw. What do you think will happen? Just as the balloon will attract the wall, it also pulls on the free swinging straw. Now try polishing other objects and bringing them close to the versorium. You might start with a plastic comb, a plastic pen or a rubber ball. The lighter weight of the straw balanced on the point of the nail will swing toward a very small charge.

Possible problems: Again, humidity is your worst enemy. Be sure the hole in the straw is large enough for the nail to move easily in. If the hole is not in the center one end will tend to droop. Snipping a tiny bit from the heavy end with a pair of scissors can quickly solve this problem. Smaller imbalances can be fixed by using the nail to make a small dent in the top of the straw, so that the point fits through the hole and into the dent.

Variations: Try rubbing pencils, pens, metals, glass, wood, crayons, etc. Also try polishing them with different cloths, rubber, plastic wrap, wax paper, and anything else you can try. Sort the items by which work best with the other. Sometimes, the straw may move away from the object. In this case, the straw has taken on a static charge. Just as two like poles of a magnet will push apart, two like static charges repel. This leads us into our next experiment.

The Discovery of Static Electricity

In 546 B.C., a greek scientist named Thales accidentally discovered static charges while polishing a piece of amber. As he rubbed the amber, he noticed that it would attract bits of string. The

---

of rock formations in the United States for those interested in rock exploration. He would even like to compile a fiction satire entitled "Fieldguide for Windshield Entomology" along the lines of the "Far Side" cartoons.

- Other ideas for summer work include: computer consulting (which he has done for his father-in-law's company); all phases of desktop publishing; and summer field camps (conducted through museums and consisting of three-day trips for students from fifth grade to high school levels, emphasizing nature, fossils, caves, canoeing, hikes, and night exploration).

Financial Data

Robert began the SEC with only $10,000, a new Ford station wagon, and his luck. He had enough operating money for one month and depended on revenue from shows each week to continue the next week's travel. Initially he traveled alone and economized by staying in low-budget motels when possible and taking along a microwave oven to "cook" frozen dinners. He filled in the gaps in his show schedule by working in computer consulting and desktop publishing, primarily for clients of Lisa's dad. Because of his skill at computer system consulting, he was able to

Exhibit 3   *Continued*

word electricity comes from *elektron,* the greek word for amber. We can recreate Thales' experiment by polishing a balloon with a piece of wool. Inflate the balloon and tie it off. Now rub it briskly with the wool. After polishing for a minute or so, place the balloon against the wall and release it. If you have generated enough static, the balloon will stick.

How it works: As you rub the balloon, you transfer tiny pieces of atoms called electrons from the balloon to the cloth. These electrons have a negative charge. Just as a magnet has a north and south pole, static charges are positive and negative. By removing negative charges from the balloon, you leave it with a positive charge. By adding these charges to the cloth, it will become negative. Just as the north and south poles of magnets will stick together, positive and negative charges attract.

Why does the positive balloon stick to the uncharged wall? The wall is made of an even number of positive and negative charges. As you bring the positive balloon close to it, the negative charges are attracted to the surface, forming a oppositely charged spot for the balloon to stick.

Possible problems: The major problem you might encounter is humidity. The more moisture there is in the air, the harder it will be to generate the static charge. A bright, cold winter day is the best for static experiments. Hot, humid days and rainy weather are the worst. Be sure your piece of wool is dry and clean. If you must work in damp weather, a hair dryer applied to the balloon, wool and wall will help.

Variations: Try rubbing the balloon with other substances. Some of the things you might try are hair, different types of cloth, plastics, wood, etc. Sort the items in your classroom into groups of those that charge the balloon and those that don't. Find out which things you can get the balloon to stick to. You may be able to pick up string, bits of paper or even lift the hair on your head. Will the balloon stick to wood, metal, plastic or glass? How long will the balloon stay? This depends on humidity and the surface. It may vary from a few seconds to a day or two.

obtain a few days, or a few weeks', work when he was in Memphis. Robert estimated that he could earn about $30,000 per year working full time as a computer consultant for his father-in-law. (This job continues to be available for him if he ever wants to pursue it full time.)

During the first year he drove from coast to coast in order to build his reputation in as many parts of the country as possible. This caused expenses to be very high. However, he was able to take a tax loss and received a nice refund. This he invested in a pickup truck with a cover for his equipment. This improved the traveling conditions and made loading and unloading easier.

The second year proved that a good reputation does generate shows, since most bookings were in the same cities as the previous year's shows. In addition, more teachers voiced an interest in workshops, and this added income, particularly for the month of August. Also, museum interest began to increase. Museums were finding that shows would increase their attendance figures and attendance figures would increase their operating budgets.

Robert found that more money could be made in a week of shows (for five days) at schools, but travel expenses almost balanced out the increase in profits. However, bookings at a museum eliminated the possibility of individual shows in the area schools because the school groups all came to the museum to see the show.

At the end of year two, Robert is still operating at a loss. Mileage and hotel costs are his primary expenses. Travel days represent days without income. A summary of his earnings and expenses is presented below.

Year 1—Summary

Began with: $10,000 and a new station wagon
Spent: $8,000 on equipment and supplies
Revenue: $4,000 from shows
               $5,000 from computer consulting

(Was able to take a tax loss and got a large refund.)

Year 2—Summary

Revenue: $6,000 from shows
               $3,000 from computer consulting
               $1,000 from workshops
Financed a pickup truck and topper
Began planning rock/fossil kits
Began writing teacher's manuals
Still took a business loss on income.

Year 3—Projections

Revenue: $8,000 from shows
               $4,000 from museums
               $1,000 from workshops
                 $600 from teacher's manuals
                 $200 from rock/fossil kits
               $1,500 from trade shows
Planned Expenditures: travel trailers, van, equipment updates and modifications.

The Science Education Company

Robert is currently completing Phase I and approaching Phase II of his business plan. At this time, he *is* the company. He does all the presentations, setups, teardowns, equipment design, construction, repair, and transportation. Marketing, scheduling, public relations, and accounting are done on his Macintosh and Apple II computers. The Mac allows him to format his fliers, while minimizing costs and maximizing the control of their appearance. His few experiments with contracting portions of his work have been unsatisfactory. Robert admits that he doesn't trust anyone else to do the work for him. If he does it himself, he knows it will be done correctly.

The bulk mail duties require more time and organization than he has or is willing to devote to the task. He doesn't like the paperwork involved—even if it can be done on the computer. He finds any way to put off routine tasks such as preparing his expense reports. He hates being behind a desk and he prefers to be active and performing in the spotlight. Lisa had mentioned that sometimes a small thing, like getting a map of a city, could save Robert valuable time spent looking for a school from word-of-mouth directions.

The Future

Robert is at a crossroads in his business. He appears to have grown out of the introductory phase where he, the entrepreneur, seems happiest. "What do you think I should do? If my business grows, as I want it to, I'm afraid I'll lose control and be bogged down by the logistics of planning and the bureaucracy of a growing business," Robert had explained to Michelle. "If it doesn't grow soon, perhaps within the next six months, I will have to rethink my future because I lack the money to continue, especially with the travel expenses and replacement parts costs," he had added.

Michelle pondered Robert's dilemma, then she asked him to discuss his own personal goals. "Well," he stated, "my prime goals are to work at the things I like— teaching science, traveling extensively, earning enough money to be comfortable but not rich, and exciting as many people as I can about the world of science. I love the spotlight and am happiest when I am incredibly busy. I hate paperwork, but I like working with computers enough to keep up with it."

Robert agreed that he is almost at the point where he could keep a second show busy. The first step is finding the right person. "I need someone who likes to travel (ten months a year), has a strong rapport with people, and especially children, a science background (necessary for fielding questions), and can maintain and repair the equipment. I also need a way to insure that this person doesn't steal the show. While the show is copyrighted, with a simple rewrite of the script they could have their own show," Robert had explained. Currently he is visiting each area for a three- to four-week period. The electricity show schedule is as follows:

Month	Show Location
January	Florida
February and March	Louisiana, Mississippi, Alabama, and the Gulf Coast
April	Carolinas and North Georgia
May	New Mexico, Utah, Idaho
June to August	Museum bookings, field programs, and teacher workshops (various locations)
September	Memphis
October	Nashville
November	Missouri
December	Memphis

April is the busiest month because most schools want him to perform during their scheduled science fairs. Also, January and February are key months. The weather is bad and schools don't schedule field trips during this time and instead rely on in-house performances to entertain students.

He feels that a change to smaller areas (each visited twice a year) would make better use of word-of-mouth bookings within the same school year. He also feels there is a choice between hiring additional employees or franchising the show. Another decision is the possible addition of new shows.

Robert would like to eventually have his own science television show on an educational station, similar to the "Mr. Wizard Show." He sees himself with a show in approximately 20 years (at age 52). In five years he would like to have a very polished electricity show, streamlined marketing, full-time clerical help, and at least two other traveling shows.

Robert is not in the business for money and material wealth. His dream is to make science popular again. He feels the United States has abandoned the emphasis on science and one of the reasons is because teachers don't make the courses fun, challenging, or exciting. Statistics from the 1989 International Science Study places the United States near the bottom in science education, and supports the increased need for science education. His shows and other ideas can stimulate this latent science interest. Robert is a born educator and does excite groups, regardless of his topic.

Michelle had also asked Lisa about her views of Robert's future. "Well," Lisa began, "I have serious doubts about him hiring other people to do the shows. He does not have the money to give them insurance or even a steady salary. I also feel that no one will ever do the same great show he does. He can't train them to be him. The teachers just love him and they love how he does the show even more so than the show itself. He is so excited about what he does that he has a magnetism about him. *He* sells the show and not the show itself."

Robert agreed that he would prefer not to manage other people and that he probably wouldn't do a good job of it. He felt he couldn't keep up with all the reporting requirements, social security records, and other paperwork that extra people and extra shows would generate. This would just put him right back into red tape and office politics.

The everyday duties and realities like paying bills are a big downfall for him. His expenses currently include travel (hotel and food), truck expenses (fuel and repair), and equipment maintenance. Robert travels about 55,000 miles per year. This could increase by about 5,000 miles if additional states were involved. The couple spends about 200 nights per year in hotels. About 60 percent of these nights are in tourist areas, at peak rates ($65/night or more), but this cannot be avoided. He has considered purchasing a travel trailer to use to ease some of the hotel expenses. Currently, sources for new show bookings come from word of mouth from past successful shows. He estimates that he gets about 30 percent of his new business this way. He gets a 60 percent return on his summer teaching workshops since most teachers want him to bring his show to their schools during the coming school year.

Robert admitted that he does not save money and that he does not have a savings account or a retirement plan. Robert must make enough money for their house payment ($585/month), two vehicles (payments and upkeep of $400/month), payments on the $10,000 loan from his father-in-law (payable as profits allow—no time limit or interest), possible payments on a new trailer he's considering, built-up credit card debt (approximately $5,800), self-paid medical insurance ($200/month), social security, bills for Lisa's medication and doctor visits ($100/month), house repairs (as required), veterinary bills for their dog ($100/year), large gasoline bills ($1,200/year), expenses from the trips (varies per location), and upkeep on the show equipment.

"Neither one of us wants to be rich to excess," Lisa had said, "but Robert underestimates his bills and overestimates his possible income, especially since he has so much slack time with no income between shows.

"I don't mean to make Rob and his dream sound hopeless, and I do believe in his ability to have a successful business. I just wish he wouldn't get too carried away with expansion and I wish he could afford to have someone take care of the paperwork for him.

"Robert is the commodity, and not the show. Therefore he can't hire people to clone himself. He could be happy being booked all the time without all the demands of paperwork.

"Let him always be in demand, and make enough money to be comfortable. Forget the grandiose dreams of having a huge corporation. He is not executive material, and would hate it if you handed it to him. My Dad offered him a regular job opportunity and he turned it down (once he lasted as a computer salesman for only two days.) He told me he wouldn't want a promotion at the Pink Palace Museum because he would be buried alive under the paperwork and management duties. That was a big part of him saying there was nowhere else to advance at the Pink Palace. His position there allowed him to interact with his audience and that's what he lives for! He withers when he hasn't been in front of a crowd for a week.

"I see him happiest at learning how to manage what he has and making his shows the best they can be along with having the paperwork part flow smoothly. If it ran well, and supported us, I don't see him ever being happier. If he had more he would probably lose it, or throw it all away because he'd hate it."

As Robert and Lisa had continued to explain his show and further business ideas, Michelle wondered what she should recommend to Robert. He had so many ideas but he was only one person. What could she recommend that would allow Robert to establish some growth and control over his company and yet maintain the creativity and innovation he desired? What should Phase III and Phase IV of his business be? Would a regular show schedule and fixed route increase profits? Should he spend more time cultivating museum business? Should Robert consider adding a business partner and manager to take advantage of his ideas as well as the growth opportunities available? Should he franchise his show?

Appendix 1

Robert Krampf
4508 Leatherwood
P.O. Box 17521
Memphis, TN 38117
(901) 763-4348

Work Experience

Science Education Company. (1987 to present) Owner and founder of a traveling science company. Goals are to make science popular, fun, challenging, and exciting to learn. Duties include teaching science through a traveling electricity show to students and the general public.

Computer Consultant. (Summer 1988 to present) Worked both part time and full time as a freelance computer consultant, responsible for identifying organizational needs, suggesting computer hardware and software needs, and equipment setup and employee education. Also performed laptop printing for business proposals.

Memphis Pink Palace Museum. Curator (Full time 1977 to 1987) Responsible for museum education and conducting student and visitor workshops and training. Teacher in Education Department (Part time 1974 to 1977). Responsible for teaching science classes for K–12 students and also performed duties as a rock and fossil collections geologist.

Education

Memphis State University (1977–1978). 47 semester hours toward a Bachelor's in Science. 4.0 GPA on a 4.0 scale.

University of Tennessee at Martin (1974–1977). Completed 129 credit hours toward a Bachelor's Degree in Science. 3.89 GPA on a 4.0 scale.

Diploma with Honors (1974). Fairley High School. Memphis, Tennessee. 3.9 GPA on a 4.0 scale.

Personal Information

Health:	Excellent
Marital Status:	Married to Lisa B. Krampf, no children
Hobbies:	Science, teaching, fossils, traveling
Travel:	Willing to travel and relocate

CASE • *Kitchen Made Pies—Revised*

James J. Chrisman, University of Calgary
Fred L. Fry, Bradley University
Charles W. Hofer, University of Georgia

In late 1981, Paul Dubicki, owner and president of Kitchen Made Pies (KMP), was faced with a difficult problem. Company sales had stagnated since 1975, and the firm was about to suffer its fourth straight year of losses (see Exhibit 1). Further compounding this problem were unfavorable economic and industry conditions, both locally and nationally, as well as difficulties with certain customers and creditors. In addition, KMP's balance sheet showed a deficit equity position (see Exhibit 2), which limited the range of feasible alternatives available to turn the situation around. In spite of these concerns, Mr. Dubicki was determined to return the business to profitability, and was confident that this task could be accomplished if he could only get away from day-to-day decision making.

When commenting on the current situation at Kitchen Made, Mr. Dubicki emphasized that volume was the key to success:

> We must increase our customer base and we must somehow encourage our present distributors to provide the promotional support retailers need to sell our products. One well-publicized special can sell more pies in one day than can be sold in a normal week without one. That's what I'd like to concentrate on, but every day something else comes up around here.

The remainder of this case discusses the situation facing Kitchen Made Pies in late 1981. First, a brief description of KMP's history is presented. This is followed

Exhibit 1
KMP Operating Results 1971–1981 (Dollars in Thousands)

	Sales	Profits		Production						Selling*		Administration	
				Materials		Labor		Overhead*					
1971	$ 844	$ 14	1.7%	$432.1	51.2%	$253.2	30.0%	$ 64.1	7.6%	$24.5	2.9%	$ 83.6	9.9%
1972	955	8	0.8%	482.3	50.5%	279.8	29.3%	67.8	7.1%	26.7	2.8%	90.7	9.5%
1973	1,246	24	1.9%	656.6	52.7%	306.5	24.6%	110.9	8.9%	34.9	2.8%	114.6	9.2%
1974	1,453	18	1.2%	828.2	57.0%	324.0	22.3%	135.1	9.3%	36.3	2.5%	111.9	7.7%
1975	1,604	110	6.9%	864.6	53.9%	332.0	20.7%	150.8	9.4%	35.3	2.2%	110.7	6.9%
1976	1,580	109	6.9%	771.0	48.8%	363.4	23.0%	178.5	11.3%	41.1	2.6%	116.9	7.4%
1977	1,642	7	0.4%	802.9	48.9%	426.9	26.0%	221.7	13.5%	44.3	2.7%	139.6	8.5%
1978	1,608	−24	−1.5%	818.5	50.9%	422.9	26.3%	204.2	12.7%	35.4	2.2%	151.2	9.4%
1979	1,601	−58	−3.6%	810.1	50.6%	432.3	27.0%	209.7	13.1%	44.8	2.8%	160.1	10.0%
1980	1,506	−91	−6.0%	772.6	51.3%	426.2	28.3%	192.8	12.8%	49.7	3.3%	155.1	10.3%
1981	1,635	−178	−10.9%	887.8	54.3%	452.9	27.7%	220.7	13.5%	67.0	4.1%	183.1	11.2%

*Includes both fixed and variable costs.

Note: All cost figures are not strictly comparable due to changes in allocation procedures, though these changes were not substantial in nature.

Source: KMP's internal data, 1981.

Exhibit 2   KMP Balance Sheet, 1981

Assets (dollars in thousands)		Liabilities and Equity	
Current:		*Current:*	
Cash	$ 2	Accounts payable	$291
Accounts receivable	163	Unsecured bank note	70
Inventory	137	Accrued payroll and taxes	25
Prepaid expenses	17	Note — F. Dubicki	8
Total current assets	$319	Total current liabilities	$394
Fixed Assets: (after depreciation)		*Long-Term Liabilities:*	
Leasehold improvements	$ 1	Bank note on truck	$ 15
Machinery and equipment	48	Bank note on equipment	12
Autos and trucks	28		
Total fixed assets	77	Total long-term liabilities	$ 27
TOTAL ASSETS	$396	TOTAL LIABILITIES	$421
		EQUITY (deficit)	$ (25)
		TOTAL LIABILITIES AND EQUITY	$396

Source: KMP's internal data, 1981.

by a general discussion of the baking industry; the pie segment in particular. Next, a description of the local and national environment in 1981 is provided, after which Kitchen Made's current operations are discussed. Finally, a brief description of KMP's future as seen by Mr. Dubicki is presented.

Company History

In 1981, Kitchen Made Pies was a regional producer of a wide variety of pies, as well as other bakery products. Located in Peoria, Illinois, the firm traced its history back 30 years. The company was founded by Frank Dubicki, the father of the current owner, and had been run by the Dubicki family throughout its existence.

Paul Dubicki grew up and worked for his father in the bakery business, but was not very interested in pursuing a career with the firm in his youth. After leaving the business to attend college and work on his own, Paul returned in 1968 to work for his father and later become, along with his brother, David Dubicki, a minority stockholder. During this time, Paul was dissatisfied because he never seemed able to get away from line operations and other day-to-day aspects of the business. Furthermore, he felt that the true market potential of the firm had never been realized due to his father's persistent reliance upon one customer, Dean's Distributing, for the bulk of KMP's sales. Paul did not believe Dean's served Kitchen Made's needs particularly well, and that future growth depended upon an expanded, and perhaps more selective, customer base. However, the elder Dubicki remained firm in his convictions and the status quo at KMP was maintained throughout the 1970s.

In early 1981, the elder Dubicki was persuaded by Paul to sell out, though he did retain ownership of the company's land and facilities. This sale was accomplished through a redemption of Frank Dubicki's stock by the corporation in a transaction that also eliminated his sizeable debt to the corporation. At the same time, David voluntarily gave his share of the business to his brother, leaving Paul as the sole owner. In this context it should be noted that David Dubicki never showed much interest in the business and was not directly involved in its operation at the time of his exit.

Upon assuming full control, Paul Dubicki immediately set about changing and updating the firm's various operational procedures, and established for the first time a commitment to strategic planning. Unfortunately, problems such as delinquent accounts and lagging sales, which had built over a long period of time, had also become very serious problems.

The Baking Industry

General Description

The baking industry can be divided into two broad SIC code categories: bread, cakes, and related products (SIC Code #2051), which includes pies (SIC Code #20515), and cookies and crackers (SIC Code #2052). The latter category will not be discussed further in this case, however. According to the 1977 *U.S. Census* of manufacturers:

> This industry [SIC Code #2051] comprises establishments primarily engaged in the manufacture of bread, cakes, and other "perishable" bakery products. Establishments manufacturing bakery products for sale primarily through one or more nonbaking retail outlets are included in this industry [p. 20E-2].

Baked goods have been produced and consumed by individuals all over the world for hundreds of years. Traditionally, baking has been a trade occupation, with nearly every community having at least one local baker in the area. Baking has also been done in the home for many generations. Thus, the baking business has always had a distinctly local flavor and orientation. In fact, it was not until around the turn of the century that technological advances, such as refrigeration and food preservatives, permitted baked goods (and other food products) to be transported any distance.

Even in 1981 transportation costs and the perishable nature of baked goods were significant barriers to industry consolidation. As a result, the baking industry remained fragmented, although less so than in earlier periods. Thus, there were only moderate increases between 1972 and 1977 in the concentration ratios for the top 4 firms (29 percent to 33 percent), top 8 firms (39 percent to 40 percent), and the top 50 firms (62 percent to 68 percent) in the bread, cake, and related products industries. Furthermore, during the same period, the number of establishments employing less than 20 workers increased, while the total number of competitors decreased almost 8 percent. These trends, which resulted in fewer medium-sized bakers, implied that large firms with internal delivery capabilities, and smaller firms that emphasized local business, possessed certain cost and/or market advantages. Some industry observers also felt that the recurring energy shortages would accentuate this development.

Exhibit 3 provides a composite of the bread, cake, and related products segment of the baking industry as of 1977.

Current Conditions[1]

Though the outlook for the baking industry was helped considerably in 1981 by softening sugar prices and stabilized wheat prices, overall prospects were somewhat uncertain due to the recessionary conditions in the U.S. economy and recent shortages of certain essential ingredients such as sugar. Exhibit 4 provides producer and consumer price indexes for selected commodities for the years 1970 and 1975–1981. The baking industry (with the possible exception of breads), and particularly the pie and cake segment, seemed likely to suffer because purchases of these products tended to be more discretionary in nature than other foodstuffs. When the economy declines, it is usually discretionary items that consumers cut back on first. Indeed, as Exhibit 5 indicates, sales in the mature bread, cake, and related products segment

Exhibit 3
Bread, Cake, and Related Products Industry Statistics, 1977

SIC Code 2051

Establishments (total)	3,062
1–19 employees	1,945
20–99 employees	561
More than 100 employees	556

Total number of employees (office, production, etc.)	178,000
Total payrolls	$2,335,800,000
Cost of materials	$3,909,000,000
Value of shipments	$9,274,900,000

Inventories

	Beginning	Ending
Total	$220,600,000	$235,100,000
Finished goods	22,000,000	25,000,000
Work in process	2,100,000	3,700,000
Raw materials	196,500,000	206,400,000
Capital expenditures	$303,800,000	

Source: *U.S. Census of Manufacturers,* 1977, p. 20E–10.

[1]The majority of the discussion in this section was drawn from the *U. S. Industry Outlook,* 1980 and 1981.

Exhibit 4   **Producer and Consumer Price Index for Commodities, 1970, 1975–1981**

	Producer Price Index (1967 = 100)							
	1970	1975	1976	1977	1978	1979	1980	1981
All commodities	110.4	174.9	183.0	194.2	209.3	235.6	268.8	293.4
Processed food and feeds	112.1	182.6	178.0	186.1	202.6	222.5	241.2	248.7
Cereal and bakery products	107.7	178.0	172.1	173.4	190.3	210.3	236.0	255.5
Grains (including wheat)	98.8	223.9	205.9	165.0	182.5	214.8	239.0	248.4
Processed fruits and vegetables	110.6	169.8	170.2	187.4	202.6	221.9	228.7	261.2
Sugar and confectionary	115.8	254.3	190.9	177.4	197.8	214.7	322.5	275.9

	Consumer Price Index (1967 = 100)							
	1970	1975	1976	1977	1978	1979	1980	1981
All items	116.3	161.2	170.5	181.5	195.4	217.4	246.8	272.4
Food	114.9	175.4	180.8	192.2	211.4	234.5	254.6	274.6
Food at home	113.7	175.8	179.5	190.2	210.2	232.9	251.5	269.9
Food away from home	119.9	163.0	169.4	175.4	189.4	208.5	231.1	254.9
Sugar and sweets	115.1	246.2	218.2	229.4	257.5	277.6	341.3	368.3
Cereal and bakery products	108.9	184.8	180.6	183.5	199.9	220.1	246.4	271.1

Source: *U.S. Statistical Abstract,* 1982, p. 456.

Exhibit 5   **Value of Shipments: Bread, Cake, and Related Products + Pies, Fruit and Custard, Except Frozen**

Bread, Cake, and Related Products (in millions of dollars)

SIC #2051

	1975	1976	1977	1978	1979	1980
Industry value of shipment[1]	9,059	9,512	9,275	9,504	10,360	11,500
Product value of shipment[2]	7,727	8,084	7,966	8,170	9,000	9,930
Change in producer price index	+1.6%	+2.8%	+1.3%	+13.4%	+12.1%	+12.4%

Pies, Fruit and Custard, Except Frozen (value in millions of dollars; quantities in thousands of tons)

SIC #20515

	1967	1972	1973	1974	1975	1976	1977
Product value of shipments[3]	226.7	224.2	254.8	326.0	319.0	347.6	297.1
Quantities shipped	NA	574.5	NA	NA	NA	NA	498.0

[1]Value of all products, services sold by the bread, cake, and related products industry (SIC 2051).

[2]Value of all shipments of bread, cake, and related products produced by all industries.

[3]Value of all shipments of fruit and custard pies (except frozen) produced by all industries.

NA = information not available.

Sources: *U.S. Industrial Outlook,* 1981, p. 391; and *U.S. Census of Manufacturers,* 1977, p. 20E–18.

had been somewhat erratic during the 1975–1980 time period. As this exhibit also shows, the pie industry had done even worse.

Several other emerging trends also threatened to upset whatever balance currently existed in the industry. More and more consumers appeared to be cutting down on sweets and sugar intake for health and weight reasons. Additionally, the average age of the population was increasing due to the demographic changes resulting from the 1950s and 1960s baby boom (see Exhibit 6). Since people's eating habits and preferences tend to change as they grow older, this trend could significantly affect the industry's sales and product mix.

Other factors which could affect the outlook and subsequent performance of the baking industry were recent trends toward eating out and the emerging popularity of prepared foods. In the fast-paced world of the 1980s, people no longer had as much time to cook their own meals. Increases in the number of single households (see Exhibit 6) and the growing participation of women in the work force had exacerbated these trends. According to the *U. S. Industrial Outlook,* 1981:

> The growing trend among Americans toward eating out has been good for the bakery foods industry because all types of restaurants serve bakery foods. Fast-food outlets are major users of buns and rolls but also serve other bakery goods. Conventional restaurants serve all types of bakery foods including buns, rolls, variety breads and sweet goods. [p. 392]

It should be noted, however, that according to Mr. Dubicki, fast-food chains, which were gaining in popularity, usually purchased desserts on a nationwide basis and did not like to buy from local dessert manufacturers.

Exhibit 6   **U.S. Population and Household Demographics (1960–1981)**

	Total Population	Percentage under 18 Years	Percentage 18–34 Years	Percentage 35–54 Years	Percentage over 55 Years
1960	180,671,000	35.7	21.6	24.8	17.8
1970	205,052,000	34.1	24.4	22.7	18.9
1980	227,658,000	28.0	29.8	21.4	20.9
1981	229,807,000	27.5	30.3	21.3	20.9

Households	1960	1970	1980	1981
Total number of households	52,600,000	62,900,000	80,800,000	82,400,000
1-person households	13.1%	17.0%	22.7%	23.0%
2-person households	27.8%	28.8%	31.4%	31.3%
3-person households	18.9%	17.3%	17.5%	17.7%
4-person households	17.6%	15.8%	15.7%	15.5%
5-person households	11.5%	10.4%	7.5%	7.4%
6-person households	5.7%	5.6%	3.1%	3.1%
7-or-more-person households	5.4%	5.1%	2.2%	2.0%
Average number of persons per household	3.33	3.14	2.76	2.73

Source: *U.S. Statistical Abstract,* 1982.

Government regulation was also a potentially serious concern for bakers. Recent controversies included the issue of what natural and organic foods really meant (and when foods could be advertised as such) as well as product labeling regulations. No specific projections on the effects of these legislative activities could be made in regard to industry participants, although costs were expected to increase as a result, and hence inefficient producers might face difficulties.

Frozen bakery products were yet another area of concern for industry participants. Though the overall trend had been one of increasing sales of frozen bakery goods (see Exhibit 7), and many grocers saw significant advances for a number of frozen products in the 1980s, at least two factors threatened to constrain frozen food sales growth. First of all, consumers seemed to view frozen foods as being more expensive than fresh or canned items. Secondly, grocers were hesitant to expand frozen food selections in the supermarket due to high energy costs, which, no average, actually exceeded the cost of rent in 1980 [*Progressive Grocer,* April 1981]. Therefore, the future of frozen food sales in general, and frozen pie sales in particular, remained in doubt.

Value Added in the Baking Industry

The value added chain in the baking industry starts, of course, with the farmer who grows the grains, fruit, and other products which make up the baked good, in this case, pies. Farmers represented the closest facsimile to a purely competitive market existing in the U.S. economy, thus farmers were price-takers rather than price-makers. As a result, the effects of farmers' activities on conditions in the baking industry were limited to the quantity of goods brought to market (which in itself largely determines prices, but was uncontrollable by the individual farmer unless one or more decided to withhold their produce—an infrequent occurrence) and the overall quality of these goods.

The farmers sold their products to food processors such as sugar refineries and flour mills which transformed the raw foodstuffs into the actual material used in the bakeries. Due to economies of scale, and the fragmented nature of the baking industry, these suppliers tended to be larger than many of their customers (though this was not always the case) and hence enjoyed relative power in regard to price and service agreements. It should be noted that many of the larger firms involved

Exhibit 7	Sales Records of Frozen Foods, 1979			
Categories	Millions of Dollars	Percent Change versus 1974	Percent Change versus 1978	Percentage of Total
Total, all frozen foods	$7,643.8	+73%	+ 9.9%	100%
Baked goods	$ 860.8	+70.8%	+10%	11.2%
Sweet goods	$ 437.0	+50.2%	+ 6.1%	5.7%
Pies	$ 229.9	+66.6%	+14.5%	3.0%

Source: "Grocery Retailing in the 1980s," *Progressive Grocer,* 1980, p. 96.

Exhibit 8
Frozen Food Predictions for the 1980s: Survey of Buyers/Merchandisers*

"Outstanding Advances"

Boilable pouch products	Vegetables, prepared
Pizza	Dairy toppings
Frozen meats, poultry	Vegetables, reg. box
Premium quality	Sweet goods
Private label	Dessert pies
Vegetables, reg. poly	Non-orange juices
Fish, seafood	

"Good Advances"

Single-dish entries
Single serving
Orange juice
Frozen meat, poultry
Diet/low calorie
Family servings
Potatoes
Nationality foods
Breakfast items
Entrees
Ice cream

"Average Advances"

Pot pies
Fruits
Bread, rolls
Margarine
Miscellaneous desserts
Snacks
Regular dinners
Pet foods

"Decline Anticipated"

Generic labels

*Products ranked in descending order.

Source: "Grocery Retailing in the 1980s," *Progressive Grocer,* 1980, p. 92.

in the baking industry were vertically integrated backward into the food processing business, thus enjoying potential cost advantages over nonintegrated rivals.

The processed foodstuffs were the basic raw materials for the competitors in the baking industry who will be described in the following section. Once the baked product was produced it had to be transported, distributed, and sold to the consumer. To reach the ultimate consumer, two (though in some cases only one) intermediate links in the value added chain intervene after the baked goods were prepared.

Producers of baked goods usually sold their products to distributors [75 percent of sales according to *Progressive Grocers,* 1980] though some made direct deliveries to retail or institutional customers. Since distributors contributed so substantially to the value added chain it is useful to understand the types of distribution, their cost structures, and their basic strategies.

Many competitors in the baking industry were forward integrated into the distribution and retail end of the value added chain. However, this discussion will focus on the activities of independent distributors, bearing in mind their operations were somewhat similar (though not entirely so) to vertically integrated competitors.

There were three basic types of independent distributors or wholesalers. Voluntary wholesalers sponsor retailers who belonged to voluntary merchandising groups such as IGA (Independent Grocers Association) or Red and White, and did virtually all business with this related buying group. Cooperative wholesalers were actually owned (wholly or partially) by (generally independent) retail grocers and specifically served the needs of these customers. Certified Grocers and Associated Grocers were two examples of wholesale buying groups organized by retailers. Unaffiliated wholesalers, as the name suggests, did business with unaffiliated independent grocers and also served some of the needs of the large food chains, as well. All these types of distributors provided grocers with a wide range of food products, including pies. Some smaller concerns concentrated on certain food lines such as baked goods, but many dealt with the full range of food products sold in grocery stores. Exhibit 9 provides statistics on wholesaler operating characteristics in 1980.

Distributors used two basic methods to sell products to grocers. Some sold on a guaranteed basis with unsold products returned to the dealer at no charge. Others sold products unguaranteed, i.e., grocers assumed full responsibility for all products they bought. As might be expected, profit margins for the two methods differed. Grocers usually made about 23–25 percent on guaranteed sales, while unguaranteed sales yielded margins of approximately 35–40 percent. However, because of the inherent risks involved in unguaranteed purchases, many grocers preferred the lower-but-safer profit margins of guaranteed arrangements, especially when dealing with unaffiliated "door-to-store" distributors. Nonguaranteed sales worked well, and were most commonly used, through efficient "drop shipment" techniques sometimes used by break bakers.

Exhibit 9	Wholesaler Operations Review, 1980		
	Voluntary	**Co-op**	**Unaffiliated**
Distribution centers per firm	1.6	1.7	1.3
Average size in square feet	226,000	227,000	38,000
Annual turnover	15.9	16.1	11.0
Service level to store	94.9%	94.9%	88.3%
Manufacturers' service level	93.9%	89.9%	86.7%
Sale per square foot	$509	$472	$187
Average sales	$187,495,000	$223,329,000	$9,614,000
Gross margin	7.4%	6.5%	9.2%
Net profits (BT)	1.6%	1.4%	1.6%
Expenses (as Percent of Sales)			
Payroll	3.74%	4.08%	6.15%
Transportation	.15%	.17%	.25%
Utilities	.22%	.20%	.40%
Interest	.36%	.37%	.50%
Insurance	.17%	.16%	.55%
Goods	92.6%	93.5%	90.8%
Business (as Percent of Sales)			
Supermarkets	63%	68%	26%
Convenience stores	16%	9%	11%
Small stores	21%	23%	63%

Source: *Progressive Grocer,* April 1981.

Door-to-store distributors accumulated individual orders daily and delivered merchandise direct from the baker to the grocer. On the other hand, drop shipments involved larger orders which were taken first to warehouses for later delivery to individual stores. For example, drop ship distributors, such as Eisner's (a current customer of KMP), sold direct to their own or an affiliated grocery chain and thus enjoyed profits on both the delivery and retail end. According to Mr. Dubicki, this was an important competitive advantage since 40–50 percent of the retail product cost was in distribution. Another distinguishing feature separating drop shippers and door-to-store distributors was the greater willingness of the former to provide the promotional support necessary to sell the food products. This in part explained the willingness of grocers to make unguaranteed purchases with drop shippers. Due to these factors, Mr. Dubicki expressed a desire to concentrate on doing business with this type of customer (distributor).

Although many pies were sold to institutional customers and restaurants, the last link in the value added chain for the baking industry was usually the retail grocer, who sold the bakery product to the ultimate customer. Grocers sold pies to the consumer in at least three ways. Some supermarkets depended on sales of prepackaged pies which were bought from an outside supplier and sold on the premises. Prepackaged pies could be either fresh or frozen, though frozen pie purchases were more common due to the limited shelf life (approximately 2–4 days) of fresh pies.

Many stores had taken different approaches. In-store bakeries were gaining popularity not only because of the higher profit margins available but also because they attracted consumers into the store who bought other things in addition to baked goods. Some grocers ran "scratch" operations, that is, bakery goods were made and baked at the store, while some grocers ran "bake-off" operations, that is, baked foods were bought from an outside supplier (prebaked or unbaked) and baked or rebaked on the premises. Though some supermarkets employed one method or the other, it was not uncommon to find pies or other bakery products sold via a combination of these methods in a single store. [*U.S. Industrial Outlook,* 1980] It should be noted that in-store bakeries with scratch operations made their own pies, thus were not customers for firms such as KMP. In-store bakeries with bake-off operations, however, did buy pies (mainly fresh).

The overall trend for in-store bakeries was on the upswing but 1981 saw a reversal to this trend. Bakery departments and delicatessens offered grocers the highest profit margins but their percentage contribution to total sales fell in 1981 compared to 1980 (see Exhibit 10) according to statistics compiled by the National Association of Retail Grocers. Furthermore, the *Progressive Grocer's* annual survey of supermarket operations revealed that among sample respondents, the percentage operating on-premises bake-off bakeries (1979—26 percent, 1980—24 percent) and scratch bakeries (1979—17 percent, 1980—15 percent) declined.

Competitors

Kitchen Made Pies competed against a variety of firms that did business both regionally and nationally. Some rivals made a full line of pies. Additionally, some firms were also diversified into breads and other bakery products. Others had been

Exhibit 10	Grocer Sales and Profit Mix

	1981	1980	Trend
Sales Mix			
Grocery	65.9%	66.1%	(.3%)
Meat	19.9%	20.6%	(3.5%)
Produce	6.6%	6.3%	4.8%
Bakery	2.9%	3.8%	(31.0%)
Delicatessen	3.3%	3.6%	(9.1%)
Gross Profit			
Grocery	18.8%	17.9%	5.0%
Meat	20.8%	19.9%	4.5%
Produce	28.7%	27.7%	3.6%
Bakery	41.9%	39.3%	6.6%
Delicatessen	40.1%	36.7%	9.3%
Total Store	20.2%	19.6%	3.1%

	Bakery Sales (Percentage of Total Sales)				Bakery Gross Profit		
	High	Low	Average		High	Low	Average
1981	5.0%	1.4%	2.9%	1981	55.6%	34.3%	41.9%
1980	5.4%	.9%	3.8%	1980	52.5%	16.7%	39.3%
1979	3.7%	2.1%	2.9%	1979	54.6%	40.8%	48.1%

Source: "1981 Financial Analysis," National Association of Retail Grocers of the U.S., pp. 1, 12, 16.

successful concentrating on specific sizes or types of pies which allowed longer production runs, lower inventories, and thus lower costs in some cases. Mr. Dubicki felt, however, that Kitchen Made's full-line strategy gave the firm an advantage over competitors in attracting new customers and protected sales from changes in consumer taste.

Kitchen Made had no direct competition located in the Peoria area although it did compete against a variety of firms for local as well as regional business. In some cases the firm also competed against its own customers who possessed in-house baking capabilities. Most independent companies primarily engaged in pie production were relatively small (see Exhibit 11 for summary statistics on establishments providing fresh pies). Other competitors were either divisions, or parts of divisions, for large, diversified food manufacturers.

By far the largest competitor for KMP was Mrs. Smith's Frozen Food Company, a division of Kellogg's. Mrs. Smith produced and distributed frozen dessert pies (usually 8″ or 10″ sizes), pie shells, and frozen dessert and entree crepes nationwide, and in some areas fresh baked pies and other pastries. Other products included "Eggo" frozen waffles and nondairy whipped toppings. These products were sold to both retail (grocer, restaurants) and institutional (hospitals, universities) customers. Mrs. Smith's was based in Pottstown, Pennsylvania, and in addition had plants in Morgantown, York, and Philadelphia, Pennsylvania; McMinnville, Oregon;

Exhibit 11

Pies, Fruit and Custard, Except Frozen

1977 Summary Statistics (dollars in millions)
SIC 20515

	Number of Establishments	Number of Employees	Payroll	Cost of Materials	Value of Shipments
Establishments with this product class primary	44	3,700	$47.9	$101.7	212.3
Establishments with 75% specialization or more in class	26	2,000	$26.3	$48.3	109.8

Source: *U.S. Census of Manufacturers,* 1977, p. 20E-15.

Atlanta, Georgia; San Jose, California; Silver Springs, Maryland; Blue Anchor, New Jersey; and Arlington, Tennessee. Total sales in 1981 were approximately $150 million, and the company employed about 2,300 individuals.

Chef Pierre was another nationwide producer of frozen 8″ and 10″ pies. Owned by Consolidated Foods Corporation (1981 corporate sales $5.6 billion, profit $140 million) since 1978, Chef Pierre also prepared other frozen desserts through independent brokers and distributors. Chef Pierre's primary market was the midwestern United States which was mainly served by the company's 270,000 square foot facility in Traverse City, Michigan. Though no sales figures were obtainable for this distinct operation alone, Consolidated's frozen food operations, of which Chef Pierre was a part (along with Booth fisheries Corp., Idaho Frozen Food Corp., Popsicle Industries, Inc., and Kitchens of Sara Lee, Inc.), registered 1980 and 1981 sales of $598 million and $643 million, respectively. Pretax income in 1981 for Consolidated's frozen foods division was $28 million as opposed to $32 million in 1980.

KMP also competed against at least three significant regional rivals for its pie business. Shenandoah Pies, with its location and markets in St. Louis, Missouri, was one of KMP's chief rivals in this area. Shenandoah made a full line of fresh pies which it sold to both retail and institutional customers.

In the Chicago, Illinois, area, KMP competed against Fasano Pies, which supplied retail and institutional customers east of the Rocky Mountains with 9″ fresh pies and 8″ and 10″ frozen pies. Fasano employed approximately 200 persons and had 1981 sales of $12 million. Fasano, like Kitchen Made, had been experiencing financing difficulties.

Blue Bird Baking Co., located in Dayton, Ohio, was a regional producer of 4″ and 8″ fresh pies which it sold to Midwestern retail customers. Blue Bird was the largest of KMP's regional rivals with 1981 sales of $15 million. Employment levels at Blue Bird during this time period were approximately 200 persons.

In summary, competitors seemed to follow a full line or limited line approach. Additionally, most seemed to concentrate on either fresh or frozen products. For the most part, larger firms seemed to offer a full line of frozen pies nationally while smaller firms emphasized limited lines of fresh pies in regional markets. No matter what strategy employed, efficiency in product and purchasing was extremely important since the cost of raw material (42 percent of sales in 1972 and 1977) and labor (28 percent of sales in 1972, 35 percent in 1977) amounted to over 2/3 of total pie revenues. Since the larger firms had facilities for long, simultaneous production runs of many pies, flavors, and sizes, and could take advantage of purchasing economics, a full line strategy was feasible. Smaller firms without such capabilities had to be content with serving niches in the marketplace, both in varieties and customer coverage, because in order to be reasonably cost competitive they had to be able to match to a certain degree the economies of their more powerful competitors. The only way this could be accomplished was by concentrating on a limited line strategy.

The Peoria Area Environment

The Peoria area, like most Midwestern cities, had shown little or no growth in the past decade, as the U.S. population shifted to the Southwest. Peoria itself showed a population decline according to the 1980 census, although the number of households increased. Exhibit 12 provides summary demographic statistics for the Peoria area.

Exhibit 12   **Peoria Area Demographics Population in Thousands[1]**

	Census			Preliminary Census	Projected Total	
	1950	1960	1970	1980	1990	2000
City	111.9	103.2	127.0	121.4	126.0	129.7
Metro area	271.8	313.4	342.0	360.6	380.2	401.2

Population Characteristics[2]	Metropolitan Peoria	Total United States
Male	48.6%	48.7%
Female	51.4%	51.3%
Children under 18	34.9%	34.3%
Median age	28.2 years	28.1 years

Labor data — Peoria Metropolitan Area, March 1980[1]

Civilian labor force	172,250
Unemployment	12,725
Percent of unemployment	7.4%
Manufacturing	51,500
Nonmanufacturing	83,400
Total government employees	17,200
Agricultural employees	3,700
Retail trade	26,800

[1]Source: "Peoria Profile," Peoria Area Chamber of Commerce, September 1980.

[2]Source: *Journal Star* research in, "Peoria: Illinois' Other Prime Market," 1980.

The economy in Peoria had traditionally been solid due to the dominant influence of Caterpillar Tractor Co., a Pabst Brewing plant, a Hiram-Walker distillery, a number of other medium-sized manufacturing facilities, and a host of smaller plants—many of which were suppliers of Caterpillar (see Exhibit 13). As a result, Peoria wage rates and median income had consistently ranked in the top 20 cities in the nation. Many Peorians believed that "Peoria doesn't have recessions."

That appeared to have changed in the last few years, however. A 12-week strike in the fall of 1979 idled many of the 30,000 + Peoria area Caterpillar workers and did far more damage to the many suppliers and other businesses that depended either directly or indirectly on the firm. In addition the Hiram-Walker plant and a Colonial Baking (bread) facility closed in 1981, the Pabst plant was scheduled to close in March 1982, and Caterpillar, for the first time in 20 years, laid off substantial numbers of workers in 1981. As a result, Peoria, which had escaped the impact of the extended recession which started around the end of the 1970s, began to suffer. Unemployment rates reached double-digit levels, with no relief in sight.

Exhibit 13   **Peoria Area Companies**

200–299 Employees

Allied Mills
Belwood Nursing Home
Carson, Pirie, Scott & Co.
Central Telephone
Commonwealth Edison
East Peoria City
Equitable Life
Federal Warehouse
First Federal Savings
First National Bank
Great Central Insurance
H. C. Products
Chris Hoerr & Co.
Hopedale Hospital
Illinois Mutual Insurance
IBM
Jefferson Bank
V. Jobst
Jumer's Castle Lodge
Lum's, Inc.
Metamora Woodworking, Metamora
Morton Metalcraft, Morton
Natkin Co.
J. C. Penney, Pekin
J. C. Penney, Peoria
Pekin City
Peoria Library
Peoria Hilton Hotel
Ramada Inn

Rock Island Lines
Ben Schwartz Markets
Sealtest
Sprinkman Industries
Szold's, Inc.
Thompson Food Basket
Toledo, Peoria & Western R.R.
West Central Utilities
Zaborac Electric

300–399 Employees

Ashland Chemical
Cohen Furniture
Cullinan & Sons
East Peoria High School
East Peoria Schools
Farm Supply Services
Interstate Bakeries
Lexington House
Libby, McNeil & Libby
Limestone High School, Bartonville
McDougal-Hartman
Montgomery Ward
Morton Building
Morton Schools, Morton
L. R. Nelson
Ozark Airline
Pekin Insurance, Pekin
UNARCO

It was possible that these events would have significant impact on the sales of pies and other desserts in the Peoria area. For instance, Caterpillar (not a customer of KMP) used less than half as many pies in 1981 as it did ten years before. Similar problems were expected in regard to other institutional, and possibly retail, markets in the future. Exhibits 14 and 15 provide statistics and listings of the major wholesalers and retail grocers in the Peoria area, respectively.

Kitchen Made Pies' Current Operations

Product Line

Kitchen Made Pies, as the name implies, was primarily engaged in pie baking. The company made a full line of pies, some on a regular basis, some seasonally. Exhibit 16 lists all major sizes and flavors of pies produced by Kitchen Made, as well as other bakery products which the firm made.

Kitchen Made sold both fresh and frozen pies, though the former was preferred by Mr. Dubicki due to better turnover and more predictable ordering on the part

---

Exhibit 13   *continued*

Venture Stores
Zeller Zone Center

400–499 Employees
Bemis Co.
Bergner's, Inc.
Fleming & Potter
Journal Star
Pekin Schools, Pekin
U.S. Regional Lab

500–599 Employees
American Distilling
Commercial National Bank
Foster-Gallagher
Pekin Memorial Hospital
Peoria & Pekin Union
Sears, Roebuck & Co.

600–699 Employees
Bradley University
C. Iber & Sons
C.P.C. International
Illinois Bell Telephone
Illinois Central College
Kroger Co., E. Peoria
City of Peoria
Proctor Hospital
U.S. Post Office

Over 699 Employees
Caterpillar Tractor Co.
Central Illinois Light Co.
Keystone Steel
Methodist Hospital
Pabst Brewing
Peoria Dist. #150 Schools
St. Francis Hospital
Wabco

Estimated Major Industry Work Schedules

	1st Shift	Percentage	2nd Shift	Percentage	3rd Shift	Percentage	Total
Caterpillar	24,300	67	7,200	20	4,800	13	36,300
Keystone	1,300	47	800	29	650	24	2,750
Pabst	334	48	192	27	175	25	701
Total	25,934	65	8,192	21	5,625	14	39,751

Source: *Journal Star* research in "Peoria: Illinois' Other Prime Market," 1980.

Exhibit 14   **Peoria Area Food Wholesalers and Statistics**

Major Local Grocery Wholesalers		Major Local Food Brokers	
Calihan Co.	Peoria Packing Co.	Block & Lieb, Inc.	Mild American Marketing
Chris Hoerr & Son So.	Rashid Provision Co., Inc.	Calkins & Co.	Myles Young, Inc.
Illinois Fruit & Produce Corp.	Schmidt Brothers Produce	Conneely Brokerage Co.	Pavey & Co.
Leu Collins Inc.	SuperValu Stores, Inc.	Glatz Bros., Inc.	Peoria Marketing Corp.
Geo. O. Pasquel Co.	Waugh Frozen Food Co.	Hockenberg-Rubin Co.	Pioneer Food Sales
Peoria Cash & Carry	Winkler's Meats	M. J. Holland, Inc.	Professional Marketers, Inc.
		R. Kinsinger Co.	E. Skinner, Inc.
		E. L. Menges Brokerage Co.	M. L. Underwood
			James A. Woodhouse Co.

	All Establishments			Establishments with Payroll	
		Operated by Unincorporated Business			Paid Employees for Week
Types of customers	Number	Sole Proprietorships (number)	Partnerships (number)	Number	(number)
Food stores	332	151	30	261	3,198
Grocery stores	207	91	19	175	2,666
All other	125	50	11	86	532
Eating and drinking places	640	343	55	538	4,934
Eating places	384	195	31	344	4,239

Source: "Peoria: Illinois' Other Prime Market," Peoria Area Chamber of Commerce, 1980.

---

of customers. One problem which restricted frozen pie sales was limited freezer space. Kitchen Made had only enough capacity to store 3,500 pies at one time. Since this represented the maximum amount of pies per day it could freeze, frozen pie sales were limited to this volume. Due to current sales mixes, KMP did not usually utilize its full storage capacity.

The Dubickis had long been proud of the fact that they used only the highest-quality ingredients in Kitchen Made products. Mr. Dubicki strongly believed that Kitchen Made pies tasted better than competitors' products, and that customers recognized this difference. Mr. Dubicki viewed this quality, however, as a major strength, especially to maintain repeat business. Still he conceded that many times customers were more concerned with price. But in the end Mr. Dubicki believed KMP's superior quality would win out through development of loyal KMP customers.

Kitchen Made pies were usually more expensive than the competitions', although prices at KMP had remained stable over the last several years, and in fact were the same in 1981 as they were in 1980. Exhibit 17 shows the relative prices for the various types of pies made by Kitchen Made. Management was particularly pleased with their high top meringue pie. Because of its superior looks and acceptance

| Exhibit 15 | Peoria Area Retail Grocers Statistics and Competitors |

Retail Sales by Store Group

| | Food Stores | | | Eating and Drinking Places |
Metro Area	Total Retail Sales ($000)	Total ($000)	Supermarkets ($000)	Total ($000)
Peoria S.M.S.A.	1,372,088	246,732	229,337	117,013
Peoria County	894,761	129,410	121,930	74,185
Tazewell County	407,459	103,601	95,499	37,057
Woodford County	69,868	13,721	11,908	5,771

Retail Sales by Merchandise Line

| | Groceries and Other Foods | |
Metro Area	All Stores ($000)	Food Stores ($000)
Peoria S.M.S.A.	215,334	202,892

Major Food Chain Stores	Number of Stores
A & P	1
Ben Schwartz (IGA)	6
Cardinal	4
Convenient Food Mart	15
Del Farm	4
Eagle	3
IGA	10
Kroger	10
Mr. K's	3
Randall's	1
Red Fox	22
Thompson Food Basket	8
Vogels	2

Source: "Peoria: Illinois' Other Prime Market," Peoria Area Chamber of Commerce, 1980.

by consumers, the price charged was much higher than the regular meringue, while costs were almost identical. Thus, profit margins were significantly higher.

Markets/Consumers

The majority of Kitchen Made's sales were made to food/bakery distributors that basically supplied two major markets. One was the institutional market which consisted of restaurants, as well as university, hospital, corporate, and government

Exhibit 16		Pie Categories	

4″	8″	9″	Other
Apple*	Apple*	Apple*	8″ cakes
Blackberry*	Applecrum	Applecrum	10″ cakes
Cherry*	Black raspberry	Blackberry*	Sheet cakes
Chocolate*		Black raspberry	Shortcake
	Cherry*	Boston	
Coconut*	Chocolate*	Cherry*	
Lemon*			
Peach*	Coconut*	Chocolate Boston	
Pineapple*	Lemon*		
	Peach*	Peach*	
	Pineapple*	Pineapple*	
	Pumpkin*	Pumpkin	
		Walnut	
	Banana meringue (HT + R)		
	Chocolate meringue (HT + R)	Banana meringue (R)	
	Coconut meringue (HT + R)	Chocolate meringue (R)	
	Lemon meringue (HT + R)	Coconut meringue (R)	
		Lemon meringue (R)	
		Banana whip	
		Chocolate whip	
		Coconut whip	
		Lemon whip	
		Pumpkin whip	

Notes: HT = high tops; R = regular.
   *Made on a regular basis.

cafeterias. The other was the retail market which included grocery stores and convenience outlets. The retail segment of KMP's market was susceptible to change in the economy, as was the institutional side. However, some segments of the institutional market, such as hospital cafeterias, did not always reflect economic variabilities.

Kitchen Made's total sales were almost evenly split between the two markets. The institutional market accounted for the majority of cake and 9″ pie sales, while the retail market bought mainly 4″ and 8″ pies. Most distributors concentrated on one market or the other, thus determining the type of products they purchased.

Exhibit 17		Kitchen Made Pies Wholesale Pie Prices	

4″ pies	$.25	8″ regular meringue	$.90	9″ fruit pies	$1.30
		8″ high top meringue	$1.40	9″ whips	$1.30
		8″ fruit pies	$1.00	9″ meringue	$1.25
				9″ specialty	$1.60
				9″ walnut	$2.00
				9″ cherry	$2.25

Buying motives for both markets varied depending upon the customer and market area involved. Some customers were very conscious of price, especially in institutional markets, while others—most notably restaurants and grocers—sometimes were more interested in quality or promotional support.

Kitchen Made's products were sold in the Peoria and St. Louis areas, but the firm also served customers in other parts of Missouri and Illinois, as well as in Iowa and Wisconsin. Major distributors of Kitchen Made products, as well as their served markets, are provided in Exhibit 18.

Besides the differences in buying motives and the type of products purchased by the two end markets, there were several other features which differentiated them from each other. Institutional markets frequently preferred frozen pies because of buying habits (institutional customers often bought to satisfy monthly needs) which prevented extensive use of fresh varieties. In contrast, turnover was a way of life in the grocery business. Thus retail customers usually preferred to make weekly or biweekly purchases. Mr. Dubicki believed retail customers liked fresh pies better because they could be put directly on the shelf, which eliminated storage, thawing, and the extra work involved in moving and stocking products twice. However, fresh pies in the grocery stores sold best through the in-store bakeries which connoted greater "freshness" to the ultimate consumer than other store locations.

In addition, retailers depended heavily upon promotional assistance for sales. In fact, one of the primary reasons Dean's Distributing, which at one time accounted for almost all of KMP's sales, became a less important customer for Kitchen Made and was not a factor in the Peoria retail market was that it refused to offer grocers this type of support. Since Dean's still accounted for 40 percent of KMP's sales as of 1981, the result was that Kitchen Made had virtually no representation in the local retail market. This was a major problem according to Mr. Dubicki because he saw retail customers as more desirable than institutional customers, and therefore wished to focus on the former. Mr. Dubicki also had been attempting to attract business from drop ship distributors because of the reduced price for retailers, and hence consumers. This, he felt, could help circumvent the higher prices charged

Exhibit 18
Percentage of Breakdowns of KMP Sales by Customer

Customer	Percentage of KMP Sales	Customer Type
Dean's Distributing	40%	Institutional
McCormick Distributing	10%	Institutional
Lowenberg	11%	Retail
Eisner's	8%	Retail
Master Snack & New Process	13%	Retail
Edwards	4%	Retail
Other	14%	Retail

for Kitchen Made products on the wholesale end. Furthermore, since drop shippers usually ordered larger quantities, Mr. Dubicki believed that longer production runs, and therefore lower costs, were possible.

In addition to sales to bakery wholesalers, Kitchen Made also operated its own delivery truck which was used primarily to deliver specialty or rush orders. No plans had been made to expand this portion of the operation.

Production

Baking and production techniques at Kitchen Made were relatively simple, though not without their own special problems. In most instances, pie crusts and fillings were made on KMP's only assembly line. One person operated the dough machine which flattened the dough and rolled enough out to make one crust. Next, the dough was passed to a second person who placed it into a pie pan. The machine then pressed the dough into the pan. Afterward, the crust passed under a filling machine which was set according to the size of the pie being made. After the crust was filled with the desired ingredients, the pie moved to another station where the top crust was molded onto the sides of the pie pan and the excess dough removed. This excess was transported by conveyor back to the dough machine.

All fruit pies were put together by the method described above, but cream pies were filled by hand. Mr. Dubicki intended to make all of Kitchen Made's pie products on the assembly line in the near future.

A major problem associated with production was the frequent conversions required each time the size or the flavor of the pies was changed. It took approximately 15–20 minutes to change over to a different size pie, and 4–5 minutes to change the type of ingredient. Size changes usually occurred twice a day (from 4″ to 8″ to 9″), but ingredients had to be changed 20–25 times per day depending upon the production schedule. It should be mentioned that a more efficient pie machine was available, but would be expensive ($150,000), and would require longer production runs to be efficient according to Mr. Dubicki. However, no explicit cost analysis had been conducted.

Once the pies were assembled, they were placed on racks and wheeled over to the ovens for baking. All fresh pies were baked. However, whether frozen pies were baked or not depended on customer preference. After baking, the pies were again placed upon racks and wheeled over to their appropriate packaging area. All pies were packaged in plain paper boxes with the Kitchen Made logo printed on the sides and top. Once packaged the pies were stacked within easy access of the shipping docks for convenient loading.

One way to reduce production costs would have been to limit the numbers of different types of pies made. However, Mr. Dubicki was concerned that this move could hurt the firm because he felt many retail and institutional buyers preferred to buy full lines of products from the same supplier. Despite this perceived concern, substantial savings were available by limiting pie varieties. For example, with full crews, Kitchen Made baked a little more than $30,000 worth of pies and cakes per week. In some instances, when the firm received a special order, a half crew would be brought in on an unscheduled shift. On these days, production reached as high as $10,000.

Recently, the first production manager, not a member of the Dubicki family, was appointed from off the shop floor. Despite opening up this new position, Mr. Dubicki had continued to spend a significant portion of his time in the shop. The production manager helped mainly in a supervisory role. Mr. Dubicki expressed confidence in her ability, but was concerned with her failure to delegate work assignments and responsibilities.

One positive recent development was the ability of Mr. Dubicki to reduce raw materials inventory. Though done as much out of necessity as out of design, the move nonetheless helped in many respects. In the past, ingredients such as fillings, flour, sugar, etc., were often bought in six-month quantities. In 1981, the firm tried to buy only what it needed for one or two weeks, except in special cases when supplies were hard to find or favorable price breaks could be obtained.

Exhibit 19 provides a rough sketch of Kitchen Made Pies' plant layout in 1981.

Financial Information

Given Kitchen Made's current product mix, sales of approximately $35,000 per week ($1,820,000 per year) were needed to break even, according to Mr. Dubicki. Variable expenses (materials and labor) were estimated to be about 85 percent of sales revenue. Exhibit 20 provides a rough breakdown of sales and operating profits by product line in percentages and dollar amounts. The 4″ pies and the cakes were the biggest money-makers according to Mr. Dubicki, with margins on the 8″ and 9″ varieties substantially lower.

Because of weak sales over the past several years, the financial condition of Kitchen Made had deteriorated. Exhibit 1 provides the operating results for the years 1971 through 1981. Exhibit 2 shows the balance sheet for 1981. Exhibit 21 presents the computable financial ratios for Kitchen Made as compared to industry averages for SIC code 2051 business (i.e., bread, cake, and related products) with sales of under $50 million.

Besides the apparent liquidity and solvency problems indicated by these statements, several other events served to increase their seriousness. The most immediate problem related to the bank note which had currently come due. Kitchen Made had an agreement with a local banking institution which allowed it to borrow $70,000 on a program resembling revolving credit. Kitchen Made paid only interest on this loan with the principal due in lump sum at the end of the borrowing period. Mr. Dubicki had hoped to refinance the loan, but the attitude of the bank caused him great concern and dissatisfaction. One major complaint was that despite sometimes keeping as much as $20,000 to $30,000 in cash in its checking account at the bank, KMP received no interest relief. Furthermore, when discussing the possibility of refinancing the loan, Mr. Dubicki was informed that in the future he would be required to sign a second mortgage on his house to secure the note. Without renewal, the firm would be faced with a considerable liquidity problem. However, Mr. Dubicki was hopeful that other Peoria area banks would welcome Kitchen Made's business if his present bank did not choose to continue their current relationship. It must be understood that this note was not secured in any way, and arrangements to place the bank in a secured position with options for renewal were possible, though not a certainty.

Exhibit 19   **KMP Plant Layout (Rough Sketch)**

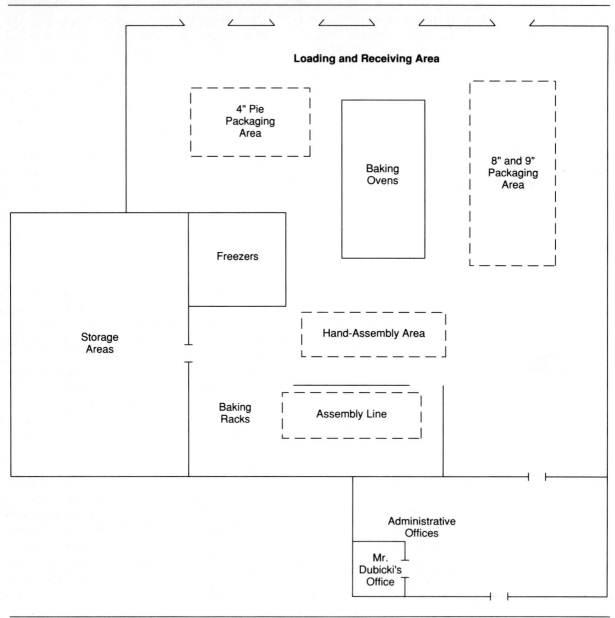

Another problem causing concern was slow payments by some customers. Most firms paid on time, and some such as Lowenberg and Eisner's consistently took advantage of discounts for early payment (usual terms are 2 percent/10 days, net/ 30 days). The major delinquent was Dean's Distributing. Dean's currently owed back payments amounting to $60,000. Mr. Dubicki felt most of this account was

Exhibit 20	Sales/Operating Profits by Product Lines, Last 12 Months

	Sales Revenues		Gross Profits		
Product	Dollar	Percent of Total	Dollars	Percent	Gross Profit Margin
4-inch pie	$ 536,000	33.5%	$147,600	61.5%	27.5%
8-inch pie	296,000	18.5	24,700	10.3	8.3
9-inch pie	704,000	44.0	50,400	21.0	7.2
Cakes	64,000	4.0	17,300	7.2	27.0
Total	$1,600,000	100.0%	$240,000	100.0%	15.0%

Wholesale Pie Prices for Kitchen Made Pies

4-inch pies	$.25	8-inch regular meringue	$.90	9-inch fruit pies	$1.30
		8-inch high-top meringue	$1.40	9-inch whips	$1.30
		8-inch fruit pies	$1.00	9-inch meringue	$1.25
				9-inch specialty	$1.60
				9-inch walnut	$2.00
				9-inch cherry	$2.25

uncollectible, but had not, as of yet, written this amount off the company's books. Mr. Dubicki expressed a desire to eliminate or substantially cut back on the business done with this customer, but despite unfavorable relations and poor payment record, Dean's still accounted for a large portion of sales. Thus Mr. Dubicki felt Kitchen Made needed to continue to do business with this customer to maintain sales levels. However, all dealings were now conducted strictly on a cash basis with this firm and at least a portion of the overdue account was being gradually paid off.

Exhibit 21
Selected Company and Industry Financial Ratios, 1981

	Industry SIC Code 2051	Kitchen Made Pies
Current ratio	.76	.81 (without Dean's .66)
Net profit/sales	3.8%	Negative
Net profit/total assets	6.5%	Negative
Net profit/equity	19.5%	Negative
Sales/equity	7.6x	Negative
Sales/total assets	2.5x	4.1x
Collection period	14 days	36 (without Dean's 23)
Sales/working capital	8.8x	Negative
Sales/inventory	53.3x	11.9x
Fixed assets/equity	131.6%	Negative
Total debt/equity	201.7%	Negative

Source: *Key Business Ratios 1981*, Dun & Bradstreet.

In spite of these financial difficulties, Mr. Dubicki indicated that Kitchen Made had been able to keep up-to-date on most of its current payables and pay small amounts on older accounts. Thus, while the situation was far from ideal and the firm was very vulnerable to unforeseen events, Mr. Dubicki believed liquidity was probably not a life-or-death concern at the moment. However, he did realize that any further decline in this condition could be extremely hazardous and potentially fatal.

Management and Organization

Most of the managerial activities at Kitchen Made Pies were handled directly by Mr. Dubicki. Besides the production manager, Ms. Barbara Britt, the only other management personnel were Ms. Charolete Watson, office manager, and Mr. Lonnie Beard, the sales promotion manager. Mr. Beard was responsible for making sure products were stocked and advertised properly at the individual stores which he visited periodically. Mr. Dubicki, besides being president and owner, also acted as general manager, sales and distribution manager, prepared projected cash flow statements, searched for new accounts, and handled many other day-to-day activities. About the only activity he was not directly involved with was the actual assembly of the pies.

Kitchen Made currently employed about 30 production workers whose responsibilities were more or less evenly split among preparation and assembly, baking, packaging, and other duties such as shipping and receiving. The shop was unionized and paid wages (about $7.25 per hour) comparable to other like-sized area firms. In addition to production and office personnel, Kitchen Made also employed several maintenance workers, a truck driver, and a half-dozen office workers.

Mr. Dubicki's View of the Future

Though the current situation at Kitchen Made Pies was far from ideal, Mr. Dubicki had expressed a commitment to planning and had made some long-needed improvements in operations such as inventory reduction. Furthermore, he believed that the good employee relations which he had developed would facilitate some of the changes being considered. Naturally, Mr. Dubicki recognized that there were many questions yet to be answered and that the answers to these questions could determine the company's fate in the future. Despite all of these problems, however, Mr. Dubicki remained confident. In his own words:

> We have been actively soliciting new accounts, reduced our dependence on Dean's and improved production methods and controls. I'm optimistic about our future. But then again, isn't that the only way I can feel?

The Business Plan Process

Key Topics

- Defining a Business Plan
- Benefits of a Business Plan
- Development of a Well-Conceived Plan
- Data Sources

Comprehensive Entrepreneurial Cases

- Shadow Brewing Company
- The Benjamin Sandman Children's Bookstore

Defining a Business Plan

A **business plan** is a written document that details a proposed venture. It must illustrate current status, expected needs, and projected results of the new business.[1] Every aspect of the venture needs to be described: the project, marketing, research and development, manufacturing, management, critical risks, financing, and milestones or timetable. A description of all of these facets of the proposed venture is necessary to give a clear picture of what that venture is, where it is projected to go, and how the entrepreneur plans to get it there. In other words, the business plan is the entrepreneur's road map for a successful enterprise.[2]

The business plan is also referred to as a venture plan, or a loan proposal, or an investment prospectus. Whatever its name, a business plan is the document that is initially required by any financial source, and one that allows the entrepreneur entrance into the investment-seeking process. Although it may be utilized as a working document once the venture is established, the major purpose of the business plan is to encapsulate strategic developments of the project in a comprehensive document for outside investors to scrutinize.

The business plan describes to potential investors and financial sources all of the events that may affect the venture being proposed, which includes various projected actions of the venture and their associated revenues and costs. It is vital that the assumptions upon which the plan is being based are explicitly stated. For

---

[1]Fred L. Fry and Charles R. Stoner, "Business Plans: Two Major Types," *Journal of Small Business Management* (January 1985): 1–6.

[2]Donald F. Kuratko and Arnold Cirtin, "Developing a Business Plan for Your Clients," *National Public Accountant* (January 1990): 24–28.

example, increases or decreases in the market or upswings or downswings in the economy during the start-up period of the new venture should be stated.

The emphasis of the business plan should always be the final implementation of the venture. In other words, it is not just the writing of an effective plan that is important, but also the translation of that plan into a successful enterprise.[3]

Thus, a business plan should:

- Describe every aspect of a particular business
- Include a marketing plan
- Clarify and outline financial needs
- Identify potential obstacles and alternative solutions
- Serve as a communication tool for all financial and professional sources

The business plan is the major tool used to guide the formation of the venture, as well as the primary document needed to manage it. But it is also more than a written document; it is a process that begins when entrepreneurs gather information and then continues as projections are made, implemented, measured, and updated; that is, it is an ongoing process.

Benefits of a Business Plan

The entire business-planning process forces an entrepreneur to analyze all aspects of the venture and prepare effective strategies to deal with the uncertainties that will undoubtedly arise. Thus, a business plan may help an entrepreneur avoid a project that is doomed to failure. As one researcher states, "If your proposed venture is marginal at best, the business plan will show you why and may help you avoid paying the high tuition of business failure. It is far cheaper not to begin an ill-fated business than to learn by experience what your business plan could have taught you at a cost of several hours of concentrated work."[4]

The benefits derived from a business plan for both the entrepreneur and the financial sources that evaluate it are discussed next.

Financing   Venture capitalists and most banks require business plans. Generally, when our national economy declines, it becomes more difficult to obtain financing, and financiers increase their demands for documentation. Many entrepreneurs say that they write business plans only because their bankers or venture capitalists require them to.

Increased Knowledge   Many of these same entrepreneurs also say that the process of actually putting the plan together is just as important as obtaining financing. Writing the plan forces them to view the business critically, objectively, and thoroughly.

---

[3]James W. Henderson, *Obtaining Venture Financing* (Lexington, MA: Lexington Books, 1988), 13–14.

[4]Joseph R. Mancuso, *How to Write a Winning Business Plan* (Englewood Cliffs, NJ: Prentice-Hall, 1985), 44.

Preventing Poor Investments   Business plans help entrepreneurs avoid projects that are poor investments. It is better not to begin a business that is destined to become a failed investment than to learn by experience what your business plan could have taught you.

Planning   Business plans force you to plan. Because all aspects of the venture must be addressed in the plan, the entrepreneur develops and examines operating strategies and their expected results. Goals and objectives are quantified so that forecasts can be compared with actual results. This type of planning can help keep you on track.[5]

It should be noted that entrepreneurs who prepare all or most of the business plan themselves are the ones who tend to benefit the most. Those who delegate this job tend to gain the least. If an entrepreneurial team is involved in planning, then all of the key members should help write the plan, although it is important that the lead entrepreneur understand each member's contribution. If consultants are sought to help prepare a business plan, the entrepreneur must remain the driving force behind the plan. Seeking the advice and assistance of outside professionals is always wise, but entrepreneurs need to understand every aspect of the business plan because it is they, and not the consultants, who come under the scrutiny of financial sources. Thus, the business plan stands as the entrepreneur's description and prediction for his or her venture and it must be defended by the entrepreneur; simply put, it is the entrepreneur's responsibility.

Developing a Well-Conceived Business Plan

Most investors agree that only a well-conceived, well-developed business plan can gather the necessary support that eventually leads to financing. The business plan must describe the new venture with excitement and yet with complete accuracy.

The Components

A brief description of the ten components of a business plan are presented next.[6]

Executive Summary   This is the most important section because it has to convince the reader that the business will succeed. In no more than three pages you should summarize the highlights of the rest of the plan.

The Executive Summary must be able to stand on its own; it should not simply be an introduction to the rest of the business plan. Investors who review many business plans may read only the Executive Summary, so if it cannot gain the investor's confidence on its own, the plan will be rejected and will never be read in its entirety.

---

[5]See Donald F. Kuratko, "Demystifying the Business Plan Process: An Introductory Guide," *Small Business Forum* (Winter 1991): 33–40.

[6]See Donald F. Kuratko and Richard M. Hodgetts, *Entrepreneurship: A Contemporary Approach,* 2d ed. (Fort Worth, TX: Dryden/HBJ Publishers, 1992), 222–316.

This section should discuss who will purchase the product or service, how much money is required for start up, and what the payback is expected to be. You should also explain why you are uniquely qualified and skilled to manage the business.

Because this section summarizes the plan, it is often best to write it last.

Description of the Business   This section should provide background information about your industry, a history of your company, and a general description of your new product or service. Your product or service should be described in terms of its unique qualities and value to consumers.

Specific **short-** and **long-term objectives** must be defined. Clearly state what sales, market share, and profitability objectives you want your business to achieve.

Marketing   Two major parts comprise the marketing section. The first is **research and analysis.** Here you should explain who will buy the product or service, or, in other words, identify your target market. Measure your market size and trends and estimate the market share you expect to capture. Be sure to include support for your sales projections. For example, if your figures are based on published marketing research data, be sure to cite the source. Do your best to make realistic and credible projections. Describe your competition in considerable detail, identifying their strengths and weaknesses. Finally, explain how you will be better than your competitors.

The second part is your **marketing plan.** This critical section should include your market strategy, sales and distribution, pricing, advertising, promotion, and public awareness. You should also demonstrate how your pricing strategy will result in a profit, identify your advertising plans, and include cost estimates to validate the proposed strategy.

Research, Design, and Development   This section includes **developmental research** leading to the design of the product. Industrial design is an art form that has successfully found its way into business, and it should not be neglected. Technical research results should be evaluated. Include the costs of research, testing, and development. Explain carefully what has already been accomplished (e.g., prototype development, lab testing, early development). Finally, mention any research or technical assistance that has been provided for you.

Manufacturing   Explain the process steps to be used to produce your product or service. A simple flowchart is often used to show how a product will be assembled. This section should also describe the advantages of your location in terms of zoning, tax laws, wage rates, labor availability, and proximity to suppliers and transportation systems. The requirements and costs of your production facilities and equipment should also be outlined in this section. (Be careful—too many entrepreneurs underestimate this part.)

Organization   Start by describing the **management team,** their unique qualifications, and how you will compensate them (including salaries, employment agreements, stock purchase plans, levels of ownership, and other considerations).

Discuss how your organization will be structured and consider including a diagram illustrating who will report to whom. Also include a discussion of the potential contribution of the board of directors, advisors, and consultants. Finally, carefully describe the legal structure of your venture (i.e., sole proprietorship, partnership, or corporation).

Critical Risks   Discuss **potential risks** before investors point them out. Outside consultants can often help identify risks and recommend alternative courses of action. Here are some examples of potential risks: price-cutting by competitors; potentially unfavorable industrywide trends; design or manufacturing costs that could exceed estimates; sales projections that are not achieved; production development schedules that are not met; difficulties or long lead times in procuring parts or raw materials; and greater-than-expected innovation and development costs needed to keep pace with new competition. The main objective of this section is to show that you can anticipate and control (to a reasonable degree) your risks.

Financial   This section of the business plan will be closely scrutinized by potential investors, so it is imperative that you give it the attention it deserves. Three key financial statements must be presented: a **balance sheet,** an **income statement,** and a **cash flow statement.** These statements typically cover a three-year period. Be sure you state all the assumptions you made when calculating the figures.

Determine the stages at which your business will require external financing and identify the expected financing sources (both debt and equity). Also, clearly show what return on investment these sources will achieve if they invest in your business. The final item to include is a break-even chart, which should show what level of sales will be required to cover all costs.

If the work is done well, the financial statements should represent the actual financial achievements expected from the business plan. They also provide a standard by which to measure the actual results of operating the enterprise and become a very valuable tool for managing and controlling the business in the first few years.

Milestone Schedule   This is another important segment of the business plan because it requires determining what tasks must be accomplished to achieve your objectives. Milestones and deadlines should be established and monitored while the venture is in progress. Each milestone is related to all of the others and together they comprise a network of the entire project.

Appendix   This section includes important background information that was not included in the other sections. It should include such items as resumes of the management team, names of references and advisors, drawings, documents, agreements, and any materials that support the plan. You may also wish to add a bibliography of the sources from which you drew information.

Table 3.1 provides a complete outline of a business plan's components. This checklist is presented in a question format to help you assess the thoroughness of the plan.

Acquiring information will probably be the most time-consuming part of the business-plan process. Following is a brief sampling of types of sources that may help you find the kind of information you will need.

Table 3.1   **A Business Plan Checklist: Key Questions to Answer**

I. Executive Summary

a. Why will the business succeed?
b. What do you want to start (or change)?
c. How much money is required?
d. What is the return on the investment?
e. Why is the venture a good risk?

II. Business Description

a. What type of business are you planning?
b. What products or services will you sell?
c. What type of opportunity is it (new, part-time, expansion, seasonal, year-round)?
d. Why does it promise to be successful?
e. What is the growth potential?
f. How is it unique?

III. Marketing

a. Who are your potential customers?
b. How large is the market?
c. Who are your competitors? How are their businesses positioned?
d. What market share do you anticipate?
e. How will you price your product or service?
f. What advertising and promotional strategies will you use?

IV. Research, Design, and Development

a. Have you carefully described your design or development?
b. What technical assistance have you received?
c. What research needs do you anticipate?
d. Are the costs involved in research and design reasonable?

V. Manufacturing

a. Where will the business be located? Why?
b. What steps are required to produce your product or service?
c. What are your needs for production (e.g., facilities and equipment)?
d. Who will be your suppliers?
e. What type of transportation is available?
f. What is the supply of available labor?
g. What will it cost to produce your product or service?

VI. Organization

a. Who will manage the business?

b. What qualifications do you have?
c. How many employees will you need? What will they do?
d. How will you structure your organization?
e. What are your plans for employee salaries, wages, and benefits?
f. What consultants or specialists will you need? How will you use them?
g. What legal form of ownership will you choose? Why?
h. What licenses and permits will you need?

VII. Critical Risks

a. What potential problems could arise?
b. How likely are they?
c. How do you plan to manage these potential problems?

VIII. Financial

a. What is your total estimated business income for the first year? Monthly for the first year? Quarterly for the second and third years?
b. What will it cost you to open the business?
c. What will your personal monthly financial needs be?
d. What sales volume will you need in order to make a profit during the first three years?
e. What will be the break-even point?
f. What will be your projected assets, liabilities, and net worth on the day before you expect to open?
g. What are your total financial needs?
h. What are your potential funding sources? How will you spend it?
i. How will the loans be secured?

IX. Milestone Schedule

a. What timing have you projected for this project?
b. How have you set your objectives?
c. Have you set up your deadlines for each stage of your venture?
d. Is there a relationship between events in this venture?

X. Appendix

a. Have you included all important documents, drawings, agreements, and references?

Source: Donald F. Kuratko, "Demystifying the Business Plan Process: An Introductory Guide," *Small Business Forum* (Winter 1990): 36.

Data Sources for Your Business Plan

Some sources of internal data include:

- Accounting records
- Marketing studies
- Customer complaint files

- Sales records
- Other company records

Some sources of external data include:

- American Statistics Index
- Business Information Sources
- Consultants and Consulting Organizations Directory
- Directories in Print
- Directory of Industry Data Sources
- Directory of On-Line Databases
- Encyclopedia of Associations
- Encyclopedia of Business Information Sources
- Small Business Sourcebook
- Statistical Reference Index
- General guides (which provide direction on where to look for data on a particular topic)

Some indexes to books and articles include:

- Applied Technology and Sciences Index
- Books in Print
- Business Periodicals Index
- Computer Database Information Searches
- Reader's Guide to Periodical Literature
- Standard Periodical Directory
- Wall Street Journal Index

Some government publications include:

- Census reports (agriculture, construction, housing, manufacturers, mineral industries, population, retail trade, service industries, transportation, wholesale trade)
- County and City Data Book
- County Business Patterns
- Economic Indicators
- Guide to Foreign Trade Statistics
- Guide to Industrial Statistics
- U.S. Industrial Outlook

Some organizations and people include:

- American Marketing Association
- Friends, relatives, and other small-business owners
- Librarians
- Local Chamber of Commerce offices
- Local and regional newspapers
- Marketing research firms
- Small Business Development Centers (SBDCs)
- State, local, and federal government offices
- Trade associations
- Universities

Guidelines to Remember

The following points are a collection of recommendations by experts in venture capital and new-venture development.[7] These guidelines are presented as tips for successful business-plan development and should be adhered to so others will understand the importance of the various plan segments you are presenting. (Table 3.2 provides helpful hints for each segment of the plan.)

Keep the Plan Reasonably Short   Business plan readers are important people who refuse to waste time. Therefore, entrepreneurs should explain the venture not only carefully and clearly, but also concisely. (The plan should be no more than 40 pages long, excluding appendix.)

Appropriately Organize and Package the Plan   A table of contents, an executive summary, an appendix, exhibits, graphs, proper grammar, a logical arrangement of segments, and overall neatness are critical elements in the effective presentation of a business plan.

Orient the Plan toward the Future   Entrepreneurs should attempt to create an exciting plan by outlining trends and forecasts that describe what the venture intends to do and what the opportunities are for the use of the product or service.

Avoid Exaggeration   Sales potentials, revenue estimates, and the venture's potential growth should not be inflated. Many times best-case, worst-case, and probable-case scenarios should be developed. Documentation and research are vital to the credibility of the plan.

Highlight Critical Risks   The critical risks segment of the business plan is important because it demonstrates the entrepreneur's ability to analyze potential problems and develop alternative courses of action.

Present Evidence of an Effective Entrepreneurial Team   The management segment of the business plan should clearly identify the skills of each key person as well as demonstrate how all such persons can effectively work together as a team to manage the venture.

Do Not Overdiversify   Focus the attention of the plan on one main opportunity for the venture. A new business should not attempt to create multiple markets or pursue multiple ventures until it has successfully developed one main strength.

---

[7]These guidelines are adapted from Jeffry A. Timmons, "A Business Plan Is More Than a Financing Device," *Harvard Business Review* (March–April 1980): 25–35; W. Keith Schilit, "How to Write a Winning Business Plan," *Business Horizons* (September–October 1987): 13–22; and Donald F. Kuratko and Ray V. Montagno, *The Entrepreneur's Guide to Venture Formation* (Muncie, IN: Center for Entrepreneurial Resources, Ball State University, 1986): 33–34.

Table 3.2	Helpful Hints for Writing the Business Plan

Summary

No more than three pages.

This is the most crucial part of your plan because it must capture the reader's interest.

What, how, why, where, etc. must be summarized.

Complete this part *after* the finished business plan has been written.

Business Description Segment

The name of the business.

A background of the industry with history of the company (if any) should be covered here.

The potential of the new venture should be described clearly.

Any unique or distinctive features of the venture should be spelled out.

Marketing Segment

Convince investors that sales projections and competition can be met.

Market studies should be used and disclosed.

Identify target market, market position, and market share.

Evaluate *all* competition and specifically cover "why" and "how" you will be better than the competitors.

Identify all market sources and assistance used for this segment.

Demonstrate pricing strategy since your price must penetrate and maintain a market share to *produce profits*. Thus, "lowest" price is *not* necessarily the "best" price.

Identify your advertising plans with cost estimates to validate the proposed strategy.

Research, Design, and Development Segment

Cover the *extent* and *costs* involved in needed research, testing, or development.

Explain carefully what has been accomplished *already* (prototype, lab testing, early development).

Mention any research or technical assistance that has been provided for you.

Manufacturing Segment

Provide the advantages of your location (zoning, tax laws, wage rates).

List the production needs in terms of facilities (plant, storage, office space) and equipment (machinery, furnishings, supplies).

Describe the access to transportation (for shipping and receiving).

Explain proximity to your suppliers.

Mention the availability of labor in your location.

Provide estimates of manufacturing costs—be careful, too many entrepreneurs "underestimate" their costs.

Management Segment

Provide resumes of all key people in the management of the venture.

Carefully describe the legal structure of the venture (sole proprietorship, partnership, or corporation).

Cover the added assistance (if any) of advisers, consultants, and directors.

Provide information on how everyone is to be compensated. (How much, also.)

(continued)

Table 3.2   *continued*

Critical Risks Segment

Discuss potential risks *before* investors point them out. Some examples include:

Price-cutting by competitors.

Potentially unfavorable industrywide trends.

Design or manufacturing costs in excess of estimates.

Sales projections not achieved.

Product development schedules not met.

Difficulties or long lead times encountered in the procurement of parts or raw materials.

Larger-than-expected innovation and development costs to stay competitive.

Alternative courses of action.

Financial Segment

Provide statements.

Describe the needed sources for your funds and the uses you intend for the money.

Provide a budget.

Create stages of financing for purposes of allowing evaluation by investors at various points.

Milestone Schedule Segment

Provide a timetable or chart to demonstrate when each phase of the venture is to be completed. This shows the relationship of events and provides a deadline for accomplishment.

Source: Donald F. Kuratko and Ray V. Montagno, *The Entrepreneur's Guide to Venture Formation* (Muncie, IN: Center for Entrepreneurial Resources, Ball State University, 1986): 33–34. Reprinted with permission.

Identify the Target Market   Substantiate the marketability of the venture's product or service by identifying the particular customer niche that is being sought. This segment of the business plan is pivotal to the success of the other parts. Market research must be included to demonstrate *how* this market segment has been identified.

Write the Plan in the Third Person   Rather than continually stating "I," "we," or "us," the entrepreneur should phrase everything as "he," "they," or "them." In other words, avoid personalizing the plan and keep the writing objective.

Capture the Reader's Interest   Because a small percentage of the business plans that are submitted to investors are actually funded, entrepreneurs need to capture the reader's interest right away by emphasizing the venture's uniqueness. Use the title page and executive summary as key tools for capturing the reader's attention and creating a desire to read more.

Preparing a business plan will not guarantee success or remove risk or uncertainty, and it will not always result in financing. But business plans can help entrepreneurs make informed decisions. For this reason alone they almost always prove to be a good investment of time and effort.

CASE

CASE • *Shadow Brewing Company*

Darin M. Floyd, Ball State University

Table of Contents

I. Executive Summary

A. Statement of Purpose

The following financial proposal has been prepared by Darin Floyd in order to obtain financing for the Shadow Brewing Company (the Company) in the amount of $594,000. Through the offering of preferred stock, Mr. Floyd feels he will gain this funding, which is essential for the start-up and operational success of the Carmel, Indiana-based microbrewery. Investors will watch their equity in the Company steadily grow over the first three to five years. Investors could receive additional large gains from the Company if expansion is created through franchising. Once the Company has proven its products and processes, the Company will take the necessary steps needed to ensure franchise operations. These steps will begin, again, once it is a proven concept. The ROI and financials in this document do not contain any revenues from franchising or its fees.

Mr. Darin Floyd will invest $161,000 of his own capital into the business, and his father, Mr. William Floyd, will invest $50,000. The remainder is to be raised through the stock offering, with shares to be sold at $5.00 each.

Sources and Applications of Funding

Sources

D. Floyd's investment	$161,000.00
W. Floyd's investment	50,000.00
Stock offering	594,000.00
Total	$805,000.00

Applications

Equipment (first year)	$455,951.00
Cash for working capital	349,049.00
Total	$805,000.00

More financial information can be found in the Financial Explanations.

B. Summary Description of the Company

The Shadow Brewing Company is positioning itself as an aggressive, state-of-the-art facility within the growing microbrewing industry. With proper management and guidance, the Company expects its sales and profit levels to reach the following:

Year	Gross Sales	Gross Margin	Net Profit	Owner's Equity
One	$ 147,574.00	$132,136.00	$(194,281.57)	$ 531,245.30
Two	620,025.00	505,159.00	76,442.00	611,581.00
Three	923,785.00	723,720.00	253,102.00	864,683.00
Four	1,067,327.00	834,141.00	272,927.00	1,137,609.00
Five	1,175,474.00	918,661.00	307,133.00	1,444,743.00

Marketing will be carried out through various means of promotions, such as taste tests, tours of the brewery, print, and also radio media. The Company hopes that most of its marketing will be done by word of mouth. After speaking with many other microbreweries, the Company found that this is the best and most stable means for achieving sales goals.

Mr. Darin Floyd will be president and chief executive officer of the Company, with 20 percent ownership. He will also design and brew all of the Company's products. There will eventually be a sales staff of three people, excluding Mr. Floyd, and a delivery driver, bringing total employment to five individuals. Mr. William Floyd will serve as chairman of the board.

This business plan will serve as a formal outline for start-up and the first four years of operation and will continually be updated for future use.

II. Business Description

A. Image of the Shadow Brewing Company

Shadow Brewing Company will be positioned as a state-of-the-art facility, with heavy emphasis on aesthetics as well as stringent quality control measures, which produces only the finest products. The Company's success will be achieved by using the latest technology, such as turn-key brewing equipment, computer-monitored systems, and customized ingredients. The Company will produce Wheat, Ale, and Pilsner products, each with a distinctive taste, to appeal to different consumer preferences, demonstrating the Company's dedication to and awareness of consumer trends.

This image will be carried out in every aspect of operations, from the initial recipe stage, all the way through to the packaging of the product. Taste tests will be performed to determine greatest consumer appeal in the recipe stage. Through the use of high-quality ingredients, such as various multirow grains and customized malts, premium beers will be produced. Quality control (QC) and quality assurance (QA) will be the hallmark throughout the production, bottling, and packaging stages. Visible graphic design and variances of packaging will be employed to distinguish the Company's products. Throughout these stages, customer service will be dedicated to excellence, with each employee paying close attention to his respective and prospective clients.

B. *Objectives*

1. Long-Term Objectives   Shadow Brewing Company's foremost and enduring objective will be to produce high-quality beer products which suit the tastes of Shadow's Indianapolis-based market. Another long-term objective for the Company is to establish a customer base of at least 10,000 loyal consumers within five years; specifically, to have a data base with customers' names, addresses, and other vital information. From this, consumer trends can be more precisely followed, allowing the Company to make any necessary alterations to either product or service.

2. Short-Term Objectives   Two of the most important short-term objectives for the Company are to obtain cash flow break-even and initial consumer recognition, appeal, and acceptance. This is critical to any brewer who wants its name to be associated with a great product, not the stigma attached to a poor one, and compels the Company to do extensive research and taste testing to assure its recognition, appeal, and acceptance. The Company's initial sales objective will be $147,000 in sales in year one, and $620,000 by year two.

C. *Shadow Brewing Company's Advantages*

Several advantages set the Company apart from other microbrewers, especially its primary competitor, the Indianapolis Brewing Company. First, Shadow will have a brewmaster, Darin Floyd, trained at the Siebel Institute of Technology, a world-renowned institution, who will be able to create more precise recipes and follow stricter quality measures.

Second, the Shadow Brewing Company will have a capacity of 5,000 barrels a year, much larger than most micros (average capacity is 2,365 barrels per year).[1] This allows for greater distribution and the ability to produce a wider range of products.

Third, the equipment that the Company will be using is, as mentioned earlier, of a "high-tech" nature, allowing for better QC and QA, and less labor involvement, and thus allowing for improved profit margins and less variance in taste and product quality. In addition, the processes can be monitored and evaluated to determine capacity usage and effectiveness, something only a handful of micros currently do.

D. Proprietor's Background

Darin M. Floyd has demonstrated overwhelming interest in the brewing industry. In high school, Mr. Floyd began researching the industry, focusing specifically on microbreweries and brewpubs. He began a seven-year career in the restaurant business, participating in all phases of the business.

Throughout his college career, Mr. Floyd continued to research the microbrewing industry. In 1988 he attended a brewpub convention in Schaumburg, Illinois, and by 1991 he had visited five brewpubs, three large breweries, three micros, and three beverage-related trade shows. At each visit he either held discussions with an executive or with a brewmaster, gaining valuable insight into the industry and the respective businesses.

Toward the end of 1990, Mr. Floyd began the development of this business proposal. In addition, in late 1991 Mr. Floyd attended the world-renowned Siebel Institute of Technology (United States Brewer's Academy) in their masters-equivalent program. The program, located in Chicago, started in September and continued through November, covering every aspect of the brewing process.

Upon graduation from Siebel's, Mr. Floyd began his Brewmaster Apprenticeship at Weinkeller Brewery in Berwyn, Illinois. As part of his ongoing study, Mr. Floyd was fortunate enough to help establish a second Weinkeller in Westmont, Illinois. By doing so, Mr. Floyd learned firsthand everything that it takes to construct a brewery. In addition, Mr. Floyd has assumed responsibility for the smooth operation of both Weinkeller Brewpubs.

Bill Floyd has held several executive-level positions in marketing, sales, and operations for the Burroughs Corporation, Recognition Equipment, and ShipNet Systems, Inc. and is currently the president of Information Profit Group, a company he founded.

III. Product Description

Shadow will produce three main products: a wheat beer, an ale, and a Pilsner. The wheat beer is pale in color, less in alcohol content and calories, but has a distinct wheat taste. The ale will follow the "Deusseldorfer" style beer made in Germany, rich in flavor and amber in color. The Pilsner, a Czechoslovakian beer, will be Shadow's "flagship" beer, produced as a nouveau-lager, stronger and more bodied than the typical "American beer," with more hop flavor.

All of Shadow's products will follow the old-world brewing standard, "Reinheitsgebot," the German Purity Law of 1516, which permits only malted barley, hops, yeast, and water as ingredients. In addition, there will be no additives, adjuncts, or chemical preservatives. Beers with adjuncts such as syrup, corn, or rice produce more fusel oils and higher alcohols, which promote headache and hangover. This is not the case with Shadow beers, all malt beverages with plenty of body to go with the alcohol.

Since Shadow's products are all natural, they will be marketed as such. Following are the daily requirements and percent fulfilled by a liter of beer for male adults.

There are approximately 14 calories per ounce in an all-malt beer, or 168 calories per 12-ounce bottle.

Nutrient	R.D.A. Mg/Day	Mg/1	R.D.A./Liter	Percent/Liter
Protein	56,000	4,800	11,090	43
Calcium	800	60	158	38
Phosphorus	800	250	158	158
Iron	10	.03	2	2
Magnesium	350	80	69	116
Thiamine	1.4	.05	.277	18
Riboflavin	1.6	.7	.317	220
Niacin	18	6.8	3.57	190
Pantothenic Acid	.5	.7	.99	71
Vitamin B-6	2	.76	.40	190
Folacin	.4	.7	.079	886
Vitamin B-12	.003	.0099	.00059	1,678

One liter of beer is 18 percent of a person's calories and supplies:

37.8% of the niacin needs	175% of the folacin needs
38% of the B-6 needs	330% of the B-12 needs
43.8% of the riboflavin needs	

In other words, beer is a good source of the above, and of magnesium and phosphorus, but is a poor source of calcium, iron, thiamine, and pantothenic acid. Beer is very low in sodium, at less than 35mg per 12 ounces per the FDA standard (for those who must watch their sodium) and high in potassium.

IV. Industry Description

With 60 million adults drinking beer (35 percent of the adult population), the U.S. brewing industry is a $40 billion market. However, the overall beer industry is near stagnant, with less than 0.3 percent growth. One of the reasons for this slowed growth is the pricing trends. Contrary to popular opinion, the beer industry is price elastic, meaning that increases in prices bring decreases in volume. Part of these increased prices stem from government taxation. On January 1, 1991, federal excise taxes doubled on large brewers, from $9 a barrel to $18 a barrel, and the tax burden has been felt by the consumers. Still, the breweries say they don't foresee their customers substantially reducing their purchases of beer in the face of these price increases.[2]

As a result of the consumers' apparent price sensitivity, the inflation rate for alcoholic beverages has been moderate (in 1989 the consumer price index for alcoholic beverages rose 4.1 percent, compared to a 4.8 percent rise for all other items). This below-average price inflation underlines the potential for heightened future competition.[3]

Another reason for slowed growth in the beer industry is consumer preference, which appears to outweigh economic factors. Throughout the 1960s and the 1970s, the beer industry grew rapidly, despite various recessions. During the recession of the early 1980s, however, beer consumption slowed, and during the strong period of economic growth in the late 1980s, beer consumption was relatively flat.[4]

This can partly be explained by the consumers' trend toward healthier products and perhaps a somewhat reduced social acceptance of drinking. Drinking in moderation seems to be the trend, and rightfully so, considering less social acceptance and strict antiinebriation laws.

Despite these factors, the brewers are optimistic that with the introduction of new low-calorie and low-alcohol beers, they should be able to hold their ground. In fact, they are confident that their consumers won't trade down from premium-priced beers.[5]

A. Imported Beer Industry

In 1970, imported beer was an insignificant portion of the U.S. beer consumption, accounting for less than 1.0 percent of the market. By 1987, however, market share had expanded to 5.0 percent. Since then, a weaker dollar has slowed imported beer growth. In 1988 imports still had 5.0 percent of the market, but this fell to 4.5 percent in 1989. Of those who drink beer, 16.5 percent are considered import drinkers, on a national scale.[6]

At least 50 percent of import volume comes from on-premises consumption, including restaurants and bars, versus 30 percent for domestic beers.[7] As mentioned above, the social and legal pressures against alcohol abuse are growing, but due to their on-premise consumption, have a disproportionate greater effect on imported beers, cutting into their greatest market.

B. Microbrewing Industry

Of the flat and declining markets within the brewing industry, only one segment has shown significant growth: the microbrewing segment. Total production of micros and brewpubs was over 250,000 barrels in 1990, up 45 percent from the previous year (see Exhibit 1). During each of the past three years, an average of more than 16 microbreweries and 55 brewpubs have opened around the nation (see Exhibit 2). The top 30 producers averaged 26 percent growth, with only three selling less beer in 1990 than in 1989. In 1985, there were only 21 microbreweries operating, and in 1990 there were 84.[8] This growth indicates that microbrewery products not only are gaining wider acceptance with the public, but also indicates that locally made products and small businesses are gaining favor with consumers. The 1990s offer emerging opportunities for the microbrewing industry. There is the potential for some 500 micros and brewpubs nationwide by the middle of the decade.[9]

Microbrewers are generally focusing their marketing attention on the imported beer market because their beers are at the upper end of the beer market, where imports sell.

V. Marketing Section
A. Competition

1. Direct Competition   Shadow Brewing Company's direct competitor in its served market will be the Indianapolis Brewing Company (IBC), whose primary products are Duesseldorfer Draft Ale, Main Street Lager, and Main Street Pilsner.

Exhibit 1

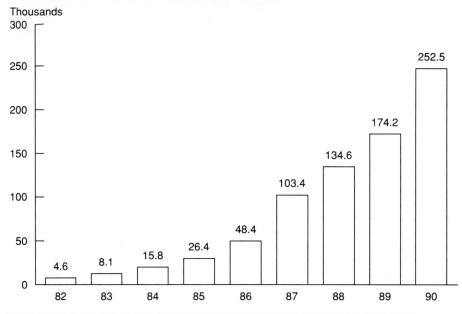

TAXABLE PRODUCTION OF US MICROBREWERIES
(Figured in US Barrels)

These are available in bottles as well as draft. IBC is located at 33rd and Post Road on the east side of Indianapolis. It has a brewing capacity of 1,700 barrels per year and a bottling capacity of about 15,000 cases per year. Its distribution is done by its four-person sales staff who directly market IBC's products.

IBC was encouraged to drop both of its Main Street Lines due to their lack of consumer appeal and lagging sales by a marketing group from Indiana University. Overall, IBC poses little threat, if any, to Shadow. Having another microbrewer in the area only enhances the public's awareness of the products.

2. Indirect Competition   The Company's primary competition will come from the imported beer segment. These are the higher-end beers that Shadow will be competing with for shelf space and price. The leading imports are listed below, and average $6.46 per six-pack.

Top 10 Imported Beer Brands

1. Heineken (Netherlands)
2. Molson (Canada)
3. Beck's (Germany)
4. Moosehead (Canada)
5. Corona (Mexico)
6. St. Pauli Girl (Germany)
7. Dos Equis (Mexico)
8. Foster's Lager (Australia)
9. Amstel Light (Netherlands)
10. Labatt (Canada)

Exhibit 2

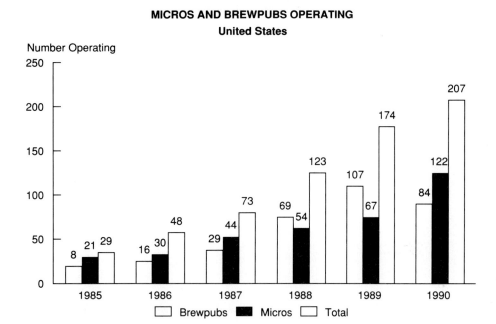

The Company's market surveys indicate these imports average 9.0 percent of beer sales in liquor stores and 16 percent in other retail outlets. In addition, the average liquor store carries 30 different imports, while other retailers carry 6.

Although the Company will be competing with imports, there are some super-premium beers and newly introduced products that may sway a consumer. For instance, Michelob products are fairly big sellers, as well as new products like Bud Dry and Miller Genuine Draft Light. These products average $4.08 per six-pack and make up 11 percent of beer sales in liquor stores and 10 percent in retail outlets. The average number of super-premiums carried by liquor stores is seven, and other retailers carry four.

B. Research and Analysis

1. **Target Market**   The focus of both time and financial commitment will be dedicated to attracting those consumers who currently spend money on imported beers. Since the Company will sell the majority of its products through retailers, it will target those retail outlets in the Indianapolis and surrounding areas that cater to the upper-end consumer, those people between the ages of 24 and 54, earning $30,000 a year or more, and professional and college educated. Of course, this only represents the majority of the consumers who will purchase Shadow's beer, but others not included in this area will purchase it as well (see Appendix A).

2. Market Size   According to the national average, 16.5 percent of beer drinkers are imported beer consumers, meaning a projected market of Indianapolis and surrounding area import consumers at 281,972. After further research, however, the Company found Indianapolis to be below average, with 12 percent import beer consumers, or 206,452 people. Although this market is below the "norm," the Company feels such a potential customer base will easily suffice as a market base.

3. Expected Market Share   Market surveys, conducted by the Company of liquor stores, restaurants, and bars in the Indianapolis and surrounding areas, indicate actual (initial) purchases of 2,140 cases per month and 176 kegs per month, generating sales of $500,200 per year. This is the average price the market segment is willing to pay upon introduction of products (see Appendix B).

Survey Results (Averages)

Items Sold	Price		Total Sales
Kegs— 176	$45.21		$ 7,956.96
Cases—2,140	15.76		33,726.40
		Total monthly	$ 41,683.36
		Total yearly	$500,200.32

Same Amount Sold at Company Prices

Kegs— 176	$75.00		$ 3,200.00
Cases—2,140	18.00		38,520.00
		Total monthly	$ 51,720.00
		Total yearly	$620,640.00

Proportional Amount Sold at Company Prices

Kegs— 106	$75.00		$ 7,950.00
Cases—1,874	18.00		33,732.00
		Total monthly	$ 41,682.00
		Total yearly	$500,184.00

Based on this research, the Company expects to capture at least 4 percent of the Indianapolis import market within the first three years, which would more than account for the sales level of $924,000. Shadow's objective, however, is to capture 5 percent within five years based on current market analysis and the projected growth both in the Indianapolis area and in the import beer market.

C. Marketing Plan

1. Taste Tests   Once the brewing equipment has been installed, small batches of various beers will be produced. Local taste testings will then be set up with various retailers to establish current taste trends in the Indianapolis market. This is an essential process because it allows the Company to determine specific recipes that are the most appealing to consumers, without going to the expense of producing large batches of beer that may, or may not, sell in the marketplace. This is also important to the Company's recognition as a new local brewer. With help from retailers and other media, this will be one of the most cost effective ways of advertising.

2. Direct Sales   Once specific recipes have been produced, sales associates will begin to market the Company's products to various retailers. The retailers that will be targeted first will be restaurants, bars, and other operations that serve draft beer, *not* liquor stores. This practice is used by many micros in the initial start-up phase of operations, primarily for two reasons. First, by distributing draft beer to restaurants and the like, more customers will have the opportunity to be aware of the products and to try them. Second, this defers capital outlays that are necessary to purchase the bottling and packaging equipment. This method of sales has proven to be the most cost effective way of sales for small brewers in the past simply because the accounts can be more personally controlled, and the consumer won't see an increased cost in Shadow's products due to a distributor's cost of sales.

In order to encourage retailers to carry Shadow's lines, sales associates will take samples of the different products into each establishment in order for the owners and/or staff to taste. By doing so, the retailer can determine if certain brands will sell in their respective establishments, and the sales associate will know how much the retailer might want to purchase on a trial basis.

3. Point-of-Sale Displays   Once store owners agree to carry Shadow's products, point-of-sale displays will be set up. For liquor stores, posters will be hung for sale, as well as T-shirts and baseball caps bearing the Shadow name and logo. In addition, the Company will place clear display decals on the coolers that bear the Shadow name and logo. Restaurants will have some posters for sale, but will also have table tents and drink coasters set up throughout the various establishments. Through point-of-sale methods, Shadow hopes to increase the awareness and consumption of its products quickly throughout its sales areas.

4. Local Promotions   In addition to the initial taste testings, these events will be continued at those retailers carrying Shadow's products. The Company feels that such events place personal emphasis on the products and customer service, while at the same time boosting their overall recognition. Another promotional idea will be to have a postcard within each six-pack that asks the purchaser for various information. These cards, when returned to Shadow, will be put into a customer data base. This data base will help Shadow better monitor its market and will act as a large mailing list for future promotional ideas.

5. Tours for the public   Free tours to the public will be provided every Saturday and by appointment for larger groups. This is an excellent way to attract potential consumers because they actually get to view the production facility and sample the products. This should allow Shadow to gain some on-site sales from the visitors as well.

6. Local Recognition   Throughout all stages, local recognition via articles, interviews, and other means of "focused" advertising will be achieved. In addition, Shadow will send its products to those individuals who may enable further recognition, such as the mayor of Indianapolis, the Colts football team, and the like. Again, word of mouth will be the most important means of advertising.

7. Limited Advertising   Although Shadow feels that direct marketing is the most appropriate means of sale for its products, some monies will be allocated to advertising. Initially, advertising will be used in various media to acknowledge special events by the Company. In the future, if deemed appropriate, advertising will be used to promote the Company's products in the more traditional fashion of print and radio advertisements.

VI. Manufacturing Segment

A. Technical Description of the Brewing Process

The brewing process is somewhat technical concerning chemical equations, elemental breakdowns, and the like, but is basically a seven-stage process: malting, mashing, brewing, fermenting, aging, carbonating, and packaging.

In the malting stage, grain is soaked in water and allowed to germinate in order to unbind amylase, the enzyme that converts starch into sugar when beer is cooked. After grains and enzymes are cooked together in the mashing stage, the spent grains are filtered out, and the resulting liquid, called wort, is brewed, along with a few hops per barrel. Hops give the beer its faintly bitter flavor and stop the enzyme conversion of starch to sugar.

After the wort is cooled and filtered and the spent hops strained out, Shadow will add its own strains of yeast to convert the sugars to alcohol and carbon dioxide. The next step, lagering (which means "to store"), allows the yeast to settle out, after which the beer is again filtered. After filtering, the beer is then bottled, canned or kegged, and packaged for distribution.

B. Location

The Shadow Brewing Company will be located in Kirby Plaza North, a light manufacturing area of Carmel's industrial park. The facility will be housed in a newly built complex owned by Jon Kirby Realtors. Carmel, on the near north side of Indianapolis, has access to various routes such as Meridian Street, Keystone Ave, Indiana Highway 431, 116th Street, I-69, and 1-465. (See map, Appendix C.)

Monthly rent for the 8,000 square-foot facility is $5,333 or $8.00 per square foot (triple net). Of this $8.00, $.75 is used to cover property taxes, signage, parking lot maintenance, office renovation, and miscellaneous expenses incurred by the owner.

Carmel was chosen as the Company's location for two primary reasons. The first is due to accessibility and close proximity to Indianapolis. Second, Carmel is considered a "progressive" community by many, and the Company wishes to be positioned in just such a community.

C. Distribution

From this location, the Company will be able to market and distribute its products with ease. There will be three sales associates and one delivery driver, all of whom will ensure that timely sales and deliveries are met. Shadow's distribution of products will start in the heart of Carmel and generate out, encompassing the Indianapolis area at first, and then expanding into other cities such as Lafayette, Bloomington, and Muncie. This, however, is dependent upon the Company's capacity; the Company wishes to remain at a 5,000-barrel capacity for the immediate future.

D. Equipment Specifications and Space Requirements

As mentioned before, the space requirements for Shadow Brewing Company will be 8,000 square feet; 1,500 will be used for office and laboratory space, and the remaining 6,500 will be used for the brewing area. (See Appendix D.)

1. Brewery

a. Brewing Equipment   This equipment will be able to produce 5,000 barrels a year through a continuous operation. For example, a lager will be produced within three weeks and an ale in two. By using this system, designed and installed by Pub Brewing Company, Shadow will utilize the full capacity of the equipment. In addition, this system can be easily expanded for future capacity needs. Aesthetically, the Brewhouse equipment will be copper covered, complementing the facility's copper roof (see Appendix E).

The system is equipped with sensors that monitor the different aspects of the brewing process such as pressure, volume, and temperature ranges. Should any of these vary, the system will adjust the variance to the appropriate setting. The cost of this system is $360,000, including manufacture, installation, and technical support. The space requirement for this equipment is about 2,500 square feet.

b. Refrigeration   Refrigeration plays a large role in the freshness of beer. Since Shadow will not pasteurize its products, refrigeration is required to keep the beer as fresh as possible (which is up to 90 days). Once the product is packaged, it will be stored in a 450-square-foot cooler that will keep the products at a constant 35 degrees fahrenheit. The cooler will be able to accommodate a forklift moving within the unit, which will be able to store 384 cases and 64 keys, or a mix thereof. The cost of this unit will be $19,800, including manufacture, delivery, and installation. Space requirement for this unit is 475 square feet.

c. Keg Cleaning and Filling Equipment   Because Shadow will initially only sell draft beer, a keg cleaning and filling unit will be needed. Shadow will design a single-head keg washer and single-head keg filler capable of washing and filling 10–15 kegs per hour. This system should cost no more than $1,000. The system will require about 120 square feet of space, including keg storage.

d. Bottling and Packaging Equipment   This equipment is made up of the following: a 16-valve liquid filling unit, a crown capping unit, a rinser, and a labeler. This system, although large (having an approximate capacity to fill 200,000 cases per year), is one of the best and smallest commercial systems available today. Should Shadow ever choose to expand its brewing operations, there will be no need for future capital requirements for this system.

The costs for each unit are as follows:

Filling unit	$25,000.00
Capping and labeling unit	53,972.00
Rinsing unit	5,000.00
Total	$73,972.00

The space requirement for the entire unit will be approximately 300 square feet.

e. Grain-Handling System   In order for the Company to more closely monitor the ingredients of its products, a grain-handling system will be installed. Included in the system will be a Four Roll Malt Mill, Malt Auger and Hopper, and Grist Auger and Hopper. The system is from Ingersoll-Rand Process Equipment and will cost almost $4,000 by the time it is installed. The entire system will require approximately 500 square feet, including grain storage.

2. Beverage Truck and Forklift   A gas-powered forklift will be needed to move materials within the facility and to and from the loading dock. The cost of the forklift, which will be purchased from Caterpillar (new), is $14,611 delivered.

The delivery truck that Shadow will be using is relatively small, capable of holding 500 cases. The refrigerated unit is considered to be adequate transportation for the distribution of products throughout the Indianapolis area. The beverage truck (also new) will cost $28,000, purchased from Isuzu.

3. Laboratory Equipment   Shadow will have a laboratory in its office area that will serve many purposes such as formula development and quality control and quality assurance tests, along with producing test samples of the products. The costs for the QC and QA equipment, made by Lumac, are $7,000 plus $120 per each 10pac test package. Additional equipment should be covered by $5,000.

4. Miscellaneous Items

Item (Quantity)	Total Cost
Kegs (300)	$ 6,000.00
Grain and malt bins — first year (4)	540.00
Grain and malt bins — second year (4)	540.00
Office Equipment and miscellaneous — first year	4,000.00
Office Equipment and miscellaneous — second year	4,000.00
Computers and software	6,000.00
Total first year	$16,540.00
Total second year	$ 4,540.00
Totals	$17,080.00

E. *Suppliers and Manufacturing Costs*

In addition to the above equipment, Shadow will have various suppliers that will satisfy its production needs. The following table shows the suppliers' name, product, location, and respective cost, broken down into manufacturing cost per item and product.

Item	Supplier	Cost/Item	Case Cost	Keg Cost
6-pak holders	Boise Cascade	$ .34	$1.36	
Bottles	Anchor Glass Co.	.11	2.64	
Bottle caps	Crown Caps	.005	.12	
Malt (100lb)	Briese Malting Co.	20.00	.85	$ 6.18
Hops (5lb)	John I. Hass	6.00	.03	.20
Bottle labels	Colony Printing	.01	.48	
Sales commission		10%	1.80	7.50
Fed and state taxes		.34/gallon	.76	5.27
Transportation			.12	.83
Utilities			.15	.97
Packaging			.33	1.00
Total			$8.64	$21.95

F. *Labor Supply*

Although the Company will seek its employment needs through private means, there are alternative labor sources, should they be required. Butler University and I.U.P.U.I., located near Carmel, are two colleges that would be able to provide students for part-time or weekend help. In addition, Carmel High School has a work-release program for its students during the school year, and offers local businesses the opportunity to solicit summer employment during the year.

VII. Management

A. *Key Management Personnel*

Mr. Darin Floyd will be the president and majority stockholder of the Shadow Brewing Company. Mr. Floyd's duties will include the actual brewing of the beer (the "Brewmaster"), director of sales and marketing, general manager and administrator, and operational coordinator for the delivery and bottling processes. Mr. Floyd realizes that these duties are varied and entail a great amount of effort and responsibility and feels he can readily accomplish these tasks.

In the preoperations stage, Mr. Floyd will search for a candidate to act as operational director. This individual's responsibility will be to assist Mr. Floyd with his various duties, and specifically to move into an executive sales position once the Company is into full operations. This person will hire two additional salespersons within the first year, and a delivery driver by the beginning of the second.

Responsibilities of the sales representatives include the sale of Company products and any additional market research (and marketing) that may be required. All

Organizational Chart

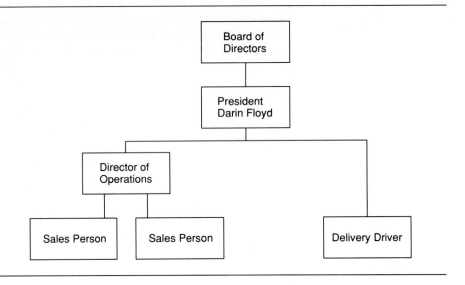

salespeople will be placed on a commissioned salary with a retrievable draw issued to them biweekly. This draw acts as an advance to their sales commission. By February of the second year, a delivery driver will be hired to deliver products to respective customers on a weekly schedule. This individual will also assist Mr. Floyd in the bottling phase of operations.

B. Legal Structure

The Shadow Brewing Company will be established as a "C" Corporation. The Company will be subject to Federal Regulation D, Rule 505, and Indiana Code 23.2.1.2(b)10 Security Laws, concerning the sale of its preferred stock. Under these laws, the Company may sell shares to up to 35 individuals, excluding exempt persons. Exempt persons include lending institutions and those individuals with a net worth exceeding $1 million. Under these laws the Company is not required to register with the Securities Exchange Commission, but is required to file a Securities Law Compliance Document.

Employment contracts will be developed by the Company's attorneys and will include the following: scheduled compensation and benefit agreements; options to purchase stock at a later date; and employment conditions subject to a quarterly review. Any additions to the employment contracts will be included when necessary.

Ownership in the Company is determined by stock purchases. Mr. Darin Floyd will purchase 20 percent of the authorized stock, and his father, Mr. William Floyd, will purchase 6.5 percent of the stock. The remaining stock will be offered for sale to both private individuals and exempt parties for $5.00 per share. As will be stated in the Stock Agreement, no individual, other than Mr. Darin Floyd, will own more than 15 percent of the available stock at the initial offering, allowing the Company to attract more investors.

C. Board of Directors, Advisors, and Consultants

Currently, the Company has only two members on its board—Darin and William Floyd. The Company hopes to attract those investors who will be the most beneficial to the management and success of Shadow Brewing Company. Stockholders will vote on board members according to their ownership in the Company.

Representing the Company is the law firm of Ice, Miller, Donadio and Ryan, located in Indianapolis. This firm will assume all legal responsibilities concerning the success of the Company. Ernst & Young, the Company's accounting firm, will be responsible for quarterly financial statements and income tax compilation. Insurance will be provided by Larue Insurance, located in Greenwood, Indiana. Primary advisory sources that have been, and may continue to be, used are listed below:

Name	Position	Company	Capacity
William Floyd	President, Owner	Information Profit Group	Finance
Robert Meneely	Retired President	Guerdon Homes	Finance
Ken Pavichevich	President, Owner	Pavichevich Brewing	Operations
Kim Renfro	General Manager	I.B.C.	Management
Jeff Davis	Zoning President	Carmel Community	Zoning
Arnie Winograd	President, Owner	J. V. Northwest	Operations
Jack Murphy	Vice-Chairman	A.B.C.	Legal
D. Anderson	Captain	Indiana Excise Division	Tax/Legal
Wallace Weakley	Judge	Hamilton County, Indiana	Legal
Bill Siebel	President, Owner	J. E. Siebel Sons	Operations
Dave Ryder	Consultant	J. E. Siebel Sons	Operations
Ted Konis	Consultant	J. E. Siebel Sons	Finance
Udo Harttung	President, Owner	Weinkeller Breweries	Operations
Fred Huber	President, Owner	Huber Breweries	Operations

D. Licenses, Permits, and Regulations

As mentioned earlier, the Company's attorneys will be responsible for all of the necessary paperwork, registrations, permits, and licenses. These will include the Brewer's Permit, Brewer's Bonds, Corporate Charter, Incorporation of the Company, Securities Agreements and related papers, Stockholders' Agreements, and Employee contracts.

VIII. Critical Risks

A. Surveys

Although the Company has performed due diligence researching its market, especially concerning its surveys, the results may not reflect an exact picture of the marketplace. However, there are two reasons why this should not affect sales projections. First, the surveys indicate initial purchases (of those stores contacted) that were thought to be accurate by the managers and owners of the respective establishments. Some may be high estimates, while at the same time some may be low estimates. The second reason the survey results need not be scrutinized is due to the Company's secondary research concerning the market size. This research indicates a large market base, over 200,000 people, who are potential end consumers of Shadow's products. If 4.0 percent were to purchase the equivalent of one case of the Company's beer during the first year, this would easily justify the first year's sales.

B. Sales Staff

The Company's primary path to profit is direct sales through the use of its sales staff. These individuals must be properly trained in order to project the proper image for the Company and to meet sales quotas. In order to ensure that quotas are met, the sales staff will be transitioned into a commission schedule over the first two years, with monthly quotas along the way. Because the Company is dependent on direct sales, every effort will be made to cultivate an outstanding, dependable sales force.

C. Failure of Products after Introduction

Even though the Company has taken large preventative steps to keep this from happening, it is still possible for a product line (or lines) to fail, despite initial demand. The Company feels that if such a situation should arise, immediate action would have to be taken. First, all remaining inventory would have to be sold (at a discount) to minimize losses. Next, more research and taste testing would have to be done, and finally a new product would be introduced. During the above situation, Shadow would try to increase production and sales of the other line(s) that are selling well in order to keep operating efficiency as high as possible.

D. Capacity

One of the largest problems faced by microbreweries is that of expansion. Many micros start out with a very small capacity and find that they need to increase due to both consumer demand and overhead. If a microbrewer can intelligently expand its operation within the same complex, it will see value-added profits from the additional beer sales. The Company already has a relatively large capacity of 5,000 barrels a year and wishes to stay at this level, at least for the immediate future. If, however, expansion is deemed necessary by the Company, the equipment would be purchased and then added to the existing equipment. This can readily be accomplished due to the existing equipment's design, which is capable of expansion.

E. Advertising Effectiveness

As mentioned earlier, one of the Company's primary objectives is initial consumer recognition, appeal, and acceptance. The various ways mentioned for advertising by the Company are word of mouth, point-of-purchase displays, taste testing, tours, and local promotion by the media. Although the Company feels these media will suit its advertising needs, additional monies may be spent at a later date if the Company feels it will increase sales.

F. Legislation

Both state and federal agencies have made many changes concerning the taxation on alcoholic beverages, primarily for the larger breweries. As of now, these agencies have tried to keep such taxation low for the smaller breweries in order for them to be able to compete. For the foreseeable future, these agencies will continue to do so. However, if increased taxation should fall on the micros, the Company would have to raise its prices in order to meet its margins. The Company would take every measure available to make these price increases proportionate to tax increases, while at the same time trying to keep market share. A few methods that could be available at such time would be internal cost cutting and offering discounts to retailers for larger purchases.

G. Undercapitalization

As with any new venture, undercapitalization can create irreversible damage. The Shadow Brewing Company understands this, and thus has set up a staged offering of stock. Initial capital requirements are crucial to the success of the Company's future and to the investor's rate of return. Once the initial capital has been acquired, there should be no immediate problems that would dictate the Company's demise.

IX. Preoperations

A. Cash Flow Statement

CASH FLOW PRE-OPERATIONS

	Quarter 1			Quarter 2			Quarter 3			Quarter 4			YEAR TOTAL
	JAN	FEB	MAR	APR	MAY	JUN	JUL	AUG	SEP	OCT	NOV	DEC	
BEGINNING BALANCE	$161,000.00	$157,760.00	$154,980.13	$152,192.16	$149,396.05	$158,291.79	$163,439.48	$169,302.17	$77,581.97	$542,769.25	$440,613.33	$332,309.45	$161,000.00
INCOME													
Interest Income	$0.00	$460.13	$452.03	$443.89	$435.74	$461.68	$476.70	$493.80	$226.28	$1,583.06	$1,286.12	$970.42	$7,288.87
Income From Sale of Stock	$0.00	$0.00	$0.00	$0.00	$16,700.00	$16,700.00	$16,600.00	$94,000.00	$500,000.00	$0.00	$0.00	$0.00	$644,000.00
CASH AVAILABLE	$161,000.00	$158,220.13	$155,432.16	$152,636.05	$166,531.79	$175,453.48	$180,516.17	$263,795.97	$577,806.25	$544,352.33	$441,898.45	$333,279.87	$812,288.87
CASH DISBURSEMENTS													
Rent	$0.00	$0.00	$0.00	$0.00	$0.00	$0.00	$0.00	$0.00	$0.00	$0.00	$0.00	$0.00	$0.00
Owners Salary	$2,000.00	$2,000.00	$2,000.00	$2,000.00	$2,000.00	$2,000.00	$2,000.00	$2,000.00	$2,000.00	$2,000.00	$2,000.00	$2,000.00	$24,000.00
Employee's Salary	$0.00	$0.00	$0.00	$0.00	$0.00	$1,800.00	$1,800.00	$1,800.00	$1,800.00	$1,800.00	$1,800.00	$1,800.00	$12,600.00
Driver's Salary	$0.00	$0.00	$0.00	$0.00	$0.00	$0.00	$0.00	$0.00	$0.00	$0.00	$0.00	$0.00	$0.00
Employee Incentive Pay	$230.00	$230.00	$230.00	$230.00	$230.00	$437.00	$437.00	$437.00	$437.00	$437.00	$437.00	$437.00	$4,209.00
Payroll Tax / Fringe Benefits	$0.00	$0.00	$0.00	$0.00	$0.00	$0.00	$0.00	$0.00	$0.00	$0.00	$0.00	$0.00	$0.00
Other Taxes	$0.00	$0.00	$0.00	$0.00	$0.00	$0.00	$0.00	$0.00	$0.00	$0.00	$0.00	$0.00	$0.00
Payroll Service	$0.00	$0.00	$0.00	$0.00	$0.00	$0.00	$0.00	$0.00	$0.00	$0.00	$850.00	$850.00	$1,700.00
Utilities	$200.00	$200.00	$200.00	$200.00	$200.00	$1,167.00	$1,167.00	$1,167.00	$1,167.00	$1,167.00	$1,167.00	$1,167.00	$9,169.00
Insurance	$0.00	$0.00	$0.00	$0.00	$0.00	$0.00	$0.00	$0.00	$0.00	$2,750.00	$2,750.00	$2,720.00	$8,220.00
Advertising	$0.00	$0.00	$0.00	$0.00	$0.00	$0.00	$0.00	$0.00	$0.00	$0.00	$0.00	$0.00	$0.00
Miscellaneous	$225.00	$225.00	$225.00	$225.00	$225.00	$225.00	$225.00	$225.00	$250.00	$0.00	$0.00	$0.00	$2,050.00
Telephone	$200.00	$200.00	$200.00	$200.00	$200.00	$200.00	$200.00	$200.00	$200.00	$200.00	$200.00	$200.00	$2,400.00
Fuel Expense	$300.00	$300.00	$300.00	$300.00	$300.00	$300.00	$300.00	$300.00	$300.00	$300.00	$300.00	$300.00	$3,600.00
Equipment Purchases	$0.00	$0.00	$0.00	$0.00	$0.00	$0.00	$0.00	$180,000.00	$28,000.00	$95,000.00	$100,000.00	$52,951.00	$455,951.00
Long Term Loan Interest	$0.00	$0.00	$0.00	$0.00	$0.00	$0.00	$0.00	$0.00	$0.00	$0.00	$0.00	$0.00	$0.00
Legal / Accounting Fees	$0.00	$0.00	$0.00	$0.00	$5,000.00	$5,800.00	$5,000.00	$0.00	$800.00	$0.00	$0.00	$1,200.00	$17,800.00
Maintenance - Equipment	$0.00	$0.00	$0.00	$0.00	$0.00	$0.00	$0.00	$0.00	$0.00	$0.00	$0.00	$0.00	$0.00
Trade Association Dues	$85.00	$85.00	$85.00	$85.00	$85.00	$85.00	$85.00	$85.00	$85.00	$85.00	$85.00	$85.00	$1,020.00
Accounts Payable / Inventory	$0.00	$0.00	$0.00	$0.00	$0.00	$0.00	$0.00	$0.00	$0.00	$0.00	$0.00	$0.00	$0.00
Loan Payment - Principle	$0.00	$0.00	$0.00	$0.00	$0.00	$0.00	$0.00	$0.00	$0.00	$0.00	$0.00	$0.00	$0.00
Dividends Paid	$0.00	$0.00	$0.00	$0.00	$0.00	$0.00	$0.00	$0.00	$0.00	$0.00	$0.00	$0.00	$0.00
Taxes Payable	0.00	0.00	$0.00	0.00	0.00	0.00	0.00	0.00	0.00	0.00	0.00	0.00	0.00
Property Taxes Payable	$0.00	$0.00	$0.00	$0.00	$0.00	$0.00	$0.00	$0.00	$0.00	$0.00	$0.00	$0.00	$0.00
Total Cash Outlay	$3,240.00	$3,240.00	$3,240.00	$3,240.00	$8,240.00	$12,014.00	$11,214.00	$186,214.00	$35,039.00	$103,739.00	$109,589.00	$63,710.00	$542,719.00
ENDING CASH BALANCE	$157,760.00	$154,980.13	$152,192.16	$149,396.05	$158,291.79	$163,439.48	$169,302.17	$77,581.97	$542,769.25	$440,613.33	$332,309.45	$269,569.87	$269,569.87
NET CASH FLOW	-$3,240.00	-$3,240.00	-$3,240.00	-$3,240.00	$8,460.00	$4,686.00	$5,386.00	-$92,214.00	$464,961.00	-$103,739.00	-$109,589.00	-$63,710.00	$101,281.00

X. Year One Financial Statements

A. Income Statement; B. Cash Flow Statement; and C. Balance Sheet

INCOME STATEMENT YEAR ONE

	Quarter 1			Quarter 2			Quarter 3			Quarter 4			FIRST YEAR TOTAL	% OF SALES
	JAN	FEB	MAR	APR	MAY	JUN	JUL	AUG	SEP	OCT	NOV	DEC		
INCOME														
Case Sales	$0.00	$0.00	$0.00	$0.00	$0.00	$0.00	$0.00	$0.00	$0.00	$0.00	$0.00	$0.00	$0.00	0.00%
Keg Sales	$0.00	$0.00	$2,000.00	$4,500.00	$7,500.00	$13,200.00	$15,927.00	$17,569.00	$18,447.00	$19,287.00	$23,469.00	$25,675.00	$147,574.00	100.00%
Total sales	$0.00	$0.00	$2,000.00	$4,500.00	$7,500.00	$13,200.00	$15,927.00	$17,569.00	$18,447.00	$19,287.00	$23,469.00	$25,675.00	$147,574.00	100.00%
Less Cost of Sales	$1,000.00	$1,000.00	$1,000.00	$1,187.00	$598.13	$1,052.70	$1,270.18	$1,401.13	$1,471.15	$1,536.14	$1,871.65	$2,047.58	$15,437.65	10.46%
Gross Margin	$-1,000.00	$-1,000.00	$1,000.00	$3,313.00	$6,901.88	$12,147.30	$14,656.82	$16,167.87	$16,975.85	$17,748.86	$21,597.35	$23,627.42	$132,136.35	89.54%
Plus interest income	$961.98	$716.80	$658.75	$605.57	$556.80	$521.56	$499.70	$486.95	$478.13	$469.29	$465.19	$471.29	$6,892.00	
TOTAL OPERATING INCOME	$-38.02	$-283.20	$1,658.75	$3,918.57	$7,458.68	$12,668.86	$15,156.52	$16,654.82	$17,453.98	$18,218.15	$22,062.54	$24,098.71	$139,028.35	
OPERATING EXPENSES														
Rent	$5,333.33	$5,333.33	$5,333.33	$5,333.33	$5,333.33	$5,333.33	$5,333.33	$5,333.33	$5,333.33	$5,333.33	$5,333.33	$5,333.33	$63,999.96	43.37%
Owners Salary	$2,000.00	$2,000.00	$2,000.00	$2,000.00	$2,000.00	$2,000.00	$2,000.00	$2,000.00	$2,000.00	$2,000.00	$2,000.00	$2,000.00	$24,000.00	16.26%
Employee's Salary	$3,600.00	$3,600.00	$3,600.00	$3,600.00	$3,200.00	$3,000.00	$2,800.00	$2,600.00	$2,400.00	$2,200.00	$2,000.00	$3,600.00	$36,200.00	24.53%
Driver's Salary	$0.00	$0.00	$0.00	$0.00	$0.00	$0.00	$0.00	$0.00	$0.00	$0.00	$0.00	$0.00	$0.00	0.00%
Payroll Tax / Fringe Benefits	$644.00	$644.00	$667.00	$682.81	$662.69	$688.85	$689.37	$690.53	$665.11	$649.35	$662.42	$865.45	$8,201.58	5.56%
Employee Incentive Pay	$0.00	$0.00	$200.00	$337.50	$562.50	$990.00	$1,194.53	$1,317.68	$1,383.53	$1,446.53	$1,760.18	$1,925.63	$11,118.05	7.53%
Property Tax Expense	$0.00	$0.00	$1,278.58	$1,278.58	$1,278.58	$1,278.58	$1,278.58	$1,278.58	$1,278.58	$1,278.58	$1,278.58	$1,278.58	$12,785.80	8.66%
Other Taxes	$0.00	$0.00	$143.80	$323.55	$539.25	$949.08	$1,145.15	$1,263.21	$1,326.34	$1,386.74	$1,687.42	$1,846.03	$10,610.57	7.19%
Utilities	$600.00	$700.00	$750.00	$795.00	$835.00	$885.00	$888.00	$891.50	$894.75	$900.00	$904.00	$910.00	$9,953.25	6.74%
Insurance	$1,167.00	$1,167.00	$1,167.00	$1,167.00	$1,167.00	$1,167.00	$1,167.00	$1,167.00	$1,167.00	$1,167.00	$1,167.00	$1,167.00	$14,004.00	9.49%
Fuel Expense	$100.00	$100.00	$100.00	$110.00	$110.00	$100.00	$100.00	$100.00	$100.00	$100.00	$100.00	$130.00	$1,250.00	0.85%
Advertising	$5,000.00	$4,500.00	$4,000.00	$4,500.00	$3,500.00	$2,750.00	$2,500.00	$2,500.00	$2,500.00	$2,500.00	$2,500.00	$2,500.00	$39,250.00	26.60%
Payroll Service	$44.00	$44.00	$44.00	$44.00	$44.00	$44.00	$44.00	$44.00	$44.00	$44.00	$44.00	$56.75	$540.75	0.37%
Long Term Loan Interest	$0.00	$0.00	$0.00	$0.00	$0.00	$0.00	$0.00	$0.00	$0.00	$0.00	$0.00	$0.00	$0.00	0.00%
Miscellaneous	$1,250.00	$1,500.00	$1,750.00	$1,000.00	$750.00	$500.00	$500.00	$500.00	$500.00	$500.00	$500.00	$500.00	$9,750.00	6.61%
Telephone	$350.00	$245.00	$250.00	$250.00	$250.00	$250.00	$250.00	$250.00	$250.00	$250.00	$250.00	$250.00	$3,095.00	2.10%
Legal / Accounting Fees	$1,500.00	$350.00	$200.00	$800.00	$0.00	$800.00	$0.00	$0.00	$800.00	$0.00	$0.00	$1,200.00	$5,650.00	3.83%
Maintenance - Equipment	$100.00	$100.00	$100.00	$100.00	$100.00	$100.00	$100.00	$100.00	$100.00	$100.00	$100.00	$100.00	$1,200.00	0.81%
Depreciation	$6,686.52	$6,686.52	$6,686.52	$6,686.52	$6,686.52	$6,686.52	$6,686.52	$6,686.52	$6,686.52	$6,686.52	$6,686.52	$6,686.52	$80,238.24	54.37%
Trade Association Dues	$85.00	$85.00	$85.00	$85.00	$85.00	$85.00	$85.00	$85.00	$85.00	$85.00	$85.00	$85.00	$1,020.00	0.69%
Total Expense	$28,459.85	$27,054.85	$28,355.23	$29,093.29	$27,103.87	$27,607.36	$26,761.48	$26,797.35	$27,514.15	$26,827.04	$27,058.45	$30,434.28	$332,867.20	225.56%
PROFIT BEFORE TAXES	$-28,497.87	$-27,338.05	$-26,696.48	$-25,174.72	$-19,645.19	$-14,938.50	$-11,604.96	$-10,142.52	$-10,060.17	$-8,408.89	$-4,995.91	$-6,335.58	$-193,838.85	-131.35%
TAXES														
State Taxes	$0.00	$0.00	$6.00	$13.50	$22.50	$39.60	$47.78	$52.71	$55.34	$57.86	$70.41	$77.03	$442.72	
Federal Taxes	$0.00	$0.00	$0.00	$0.00	$0.00	$0.00	$0.00	$0.00	$0.00	$0.00	$0.00	$0.00	$0.00	
Total Taxes	$0.00	$0.00	$6.00	$13.50	$22.50	$39.60	$47.78	$52.71	$55.34	$57.86	$70.41	$77.03	$442.72	0.00%
NET PROFIT AFTER TAXES (NPAT)	$-28,497.87	$-27,338.05	$-26,696.48	$-25,188.22	$-19,667.69	$-14,978.10	$-11,652.74	$-10,195.23	$-10,115.51	$-8,466.75	$-5,066.32	$-6,412.60	$-194,281.57	-131.65%

139

CASH FLOW YEAR ONE

	Quarter 1			Quarter 2			Quarter 3			Quarter 4			FIRST YEAR TOTAL	% OF SALES
	JAN	FEB	MAR	APR	MAY	JUN	JUL	AUG	SEP	OCT	NOV	DEC		
BEGINNING BALANCE	$269,569.87	$245,758.52	$225,856.99	$207,625.61	$190,902.99	$178,821.02	$171,324.72	$166,955.04	$163,928.75	$160,898.99	$159,493.34	$161,584.18	$269,569.87	
INCOME														
Interest Income	$981.98	$716.80	$658.75	$605.57	$556.80	$521.56	$499.70	$486.95	$478.13	$469.29	$465.19	$471.29	$6,892.00	
Cash Sales	$0.00	$0.00	$2,000.00	$4,500.00	$7,500.00	$13,200.00	$15,927.00	$17,569.00	$18,447.00	$19,287.00	$23,469.00	$25,875.00	$147,574.00	
CASH AVAILABLE	$270,531.85	$246,475.32	$228,515.74	$212,731.18	$198,959.79	$192,542.58	$187,751.42	$185,010.99	$182,853.87	$180,655.28	$183,427.53	$187,730.47	$424,035.87	
CASH DISBURSEMENTS														
Rent	$5,333.33	$5,333.33	$5,333.33	$5,333.33	$5,333.33	$5,333.33	$5,333.33	$5,333.33	$5,333.33	$5,333.33	$5,333.33	$5,333.33	$63,999.96	43.37%
Owners Salary	$2,000.00	$2,000.00	$2,000.00	$2,000.00	$2,000.00	$2,000.00	$2,000.00	$2,000.00	$2,000.00	$2,000.00	$2,000.00	$2,000.00	$24,000.00	16.26%
Employee's Salary	$3,600.00	$3,600.00	$3,600.00	$3,600.00	$3,200.00	$3,000.00	$2,800.00	$2,600.00	$2,400.00	$2,200.00	$2,000.00	$3,600.00	$36,200.00	24.53%
Driver's Salary	$0.00	$0.00	$0.00	$0.00	$0.00	$0.00	$0.00	$0.00	$0.00	$0.00	$0.00	$0.00	$0.00	0.00%
Employee Incentive Pay	$0.00	$0.00	$500.00	$337.50	$562.50	$990.00	$1,191.52	$1,317.58	$1,333.52	$1,446.53	$1,750.13	$1,825.63	$11,116.05	7.53%
Payroll Tax / Fringe Benefits	$844.00	$844.00	$967.00	$882.81	$662.69	$688.85	$689.37	$680.53	$665.11	$649.35	$662.42	$865.45	$8,201.58	5.56%
Other Taxes	$0.00	$0.00	$143.80	$323.55	$539.25	$949.08	$1,145.15	$1,263.21	$1,326.34	$1,386.74	$1,587.42	$1,846.03	$10,610.57	7.19%
Payroll Service	$44.00	$44.00	$44.00	$44.00	$44.00	$44.00	$44.00	$44.00	$44.00	$44.00	$44.00	$55.75	$540.75	0.37%
Utilities	$600.00	$700.00	$750.00	$795.00	$835.00	$885.00	$888.00	$961.50	$894.75	$900.00	$904.00	$910.00	$9,953.25	6.74%
Insurance	$1,167.00	$1,167.00	$1,167.00	$1,167.00	$1,167.00	$1,167.00	$1,167.00	$1,167.00	$1,167.00	$1,167.00	$1,167.00	$1,167.00	$14,004.00	9.49%
Advertising	$5,000.00	$4,500.00	$4,000.00	$4,500.00	$3,500.00	$2,750.00	$2,500.00	$2,500.00	$2,500.00	$2,500.00	$2,500.00	$2,500.00	$39,250.00	26.60%
Miscellaneous	$1,250.00	$250.00	$250.00	$250.00	$750.00	$500.00	$500.00	$500.00	$500.00	$500.00	$500.00	$500.00	$6,250.00	4.24%
Telephone	$350.00	$245.00	$250.00	$250.00	$250.00	$250.00	$250.00	$250.00	$250.00	$250.00	$250.00	$250.00	$3,095.00	2.10%
Fuel Expense	$100.00	$100.00	$100.00	$110.00	$110.00	$100.00	$100.00	$100.00	$100.00	$100.00	$100.00	$130.00	$1,250.00	0.85%
Equipment Purchases	$0.00	$0.00	$0.00	$0.00	$0.00	$0.00	$0.00	$0.00	$0.00	$0.00	$0.00	$0.00	$0.00	0.00%
Long Term Loan Interest	$0.00	$0.00	$0.00	$0.00	$0.00	$0.00	$0.00	$0.00	$0.00	$0.00	$0.00	$0.00	$0.00	0.00%
Legal / Accounting Fees	$1,500.00	$350.00	$200.00	$800.00	$0.00	$800.00	$0.00	$800.00	$800.00	$0.00	$0.00	$1,200.00	$5,650.00	3.83%
Maintenance - Equipment	$100.00	$100.00	$100.00	$100.00	$100.00	$100.00	$100.00	$100.00	$100.00	$100.00	$100.00	$100.00	$1,200.00	0.81%
Trade Association Dues	$85.00	$85.00	$85.00	$85.00	$85.00	$85.00	$85.00	$85.00	$85.00	$85.00	$85.00	$85.00	$1,020.00	0.69%
Accounts Payable / Inventory	$3,000.00	$1,500.00	$2,000.00	$1,450.00	$1,000.00	$1,500.00	$2,000.00	$2,250.00	$2,250.00	$2,500.00	$2,750.00	$2,500.00	$24,700.00	16.74%
Loan Payment - Principle	$1,500.00	$0.00	$0.00	$0.00	$0.00	$0.00	$0.00	$0.00	$0.00	$0.00	$0.00	$0.00	$0.00	0.00%
Dividends Paid	$0.00	$0.00	$0.00	$0.00	$0.00	$0.00	$0.00	$0.00	$0.00	$0.00	$0.00	$0.00	$0.00	0.00%
Taxes Payable	$0.00	$0.00	$6.00	$0.00	$0.00	$75.60	$0.00	$0.00	$155.83	$0.00	$0.00	$172.76	$410.19	0.28%
Proprty Taxes Payable	$0.00	$0.00	$0.00	$0.00	$0.00	$0.00	$0.00	$0.00	$0.00	$0.00	$0.00	$0.00	$0.00	0.00%
Total Cash Outlay	$24,773.33	$20,618.33	$20,890.13	$21,828.19	$20,138.77	$21,217.86	$20,796.38	$21,082.25	$21,954.88	$21,161.94	$21,843.35	$25,141.94	$261,447.35	177.16%
ENDING CASH BALANCE	$245,758.52	$225,856.99	$207,625.61	$190,902.99	$178,821.02	$171,324.72	$166,955.04	$163,928.75	$160,898.99	$159,493.34	$161,584.18	$162,588.53	$162,588.53	
NET CASH FLOW	$-24,773.33	$-20,618.33	$-18,890.13	$-17,328.19	$-12,638.77	$-8,017.86	$-4,869.38	$-3,513.25	$-3,507.88	$-1,874.94	$1,625.65	$533.08	$-113,873.35	

BALANCE SHEET YEAR ONE

	Beginning Balance – 1/1/93	Quarter 1 JAN	Quarter 1 FEB	Quarter 1 MAR	Quarter 2 APR	Quarter 2 MAY	Quarter 2 JUN	Quarter 3 JUL	Quarter 3 AUG	Quarter 3 SEP	Quarter 4 OCT	Quarter 4 NOV	Quarter 4 DEC	% OF SALES
ASSETS														
CURRENT														
Cash	$269,569.87	$245,759.52	$225,856.99	$207,625.61	$190,902.99	$178,821.02	$171,324.72	$166,955.04	$163,928.75	$160,896.99	$159,493.34	$161,584.18	$162,566.53	29.89%
Inventory	$0.00	$2,000.00	$1,250.00	$750.00	$263.00	$664.88	$1,112.18	$1,842.00	$2,690.87	$3,469.72	$4,431.58	$5,309.93	$5,762.35	1.06%
Supplies	$0.00	$0.00	$0.00	$0.00	$0.00	$0.00	$0.00	$0.00	$0.00	$0.00	$0.00	$0.00	$0.00	0.00%
TOTAL CURRENT	$269,569.87	$247,759.52	$227,106.99	$208,375.61	$191,165.99	$179,485.90	$172,436.90	$168,797.04	$166,619.61	$164,366.71	$163,924.92	$166,894.11	$168,350.87	30.95%
LONG TERM														
Equipment Fixtures	$421,951.00	$421,951.00	$421,951.00	$421,951.00	$421,951.00	$421,951.00	$421,951.00	$421,951.00	$421,951.00	$421,951.00	$421,951.00	$421,951.00	$421,951.00	
Vehicles	$28,000.00	$28,000.00	$28,000.00	$28,000.00	$28,000.00	$28,000.00	$28,000.00	$28,000.00	$28,000.00	$28,000.00	$28,000.00	$28,000.00	$28,000.00	
Computers	$6,000.00	$6,000.00	$6,000.00	$6,000.00	$6,000.00	$6,000.00	$6,000.00	$6,000.00	$6,000.00	$6,000.00	$6,000.00	$6,000.00	$6,000.00	
TOTAL LONG TERM	$455,951.00	$455,951.00	$455,951.00	$455,951.00	$455,951.00	$455,951.00	$455,951.00	$455,951.00	$455,951.00	$455,951.00	$455,951.00	$455,951.00	$455,951.00	
Less Accumulated Depreciation	$0.00	$6,666.52	$13,373.04	$20,059.56	$26,746.08	$33,432.60	$40,119.12	$46,805.64	$53,492.16	$60,178.68	$66,865.20	$73,551.72	$80,270.77	
Net Long Term Assets	$455,951.00	$449,284.48	$442,577.96	$435,891.44	$429,204.92	$422,518.40	$415,831.88	$409,145.36	$402,458.84	$395,772.32	$389,085.80	$382,399.28	$375,680.23	69.05%
TOTAL ASSETS	$725,520.87	$697,023.00	$669,684.95	$644,267.05	$620,370.91	$602,004.30	$588,268.78	$577,942.40	$569,078.45	$560,141.03	$553,010.72	$549,293.39	$544,031.10	100.00%
CURRENT LIABILITIES														
Property Tax Payable	$0.00	$0.00	$0.00	$1,278.58	$2,557.16	$3,835.74	$5,114.32	$6,392.90	$7,671.48	$8,950.06	$10,228.64	$11,507.22	$12,785.80	
Income Tax payable	$0.00	$0.00	$0.00	$0.00	$13.50	$36.00	$0.00	$47.78	$100.49	$0.00	$57.86	$128.27	$0.00	
TOTAL CURRENT	$0.00	$0.00	$0.00	$1,278.58	$2,570.66	$3,871.74	$5,114.32	$6,440.68	$7,771.97	$8,950.06	$10,286.50	$11,635.49	$12,785.80	
TOTAL LIABILITIES	$0.00	$0.00	$0.00	$1,278.58	$2,570.66	$3,871.74	$5,114.32	$6,440.68	$7,771.97	$8,950.06	$10,286.50	$11,635.49	$12,785.80	2.35%
OWNERS EQUITY														
Beginning Equity	$725,520.87	$725,520.87	$697,023.00	$669,684.95	$642,988.47	$617,800.25	$598,132.56	$583,154.46	$571,501.72	$561,306.49	$551,190.97	$542,724.22	$537,657.90	
Add (NPAT)	$0.00	$-28,497.87	$-27,338.05	$-26,696.48	$-25,188.22	$-19,667.69	$-14,978.10	$-11,652.74	$-10,195.23	$-10,115.51	$-8,466.75	$-5,066.32	$-6,412.60	
Less Dividends Paid	$0.00	$0.00	$0.00	$0.00	$0.00	$0.00	$0.00	$0.00	$0.00	$0.00	$0.00	$0.00	$0.00	
TOTAL OWNERS EQUITY	$725,520.87	$697,023.00	$669,684.95	$642,988.47	$617,800.25	$598,132.56	$583,154.46	$571,501.72	$561,306.49	$551,190.97	$542,724.22	$537,657.90	$531,245.30	97.65%
TOTAL LIABILITIES & EQUITY	$725,520.87	$697,023.00	$669,684.95	$644,267.05	$620,370.91	$602,004.30	$588,268.78	$577,942.40	$569,078.45	$560,141.03	$553,010.72	$549,293.39	$544,031.10	100.00%

XI. Year Two Financial Statements

A. Income Statement; B. Cash Flow Statement; and C. Balance Sheet

INCOME STATEMENT YEAR TWO

	Quarter 1			Quarter 2			Quarter 3			Quarter 4			YEAR TWO TOTAL	% OF SALES
	JAN	FEB	MAR	APR	MAY	JUN	JUL	AUG	SEP	OCT	NOV	DEC		
INCOME														
Case Sales	$0.00	$5,400.00	$10,800.00	$21,600.00	$23,760.00	$26,136.00	$28,749.60	$31,624.56	$33,522.03	$34,862.91	$36,257.43	$38,432.88	$291,145.42	46.96%
Keg Sales	$25,931.75	$26,191.07	$26,452.98	$26,717.51	$26,984.68	$27,254.53	$27,527.08	$27,802.35	$28,080.37	$28,361.17	$28,644.78	$28,931.23	$328,879.50	53.04%
Total sales	$25,931.75	$31,591.07	$37,252.98	$48,317.51	$50,744.68	$53,390.53	$56,276.68	$59,426.91	$61,602.40	$63,224.09	$64,902.22	$67,364.11	$620,024.92	
Less Cost of Sales	$2,058.06	$3,732.74	$5,397.63	$8,706.72	$9,385.63	$10,130.51	$10,947.94	$11,845.16	$12,445.01	$12,875.62	$13,322.80	$14,007.94	$114,865.74	18.53%
Gross Margin	$23,863.69	$27,858.33	$31,855.35	$39,610.79	$41,359.05	$43,260.02	$45,328.73	$47,581.75	$49,157.40	$50,348.46	$51,579.42	$53,356.17	$505,159.17	81.47%
Plus Interest Income	$474.22	$241.52	$247.58	$257.85	$291.65	$308.08	$347.74	$398.46	$454.37	$511.30	$575.59	$621.16	$4,729.51	
TOTAL OPERATING INCOME	$24,337.91	$28,099.85	$32,102.94	$39,868.63	$41,650.71	$43,568.10	$45,676.47	$47,980.20	$49,611.77	$50,859.76	$52,155.01	$53,977.33	$509,888.68	
OPERATING EXPENSES														
Rent	$5,333.33	$5,333.33	$5,333.33	$5,333.33	$5,333.33	$5,333.33	$5,333.33	$5,333.33	$5,333.33	$5,333.33	$5,333.33	$5,333.33	$63,999.96	10.32%
Owners Salary	$2,200.00	$2,200.00	$2,200.00	$2,200.00	$2,200.00	$2,200.00	$2,200.00	$2,200.00	$2,200.00	$2,200.00	$2,200.00	$2,200.00	$26,400.00	4.26%
Employee's Salary	$3,600.00	$3,600.00	$3,400.00	$3,000.00	$2,600.00	$2,600.00	$2,400.00	$2,200.00	$2,000.00	$1,800.00	$1,800.00	$1,400.00	$30,400.00	4.90%
Driver's Salary	$0.00	$1,735.00	$1,735.00	$1,735.00	$1,735.00	$1,735.00	$1,735.00	$1,735.00	$1,735.00	$1,735.00	$1,735.00	$1,735.00	$19,085.00	3.08%
Payroll Tax / Fringe Benefits	$905.57	$1,157.16	$1,186.25	$1,242.05	$1,241.38	$1,242.72	$1,246.27	$1,252.25	$1,249.27	$1,241.19	$1,233.63	$1,233.27	$14,431.00	2.33%
Employee Incentive Pay	$2,074.54	$2,527.29	$2,980.24	$3,865.40	$4,069.57	$4,271.24	$4,502.13	$4,754.15	$4,928.19	$5,057.93	$5,192.18	$5,369.13	$49,601.99	8.00%
Property Tax Expense	$1,278.58	$1,278.58	$1,760.09	$1,760.09	$1,760.09	$1,760.09	$1,760.09	$1,760.09	$1,760.09	$1,760.09	$1,760.09	$1,760.09	$20,158.06	17.55%
Other Taxes	$1,864.49	$2,055.94	$2,247.57	$2,612.19	$2,700.52	$2,795.95	$2,899.18	$3,010.97	$3,091.88	$3,154.78	$3,219.80	$3,310.01	$32,963.09	5.32%
Utilities	$950.00	$1,110.00	$1,115.00	$1,128.00	$1,130.00	$1,132.00	$1,135.00	$1,135.00	$1,135.00	$1,135.00	$1,135.00	$1,135.00	$13,375.00	2.16%
Insurance	$1,283.00	$1,283.00	$1,283.00	$1,283.00	$1,283.00	$1,283.00	$1,283.00	$1,283.00	$1,283.00	$1,283.00	$1,283.00	$1,283.00	$15,396.00	2.48%
Fuel Expense	$150.00	$150.00	$150.00	$150.00	$150.00	$150.00	$150.00	$150.00	$150.00	$150.00	$150.00	$150.00	$1,800.00	0.29%
Advertising	$3,000.00	$3,000.00	$3,000.00	$3,000.00	$3,000.00	$3,000.00	$3,000.00	$3,000.00	$3,000.00	$3,000.00	$3,000.00	$3,000.00	$36,000.00	5.81%
Payroll Service	$56.00	$66.00	$66.00	$66.00	$66.00	$66.00	$66.00	$66.00	$66.00	$66.00	$66.00	$76.50	$792.50	0.13%
Long Term Loan Interest	$0.00	$0.00	$0.00	$0.00	$0.00	$0.00	$0.00	$0.00	$0.00	$0.00	$0.00	$0.00	$0.00	0.00%
Miscellaneous	$2,000.00	$1,000.00	$750.00	$0.00	$0.00	$500.00	$0.00	$0.00	$500.00	$500.00	$500.00	$500.00	$8,250.00	1.33%
Telephone	$250.00	$250.00	$250.00	$250.00	$250.00	$250.00	$250.00	$250.00	$250.00	$250.00	$250.00	$250.00	$3,000.00	0.48%
Legal / Accounting Fees	$225.00	$0.00	$1,000.00	$800.00	$0.00	$800.00	$0.00	$800.00	$0.00	$0.00	$0.00	$1,500.00	$5,125.00	3.47%
Maintenance - Equipment	$200.00	$200.00	$200.00	$200.00	$200.00	$200.00	$200.00	$200.00	$200.00	$200.00	$200.00	$200.00	$2,400.00	0.39%
Depreciation	$6,957.91	$6,957.91	$6,957.91	$6,957.91	$6,957.91	$6,957.91	$6,957.91	$6,957.91	$6,957.91	$6,957.91	$6,957.91	$6,957.91	$83,494.92	13.47%
Trade Association Dues	$85.00	$85.00	$85.00	$85.00	$85.00	$85.00	$85.00	$85.00	$85.00	$85.00	$85.00	$85.00	$1,020.00	0.16%
Total Expense	$32,413.42	$33,989.21	$35,699.39	$36,167.97	$35,451.80	$36,362.24	$35,702.92	$35,872.71	$36,724.47	$35,909.23	$35,900.93	$37,498.24	$427,692.53	68.98%
PROFIT BEFORE TAXES	$-8,075.52	$-5,889.36	$-3,596.45	$3,700.67	$6,198.91	$7,205.86	$9,973.55	$12,107.49	$12,887.29	$14,950.54	$16,254.08	$16,479.09	$82,196.15	13.25%
TAXES														
State Taxes	$77.80	$94.77	$111.76	$144.95	$152.23	$160.17	$168.83	$178.28	$184.81	$189.67	$194.71	$202.09	$5,753.73	
Federal Taxes	$0.00	$0.00	$0.00	$0.00	$0.00	$0.00	$0.00	$0.00	$0.00	$0.00	$0.00	$0.00	$0.00	0.00%
Total Taxes	$77.80	$94.77	$111.76	$144.95	$152.23	$160.17	$168.83	$178.28	$184.81	$189.67	$194.71	$202.09	$5,753.73	
NET PROFIT AFTER TAXES (NPAT)	$-8,153.31	$-5,984.13	$-3,708.21	$3,555.72	$6,046.68	$7,045.68	$9,804.72	$11,929.21	$12,702.49	$14,760.86	$16,059.38	$16,277.00	$76,442.42	12.33%

CASH FLOW YEAR TWO

	Quarter 1			Quarter 2			Quarter 3			Quarter 4			YEAR TWO TOTAL	% OF SALES
	JAN	FEB	MAR	APR	MAY	JUN	JUL	AUG	SEP	OCT	NOV	DEC		
BEGINNING BALANCE	$162,588.53	$82,805.56	$84,885.43	$88,404.60	$99,995.66	$105,626.72	$119,223.72	$136,613.21	$155,783.87	$175,302.25	$197,346.41	$212,969.81	$162,588.53	
INCOME														
Interest Income	$474.22	$241.52	$247.58	$257.85	$291.65	$308.08	$347.74	$398.46	$454.37	$511.30	$575.59	$621.16	$4,729.51	
Cash Sales	$25,931.75	$31,591.07	$37,252.98	$48,317.51	$50,744.68	$53,390.53	$56,276.68	$59,426.91	$61,602.40	$63,224.09	$64,902.22	$67,364.11	$620,024.92	
CASH AVAILABLE	$188,994.49	$114,638.14	$122,385.99	$136,979.95	$151,031.99	$159,325.32	$175,848.13	$196,438.58	$217,840.64	$239,037.63	$262,824.22	$280,955.08	$787,342.96	
CASH DISBURSEMENTS														
Rent	$5,333.33	$5,333.33	$5,333.33	$5,333.33	$5,333.33	$5,333.33	$5,333.33	$5,333.33	$5,333.33	$5,333.33	$5,333.33	$5,333.33	$63,999.96	10.32%
Owners Salary	$2,200.00	$2,200.00	$2,200.00	$2,200.00	$2,200.00	$2,200.00	$2,200.00	$2,200.00	$2,200.00	$2,200.00	$2,200.00	$2,200.00	$26,400.00	4.26%
Employee's Salary	$3,600.00	$3,600.00	$3,400.00	$3,000.00	$2,800.00	$2,600.00	$2,400.00	$2,200.00	$2,000.00	$1,800.00	$1,600.00	$1,400.00	$30,400.00	4.90%
Driver's Salary	$0.00	$1,735.00	$1,735.00	$1,735.00	$1,735.00	$1,735.00	$1,735.00	$1,735.00	$1,735.00	$1,735.00	$1,735.00	$1,735.00	$19,085.00	3.08%
Employee Incentive Pay	$2,074.54	$2,527.29	$2,990.24	$3,865.40	$4,059.57	$4,271.24	$4,502.13	$4,754.15	$4,928.19	$5,057.93	$5,192.18	$5,399.13	$49,601.99	8.00%
Payroll Tax / Fringe Benefits	$905.57	$1,157.16	$1,198.25	$1,242.05	$1,241.38	$1,242.72	$1,246.27	$1,252.25	$1,249.27	$1,241.19	$1,233.63	$1,233.27	$14,431.00	2.33%
Other Taxes	$1,864.49	$2,055.94	$2,247.57	$2,612.19	$2,700.52	$2,795.95	$2,899.18	$3,010.97	$3,091.68	$3,154.78	$3,219.80	$3,310.01	$32,683.09	5.32%
Payroll Service	$58.00	$66.00	$66.00	$66.00	$66.00	$66.00	$66.00	$66.00	$66.00	$66.00	$66.00	$76.50	$792.50	0.13%
Utilities	$950.00	$1,110.00	$1,115.00	$1,128.00	$1,130.00	$1,132.00	$1,135.00	$1,135.00	$1,135.00	$1,135.00	$1,135.00	$1,135.00	$13,375.00	2.16%
Insurance	$1,283.00	$1,283.00	$1,283.00	$1,283.00	$1,283.00	$1,283.00	$1,283.00	$1,283.00	$1,283.00	$1,283.00	$1,283.00	$1,283.00	$15,396.00	2.48%
Advertising	$3,000.00	$3,000.00	$3,000.00	$3,000.00	$3,000.00	$3,000.00	$3,000.00	$3,000.00	$3,000.00	$3,000.00	$3,000.00	$3,000.00	$36,000.00	5.81%
Miscellaneous	$2,000.00	$1,000.00	$750.00	$500.00	$500.00	$500.00	$500.00	$500.00	$500.00	$500.00	$500.00	$500.00	$8,250.00	1.33%
Telephone	$250.00	$250.00	$250.00	$250.00	$250.00	$250.00	$250.00	$250.00	$250.00	$250.00	$250.00	$250.00	$3,000.00	0.48%
Fuel Expense	$150.00	$150.00	$150.00	$150.00	$150.00	$150.00	$150.00	$150.00	$150.00	$150.00	$150.00	$150.00	$1,800.00	0.29%
Equipment Purchase	$78,512.00	$0.00	$0.00	$0.00	$0.00	$0.00	$0.00	$0.00	$0.00	$0.00	$0.00	$0.00	$78,512.00	12.66%
Long Term Loan Interest	$0.00	$0.00	$0.00	$0.00	$0.00	$0.00	$0.00	$0.00	$0.00	$0.00	$0.00	$0.00	$0.00	0.00%
Legal / Accounting Fees	$225.00	$0.00	$1,000.00	$800.00	$800.00	$800.00	$0.00	$0.00	$800.00	$0.00	$0.00	$1,500.00	$5,125.00	0.83%
Maintenance - Equipment	$200.00	$200.00	$200.00	$200.00	$200.00	$200.00	$200.00	$200.00	$200.00	$200.00	$200.00	$200.00	$2,400.00	0.39%
Trade Association Dues	$85.00	$85.00	$85.00	$85.00	$85.00	$85.00	$85.00	$85.00	$85.00	$85.00	$85.00	$85.00	$1,020.00	0.16%
Accounts Payable / Inventory	$3,500.00	$4,000.00	$7,000.00	$9,250.00	$11,000.00	$12,000.00	$12,250.00	$13,500.00	$14,000.00	$14,500.00	$15,000.00	$15,250.00	$131,250.00	21.17%
Loan Payment - Principle	$0.00	$0.00	$0.00	$0.00	$0.00	$0.00	$0.00	$0.00	$0.00	$0.00	$0.00	$0.00	$0.00	0.00%
Dividends Paid	$0.00	$0.00	$0.00	$0.00	$0.00	$0.00	$0.00	$0.00	$0.00	$0.00	$0.00	$0.00	$0.00	0.00%
Taxes Payable	$0.00	$0.00	$0.00	$284.33	$0.00	$457.36	$0.00	$0.00	$531.92	$0.00	$0.00	$586.47	$1,860.07	0.30%
Property Taxes Payable	$0.00	$0.00	$0.00	$0.00	$0.00	$0.00	$0.00	$0.00	$0.00	$0.00	$7,671.48	$0.00	$15,342.96	2.47%
Total Cash Outlay	$106,188.93	$29,752.72	$33,981.39	$36,984.29	$45,405.28	$40,101.60	$39,234.92	$40,854.71	$42,536.39	$41,691.23	$49,854.41	$44,616.71	$551,004.58	88.87%
ENDING CASH BALANCE	$82,805.56	$84,885.43	$88,404.60	$99,995.66	$105,626.72	$119,223.72	$136,613.21	$155,783.87	$175,302.25	$197,346.41	$212,969.81	$236,338.37	$236,338.37	
NET CASH FLOW	$-80,257.18	$1,838.35	$3,271.59	$11,333.22	$5,339.40	$13,298.93	$17,041.76	$18,772.20	$19,064.01	$21,532.86	$15,047.81	$22,747.40	$69,020.33	

143

BALANCE SHEET YEAR TWO

	Beginning Balance – 1/1/94	Quarter 1			Quarter 2			Quarter 3			Quarter 4			% OF SALES
		JAN	FEB	MAR	APR	MAY	JUN	JUL	AUG	SEP	OCT	NOV	DEC	
ASSETS														
CURRENT														
Cash	$162,568.53	$82,805.56	$84,885.43	$88,404.60	$99,995.66	$105,626.72	$119,223.72	$136,613.21	$155,763.87	$175,302.25	$197,346.41	$212,969.81	$238,338.37	43.44%
Inventory	$5,782.35	$7,194.29	$7,461.55	$9,063.93	$9,607.21	$11,221.58	$13,091.07	$14,393.13	$16,047.97	$17,602.97	$19,227.34	$20,904.55	$22,146.60	4.07%
Supplies	$0.00	$0.00	$0.00	$0.00	$0.00	$0.00	$0.00	$0.00	$0.00	$0.00	$0.00	$0.00	$0.00	0.00%
TOTAL CURRENT	$168,350.87	$89,999.85	$92,346.98	$97,468.52	$109,602.87	$116,848.29	$132,314.79	$151,006.34	$171,831.84	$192,905.21	$216,573.75	$233,874.35	$258,484.97	47.51%
LONG TERM														
Equipment Fixtures	$421,951.00	$500,463.00	$500,463.00	$500,463.00	$500,463.00	$500,463.00	$500,463.00	$500,463.00	$500,463.00	$500,463.00	$500,463.00	$500,463.00	$500,463.00	
Vehicles	$26,000.00	$26,000.00	$26,000.00	$26,000.00	$26,000.00	$26,000.00	$26,000.00	$26,000.00	$26,000.00	$26,000.00	$26,000.00	$26,000.00	$26,000.00	
Computers	$6,000.00	$6,000.00	$6,000.00	$6,000.00	$6,000.00	$6,000.00	$6,000.00	$6,000.00	$6,000.00	$6,000.00	$6,000.00	$6,000.00	$6,000.00	
TOTAL LONG TERM	$455,951.00	$534,463.00	$534,463.00	$534,463.00	$534,463.00	$534,463.00	$534,463.00	$534,463.00	$534,463.00	$534,463.00	$534,463.00	$534,463.00	$534,463.00	
Less Accumulated Depreciation	$80,270.77	$87,227.87	$94,185.78	$101,143.69	$108,101.60	$115,059.51	$122,020.56	$128,978.47	$135,936.38	$142,894.29	$149,852.20	$156,810.11	$163,768.02	
Net Long Term Assets	$375,680.23	$447,235.13	$440,277.22	$433,319.31	$426,361.40	$419,403.49	$412,442.44	$405,484.53	$398,526.62	$391,568.71	$384,610.80	$377,652.89	$370,694.98	68.14%
TOTAL ASSETS	$544,031.10	$537,234.98	$532,624.20	$530,787.83	$535,964.27	$536,251.78	$544,757.23	$556,490.87	$570,358.46	$584,473.92	$601,184.55	$611,527.24	$629,179.95	115.65%
CURRENT LIABILITIES														
Property Tax Payable	$12,785.60	$14,065.19	$15,343.77	$17,103.86	$18,863.95	$12,952.56	$14,709.51	$16,469.60	$18,229.69	$19,969.78	$21,749.87	$15,838.48	$17,598.57	
Income Tax payable	$0.00	$77.80	$172.57	$284.33	$144.95	$297.19	$0.00	$168.83	$347.11	$0.00	$189.67	$384.38	$0.00	
TOTAL CURRENT	$12,785.60	$14,142.99	$15,516.34	$17,388.19	$19,008.90	$13,249.75	$14,709.51	$16,638.43	$18,576.80	$19,969.78	$21,939.54	$16,222.86	$17,598.57	3.23%
TOTAL LIABILITIES	$12,785.60	$14,142.99	$15,516.34	$17,388.19	$19,008.90	$13,249.75	$14,709.51	$16,638.43	$18,576.80	$19,969.78	$21,939.54	$16,222.86	$17,598.57	
OWNERS EQUITY														
Beginning Equity	$537,657.90	$531,245.30	$523,091.99	$517,107.86	$513,399.64	$516,955.36	$523,002.04	$530,047.72	$539,852.44	$551,781.65	$564,484.14	$579,245.00	$595,304.38	
Add (NPAT)	$-6,412.60	$-8,153.31	$-5,984.13	$-3,708.21	$3,555.72	$6,046.68	$7,045.68	$9,804.72	$11,929.21	$12,702.49	$14,760.86	$16,059.38	$16,277.00	
Less Dividends Paid	$0.00	$0.00	$0.00	$0.00	$0.00	$0.00	$0.00	$0.00	$0.00	$0.00	$0.00	$0.00	$0.00	
TOTAL OWNERS EQUITY	$531,245.30	$523,091.99	$517,107.86	$513,399.64	$516,955.36	$523,002.04	$530,047.72	$539,852.44	$551,781.65	$564,484.14	$579,245.00	$595,304.38	$611,581.38	112.42%
TOTAL LIABILITIES & EQUITY	$544,031.10	$537,234.98	$532,624.20	$530,787.83	$535,964.26	$536,251.78	$544,757.23	$556,490.87	$570,358.45	$584,473.92	$601,184.55	$611,527.24	$629,179.95	115.65%

XII. Year Three Financial Statements

A. Income Statement; B. Cash Flow Statement; and C. Balance Sheet

INCOME STATEMENT YEAR THREE

	Quarter 1			Quarter 2			Quarter 3			Quarter 4			YEAR THREE TOTAL	% OF SALES
	JAN	FEB	MAR	APR	MAY	JUN	JUL	AUG	SEP	OCT	NOV	DEC		
INCOME														
Case Sales	$39,970.19	$40,769.60	$41,584.99	$42,416.69	$44,749.61	$45,987.09	$49,336.44	$50,323.17	$50,826.40	$51,334.87	$51,848.01	$52,366.49	$562,513.34	60.89%
Keg Sales	$29,220.54	$29,804.96	$29,953.98	$30,103.75	$30,254.27	$30,405.54	$30,557.57	$30,435.83	$30,314.57	$30,193.79	$30,073.50	$29,953.88	$361,271.97	39.11%
Total sales	$69,190.74	$70,574.55	$71,538.97	$72,520.44	$75,003.88	$77,392.63	$79,894.01	$80,758.99	$81,140.97	$81,528.46	$81,921.51	$82,320.17	$923,785.31	
Less Cost of Sales	$14,499.04	$14,789.02	$15,049.15	$15,314.30	$16,036.55	$16,729.80	$17,457.17	$17,747.87	$17,891.40	$18,036.51	$18,183.20	$18,331.49	$200,065.50	21.66%
Gross Margin	$54,691.70	$55,785.53	$56,489.82	$57,206.14	$58,967.33	$60,662.83	$62,436.84	$63,011.13	$63,249.57	$63,491.95	$63,738.31	$63,988.68	$723,719.81	78.34%
Plus interest income	$699.32	$763.86	$844.21	$923.60	$1,003.00	$1,060.17	$1,104.63	$1,201.03	$1,299.22	$1,351.44	$1,454.99	$1,529.78	$13,225.26	
TOTAL OPERATING INCOME	$55,381.02	$56,549.39	$57,334.03	$58,129.74	$59,970.33	$61,723.00	$63,541.47	$64,212.16	$64,548.79	$64,843.39	$65,193.29	$65,518.46	$736,945.07	
OPERATING EXPENSES														
Rent	$5,333.33	$5,333.33	$5,333.33	$5,333.33	$5,333.33	$5,333.33	$5,333.33	$5,333.33	$5,333.33	$5,333.33	$5,333.33	$5,333.33	$63,999.96	6.93%
Owners Salary	$2,400.00	$2,400.00	$2,400.00	$2,400.00	$2,400.00	$2,400.00	$2,400.00	$2,400.00	$2,400.00	$2,400.00	$2,400.00	$2,400.00	$28,800.00	3.12%
Employee's Salary	$1,200.00	$1,200.00	$1,200.00	$1,200.00	$1,200.00	$1,200.00	$1,200.00	$1,200.00	$1,200.00	$1,200.00	$1,200.00	$1,200.00	$14,400.00	1.56%
Driver's Salary	$1,800.00	$1,800.00	$1,800.00	$1,800.00	$1,800.00	$1,800.00	$1,800.00	$1,800.00	$1,800.00	$1,800.00	$1,800.00	$1,800.00	$21,600.00	2.34%
Payroll Tax / Fringe Benefits	$1,224.88	$1,215.06	$1,223.54	$1,232.18	$1,254.03	$1,275.06	$1,297.07	$1,304.68	$1,306.04	$1,311.45	$1,314.91	$1,318.42	$15,279.31	1.65%
Employee Incentive Pay	$5,535.26	$5,645.96	$5,723.12	$5,801.64	$6,000.31	$6,191.41	$6,391.52	$6,460.72	$6,491.28	$6,522.28	$6,553.72	$6,585.61	$73,902.82	8.00%
Property Tax Expense	$1,239.66	$1,239.66	$1,239.66	$1,239.66	$1,239.66	$1,239.66	$1,239.66	$1,239.66	$1,239.66	$1,239.66	$1,239.66	$1,239.66	$15,916.78	1.72%
Other Taxes	$3,380.00	$3,447.60	$3,484.41	$3,521.79	$3,607.27	$3,689.75	$3,775.86	$3,798.66	$3,806.06	$3,813.64	$3,821.42	$3,829.40	$43,975.88	4.76%
Utilities	$1,140.00	$1,140.00	$1,140.00	$1,140.00	$1,140.00	$1,140.00	$1,140.00	$1,140.00	$1,140.00	$1,140.00	$1,140.00	$1,140.00	$13,680.00	1.48%
Insurance	$1,283.00	$1,283.00	$1,283.00	$1,283.00	$1,283.00	$1,283.00	$1,283.00	$1,283.00	$1,283.00	$1,283.00	$1,283.00	$1,283.00	$15,396.00	1.67%
Fuel Expense	$175.00	$175.00	$175.00	$175.00	$175.00	$175.00	$175.00	$175.00	$175.00	$175.00	$175.00	$175.00	$2,100.00	0.23%
Advertising	$3,000.00	$3,000.00	$3,000.00	$3,000.00	$3,000.00	$3,000.00	$3,000.00	$3,000.00	$3,000.00	$3,000.00	$3,000.00	$3,000.00	$36,000.00	3.90%
Payroll Service	$66.00	$66.00	$66.00	$66.00	$66.00	$66.00	$66.00	$66.00	$66.00	$66.00	$66.00	$76.50	$802.50	0.09%
Long Term Loan interest	$0.00	$0.00	$0.00	$0.00	$0.00	$0.00	$0.00	$0.00	$0.00	$0.00	$0.00	$0.00	$0.00	0.00%
Miscellaneous	$500.00	$500.00	$500.00	$500.00	$500.00	$500.00	$500.00	$500.00	$500.00	$500.00	$500.00	$500.00	$6,000.00	0.65%
Telephone	$250.00	$250.00	$250.00	$250.00	$250.00	$250.00	$250.00	$250.00	$250.00	$250.00	$250.00	$250.00	$3,000.00	0.32%
Legal / Accounting Fees	$0.00	$0.00	$1,000.00	$800.00	$0.00	$800.00	$0.00	$0.00	$800.00	$0.00	$0.00	$1,500.00	$4,900.00	0.53%
Maintenance - Equipment	$250.00	$250.00	$250.00	$250.00	$250.00	$250.00	$250.00	$250.00	$250.00	$250.00	$250.00	$250.00	$3,000.00	0.32%
Depreciation	$5,329.41	$5,329.41	$5,329.41	$5,329.41	$5,329.41	$5,329.41	$5,329.41	$5,329.41	$5,329.41	$5,329.41	$5,329.41	$5,329.41	$63,952.92	6.92%
Trade Association Dues	$85.00	$85.00	$85.00	$85.00	$85.00	$85.00	$85.00	$85.00	$85.00	$85.00	$85.00	$85.00	$1,020.00	0.11%
Total Expense	$34,911.97	$34,880.45	$35,482.47	$35,407.01	$34,913.01	$36,007.61	$35,515.84	$35,615.48	$36,456.78	$35,698.77	$35,741.45	$37,295.33	$427,926.18	46.32%
PROFIT BEFORE TAXES	$20,469.05	$21,668.94	$21,851.56	$22,722.73	$25,057.31	$25,715.39	$28,025.63	$28,596.69	$28,092.01	$29,144.62	$29,451.84	$28,223.13	$309,018.89	33.45%
TAXES														
State Taxes	$207.57	$211.72	$214.62	$217.56	$225.01	$232.18	$239.68	$2,001.77	$1,966.44	$2,040.12	$2,061.63	$1,975.62	$11,593.93	
Federal Taxes	$0.00	$0.00	$0.00	$4,589.99	$5,061.58	$5,194.51	$5,661.18	$603.71	$5,674.59	$5,887.21	$5,949.27	$5,701.07	$44,323.11	
Total Taxes	$207.57	$211.72	$214.62	$4,807.55	$5,286.59	$5,426.69	$5,900.86	$2,605.48	$7,641.03	$7,927.34	$8,010.90	$7,676.69	$55,917.03	4.80%
NET PROFIT AFTER TAXES (NPAT)	$20,261.47	$21,457.22	$21,636.94	$17,915.18	$19,770.72	$20,288.70	$22,124.77	$25,991.21	$20,450.98	$21,217.28	$21,440.94	$20,546.44	$253,101.86	27.40%

CASH FLOW YEAR THREE

	Quarter 1 JAN	FEB	MAR	Quarter 2 APR	MAY	JUN	Quarter 3 JUL	AUG	SEP	Quarter 4 OCT	NOV	DEC	YEAR THREE TOTAL	% OF SALES
BEGINNING BALANCE	$236,338.37	$261,895.95	$289,443.42	$316,663.19	$343,885.38	$363,487.77	$378,731.20	$411,783.07	$445,446.69	$463,351.81	$498,852.01	$524,495.59	$236,338.37	
INCOME														
Interest Income	$689.32	$763.86	$844.21	$923.60	$1,003.00	$1,060.17	$1,104.63	$1,201.03	$1,299.22	$1,351.44	$1,454.99	$1,529.78	$13,225.26	
Cash Sales	$69,190.74	$70,574.55	$71,538.97	$72,520.44	$75,003.88	$77,392.63	$79,894.01	$80,758.99	$81,140.97	$81,528.46	$81,921.51	$82,320.17	$736,945.07	
CASH AVAILABLE	$306,218.43	$333,234.37	$361,826.60	$390,107.23	$419,892.26	$441,940.57	$459,729.85	$493,743.10	$527,886.88	$546,231.71	$582,228.51	$608,345.54	$986,508.70	
CASH DISBURSEMENTS														
Rent	$5,333.33	$5,333.33	$5,333.33	$5,333.33	$5,333.33	$5,333.33	$5,333.33	$5,333.33	$5,333.33	$5,333.33	$5,333.33	$5,333.33	$63,999.96	8.68%
Owners Salary	$2,400.00	$2,400.00	$2,400.00	$2,400.00	$2,400.00	$2,400.00	$2,400.00	$2,400.00	$2,400.00	$2,400.00	$2,400.00	$2,400.00	$28,800.00	3.91%
Employee's Salary	$1,400.00	$1,200.00	$1,200.00	$1,200.00	$1,200.00	$1,200.00	$1,200.00	$1,200.00	$1,200.00	$1,200.00	$1,200.00	$1,200.00	$14,600.00	1.98%
Driver's Salary	$1,800.00	$1,800.00	$1,800.00	$1,800.00	$1,800.00	$1,800.00	$1,800.00	$1,800.00	$1,800.00	$1,800.00	$1,800.00	$1,800.00	$21,600.00	2.93%
Employee Incentive Pay	$5,535.95	$5,545.99	$5,723.12	$5,801.64	$6,009.31	$6,121.41	$6,391.62	$6,466.72	$6,491.26	$6,522.28	$6,563.61	$6,569.61	$73,902.82	10.03%
Payroll Tax / Fringe Benefits	$1,224.88	$1,215.06	$1,223.54	$1,232.18	$1,254.03	$1,275.06	$1,297.07	$1,304.68	$1,308.04	$1,311.45	$1,314.91	$1,318.42	$15,279.31	2.07%
Other Taxes	$3,380.00	$3,447.60	$3,484.41	$3,521.79	$3,607.27	$3,689.75	$3,775.86	$3,798.68	$3,806.06	$3,813.64	$3,821.42	$3,829.40	$43,975.88	5.97%
Payroll Service	$66.00	$66.00	$66.00	$66.00	$66.00	$66.00	$66.00	$66.00	$66.00	$66.00	$66.00	$76.50	$802.50	0.11%
Utilities	$1,140.00	$1,140.00	$1,140.00	$1,140.00	$1,140.00	$1,140.00	$1,140.00	$1,140.00	$1,140.00	$1,140.00	$1,140.00	$1,140.00	$13,680.00	1.85%
Insurance	$1,283.00	$1,283.00	$1,283.00	$1,283.00	$1,283.00	$1,283.00	$1,283.00	$1,283.00	$1,283.00	$1,283.00	$1,283.00	$1,283.00	$15,396.00	2.09%
Advertising	$3,000.00	$3,000.00	$3,000.00	$3,000.00	$3,000.00	$3,000.00	$3,000.00	$3,000.00	$3,000.00	$3,000.00	$3,000.00	$3,000.00	$36,000.00	4.89%
Miscellaneous	$500.00	$500.00	$500.00	$500.00	$500.00	$500.00	$500.00	$500.00	$500.00	$500.00	$500.00	$500.00	$6,000.00	0.81%
Telephone	$250.00	$250.00	$250.00	$250.00	$250.00	$250.00	$250.00	$250.00	$250.00	$250.00	$250.00	$250.00	$3,000.00	0.41%
Fuel Expense	$175.00	$175.00	$175.00	$175.00	$175.00	$175.00	$175.00	$175.00	$175.00	$175.00	$175.00	$175.00	$2,100.00	0.28%
Equipment Purchases	$0.00	$0.00	$0.00	$0.00	$0.00	$0.00	$0.00	$0.00	$0.00	$0.00	$0.00	$0.00	$0.00	0.00%
Long Term Loan Interest	$0.00	$0.00	$0.00	$0.00	$0.00	$0.00	$0.00	$0.00	$0.00	$0.00	$0.00	$0.00	$0.00	0.00%
Legal / Accounting Fees	$0.00	$0.00	$1,000.00	$800.00	$0.00	$800.00	$0.00	$0.00	$800.00	$0.00	$0.00	$1,500.00	$4,900.00	0.66%
Maintenance - Equipment	$250.00	$250.00	$250.00	$250.00	$250.00	$250.00	$250.00	$250.00	$250.00	$250.00	$250.00	$250.00	$3,000.00	0.41%
Trade Association Dues	$85.00	$85.00	$85.00	$85.00	$85.00	$85.00	$85.00	$85.00	$85.00	$85.00	$85.00	$85.00	$1,020.00	0.14%
Accounts Payable / Inventory	$16,500.00	$16,000.00	$16,250.00	$16,750.00	$17,500.00	$18,250.00	$19,000.00	$19,250.00	$18,500.00	$18,250.00	$18,000.00	$17,750.00	$212,000.00	28.77%
Loan Payment - Principle	$0.00	$0.00	$0.00	$0.00	$0.00	$0.00	$0.00	$0.00	$0.00	$0.00	$0.00	$0.00	$0.00	0.00%
Dividends Paid	$0.00	$0.00	$0.00	$0.00	$0.00	$0.00	$0.00	$0.00	$0.00	$0.00	$0.00	$0.00	$0.00	0.00%
Taxes Payable	$0.00	$0.00	$0.00	$633.91	$0.00	$15,520.83	$0.00	$0.00	$16,147.36	$0.00	$0.00	$23,614.93	$55,917.03	7.59%
Proprty Taxes Payable	$0.00	$0.00	$0.00	$0.00	$10,560.54	$0.00	$0.00	$0.00	$0.00	$0.00	$10,560.54	$0.00	$21,121.08	2.87%
Total Cash Outlay	$44,322.47	$43,790.95	$45,163.40	$46,221.85	$56,404.48	$63,209.37	$47,946.77	$48,296.41	$64,535.07	$47,379.70	$57,732.92	$72,091.19	$637,094.59	86.45%
ENDING CASH BALANCE	$261,895.95	$289,443.42	$316,663.19	$343,885.38	$363,487.77	$378,731.20	$411,783.07	$445,446.69	$463,351.81	$498,852.01	$524,495.59	$536,254.35	$349,414.11	
NET CASH FLOW	$24,868.27	$26,783.60	$26,375.57	$26,296.59	$18,599.39	$14,183.26	$31,947.24	$32,462.59	$16,605.90	$34,148.76	$24,188.59	$10,228.99	$286,690.72	

BALANCE SHEET YEAR THREE

	Beginning Balance 1/1/95	Quarter 1			Quarter 2			Quarter 3			Quarter 4			% OF SALES
		JAN	FEB	MAR	APR	MAY	JUN	JUL	AUG	SEP	OCT	NOV	DEC	
ASSETS														
CURRENT														
Cash	$236,338.37	$261,895.95	$289,443.42	$316,663.19	$343,865.36	$363,497.77	$378,731.20	$411,783.07	$445,446.99	$463,351.81	$498,852.01	$524,495.59	$536,254.35	98.57%
Inventory	$22,146.60	$24,147.56	$25,356.54	$26,559.39	$27,995.09	$29,458.55	$30,978.75	$32,521.57	$34,023.71	$34,632.31	$34,845.60	$34,662.60	$34,061.10	6.26%
Supplies	$0.00	$0.00	$0.00	$0.00	$0.00	$0.00	$0.00	$0.00	$0.00	$0.00	$0.00	$0.00	$0.00	0.00%
TOTAL CURRENT	$258,484.97	$286,043.52	$314,801.96	$343,222.59	$371,860.47	$392,946.32	$409,709.95	$444,304.65	$479,470.40	$497,984.12	$533,697.81	$559,158.18	$570,335.45	104.84%
LONG TERM														
Equipment Fixtures	$500,463.00	$500,463.00	$500,463.00	$500,463.00	$500,463.00	$500,463.00	$500,463.00	$500,463.00	$500,463.00	$500,463.00	$500,463.00	$500,463.00	$500,463.00	
Vehicles	$26,000.00	$26,000.00	$26,000.00	$26,000.00	$26,000.00	$26,000.00	$26,000.00	$26,000.00	$26,000.00	$26,000.00	$26,000.00	$26,000.00	$26,000.00	
Computers	$8,000.00	$8,000.00	$8,000.00	$8,000.00	$8,000.00	$8,000.00	$8,000.00	$8,000.00	$8,000.00	$8,000.00	$8,000.00	$8,000.00	$8,000.00	
TOTAL LONG TERM	$534,463.00	$534,463.00	$534,463.00	$534,463.00	$534,463.00	$534,463.00	$534,463.00	$534,463.00	$534,463.00	$534,463.00	$534,463.00	$534,463.00	$534,463.00	
Less Accumulated Depreciation	$163,768.02	$169,097.43	$174,426.84	$179,756.25	$185,085.66	$190,415.07	$195,744.48	$201,073.89	$206,403.30	$211,732.71	$217,062.12	$222,391.53	$227,720.94	
Net Long Term Assets	$370,694.98	$365,365.57	$360,036.16	$354,706.75	$349,377.34	$344,047.93	$338,718.52	$333,389.11	$328,059.70	$322,730.29	$317,400.88	$312,071.47	$306,742.06	56.36%
TOTAL ASSETS	$629,179.95	$651,409.09	$674,838.12	$697,929.34	$721,257.81	$736,994.25	$748,428.47	$777,693.76	$807,530.10	$820,714.41	$851,098.69	$871,229.65	$877,077.51	161.22%
CURRENT LIABILITIES														
Property Tax Payable	$17,598.57	$19,358.66	$21,118.75	$22,358.41	$23,598.07	$14,277.19	$15,516.85	$16,756.51	$17,996.17	$19,235.83	$20,475.49	$11,154.61	$12,394.27	
Income Tax payable	$0.00	$207.57	$419.30	$653.91	$4,807.55	$10,094.14	$0.00	$5,900.86	$8,506.33	$0.00	$7,927.34	$15,938.24	$0.00	
TOTAL CURRENT	$0.00	$19,566.23	$21,538.05	$22,992.32	$28,406.62	$24,371.33	$15,516.85	$22,657.37	$26,502.50	$19,235.83	$28,402.83	$27,092.85	$12,394.27	
TOTAL LIABILITIES	$17,598.57	$19,566.23	$21,538.05	$22,992.32	$28,406.62	$24,371.33	$15,516.85	$22,657.37	$26,502.50	$19,235.83	$28,402.83	$27,092.85	$12,394.27	2.28%
OWNERS EQUITY														
Beginning Equity	$595,304.38	$611,581.38	$631,842.85	$653,300.07	$674,937.01	$692,852.19	$712,622.91	$732,911.62	$755,036.39	$781,027.60	$801,478.58	$822,695.86	$844,136.80	
Add (NPAT)	$16,277.00	$20,261.47	$21,457.22	$21,636.94	$17,915.18	$19,770.72	$20,288.70	$22,124.77	$25,991.21	$20,450.98	$21,217.28	$21,440.94	$20,546.44	
Less Dividends Paid	$0.00	$0.00	$0.00	$0.00	$0.00	$0.00	$0.00	$0.00	$0.00	$0.00	$0.00	$0.00	$0.00	
TOTAL OWNERS EQUITY	$611,581.38	$631,842.85	$653,300.07	$674,937.01	$692,852.19	$712,622.91	$732,911.62	$755,036.39	$781,027.60	$801,478.58	$822,695.86	$844,136.80	$864,683.24	158.94%
TOTAL LIABILITIES & EQUITY	$629,179.95	$651,409.08	$674,838.11	$697,929.33	$721,257.81	$736,994.25	$748,428.47	$777,693.75	$807,530.10	$820,714.41	$851,098.69	$871,229.65	$877,077.51	161.22%

XIII. Year Four Financial Statements

A. Income Statement; B. Cash Flow Statement; and C. Balance Sheet

INCOME STATEMENT YEAR FOUR

	Quarter 1			Quarter 2			Quarter 3			Quarter 4			YEAR FOUR TOTAL	% OF SALES
	JAN	FEB	MAR	APR	MAY	JUN	JUL	AUG	SEP	OCT	NOV	DEC		
INCOME														
Case Sales	$52,628.32	$53,154.61	$53,686.15	$54,223.02	$54,785.25	$55,312.90	$55,866.03	$56,424.69	$56,143.97	$55,864.64	$55,586.71	$55,310.16	$658,986.44	61.74%
Keg Sales	$30,103.45	$30,404.49	$30,708.53	$32,243.96	$33,856.16	$35,548.96	$37,326.41	$39,192.73	$37,326.41	$35,548.96	$33,856.16	$32,243.96	$408,360.17	38.26%
Total sales	$82,731.78	$83,559.09	$84,394.68	$86,466.97	$88,621.40	$90,861.86	$93,192.44	$95,617.42	$93,470.38	$91,413.61	$89,442.87	$87,554.12	$1,067,326.61	
Less Cost of Sales	$18,423.15	$18,607.38	$18,793.46	$19,079.35	$19,373.00	$19,674.73	$19,984.88	$20,303.80	$20,069.50	$19,842.71	$19,623.09	$19,410.33	$233,185.39	21.85%
Gross Margin	$64,308.62	$64,951.71	$65,601.23	$67,387.62	$69,248.40	$71,187.13	$73,207.55	$75,313.62	$73,400.88	$71,570.90	$69,819.77	$68,143.79	$834,141.22	78.15%
Plus Interest Income	$1,564.08	$1,730.01	$1,855.56	$1,947.78	$1,953.34	$2,008.29	$2,025.79	$2,164.07	$2,308.70	$2,302.36	$2,437.11	$2,545.74	$24,842.79	
TOTAL OPERATING INCOME	$65,872.70	$66,681.72	$67,456.78	$69,335.39	$71,201.74	$73,195.41	$75,233.35	$77,477.68	$75,709.58	$73,873.25	$72,256.88	$70,689.53	$858,984.01	
OPERATING EXPENSES														
Rent	$5,333.33	$5,333.33	$5,333.33	$5,333.33	$5,333.33	$5,333.33	$5,333.33	$5,333.33	$5,333.33	$5,333.33	$5,333.33	$5,333.33	$63,999.96	6.00%
Owners Salary	$2,600.00	$2,600.00	$2,600.00	$2,600.00	$2,600.00	$2,600.00	$2,600.00	$2,600.00	$2,600.00	$2,600.00	$2,600.00	$2,600.00	$31,200.00	2.92%
Employee's Salary	$1,200.00	$1,200.00	$1,200.00	$1,200.00	$1,200.00	$1,200.00	$1,200.00	$1,200.00	$1,200.00	$1,200.00	$1,200.00	$1,200.00	$14,400.00	1.35%
Driver's Salary	$1,980.00	$1,980.00	$1,980.00	$1,980.00	$1,980.00	$1,980.00	$1,980.00	$1,980.00	$1,980.00	$1,980.00	$1,980.00	$1,980.00	$23,760.00	2.23%
Payroll Tax / Fringe Benefits	$1,409.34	$1,417.08	$1,424.69	$1,444.27	$1,464.41	$1,485.36	$1,507.15	$1,529.82	$1,509.75	$1,490.52	$1,472.09	$1,454.43	$17,609.10	1.65%
Employee Incentive Pay	$7,032.20	$7,102.52	$7,173.55	$7,349.69	$7,532.82	$7,723.26	$7,921.36	$8,127.48	$7,944.96	$7,770.18	$7,602.64	$7,442.10	$90,722.76	8.50%
Property Tax Expense	$1,239.66	$1,239.66	$997.28	$997.28	$997.28	$997.28	$997.28	$997.28	$997.28	$997.28	$997.28	$997.28	$12,452.12	5.34%
Other Taxes	$3,848.54	$3,887.03	$3,925.90	$4,053.48	$4,198.75	$4,325.98	$4,471.48	$4,623.55	$4,480.38	$4,343.64	$4,213.03	$4,088.27	$50,448.02	4.73%
Utilities	$1,140.00	$1,140.00	$1,140.00	$1,140.00	$1,140.00	$1,140.00	$1,140.00	$1,140.00	$1,140.00	$1,140.00	$1,140.00	$1,140.00	$13,680.00	1.28%
Insurance	$1,300.00	$1,300.00	$1,300.00	$1,300.00	$1,300.00	$1,300.00	$1,300.00	$1,300.00	$1,300.00	$1,300.00	$1,300.00	$1,300.00	$15,600.00	1.46%
Fuel Expense	$185.00	$185.00	$185.00	$185.00	$185.00	$185.00	$185.00	$185.00	$185.00	$185.00	$185.00	$185.00	$2,220.00	0.21%
Advertising	$500.00	$500.00	$500.00	$500.00	$500.00	$500.00	$500.00	$500.00	$500.00	$500.00	$500.00	$500.00	$6,000.00	0.56%
Payroll Service	$66.00	$66.00	$66.00	$66.00	$66.00	$66.00	$66.00	$66.00	$66.00	$66.00	$66.00	$76.50	$802.50	0.08%
Long Term Loan Interest	$0.00	$0.00	$0.00	$0.00	$0.00	$0.00	$0.00	$0.00	$0.00	$0.00	$0.00	$0.00	$0.00	0.00%
Miscellaneous	$225.00	$225.00	$225.00	$225.00	$225.00	$225.00	$225.00	$225.00	$225.00	$225.00	$225.00	$225.00	$2,700.00	0.25%
Telephone	$200.00	$200.00	$200.00	$200.00	$200.00	$200.00	$200.00	$200.00	$200.00	$200.00	$200.00	$200.00	$2,400.00	0.22%
Legal / Accounting Fees	$0.00	$0.00	$1,000.00	$800.00	$0.00	$800.00	$0.00	$0.00	$900.00	$0.00	$0.00	$0.00	$4,900.00	0.45%
Maintenance - Equipment	$300.00	$300.00	$300.00	$300.00	$300.00	$300.00	$300.00	$300.00	$300.00	$300.00	$300.00	$1,500.00	$3,600.00	0.34%
Depreciation	$4,164.83	$4,164.83	$4,164.83	$4,164.83	$4,164.83	$4,164.83	$4,164.83	$4,164.83	$4,164.83	$4,164.83	$4,164.83	$4,164.83	$49,977.96	4.68%
Trade Association Dues	$85.00	$85.00	$85.00	$85.00	$85.00	$85.00	$85.00	$85.00	$85.00	$85.00	$85.00	$85.00	$1,020.00	0.10%
Total Expense	$32,808.91	$32,925.45	$33,800.75	$33,923.88	$33,460.41	$34,611.04	$34,176.43	$34,557.29	$35,011.55	$33,880.75	$33,564.21	$34,771.74	$407,492.43	38.18%
PROFIT BEFORE TAXES	$33,063.79	$33,756.27	$33,656.01	$35,411.50	$37,741.32	$38,584.37	$41,056.92	$42,920.39	$40,698.03	$39,992.50	$38,692.68	$35,917.79	$451,491.58	42.30%
TAXES														
State Taxes	$2,314.47	$2,362.94	$2,355.92	$2,478.81	$2,641.89	$2,700.91	$2,873.98	$3,004.43	$2,848.86	$2,799.48	$2,708.49	$2,514.25	$31,604.41	
Federal Taxes	$10,762.26	$10,987.67	$10,955.03	$11,526.44	$12,284.80	$12,559.21	$13,364.03	$13,970.59	$13,247.21	$13,017.56	$12,594.47	$11,691.24	$146,960.51	
Total Taxes	$13,076.73	$13,350.60	$13,310.95	$14,005.25	$14,926.69	$15,260.12	$16,238.01	$16,975.01	$16,096.07	$15,817.03	$15,302.95	$14,205.49	$178,564.92	13.77%
NET PROFIT AFTER TAXES (NPAT)	$19,987.06	$20,405.66	$20,345.06	$21,406.25	$22,814.63	$23,324.25	$24,818.91	$25,945.38	$24,601.96	$24,175.47	$23,389.72	$21,712.30	$272,926.66	25.57%

CASH FLOW YEAR FOUR

	Quarter 1			Quarter 2			Quarter 3			Quarter 4			YEAR FOUR TOTAL	% OF SALES
	JAN	FEB	MAR	APR	MAY	JUN	JUL	AUG	SEP	OCT	NOV	DEC		
BEGINNING BALANCE	$536,254.35	$593,145.78	$636,191.03	$667,802.61	$669,717.29	$688,555.76	$694,557.55	$741,965.20	$791,555.25	$789,379.52	$835,580.58	$872,824.23	$536,254.35	
INCOME														
Interest Income	$1,564.08	$1,790.01	$1,855.58	$1,947.76	$1,953.34	$2,008.29	$2,025.79	$2,184.07	$2,308.70	$2,302.36	$2,437.11	$2,545.74	$24,842.79	
Cash Sales	$82,731.78	$83,559.09	$84,394.68	$86,466.97	$88,521.40	$90,861.86	$93,192.44	$95,617.42	$93,470.38	$91,413.61	$89,442.87	$87,554.12	$858,984.01	
CASH AVAILABLE	$620,550.20	$678,434.88	$722,441.28	$756,217.34	$760,292.03	$781,425.91	$789,775.78	$839,746.69	$887,334.33	$883,095.48	$927,460.56	$962,924.09	$1,420,081.15	
CASH DISBURSEMENTS														
Rent	$5,333.33	$5,333.33	$5,333.33	$5,333.33	$5,333.33	$5,333.33	$5,333.33	$5,333.33	$5,333.33	$5,333.33	$5,333.33	$5,333.33	$63,999.96	7.45%
Owners Salary	$2,600.00	$2,600.00	$2,600.00	$2,600.00	$2,600.00	$2,600.00	$2,600.00	$2,600.00	$2,600.00	$2,600.00	$2,600.00	$2,600.00	$31,200.00	3.63%
Employee's Salary	$1,200.00	$1,200.00	$1,200.00	$1,200.00	$1,200.00	$1,200.00	$1,200.00	$1,200.00	$1,200.00	$1,200.00	$1,200.00	$1,200.00	$14,400.00	1.68%
Driver's Salary	$1,980.00	$1,980.00	$1,980.00	$1,980.00	$1,980.00	$1,980.00	$1,980.00	$1,980.00	$1,980.00	$1,980.00	$1,980.00	$1,980.00	$23,760.00	2.77%
Employee Incentive Pay	$7,032.20	$7,102.52	$7,173.55	$7,349.69	$7,532.82	$7,723.26	$7,921.36	$8,127.48	$7,944.98	$7,770.16	$7,602.64	$7,442.10	$90,722.76	10.56%
Payroll Tax / Fringe Benefits	$1,409.34	$1,417.08	$1,424.89	$1,444.27	$1,464.41	$1,485.36	$1,507.15	$1,529.82	$1,509.75	$1,490.52	$1,472.09	$1,454.43	$17,609.10	2.05%
Other Taxes	$3,848.54	$3,887.03	$3,925.90	$4,053.48	$4,186.75	$4,325.98	$4,471.48	$4,623.55	$4,480.36	$4,343.64	$4,213.03	$4,088.27	$50,448.27	5.87%
Payroll Service	$66.00	$66.00	$66.00	$66.00	$66.00	$66.00	$66.00	$66.00	$66.00	$66.00	$66.00	$78.50	$802.50	0.09%
Utilities	$1,140.00	$1,140.00	$1,140.00	$1,140.00	$1,140.00	$1,140.00	$1,140.00	$1,140.00	$1,140.00	$1,140.00	$1,140.00	$1,140.00	$13,680.00	1.59%
Insurance	$1,300.00	$1,300.00	$1,300.00	$1,300.00	$1,300.00	$1,300.00	$1,300.00	$1,300.00	$1,300.00	$1,300.00	$1,300.00	$1,300.00	$15,600.00	1.82%
Advertising	$500.00	$500.00	$500.00	$500.00	$500.00	$500.00	$500.00	$500.00	$500.00	$500.00	$500.00	$500.00	$6,000.00	0.70%
Miscellaneous	$225.00	$225.00	$225.00	$225.00	$225.00	$225.00	$225.00	$225.00	$225.00	$225.00	$225.00	$225.00	$2,700.00	0.31%
Telephone	$200.00	$200.00	$200.00	$200.00	$200.00	$200.00	$200.00	$200.00	$200.00	$200.00	$200.00	$200.00	$2,400.00	0.28%
Fuel Expense	$185.00	$185.00	$185.00	$185.00	$185.00	$185.00	$185.00	$185.00	$185.00	$185.00	$185.00	$185.00	$2,220.00	0.26%
Equipment Purchase	$0.00	$0.00	$0.00	$0.00	$0.00	$0.00	$0.00	$0.00	$0.00	$0.00	$0.00	$0.00	$0.00	0.00%
Long Term Loan Interest	$0.00	$0.00	$0.00	$0.00	$0.00	$0.00	$0.00	$0.00	$0.00	$0.00	$0.00	$0.00	$0.00	0.00%
Legal / Accounting Fees	$0.00	$0.00	$1,000.00	$900.00	$0.00	$900.00	$0.00	$0.00	$900.00	$0.00	$0.00	$900.00	$4,900.00	0.57%
Maintenance - Equipment	$300.00	$300.00	$300.00	$300.00	$300.00	$300.00	$300.00	$300.00	$300.00	$300.00	$300.00	$300.00	$3,600.00	0.42%
Trade Association Dues	$85.00	$85.00	$85.00	$85.00	$85.00	$85.00	$85.00	$85.00	$85.00	$85.00	$85.00	$85.00	$1,020.00	0.12%
Accounts Payable / Inventory	$0.00	$14,722.89	$26,000.00	$18,000.00	$36,000.00	$13,227.37	$18,796.26	$18,796.26	$18,796.27	$18,796.26	$18,796.27	$16,296.26	$218,227.84	25.41%
Loan Payment - Principle	$0.00	$0.00	$0.00	$0.00	$0.00	$0.00	$0.00	$0.00	$0.00	$0.00	$0.00	$0.00	$0.00	0.00%
Dividends Paid	$0.00	$0.00	$0.00	$0.00	$0.00	$0.00	$0.00	$0.00	$0.00	$0.00	$0.00	$0.00	$0.00	0.00%
Taxes Payable	$0.00	$0.00	$0.00	$39,738.28	$0.00	$44,192.06	$0.00	$0.00	$49,309.10	$0.00	$0.00	$45,325.47	$178,564.92	20.79%
Proprty Taxes Payable	$0.00	$0.00	$0.00	$0.00	$7,437.96	$0.00	$0.00	$0.00	$0.00	$0.00	$7,437.96	$0.00	$14,875.92	1.73%
Total Cash Outlay	$27,404.42	$42,243.85	$54,638.67	$86,500.05	$71,736.28	$86,868.36	$47,810.58	$48,191.44	$97,954.80	$47,514.90	$54,636.33	$91,231.36	$756,731.03	88.10%
ENDING CASH BALANCE	$593,145.78	$636,191.03	$667,802.61	$669,717.29	$688,555.76	$694,557.55	$741,965.20	$791,555.25	$789,379.52	$835,580.58	$872,824.23	$871,692.72	$663,350.12	
NET CASH FLOW	$55,327.36	$41,315.24	$29,756.02	$-33.08	$16,885.14	$3,993.50	$45,381.86	$47,425.98	$-4,484.43	$43,898.70	$34,806.54	$-3,677.24	$310,595.58	

149

BALANCE SHEET YEAR FOUR

	Beginning Balance 1/1/98	Quarter 1			Quarter 2			Quarter 3			Quarter 4			% OF SALES
		JAN	FEB	MAR	APR	MAY	JUN	JUL	AUG	SEP	OCT	NOV	DEC	
ASSETS														
CURRENT														
Cash	$538,254.35	$560,145.78	$636,191.03	$687,802.61	$669,717.29	$688,555.76	$694,557.55	$741,965.20	$791,555.26	$789,379.52	$835,590.58	$872,824.23	$871,692.72	160.23%
Inventory	$34,081.10	$15,657.95	$11,773.46	$18,960.00	$17,900.65	$34,527.65	$28,080.28	$26,891.66	$25,384.12	$24,110.89	$23,054.44	$22,237.62	$19,123.56	3.52%
Supplies	$0.00	$0.00	$0.00	$0.00	$0.00	$0.00	$0.00	$0.00	$0.00	$0.00	$0.00	$0.00	$0.00	0.00%
TOTAL CURRENT	$570,335.45	$608,803.74	$847,964.49	$666,762.61	$687,617.94	$723,083.41	$722,637.83	$768,856.86	$816,939.38	$813,490.41	$858,645.02	$895,061.85	$890,816.27	163.74%
LONG TERM														
Equipment Fixtures	$500,463.00	$500,463.00	$500,463.00	$500,463.00	$500,463.00	$500,463.00	$500,463.00	$500,463.00	$500,463.00	$500,463.00	$500,463.00	$500,463.00	$500,463.00	
Vehicles	$28,000.00	$28,000.00	$28,000.00	$28,000.00	$28,000.00	$28,000.00	$28,000.00	$28,000.00	$28,000.00	$28,000.00	$28,000.00	$28,000.00	$28,000.00	
Computers	$6,000.00	$6,000.00	$6,000.00	$6,000.00	$6,000.00	$6,000.00	$6,000.00	$6,000.00	$6,000.00	$6,000.00	$6,000.00	$6,000.00	$6,000.00	
TOTAL LONG TERM	$534,463.00	$534,463.00	$534,463.00	$534,463.00	$534,463.00	$534,463.00	$534,463.00	$534,463.00	$534,463.00	$534,463.00	$534,463.00	$534,463.00	$534,463.00	
Less Accumulated Depreciation	$227,720.94	$231,886.77	$236,050.60	$240,215.43	$244,360.28	$248,545.09	$252,709.92	$256,874.75	$261,039.58	$265,204.41	$269,369.24	$273,534.07	$277,698.90	
Net Long Term Assets	$306,742.06	$302,577.23	$298,412.40	$294,247.57	$290,082.74	$285,917.91	$281,753.08	$277,588.25	$273,423.42	$269,258.59	$265,093.76	$260,928.93	$256,764.10	47.20%
TOTAL ASSETS	$877,077.51	$911,380.97	$946,376.89	$961,030.18	$977,700.68	$1,009,001.32	$1,004,390.91	$1,046,445.11	$1,090,362.76	$1,082,749.00	$1,123,738.78	$1,155,990.78	$1,147,580.37	210.94%
CURRENT LIABILITIES														
Property Tax Payable	$12,384.27	$13,633.93	$14,873.59	$15,870.87	$16,868.15	$10,427.47	$11,424.75	$12,422.03	$13,419.31	$14,416.59	$15,413.87	$8,973.19	$9,970.47	
Income Tax payable	$0.00	$13,076.73	$26,427.33	$39,738.28	$14,005.25	$28,931.94	$0.00	$16,238.01	$33,213.03	$0.00	$15,817.03	$31,119.99	$0.00	
TOTAL CURRENT	$0.00	$26,710.66	$41,300.92	$55,609.15	$30,873.40	$39,359.41	$11,424.75	$28,660.04	$46,632.34	$14,416.59	$31,230.90	$40,093.18	$9,970.47	
TOTAL LIABILITIES	$12,384.27	$26,710.66	$41,300.92	$55,609.15	$30,873.40	$39,359.41	$11,424.75	$28,660.04	$46,632.34	$14,416.59	$31,230.90	$40,093.18	$9,970.47	1.83%
OWNERS EQUITY														
Beginning Equity	$844,138.90	$864,683.24	$884,670.30	$905,075.97	$925,421.02	$946,827.26	$969,641.91	$992,966.16	$1,017,785.07	$1,043,730.45	$1,068,332.41	$1,092,507.87	$1,115,897.60	
Add (NPAT)	$20,546.44	$19,987.06	$20,405.68	$20,345.06	$21,406.25	$22,814.63	$23,324.25	$24,818.91	$25,945.38	$24,601.96	$24,175.47	$23,398.72	$21,712.30	
Less Dividends Paid	$0.00	$0.00	$0.00	$0.00	$0.00	$0.00	$0.00	$0.00	$0.00	$0.00	$0.00	$0.00	$0.00	
TOTAL OWNERS EQUITY	$864,683.24	$884,670.30	$905,075.97	$925,421.02	$946,827.26	$969,641.91	$992,966.16	$1,017,785.07	$1,043,730.45	$1,068,332.41	$1,092,507.87	$1,115,897.60	$1,137,609.90	209.11%
TOTAL LIABILITIES & EQUITY	$877,077.51	$911,380.96	$946,376.89	$961,030.18	$977,700.68	$1,009,001.32	$1,004,390.91	$1,046,445.11	$1,090,362.78	$1,082,749.00	$1,123,738.78	$1,155,990.77	$1,147,580.37	210.94%

XIV. Financial Explanations

A. Preoperational Assumptions (Cash Flow)

This cash flow statement is provided to give a clear picture as to where monies are allocated before operation, and to show when said monies need to be collected.

- **Interest income**—Interest income is obtained monthly at a rate of 3.5 percent.
- **Stock/equity income**—This shows the Company's funding, step by step. Mr. Darin Floyd invests $161,000 in January of 1992. His father, Mr. William Floyd, invests a total of $50,000 from May until July. The offering of stock and sale of the stock need to be complete by November 1992.
- **Owner's pay**—Mr. Floyd will be paid $2,000 per month while he raises investors and prepares for operations.
- **Employee's salary**—The Company will hire an operational director to assist Mr. Floyd with his preoperational duties.
- **Payroll tax/fringe benefits**—Figured at 11.5 percent of salaries.
- **Insurance**—This insurance only covers employees prior to operational phase.
- **Miscellaneous**—Covers mostly incidental costs not covered in other areas.
- **Telephone**—In order to contact potential investors and suppliers, $400 has been allocated each month for this expense.
- **Fuel expense**—Mr. Floyd expects to do a great deal of traveling each month to visit with prospective investors and to meet with advisors.
- **Equipment purchases**—In order for the proper equipment to be installed before operations, certain amounts must be prepaid to the manufacturers. In addition, some office equipment, computers, delivery truck, and the forklift are also purchased before operations.
- **Travel expense**—If traveling by car is not feasible, Mr. Floyd will travel by plane. This expense also includes any hotel accommodations that may be required.
- **Legal/accounting fees**—Provided by Ice, Miller, Donadio and Ryan Attorneys. The fees total $15,000 (to be paid over a four-month period) and include Incorporation, Corporate Charter, Securities Arrangements, Stock Agreements, Employment Contracts, and any other registrations required by the Company prior to operation. Accounting fees were provided by Ernst & Young.

B. Operational Financial Statements

1. Income Statement

- **Sales**—First year are conservatively based. The Company realizes that sales cannot start at a high level, even though there may be an initial demand. First-year sales allow for the sales staff to acquire accounts at a reasonable rate. Second-year sales are based on market surveys and do include the sale of cases of beer. The Company feels that with the addition of the bottling line, these sales levels can be reached at a relatively progressive rate. Subsequent years are based on capacity; the company wishes to keep its proportion of draft to case sales around 50 percent each. Price increases at 4 percent per year were implemented. Seasonal variations were included in later years.

- **Interest income**—Taken from the cash flow statement. It is calculated by taking the beginning cash balance per month, multiplied by a 3.5 percent interest rate, and divided by 12 to achieve the monthly interest income.
- **Cost of goods sold**—For keg sales equals 27.55 percent, which covers ingredients; for cases equals 30.44 percent, which includes bottles, labels, caps, holders, and ingredients.
- **Rent**—Figured at $8 per square foot (triple net) multiplied by the 8,000 square feet, per annum, that the Company will need for operations. This includes taxes, maintenance, signage, and other items associated with the leasing of the property.
- **Owner's pay**—Mr. Floyd will be paid a $24,000 salary the first year, with a 10 percent yearly increase thereafter.
- **Employee's salaries**—Because sales will not begin to level until the third year, the salespeople will be given a salary/commission package that should average $22,900 the first year, $25,000 the second, $26,600 the third, $28,000 the fourth, and $29,385 the fifth.
- **Driver's salary**—Beginning in year two, this individual will be paid a monthly salary of $1,735, with a yearly increase of roughly 10 percent.
- **Payroll tax/fringe benefits**—This is figured monthly at 11.5 percent of all salaries and commission paid.
- **Employee incentive pay**—Salespeople receive a 10 percent commission on their sales. This figure takes into account Mr. Floyd's sales efforts as well, assuming he sells 25 percent the first year, 20 percent the second, 15 percent the third, and 10 percent from there on. Mr. Floyd, however, receives no commission pay.
- **Property taxes**—Assessed in March by adding the book value of equipment to February's ending inventory. The sum is then divided by 3, multiplied by 10 percent, and then divided by 12 to get the monthly expense. This expense is accrued, where half is paid in the following May and the other half is paid in November.
- **Other taxes**—Incurred by operations are the federal and state taxes for producing beer. The federal tax is $7 per barrel, while the state tax is $.115 per gallon. This is figured once the product becomes sellable, i.e., when it is kegged or bottled. This tax is collected monthly.
- **Utilities**—Include water, electricity, and gas and were figured by using the Indianapolis Brewing Company's (IBC) utility bill and then increased by 20 percent. IBC has the same size building.
- **Insurance**—Figured at $14,000 per year for liability, key-man disability and life, workmen's compensation, and other coverage. This was based on IBC's rates, which has six employees.
- **Fuel expense**—Includes the travel done in the early months of operations to taste testings and local promotions, and is expensed later for the forklift and delivery truck.
- **Advertising**—Initially, the Company will spend $3,000 to have certain items made up, such as coasters and table-tents, for local promotions. Monthly advertising figures thereafter are $2,500, which would include posters, T-shirts,

hats, and more of the above. Approximately half will go toward radio and print ads. More money may be allocated if necessary.

- **Payroll service**—Figures provided by Automated Data Processing (ADP) per employee, as hired.
- **Miscellaneous**—Items such as petty cash, office supplies, and minor purchases, based on IBC's miscellaneous expense of $200 per month. *Note:* During the early months of the first two years in operation, great amounts of monies are allocated to this expense; this is to cover any cost overruns that may be incurred during installation of equipment.
- **Telephone**—Based on a monthly service fee of $145 for a two-line system, with $100 in long distance per month. The hookup fee, $114, is expensed in January. Figures were obtained from Indiana Bell.
- **Legal/accounting fees**—Provided by Ernst & Young and include quarterly balance checks at $800 each; fourth quarter financial summation for $1,500; and tax preparation in March for $1,000.
- **Equipment/maintenance**—Monthly figures were provided by Pub Brewing Company and Nissan Forklifts for the first year which equal $80 and $20, respectively. After the first year, this expense grows due to additional equipment purchases and the actual depreciation of the equipment.
- **Depreciation**—Expensed monthly according to the double-declining balance method.
- **Trade association dues**—$1,000 per year for the Microbrewers Association, Master Brewer's Association, and includes monthly publications from each. This also includes subscriptions to four other trade magazines.
- **State taxes**—Figured at .3 percent of gross sales while the Company is at a loss, and 7 percent of net profit after the Company has carried forward its losses and is showing a profit, which is in August of the third year of operations. State tax is accrued and then paid out quarterly.
- **Federal taxes**—No federal taxes are paid until the Company shows a profit, again, in August of the third year, due to carrying its losses forward. Monthly tax rates are based on yearly income projections and divided by the appropriate amount of months. All figures take into account the appropriate tax rates.

2. Cash Flow The beginning cash balance for year one starts with the $269,569.87, the amount left after equipment purchases.

- **Accounts payable/inventory**—Although this is not a credit account, the Company will pay its debts as they are incurred (within that month).
- **Dividends paid**—There are no dividends paid within the first five years.

XV. Milestone Schedule

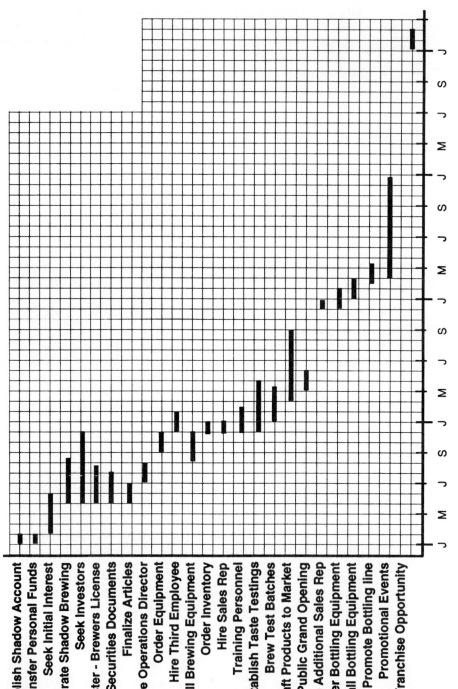

William E. Floyd

December 18, 1991

Mr. Darin M. Floyd
1123 West Wayne
Suite 124
Muncie, IN 47303

Dear Darin,

After watching an idea become a dream and then evolve into a burning desire, it is my pleasure to provide this document. It is my intent to furnish $50,000 in seed capital to begin the initial stages of funding for the Shadow Brewing Company®.

This money should be utilized for the initial formulation of the Company and its pro-rata share converted into preferred stock. As you have requested, the payments are staged over three months. Beginning May 1, 1992, I will send you $16,700 for two months and the balance of $16,600 in July.

I wish you well as you continue your venture to brew the best beer in the mid-west. As always, I remain your loving father and ardent supporter.

Warm personal regards,

W.E.Floyd
President
Information Profit group

Information Profit group
2110 Shetland   •   Inverness, Illinois 60010   •   708-382-7035

IMPORT BEER CONSUMERS

TOWN/CITY	ZIP CODE	20-24	25-34	35-44	45-54	55-64	65+	TOTAL
ALEXANDRIA	46001	82	503	296	144	83	85	1,193
ANDERSON	46011	348	1,899	1,266	650	336	327	4,825
ANDERSON1	46012	94	871	357	173	103	119	1,718
ANDERSON2	46013	45	325	199	93	64	69	796
ANDERSON3	46014	73	579	333	133	92	122	1,332
ANDERSON4	46016	28	270	115	43	25	41	521
ANDERSON5	46017	23	146	83	42	22	20	337
ARCADIA	46030	43	287	190	84	41	40	686
ARLINGTON	46104	10	55	31	17	10	11	134
ATLANTA	46031	25	152	98	49	23	23	370
BAINBRIDGE	46105	26	164	85	48	29	24	376
BARGERSVILLE	46106	26	167	95	51	25	22	387
BEECH GROVE	46107	62	470	235	112	78	85	1,041
BOGGSTOWN	46110	21	109	76	45	18	13	281
BROOKLYN	46111	31	160	103	54	25	23	396
BROWNSBURG	46112	165	843	632	340	143	101	2,225
BROWNSTOWN	47220	36	237	130	67	39	44	554
BURNEY	47222	0	1	1	1	0	0	3
BUTLERVILLE	47223	8	37	20	14	6	7	91
CAMBY	46113	16	96	72	29	15	9	239
CANAAN	47224	8	48	23	13	5	7	104
CARMEL	46032	331	1,621	1,058	723	321	191	4,245
CARTHAGE	46115	17	100	54	28	16	17	232
CENTERVILLE	47330	64	381	254	132	75	77	983
CHARLOTSVILLE	46117	1	5	3	2	1	1	12
CICERO	46034	26	174	115	51	25	24	415
CLAYTON	46118	40	222	146	85	39	33	565
CLOATSVILLE	46121	13	78	44	41	11	12	201
CLOVERDALE	46120	40	225	117	144	37	38	602
COLFAX	46035	5	33	15	9	5	5	72
COLUMBUS	47201	412	2,434	1,612	842	403	356	6,059
COLUMBUS1	47203	64	420	271	136	69	68	1,027
CONNERSVILLE	47331	209	1,213	770	358	202	224	2,975
DALEVILLE	47334	38	182	133	72	44	33	502
DANVILLE	46122	198	1,113	782	411	181	152	2,837
EDINBURGH	46124	38	228	130	60	31	31	518
ELWOOD	46036	106	653	366	185	98	122	1,529
FAIRLAND	46126	47	248	170	99	43	31	638
FALMOUTH	46127	3	30	15	7	3	5	63
FILLMORE	46128	17	102	57	29	18	15	239
FISHERS	46038	47	255	243	108	41	25	718
FOREST	46039	6	40	25	13	6	6	96
FORTVILLE	46040	43	221	142	82	37	32	557
FOUNTAINTOWN	46130	17	105	54	33	15	15	239
FRANKFORT	46041	151	1,054	615	296	179	213	2,508
FRANKLIN	46131	90	713	343	165	89	108	1,507
FRANKTON	46044	33	200	119	66	38	35	490
GLENWOOD	46133	3	15	9	5	2	3	36
GREENCASTLE	46135	102	949	250	146	89	104	1,640
GREENFIELD	46140	255	1,401	874	478	217	190	3,416
GREENSBURG	47240	143	940	520	253	135	163	2,154
GREENWOOD	46142	344	1,909	1,410	704	299	216	4,883
GREENWOOD1	46143	114	756	475	230	111	90	1,776
HANOVER	47243	51	466	157	74	32	36	817
HOMER	46146	14	101	51	26	16	19	227
HOPE	47246	34	214	123	56	25	27	479
INDIANAPOLIS	46201	257	2,115	1,164	420	266	352	4,573
INDIANAPOLIS1	46202	134	1,135	545	216	168	251	2,448
INDIANAPOLIS2	46203	354	2,786	1,322	593	376	437	5,870
INDIANAPOLIS3	46204	9	129	80	40	34	60	352
INDIANAPOLIS4	46205	282	2,245	1,372	445	260	322	4,926
INDIANAPOLIS5	46208	278	2,010	1,036	456	306	381	4,466
INDIANAPOLIS6	46214	134	1,194	724	275	146	129	2,603
INDIANAPOLIS7	46216	5	75	28	7	1	0	116
INDIANAPOLIS8	46217	136	943	564	281	166	138	2,227
INDIANAPOLIS9	46218	392	2,509	1,150	581	324	304	5,260
INDIANAPOLIS10	46219	270	2,028	1,257	550	391	491	4,986
INDIANAPOLIS11	46220	198	1,446	1,379	473	289	401	4,187
INDIANAPOLIS12	46221	45	351	159	71	46	55	727
INDIANAPOLIS13	46222	268	2,423	1,350	426	292	340	5,100
INDIANAPOLIS14	46224	159	1,808	1,033	329	228	205	3,761
INDIANAPOLIS15	46225	51	439	210	87	58	79	923
INDIANAPOLIS16	46226	375	2,841	1,811	741	418	333	6,520
INDIANAPOLIS17	46227	296	2,623	1,386	612	386	411	5,715
INDIANAPOLIS18	46229	202	1,430	876	368	173	115	3,164
INDIANAPOLIS19	46231	67	426	282	136	61	51	1,023

IMPORT BEER CONSUMERS

	ZIP CODE	20-24	25-34	35-44	45-54	55-64	65+	TOTAL
INDIANAPOLIS20	46234	50	330	215	107	46	29	777
INDIANAPOLIS21	46236	177	1,564	983	323	149	114	3,312
INDIANAPOLIS22	46237	185	1,310	900	372	191	169	3,127
INDIANAPOLIS23	46239	97	619	358	207	126	108	1,515
INDIANAPOLIS24	46240	96	700	464	219	149	167	1,795
INDIANAPOLIS26	46241	331	2,404	1,349	596	344	307	5,331
INDIANAPOLIS26	46250	82	583	391	188	113	79	1,436
INDIANAPOLIS27	46254	118	1,035	714	202	89	62	2,221
INDIANAPOLIS28	46256	84	545	390	199	100	51	1,370
INDIANAPOLIS29	46259	45	229	194	91	39	26	624
INDIANAPOLIS30	46260	229	1,731	1,200	489	251	245	4,125
INDIANAPOLIS31	46268	50	343	276	113	56	51	890
INDIANAPOLIS32	46278	26	169	111	69	36	25	437
INDIANAPOLIS33	46280	35	208	145	76	41	32	538
INDIANAPOLIS34	46290	2	12	10	5	3	2	34
INGALLS	46048	22	147	83	45	25	19	340
JAMESTOWN	46147	20	125	71	43	18	18	295
KEMPTON	46049	12	63	40	25	11	12	164
KIRKLIN	46050	14	87	52	27	15	17	213
KNIGHTSTOWN	46148	30	179	100	57	31	31	428
LAPEL	46051	35	182	126	63	36	38	480
LEBANON	46052	136	942	570	273	144	164	2,229
LIZTON	46149	9	47	29	18	8	8	119
MADISON	47250	145	980	581	276	176	207	2,366
MANILLA	46150	20	109	67	38	17	16	267
MARKLEVILLE	46056	34	190	127	72	37	30	490
MARTINSVILLE	46151	220	1,301	773	411	200	193	3,099
MAYS	46155	17	67	19	13	5	7	128
McCORDSVILLE	46055	25	118	86	49	21	17	315
MICHIGANTOWN	46057	20	98	70	30	16	20	255
MILROY	46156	19	115	55	29	15	16	250
MONROVIA	46157	43	232	150	83	38	33	578
MOORESVILLE	46158	141	824	483	282	130	96	1,937
MORGANTOWN	46160	43	214	141	76	37	39	550
MORRISTOWN	46161	16	103	52	31	14	14	231
MULBERRY	46058	13	79	49	25	12	17	195
MUNCIE	47302	242	1,621	917	440	260	273	3,754
MUNCIE1	47303	209	1,798	805	383	197	212	3,604
MUNCIE2	47304	329	1,440	635	300	177	188	3,069
MUNCIE3	47305	29	373	141	50	29	40	662
NEEDHAM	46162	26	217	91	50	28	27	439
NEW PALESTINE	46163	77	408	274	165	70	57	1,052
NINEVEH	46164	22	225	70	40	23	23	402
NOBLESVILLE	46060	217	1,304	858	473	212	175	3,239
NORTH SALEM	46165	16	87	53	33	14	14	216
NORTH VERNON	47265	118	710	419	198	98	107	1,649
PARAGON	46166	14	68	36	25	11	10	164
PENDLETON	46064	164	837	490	268	128	90	1,977
PITTSBORO	46167	29	146	111	57	23	22	389
PLAINFIELD	46168	133	1,113	558	270	140	234	2,449
PUTNAMVILLE	46170	38	226	99	41	21	14	439
ROSSVILLE	46065	18	98	62	32	16	20	247
SCIPIO	47273	40	215	125	69	28	25	502
SEYMOUR	47274	150	996	621	282	157	177	2,384
SHARPSVILLE	46068	31	165	116	60	29	26	429
SHERIDAN	46069	94	546	359	197	89	89	1,375
SUMMITVILLE	46070	10	51	31	17	9	9	127
THORNTOWN	46071	35	215	120	69	33	34	506
TIPTON	46072	57	400	218	116	67	78	937
WESTFIELD	46074	86	521	332	168	69	60	1,236
WHITESTOWN	46075	8	50	29	18	8	7	120
WINDFALL	46076	11	64	36	20	10	11	152
ZIONSVILLE	46077	47	249	177	107	44	35	660
TOTALS		13,091	89,308	52,905	24,592	13,259	13,297	206,452

TOTAL POPULATION	1,708,924.00
TOTAL TARGET MARKET	430,709.37
IMPORTED BEER	71,067.05
IMPORT BEER CONSUMERS	206,452.49

APPENDIX B   Survey Results

Question	Average Answer	
Basic Sales and Price Survey	Restaurant Bar	Liquor Store
1. Years they have been in business	11	15
2. Percent of beer sales to total alcohol sales	63%	58%
3. Percent of popularly priced beer sold	7%	22%
4. Percent of premium-priced beer sold	66%	58%
5. Percent of super-premium-priced beer sold	10%	11%
6. Percent of import beer sold	17%	9%
7. How many different imports do they carry	6	30
8. How many super-premiums do they carry	4	7
9. Average price of a premium 12 oz. glass	$1.57	$3.68
10. Average price of a super-premium 12 oz. glass	$1.82	$4.08
11. Average price of an imported 12 oz. glass	$2.56	$6.48
12. Do they carry any microbrewed beer (%Yes)	24%	45%
13. If yes, what is the price of an average 12 oz. glass	$2.21	$5.68
14. Do they buy kegs of super-premium beer (%Yes)	36%	42%
15. If yes, what is the average price per keg	$41.67	$52.73
Microbeer Questionnaire		
16. Would you sell a microbeer made in Indiana (%Yes)	55%	81%
17. If yes, how much would *you* pay per case	$16.06	$15.45
18. If yes, how much would *you* pay per keg	$46.75	$43.67
19. How many cases would you purchase per month	8	23
20. How many kegs would you purchase per month	8	8
Opinion		
21. Average age of import beer consumer	32	29
22. Do *you* think there is a market for a microbeer made and sold in Indiana (%Yes)	96%	100%

APPENDIX C

Carmel Shopper's Guide

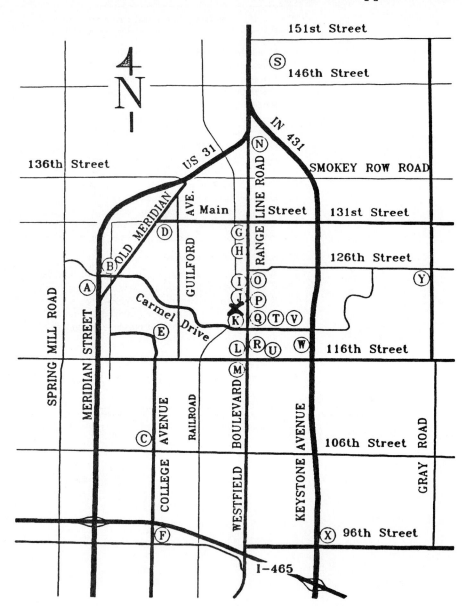

A   Meridian Park Shoppes
B   Tedco (proposed)
C   Home Place
D   Carmel Shopping Center
E   Wholesale Club
F   96th & College
G   Lumberyard Mall
H   Elliot's Mohawk Plaza
I   Carmel Plaza
J   Carmel Gate
K   Kirby Park
L   The Center
M   The Corner
N   North Range Line Road
O   Mohawk Landing
P   Shoshone Place
Q   Hunter's Quest
R   Carmel Walk
S   Simon Mall (proposed)
T   Hunter's Run
U   Woodland Shoppes
V   Marsh Plaza
W   Keystone Square
X   96th & Keystone
Y   Brookshire Shops

APPENDIX D

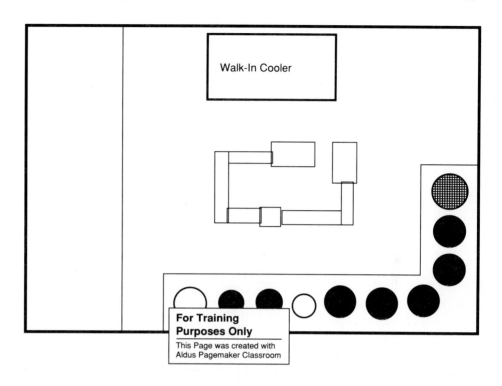

Walk-In Cooler

For Training Purposes Only
This Page was created with
Aldus Pagemaker Classroom

APPENDIX E

Section V—Pricing

A. Brewing Equipment

(1)	35-barrel mash mixer/kettle
(1)	42-barrel lauter tun
(5)	77.4-barrel fermenters
(1)	69.5-barrel finished beer tank
(1)	72-barrel hot water tank
(1)	72-barrel cold water tank
(1)	Yeast buggy
(1)	Mild steel brewer's platform
(1)	40-barrel whirlpool

$208,268.00

B. Support Equipment

(1)	Steam plant 60 BHP
(1)	Glycol unit 20 HP
(1)	Sterile pad filter 60 BBL
(1)	DE pressure leaf filter
(1)	Heat exchanger AT-10
(1)	Grain mill 1650# per hour
(7)	Triclover pumps
(1)	Grist case on load cells with digital display
(1)	15′ conveyor
(2)	Temperature control stations

$108,307.00

C. Accessories (Totals)

(37)	1½″ butterfly valves
(3)	1½″ throttle valve
(5)	Thermometer 0–250 degrees fahrenheit
(2)	1½″ sight glass—in line
(1)	Aerator—1½″
(150′)	Brewery hose 1½″
(20)	Hose barbs 1½″

(continued)

Section V *continued*

(1)	Carbonating stone	(8)	3″ gaskets triclover	
(9)	Sample port	(4)	3″ clamps triclover	
(9)	Pressure/vacuum relief			$ 19,313.00
(9)	Vacuum relief			
(9)	Pressure gauge 0–30 PSI		**D. Installation/training**	$ 15,000.00
(9)	CO2 connector—quick disconnect			
(13)	CIP—360 degrees		**E. Freight**	9,112.00
(135)	1½″ clamps triclover			
(135)	1½″ gaskets triclover		Total Brewery Cost	$360,000.00

Notes

1. Annual Industry Review, Institute for Brewing Studies, March–April 1990, 8–16.

2. Standard & Poor's Industry Surveys, December 6, 1990, F1–F39.

3. Ibid.

4. Ibid.

5. Standard & Poor's Industry Surveys, December 6, 1990.

6. Simmons Market Research Bureau, Inc., Alcoholic Beverages 1989, Section P–17, 1–233.

7. Standard & Poor's Industry Surveys.

8. Annual Industry Review.

9. Beer Business Cycle, Institute for Brewing Studies, March–April 1990, 19–21.

C A S E • *The Benjamin Sandman Children's Bookstore*

Jack B. Hess III, Ball State University

Table of Contents

I. Summary

A. *Statement of Purpose*

This business plan has been developed to obtain a five-year, 11.5 percent annual interest rate loan of $80,000 and a $10,000 line of credit with an annual interest rate of 11.5 percent. The plan has also been formulated to help secure $16,800 worth of equity financing through two private placements of common stock valued at $8,400 per placement. After this financing is secured, this document will serve as a financial outline and operational plan for the first four years of the venture's operation.

B. *Description of The Benjamin Sandman Children's Bookstore*

The Benjamin Sandman Children's Bookstore is a retail establishment that will specialize in the manufacture and sale of children's books, writing development products, videotapes, and stuffed toys to the members of the children's consumer market. The venture will be legally structured as an S corporation in May of 1992 by its proprietor, Mr. Jack B. Hess III, and it will commence operations on July 1, 1992. The Benjamin Sandman Children's Bookstore will be located at the Clearwater Crossing retail development on 82nd Street and Dean Road in Indianapolis, Indiana, and will be positioned within 50 feet of Baby Superstore, the state's largest retailer of children's clothing and furnishings.

C. The Benjamin Sandman Product Line

The Benjamin Sandman Children's Bookstore will design, manufacture, and market its own line of story books and writing development products under the Benjamin Sandman brand name by utilizing the product concepts of Mr. Hess and the talents of various freelance artists. These original products will be available at no other retail store and, if successful, will give this venture a unique and competitive edge in the marketplace. Also, by implementing such a concept, this venture will possess the exclusive intellectual right to reproduce the Benjamin Sandman characters in developing original promotional/advertising campaigns and in creating a unique and identifiable store atmosphere.

D. The Opportunity

The tremendous growth of both the children's book industry and the Lake Clearwater area provides an exceptional opportunity for The Benjamin Sandman Children's Bookstore. Not only have sales for children's books more than doubled since 1985, but children's-only bookstores are blossoming by the hundreds with one of the lowest failure rates out of all specialty bookstores. Moreover, the Lake Clearwater area provides the ideal community in which to locate a children's bookstore. Within a five-mile radius of the Lake Clearwater area lies the highest per capita and average family income levels in the entire state of Indiana. This extraordinary amount of disposable income provides the perfect economic base to support a unique retail venture of this type.

E. The Niche

In an attempt to carve out its niche in the current children's market, The Benjamin Sandman Children's Bookstore will attack the competition by providing the consumer with an identifiable store image, knowledgeable sales staff, large inventory selection, and unique product innovations. The two key elements of knowledge and selection are aimed at competing with the chain bookstores that are limited in what they can offer the consumer due to their general inventory requirements. The remaining two elements of image and product innovation are aimed at competing with the children's bookstores in the community that will be unable to obtain the offerings that this venture will provide. These key elements should help The Benjamin Sandman Children's Bookstore to establish and maintain the loyalty of its customers.

F. Financial Summary

In order to commence operations, this venture will require $121,000, preferably obtained from an $80,000 long-term bank loan, $16,800 in shareholders' equity, and $24,200, which Mr. Hess will personally bring into the business. Once the initial capitalization is secured, the acquired assets will be used as collateral on the long-term note and the operational activity of this venture should generate enough earnings to provide a solid return to both debt and equity investors. By the fourth year of operation, The Benjamin Sandman Children's Bookstore is projected to generate over $261,000 in sales revenues and over $13,000 in before-tax profits. This level of performance will provide a return on investment of 11.5 percent and a 22.7 percent rate of return on the shareholders' equity as documented by the pro forma financial statements found in this plan. Based on these assumptions, it is clear that The Benjamin Sandman Children's Bookstore will provide potential investors with an excellent opportunity to invest in a unique venture concept while earning a sound financial return.

II. Business Description Segment

A. Mission Statement

The mission of The Benjamin Sandman Children's Bookstore is to provide a wide selection of children's books, videotapes, and stuffed toys, as well as quality customer service, to the citizens of its surrounding community. The venture will sell not only children's products that are produced by established publishers and manufacturers, but it will also sell its own original line of books and other various supporting products under the Benjamin Sandman brand name. In this way, the venture will utilize the talent of local writers and artists in order to bring a unique line of products to the customer which are the exclusive domain of The Benjamin Sandman Children's Bookstore. The Benjamin Sandman brand name will be more than just a marketing tool aimed at unifying the products of various freelance writers and artists; rather, it will come to represent a quality line of children's products and customer services provided by the venture.

B. Industry Background

The current status of the children's book industry is one of extraordinary growth. From 1985 to 1990, children's book sales more than doubled.[1] The growth in the industry, on both the publishing and the retailing ends, is the result of many factors converging at the same time. First, many independent booksellers recognized the need to differentiate themselves from the chain stores by specializing in smaller market segments. Also, as American Bookseller Association President Ed Morrow stated, "When you put it all together—the demographics of the population bulge, and the fact that much more than in the past, parents are oriented toward education—it's one phenomenon reinforcing the other."[2]

Evidence of a renaissance in children's books is everywhere. Children's-only bookstores, all but unheard of 15 years ago, have mushroomed by the hundreds.

The boom in children's books has been further aided by curriculum changes in schools that supplement textbooks with literature, and the abundance of a well-educated generation of parents who have begun reading to their children at a very young age. Because of such a renaissance, the children's book industry has been experiencing a phenomenal rate of growth of over 15 percent a year since 1985.[3]

Although children's books will be the primary product line of The Benjamin Sandman Children's Bookstore, complementary sidelines that will be sold by the venture, such as children's videotapes and stuffed toys, are also experiencing growth in their respective industries. In the volatile world of video, the children's category is clearly emerging as the strongest and most profitable market niche.[4] Moreover, the number of children that will be enrolled in the kindergarten to eighth grade level will peak in 1996,[5] making the 1990s the perfect time for the start-up of a venture specializing in children's books and related products.

Not only does the current status of the children's book industry seem rooted in opportunity and growth, but the future seems equally as bright. According to a study conducted by the Book Industry Study Group, the projected sales of children's books are expected to continue rising to over $1.5 billion in 1994, a 30 percent increase over the 1992 projections.[6] Most experts at *Publishers Weekly* magazine agree that the most significant operational trends within the children's bookstore industry will consist of existing stores opening up second locations and the relocation of these stores to larger spaces.[7]

C. The Company

The Benjamin Sandman Children's Bookstore will commence operations on July 1, 1992. This date was chosen for several reasons. First, the peak periods for children's bookstores are traditionally the holiday season, running from October through New Year's Day, and the Easter/Passover period in the spring.[8] By opening on this date, the venture could correct any operational problems which may arise early on and therefore be equipped to handle the peak revenue periods which would occur later in the operating year. Second, this two-month time frame would give the venture the needed time for expansion of its own product line and the opportunity to compile the needed inventory requirements. Book publishers need advance order time, especially for new clients. Therefore, purchasing lead times for inventory orders in the book industry can run anywhere from six to eight weeks.[9] In other words, this two-month start-up period would help to ensure that many, if not all, of the inventory orders would be filled by the large number of publishers that would have to be utilized.

The Benjamin Sandman Children's Bookstore will be located in Indianapolis, Indiana, at the Clearwater Crossing development on East 82nd Street and Dean Road. Fronted on busy 82nd Street, a major artery of the affluent north side, Clearwater Crossing provides easy access and excellent visibility for the venture.

D. Short- and Long-Term Objectives

The short-term objective of The Benjamin Sandman Children's Bookstore is to develop an effective marketing program which will allow the venture to compete with the local independent and chain bookstores in the children's book and related product market niche. The first two years of the venture's operation will be the allocated time frame in order to achieve this objective. After the venture establishes its competitive position within the community and reaches its expected market share potential, it will then, through the next 2 to 4 years of operation, pursue the long-term objective of expanding its own line of products. The fulfillment of this objective will allow the venture to realize both higher profit levels and a higher degree of uniqueness and originality.

E. Uniqueness and Advantages of the Venture

Because The Benjamin Sandman Children's Bookstore will develop and sell its own line of products, it will be truly unique from its competitors. This uniqueness will be enforced by the publication copyrights already owned by the proprietors in addition to any future copyrights that will be obtained through new-product developments. In fact, The Benjamin Sandman Children's Bookstore will be the only children's bookstore in the city of Indianapolis, not to mention the only venture out of its direct competitors, to develop and sell its own offerings.

There are four distinct advantages that the venture will realize by implementing such a concept. First, the venture will provide jobs to local writers and artists, allowing them to gain exposure and express their talents to their community. Second, the consumer will be able to identify the venture's product line within the context of the store itself due to the use of the Benjamin Sandman brand name. Third, greater profit margins will be experienced by the venture in selling its own products rather than selling only currently published books. Profit margins for books are very tight when compared to other products. While toys and games are marked up 50 percent, books only have a 40 percent markup.[10] Books that are the property of the venture, however, can be produced by a local printer for a much lower cost than buying books from an established publisher. Therefore, by gradually expanding the venture's product line, a greater composition of its own products will comprise the store's inventory and thus greater profit margins will be realized. Fourth, the venture will be able to use its intellectual property in the form of copyrights to build a distinct competitive advantage. In this regard, the venture will have a collection of products that are unaccessible to the competition and that can be used for the exclusive marketing purposes of the venture. For instance, Mr. Hess plans to have a freelance artist, Mrs. Judith Hess, reproduce many of their illustrated characters into three-dimensional models. The characters will then be placed within the front window and throughout the store itself in order to attract young children, promote the venture's products, and make the interior of the venture identifiable and unique.

III. Marketing Segment

A. Research and Analysis

1. **Target Market**   Defining a target market for a children's store is a difficult task. While the child has the unsatisfied needs for the products and services, it is the parent or immediate family member who ultimately controls the purse strings or the purchasing power. Therefore, the target market for The Benjamin Sandman

Children's Bookstore is actually a synthesis between two separate subgroups. In order to integrate both of these subgroups into the venture's marketing efforts, this plan will analyze the child's immediate family as the venture's target market since it controls the purchasing decisions and the buying power. Furthermore, the children, who comprise the second target market subgroup, will be utilized to determine the size and trends of the market in which the venture will operate since they dictate the need for such a concept. Both of these subgroups will then be the focus of attention within the discussion of the venture's marketing plan which will further integrate the two subgroups into one homogeneous target market.

Market/Venture Survey   In order to study who buys children's books and why, a market survey was conducted to analyze and measure the demographic and psychographic variables of the venture's target market. On February 3, 1992, two separate kindergarten classes were chosen as a sampling group for the market study. With the assistance of Mrs. Naomi Anderson, a kindergarten teacher at the Woodbrook Elementary School, 40 surveys were distributed to the parents of her students as they picked up their children. Woodbrook Elementary is located within Clay Township in Hamilton County and is approximately three miles north of the proposed location for the venture.

In addition, with the assistance of Susan Sherman, a kindergarten teacher at Centralized Kindergarten at Lawrence North High School, 40 surveys were also distributed to the parents of her students. Centralized Kindergarten is located within Lawrence Township in Marion County and is approximately three miles east of the proposed location for the venture. Out of the 80 surveys distributed, 68 were returned for an excellent response rate of 85 percent. A complete analysis of this survey can be found in Appendix A; however, the following is a summary of the most important survey conclusions:

- Out of the 68 surveys returned, only 2 stated that they did not purchase children's books. Therefore, approximately 97 percent of the respondents do in fact buy books for their children; however, a conservative estimate of only 90 percent will be used in the market calculations.
- The mother of the child was the primary buyer of children's books in 76 percent of the families—more than all of the other classifications combined.
- 48 percent of the respondents were between the ages of 26 and 30 years old while approximately 24 percent were between the ages of 31 and 35 years old—the highest two categories.
- The most important criteria cited when buying a children's book was its content by 38 percent of the respondents; price was next with 32 percent of the respondents.
- The average amount of money spent on children's books per child in a year was $62.50.
- Respondents felt that the surrounding bookstores needed to most improve their customer service (34 percent of the respondents) and their selection of children's books (26 percent). The venture will therefore develop a quality customer service program and will offer a wide selection of inventory to its customers.
- Approximately 80 percent of the respondents said they normally travel only one to five miles to purchase children's books while approximately 20 percent

said they travel six miles or more. This occurrence is probably the result of this area being one of the largest retail districts in the state of Indiana. Customers do not have to travel as far to get the products they need; therefore they tend to patronize the stores with the most convenient locations. For this reason, the size of the market will be based upon a primary and a secondary market analysis.

- In general terms, the respondents perceived that story books and reading/writing development products were the most beneficial items that contributed to their child's development, all of which averaged a four or greater on a scale of one to five. Therefore, future product developments of the venture will be reflective of this fact.

- The most beneficial services cited in selecting products for children were newsletters on new products, a story-telling hour at a children's store, and the ability to preview videotapes at the store. Because of their high ranking, these services will be offered by The Benjamin Sandman Children's Bookstore and will be discussed in more detail within the venture's marketing plan.

With these responses in mind, a few conclusions can be formed about the target market for this venture. First, the primary buyers of children's books are women who are usually the mother of the child, with the majority being between the age of 26 and 35. Second, the majority of these buyers do not travel more than five miles to purchase books for their children due to the number of retailers and the size of the selling district. Third, most of these buyers shop for book quality and content over price and usually spend around $62 on each child a year in acquiring children's books. Fourth, these buyers would like to see a greater number of customer services and a wider selection of educational development products in the stores that they patronize when buying children's books.

Market/Product Survey   In addition to the market/venture survey that was conducted, a second survey was distributed in order to measure the attitudes and perceptions of the target market toward the venture's own product line. On March 2, 1992, 18 children and their mothers were approached at the Lawrence Public Library Branch on Hague Road in Indianapolis, Indiana. The mother of the child was given a copy of the children's book, *Tipett Strauss,* by Benjamin Sandman, which represents a sampling of the attributes and quality that will be present in all of the venture's products. After receiving the book, the mother was asked to preview the product and to then answer a few questions on the provided market/product survey. The survey then instructed the mother to either read the book to her child or give it to the child to preview for him- or herself. Once the child was adequately exposed to the product, the mother was instructed to answer the questions found on the second page of the survey. This market/product survey was therefore designed to measure the attitudes and perceptions of both customer subgroups (the parents and their children), thus determining the product's acceptability and desirability to the venture's target market. While a complete analysis is produced in Appendix A, the following is a summary of the survey's findings:

- On a scale of one to four, with a four being best, the mothers ranked the attributes of story content, illustration, layout, and product appeal at an average of 3 or greater with an overall average quality rating of a 3.4.

- Based on the same four-point scale, similar results were found regarding the mother's perception on how her child felt about the same attributes with an overall average rating of 3.3.
- 72 percent of the responding mothers cited that they would indeed purchase such a product for their child.
- 77 percent of the respondents said that they would be interested in seeing more products like the one that they previewed.
- 44 percent of the mothers reported that they believed their child really enjoyed the book, while 29 percent felt that their child liked the book.
- Out of the responding mothers, 22 percent cited that they would be willing to pay $5 to $9.99 for the product while 35 percent cited that they would be willing to pay $10 to $14.99 for the product—the highest two percentages of the six categories.

Assuming that these 18 parents and their children represent an accurate sample of this venture's target market, there seems to be a high level of acceptability toward the product that was tested. Because Mr. Hess will personally assure that all future product developments are at an equal or greater quality level than the tested product, there should be a continued high level of desirability for the products produced by The Benjamin Sandman Children's Bookstore. In fact, all of the attributes of the tested book were highly regarded by both of the target market subgroups. Not only did three out of four respondents cite that they would like to see more products like this in the future, but the same approximate ratio of respondents indicated that they would indeed purchase such a product for their child.

2. Market Size and Trends   The market size for The Benjamin Sandman Children's Bookstore will be based upon both a primary and a secondary market analysis. The reason for using this segmented approach is derived from the primary market research that was presented earlier. According to the market/venture survey, approximately 80 percent of the respondents indicated that they normally travel five miles or less to purchase children's books. While this represents a large segment of the venture's market, there is still a smaller, yet profitable, segment that is located beyond the initial five-mile radius. For these reasons, the primary market for The Benjamin Sandman Children's Bookstore will include all members of the target market who are within a five-mile radius of the proposed location for the venture and will represent approximately 80 percent of all revenues. Conversely, the venture's secondary market will include those members of the target market who live more than five miles from the proposed location and will represent the remaining 20 percent of the sales revenues.

Primary Market Size   In 1990, within a five-mile radius of the proposed location, there were approximately 24,815 children present from the ages of 0 to 13. These children represent over 45,000 families in the area and, according to an Urban Decision marketing report, will increase in number by over 14 percent by the year 1993. Also, these families possess an average family income of over $60,736, which demonstrates the immense buying power that exists in this market. In fact, according to the 1988 census updates, Hamilton county, which will comprise a large segment of this venture's market, had a per capita income of $16,360, the highest per capita income level in the state of Indiana.[11] Furthermore, it is estimated that these families will earn, on average, more than $67,732 in family income by the year 1993, an 11 percent increase over the 1990 estimates.

Besides its great buying power potential, this market shows many signs of immense growth as indicated by the current surrounding developments. In 1989, Lincoln Properties constructed the Lake Shore development which contains over 740 apartment units and is immediately east of the proposed site. Following this development in 1991 was the construction of River Road Courts, a living complex containing over 742 apartment units located immediately north of the site. Future growth of this market is currently being demonstrated by the Lake Clearwater development which is immediately south of the proposed site. According to the Jonathan Real Estate Company, this development will be complete in 1994 and will include $100,000 to $500,000 condominium units that are currently under construction. Table 1 illustrates this venture's primary market size in both units (children's books) and dollars.

Secondary Market Size   The secondary market for The Benjamin Sandman Children's Bookstore consists of those members of the target market who live in a radius of five to ten miles of the proposed site. The number of children within a ten-mile radius in 1990 was estimated to be 103,467. If the number of children in a five-mile radius, which is 24,815, is subtracted from the ten-mile figure, the total number of children who therefore compose this venture's secondary market is 78,652. These children represent more than 101,822 families that earn, on average, more than $48,653 in family income (a weighted average between the five- and ten-mile figures) and are expected to grow in number by more than 6 percent by 1993.[12]

Elementary school enrollment trends are a good indicator of this market's size and growth potential. There are essentially three school systems that are within

Table 1	Primary Market Size	
	Children ages 0–13 in a five-mile radius	24,815
	Average dollars spent per child per year (market/venture survey, question # 4)	$62.50
	Average price for a children's book – 1990: (see Exhibit 1 for calculations)	$8.28

According to the market/venture survey results, 97% of parents buy books for their children; however, to be conservative, assume only 90% buy children's books:

90% of 24,815 children = 22,333 children whose parents buy children's books

Primary Market Size for Children's Books

Dollars	22,333 × $62.50	=	$1,395,812
Units	$1,395,812/$8.28	=	168,576 children's books

**Exhibit 1
Calculation for the Average Price of a Children's
Book**

Data

Juvenile hardcover average per-volume price	$12.92[1]
Juvenile mass market paperback average per-volume price	3.63[2]
Juvenile trade paperback average per-volume price	6.75[2]
Juvenile paperback average per-volume price (($3.63 + $6.75)/2 = $5.19)	5.19
Average children's bookstore percent of hardcover inventory	40%[3]
Average children's bookstore percent of softcover inventory	60%[3]

Calculations

			weighted average		
Hardcover average:	$12.92	×	40.00%	=	5.17
Paperback average:	5.19	×	60.00%	=	3.11
		Average price for a juvenile book			$ 8.28

Sources: 1. 1990 Facts and Figures, *Publishers Weekly*, March 8, 1991, 38. 2. 1990 Facts and Figures, *Publishers Weekly*, March 8, 1991, 39. 3. Children's Bookselling Survey, *Publishers Weekly*, January 13, 1992, 27.

the scope of this market: Lawrence Township, Washington Township, and the Carmel Clay School system. From 1985 to 1990, each of these townships experienced considerable growth in school enrollment ranging from Washington Township's growth of 13 percent, Lawrence Township's growth of 19 percent, to Carmel Clay's growth of over 35 percent.[13] According to Dr. Robert Hartman, the superintendent of the Carmel Clay Schools, this township's high level of enrollment growth is expected to continue at this rate until well into 1996. Furthermore, according to Dr. Percy Clark, the superintendent of the Lawrence Township Schools, kindergarten enrollment is expected to increase by over 25 percent in this township until the end of the decade. Table 2 illustrates this venture's secondary market size in both units (children's books) and dollars.

3. Competition

Direct Competition   The Benjamin Sandman Children's Bookstore will initially face three direct competitors in the northern region of Indianapolis. These competitors include Kids Ink Children's Bookstores, Treehouse Tales Children's Bookstore, and Create-a-Book Children's Bookseller.

Kids Ink is the oldest and largest competitor currently operating three locations with a fourth site under planning in the Lafayette Square area on the west side of

Table 2	Secondary Market Size

Children ages 0–13 in a ten-mile radius	103,457
Minus children ages 0–13 in a five-mile radius	24,815
Number of children in the secondary market	78,652
Average dollars spent per child per year (market/venture survey, question # 4)	$62.50
Average price for a children's book — 1990	$8.28

According to the market/venture survey results, 97% of parents buy books for their children; however, to be conservative, assume only 90% buy children's books:

90% of 78,652 children = 70,786 children whose parents buy children's books

Secondary Market Size for Children's Books

Dollars	70,786 × $62.50	=	$4,424,125
Units	$4,424,125/$8.28	=	534,314 children's books

Indianapolis. The three stores are located at 13632 North Meridian Street, 241 West Main Greenwood, and 5619 North Illinois Street. Out of the three locations, the North Meridian store will create the most competitive pressure to this venture since it is located in the northern region of Carmel, Indiana—a major market community of The Benjamin Sandman Children's Bookstore. Kids Ink has many strengths including the largest selection of children's books in the area, special customer services, and extra promotional activities related to school book fairs. On the other hand, the North Meridian store and the North Illinois store both suffer from poor location visibility and the store atmosphere at each of the three locations is akin to a library rather than a place that creates an exciting atmosphere for a child.

Treehouse Tales is located at 1490 East 86th Street, approximately four miles west of the proposed site for this venture. Because it is the closest of all direct competitors, it will most definitely pose the greatest competitive threat to The Benjamin Sandman Children's Bookstore. The strength of this store lies in its customer service. Mrs. Debra Hipes, the proprietor and manager of the store, is an experienced school teacher with a degree in children's literature, making her knowledge and expertise an extreme asset of this competitor. Also, the store atmosphere of Treehouse Tales is far superior and more conducive to entertaining children than the three Kids Ink stores. While these are strong advantages for Treehouse Tales, the store hours of the business are a major limiting factor. The store is not open on any day with the exception of Thursday past 5:30 p.m. and it is closed on Sundays. These store hours therefore restrict families in which both parents work, which is a variable that dominates this particular market area. Besides inconvenient store hours, this venture has poor location visibility and is also very hard to access off the main artery of East 86th Street.

Create-a-Book is a service offered by the larger store called The Reading Railroad which is located within Union Station in downtown Indianapolis. This store offers customized children's books with a child's name and hometown integrated within the text of a previously illustrated book design. Even though this store is more than 10 miles away from the proposed site for The Benjamin Sandman Children's Bookstore, it is still a competitive pressure due to the immense popularity that these books have experienced over the last three years. These customized books are highly sought after gift items and customers are willing to drive the extra distance in order to obtain them. This store's major strength lies in its location. Union Station is a central shopping location in Indianapolis and offers much pedestrian traffic flow. The main weakness of this store, however, is its selection. Because it only offers 12 titles, it limits the return of repeat customers. The following chart analyzes some of the attributes for these direct competitors:

Attribute	Kids Ink	Treehouse Tales	Create-a-Book
Status	Chain	Independent	Independent
Selection	15,000 titles	8,000 titles	12 customized titles
Store hours	10a–8p M–Sat	10a–5:30p M–W,F,Sat	11a–9p M–F
	1p–5p Sun	10a–7p Th	11a–10p Sat & Sun
Knowledgeable staff	Yes	Yes	No
Story-telling hour	Yes	No	Yes
Square feet	1,600	1,400	800
Atmosphere	Average	Excellent	Average
Location	Average	Average	Excellent
Newsletter	Yes	No	No
Own product line	No	No	No

Indirect Competition   Because of their extreme proximity to The Benjamin Sandman Children's Bookstore, the indirect competitors of this venture could possibly influence its operations more than its direct competitors. There are approximately four general bookstores that carry children's books within a five-mile radius: B. Dalton Bookseller, Borders Book Shop, Coopersmith's Bookshoppe, and Waldenbooks. Although B. Dalton and Waldenbooks carry the fewest number of children's book titles, they together control more than half the share of the primary market due to their excellent Castleton Square Mall locations and their respectable chain-store status. An additional strength of these two competitors lies in their buying power. Because their national headquarters buys the inventory for each of the outlets, they are able to experience economies of scale and purchase quantity discounts. This fact means that these stores can often lower their prices to combat competitive pressures and still obtain a respectable gross margin on the products—a luxury that a children's-only store cannot experience. The weakness of these competitors, however, is their small inventory selection of children's books and their lack of a knowledgeable staff regarding children's products.

Borders is located at 5612 Castleton Corner in Indianapolis behind Castleton Square Mall. This store is one of the largest bookstores in the state of Indiana in both selling area (16,000 square feet) and general inventory size (over 100,000 book titles). Because of its large selection and superb customer services, this competitor has tremendous customer drawing power and provides, for most parents, an excellent one-stop shopping opportunity for purchasing both books for themselves and their children. The one weakness this store has is that it lacks a staff that is knowledgeable in the field of children's authors and publishers and the fact that its inventory of children's books is still smaller than all of the children's-only bookstores in the area.

Coopersmith's is the newest entry into the book market, opening in 1990 and located on the ground floor of the Keystone at the Crossing Mall. Although this competitor has fewer children's titles than Borders, it still offers more than B. Dalton and Waldenbooks, making it an attractive draw to customers who live in the Keystone area. Coopersmith's has the same approximate number of general book titles as the two chain stores; however, because it is an independent operator, it lacks the same purchasing power as the chains, making it less competitive on the pricing front. The following chart analyzes some of the most important attributes of these indirect competitors:

Attribute	B. Dalton	Borders	Coopersmith's	Waldenbooks
Status	Chain	Independent	Independent	Chain
Number of titles	25,000	100,000	25,000	30,000
Children's titles	1,500	5,000	2,000	1,700
Telephone orders	Yes	Yes	Yes	Yes
Gift certificates	Yes	Yes	No	Yes
Special orders	Yes	Yes	Yes	Yes
Credit cards	Yes	Yes	Yes	Yes
Audiotapes	Yes	Yes	No	No
Videotapes	Yes	No	Yes	No
Store hours	10a–9p M–Sat	9a–9p M–Sat	10a–8:30p M–F	10a–9p M–Sat
	12p–6p Sun	11a–5p Sun	10a–6p Sat	12p–6p Sun
			12p–5p Sun	
Newsletter	No	Yes	No	No
Own product line	No	No	No	No
Service	Average	Excellent	Average	Average
Atmosphere	Average	Excellent	Excellent	Average
Location	Excellent	Excellent	Average	Excellent
Visibility	Excellent	Average	Average	Excellent

4. Sales Forecast and Market Share   The sales forecast for The Benjamin Sandman Children's Bookstore will be based upon an ongoing Cahners Publishing survey which has studied the operations of over 87 children's-only bookstores over the past three years (see Exhibit 2). According to the survey, the average annual sales in 1990 for a children's-only bookstore were $179.3 per square foot. In order to further refine this estimate to reflect the region in which this venture will operate, Diane Roback, the editor of the Cahners Publishing survey, was contacted. Based on a phone conversation with Ms. Roback, it was determined that the average annual sales in 1990 for a children's-only bookstore in the east north central region, which includes Indiana, Illinois, Michigan, Wisconsin, and Ohio, were $175.9 per square foot (the sales figures for Indiana alone were not available for reasons of business confidentiality). Because this figure represents the same approximate region, selling area (1,180 square feet), and inventory composition (75 percent children's books/25 percent sideline items) as The Benjamin Sandman Children's Bookstore, it will be utilized to determine the first year's sales estimate for the venture.

Exhibit 2   **Trends in the Children's Bookstore Market**

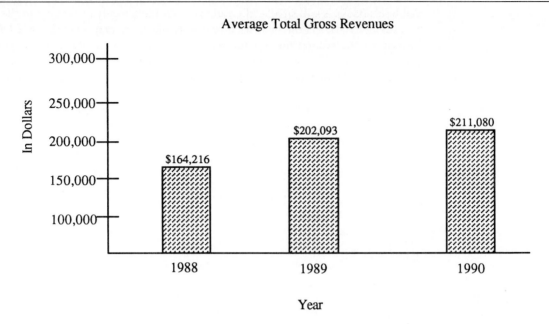

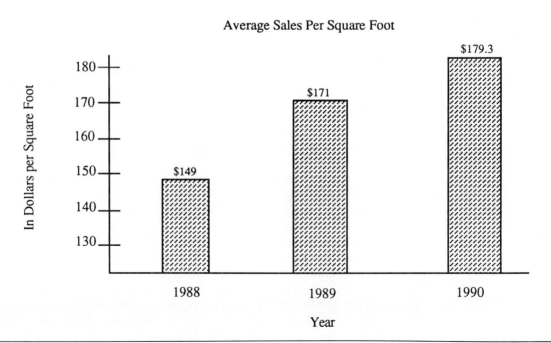

Source: Cahners Publishing surveys printed in *Publishers Weekly*, November 24, 1989; November 20, 1990; January 13, 1992.

Although the proposed venture site contains 1,600 square feet of layout area, the following floor plan diagram illustrates that only 1,200 square feet will be available for actual selling area (see Exhibit 3). Also, the sales per square foot will reflect the same annual growth rate that exists in the children's bookstore industry based on the Cahners Publishing survey, which is approximately 5.5 percent per year. This rate of growth is expected to remain stable at this level by most experts throughout the next three years.[14] With these facts in mind, the 1990 sales-per-square-foot estimate will be raised by 5.5 percent (to a level of $185.5/square feet) to represent a more current and accurate sales forecast for the venture. Consequently, a venture of this type and size should expect an annual sales level of $222,600 ($185.5 × 1,200 square feet). However, because it will take the venture a fair amount of time to build a clientele and to create its anticipated store image in the mind of the consumer, this figure will be reduced by one-and-a-half year's growth of 8 percent to make the first year's sales estimate both realistic and conservative. The following table documents the sales forecast for The Benjamin Sandman Children's Bookstore:

Sales Forecast

	Year 1	Year 2	Year 3	Year 4
Sales/square feet	$185.5	$195.7	$206.4	$217.7
Annual sales	$204,790*	$234,840	$247,680	$261,240

*Reduced by one-and-a-half year's growth of the sales/sq.ft. figure.

Sales Forecast Justification   The sales forecast for The Benjamin Sandman Children's Bookstore is justified as being both realistic and conservative when compared to the American Bookseller Association's ABACUS study. The ABACUS study is a financial survey of member bookstores based on 1989 operations conducted by the accounting firm of Ernst & Young. Based on the survey's results, specialty stores, which include children's bookstores, had sales per selling square foot of $266 and averaged an inventory turnover rate of 3.2 times. Based on these figures, the following calculations could be made:

$$1,200 \text{ square selling feet} \times \$266 = \$319,200$$
$$8,500 \text{ titles} \times 3.2 \text{ times} \times \$8.28 = \$225,216$$

Therefore, the annual sales based on these estimates would fall somewhere between $225,000 to $319,200 for an established specialty bookstore, making the forecast for The Benjamin Sandman Children's Bookstore both in line and fairly conservative when compared with these figures. (See Exhibit 4.)

As stated earlier, 80 percent of the venture's revenues will be represented by the primary market and the remaining 20 percent will be obtained from the secondary market. Accordingly, the primary market share for this venture was calculated by taking 80 percent of the annual sales and dividing it by the primary market size. Then, the secondary market share was derived by taking the remaining 20 percent of the sales revenues and dividing it by the secondary market size. In order to calculate the market share for the next three years, the size of the primary

Exhibit 3   Floor Plan for The Benjamin Sandman Children's Bookstore

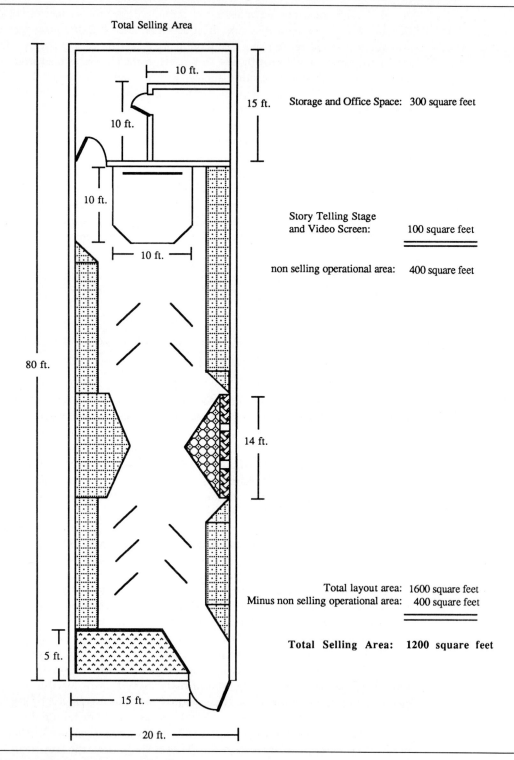

Total Selling Area

10 ft.

15 ft.   Storage and Office Space: 300 square feet

10 ft.

10 ft.

10 ft.

Story Telling Stage
and Video Screen: 100 square feet

non selling operational area: 400 square feet

80 ft.

14 ft.

Total layout area: 1600 square feet
Minus non selling operational area: 400 square feet

Total Selling Area: 1200 square feet

5 ft.

15 ft.

20 ft.

Exhibit 4

The Benjamin Sandman Children's Bookstore Sales Breakdown in Children's Book Units for the First Year

---

Sales year one	$204,790
Average price for a children's book	$8.28

Books as percent of sales: 75%   × $204,790 = $153,590

Sales in units for year one	($153,590/$8.28)	= 18,549 books a year
Books sold per week	(18,549/51 weeks)	= 363 books a week
Books sold per day	(363/7 days)	= 51 books a day
Books sold per hour	(51/average of 8 hours)	= 6.4 books an hour

---

According to the Cahners Publishing Survey, January 13, 1992, the average number of children's books purchased per customer for a children's-only bookstore was 3.5; therefore,

6.4 books an hour/3.5 books per customer = 1.8 customers per hour

Based on an observation for a one-hour weekday period of Treehouse Tales and the North Meridian Kids Inc. Bookstore on Thursday March 5, 1992, each store generated the following customer totals: Treehouse Tales—3 customers per hour; Kids Inc.—5 customers per hour.

Based on these findings of an average of only 1.8 customers per store hour, it is apparent that The Benjamin Sandman Children's Bookstore should be able to meet its first-year book sales estimate.

---

and secondary markets was increased by their respective growth rates. Because the primary market was expected to grow by 14 percent over a three-year period in the market size analysis, the dollar forecast of its market size was increased by 4 percent a year. Consequently, the secondary market was expected to grow by 6 percent over the three-year period, thus its dollar forecast was increased by 2 percent a year. A summary of these calculations is presented in Exhibit 5.

B. Marketing Plan

1. Market Strategy   The marketing philosophy for The Benjamin Sandman Children's Bookstore is to provide the customer with a unique and innovative line of products and customer services that will carve out a modest, yet profitable, niche in the children's book and educational product markets. The focus of the program will be aimed at both the parents and the children themselves in order to integrate the two target subgroups into one homogeneous market. The Benjamin Sandman Children's Bookstore plans to exploit this market niche and obtain the loyalty of its initial and future customers by creating the following venture image, product developments, and value-added services.

Venture Image   The image of the venture itself will be very unique from any of the direct or indirect competitors in the market. The front window of the store will be filled with three-dimensional character models from the book, *Tipett Strauss* (written by Mr. Hess), which will be brought to life with motion by electric motors, a trait that attracts young children (see artist rendition in Exhibit 6). Also, the

Exhibit 5	Market Share Calculations

	Year 1	Year 2	Year 3	Year 4
Market Growth (in dollars)				
Primary (4% growth)	$1,395,812	$1,451,644	$1,509,709	$1,570,098
Secondary (2% growth)	4,424,125	4,512,607	4,602,859	4,694,916

Market Share

	Primary Market	Secondary Market
Year 1	$\dfrac{\$163,832}{\$1,395,812} = 11.7\%$	$\dfrac{\$40,958}{\$4,424,125} = .92\%$
Year 2	$\dfrac{\$187,872}{\$1,451,644} = 12.9\%$	$\dfrac{\$46,968}{\$4,512,607} = 1.0\%$
Year 3	$\dfrac{\$198,144}{\$1,509,709} = 13.1\%$	$\dfrac{\$49,536}{\$4,602,859} = 1.05\%$
Year 4	$\dfrac{\$208,992}{\$1,570,098} = 13.3\%$	$\dfrac{\$52,248}{\$4,694,916} = 1.1\%$

ceilings of the store will not be finished with the standard acoustic panels at the ten-foot height, but will be left open in order to create a wide open store appearance. Then, due to the extra ceiling space, additional characters from the Benjamin Sandman story books will be placed upon the top of the bookcases and cash register to give the store a Disneyesque atmosphere. The purposes of displaying the three-dimensional characters throughout the store are to (1) create an atmosphere conducive to entertaining and attracting young children, (2) promote the venture's own Benjamin Sandman product line, and (3) make the image of this venture truly identifiable. Besides these attractions, the store will also contain a children's play and reading area for the parents' convenience while they shop (Location #8 on floor plan), and in the back of the store there will be a story-telling stage which will be utilized during the promotional story-telling hour provided for the children. Moreover, at the back of the store, located behind the story-telling stage, there will be positioned a large video screen and projector which will play children's videos—a strategy that will add to the store's moving atmosphere, as well as promote the videotape products (Locations 3 and 4 on floor plan).

Merchandise   The Benjamin Sandman Children's Bookstore will carry approximately 8,500 children's book titles in addition to its own line of products. The store will also carry 40 children's video titles and over 30 different types of stuffed toys from the Manhattan Toy Company. This inventory level will allow the store to have plenty of room for its own expanding product line while still remaining very competitive in terms of selection with the other children's bookstores in the area. Previous marketing research has found that shopping customers usually drift to

Exhibit 6 Artist Rendition of Store Front and Window

the right after entering the front door of a retail store.[15] Due to this fact, products with the highest gross margins will be placed in the front of the store on the right-hand side. Therefore, the Benjamin Sandman product line, which has the highest gross margin, will be placed in the right, front corner of the store along with picture/toddler books (having the second highest gross margin) being placed in the left, front corner. The placement of the remaining children's book categories, as well as the sideline products, are located on the merchandise diagram along with a description of the children's book classifications in the floor plan.

The Product Line   The Benjamin Sandman product line will initially consist of two separate categories: story books and writing development products. Each story book has been and will be designed with a consistent format, making the products identifiable as a collection. The text of each book is written in a rhymed couplet meter which is printed in large, easy-to-read letters and conveys the virtues of happiness, humor, and moral issues. The illustrations consist of bright, hand-painted watercolors which quickly attract the eye of both the child and the parent as a customer. The majority of these books will be created by Mr. Hess himself; however, in order to facilitate and expand the product line at a greater rate, various freelance artists, such as Susan Moore, Judith Hess, and Andrea Eberbach, will be commissioned to illustrate a number of the titles. Although a different group of artists and writers may work on each book, all of the products will be required to meet a consistent high level of quality and each will possess the pen name of Benjamin Sandman as the author. This marketing strategy will hopefully allow the customer to identify the individual book as a part of a larger collection and as a creation of the store itself.

The next product category consists of writing development products which are an exclusive creation of the Benjamin Sandman venture. These products consist of a three-dimensional character or story scene which is accompanied by a book with empty pages and a pencil. The child is encouraged by the product to write a story in the book about the character or scene, thus allowing the children to practice writing skills, develop creative ideas, and feel a sense of accomplishment in creating something on their own. After the pages are full, they simply slide out, allowing the story to be kept, and a new set of pages slide into the book binding, allowing it to be reused. This product creation is an attempt to fulfill the needs of the parents who responded to the market/venture survey indicating that writing development products greatly contributed to their child's growth.

The Customer Services   The niche for this venture will be created not only with its unique image and product line, but also by an array of value-added services including special product orders, videotape previewing, and a knowledgeable staff. Because it will represent a large number of children's book publishers, The Benjamin Sandman Children's Bookstore will be able to special-order any products that it does not have in its current inventory, thus providing the customer with a larger selection of children's products and the ability to obtain less popular titles. Many parents have indicated that they would like the opportunity to preview videotapes for their children before making the final purchase, thereby screening the product for its content of quality, violence, and educational features. Because of its ability to show videotapes on a large screen, this venture will be able to accommodate these parents and allow them to preview any videotapes they so desire before making the purchase decision. Also, this venture plans to have one of the most knowledgeable staffs regarding children's books in the area. This strategy will be implemented by hiring two individuals who have expressed commitment to this venture, Mr. Mike Wilkey and Mrs. Cindy Shirey. Mr. Wilkey has extensive experience in retail bookselling and was a previous employee of Borders Book Shop—an indirect competitor of this venture. Mrs. Shirey is an experienced elementary school teacher and the author of several children's books with much expertise in the field of children's issues.

2. Pricing Policy Unlike most industries, the book industry functions on the basis of suggested retail price to such an extent that the prices are actually printed on the book itself. Unless there are substantial competitive pressures, most book retailers sell the products at their suggested retail price and attempt instead to gain customers through image and service. This is true because, as stated earlier, there is very little room to lower the price of a book due to its tight gross margin. Therefore, The Benjamin Sandman Children's Bookstore will sell all published books and sideline items at their suggested retail price unless there is a substantial quantity order made by a particular customer, in which a discount on the total order price will be made (say, in the case of a school educator buying literature for a class). This pricing policy will produce an average gross margin of about 40 percent on the sales revenues of these products.

The pricing concept for the venture's own product line was derived from the primary market/product survey that was conducted. According to the survey, more than half of the respondents indicated that they would pay between $5 and $14.99 for the test product. Consequently, the price for Benjamin Sandman story books will initially be set at $9.99 and will be adjusted accordingly based on future market tests, surveys, and customer reactions. This pricing strategy will allow the venture to realize a gross margin of over 50 percent on its Benjamin Sandman story book purchases (see Exhibit 7 for calculations).

The pricing concept for the venture's writing development products will vary from creation to creation on whether the set consists of an individual character or an entire story scene. The price for an individual character will range from $9.99 to $19.99 and the price for an entire story scene will range from $14.99 to $39.99. Like its sales price, the gross margin produced by this product will vary from set to set depending on its selling price and its material and labor costs.

3. Advertising and Promotions The chief promotional tool implemented by this venture will be its story-telling hour. Each Saturday afternoon, at one o'clock, one of the employees will present a group of new products to the participating children and their parents, allowing them to select two or three of the titles to be read. As the employee reads the text of the book, the book's illustrations will be displayed on the store's video screen located behind the story-telling stage, allowing the participants to better view the product. This story-telling hour will be an important promotional tool, allowing the venture to (1) attract potential customers of the target market to the store location, (2) offer the children and their parents the opportunity to preview new merchandise, and (3) promote the venture's image, product line, and customer services.

The Benjamin Sandman Children's Bookstore will utilize three different types of media for its advertising campaign: newsletters, magazines, and newspapers. Each advertising program for the venture will be designed utilizing the published Self Regulatory Guidelines for Children's Advertising developed by the Children's Advertising Review Unit of the Council of Better Business Bureaus. The function of the Guidelines is to delineate those areas that need particular attention to help avoid deceptive advertising messages to children. The intent is to help advertisers deal sensitively and honestly with children and is not meant to deprive them, or children, of the benefits of innovative advertising approaches.[16]

Exhibit 7   **Manufacturing Cost Data**

Initial Inventory	Additional Inventory Lots

Data

3 book titles × 1,000 copies of each title = 3,000 printed books

Fixed printing costs	$5,000 for start-up plates and first 1,000 copies
Variable printing costs	$3,000 per additional 1,000 book units 2,000 needed to reach the 3,000 needed units
Total variable costs	$3,000 × (2 units of 1,000) = $6,000
Artwork labor costs	($70 per illustration × 15 illustrations per book) × 3 books = $3,150

Calculations

$$\text{Total cost for 3,000 books} = \frac{\text{Total fixed} + \text{Total variable}}{\$8,150 + \$6,000} = \$14,150$$

Cost per unit = $14,150/3,000 units = $4.71 per unit

$$\text{Gross margin} = \frac{(\text{Retail price per unit} - \text{Cost per unit})}{\text{Retail price}}$$
$$\frac{(\$9.99 - \$4.71)}{\$9.99}$$
$$= 53\%$$

Data

3 book titles × 333 copies = 1,000 printed books

Fixed printing costs	$300 for tooling set-up
Variable printing costs	$3,000 per additional 1,000 books units

Calculations

$$\text{Total cost for 1,000 books} = \frac{\text{Total fixed} + \text{Total variable}}{\$300 + \$3,000} = \$3,300$$

Cost per unit = $3,300/1,000 units = $3.30 per unit

$$\text{Gross margin} = \frac{(\text{Retail price per unit} - \text{Cost per unit})}{\text{Retail price}}$$
$$\frac{(\$9.99 - \$3.30)}{\$9.99}$$
$$= 67\%$$

Source: All cost estimates supplied by the Shepard-Poorman Printing Company, 7301 North Woodland Drive, Indianapolis, IN 46268. All artistic rates supplied by Susan Moore, Commercial Artist, Indianapolis, Indiana.

The first advertising program will consist of a venture newsletter. The *Benjamin Sandman Newsletter* will act as a direct communication between the store and its target market, reinforcing the image of the store as having much more to offer than the children's department of a chain bookstore. The mailing list for this newsletter will be constructed utilizing the customer information collected upon each sales purchase and will be mailed to these customers four times a year—every three months. The cost of this program, including printing and mailing expenses, will constitute approximately 10 percent of the advertising budget which was an estimate derived from a discussion with Mrs. Shirley Mullin, the proprietor of the North Meridian Street Kids Ink Children's Bookstore.

The second advertising program for this venture will consist of magazine media. The chosen source for this program will be the *Indianapolis Monthly* magazine which currently has a monthly circulation rate of 45,850 copies. This publication will provide an excellent vehicle for advertising to the venture's target market since it aims toward adults in the early family development stages and since more than 72 percent of its subscribers live on the north side of Indianapolis—the approximate area surrounding the proposed location for this venture. Six advertisements per year, approximately 1/6 of a page, will be allocated to the publication—four during the store's peak selling seasons (October, November, December, and April) and two during the initial opening months of the venture.

Indy's Child Inc. newspaper will be utilized as the third type of media in the venture's advertising strategy. This newspaper circulates to more than 45,000 kids and their parents in the north and central regions of Indianapolis, making it the perfect vehicle for communicating with the two subgroups of the venture's target market. An advertisement for The Benjamin Sandman Children's Bookstore will be placed in this newspaper every month of the year, including six 3 × 5 inch and six 2 3/8 × 2 3/8 inch advertisements. For the grand opening of the store, two additional advertisements will be placed in the *Indianapolis Star*'s Lifestyle section each Sunday of the grand opening month. The Lifestyle section has a current circulation of 413,346 copies and was chosen because it is typically the section which attracts the greatest number of female readers.

In addition to these programs, a telephone listing printed in red superbold print will be purchased in the Ameritech Yellow Pages. Not only has red print been proven in several marketing studies to attract a reader's attention over black print, but the listing for The Benjamin Sandman Children's Bookstore should be the only red superbold listing on its respective bookstore page. The three proposed advertisements shown in Exhibit 8 illustrate the same approximate size and methods that will be employed in targeting both the parents and their children in the venture's marketing efforts. Figure 1 is the proposed advertisement that will appear in *Indy's Child Inc.* and in *Indianapolis Monthly* that will target the parent subgroup. Figure 2 will appear in *Indy's Child Inc.* and will be focused more toward the children's market subgroup. Figure 3, on the other hand, is the proposed 3 × 5 inch advertisement that will run in the *Indy's Child Inc.* newspaper. This size of advertisement will give The Benjamin Sandman Children's Bookstore the largest space of all children's bookstores that periodically advertise in this newspaper. The cost analysis for the venture's various advertising programs is presented in Table 3.

IV. Operations Segment

A. *Location Analysis*

The proposed site for The Benjamin Sandman Children's Bookstore is located at the Clearwater Crossing mixed-use development on 82nd Street and Dean Road in Indianapolis, Indiana. Besides the site's excellent location, amenities, and access, it provides a perfect blend of complementary retailers to this venture being positioned within walking distance of two children's clothing and furniture stores. Baby Superstore will be less than 50 feet away from this venture and is the largest children's furniture and clothing store in Indiana, containing over 26,000 square feet of retail selling area. This fact makes Baby Superstore an excellent draw of customers to the Lake Clearwater area who compose the target market for The Benjamin Sandman Children's Bookstore. Furthermore, this site is just 200 yards west of Chocolate Soup Children's Clothing Store located in Sourwine's River's

Exhibit 8

WE ARE BUILDING YOUR CHILD'S FUTURE... ONE BOOK AT A TIME!

The
Benjamin   Sandman
Children's Bookstore

82nd Street and Dean Road
Indianapolis, IN

Come See Our Original Line Of Children's Books

Figure 1

HELLO KIDS

I am Benjamin Sandman and you can read more about me and my friends at

THE BENJAMIN SANDMAN CHILDREN'S BOOKSTORE

82nd Street and Dean Road
Indianapolis, IN

Figure 2

GRAND OPENING!!

The
Benjamin   Sandman
Children's Bookstore

August 1, 1992

The only children's bookstore in Indianapolis that has its own line of children's books and products.

Also featuring:
8,500 children's book titles

Story telling hour every Saturday

A knowledgeable staff

Newsletter on new products

Video Tape Previewing

Special Orders

82nd Street and Dean Road
Indianapolis, IN

Figure 3

Table 3	Advertising Cost Analysis		
Media Type	**Rate**	**Total Cost**	**CPM***
Indianapolis Monthly	6 ads @ $390 Ad size: 1/6 page	$2,340	$8.59
Indy's Child Inc.	6 ads @ $225 Ad size: 3 × 5 inches	1,350	5.00
	6 ads @ $75 Ad size: 2⅜ × 2⅜ inches	450	1.66
Indianapolis Star	2 ads @ $320 Ad size: 1 column by 2½ inches Lifestyle Section	640	.77
Ameritech Yellowpages	1 listing in red superbold print — $90 per month	1,080	
Newsletter	Estimated 10% of budget size: 2 pages	$ 610	
	Total First Year Advertising Cost	$6,470	

*CPM: Contact cost per thousand — ad rate divided by the circulation rate in thousands.

Edge development. These two complementary children's stores, along with The Benjamin Sandman Children's Bookstore, could possibly make this site a dominant shopping area for the customers of children's products.

The location of this site is exceptional, being positioned at the center of residential and commercial activity in Indianapolis. Clearwater Crossing is the final phase of the Lake Clearwater development on the north side of the city—a mixed-use project containing both business and retail units built around the largest private lake in Marion County. Lake Clearwater consists of three residential communities, the Clearwater Shoppes development, and Lake Clearwater Office Park, all of which are adjacent to Clearwater Crossing. Moreover, this site is midway between the two largest developments in the metropolitan area: Castleton Square and Keystone at the Crossing. This means that within a two-mile radius of this site there is the widest array of shopping facilities, restaurants, and hotels in Indianapolis, with over 3 million feet of retail space, 100 restaurants, and hundreds of rooms. Also, the Indianapolis Department of Transportation estimates that, on average, more than 26,053 cars pass by this site each day, making it one of the highest-ranked retail districts in terms of commuter traffic in the city.

Besides its attractive location, this site provides easy access from most parts of Indianapolis. Two ramps for the I-465 beltway are within a mile of Clearwater Crossing at either Keystone Avenue or Allisonville Road and this location makes it easy to reach the development without the congestion and other traffic problems. Also, 82nd Street has been widened to five lanes and a traffic signal at the intersection of this street and Dean Road provides excellent access to the development. The

Skinner-Broadbent Company, which is the developer of the Clearwater Crossing facility, has proposed a leasing arrangement and a standard finish for this type of business. In addition to this proposal, the general contracting firm of Shiel and Sexton will provide the leasehold improvements on the facility including the store's story-telling stage, bookshelves, cash register fixture, and front window display case.

B. Inventory

As stated earlier, The Benjamin Sandman Children's Bookstore will initially carry 8,500 children's titles in addition to its product line. The average cost for each title has been computed using two methods: the cost method and the markup method (both computations can be found in Exhibit 9). Based on these calculations, it was determined that the average cost of a children's title is approximately $4.96; therefore, the inventory cost for 8,500 children's titles would be $42,160 (8,500 × $4.96). Because children's books will represent around 75 percent of the venture's inventory composition, it will consequently represent 75 percent of the inventory cost. The remaining inventory portion will consist of sideline items such as children's

---

Exhibit 9   **Average Cost of a Children's Title**

Cost Method

Cost of goods sold percentage for children's title	60%
Average retail price for children's title	$8.28

Average cost of children's title = Average retail price × Cost of goods sold percentage

$$= \quad \$8.28 \quad \times \quad 60\%$$

$$= \quad \$4.96$$

Markup Method

$$\text{Markup} = \frac{(\text{sales price per unit} - \text{Cost per unit})}{\text{Cost per unit}}$$

Can be expressed as:

Sales price per unit = markup (cost per unit) + Cost per unit

Where:
Sales price per unit: $8.28
Markup percent at 40% margin: .667
Solve for cost per unit

$$\text{Sales price per unit} = \quad .667 \quad (\text{Cost per unit}) + \text{Cost per unit}$$

$$\$8.28 \quad = \quad 1.667 \quad \text{Cost per unit}$$

$$\$4.96 \quad = \quad \text{Cost per unit}$$

---

videos and stuffed toys that will be valued at approximately 25 percent of the total inventory cost. In addition to these products which are produced by established manufacturers and publishers, an inventory allotment of $14,150 worth of products from The Benjamin Sandman Press will be manufactured and included in the initial inventory cost. A description of these goods, along with their respective cost breakdowns, can be found in the following manufacturing section. The following table illustrates the initial inventory cost breakdown for The Benjamin Sandman Children's Bookstore:

Initial Inventory Cost

8,500 children's titles	$42,160	(75%)
Sideline items	$14,340	(25%)
Plus Benjamin Sandman Press	$14,150	
Total initial inventory cost	$70,650	

Inventory Purchases   Inventory purchases for The Benjamin Sandman Children's Bookstore will occur on a monthly basis and will reflect the cyclical nature of this venture's revenues. In other words, monthly inventory purchases in September, October, and November will be at a greater level than the postholiday or slower summer months in order to keep inventory requirements at their desired levels. This type of seasonal purchasing will satisfy two objectives. First, a smaller, but adequate, inventory level will be present during the slower selling months of the fiscal year in order to keep inventory carrying costs to a minimum. Second, an inventory level that includes over 15 percent of the top-selling titles being doubled-stocked (two copies of one title) will occur in the prime selling holiday months when a large amount of inventory is most needed.

Inventory Control   Because inventory control is a vital process in any bookstore, The Benjamin Sandman Children's Bookstore will utilize a perpetual computerized inventory control system. Although this system requires more of a time commitment to maintain than a periodic system (where the books are counted at a fixed interval of time), it will fulfill three objectives. First, top-selling titles should always be in stock since their sale is immediately recognized by the system. Second, books that are not selling well can be tracked through the master inventory ledger and can be returned to the publisher. Third, this computerized system will provide up-to-the-minute details at the touch of a key on what titles are in stock in order to better assist the customer.

Inventory Selection   Due to the immense number of children's book titles from which to choose and due to the fact that Mr. Hess has a limited knowledge of children's titles, a children's book consultant will be employed by The Benjamin Sandman Children's Bookstore. This consultant will be utilized once every quarter of the fiscal year to screen and suggest new children's titles based on their illustration, content, and subject matter. Mrs. Cindy Shirey, who was mentioned in the marketing section as a key knowledgeable staff member, will initially act as the consultant to this venture. Not only will her knowledge and expertise prove to be a valuable asset to this venture, but her work as a school teacher will allow Mrs. Shirey to become a strong liaison between the local school curriculums and the inventory content of The Benjamin Sandman Children's Bookstore.

C. Suppliers

Initially, this venture will deal with three different classes of suppliers: book suppliers, sideline suppliers, and store suppliers.

Book Suppliers   This venture will ultimately deal with over a hundred different book publishers as a supply for its inventory needs. Dealing with individual publishers is a standard in the specialty bookstore industry because of the lack of regional distributors and wholesalers. The few distributors that do exist are basically in the order fulfillment business—accepting orders for a single title at a reasonable discount. While these distributors are suitable for this venture's special-order requirements, it is the publishers themselves that must be utilized in order to get the desired book titles and quantity levels that a specialty bookstore requires.

Until recently, each book publishing company had different arrangements for payments, shipping, and returns of unsold books, making retailer/publisher relationships a virtual nightmare. Within the last four years, however, the smaller publishing houses in the industry have begun to align their purchase terms with the standards set by the larger publishing firms. Currently, Bantam Doubleday Dell and Western Publishing, which are considered to be the largest children's book publishers, have been the model for establishing purchase terms and arrangements. These terms include 60 days of credit before payments are due on any purchases, but no cash discounts for early payment. Rather than cash discounts, most publishers offer quantity discounts on any purchase orders. Most of these discounts are only applicable to the larger chain bookstores, and for this reason they will not apply to many of the purchase orders made by this venture.

Sideline Suppliers   Two companies will initially be used as suppliers for this venture's sideline inventory requirements: G & S Distributors and The Manhattan Toy Company. G & S Distributors, located at 3709 North Shadeland Avenue in Indianapolis, Indiana, carries over 100,000 videotape titles—1,200 of which are current children's video titles. The Manhattan Toy Company, located in New York, will be utilized as a supplier of stuffed toys to this venture since it produces one of the most popular lines of stuffed bears and dinosaurs currently available.

Store Suppliers   The supplier of store supplies (paper bags, pricing labels, gift certificates, etc.) will be the Booksellers Order Service which is a division of the American Booksellers Association (ABA). Although this service is quite a distance away, located in Tarrytown, New York, it sells a wide array of store supplies to members of the ABA at a discount, making it an attractive supplier to this venture.

D. Manufacturing   The Benjamin Sandman product line, although developed by Mr. Hess and other freelance artists, will be manufactured in color commercial print by The Shepard-Poorman Printing Company. The proposed manufacturing schedule for this venture will be developed in four initial phases. Each phase will consist of the development, design, and printing of three original children's book titles and will operate within the time frame of one fiscal year for the completion of the phase. Additionally, each phase will commence in July of every year in order to ensure that the manufactured units are ready for sale in the peak holiday seasons.

Because printing plates are needed for an initial allotment of inventory to be produced, the fixed costs for these beginning inventory lots are fairly high. However, since these plates are used again in the process of any future printing runs, the additional inventory lots are produced at a much greater gross margin than the original inventory lot. It is this fact that makes this concept very profitable beginning in the fourth year of operation when these additional inventory lots can be sold. The table below displays the gross margin for the Benjamin Sandman story books on the initial inventory lot (labeled as Lot 1) as compared with additional inventory orders (labeled as Lot 2):

Gross Margin on Manufactured Units

	Gross Margin	Cost Factor		
Lot 1	53%	47%	=	100%
Lot 2 +	67%	33%	=	100%

Phase Development   The first phase of product development will be funded by the initial start-up capital raised for this venture. This cash outlay will be for $14,150 and will cover the fixed printing and artistic labor costs, as well as the additional variable costs. This first phase will produce three original book titles with 1,000 copies of each title (considered a minimum printing run). The remaining three phases documented in this plan will be funded based on Shepard-Poorman's delayed billing program. This program allows smaller businesses to pay only the fixed portion of the printing costs up front. The remaining variable printing costs are broken down into two separate payments. These payments are payable within 60 days of one another after the first fixed cost payment is made. Table 4 illustrates the scope of this program and the details of the payment schedule.

Cost of Goods Sold   Because the products created by this venture can be sold below the cost of its other inventory offerings, a weighted average between the cost of these products has been computed. To begin with, an exponential growth curve was chosen from a family of curves that seemed to best fit the sales potential of the Benjamin Sandman product line. This curve, shown in Exhibit 10, produces the following figures which, at each point in time, represent the percentage that the Benjamin Sandman product line will represent of the total sales forecast:

Benjamin Sandman Product Line as a Percentage of Total Sales Revenue

Year 1	Year 2	Year 3	Year 4
2.1%	6.5%	12.5%	20.0%

Table 4		Phase Development Payment Schedule		
	Payment	**Allocation Date**	**Source**
Phase 1	$14,150	July/Year 1	Start-up capital
Phase 2	$8,150	July/Year 2	Working capital
	$3,000	September/Year 2	Working capital
	$3,000	November/Year 2	Working capital
Phase 3	$8,150	July/Year 3	Working capital
	$3,000	September/Year 3	Working capital
	$3,000	November/Year 3	Working capital
Phase 4	$8,150	July/Year 4	Working capital
	$3,000	September/Year 4	Working capital
	$3,000	November/Year 4	Working capital
Additional Lots	$3,300	December/Year 4	Working capital
	$3,300	February/Year 4	Working capital

These estimates show that the Benjamin Sandman product line will only represent around 2 percent of the first year's sales forecast; however, by the fourth year, these products will represent almost 20 percent of the venture's revenues. By the fourth year of operation, both phases one and two should be in their second printing and these units will therefore be sold at their respective higher gross margin levels. In order to properly reflect these different inventory costs into the estimated cost of goods for the Benjamin Sandman product line, a weighted average was taken between the various inventory lots at their respective cost factors. As a final calculation, the cost of any Benjamin Sandman product sold was taken as a percent of the total sales forecast based on the projected growth percentages. The following table shows a summary of the cost of goods sold as a percent of sales that will be used in the pro forma financial statements:

Cost of Goods Sold
(Percentage of Sales Dollars)

Year 1	Year 2	Year 3	Year 4
59%	59%	58%	57%

V. Management Segment

A. *Legal Structure*

The legal and business structure of The Benjamin Sandman Children's Bookstore will be established and operated as an S Corporation. This corporation will initially

| Exhibit 10 | Benjamin Sandman Product Line as a Percentage of Total Sales Revenue (Based on Growth Curve of % Growth = $aT^{1.6}$) |

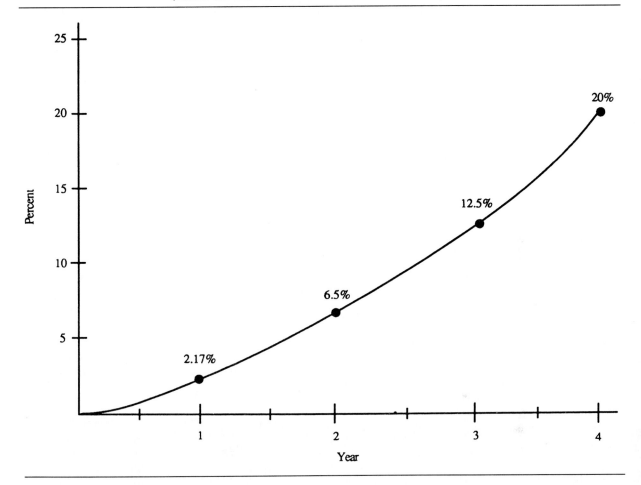

authorize 100,000 shares of common stock with a par value of $1 per share. Out of the 100,000 authorized shares, 41,000 shares will be issued to three shareholders receiving the following equity interest:

Shareholder	Investment	Shares Owned	Percent Interest
Mr. Jack B. Hess III	$24,200	24,200	60%
Mr. Michael S. Wilkey	$ 8,400	8,400	20%
Mr. Jack B. Hess, Jr.	$ 8,400	8,400	20%
Total	$41,000	41,000	100%

These three shareholders will compose the board of directors and will determine the overall strategy and future plans for this venture. Mr. Jack B. Hess III will preside as president of the board and any voting rights will be based on the premise of one vote per share of common stock as issued above. This legal structure was chosen because it (1) avoids the double taxation of the regular corporation by being taxed at only the shareholder level, (2) allows the shareholders to use first-year losses to offset taxable income, and (3) allows financial activity to be kept confidential with only a report going to the IRS to indicate the shareholders' income.

B. Key Personnel

The following is a summary of the key personnel and their responsibilities and key attributes:

Jack B. Hess III, President, General Manager, and Director of Product Development

Proprietor's Background   Mr. Jack B. Hess III graduated cum laude from the award-winning Ball State University Entrepreneurship Program where he honed his skills in the operation of a small-business venture. Mr. Hess was a consistent Dean's List student, holding a 3.78 grade point average overall with a 3.82 grade point average in his major and was admitted to four scholastic honor societies while attending Ball State University. In addition to his academic involvement, Mr. Hess participated in a community entertainment group and was a member of the Association of Collegiate Entrepreneurs (ACE). His previous work experience has been mostly in the retail sector, giving him a good working knowledge into the operations of a retail establishment.

Proprietor's Responsibilities   As proprietor, Mr. Hess will be responsible for the overall operation of The Benjamin Sandman Children's Bookstore, overseeing the construction of the store's interior, hiring personnel, maintaining inventory requirements, and supervising the day-to-day sales activities. In addition, Mr. Hess will oversee any new-product developments that will be produced under the Benjamin Sandman brand name, acting as the major creator, inspector, and activity coordinator of the project. Mr. Hess hopes to build upon the exceptional feedback that has been obtained from the test market survey of the target market and intends to constantly enhance new-product developments to reflect the wants and desires of this market. The future vision of Mr. Hess is to develop a highly desirable store atmosphere and product line in a standardized setting that will allow this venture to be the model for a proposed franchising opportunity.

Mr. Michael S. Wilkey, Sales Manager   Mr. Wilkey will be responsible for sales activity of The Benjamin Sandman Children's Bookstore. He will assist potential customers in making purchases and will promote the venture's own product line as an original creation that can be obtained at no other children's store. Also, Mr. Wilkey will conduct the venture's story-telling hour that will be held each Saturday.

Not only will he present and read the selected story, but he will also put together the video presentations that will accompany the promotional event. Mr. Wilkey was a former employee of Border's Bookstore, a major indirect competitor of this venture, and will bring his knowledge and experience in retail book selling to the operations of this venture.

Mrs. Cindy Shirey, Children's Book Consultant   Mrs. Shirey will be responsible for providing assistance to the general manager in selecting the children's book titles that will comprise the inventory of this venture. Her services will be required each quarter of the fiscal year; however, Mr. Hess will keep in close contact with Mrs. Shirey to track the most recent trends in children's books. Mrs. Shirey is a certified teacher, graduating from Stephen F. Austin University in Nacogdoches, Texas, and has a degree in special education with a minor in psychology. Besides her academic training and teaching experience, Mrs. Shirey is an experienced writer of several children's books and will be a contributing author to the venture's own product line.

C. Professional Support

The following will act on a consulting basis for The Benjamin Sandman Children's Bookstore:

- Accountant/CPA: Tom Hicks, Carmel, Indiana
- Insurance: Billy Hill, Indianapolis, Indiana
- Legal Counsel: Larry Lawhead, Indianapolis, Indiana
- Commercial Banker: Cynthia Williams, Indianapolis, Indiana

VI. Critical Risks

The following risks have been identified as potential problem areas for the operation of this venture.

A. Limited Product Acceptance

Although a sample product of this venture was tested and the respondents' attitudes seemed very positive toward the nature of the product, customer responses may not replicate the results of the test market survey. If this situation develops, a new test market study will be conducted and the results of the survey will be used to make any adjustments that are necessary in the next manufacturing phase.

B. Market Niche Too Narrow

Many parents who purchase books for their children are also serious readers themselves and enjoy general bookstores that provide both children's and adult selections. In order to combat this perception, advertising campaigns will be focused around building awareness that this venture has more children's titles and a more knowledgeable sales staff than the ordinary chain bookstore.

C. Venture Liability

Because this venture will deal with a great number of children, there is an increased chance for injury on the premises of the business. In order to deal with this risk, a special liability policy designed for retail operations dealing with children will be purchased from Mr. Billy Hill of State Farm Insurance. Also, because of the special leasehold improvements that were requested by Mr. Hess, all of the bookshelf fixtures will be built into the existing wall of the building to ensure that nothing heavy inside the venture could fall or be pulled over.

D. Competition

Competitors could be a big threat to this venture since they are well established in the community with a steady clientele and possess much experience in the industry. In order to combat this pressure, this venture will use its unique store image, experienced staff, promotional campaigns, and product innovation to build and maintain a profitable and stable niche in the children's product market.

E. Management Experience

Mr. Hess lacks experience in operating a retail bookstore/children's store and this may adversely affect the operations of the venture. Because of this fact, Mr. Hess will hire a book consultant, mentioned in the key personnel section, as an advisor of inventory selection. Also, as a member of the American Booksellers Association, this venture will be able to utilize the association's consulting department which advises new businesses on operating matters.

F. Inventory Control

Because this venture will deal with hundreds of suppliers, each with their own terms, the possibility of missing payments is very high. In order to ensure that this does not happen, The Benjamin Sandman Children's Bookstore will develop its computerized inventory system to flag suppliers on a daily basis that require attention in terms of purchase payments. This will allow the venture to make its payments while building a good credit history and controlling its operating cash flow.

G. Rising Manufacturing Costs

Although printing costs have not increased at a substantial rate over the last few years, many elements could influence these costs in the future. In case these costs do increase at an abnormal rate, two backup manufacturers have been selected as a secondary printing source. Also, this venture has a $10,000 line of credit which can be tapped in order to cover these rising costs and still maintain a positive cash balance.

H. Incorrect Sales Projections

In the case where the forecasted sales projections are wrong, two alternatives exist. First, a $10,000 line of credit can be utilized in order to cover cash shortages in meeting liability expenses until different financing can be obtained. Second, a manufacturing phase can be delayed until such time that sufficient sales revenues are generated, thus providing a large sum of capital to tap.

VII. Milestone Segment

A. Timetable for Venture Start-Up

	May 1–15	May 16–31	June 1–15	June 16–30
1.	____			
2.	_____			
3.	____			
4.	_____			
5.			_____	
6.				_____

1. *May 1 to May 8:* Finish securing long-term note and private placement of equity; meet with lawyer to verify legal documents.
2. *May 1 to June 20:* Meet with book consultant and begin to order inventory.
3. *May 10 to May 15:* Acquire computer system and begin software development for inventory control system.
4. *May 15 to May 31:* Place order with Shepard-Poorman Communications for Benjamin Sandman manufactured units; secure building permits; submit application with Indiana National Bank for line of credit.
5. *June 1 to June 20:* Receive finished Benjamin Sandman units; make first rent deposit with Skinner-Broadbent; Shiel-Sexton begins construction on store's interior to be completed by June 19; submit forms with publishers for purchasing credit; verify order status on undelivered inventory; pay utility and phone deposits and connection fees.
6. *June 15 to June 30:* Acquire equipment, furniture, and character models; officially hire and train sales manager; coordinate all publicity and advertising media for grand opening.
7. *July 1, 1992:* First day of venture operation.

VIII. Financial Segment

A. *Financial Forecast*

This section explains how the figures were derived in the development of the following pro forma financial statements.

1. Income Statement Assumptions

1. **Total sales:** Sales for the first four years of operation were taken from the projections developed in the marketing segment of this business plan. The monthly estimates follow the seasonal trends that exist in the industry, with the peak selling seasons occurring in October, November, and December and again in the Easter/Passover month of April.

2. **Cost of goods sold:** The cost of goods sold projections were calculated in the manufacturing section of this plan as a weighted average between the venture's own products at production cost and the cost of the other inventory items which were estimated to be 60 percent of sales. (Sixty percent is the average cost of goods sold as a percent of sales cited in both the ABACUS Financial Bookstore Survey and the Entrepreneur Group's Business Start-Up Guide.)

3. **Beginning inventory:** This figure represents the inventory cost in dollars on the first day of each month (derived from the ending inventory cost of the previous month) and includes the venture's own products in the total estimate.

4. **Merchandise purchases:** This purchase figure is the cost of inventory purchases in dollars that occurs in each month. These purchases were based on a budget that allocated more funds to the peak selling seasons in order to keep inventory levels at an adequate level relative to consumer demand.

5. **Returns at cost:** Returns at cost were estimated at around 3 percent of sales based on the average figure for specialty bookstores in the ABACUS operations survey of member bookstores. Because of the time required in determining slow-selling titles, no returns will occur in year one until six months into the fiscal year.

6. **Manufactured units:** This figure represents the cost of any manufactured units for the Benjamin Sandman product line that are produced during the fiscal year.

7. **Total adjusted inventory:** This figure is the inventory level produced by taking the beginning inventory level and adding any purchases, less any returns, plus any manufactured units.

8. **Ending inventory:** This figure represents the inventory value in dollars after the cost of goods sold is subtracted from the adjusted inventory level and represents the beginning inventory figure for the following month.

9. **Gross margin:** Calculated by taking Total Sales (line 1) and subtracting the Cost of Goods Sold (line 2).

10. **Owner's compensation:** This figure is the compensation that Mr. Hess will receive as proprietor and general manager for this venture. This estimate is projected to increase by 10 percent a year and includes all applicable FICA, state, and federal unemployment taxes.

11. **Wages: employees:** This figure includes the sales manager wages of $13,500. This salary will increase by 10 percent each year and includes all applicable FICA, state, and federal unemployment taxes.

12. **Consulting fees:** This value is the salary for the children's book consultant paid on a quarterly basis beginning in July; however, the first payment will be distributed in May when the initial inventory is selected. This fee will increase by 10 percent in the third year and does not include any payroll taxes since the consultant will be defined as an independent contractor of this venture.

13. **Rent:** Rent for the first year was taken from a written estimate from the Skinner-Broadbent Development Company. This estimate was for $15 per square foot plus a net term of $2.14 on a 1,600-square-foot facility. A 5 percent annual increase is anticipated for this expense based on the trend that has occurred in Skinner-Broadbent's rent increases over the last two years.

14. **Utilities:** The first year's utility rate of $380 per month was based on two estimates from Public Service Indiana of the retail establishments located on each side of the proposed site for this venture. This expense is anticipated to increase by 5 percent a year.

15. **Advertising:** Expenses for advertising are based upon the estimated ad rates of the media discussed in the marketing section of this plan. The first year's expense will be for $6,470 and will be allocated in the months in which the particular advertising media is utilized. All subsequent advertising expenses will fall in line with the industry average of 1.6 percent of sales based on the ABACUS Financial Survey for specialty bookstores.

16. **Telephone:** The first year's telephone expense was based on an oral estimate from Ameritech of the approximate expenses of other retailers in the district in which this venture will operate. It is anticipated that this expense will increase by 5 percent a year.

17. **Legal/accounting services:** The initial legal expense of $1,260 will be disbursed in May so a lawyer can establish the incorporation agreements and the work for hire documents that will be required for the store to legally own any work created by a freelance artist. This estimate was based on an oral estimate from Larry Lawhead and will be a one-time expense. The accounting service expense was taken from an oral estimate from Tom Hicks, CPA. This estimate includes a $30 monthly computerized bookkeeping service and a $60 expense for tax preparation allocated in January of each year. This fee will increase by 5 percent in the third year of operation.

18. **Supplies:** This supplies expense was based on an average monthly estimate from the Booksellers Order Service of supply purchases made by a store at this sales level. This expense is expected to increase by 5 percent a year.

19. **Depreciation:** Depreciation was calculated for the leasehold improvements and the computer equipment by using a straight-line method over five years. The Furniture and Fixtures and the Character Models were depreciated by using a straight-line method over seven years. Half of the total depreciation value will be allocated in year one, while the entire value will be expensed in years two through four.

20. **Insurance:** Insurance expense was taken based on a written estimate from State Farm Insurance and includes the premiums for both the worker's compensation and business liability policies. This expense will be paid to State Farm on a quarterly basis beginning in July.

21. **Credit card service charges:** For this venture, it was assumed, based upon the ABACUS Financial survey, that 20 percent of the total sales figure would be credit card sales. For this reason, a credit card service charge of 5 percent was assessed to 20 percent of each month's total sales estimate.

22. **Dues and subscriptions:** Each year dues of $117 will be paid to the American Booksellers Association and the remaining amount of this expense will be disbursed for various educational magazine subscriptions.

23. **Miscellaneous office expense:** This expense consists of a petty cash account for office supplies and postage. This expense is expected to increase by 5 percent a year.

24. **Maintenance:** Store cleaning and repair requirements are estimated at $50 a month and are expected to increase by 5 percent a year.

25. **Inventory/property tax:** Inventory and property tax has been expensed starting in March of year one, the date of the first assessment. The amount of the expense for each year was calculated by adding the inventory dollar amount to the net book value of the fixed assets on March 1, dividing this number by three, and taking this number times 10 percent. Although 12 equal payments are expensed each month beginning in March of year one, two equal payments of half the total tax due are disbursed during May and November of the year following the assessment.

26. **Other expenses:** This expense includes interest payments on the long-term note and an annual service charge of $50 for the established line of credit allocated each year in the month of January. Because sales tax was not used in the revenue calculations, no calculations have been made for this expense.

27. **Tax distributions to shareholders:** Enough of this venture's earnings will be distributed to the three shareholders to cover any personal income tax liabilities incurred. Tax rates of 5 percent for state income tax and 15 percent for federal income tax have been used in these calculations and all distributions will be made in April, June, September, and December.

2. Cash Flow Statement Assumptions

1. **Cash balance, beginning:** This balance figure is the amount of cash that is available on the first day of each month derived from the ending cash balance of the preceding month. The initial cash balance in the base period (June 30) of year one is the result of the working capital obtained from the initial financing of this venture minus two loan payments of $1,759 disbursed in the months of May and June when the loan is acquired.

2. **Sales receipts:** It is anticipated that 80 percent of all sales will be on a cash basis payable at the time of the sale. The remaining 20 percent of the sales will be paid by credit card and will also be collected in the month of the sales purchase.

3. **Line of credit:** A $10,000 open line of credit at 11.5 percent interest will be established at Indiana National Bank in Indianapolis to meet any unexpected financial needs. This figure therefore represents the monthly charges made against this account to meet any capital requirements.

4. **Returns at cost:** It is expected, based on industry trends, that all book returns stated in the income statement will be collected in the form of a check from the respective publishing company in the month the return is filed.

5. **Purchase inventory:** It is assumed that cash disbursements for this venture's inventory purchases will be allocated 60 days after the receipt of the order. This type of purchasing credit is typical in the retail bookselling industry and was discussed in the operations segment of this plan.

6. **Purchase equipment:** This account represents the value of any additional equipment that is purchased by this venture after its initial equipment acquisitions.

7. **Manufacturing costs:** This cost figure represents the cash outlay to Shepard-Poorman Communications and any freelance artists who are employed in coproducing the venture's own product line. As documented in the manufacturing section of this plan, all fixed costs will be disbursed when the finished products are received. The remaining variable manufacturing costs will be disbursed 60 days of one another after the fixed payment is made. Additional inventory allotment orders, found in December and February of year four, will be paid in full when the finished units are received.

8. **Incurred operating expense:** This figure represents the total operating expense of each month found on the income statement minus the noncash expense of depreciation and the inventory/property tax expense which is detailed in a separate section of the cash disbursements section.

9. **Principal repayment:** These amounts are the cash disbursed for the principal repayment of the five-year long-term note at 11.5 percent interest and the $10,000 established line of credit at the same interest rate.

10. **Interest on debt:** These values represent the interest payable on a monthly basis for the long-term note. The interest on the line of credit was computed from the balance that was outstanding in each month and the $50 maintenance/service charge for this credit line is disbursed under this account in January of each year.

11. **Taxes payable:** Taxes are disbursed in the months of April, June, September, and December for the income tax liability the corporation's shareholders will experience. Additionally, taxes are disbursed in the months of May and November for the inventory/property tax liability that is assessed in March of the previous year.

12. **Cash balance, ending:** This value is computed by taking the beginning cash balance of each month, adding the total cash received, and subtracting the total cash disbursements. This cash value then becomes the beginning cash balance for the following month.

3. Balance Sheet Assumptions

1. **Cash:** The cash balance is taken directly from the ending cash balance shown on the cash flow statement of the respective year. The minimum cash balance required by the management of this venture will be $1,200; therefore, the available line of credit will be utilized any time the ending cash balance falls below this level.

2. **Inventory:** An initial inventory valued at $70,650 ($56,500 worth of published children's books, videos, and stuffed toys and $14,150 worth of Benjamin Sandman products) will be purchased in May and June of year one. The remaining inventory levels for each month are taken directly from the ending inventory balance shown on the income statement.

3. **Fixed assets:** All equipment, furniture, and fixtures ($5,673) will be paid for in June of the first year of operation. The American Eagle computer system, which will be utilized for this venture's inventory control needs, will be purchased and paid for in May of year one. Fifteen three-dimensional character models from the venture's own books will be designed and created by Mrs. Judith Hess. These models will be created in two phases. The first phase of ten characters will be ready by the time the store opens. The second phase of five characters will be produced over the first three months of the store's operation. While these models will be delivered in two phases, they will be paid for ($3,200) up front in the month of June.

    Because of the special leasehold improvements required by this venture, the Shiel-Sexton Construction Company Inc., a general contractor specializing in retail interiors, will provide the improvements on the facility. Due to the fact that the lease expense includes a provision credit for such improvements, the leasing firm of Skinner-Broadbent has agreed to pay for half of the improvement costs up to $20,000. Based on the estimate of $38,605 supplied by Shiel-Sexton, The Benjamin Sandman Children's Bookstore will pay $19,302 in June for these improvements and the Skinner-Broadbent Company will pay the remaining balance for the project.

4. **Accounts payable:** This value represents the cumulative accrued inventory purchases that are payable within 60 days upon receipt of each order. Also, any principal amounts on the line of credit are allocated to this current liability account.

5. **Taxes payable:** This value contains the accrued inventory/property taxes and the shareholders' income tax liability that have been expensed but not yet paid.

6. **Long-term note:** This amount represents the principal portion of the long-term note that still remains to be paid taken directly from the loan schedule.

7. **Contributed capital:** This value represents the total amount of funds that have been contributed by the three shareholders and remains constant over the life of the projections.

8. **Retained earnings:** This figure represents the cumulative net profits for the venture over the duration of the projections.

B. Sources and Use of Funds

1. Source of Capital Funds   In accordance with the projected income statements and cash flow projections contained at the end of this financial section, The Benjamin Sandman Children's Bookstore will need approximately $121,000 in order to commence operations and have an adequate level of capital available. Due to this fact, Mr. Hess is seeking a five-year, 11.5 percent annual interest rate loan for $80,000 and an 11.5 percent, $10,000 line of credit. In addition to this loan, $41,000 in equity will be raised through the issuance of 41,000 shares of common stock to three shareholders as documented in the management section of this plan. Out of the three potential shareholders, Mr. Hess and Mr. Wilkey will be employees of the venture and have agreed to reinvest any profits back into the company in the form of retained earnings. The remaining shareholder, Mr. Jack B. Hess, Jr., has agreed not to accept any quarterly dividends; rather, he plans on selling his interest

Table 5   **Use of Capital Funds**

Use of Funds	Amount	Estimate Source	Location
Working capital	$ 11,000		
Initial inventory	56,500	Inventory section	
Supplies			
Office supplies	150	Booksellers Order Service	Tarrytown, New York
Packaging/shipping supplies	75	Booksellers Order Service	Tarrytown, New York
Store supplies	300	Booksellers Order Service	Tarrytown, New York
Equipment			
Cash register	675	NCR Business Machines	Indianapolis, Indiana
Security system	1,120	Honeywell Protection Systems	Indianapolis, Indiana
Computer System	1,800	CompuAge Computer systems	Muncie, Indiana
Furniture			
Chairs	300		
Office furniture	350	Office Depot	Indianapolis, Indiana
Fixtures	3,228	Wert Fixtures and Display Supply	Indianapolis, Indiana
Leasehold improvements	19,302	Shiel & Sexton General Contractors	Indianapolis, Indiana
Character models	3,200		
Signage	1,400	Skinner-Broadbent Developments	Indianapolis, Indiana
Rent	4,570	Skinner-Broadbent Developments	Indianapolis, Indiana
Utilities	460	Public Service Indiana	Indianapolis, Indiana
Telephone	250	Indiana Bell	Indianapolis, Indiana
Professional services	1,260	Larry Lawhead/Tom Hicks	Indianapolis, Indiana
Licenses	50	License Bureau	Indianapolis, Indiana
Initial consulting fee	400	Consultant and Business Report	
Video screen	460	Video Concepts	Indianapolis, Indiana
Manufactured units	14,150	Shepard-Poorman Communications	Indianapolis, Indiana
Total	$121,000		

in the company in year five for a capital gain based on the build-up in equity that is stated in the financial projections.

2. Use of the Capital Funds   Table 5 illustrates the detailed use of capital funds raised for this venture. All assets, with the exception of the venture's own product line inventory and the character models, will be used as collateral for the $80,000 loan. In addition, the parents of Mr. Hess have agreed to sign for any amount of the loan that is not adequately covered by the available assets.

A financial analysis for The Benjamin Sandman Children's Bookstore has been conducted based on the assumed level and types of financing that have been described. The projected financial performance of this venture, as illustrated by a summary of selected financial ratios, a break-even analysis, and a complete set of pro forma financial statements can be found on the following pages.

The Benjamin Sandman Children's Bookstore
Ratio and Break Even Analysis

	Year One	Year Two	Year Three	Year Four	Industry '90 Median
Liquidity Ratios:					
Current Ratio	4.4	3.2	2.9	2.8	2.0
Quick Ratio	0.9	0.5	0.4	0.5	0.4
Coverage Ratios:					
Ebit/Interest	0.6	1.5	2.6	5.2	2.0
Leverage Ratios:					
Debt/Net Worth	3.1	2.5	1.7	0.9	3.6
Operating Ratios:					
Inventory Turnover	1.8	1.9	2.0	2.3	2.7
Sales/ Net Fixed Assets	7.1	9.6	13.0	19.0	16.6
Sales/ Total Assets	1.7	2.0	2.3	2.5	2.1
Profitablity Ratios:					
Return on Investment	-3.0%	3.1%	6.5%	11.5%	
Earnings per Share	($0.08)	$0.08	$0.16	$0.26	
Return on Owner's Equity	-13.0%	11.0%	17.5%	22.7%	
Key Measures:					
Total Sales	$204,790	$234,840	$247,680	$261,240	
Sandman Product Sales	$4,434	$15,264	$30,960	$52,248	
Net Profits Before Taxes	($3,529)	$3,369	$7,954	$13,419	
Net Profits After Taxes	($3,529)	$3,369	$6,454	$10,836	
Cost of Goods Sold (%)	59%	59%	58%	57%	
Manufacturing Costs	$14,150	$14,150	$14,150	$20,750	
Break Even Point:					
Sales Estimate	$204,790	$234,840	$247,680	$261,240	
Avg. Sales Price per Unit	$8.28	$8.28	$8.28	$8.28	
Estimated Sales in Units	24,733	28,362	29,913	31,550	
Variable Costs:					
Cost of Goods Sold	$120,826	$138,556	$143,654	$148,907	
Advertising	$6,470	$4,200	$4,500	$4,500	
Supplies	$1,200	$1,260	$1,320	$1,380	
Credit Card Expense	$2,048	$2,348	$2,477	$2,612	
Misc. Office Expense	$600	$624	$648	$672	
Maintenance	$600	$624	$648	$672	
Total Variable Costs	$131,744	$147,612	$153,247	$158,743	
Variable Cost per Unit	$5.32	$5.20	$5.12	$5.03	
Fixed Costs	$76,575	$83,859	$86,479	$89,078	
Break Even Point:					
Units	25,870	27,227	27,366	27,408	
Dollars	$214,203	$225,439	$226,597	$226,938	

The Benjamin Sandman Children's Bookstore
Income Statement
Year One

	July	August	September	October	November	December	January	February	March	April	May	June	Total
Total Sales	$11,000	$14,000	$15,000	$17,000	$23,790	$26,000	$16,000	$16,000	$16,000	$18,000	$16,000	$16,000	$204,790
Less: Cost of Goods Sold	$6,490	$8,260	$8,850	$10,030	$14,036	$15,340	$9,440	$9,440	$9,440	$10,620	$9,440	$9,440	$120,826
Beginning Inventory	$70,650	$72,160	$71,900	$75,050	$77,020	$73,984	$69,644	$69,692	$69,740	$69,788	$68,656	$67,704	
Merchandise Purchases	$8,000	$8,000	$12,000	$12,000	$11,000	$11,000	$10,000	$10,000	$10,000	$10,000	$9,000	$9,000	$120,000
Less: Returns at Cost							$512	$512	$512	$512	$512	$512	$3,072
Manufactured Units													$0
Total Adjusted Inventory	$78,650	$80,160	$83,900	$87,050	$88,020	$84,984	$79,132	$79,180	$79,228	$79,276	$77,144	$76,192	
Ending Inventory	$72,160	$71,900	$75,050	$77,020	$73,984	$69,644	$69,692	$69,740	$69,788	$68,656	$67,704	$66,752	
Gross Margin	$4,510	$5,740	$6,150	$6,970	$9,754	$10,660	$6,560	$6,560	$6,560	$7,380	$6,560	$6,560	$83,964
Less Expenses:													
Owner's Compensation	$1,250	$1,250	$1,250	$1,250	$1,250	$1,250	$1,250	$1,250	$1,250	$1,250	$1,250	$1,250	$15,000
Wages: Employees	$1,125	$1,125	$1,125	$1,125	$1,125	$1,125	$1,125	$1,125	$1,125	$1,125	$1,125	$1,125	$13,500
Consulting Fees	$400			$400			$400			$400			$1,600
Rent	$2,285	$2,285	$2,285	$2,285	$2,285	$2,285	$2,285	$2,285	$2,285	$2,285	$2,285	$2,285	$27,420
Utilities	$380	$380	$380	$380	$380	$380	$380	$380	$380	$380	$380	$380	$4,560
Advertising	$705	$1,345	$165	$705	$705	$705	$470	$165	$165	$1,010	$165	$165	$6,470
Telephone	$70	$70	$70	$70	$70	$70	$70	$70	$70	$70	$70	$70	$840
Legal/Accounting Services	$30	$30	$30	$30	$30	$30	$90	$30	$30	$30	$30	$30	$420
Supplies	$100	$100	$100	$100	$100	$100	$100	$100	$100	$100	$100	$100	$1,200
Depreciation	$229	$229	$229	$229	$229	$229	$229	$229	$229	$229	$229	$229	$2,748
Insurance	$217			$217			$217			$217			$868
Credit Card Service Charges	$110	$140	$150	$170	$238	$260	$160	$160	$160	$180	$160	$160	$2,048
Dues and Subscriptions	$117			$30	$30								$177
Misc. Office Expense	$50	$50	$50	$50	$50	$50	$50	$50	$50	$50	$50	$50	$600
Maintenance	$50	$50	$50	$50	$50	$50	$50	$50	$50	$50	$50	$50	$600
Inventory/Property Tax									$272	$272	$272	$272	$1,088
Total Operating Expense	$7,118	$7,054	$5,884	$7,091	$6,542	$6,534	$6,876	$5,894	$6,166	$7,648	$6,166	$6,166	$79,139
Operating Income	($2,608)	($1,314)	$266	($121)	$3,212	$4,126	($316)	$666	$394	($268)	$394	$394	$4,825
Other Expenses	$747	$737	$728	$718	$708	$698	$737	$677	$667	$656	$646	$635	$8,354
Net Income Before Taxes	($3,355)	($2,051)	($462)	($839)	$2,504	$3,428	($1,053)	($11)	($273)	($924)	($252)	($241)	($3,529)
Tax Distrib. to Shareholders													
Net Income	($3,355)	($2,051)	($462)	($839)	$2,504	$3,428	($1,053)	($11)	($273)	($924)	($252)	($241)	($3,529)

The Benjamin Sandman Children's Bookstore

Income Statement

Year Two

	July	August	September	October	November	December	January	February	March	April	May	June	Total
Total Sales	$18,000	$18,000	$18,000	$20,000	$23,843	$26,000	$18,000	$18,000	$18,000	$21,000	$18,000	$18,000	$234,840
Less: Cost of Goods Sold													
Beginning Inventory	$10,620	$10,620	$10,620	$11,800	$14,066	$15,340	$10,620	$10,620	$10,620	$12,390	$10,620	$10,620	$138,556
Merchandise Purchases	$66,752	$78,697	$76,492	$78,287	$78,902	$77,251	$74,326	$75,121	$75,916	$76,711	$75,736	$74,531	
Less: Returns at Cost	$9,000	$9,000	$13,000	$13,000	$13,000	$13,000	$12,000	$12,000	$12,000	$12,000	$10,000	$10,000	$138,000
Manufactured Units	$585	$585	$585	$585	$585	$585	$585	$585	$585	$585	$585	$585	$7,020
	$14,150												$14,150
Total Adjusted Inventory	$89,317	$87,112	$88,907	$90,702	$91,317	$89,666	$85,741	$86,536	$87,331	$88,126	$85,151	$83,946	
Ending Inventory	$78,697	$76,492	$78,287	$78,902	$77,251	$74,326	$75,121	$75,916	$76,711	$75,736	$74,531	$73,326	
Gross Margin	$7,380	$7,380	$7,380	$8,200	$9,774	$10,660	$7,380	$7,380	$7,380	$8,610	$7,380	$7,380	$96,284
Less Expenses:													
Owner's Compensation	$1,375	$1,375	$1,375	$1,375	$1,375	$1,375	$1,375	$1,375	$1,375	$1,375	$1,375	$1,375	$16,500
Wages: Employees	$1,237	$1,237	$1,237	$1,237	$1,237	$1,237	$1,237	$1,237	$1,237	$1,237	$1,237	$1,237	$14,844
Consulting Fees	$400			$400			$400			$400			$1,600
Rent	$2,350	$2,350	$2,350	$2,350	$2,350	$2,350	$2,350	$2,350	$2,350	$2,350	$2,350	$2,350	$28,200
Utilities	$400	$400	$400	$400	$400	$400	$400	$400	$400	$400	$400	$400	$4,800
Advertising	$250	$250	$250	$450	$450	$450	$250	$250	$450	$450	$350	$350	$4,200
Telephone	$74	$74	$74	$74	$74	$74	$74	$74	$74	$74	$74	$74	$888
Legal/Accounting Services	$30	$30	$30	$30	$30	$30	$90	$30	$30	$30	$30	$30	$420
Supplies	$105	$105	$105	$105	$105	$105	$105	$105	$105	$105	$105	$105	$1,260
Depreciation	$457	$457	$457	$457	$457	$457	$457	$457	$457	$457	$457	$457	$5,484
Insurance	$217			$217			$217			$217			$868
Credit Card Service Charges	$180	$180	$180	$200	$238	$260	$180	$180	$180	$210	$180	$180	$2,348
Dues and Subscriptions	$117			$30	$30								$177
Misc. Office Expense	$52	$52	$52	$52	$52	$52	$52	$52	$52	$52	$52	$52	$624
Maintenance	$52	$52	$52	$52	$52	$52	$52	$52	$52	$52	$52	$52	$624
Inventory/Property Tax	$272	$272	$272	$272	$272	$272	$272	$272	$275	$275	$275	$275	$3,276
Total Operating Expense	$7,568	$6,834	$6,834	$7,701	$7,122	$7,114	$7,511	$6,834	$7,037	$7,684	$6,937	$6,937	$86,113
Operating Income	($188)	$546	$546	$499	$2,652	$3,546	($131)	$546	$343	$926	$443	$443	$10,171
Other Expenses	$624	$614	$603	$591	$580	$569	$608	$546	$534	$523	$511	$499	$6,802
Net Income Before Taxes	($812)	($68)	($57)	($92)	$2,072	$2,977	($739)	$0	($191)	$403	($68)	($56)	$3,369
Tax Distrib. to Shareholders													$0
Net Income	($812)	($68)	($57)	($92)	$2,072	$2,977	($739)	$0	($191)	$403	($68)	($56)	$3,369

The Benjamin Sandman Children's Bookstore
Income Statement
Year Three

	July	August	September	October	November	December	January	February	March	April	May	June	Total
Total Sales	$19,000	$19,000	$19,000	$21,000	$24,680	$28,000	$19,000	$19,000	$19,000	$22,000	$19,000	$19,000	$247,680
Less: Cost of Goods Sold	$11,020	$11,020	$11,020	$12,180	$14,314	$16,240	$11,020	$11,020	$11,020	$12,760	$11,020	$11,020	$143,654
Beginning Inventory	$73,326	$85,837	$84,198	$84,559	$83,760	$80,827	$75,968	$75,329	$74,690	$75,051	$73,672	$73,033	
Merchandise Purchases	$10,000	$10,000	$12,000	$12,000	$12,000	$12,000	$11,000	$11,000	$12,000	$12,000	$11,000	$11,000	$136,000
Less: Returns at Cost	$619	$619	$619	$619	$619	$619	$619	$619	$619	$619	$619	$619	$7,428
Manufactured Units	$14,150												$14,150
Total Adjusted Inventory	$96,857	$95,218	$95,579	$95,940	$95,141	$92,208	$86,349	$85,710	$86,071	$86,432	$84,053	$83,414	
Ending Inventory	$85,837	$84,198	$84,559	$83,760	$80,827	$75,968	$75,329	$74,690	$75,051	$73,672	$73,033	$72,394	
Gross Margin	$7,980	$7,980	$7,980	$8,820	$10,366	$11,760	$7,980	$7,980	$7,980	$9,240	$7,980	$7,980	$104,026
Less Expenses:													
Owner's Compensation	$1,512	$1,512	$1,512	$1,512	$1,512	$1,512	$1,512	$1,512	$1,512	$1,512	$1,512	$1,512	$18,144
Wages: Employees	$1,360	$1,360	$1,360	$1,360	$1,360	$1,360	$1,360	$1,360	$1,360	$1,360	$1,360	$1,360	$16,320
Consulting Fees	$440			$440			$440			$440			$1,760
Rent	$2,420	$2,420	$2,420	$2,420	$2,420	$2,420	$2,420	$2,420	$2,420	$2,420	$2,420	$2,420	$29,040
Utilities	$420	$420	$420	$420	$420	$420	$420	$420	$420	$420	$420	$420	$5,040
Advertising	$275	$275	$275	$475	$475	$475	$275	$275	$475	$475	$375	$375	$4,500
Telephone	$77	$77	$77	$77	$77	$77	$77	$77	$77	$77	$77	$77	$924
Legal/Accounting Services	$32	$32	$32	$32	$32	$32	$92	$32	$32	$32	$32	$32	$444
Supplies	$110	$110	$110	$110	$110	$110	$110	$110	$110	$110	$110	$110	$1,320
Depreciation	$457	$457	$457	$457	$457	$457	$457	$457	$457	$457	$457	$457	$5,484
Insurance	$217			$217			$217			$217			$868
Credit Card Service Charges	$190	$190	$190	$210	$247	$280	$190	$190	$190	$220	$190	$190	$2,477
Dues and Subscriptions	$117			$30	$30								$177
Misc. Office Expense	$54	$54	$54	$54	$54	$54	$54	$54	$54	$54	$54	$54	$648
Maintenance	$54	$54	$54	$54	$54	$54	$54	$54	$54	$54	$54	$54	$648
Inventory/Property Tax	$275	$275	$275	$275	$275	$275	$275	$275	$254	$254	$254	$254	$3,216
Total Operating Expense	$8,010	$7,236	$7,236	$8,143	$7,523	$7,526	$7,953	$7,236	$7,415	$8,102	$7,315	$7,315	$91,010
Operating Income	($30)	$744	$744	$677	$2,843	$4,234	$27	$744	$565	$1,138	$665	$665	$13,016
Other Expenses	$487	$475	$462	$450	$437	$425	$462	$399	$386	$373	$360	$346	$5,062
Net Income Before Taxes	($517)	$269	$282	$227	$2,406	$3,809	($435)	$345	$179	$765	$305	$319	$7,954
Tax Distrib. to Shareholders				$19	$463	$734			$17	$147	$59	$61	$1,500
Net Income	($517)	$269	$282	$208	$1,943	$3,075	($435)	$345	$162	$618	$246	$258	$6,454

The Benjamin Sandman Children's Bookstore
Income Statement
Year Four

	July	August	September	October	November	December	January	February	March	April	May	June	Total
Total Sales	$19,000	$19,000	$19,000	$23,000	$26,240	$32,000	$20,000	$20,000	$20,000	$25,000	$19,000	$19,000	$261,240
Less: Cost of Goods Sold	$10,830	$10,830	$10,830	$13,110	$14,957	$18,240	$11,400	$11,400	$11,400	$14,250	$10,830	$10,830	$148,907
Beginning Inventory	$72,394	$85,064	$83,584	$84,104	$82,344	$78,737	$73,147	$71,097	$72,347	$71,297	$67,397	$66,917	
Merchandise Purchases	$10,000	$10,000	$12,000	$12,000	$12,000	$10,000	$10,000	$10,000	$11,000	$11,000	$11,000	$11,000	$130,000
Less: Returns at Cost	$650	$650	$650	$650	$650	$650	$650	$650	$650	$650	$650	$650	$7,800
Manufactured Units	$14,150					$3,300		$3,300					$20,750
Total Adjusted Inventory	$95,894	$94,414	$94,934	$95,454	$93,694	$91,387	$82,497	$83,747	$82,697	$81,647	$77,747	$77,267	
Ending Inventory	$85,064	$83,584	$84,104	$82,344	$78,737	$73,147	$71,097	$72,347	$71,297	$67,397	$66,917	$66,437	
Gross Margin	$8,170	$8,170	$8,170	$9,890	$11,283	$13,760	$8,600	$8,600	$8,600	$10,750	$8,170	$8,170	$112,233
Less Expenses:													
Owner's Compensation	$1,660	$1,660	$1,660	$1,660	$1,660	$1,660	$1,660	$1,660	$1,660	$1,660	$1,660	$1,660	$19,920
Wages: Employees	$1,496	$1,496	$1,496	$1,496	$1,496	$1,496	$1,496	$1,496	$1,496	$1,496	$1,496	$1,496	$17,952
Consulting Fees	$440			$440			$440			$440			$1,760
Rent	$2,492	$2,492	$2,492	$2,492	$2,492	$2,492	$2,492	$2,492	$2,492	$2,492	$2,492	$2,492	$29,904
Utilities	$460	$460	$460	$460	$460	$460	$460	$460	$460	$460	$460	$460	$5,520
Advertising	$275	$275	$275	$475	$475	$475	$275	$275	$475	$475	$375	$375	$4,500
Telephone	$80	$80	$80	$80	$80	$80	$80	$80	$80	$80	$80	$80	$960
Legal/Accounting Services	$32	$32	$32	$32	$32	$32	$92	$32	$32	$32	$32	$32	$444
Supplies	$115	$115	$115	$115	$115	$115	$115	$115	$115	$115	$115	$115	$1,380
Depreciation	$457	$457	$457	$457	$457	$457	$457	$457	$457	$457	$457	$457	$5,484
Insurance	$217			$217			$217			$217			$868
Credit Card Service Charges	$190	$190	$190	$230	$262	$320	$200	$200	$200	$250	$190	$190	$2,612
Dues and Subscriptions	$117			$30	$30								$177
Misc. Office Expense	$56	$56	$56	$56	$56	$56	$56	$56	$56	$56	$56	$56	$672
Maintenance	$56	$56	$56	$56	$56	$56	$56	$56	$56	$56	$56	$56	$672
Inventory/Property Tax	$254	$254	$254	$254	$254	$254	$254	$254	$254	$234	$234	$234	$2,968
Total Operating Expense	$8,397	$7,623	$7,623	$8,550	$7,925	$7,953	$8,350	$7,633	$7,813	$8,520	$7,703	$7,703	$95,793
Operating Income	($227)	$547	$547	$1,340	$3,358	$5,807	$250	$967	$787	$2,230	$467	$467	$16,540
Other Expenses	$333	$319	$305	$301	$277	$263	$299	$234	$220	$205	$190	$175	$3,121
Net Income Before Taxes	($560)	$228	$242	$1,039	$3,081	$5,544	($49)	$733	$567	$2,025	$277	$292	$13,419
Tax Distrib. to Shareholders				$182	$593	$1,067		$132	$109	$390	$53	$57	$2,583
Net Income	($560)	$228	$242	$857	$2,488	$4,477	($49)	$601	$458	$1,635	$224	$235	$10,836

The Benjamin Sandman Children's Bookstore
Cash Flow Statement
Year One

	July	August	September	October	November	December	January	February	March	April	May	June	Total
Cash Balance, Beginning	$7,482	$9,835	$15,252	$14,838	$15,218	$18,937	$24,874	$21,931	$20,020	$19,109	$18,716	$17,805	
Plus Cash Receipts:													
Sales Receipts	$11,000	$14,000	$15,000	$17,000	$23,790	$26,000	$16,000	$16,000	$16,000	$18,000	$16,000	$16,000	$204,790
Line of Credit													$0
Returns at Cost							$512	$512	$512	$512	$512	$512	$3,072
Total Cash Received	$11,000	$14,000	$15,000	$17,000	$23,790	$26,000	$16,512	$16,512	$16,512	$18,512	$16,512	$16,512	$207,862
Less Cash Disbursed:													
Purchase Inventory			$8,000	$8,000	$12,000	$12,000	$11,000	$11,000	$10,000	$10,000	$10,000	$10,000	$102,000
Purchase Equipment													$0
Manufacturing Cost													$0
Incurred Operating Expense	$6,889	$6,825	$5,655	$6,862	$6,313	$6,305	$6,647	$5,665	$5,665	$7,147	$5,665	$5,665	$75,303
Principal Repayment:													
Long term debt	$1,011	$1,021	$1,031	$1,040	$1,050	$1,060	$1,071	$1,081	$1,091	$1,102	$1,112	$1,123	$12,793
Line of credit													$0
Interest on Debt:													
Long term debt	$747	$737	$728	$718	$708	$698	$687	$677	$667	$656	$646	$635	$8,304
Line of credit							$50						$50
Taxes Payable													
Tax Distrib. to Shareholders													$0
Inventory/Property Tax													$0
Total Disbursements	$8,647	$8,583	$15,414	$16,620	$20,071	$20,063	$19,455	$18,423	$17,423	$18,905	$17,423	$17,423	$198,450
Cash Balance, Ending	$9,835	$15,252	$14,838	$15,218	$18,937	$24,874	$21,931	$20,020	$19,109	$18,716	$17,805	$16,894	

The Benjamin Sandman Children's Bookstore
Cash Flow Statement
Year Two

	July	August	September	October	November	December	January	February	March	April	May	June	Total
Cash Balance, Beginning	$16,894	$9,732	$11,453	$9,174	$11,029	$12,303	$18,745	$16,739	$15,461	$14,963	$16,858	$13,848	
Plus Cash Receipts:													
Sales Receipts	$18,000	$18,000	$18,000	$20,000	$23,840	$26,000	$18,000	$18,000	$18,000	$21,000	$18,000	$18,000	$234,840
Line of Credit													$0
Returns at Cost	$585	$585	$585	$585	$585	$585	$585	$585	$585	$585	$585	$585	$7,020
Total Cash Received	$18,585	$18,585	$18,585	$20,585	$24,425	$26,585	$18,585	$18,585	$18,585	$21,585	$18,585	$18,585	$241,860
Less Cash Disbursed:													
Purchase Inventory	$9,000	$9,000	$10,000	$10,000	$12,000	$12,000	$12,000	$12,000	$11,000	$11,000	$12,000	$12,000	$132,000
Purchase Equipment													$0
Manufacturing Cost	$8,150		$3,000		$3,000								$14,150
Incurred Operating Expense	$6,839	$6,105	$6,105	$6,972	$6,393	$6,385	$6,782	$6,105	$6,305	$6,952	$6,205	$6,205	$77,353
Principal Repayment:													
Long term debt	$1,134	$1,145	$1,156	$1,167	$1,178	$1,189	$1,201	$1,212	$1,224	$1,235	$1,247	$1,259	$14,347
Line of credit													$0
Interest on Debt:													
Long term debt	$624	$614	$603	$591	$580	$569	$558	$546	$534	$523	$511	$499	$6,752
Line of credit							$50						$50
Taxes Payable													
Tax Distrib. to Shareholders													$0
Inventory/Property Tax											$1,632		$1,632
Total Disbursements	$25,747	$16,864	$20,864	$18,730	$23,151	$20,143	$20,591	$19,863	$19,063	$19,710	$21,595	$19,963	$246,284
Cash Balance, Ending	$9,732	$11,453	$9,174	$11,029	$12,303	$18,745	$16,739	$15,461	$14,963	$16,858	$13,848	$12,470	

The Benjamin Sandman Children's Bookstore
Cash Flow Statement
Year Three

	July	August	September	October	November	December	January	February	March	April	May	June	Total
Cash Balance, Beginning	$12,470	$4,903	$6,260	$4,617	$7,067	$7,185	$14,036	$12,626	$11,983	$12,140	$14,593	$12,200	
Plus Cash Receipts:													
Sales Receipts	$19,000	$19,000	$19,000	$21,000	$24,680	$28,000	$19,000	$19,000	$19,000	$22,000	$19,000	$19,000	$247,680
Line of Credit													$0
Returns at Cost	$619	$619	$619	$619	$619	$619	$619	$619	$619	$619	$619	$619	$7,428
Total Cash Received	$19,619	$19,619	$19,619	$21,619	$25,299	$28,619	$19,619	$19,619	$19,619	$22,619	$19,619	$19,619	$255,108
Less Cash Disbursed:													
Purchase Inventory	$10,000	$10,000	$10,000	$10,000	$12,000	$12,000	$12,000	$12,000	$11,000	$11,000	$12,000	$12,000	$134,000
Purchase Equipment													$0
Manufacturing Cost	$8,150		$3,000		$3,000								$14,150
Incurred Operating Expense	$7,278	$6,504	$6,504	$7,411	$6,791	$6,794	$7,221	$6,504	$6,704	$7,391	$6,604	$6,604	$82,310
Principal Repayment													
Long term debt	$1,271	$1,283	$1,296	$1,308	$1,321	$1,333	$1,346	$1,359	$1,372	$1,385	$1,398	$1,412	$16,084
Line of credit													$0
Interest on Debt:													
Long term debt	$487	$475	$462	$450	$437	$425	$412	$399	$386	$373	$360	$346	$5,012
Line of credit							$50						$50
Taxes Payable						$1,216				$17		$267	$1,500
Tax Distrib. to Shareholders													
Inventory/Property Tax					$1,632						$1,650		$3,282
Total Disbursements	$27,186	$18,262	$21,262	$19,169	$25,181	$21,768	$21,029	$20,262	$19,462	$20,166	$22,012	$20,629	$256,388
Cash Balance, Ending	$4,903	$6,260	$4,617	$7,067	$7,185	$14,036	$12,626	$11,983	$12,140	$14,593	$12,200	$11,190	

The Benjamin Sandman Children's Bookstore
Cash Flow Statement
Year Four

	July	August	September	October	November	December	January	February	March	April	May	June	Total
Cash Balance, Beginning	$11,190	$2,246	$2,226	$1,200	$4,249	$5,517	$12,045	$11,248	$9,918	$11,688	$17,510	$15,866	
Plus Cash Receipts:													
Sales Receipts	$19,000	$19,000	$19,000	$23,000	$26,240	$32,000	$20,000	$20,000	$20,000	$25,000	$19,000	$19,000	$261,240
Line of Credit			$994										$994
Returns at Cost	$650	$650	$650	$650	$650	$650	$650	$650	$650	$650	$650	$650	$7,800
Total Cash Received	$19,650	$19,650	$20,644	$23,650	$26,890	$32,650	$20,650	$20,650	$20,650	$25,650	$19,650	$19,650	$270,034
Less Cash Disbursed:													
Purchase Inventory	$11,000	$11,000	$10,000	$10,000	$12,000	$12,000	$12,000	$10,000	$10,000	$10,000	$11,000	$11,000	$130,000
Purchase Equipment													$0
Manufacturing Cost	$8,150		$3,000		$3,000	$3,300		$3,300					$20,750
Incurred Operating Expense	$7,686	$6,912	$6,912	$7,839	$7,214	$7,242	$7,639	$6,922	$7,122	$7,829	$7,012	$7,012	$87,341
Principal Repayment:													
Long term debt	$1,425	$1,439	$1,453	$1,467	$1,481	$1,495	$1,509	$1,524	$1,538	$1,553	$1,568	$1,583	$18,035
Line of credit				$994									$994
Interest on Debt													
Long term debt	$333	$319	$305	$291	$277	$263	$249	$234	$220	$205	$190	$175	$3,061
Line of credit				$10			$50						$60
Taxes Payable													
Tax Distrib. to Shareholders						$1,822				$241		$500	$2,563
Inventory/Property Tax					$1,650						$1,524		$3,174
Total Disbursements	$28,594	$19,670	$21,670	$20,601	$25,622	$26,122	$21,447	$21,980	$18,880	$19,828	$21,294	$20,270	$265,978
Cash Balance, Ending	$2,246	$2,226	$1,200	$4,249	$5,517	$12,045	$11,248	$9,918	$11,688	$17,510	$15,866	$15,246	

The Benjamin Sandman Children's Bookstore
Balance Sheet
Year One

	Base Per.	July	August	September	October	November	December	January	February	March	April	May	June
Assets													
Current													
Cash	$7,482	$9,835	$15,252	$14,838	$15,218	$18,937	$24,874	$21,931	$20,020	$19,109	$18,716	$17,805	$16,894
Inventory	$70,650	$72,160	$71,900	$75,050	$77,020	$73,984	$69,644	$69,692	$69,740	$69,788	$68,656	$67,704	$66,752
Supplies	$525	$525	$525	$525	$525	$525	$525	$525	$525	$525	$525	$525	$525
Total Current	$78,657	$82,520	$87,677	$90,413	$92,763	$93,446	$95,043	$92,148	$90,285	$89,422	$87,897	$86,034	$84,171
Fixed													
Equipment & Furniture	$5,673	$5,673	$5,673	$5,673	$5,673	$5,673	$5,673	$5,673	$5,673	$5,673	$5,673	$5,673	$5,673
Less Accumulated Deprec.		$34	$68	$101	$135	$169	$202	$236	$270	$304	$337	$371	$405
Net Furniture and Equip.		$5,639	$5,605	$5,572	$5,538	$5,504	$5,471	$5,437	$5,403	$5,369	$5,336	$5,302	$5,268
Computer System	$1,800	$1,800	$1,800	$1,800	$1,800	$1,800	$1,800	$1,800	$1,800	$1,800	$1,800	$1,800	$1,800
Less Accumulated Deprec.		$15	$30	$45	$60	$75	$90	$105	$120	$135	$150	$165	$180
Net Computer System		$1,785	$1,770	$1,755	$1,740	$1,725	$1,710	$1,695	$1,680	$1,665	$1,650	$1,635	$1,620
Leasehold Improvements	$19,302	$19,302	$19,302	$19,302	$19,302	$19,302	$19,302	$19,302	$19,302	$19,302	$19,302	$19,302	$19,302
Less Accumulated Deprec.		$161	$323	$484	$646	$807	$969	$1,130	$1,292	$1,453	$1,615	$1,776	$1,937
Net Leasehold		$19,141	$18,980	$18,818	$18,657	$18,495	$18,334	$18,172	$18,011	$17,849	$17,688	$17,526	$17,365
Character Models	$3,200	$3,200	$3,200	$3,200	$3,200	$3,200	$3,200	$3,200	$3,200	$3,200	$3,200	$3,200	$3,200
Less Accumulated Deprec.		$19	$38	$57	$76	$95	$114	$133	$152	$171	$190	$209	$228
Net Character Models		$3,181	$3,162	$3,143	$3,124	$3,105	$3,086	$3,067	$3,048	$3,029	$3,010	$2,991	$2,972
Total Fixed	$29,975	$29,746	$29,517	$29,288	$29,058	$28,829	$28,600	$28,371	$28,142	$27,912	$27,683	$27,454	$27,225
Total Assets	$108,632	$112,266	$117,194	$119,701	$121,821	$122,275	$123,643	$120,519	$118,427	$117,334	$115,580	$113,488	$111,396
Liabilities & Equity													
Current													
Accounts Payable		$8,000	$16,000	$20,000	$24,000	$23,000	$22,000	$21,000	$20,000	$20,000	$20,000	$19,000	$18,000
Taxes Payable										$272	$544	$816	$1,088
Long Term													
Long Term Note	$78,005	$76,994	$75,973	$74,942	$73,901	$72,851	$71,791	$70,720	$69,639	$68,547	$67,445	$66,333	$65,210
Owner's Equity													
Contributed Capital	$41,000	$41,000	$41,000	$41,000	$41,000	$41,000	$41,000	$41,000	$41,000	$41,000	$41,000	$41,000	$41,000
Retained Earnings	($10,373)	($13,728)	($15,779)	($16,241)	($17,080)	($14,576)	($11,148)	($12,201)	($12,212)	($12,485)	($13,409)	($13,661)	($13,902)
Total Liabilities and Equity	$108,632	$112,266	$117,194	$119,701	$121,821	$122,275	$123,643	$120,519	$118,427	$117,334	$115,580	$113,488	$111,396

The Benjamin Sandman Children's Bookstore
Balance Sheet
Year Two

	July	August	September	October	November	December	January	February	March	April	May	June
Assets												
Current												
Cash	$9,732	$11,453	$9,174	$11,029	$12,303	$18,745	$16,739	$15,461	$14,983	$16,858	$13,848	$12,470
Inventory	$78,697	$76,492	$78,287	$78,902	$77,251	$74,326	$75,121	$75,916	$76,711	$75,736	$74,531	$73,326
Supplies	$525	$525	$525	$525	$525	$525	$525	$525	$525	$525	$525	$525
Total Current	$88,954	$88,470	$87,986	$90,456	$90,079	$93,596	$92,385	$91,902	$92,219	$93,119	$88,904	$86,321
Fixed												
Equipment & Furniture	$5,673	$5,673	$5,673	$5,673	$5,673	$5,673	$5,673	$5,673	$5,673	$5,673	$5,673	$5,673
Less Accumulated Deprec.	$474	$542	$609	$677	$744	$812	$879	$947	$1,014	$1,082	$1,149	$1,217
Net Furniture and Equip.	$5,199	$5,132	$5,064	$4,997	$4,929	$4,862	$4,794	$4,727	$4,659	$4,592	$4,524	$4,457
Computer System	$1,800	$1,800	$1,800	$1,800	$1,800	$1,800	$1,800	$1,800	$1,800	$1,800	$1,800	$1,800
Less Accumulated Deprec.	$210	$240	$270	$300	$330	$360	$390	$420	$450	$480	$510	$540
Net Computer System	$1,590	$1,560	$1,530	$1,500	$1,470	$1,440	$1,410	$1,380	$1,350	$1,320	$1,290	$1,260
Leasehold Improvements	$19,302	$19,302	$19,302	$19,302	$19,302	$19,302	$19,302	$19,302	$19,302	$19,302	$19,302	$19,302
Less Accumulated Deprec.	$2,260	$2,582	$2,904	$3,226	$3,548	$3,870	$4,192	$4,514	$4,836	$5,158	$5,480	$5,802
Net Leasehold	$17,042	$16,720	$16,398	$16,076	$15,754	$15,432	$15,110	$14,788	$14,466	$14,144	$13,822	$13,500
Character Models	$3,200	$3,200	$3,200	$3,200	$3,200	$3,200	$3,200	$3,200	$3,200	$3,200	$3,200	$3,200
Less Accumulated Deprec.	$266	$304	$342	$380	$418	$456	$494	$532	$570	$608	$646	$684
Net Character Models	$2,934	$2,896	$2,858	$2,820	$2,782	$2,744	$2,706	$2,668	$2,630	$2,592	$2,554	$2,516
Total Fixed	$26,765	$26,308	$25,850	$25,393	$24,935	$24,478	$24,020	$23,563	$23,105	$22,648	$22,190	$21,733
Total Assets	$115,719	$114,778	$113,836	$115,849	$115,014	$118,074	$116,405	$115,465	$115,324	$115,767	$111,094	$108,054
Liabilities & Equity												
Current												
Accounts Payable	$24,000	$24,000	$24,000	$27,000	$25,000	$26,000	$26,000	$26,000	$27,000	$28,000	$26,000	$24,000
Taxes Payable	$1,360	$1,632	$1,904	$2,176	$2,448	$2,720	$2,992	$3,264	$3,539	$3,814	$2,457	$2,732
Long Term												
Long Term Note	$64,073	$62,928	$61,771	$60,604	$59,425	$58,236	$57,034	$55,822	$54,597	$53,362	$52,114	$50,855
Owner's Equity												
Contributed Capital	$41,000	$41,000	$41,000	$41,000	$41,000	$41,000	$41,000	$41,000	$41,000	$41,000	$41,000	$41,000
Retained Earnings	($14,714)	($14,782)	($14,839)	($14,931)	($12,859)	($9,882)	($10,621)	($10,621)	($10,812)	($10,409)	($10,477)	($10,533)
Total Liabilities and Equity	$115,719	$114,778	$113,836	$115,849	$115,014	$118,074	$116,405	$115,465	$115,324	$115,767	$111,094	$108,054

The Benjamin Sandman Children's Bookstore
Balance Sheet
Year Three

	July	August	September	October	November	December	January	February	March	April	May	June
Assets												
Current												
Cash	$4,903	$6,260	$4,617	$7,067	$7,185	$14,036	$12,626	$11,983	$12,140	$14,593	$12,200	$11,190
Inventory	$85,837	$84,198	$84,559	$83,760	$80,827	$75,968	$75,329	$74,690	$75,051	$73,672	$73,033	$72,394
Supplies	$525	$525	$525	$525	$525	$525	$525	$525	$525	$525	$525	$525
Total Current	$91,265	$90,983	$89,701	$91,352	$88,537	$90,529	$88,480	$87,198	$87,716	$88,790	$85,758	$84,109
Fixed												
Equipment & Furniture	$5,673	$5,673	$5,673	$5,673	$5,673	$5,673	$5,673	$5,673	$5,673	$5,673	$5,673	$5,673
Less Accumulated Deprec.	$1,285	$1,353	$1,420	$1,488	$1,555	$1,623	$1,690	$1,758	$1,825	$1,893	$1,960	$2,028
Net Furniture and Equip.	$4,388	$4,321	$4,253	$4,186	$4,118	$4,051	$3,983	$3,916	$3,848	$3,781	$3,713	$3,646
Computer System	$1,800	$1,800	$1,800	$1,800	$1,800	$1,800	$1,800	$1,800	$1,800	$1,800	$1,800	$1,800
Less Accumulated Deprec.	$570	$600	$630	$660	$690	$720	$750	$780	$810	$840	$870	$900
Net Computer System	$1,230	$1,200	$1,170	$1,140	$1,110	$1,080	$1,050	$1,020	$990	$960	$930	$900
Leasehold Improvements	$19,302	$19,302	$19,302	$19,302	$19,302	$19,302	$19,302	$19,302	$19,302	$19,302	$19,302	$19,302
Less Accumulated Deprec.	$6,124	$6,446	$6,768	$7,090	$7,412	$7,734	$8,056	$8,378	$8,700	$9,022	$9,344	$9,666
Net Leasehold	$13,178	$12,856	$12,534	$12,212	$11,890	$11,568	$11,246	$10,924	$10,602	$10,280	$9,958	$9,636
Character Models	$3,200	$3,200	$3,200	$3,200	$3,200	$3,200	$3,200	$3,200	$3,200	$3,200	$3,200	$3,200
Less Accumulated Deprec.	$722	$760	$798	$836	$874	$912	$950	$988	$1,026	$1,064	$1,102	$1,140
Net Character Models	$2,478	$2,440	$2,402	$2,364	$2,326	$2,288	$2,250	$2,212	$2,174	$2,136	$2,098	$2,060
Total Fixed	$21,274	$20,817	$20,359	$19,902	$19,444	$18,987	$18,529	$18,072	$17,614	$17,157	$16,699	$16,242
Total Assets	$112,539	$111,800	$110,060	$111,254	$107,981	$109,516	$107,009	$105,270	$105,330	$105,947	$102,457	$100,351
Liabilities & Equity												
Current												
Accounts Payable	$30,000	$30,000	$29,000	$31,000	$28,000	$28,000	$27,000	$26,000	$27,000	$28,000	$27,000	$26,000
Taxes Payable	$3,007	$3,282	$3,557	$3,851	$2,957	$2,750	$3,025	$3,300	$3,571	$3,955	$2,618	$2,666
Long Term												
Long Term Note	$49,582	$48,299	$47,002	$45,694	$44,372	$43,039	$41,692	$40,333	$38,960	$37,575	$36,176	$34,764
Owner's Equity												
Contributed Capital	$41,000	$41,000	$41,000	$41,000	$41,000	$41,000	$41,000	$41,000	$41,000	$41,000	$41,000	$41,000
Retained Earnings	($11,050)	($10,781)	($10,499)	($10,291)	($8,348)	($5,273)	($5,708)	($5,363)	($5,201)	($4,583)	($4,337)	($4,079)
Total Liabilities and Equity	$112,539	$111,800	$110,060	$111,254	$107,981	$109,516	$107,009	$105,270	$105,330	$105,947	$102,457	$100,351

The Benjamin Sandman Children's Bookstore
Balance Sheet
Year Four

	July	August	September	October	November	December	January	February	March	April	May	June
Assets												
Current												
Cash	$2,246	$2,226	$1,200	$4,249	$5,517	$12,045	$11,248	$9,918	$11,688	$17,510	$15,866	$15,246
Inventory	$85,064	$83,584	$84,104	$82,344	$78,737	$73,147	$71,097	$72,347	$71,297	$67,397	$66,917	$66,437
Supplies	$525	$525	$525	$525	$525	$525	$525	$525	$525	$525	$525	$525
Total Current	$87,835	$86,335	$85,829	$87,118	$84,779	$85,717	$82,870	$82,790	$83,510	$85,432	$83,308	$82,208
Fixed												
Equipment & Furniture	$5,673	$5,673	$5,673	$5,673	$5,673	$5,673	$5,673	$5,673	$5,673	$5,673	$5,673	$5,673
Less Accumulated Deprec.	$2,096	$2,164	$2,231	$2,299	$2,366	$2,434	$2,501	$2,569	$2,636	$2,704	$2,771	$2,839
Net Furniture and Equip.	$3,577	$3,510	$3,442	$3,375	$3,307	$3,240	$3,172	$3,105	$3,037	$2,970	$2,902	$2,835
Computer System	$1,800	$1,800	$1,800	$1,800	$1,800	$1,800	$1,800	$1,800	$1,800	$1,800	$1,800	$1,800
Less Accumulated Deprec.	$930	$960	$990	$1,020	$1,050	$1,080	$1,110	$1,140	$1,170	$1,200	$1,230	$1,260
Net Computer System	$870	$840	$810	$780	$750	$720	$690	$660	$630	$600	$570	$540
Leasehold Improvements	$19,302	$19,302	$19,302	$19,302	$19,302	$19,302	$19,302	$19,302	$19,302	$19,302	$19,302	$19,302
Less Accumulated Deprec.	$9,988	$10,310	$10,632	$10,954	$11,276	$11,598	$11,920	$12,242	$12,564	$12,886	$13,208	$13,530
Net Leasehold	$9,314	$8,992	$8,670	$8,348	$8,026	$7,704	$7,382	$7,060	$6,738	$6,416	$6,094	$5,772
Character Models	$3,200	$3,200	$3,200	$3,200	$3,200	$3,200	$3,200	$3,200	$3,200	$3,200	$3,200	$3,200
Less Accumulated Deprec.	$1,178	$1,216	$1,254	$1,292	$1,330	$1,368	$1,406	$1,444	$1,482	$1,520	$1,558	$1,596
Net Character Models	$2,022	$1,984	$1,946	$1,908	$1,870	$1,832	$1,794	$1,756	$1,718	$1,680	$1,642	$1,604
Total Fixed	$15,783	$15,326	$14,868	$14,411	$13,953	$13,496	$13,038	$12,581	$12,123	$11,666	$11,208	$10,751
Total Assets	$103,618	$101,661	$100,697	$101,529	$98,732	$99,213	$95,908	$95,371	$95,633	$97,098	$94,516	$92,959
Liabilities & Equity												
Current												
Accounts Payable	$31,000	$30,000	$29,994	$31,000	$28,000	$26,000	$24,000	$24,000	$25,000	$26,000	$26,000	$26,000
Taxes Payable	$2,920	$3,174	$3,428	$3,864	$3,061	$2,560	$2,814	$3,200	$3,543	$3,926	$2,689	$2,480
Long Term												
Long Term Note	$33,337	$31,898	$30,444	$28,977	$27,495	$26,000	$24,490	$22,966	$21,427	$19,874	$18,305	$16,722
Owner's Equity												
Contributed Capital	$41,000	$41,000	$41,000	$41,000	$41,000	$41,000	$41,000	$41,000	$41,000	$41,000	$41,000	$41,000
Retained Earnings	($4,639)	($4,411)	($4,169)	($3,312)	($824)	$3,653	$3,604	$4,205	$4,663	$6,298	$6,522	$6,757
Total Liabilities and Equity	$103,618	$101,661	$100,697	$101,529	$98,732	$99,213	$95,908	$95,371	$95,633	$97,098	$94,516	$92,959

Notes and Works Cited

1. Diane Roback, "Children's Book Sales: Past and Future," *Publishers Weekly,* August 31, 1990, 30–31.

2. Diane Roback, "Selling Children's Books in the Bookstore," *Publishers Weekly,* November 24, 1989, 34.

3. Nancy Brooks, "Sales of Children's Books Are Growing Faster Than Any Other Category As Baby Boomers Introduce Their Youngsters to the Wonders of Reading," *Los Angeles Times,* August 13, 1989.

4. Joanne Tangorra, "Beyond Disney—Book and Music Titles Gaining Wider Popularity in Children's Video Market," *Publishers Weekly,* July 27, 1990, 195.

5. Diane Roback, "Children's Book Sales: Past and Future," *Publishers Weekly,* November 24, 1989, 31.

6. Ibid., 30.

7. Roback, "Selling Children's Books in the Bookstore," 42.

8. Kevin McLaughlin, "The Little Bookstore That Could," *Entrepreneur,* January 1989, 69.

9. Ibid., 69.

10. Ibid., 70.

11. Census Updates of Per Capita Income, 1988, Indiana, Table 1, 46.

12. Ibid.

13. Enrollment calculations made from the *1985 Report of Statistical Information for Indiana School Corporations* and the *1990 Indiana School Directory.*

14. Based on telephone conversations with Nedine Seigal of the American Booksellers Association, Diane Roback of *Publishers Weekly,* and "Future Tense: The Outlook for Children's Books in the 90's," *Publishers Weekly,* February 21, 1991.

15. The Entrepreneur Group's Small Business Start-Up Guide, 85.

16. *Self-Regulatory Guidelines for Children's Advertising,* Council of Better Business Bureaus, Inc., Children's Advertising Review Unit, 13.

APPENDIX A
Market / Venture Survey

Please check the box under the most appropriate response

1. Who is the primary buyer of children's books in your family?

Mother	Father	Grandmother	Grandfather	Other
☐	☐	☐	☐	_____
76%	8%	6%	4%	6% aunt = 2%
				friend = 4%

2. What is the approximate age of the subject in question # 1?

15-20 yrs	21-25 yrs	26-30 yrs	31-35 yrs	36-45 yrs	46-50 yrs	51 yrs & over
☐	☐	☐	☐	☐	☐	☐
2%	7%	**48%**	24%	12%	5%	2%

3. What do you feel is the most important criteria when buying a book for your child?

Price	Illustration	Content	Author's Reputation
☐	☐	☐	☐
32%	14%	**38%**	16%

4. How much money, on average, does your family spend per child for children's books in a year?

average
__$62.50__ dollars

5. Please check the one area below in which you feel that the surrounding bookstores need to most improve upon to provide you with better value and service in buying children's books :

selection	customer service	price	atmosphere	other
☐	☐	☐	☐	_____
26%	**34%**	23%	12%	5% locaion = 3 votes

6. How far do you normally travel in order to purchase books for your children?

0-2 miles	3-5 miles	6-10 miles	more than 10 miles
☐	☐	☐	☐
34%	44%	17%	5%

Please go on to the next page ⟶

7. Using the scale below, please rate how you perceive the following products in contributing to your child's development :

not important ◄──────────────────────────► very important

   1   2   3   4   5

	average		1	2	3	4	5
story books	4.0		1	2	3	◯	5
educational audiotapes	3.1		1	2	◯	4	5
educational videotapes	3.3		1	2	3◯	4	5
educational games	2.8		1	2	◯3	4	5
stuffed toys	3.0		1	2	◯	4	5
writing development products	4.2		1	2	3	4◯	5
reading development products	4.4		1	2	3	4◯	5

8. Using the scale below, please rate the following services that would help you in selecting products for your child :

not a useful service ◄──────────────────────────► a very useful service

   1   2   3   4   5

	average		1	2	3	4	5
Newsletter on new products	4.3		1	2	3	4◯	5
Story Telling Hour at a children's store	4.1		1	2	3	◯	5
Gift Wrapping Service	2.5		1	2◯	3	4	5
Mail Delivery of Products	2.7		1	2	◯3	4	5
Catalog of New Products by Mail	3.1		1	2	◯	4	5
Previewing Videotapes at store	3.9		1	2	3	◯	5
Catering Service for children's parties (gifts, paper products, decorations and cakes all in one stop)	3.0		1	2	◯	4	5

THANK YOU FOR YOUR TIME!!!

Market / Product Survey

A note to the parent :

You have been given one product from a new series of children's books. Please take a few minutes to preview the product and answer the following questions.

1. Using the scale below, please rate the following criteria of the product :

below average	average	good	very good
1	**2**	**3**	**4**

◄───────────────────────────────────────►

	average				
Content of Story	3.3	1	2	3	4
Illustration	3.5	1	2	3	4
Layout of Book	3.0	1	2	3	4
Product Appeal	3.3	1	2	3	4
Overall Quality Rating	3.4	1	2	3	4

2. Would you purchase a product such as this one for your child?

Yes	No	Unsure
☐	☐	☐
72%	10%	18%

3. If your response to question # 2 was "YES", how much would you be willing to pay for such a product?

$1.00 -$4.99	☐	11%
$5.00-$9.99	☐	22%
$10.00-$14.99	☐	35%
$15.00-$19.99	☐	16%
$20.00-$24.99	☐	11%
$25.00 or more	☐	5%

Please go on to the next page ──────────►

A note to the parent :

Now that you have taken a few minutes to evaluate the product, please either read the book to your child and/ or give it to them to preview for themselves. Please take a minute after your child has been adequately exposed to the product to answer the following questions.

1. How did the child react to the product?

Unsure	Showed little interest	Liked the product	Really enjoyed the product
☐	☐	☐	☐
22%	5%	29%	44%

2. Please list on the lines below what you felt were your child's favorite features of the product :

use of rhyme in the story = 7 votes
lesson or morale in story = 5 votes
characters = 3 votes
text size = 2 votes
illustrations = 1 vote

3. Using the scale below, please indicate your perception on how your child felt about the following criteria :

below average	average	good	very good
1	2	3	4

←————————————————————————→

	average		
Content of Story	3.2		1 2 3 ◯ 4
Illustration	3.3		1 2 3 ◯ 4
Layout of Book	3.1		1 2 3 ◯ 4
Overall Rating	3.3		1 2 3 ◯ 4

4. Would you and your child be interested in seeing more products like this one?

Yes	No	Unsure
☐	☐	☐
77%	9%	14%

THANK YOU FOR YOUR TIME AND YOUR SUPPORT OF YOUR CHILD'S FUTURE

Entrepreneurial Growth and Development

Key Topics

- Understanding the Entrepreneurial Mind
- Transition from Entrepreneurial to Managerial Style
- Managing Paradox and Contradiction
- Acquisition of a Business Venture
- Growth and Decision Making

Comprehensive Entrepreneurial Cases

- E.O. Inc.
- Clearly Canadian Beverage Corporation
- Bulldog Pizza and Spirits

Understanding the Entrepreneurial Mind

It has been noted that entrepreneurs (1) perceive an opportunity, (2) pursue this opportunity, and (3) believe that success of the venture is possible.[1] This belief that the idea is unique, that the product is strong, or that the entrepreneur possesses special knowledge or skill must be instilled into the organization itself as it grows.

The Entrepreneurial Manager

It is important for the venture's manager to maintain an open, entrepreneurial frame of mind to avoid the danger of evolving into a bureaucrat who stifles innovation.

In some cases success will affect an entrepreneur's willingness to change and innovate, and this is particularly true if the enterprise develops an environment of complacency that the entrepreneur is comfortable with. In fact, some entrepreneurs create a bureaucratic environment in which orders are issued only from the top down and change initiated at the lower levels is not tolerated.[2] As a result, no one in the venture is willing or encouraged to become innovative or entrepreneurial because the owner-founder stifles such activity.

---

[1]Howard H. Stevenson and Jose Carlos Jarillo-Mossi, "Preserving Entrepreneurship As Companies Grow," *Journal of Business Strategy* (Summer 1986): 10.

[2]Ibid., 11.

One recent study found that the entrepreneur directly affects the firm's growth orientation as measured by profitability goals, product/market goals, human resource goals, and flexibility goals.[3] If the entrepreneur hopes to maintain the creative climate that helped launch the venture in the first place, specific steps or measures must be taken.

Building the Adaptive Firm

Entrepreneurs must establish a business that remains flexible beyond start-up. An **adaptive firm** increases opportunity for its employees, initiates change, and instills employees' desire to be innovative. Several ways to build an adaptive firm are discussed next. These rules are not set in stone, but they do enhance a venture's chance of remaining adaptive and innovative through and beyond the growth state.[4]

Increase the Perception of Opportunity

This goal can be accomplished through careful job design. Objectives for which employees will be responsible should be well defined. Keeping each level of the hierarchy informed of its role in producing the final product or service is often known as "staying close to the customer."[5] Another way to increase the perception of opportunity is through a careful coordination and integration of functional areas, which allows subordinates in different functional areas to work together as a cohesive whole.

Institutionalize Change As the Venture's Goal

This entails a preference for innovation and change rather than preservation of the status quo. If opportunity is to be perceived, the environment of the enterprise must not only encourage it but must also establish it as a goal. Within this context, a desire for opportunity can exist if resources are made available and departmental barriers are reduced.

Instill the Desire to Be Innovative

Personnel's desire to pursue opportunity must be carefully nurtured. Words alone will not create this innovative climate; specific steps such as the following should be taken.

A Reward System   Explicit forms of recognition should be given to individuals who attempt innovative opportunities. For example, bonuses, awards, salary advances, and promotions should be tied directly to employees' innovative attempts.

---

[3]Vesa Routamaa and Jukka Vesalainen, "Types of Entrepreneurs and Strategic Level Goal Setting," *International Small Business Journal* (Spring 1987): 19–29. Lanny Herron and Richard B. Robinson, Jr., "A Structural Model of the Effects of Entrepreneurial Characteristics on Venture Performance," *Journal of Business Venturing* (May 1993): 281–294.

[4]Stevenson and Jarillo-Mossi, "Preserving Entrepreneurship," 13–16.

[5]Thomas J. Peters and Robert H. Waterman, Jr., *In Search of Excellence* (New York: Harper & Row, 1982).

An Environment that Allows for Failure   Fear of failure can be minimized if employees recognize that often many attempts are needed before success is achieved. This does not imply that failure is sought or desired. However, learning from failure, as opposed to expecting punishment for it, is promoted. When this type of environment exists, people become willing to accept the challenge of change and innovation.

Flexible Operations   Flexibility makes change possible and has a positive effect. If a venture remains too rigidly tied to plans or strategies, it will not be responsive to new technologies, customer changes, or environmental shifts. Innovation will not take place because it does not "fit in."

Transition from an Entrepreneurial Style to a Managerial Approach

A venture's transitional stages are complemented (or in some cases retarded) by the entrepreneur's ability to make a transition in style. A key transition occurs during a venture's growth stage when the entrepreneur shifts to a managerial style. This is not easy to do. As Hofer and Charan have noted, "Among the different transitions that are possible, probably the most difficult to achieve and also perhaps the most important for organizational development is that of moving from a one-person, entrepreneurially managed firm to one run by a functionally organized, professional management team."[6]

A number of problems can arise in making this transition, especially if the enterprise is characterized by factors such as (1) a highly centralized decision-making system, (2) an overdependence on one or two key individuals, (3) an inadequate repertoire of managerial skills and training, and (4) a paternalistic atmosphere.[7] These characteristics, while often effective in the start-up and survival phases of a new venture, pose a threat to the development of the firm during its growth stage. Quite often these characteristics inhibit the venture's development by detracting from the entrepreneur's ability to successfully manage the growth stage.

Balancing Entrepreneurial and Managerial Style

Two important points must be remembered about managing the growth stage. First, the entrepreneur of an adaptive firm needs to retain certain entrepreneurial characteristics in order to encourage innovation and creativity in his or her personnel while personally making a transition toward a more managerial style.[8] This critical entrepreneur/manager balance is extremely difficult to achieve. As Stevenson and Gumpert have noted, "Everybody wants to be innovative, flexible, and creative.

---

[6]Charles W. Hofer and Ram Charan, "The Transition to Professional Management: Mission Impossible?" *American Journal of Small Business* (Summer 1984): 3.

[7]Ibid., 4.

[8]John B. Miner, "Entrepreneurs, High Growth Entrepreneurs, and Managers: Contrasting and Overlapping Motivational Patterns," *Journal of Business Venturing* (July 1990): 221–234.

But for every Apple, Domino's, and Lotus, there are thousands of new restaurants, clothing stores, and consulting firms that presumably have tried to be innovative, to grow, and to show other characteristics that are entrepreneurial in the dynamic sense, but have failed."[9]

Remaining entrepreneurial in nature while making the transition to some of the more administrative traits is critical to successful growth of a venture.[10] Table 4.1 provides a framework for comparing the characteristics and pressures relating to five major factors: strategic orientation, commitment to seize opportunities, commitment of resources, control of resources, and management structure. Each of these five areas is critical to the balance needed to manage entrepreneurially. At the two ends of the continuum (**entrepreneurial** focus versus **administrative** focus) are specific points of view. Stevenson and Gumpert have characterized these points in question format.

The **administrative point of view:**

- What sources do I control?
- What structure determines our organization's relationship to its market?
- How can I minimize the impact of others on my ability to perform?
- What opportunity is appropriate?

The **entrepreneurial point of view:**

- Where is the opportunity?
- How do I capitalize on it?
- What resources do I need?
- How do I gain control over them?
- What structure is best?[11]

The logic behind the disparity of these questions can be presented in a number of different ways. For example, the commitment of resources in the entrepreneurial frame of mind responds to changing environmental needs, whereas the managerial point of view is focused on the reduction of risk. In the control of resources, entrepreneurs will avoid ownership because of the risk of obsolescence and the need for more flexibility, whereas managers will view the factors of efficiency and stability as being accomplished through ownership. In terms of structure, the entrepreneurial emphasis is on a need for flexibility and independence, whereas the administrative focus is on ensuring integration with a complexity of tasks, a desire for order, and controlled reward systems.

These examples of differences in focus help establish the important issues involved at both ends of the managerial spectrum. Each point of view—entrepreneurial and administrative—has important considerations that need to be balanced if effective growth is going to occur.

---

[9]Howard H. Stevenson and David E. Gumpert, "The Heart of Entrepreneurship," *Harvard Business Review* (March–April 1985): 85.

[10]Arnold C. Cooper, "Challenges in Predicting New Firm Performance," *Journal of Business Venturing* (May 1993): 241–254.

[11]Ibid., 86–87.

Table 4.1   Entrepreneurial Culture versus Administrative Culture

	Entrepreneurial Focus	
	Characteristics	Pressures
Strategic Orientation	Driven by perception of opportunity	Diminishing opportunities Rapidly changing technology, consumer economics, social values, and political rules
Commitment to Seize Opportunities	Revolutionary, with short duration	Action orientation Narrow decision windows Acceptance of reasonable risks Few decision constituencies
Commitment of Resources	Many stages, with minimal exposure at each stage	Lack of predictable resource needs Lack of control over the environment Social demands for appropriate use of resources Foreign competition Demands for more efficient use
Control of Resources	Episodic use or rent of required resources	Increased resource specialization Long resource life compared with need Risk of obsolescence Risk inherent in the identified opportunity Inflexibility of permanent commitment to resources
Management Structure	Flat, with multiple informal networks	Coordination of key noncontrolled resources Challenge to hierarchy Employees' desire for independence

Table 4.1   *continued*

	Administrative Focus	
	Characteristics	**Pressures**
	Driven by controlled resources	Social contracts
		Performance measurement criteria
		Planning systems and cycles
	Evolutionary, with long duration	Acknowledgment of multiple constituencies
		Negotiation about strategic course
		Risk reduction
		Coordination with existing resource base
	A single stage, with complete commitment out of decision	Need to reduce risk
		Incentive compensation
		Turnover in managers
		Capital budgeting systems
		Formal planning systems
	Ownership or employment of required resources	Power, status, and financial rewards
		Coordination of activity
		Efficiency measures
		Inertia and cost of change
		Industry structures
	Hierarchy	Need for clearly defined authority and responsibility
		Organizational culture
		Reward systems
		Management theory

Managing Paradox and Contradiction

When a venture experiences surges in growth, a number of structural factors begin to present multiple challenges. These factors, such as cultural elements, personnel staffing and development, as well as appraisal and rewards systems, are in constant struggle, vacillating between a rigid, bureaucratic design and a flexible, organic design. Table 4.2 depicts the conflicting designs for each element.

Research has shown that new-venture managers experiencing growth, particularly those in emerging industries, need to adopt flexible, organic structures.[12] Rigid bureaucratic structures are best suited for mature, stabilized companies. Thus, cultural elements need to emphasize a flexible design of autonomy, risk taking, and entrepreneurship. This type of culture is a renewal of the entrepreneur's original force that created the venture. Even if the entrepreneur makes a transition toward a more administrative style, as mentioned earlier, the renewal of innovation and entrepreneurship must continue to permeate the organization.[13]

In designing a flexible structure for high growth, a number of contradictory forces are at work in certain other structural factors. Consider the following structures.

Bureaucratization versus Decentralization   Increased hiring stimulates bureaucracy; firms formalize procedures as staffing doubles and triples. Employee participation and autonomy decline and internal labor markets develop. Tied to growth, however, is also an increased diversity in product offering that favors less formalized decision processes, greater decentralization, and the recognition that the firm's existing human resources lack necessary skills to manage the broadening portfolio.

Environment versus Strategy   High levels of environment turbulence and competitive conditions favor company cultures that support risk taking, autonomy, and employee participation in decision making. Firms confront competitors, however, through strategies whose implementation depends on the design of formal systems that inhibit risk taking and autonomy.

Strategic Emphasis on Quality versus Cost versus Innovation   Rapidly growing firms strive to simultaneously control costs, enhance product quality, and improve product offerings. Minimizing costs and undercutting competitors' product prices, however, are best achieved by traditional hierarchical systems of decision making and evaluations strategies. Yet, these are in contrast with the kinds of autonomous processes most likely to encourage the pursuit of product quality and innovation.[14]

---

[12]Jeffrey G. Covin and Dennis P. Slevin, "New Venture Strategic Posture, Structure, and Performance: An Industry Life Cycle Analysis," *Journal of Business Venturing* (March 1990): 123–133.

[13]Ikujiro Nonaka and Tervo Yamanovchi, "Managing Innovation as a Self-Renewing Process," *Journal of Business Venturing* (September 1989): 299–315.

[14]Charles J. Fombrun and Stefan Wally, "Structuring Small Firms for Rapid Growth," *Journal of Business Venturing* (March 1989): 107–122. *See also* Patricia P. McDougall, Richard B. Robinson, Jr. and Angelo S. DeNisi, "Modeling New Venture Performance: An Analysis of New Venture Strategy, Industry Structure, and Venture Origin," *Journal of Business Venturing* (July 1992): 267–290.

Table 4.2
Conflicting Designs of Structural Factors

Flexible Design	Bureaucratic Design
Cultural Elements	
Autonomous	Formalized
Risk taking	Risk averse
Entrepreneurial	Bureaucratic
Staffing and Development	
Technical skills	Administrative skills
Specialists	Generalists
External hiring	Internal hiring
Appraisal and Reward	
Participative	Formalized
Subjective	Objective
Equity based	Incentive based

Source: Charles J. Fombrun and Stefan Wally, "Structuring Small Firms for Rapid Growth," *Journal of Business Venturing* (March 1989): 109.

These factors emphasize the importance of managing paradox and contradiction. Growth involves the multiple challenges of controlling costs while simultaneously enhancing quality and creating new products to maintain competitive parity, and centralizing to retain control while simultaneously decentralizing to encourage the contributions of autonomous, self-managed professionals to the embryonic corporate culture. Rapidly growing firms are challenged to strike a balance between these challenges when designing their managerial systems.

Acquisition of a Business Venture

Entrepreneurial growth may be achieved through acquisition of already existing business ventures that can enhance or expand current capabilities. However, when considering acquisition, a number of key factors should be considered.

Evaluation of the Selected Venture

The first step is to evaluate specific factors of the venture being offered for sale.

- The **business environment**: The local environment for business should be analyzed to establish the venture's potential in its present location.
- **Profits, sales, and operating ratios**: The business's profit potential is a key factor in evaluating its attractiveness and in later determining a reasonable buying price. To estimate the business's potential earning power, the buyer should review past profits, sales, and operating ratios and project sales and profits for the next one to two years.

- The **business's assets:** The tangible (physical) and intangible (e.g., reputation) assets of the business need to be assessed. The assets that should be examined are:
  —Inventory (age, quality, salability, conditions).
  —Furniture, equipment, fixtures (value, condition, leased or owned).
  —Accounts receivable (age of outstanding debts, past collection periods, credit standing of customers).
  —Trademarks, patents, copyrights, business name (value, how essential to business success, degree of competitive edge).
  —Goodwill (reputation, established clientele, trusted name).

Key Questions to Ask

In addition to evaluating the major points just presented, entrepreneurs need to ask other key questions to analyze the viability of the potential purchase. These questions range from the owner's reasons for selling to the degree of competition that the business faces. The following questions highlight some of the critical areas that need to be addressed:

1. *Why is this business being sold?* It is important to establish the owner's motivation for selling. While there may be a very good reason, such as retirement or ill health, an entrepreneur needs to investigate and verify the owner's reason. If at any time the owner's stated reason for selling does not appear to be the prime motivation, then further research must be done.

2. *What is the physical condition of the business?* The overall condition of the facilities needs to be carefully assessed in order to avoid major expenses after the purchase. Sometimes owners sell a business simply to avoid remodeling the entire location.

3. *How many key personnel will remain?* To conduct a smooth transition, a purchasing entrepreneur needs to know which personnel will remain after the sale. Certain key personnel may be extremely valuable to the continuity of the venture.

4. *What is the degree of competition?* The answer to this question must cover two distinct parts: the quantity and the quality of competitors. In other words, how many competitors are there, and how strong are they?

5. *What are the conditions of the lease?* When the business is being sold but not the building or property, it is vital to know all of the conditions of the present lease. In addition, the landlord's future plans should be established regarding future lease provisions.

6. *Are there any liens against the building?* This refers to the creditors' position and the liabilities of the business. A check should be made for any delinquent payments or outstanding debt the business may have incurred.

7. *Will the owner sign a covenant not to compete?* Legal restraint of trade is the actual purpose here, because a purchaser does not want the seller reopening a firm that is in direct competition. Thus, the law allows a reasonable covenant to cover the time and distance within which the seller agrees not to compete.

8. *Are there any special licenses required?* The buyer needs to verify federal, state, or local requirements, if any, that pertain to the type of business being purchased.

9. *What are the future trends of the business?* This is an overall look at particular industry trends and how this business will fit into those trends. In addition, the financial health of the business needs to be projected.

10. *How much capital is needed to buy?* The final purchase price is not the only factor to consider. Repairs, new inventory, opening expenses, and working capital are just a few of the additional costs that should be considered.[15]

Underlying Issues

Three issues underlie the acquisition of a business: (1) the differing goals of buyer and seller, (2) the emotional bias of the seller, and (3) the reasons for acquisition.

Goals of the Buyer and Seller   Both major parties to the transaction, buyer and seller, assign different values to the enterprise because of their basic objectives. The seller will attempt to obtain the highest possible value for the business and not heed the realistic considerations of the market, the environment, or the economy. To the seller, the enterprise may represent a lifetime investment, or at the very least, one that took a lot of effort. The buyer, on the other hand, will try to pay the lowest possible price. The enterprise is regarded as an investment for the buyer and he or she must assess the profit potential. As a result, a pessimistic view often is taken. An understanding of both positions in the valuation process is important.

Emotional Bias   The second issue to consider when acquiring a business is the seller's emotional bias. Whenever someone starts a venture, nurtures it through early growth, and makes it a profitable business, there is a tendency to believe that the enterprise is worth a great deal more than outsiders believe it is worth. Entrepreneurs must therefore try to be as objective as possible in determining a fair value for the enterprise (realizing that this fair amount will be negotiable).

Reasons for the Acquisition   Some reasons for acquiring a firm are listed below.

- Developing more growth-phase products by acquiring a firm that has developed new products in the company's industry.
- Increasing the number of customers by acquiring a firm whose current customers will substantially broaden the company's customer base.
- Increasing market share by acquiring a firm in the company's industry.
- Improving or changing distribution channels by acquiring a firm with recognized superiority in the company's current distribution channel.
- Expanding the product line by acquiring a firm whose products complement and complete the company's product line.
- Developing or improving customer service operations by acquiring a firm with an established service operation, as well as a customer service network that includes the company's products.
- Reducing operating leverage and increasing absorption of fixed costs by acquiring a firm that has a lower degree of operating leverage and can absorb the company's fixed costs.

---

[15]See Richard M. Hodgetts and Donald F. Kuratko, *Effective Small Business Management,* 4th ed. (Fort Worth, TX: Dryden/HBJ Publishers, 1992), 135–138. For additional insights, see Ted S. Frost, "How to Be a Smart Buyer," *D & B Reports* (March–April 1990): 56–58.

- Using idle or excess plant capacity by acquiring a firm that can operate in the company's current plant facilities.
- Integrating vertically, either backward or forward, by acquiring a firm that is a supplier or distributor.
- Reducing inventory levels by acquiring a firm that is a customer (but not an end-user), and adjusting the inventory levels of the company to match the orders of the acquired firm.
- Reducing indirect operating costs by acquiring a firm that will allow elimination of duplicate operating costs (e.g., warehousing, distribution).
- Reducing fixed costs by acquiring a firm that will permit elimination of duplicate fixed costs (e.g., corporate and staff functional groups).[16]

In summary, it is important that the entrepreneur and all other parties involved in the acquisition objectively view the firm's operations and potential. An evaluation of the following points can assist in this process:

- A firm's potential to pay for itself in a reasonable period of time.
- The difficulties facing the new owners during the transition period.
- The amount of security or risk that is involved in the transaction; changes in interest rates.
- The effect on the value of the company if a turnaround is required.
- Fewer potential buyers than anticipated.
- Whether current managers intend to remain with the firm.[17]

Analyzing the Business

In analyzing small, closely held businesses, comparisons should not be made with larger corporations. Many factors distinguish these types of corporations, and valuation factors that have no effect on larger firms may be significant to smaller enterprises. For example, many closely held ventures have the following disadvantages:

- **Lack of management depth.** The degree of skills, versatility, and competence of managers are limited.
- **Undercapitalization.** The amount of equity invested is usually low (often indicating a high level of debt).
- **Insufficient control.** Due to the lack of management expertise and extra capital, monitoring and controlling operations can be difficult.
- **Divergent goals.** The entrepreneur often has a vision for the venture that differs from the investor's goals or stockholders' desires, thus causing internal conflicts in the firm.

These weaknesses indicate the need for careful analysis of the small business.

---

[16]"Acquisition Strategies—Part 1," *Small Business Report* 12, Issue 1 (January 1987): 34. Reprinted with permission from *Small Business Report*. *Small Business Report* is a monthly management magazine published for top executives in small and mid-size companies by Business Research and Communications, 203 Calle Del Oaks, Monterey, CA 93940.

[17]"Valuing a Closely Held Business," *The Small Business Report* (November 1986): 30–31.

Table 4.3	Decision-Making Characteristics and Stage of Growth		
	Early Stage(s)	Growth Stage	Later Stage(s)
Primary Focus	Product business	Volume production	Cost control
	Definition	Market share	Profitability
	Acquisition of resources	Viability	Future growth opportunity
	Development of market position		
Decision-making Characteristics	Informal	Transitional	Formal
	Centralized		Decentralized
	Nonspecialized		Specialized
	Short time horizon		Long and short time horizon

Source: Thomas N. Gilmore and Robert K. Kazanjian, "Clarifying Decision Making in High Growth Ventures: The Use of Responsibility Charting," *Journal of Business Venturing* (January 1989): 71.

Growth and Decision Making

The **decision-making process** is a critical issue in the growth stage of emerging ventures.[18] The focus and style of decision making in this phase is distinctive from the earlier or later stages that a venture goes through, as illustrated in Table 4.3. Also, as depicted in the table, the organizational characteristics of successful early-stage firms and of successful mature firms are quite different, as are the problems they encounter. Early-stage firms are often unable to define tasks regarding technology or market development that are characterized by high levels of uncertainty. As a result, their organizations typically demonstrate little structure in the areas of job specialization, rules, or formality. The owner is, in many instances, the sole decision maker, with communication being informal and face-to-face. The owner-founder usually integrates people, functions, and tasks by direct contact.

In contrast, mature firms that have several hundred employees can no longer manage in such a fashion. They require formality, structure, and specialization to effectively and efficiently control and direct their organization.

The transition from early-stage decision making to later-stage decision making must be effected during the growth stage, and timing is critical. Premature introduction of structure and formalities may dampen the venture's creative, entrepreneurial climate. However, if formality and structure are adopted too late, management may lose control of the organization as its size increases, leading to major dislocations of the firm and even failure.[19]

---

[18]Robin Siegel, Eric Siegel, and Ian C. MacMillan, "Characteristics Distinguishing High Growth Ventures," *Journal of Business Venturing* (March 1993): 169–180.

[19]Thomas N. Gilmore and Robert K. Kanzanjian, "Clarifying Decision Making in High Growth Ventures: The Use of Responsibility Charting," *Journal of Business Venturing* (January 1989): 69–83.

Therefore, entrepreneurs need to recognize the important transition of decision-making style during growth and learn to authorize others to make necessary decisions to address the simultaneous challenges of rapid growth. Some suggestions for handling decision making during growth follow.

One method concentrates on the use of external resources through **networking**.[20] This method involves a system in which entrepreneurs make use of resources that are external to their venture; that is, they establish personal relationships that may be used for professional assistance. The idea is to gain a competitive advantage by extending decision making and resource availability beyond the assets that are under the domain and control of the venture. For example, a firm might promise a royalty on future sales to obtain a license to use a well-known name to market a product that could not otherwise achieve recognition. The firm is obviously taking advantage of a series of resources, which in this case is all the resources needed to create a national brand that it does not own. **External resources** are those assets, physical or otherwise, that are used by the firm in its pursuit of growth and of which the firm has no direct ownership.[21] Another example is the use of outside consulting assistance in the areas of administrative or operating problems. Strategic planning, security financing, marketing, and day-to-day operational assistance are all areas in which emerging firms may seek outside assistance.[22]

Another method suggested to entrepreneurs for handling decisions during growth is called **responsibility charting**.[23] This process assumes that decision making involves multiple roles that work together in various ways at different points over time. Therefore, its three major components are decisions, roles, and types of participation. These three components are combined to form a matrix so that a respondent can assign a type of participation to each of the roles (at the top of the matrix) for a specific decision (on the left of the matrix). Responses are then analyzed either in a group setting with all participants present or by a facilitator alone when group size makes data processing unwieldy. The steps used in responsibility charting are listed in Table 4.4.

In reporting the value of this process, Gilmore and Kanzanjian state, "Responsibility charting enables better discussions of power and authority because it allows a rich range of potential solutions, rather than the win–lose dynamics that result from discussing these issues in terms of boxes and lines of a new structure.

In growth-stage ventures, team building often fails because of the influx of new executives. If responsibility charting is used to clarify major decisions, the results can orient new executives who step into key roles. Unlike a job description

[20]J. Carlos Jarillo, "Entrepreneurship and Growth: The Strategic Use of External Resources," *Journal of Business Venturing* (March 1989): 133–147. *See also* Dean Tjosvold and David Weicker, "Cooperative and Competitive Networking by Entrepreneurs: A Critical Incident Study," *Journal of Small Business Management* (January 1993): 11–21.

[21]Ibid., 135.

[22]James J. Chrisman and John Leslie, "Strategic, Administrative, and Operating Problems: The Impact of Outsiders on Small Firm Performance," *Entrepreneurship Theory and Practice* (Spring 1989): 37–48.

[23]Gilmore and Kanzanjian, "Clarifying Decision Making in High Growth Ventures," 69–83.

Table 4.4
Steps in Responsibility Charting

1. Establish initial parameters
   Decision rules
   Common language
   Creating the matrix of key decisions and roles
2. Individual balloting and tabulation of patterns
3. Discussion, clarification, negotiation
4. Agreement on allocation of responsibility
5. Monitoring and renegotiation as needed

Source: Thomas N. Gilmore and Robert K. Kanzanjian, "Clarifying Decision Making in High Growth Ventures: The Use of Responsibility Charting," *Journal of Business Venturing* (January 1989): 73.

that only communicates one's duties, the chart shows how each manager's role interacts with the many other critical processes."[24]

Whether by using networking or responsibility charting, entrepreneurs need to develop methods to handle the increasing complexities of decision making in the growth stage.

---

[24]Ibid., 81.

CASE • *E.O. Inc.*[*]

Jerry Sheppard Simon Fraser University

Carol Causti was sure of the goals and problems her family's business would attempt to address as 1991 began:

> Ask anyone in this company and you'll find E.O. Inc. has to meet three major challenges in 1991. One, how do each of us, as owners, get more time to relax from the stresses of the business? Two, how can we get over the short-term cash flow problems the business is having? Three, how do we insure that we don't expand too quickly?

In one way all the members of the Causti family agreed with Carol: the family business, E.O. Inc., faced three main challenges. However, exactly what those challenges were differed for almost each family member. Rob Causti, Carol's father and founder of E.O. Inc., indicated that the main needs of the business were (1) to secure financing for expansion of the family-owned businesses; (2) to use the borrowed funds to develop the present enterprises; and (3) to acquire real estate adjacent to some of the present property in order to allow for future expansion. Nora, Rob's wife, wanted to reduce debt, have a less stressful working environment, and fund medical insurance for all family members. Rob and Nora's sons, Jay and Ben, were in total agreement—with each other. Jay and Ben agreed that there was a need for better equipment, more personal spending money, and shorter working hours. All the family members agreed that they needed to find some way to work together toward common goals.

History of E.O. Inc.

Hard work toward a common goal and a need for money were nothing new to the Causti clan. As Carol will tell you:

> Back in '75 my parents declared bankruptcy. My parents, brothers and I packed up all we owned and headed out from Denver in an old station wagon. For a while we stayed in Miami where my Dad managed flop houses. We had to leave because drug dealers almost blew his head off. He managed a furniture manufacturing plant in Milwaukee, but left because the owners wanted him to do some shady things with the cash flows. We ended up on welfare in Everett, Washington, in 1977. My Dad then took $500 my Mom scraped together for "emergencies" and bought a run down shoe repair shop in Marysville—twenty miles from where we lived! And he'd never fixed a shoe in his life!

---

[*]Special thanks to Sharon Sheppard, John Costanzo, and two anonymous reviewers for their assistance in preparing this manuscript. © Copyright 1992, by Jerry & Sharon Sheppard.

Thus in 1977 the Shoe Shop, later to become the Shoe Shop, Inc., was born. This business was the beginning of a highly eclectic collection of businesses the Caustis would call Entrepreneurial Opportunities, Inc. or E.O. Inc.

The Shoe Shop Inc.

Rob was quickly able to learn the craft of shoe repair through a combination of good instruction from the shop's previous owner, his natural ability with the craft, and a desire to stay off welfare (not to mention Nora's threats as to what might happen should this venture fail). The whole family pitched in to help in the business: Nora learned as fast as Rob could find the time to teach her; the two eldest children, Carol and Ben, were operating the machinery before they were teenagers; Jay, the youngest, waited on customers before he was ten. The firm, through ups and downs, supported the Caustis well since they bought it. By 1981 they had four Shoe Shops in and around Marysville and Everett. Nora ran one, Ben (then 16 years old) another, Carol (at the time 19 years old) the third, and Rob ran the fourth. An emergency might send Rob to one of the other stores. This would leave 12-year-old Jay in charge of the store in his absence.

In 1982 disaster struck. Rob came down with double pneumonia. The illness was prolonged due to Rob's worn-down condition from work-related stress associated with attempting to control the activities of four different shops. Family members urged Rob to consolidate the businesses into one location. As Rob convalesced, he gave his approval to sell off excess equipment and move the best machines to one shop. Rob decided that instead of geographic expansion the business would pursue diversification of services at the one remaining location.

The Creation of E.O. Inc.

The first chance to diversify lines of business activity came when the Caustis had the opportunity to acquire a post office substation contract. The Postal Service had determined that Marysville had grown sufficiently so that additional service was needed. The Caustis were able to take advantage of the opportunity to bid on and receive the contract from the Postal Service. Stationery sales and eventually a typing service, "Secretary-in-a-Hurry," were developed in association with the Postal Service. Nora was put in charge of the postal services and Carol ran the typing service. All these services brought in more customers and so helped the shoe repair to expand. The postal, stationery, and secretarial service also increased profits by a third.

As a reflection of the more diversified lines of business pursued by the organization, Rob created E.O. Inc in 1983. The idea was the E.O. Inc. would act as a holding company for all Causti family businesses. The post office substation, Shoe Shop Inc., and Secretary-in-a-Hurry were made wholly owned subsidiaries of E.O. Inc.

Further expansion occurred in 1984 when the Caustis became lottery ticket agents. This involved instant, daily, and lotto ticket sales. A percentage commission was taken out by the company and the remaining funds were deposited in a bank trust account. Every Friday the previous calendar week's deposits were taken out of the trust account by the state via electronic funds transfer. When the lotto jackpot would get large, the amount of trust funds could get up to $25,000. The Caustis became adept at handling large sums of cash under this type of trust arrangement.

In 1985 the Caustis contracted with several local utilities to collect payments from customers. So, instead of mailing a phone or electric bill payment from the Caustis' post office, one could simply pay the bill to the Caustis as agents for the utility. The Caustis would then deposit the funds into the utility's trust account (net of an agreed-to commission) and the utility customer's payment would be recorded as paid when the Caustis mailed the list of payments to the utility at the end of the day. Thus, several trust accounts came under the Caustis' control. It was therefore necessary to make several trips daily to the bank so the cash on hand did not grow too large. Rob indicated that if they waited until the end of an average day to make the deposits they would be carrying more than $3,500 to the bank in trust deposits alone. This was an unacceptable security risk for the Caustis.

The large amount of cash running through accounts that the Caustis controlled allowed them a certain amount of clout with the bank. The bank the Caustis did business with was just across the street from the Shoe Shop. Branches of at least three large banks, and two smaller ones, were located within five minutes' drive of the shop. Since the Caustis did all their banking at a small bank, they were one of the bank's biggest customers. This allowed Rob to use the threat of going to one of the other nearby banks to obtain financing.

On the Home Front

Even with all this activity on the job the Caustis were busy at home. In 1983 Rob and Nora Causti sold their home in Everett and moved to the town of Granite Falls, about 12 miles from their Marysville store. With the proceeds from the sale they bought a trailer and made a down payment on two 10-acre lots of heavily wooded land. The contract with the previous owner (to whom the Caustis paid their mortgage) stipulated that some of the land could be cleared for a building site to construct a house. The Caustis cleared a site for the trailer and then started on the site for the home. The good timber was sold to local saw mills and the lesser quality logs were sold as firewood. The Caustis built the home themselves on one of two 10-acre parcels that made up the land. They then sold the trailer and purchased an adjacent three-acre parcel as an investment.

The Making of the Country Store Inc.

From 1985 to 1987 the businesses ran smoothly. The Caustis lived in an attractive three-bedroom home on 23 acres. Rob became bored, however, and began looking for additional business ventures. The opportunity arose to buy the property adjacent to the family's 23 acres. This property consisted of a five-acre corner lot with an old farmhouse and an additional six-acre lot.

Rob's idea was to convert the bottom of the farmhouse into a convenience store and the upper floor into office space and sleeping quarters for the two boys. This plan solved several problems. First, it gave the family an additional location from which to bring in business. Second, in the event the Shoe Shop lost its lease in 1991, the family would have ownership of a commercial property. (Moving the Shoe Shop would probably mean loss of the postal and lotto contracts, however.) Third, Rob viewed the two businesses as seasonally balancing each other out. This final observation was confirmed by Ben:

> This sounds crazy, but it's true. In bad weather people are more likely to get their shoes repaired. Folks don't realize they have holes or other problems with their shoes until they step in a puddle and their feet get wet. Summer in this part of the world is the dry season, for the shop repair business, for weather and for people. On a hot, dry day when the shoe repair business is slow, the convenience store business should be booming with hot and thirsty people!

A fourth rationale behind the purchase of the store property was it got Rob's two sons out of the house. Rob, Ben, and Jay all agreed that such a move would be for the best since Rob and the two boys almost came to blows on several occasions. "We work more than 60 hours a week and all we get for pay is room, board, and spending money; that's all. It's a lot of work without much reward," Ben complained. Ben estimated that he and Jay received about $100 per month each and that Carol received about $1,000 per month (the larger sum went to Carol since she was not living at home). Jay added:

> It's good to be out of the house since we'd rather not have to listen to Dad's B.S. all the time. He's always telling us that we don't appreciate the fact that "the business moves we make and the work we put in are for the good of the family" and "being entrepreneurial requires sacrifice and dedication," but "in the end you've really got something!" The problems I see are that *the end* is never any time in the near future and whatever *something* we're supposed to get out of all this work we don't have yet. I don't know if we ever will.

In early 1988 the farmhouse and five acres and the adjacent six-acre lot were purchased. Under Rob's direction, Ben and Jay started to rewire and replumb the building. A parking lot was put in and walls were knocked out. Ben and Jay put in 50 to 60 hours at the Shoe Shop and then worked on the future convenience store and their living quarters during their "off hours." They were driven to finish the rebuilding since upon completion they would also have a decent (or at least a less dusty) place to live. After eating dinner and taking care of the day's accounting, Carol, and sometimes Nora, would pitch in to also help on renovations.

Ben worked alone on enlarging several passageways through supporting walls of the building that became the convenience store. "I worked alone because I needed to be able to concentrate. I risked a couple of tons of 50-year-old house falling on me if I made a wrong move." The old walls are shown as dotted lines on a layout plan supplied by the Caustis. Ben also commented that mistakes on the remodeling job he did could have been fatal in a couple of ways: "If I collapse the house the falling timbers may have killed me, if they didn't then my Dad would have killed me for destroying the place." The tone of his voice indicated he did not say this in jest.

When the remodeling was completed the building became a small 1,500-square-foot convenience—groceries, milk, snack food, pop, beer, wine, video rentals, some hot food, etc. Thus, the Country Store Inc. was added to the list of E.O. Inc. enterprises. Rob Causti planned to later expand operations at the Country Store location to include gas pumps, a restaurant, hardware area, and feed and grain department. Rob planned to eventually develop this five acres into a small strip mall of E.O. Inc. enterprises and stores rented by others. The idea was to take advantage of the rural nature of Granite Falls and to create what Carol called a "New Fashioned General Store" and what Ben referred to as "The Country Mall."

A similar "Country Mall" scheme had been attempted by another entrepreneur about ten miles away but it had closed two years ago. Rob insisted that his plan would work because this other mall was on a busy main highway where people were less likely to stop and the Country Store was part of the community with long-term loyal customers. Other family members thought that the chances of developing a loyal customer base for the Country Store and the mall were fairly likely. Carol Causti's comments were typical:

> The only competition we have is an old, dirty grocery and gas store a mile down the road. Since that place opened 12 years ago the population has more than doubled in this area. The community will easily support both of us—except we plan to outdo the guy down the road. First we plan to offer more services, a cleaner, friendlier place and we'll be open 8 a.m. to 10 p.m. every day, he's only open 9 to 9.

Present Businesses

Thus, at the close of 1990, the Causti businesses included three legal entities: Shoe Shop Inc. (which included Secretary-in-a-Hurry), E.O. Inc., and the Country Store Inc. The Marysville location was the headquarters for Shoe Shop Inc. and Secretary-in-a-Hurry and the other two entities were headquartered in Granite Falls. E.O. Inc was the sole owner of all the businesses.

Shoe Shop Inc. and Secretary-in-a-Hurry

The Shoe Shop was located in the corner of a small strip mall, and the store itself was not visible from the road. The store front was about 25 feet wide and had a large sign proclaiming "Shoe Shop." Taped on the inside of two large display windows were the store's hours (8:00 a.m. to 6:00 p.m.), various notices as to the services to be found inside: Washington State Lotto, U.S. Post Office Substation, Western Union™ (added in 1990). Additionally, posters for recently arrived videos were taped on these large display windows. Since the Caustis had a ready supply of videos from the Country Store, Rob had decided that these could also be rented out from the Shoe Shop.

Inside the Shoe Shop, about 30 feet from the door, stretched from the right to left wall was the well-worn wood paneled service counter. To the left were racks of videos and to the right were two steel shelving units. The shelving units contained stationery and mailing supplies (e.g., wrapping paper for parcels, regular and padded envelopes in a variety of sizes, writing paper, pens), and shoe-related items (e.g., polish, laces, shoe horns, brushes). At the counter, no formal divisions existed, but generally one end of the counter handled the typing service and postal substation customers; the shoe repair business, utility contract payments, and video rentals were handled at the center of the counter; and the Western Union™ and lottery patrons were served at the other end of the counter. In back of the counter was an assortment of machinery: a scale for the post office, a shoe patcher (an ancient Singer sewing machine). Also, in back of the counter were repaired shoes waiting for pickup, and, of course, the cash tills. A diagram of the store layout is included at the end of this case.

There was a door behind the counter that went into the office. This office held some of the company records and the equipment for Secretary-in-a-Hurry. The door to this office was usually kept open so that people in the office could see if the counter became crowded. If more than four people were waiting at the counter, someone would come from the office to the counter to help. Rob believed that keeping the door open allowed family members to get more done and still give quality service. Another door led from the office to the back room where all the shoe repair equipment and supplies were kept. The door to the back room was usually shut to reduce noise and odors. Most of the equipment in the back room was 10 to 15 years old but still in fairly good working order. In the back room another door led outside. This outside back door was usually kept open to provide ventilation.

The Country Store Inc.

As Rob explained it, the bend in the road as one drove up to the Country Store was critical to the success of the business. He reasoned that since people had to slow down at the curve in any case, they would be more likely to stop at the store. However, getting to the store from the main road was somewhat problematic. Due to zoning requirements the parking lot entrance was not on the main road—Oak Street—but on a side road—Barley Avenue. At the corner of Oak and Barley a small brightly lit new sign stood atop a 15-foot metal pole "The Country Store."

The Country Store building was a small, neat barn red wood building with white trim. The inside of the store was brightly lit and clean. Just inside the store was the main service counter. On top of the counter was the cash register, a microwave, and some impulse purchase items. Behind the counter were cigarettes, pop machines, hot snack food facilities, and, usually, Rob Causti. Across from the counter was a window designed to spot customers at the gas pumps that were planned for the location. Under this window was a candy rack. Rob indicated that this placement was important. If he put the rack anywhere else his theft losses would be astronomical.

In spite of carefully placing small items where they could easily be seen from the counter and the careful placement of mirrors for security purposes, theft losses were twice as high as the liberal allowances Rob had originally made for such losses. The theft losses averaged approximately 4.5 percent of the cost of goods sold. The only comparable data Rob had was on supermarkets. Supermarkets had a 1.5 percent theft loss rate. Rob suspected some employees were guilty of the thefts. He felt that his minimum wage employees thought they were worth more than the wage they were paid and decided to enhance their incomes through pilferage. In the store's first four months in business two of six nonfamily staff had been fired based on theft accusations. Rob also made sure that at least one family member was working during store hours to keep an eye on other employees. All these actions did little to cut the theft rate. There was some indication from Carol the high theft rate could probably be traced to midnight raiding from Ben and Jay. As she stated: "Ben and Jay live upstairs. If *you* got the midnight munchies and there was a whole convenience store right downstairs what would *you* do? I think my dad must know, but he probably figures he can write the expense off as part of cost of goods sold."

Toward the back of the store was a full bathroom and laundry room. The laundry room contained not only the hot water heater and washer/dryer but also a kitchen sink and stove. Jay and Ben shared these facilities with the employees since there were no other bath or kitchen facilities in the building. Also in the back of the store was a room that served as a workshop while the Caustis were reconstructing the building. If the Caustis lost the lease on their other location, then this room would, in the future, be used as a shoe repair shop. Upstairs were Jay and Ben's small bedroom, as well as a large center hall area (large enough to be a room) and a large office for the records and plans of E.O. Inc. and the Country Store.

E.O. Inc and Causti Family Finances

E.O. Inc. is a holding company. Its only real purpose, according to company Treasurer Carol Causti, is to coordinate the activities and finances of the Shoe Shop, Secretary-in-a-Hurry, and the Country Store. Thus, the statements of these companies were combined into E.O. Inc.'s financial statements. The balance sheet also showed both personal and business assets and liabilities. The reason for this unusual mingling was explained by Carol Causti:

> Our bank always makes my parents sign personally for credit. The bank also demands statements of their personal and business assets and liabilities. In order to avoid complications we just put everything on the one Balance Sheet. My Dad says that if you're an entrepreneur, you have to put it all on the line. I think his view is that since we started with almost nothing, we have nothing to lose. So we try to maximize our leverage by using all available credit and sometimes even floating three or four days' worth of checks.

Other unusual items on the financial statement were the fact that the real estate properties were shown at appraised market value. The reason for this according to Rob Causti was that the bank would evaluate how much credit to extend to the Caustis based on the appraised market value of the properties rather than their historical cost. Additional notes on the financial statements were made by Carol to help the bank analyze the documents. However, she also stated that a couple points on the statements needed additional explanation:

> The minority interest in the equity section shows stock holdings for Ben and me. Mostly, we're stockholders because there are certain income tax benefits which accrue to the family and to E.O. Inc. as a Sub-S corporation. Ben and I don't really get cash dividends, but we get our bills paid by the business. Between the two of us we've racked up about $27,000 in cash advances and other bills. Of course the bills aren't exactly ours. Basically, we lent my parents the use of our

credit cards when the businesses weren't doing well a few years ago. Now the credit card bills are *slowly* being paid down. I have a bachelor's degree in management and they never taught this in *my* finance classes. Anyway, these credit card debts have allowed my Dad to accomplish what I think are his two most important goals: maximizing business leverage and making sure Ben and I don't leave the business like we often threaten to do.

E.O. Inc. and Functional Support

Below is a brief synopsis of the support functions performed by E.O. Inc. in its role as coordinator for Causti business activities.

Marketing at E.O. Inc. was minimal. Promotion was done through the Yellow Pages™, roadway signs at both locations, and word of mouth. Market research involved in the decision to open the Country Store was based on a detailed demographic report of the region surrounding the store obtained from a secretarial service client. This report had been used in 1987 as the basis to open a large supermarket about seven miles from the Country Store. Product lines the Shoe Shop carried were determined on a trial-and-error basis. (Ben: "We buy a bit of something, if it sells we buy more, if it doesn't, we don't buy any more.") Product lines carried by the Country Store were suggested by vendors and basically followed the same trial-and-error pattern.

The pricing policy at the Country Store was substantially in the hands of suppliers who suggested the appropriate mark-ups for products. Pricing at the Shoe Shop and Secretary-in-a-Hurry was determined through price comparison—i.e., what price were others charging for same services the Caustis were offering. This was done through occasional inquiries at other repair shops or typing services around Marysville and Everett. Prices were set to be competitive. (Carol: "We're not the highest priced or the lowest priced—I think people pick us because the location is convenient, but not because of the price.") One way Carol maximized this convenience for Secretary-in-a-Hurry was to offer the service at both Causti business locations (each location contributed to about half of the secretarial service's revenue). Plans to offer shoe repair services at both locations were discussed.

Logistics functions for E.O. Inc. were mostly performed by outside vendors. All products were delivered to the Country Store by vendors. Newspapers and magazines were brought daily, and the store was credited for unsold past-date publications (yesterday's newspapers, last week's weekly journals, etc.). Various beverage companies and beer distributors came twice weekly to check and restock their products in the appropriate sections. Dairy, snack food, and bakery products were checked and restocked daily by the relevant suppliers (the store again being credited for unsold past-date product). The remaining products (groceries, paper products, sundry, candy, frozen pizza, etc.) were all supplied by one large wholesaler, Marcan, who delivered once a week. Marcan was not greatly different from other wholesalers in terms of price or service, but Marcan did extend credit to the Country Store and this was the deciding factor.

The Shoe Shop suppliers came around about twice a month and supplies of polish, laces, heels, etc. were ordered when Ben saw that they were getting low. The amount of stamps, money orders, and other post office supplies that were supposed to be on hand were stipulated in the Caustis' contract with the Postal

Service. Since inventory reports were required to be filed weekly with the Postal Service, the supplies to be ordered by Nora were simply the difference between the inventory on hand and the inventory amounts stipulated in the contract. Ordering supplies for the lottery and Western Union™ operated in the same manner as for the postal supplies. Paper and typewriter ribbon purchases for Secretary-in-a-Hurry were made by Carol on an as needed basis.

Accounting and Finance In the last two weeks of the month Rob would budget for the next month using a computer spreadsheet (e.g., June's expected revenue, expenses, and capital spending are budgeted in the last two weeks of May). Typically, one month's budget was pretty similar to the next month. Expenses which did not occur every month were, on occasion, forgotten until the bill arrived (e.g., semiannual auto insurance payments). While such problems would throw the budget out of whack, Rob still preferred to only budget one month in advance since he felt it gave the firm greater flexibility. During the course of the month daily cash receipts and disbursements were recorded separately for each subsidiary. Monthly statements of cash receipts and disbursements were produced for each subsidiary at the end of the month and occasionally compared to the budget.

Management, Operations/Human Resources Rob manages the Country Store and controls the Shoe Shop by phone. Rob occasionally visited the Shoe Shop to keep employees on their toes. In Rob's absence, Nora was in charge of the postal substation and Western Union™, Jay was in charge of the lottery and video, Ben managed the shoe repair, and Carol the typing services. When people need to be shifted to different posts because of a customer backlog in one area it was Carol who made the assignments. Wages were as close to minimum wage as possible and there was no benefits package (e.g., Rob and Nora are the only employees with medical insurance).

Integration and Coordination for the companies had been done at the Caustis' dinner table. Family members gathered together most days at dinner to coordinate business efforts. Since opening the Country Store (due to Country Store staffing requirements), these meetings were impossible and now occurred only two or three times a week after the Country Store closed at 10 p.m. These meetings usually lasted about two hours and Rob chaired them. Meetings kept main E.O. Inc employees in touch with one another and made them aware of events occurring within the firm. These meetings also served as a sounding board for operational problems and as a brainstorming session for possible solutions. However, final decisions were made by Rob. Implementation was sometimes a problem if other family members did not support the final decision.

Strategic/Long-Range Planning functions were managed by Carol Causti with substantial input from Rob Causti. There were two reasons this task had fallen to Carol: (1) her bachelor's degree in business administration and (2) her typing ability. Both skills allowed her to develop quality business plans which she could present to the bank for financing. Final approval of the plan was made by Rob.

Some Notes on the Competition

Due to their busy work schedule the Caustis were only able to gather limited information on their competition. What they did know was the geographical placement of their competitors' businesses and some of the competitors' prices.

Competitors for the Country Store's business included other convenience stores and supermarkets. Causti family members also noted that other competitors included video rental stores and gas stations that were increasingly moving into the business of selling snack foods. Locations are indicated on the map of the Marysville/Granite Falls area included at the end of the case. Occasional purchases from these various competitors allowed the Caustis to keep track of competitors' prices. Rob Causti, however, felt that vendor-suggested prices were sufficiently close to the competitors' and so these vendor-suggested prices were the ones always used.

Secretarial service competitors included two people in Marysville who performed typing and copying in their home. Carol Causti stated that if people wished to travel five miles down the road to Everett they could find "half a dozen professional offices that did typing and maybe twice that many 'at home' services." It was these Everett and Marysville services Carol called to check to see if her prices were competitive.

In Marysville there were no other shoe repair shops. To use Ben's wording: "We have the shoe repair business in Marysville sewn-up." However, Ben noted that there were five to ten shops in Everett that repaired shoes and these were the ones he or Jay called to check the Shoe Shop's pricing.

The Future

In discussing the plans for the future of the Causti companies, Carol Causti, in her role as strategic planner, told of the businesses' plans for one, two, three, five, and ten years into the future. Carol began with the two priority items for the next year:

> First, we're going to try to acquire the property across the street for about $3,000 down and a purchase price of about $100,000. The people who own it are getting divorced and want to get rid of the property quickly. The house needs some work, but we can use most of the 10 acres it sits on for future development. In the meantime we can rent the place out for a bit less than the payments until we get a chance to work on the place. It may be helpful to own both corners at this intersection for the purpose of future expansion five to ten years down the line.
>
> The second thing we need to do is get the gas pumps. My dad thinks our business will really pick up when those come in. However, they cost $60,000. On the other hand, those pumps may be vital for bringing customers to support the Country Store's expansion over the next two years.

Over the longer term Carol set out some specific goals for E.O. Inc. and the rest of the Causti enterprises:

> The other important thing we'll try to do in the next three years is to arrange financing for the strip mall we're planning. We've applied to two different banks for a half million in loans. All is going according to plan: we've been turned down twice. Let me explain the plan. For us to get a loan from the U.S. Small Business Administration, the S.B.A., we need to get turned down three times by regular lending institutions. When we get three refusals we apply to the S.B.A. and get the funding at a better rate than we could probably get at the banks. We're sure that this is the kind of project they look for and will fund.
>
> Over the long run several projects will be finished. Three to five years out we'll be constructing the strip mall, expanding our present lines to fill some of the mall space, and finding tenants for the rest of the space. Six or seven years down the line we'll fix up the house across the street. We'll also begin development of the rest of that property. Over the eight-to-ten-year time frame we may acquire

a couple other rural locations for the Country Store and from there probably develop a chain of stores.

While Carol expressed these optimistic plans she also expressed some misgivings on their likelihood of occurring and her role in their implementation:

Right now I doubt things will look anything like what we're planning. We have cash flow problems *now* and added projects aren't going to help. In addition, the work load for all of us is increasing at a time when I want to spend less time at work. I've just gotten married and I want to spend more time with my husband. Ben just got engaged and he is already trying to work less hours. In the short run we may need to hire more employees but this will put further strain on our cash. Sometimes I just want to drop out of the business and become a schoolteacher.

E.O. Inc. Revenue Breakdown, December 31, 1990

	Store Breakdown		Product Line Breakdown									
Month	Store Shop	Country Store	Food	Shoe Repair	Shoe Retail	Video	Sec./Copy.	Lotto	Contract	S.S. Misc.	C.S. Other	Total
Jan.	$ 15,281	$ 8,660	$ 6,870	$ 7,000	$ 1,400	$ 1,800	$ 1,780	$ 1,105	$ 2,521	$ 1,080	$ 340	$ 23,941
Feb.	15,319	9,742	7,900	7,030	1,395	1,755	1,930	1,100	2,521	1,080	350	25,061
Mar.	14,391	10,715	8,840	6,250	1,240	1,750	2,000	1,120	2,521	960	425	25,106
Apr.	12,916	16,985	14,675	4,685	930	2,160	2,460	900	2,521	720	850	29,901
May	11,501	20,880	18,100	3,125	620	2,600	2,960	700	2,521	480	1,275	32,381
June	11,110	22,220	19,510	3,000	400	2,500	2,920	800	2,520	480	1,200	33,330
July	10,316	19,695	17,675	3,125	620	1,890	2,150	700	2,521	480	850	30,011
Aug.	11,664	17,837	15,675	3,905	775	2,025	2,300	900	2,521	600	800	29,501
Sep.	17,989	16,467	13,725	7,810	1,550	2,565	2,920	1,400	2,521	1,200	765	34,456
Oct.	24,818	15,068	11,750	12,100	2,400	3,105	3,530	2,000	2,521	1,800	680	39,886
Nov.	23,888	12,838	9,805	11,700	2,325	2,835	3,230	2,000	2,521	1,800	510	36,726
Dec.	18,032	10,518	8,225	8,370	1,845	2,015	2,570	1,230	2,520	1,320	455	28,550
Total	$187,225	$181,625	$152,750	$78,100	$15,500	$27,000	$30,750	$14,000	$30,250	$12,000	$8,500	$368,850

Approximate Percentage of $368,850 Revenue Applicable to:

	Food	Shoe Repair	Shoe Retail	Video	Sec./Copy.	Lotto	Contract	S.S. Misc.	C.S. Other	Total
Shoe Shop	—	21.2%	4.2%	3.7%	4.2%	3.8%	8.2%	3.2%	—	48.5%
Country Store	41.4%	—	—	3.7%	4.2%	—	—	—	2.2%	51.5%

Approximate Percentage of $86,000 Labor Applicable to:

	Food	Shoe Repair	Shoe Retail	Video	Sec./Copy.	Lotto	Contract	S.S. Misc.	C.S. Other	Total
Shoe Shop	—	25.0%	1.0%	3.0%	5.0%	8.0%	15.0%	1.0%	—	58.0%
Country Store	33.0%	—	—	3.0%	5.0%	—	—	—	1.0%	42.0%

Rob and Nora Causti Income Statement, December 31, 1990

		1990	1989	1988	1987
Dividend income from E.O.		$61,637	$51,730	$27,660	$30,585
Salaries from E.O.		35,000	30,000	30,000	24,000
Expenses:	Interest paid	25,960	24,400	12,720	9,900
	Loan principle paid	13,500	7,000	6,000	5,000
	Taxes	13,599	10,000	3,600	3,600
	Living expenses	43,578	40,330	35,340	36,085
	Net Income	0	0	0	0

Rob and Nora Causti and E.O. Inc. Balance Sheet, December 31, 1990

Assets	1990	1989	1988	Liabilities	1990	1989	1988
Current Assets				**Current Liabilities**			
Personal cash	$ 1,750	$ 1,500	$ 2,000	C.S. payables	$ 12,000	$ 8,000	$ 1,000
C.S. Inc. cash	500	500	500	S.S. payables	2,500	1,000	1,000
S.S. Inc. cash	(7,500)	(2,000)	(2,000)	Postal service	10,000	10,000	10,000
Trust account	12,000	10,000	7,500	Payroll taxes	2,000	2,000	1,500
Stamps	10,000	10,000	10,000	Sales tax	2,000	2,000	1,500
C.S. inventory	12,600	7,000		Trust deposits	12,000	10,000	7,500
S.S. inventory	2,650	2,700	2,700	C.S. credit line	11,000	7,500	5,000
				Cur. part LT debt	19,200	16,800	10,000
Total current	32,000	29,700	20,700	Total current	70,700	57,300	37,500
Other Assets				**Long-Term Debt**			
Improvements	35,000	30,000	7,500	Improvements	25,500	15,000	5,000
C.S. fixtures	5,000	3,500		C.S. fixtures	4,000	4,000	
S.S. equipment	7,000	7,000	7,000	S.S. equipment	6,000	4,000	2,000
Autos	5,000	5,000	5,000	Videos	10,000	4,000	4,000
Videos	10,000	5,000	5,000	LT capital lease	10,000	8,000	
C.S. misc.	500	500		Store and 5 acres	65,000	70,000	75,000
Depreciation	(17,933)	(9,000)	(6,600)	Home and 10 acres	120,000	125,000	85,000
Capital lease	15,000	11,000		10-acre parcel	25,000	27,500	30,000
Store	120,000	110,000	100,000	6-acre parcel	14,000	15,000	
Depreciation	(6,000)	(1,000)		Cur. part LT debt	(19,200)	(16,800)	(10,000)
Store 5 acres	30,000	28,000	25,000	Total LT debt	260,300	255,700	191,000
				Total liabilities	331,000	313,000	228,500
Personal	10,000	10,000	10,000	**Equity**			
Home, 10 acres	140,000	130,000	120,000	Family equity	98,067	112,200	151,100
10-acre parcel	60,000	55,000	50,000	Property equity	65,000	33,000	
3-acre parcel	12,000	11,000	10,000	Common stock	1,000	1,000	1,000
6-acre parcel	38,000	34,000	30,000	Minority contrib.	500	500	500
Other assets	463,567	430,000	360,400	Total equity	164,567	146,700	152,600
Total assets	$495,567	$459,700	$381,100	Liabilities and equity	$495,567	$459,700	$381,100

1. Equipment at the Shoe Shop fully depreciated on 12-31-89; 3–5 more years use expected from it.
2. All 1989 and 1990 cap. lease pmts., deprectn., bus. int. (less $1,700) is Country Store (C.S.).
3. Utilities for the Shoe Shop (S.S.) are $1,600 per year for 1989 and 1990.
4. The $12,000 rent expense applies to the S.S.; all improvements apply to the C.S.
5. With the exception of above expenses, all expenses are equally shared by S.S. and C.S.
6. Videos, Payroll Payable, Sales Tax Payable are half C.S. and half S.S.; auto is personal.
7. Advances from S.S. to C.S. total $105,203 at the end of 1990.
8. For 1988, 1989, and 1990, current portion of S.S. Long-Term (LT) Debt was $1,200, $2,500, $3,000, respectively; personal portion of LT debt was $5,000, $7,000, $6,000, respectively.
9. Personal tax: $4,000 of 1989 taxes and $12,000 of 1990 taxes relate to back income tax owed but not paid in 1987. Tax payments were current as of 12-31-90. C.S. losses result in a $1,650 tax benefit.

E.O. Inc. Income Statement, December 31, 1990

		1990	1989	1988	1987
Sales	Dairy foods	$ 27,000	$ 12,000	$ 0	$ 0
	Baked goods	32,000	16,500		
	Beer and wine	43,000	21,000		
	Snack foods	50,750	27,000		
	Country Store other	8,500	5,500		
	Shoe repair	78,100	62,000	72,500	67,000
	Shoe related	15,500	11,500	14,000	13,000
	Secretarial and copies	30,750	26,000	28,000	25,000
	Contract payments	30,250	25,000	25,500	22,500
	Video rental	27,000	22,500	3,000	
	Lotto commission	14,000	11,500	14,500	13,000
	Shoe Shop misc.	12,000	9,500	5,500	5,000
	Total sales	368,850	250,000	163,000	145,500
Cost of Goods Sold	Dairy foods	21,000	10,000		
	Baked goods	25,000	13,000		
	Beer and wine	32,250	16,000		
	Snack foods	37,000	20,000		
	Country Store other	6,213	4,070		
	Shoe repair	15,500	12,000	16,000	14,000
	Shoe related	9,750	7,000	9,140	7,865
	Secretarial and copies	10,500	8,000	10,000	7,500
	Total C.O.G.S.	157,213	90,070	35,140	29,365
Gross Profit		211,637	159,930	127,860	116,135
Operating Expenses	Salaries and wages	51,000	48,750	10,500	11,250
	R. & N. Causti salaries	35,000	30,000	30,000	24,000
	Rent	12,000	12,000	12,000	12,000
	Equipment lease	10,200	10,200		
	Depreciation	8,933	2,400	2,400	2,400
	Utilities	5,200	4,500	1,600	1,500
	Insurance	2,400	2,000	750	500
	Supplies and repairs	1,250	1,000	250	250
	Bank charges	1,000	750	250	250
	Legal and accounting	500	500	500	500
	Advertising	250	250	250	250
	Shoe Shop misc.	1,000	750	250	250
	Taxes	16,700	16,500	5,500	4,000
	Interest	18,700	18,000	14,250	2,000
Total Operating Expenses		164,133	147,600	78,500	59,150
Net Income		47,504	12,330	49,360	56,985
Dividends		61,637	51,730	27,660	30,585
Change in Equity		(14,133)	(39,400)	21,700	26,400

The Country Store Inc. Layout

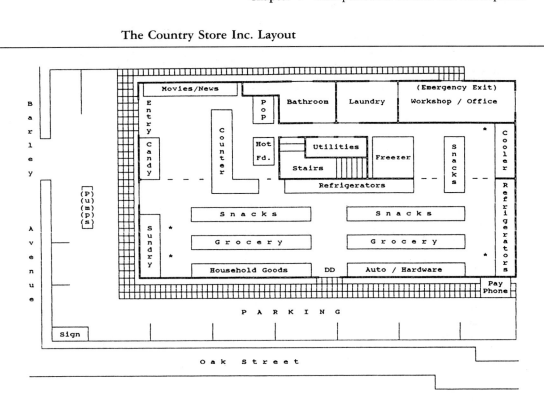

*Wide angle ceiling mirror mounted about here for security.

DD Delivery Door: used only for deliveries and locked at all other times.

The Shoe Shop Inc. Layout

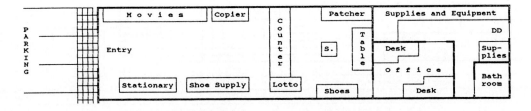

Granite Falls/Marysville Map

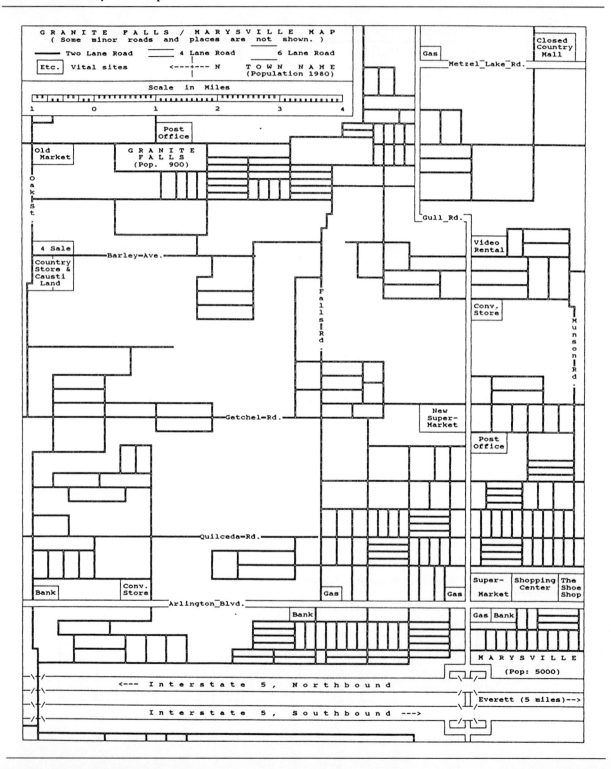

CASE • *Clearly Canadian Beverage Corporation*

Frank J. Fish

Introduction

The employees at Vancouver, B.C.-based Clearly Canadian Beverage Corporation were brimming with excitement as shares of their company, which have been ignored by Canadian and U.S. analysts, hit a new high.

The sudden attention came after Clearly Canadian's stock was selected as the top choice among growth shares in the Investment Dartboard column of *The Wall Street Journal* March 5, 1991 issue. The company was flooded with calls from analysts seeking information as the stock traded as high as $27 on the over-the-counter market; its normal trading range is between $19 and $22. New York analysts had long ignored the company and had only recently taken a more upbeat approach towards recommending the stock. Up until a few years ago, Clearly Canadian was known as International Beverage Co.—an unprofitable company with incredible sales potential.

Clearly Canadian Beverage Corp. is a small 35-person Vancouver, B.C.-based bottler run by a 44-year-old former grocery store district manager named Douglas Mason. Since launching the brand three years ago, Mason has increased sales from $8 million to $85 million.

Actually, Clearly Canadian is Mason's second branded beverage. His first was a cola soda called Jolt, which had "twice the sugar and twice the caffeine" of competing colas. In 1986, Jolt was hot; the company's shares catapulted from 2½ to 17½ (U.S.) on the Vancouver exchange—only to collapse to 2 when Jolt's sales died. (These prices are adjusted for a 2-for-7 reverse stock split in 1990.) Mason renamed the company Clearly Canadian in 1990.

Clearly Canadian was originally incorporated under the name of Cambridge Development Corporation on March 19, 1981. It changed its name to Bridgewest Development Corporation on October 28, 1983, and to BDC Industries Corp. on November 15, 1984. On September 3, 1986, the company changed its name to The Jolt Beverage Company, Ltd.

Jolt Beverage Company, Ltd. changed its name to The International Beverage Corporation on May 13, 1988. International Beverage Corporation then became the Clearly Canadian Beverage Corporation on May 14, 1990.

From its inception in 1981 to November of 1987, the company as we know it today evolved through a number of unrelated business activities, including real estate development, oil and gas exploration, new-product distribution, mining, and restaurant operations. In April of 1986, the Jolt Beverage Company reached an agreement in principle to acquire exclusive rights to distribute a new product, Jolt Cola, in Canada.

Between June 1986 and March 1987, the Jolt Beverage Company was successful in obtaining distribution in 12 states of the United States and four western Canadian provinces for the product, Jolt Cola.

In October of 1987, the rather severe stock market crash adversely affected the success of the Jolt Cola project in the United States and Canada.

The Jolt Beverage Company was forced to surrender its U.S. distribution rights for Jolt Cola for the states of Washington, Oregon, Alaska, Hawaii, Texas, Oklahoma, New Mexico, Montana, Idaho, California, Arizona, and Nevada. The forfeiture of the rights resulted for two major reasons:

1. Jolt Beverage Co., due to the financial constraints resulting from the October 1987 stock market crash, was unable to keep current with its commitments to Jolt Rochester—the inventor and sole supplier of Jolt Cola.
2. A diminishing sales performance, directly related to the company's inability to fund marketing expenditures, resulted in nonachievement of sales performance requirements and therefore the subsequent cancellation of the U.S. distribution rights.

The Jolt Beverage Co. also had the exclusive marketing, bottling, and distribution rights for Jolt Cola beverages in Canada. However, as Jolt Cola sales were diminishing in the latter part of 1988 and early 1989, the company decided to abandon the project and all inventories were liquidated by November of 1989.

Overview

Clearly Canadian is a rapidly growing marketer and distributor of Clearly Canadian brand carbonated mineral water and sparkling water beverages with natural fruit flavors. First introduced in California markets in January 1988, Clearly Canadian has quickly become the category leader in the "New Age" beverage market, the fastest-growing segment of the beverage industry. Clearly Canadian is a hybrid product designed to capitalize on the rapid growth of the $2 billion bottled water industry and the $29 billion soft drink market. Consumer demand for products perceived as upscale, healthier, natural, and containing no alcohol led New Age beverage sales to grow from $246 million in 1986 to $757 million in 1991. Clearly Canadian has grown faster than the category; in fiscal 1989, its first year, the company achieved $8 million in revenues which rose to $85 million in fiscal 1992. Clearly Canadian's record of success has been achieved with virtually no major advertising campaign and without incurring any long-term debt. Management at Clearly Canadian has been focused on making their company profitable for the short term and has not devoted a lot of time to defining a mission statement or business goals and objectives.

Management

Clearly Canadian's past and current success and future destiny are guided by a management team with vision, operating depth, and financial acumen. Rarely does one find these success factors resident in a young organization, and they imply significant and profitable corporate evolution going forward.

The company currently has eight executive officers as follows:

Name	Position
Douglas L. Mason	Chief Executive Officer and President
D. Bruce Horton	Chief Financial Officer and Secretary
Glen D. Foreman	Chief Operating Officer
Stuart R. Ross	Senior Vice-President, Administration
Ron Kendrick	Vice-President, Operations
Elliot (Swede) Ewing	Vice-President, Marketing and Sales
Nigel G. Woodall	Vice-President, Accounting and Administration
Daniel Evans	Director, Investor Relations

The company paid an aggregate of $506,708 to the company's executive officers for services rendered to the company during the company's most recently completed financial year ending June 30, 1992.

Douglas L. Mason   Mr. Mason was appointed to his present position in June of 1986. In 1984 and 1985, he was a partner with D. Bruce Horton in Continental Consulting Services. (The consulting service developed financing and marketing plans for a variety of businesses in Texas, Illinois, British Columbia, Japan, and Hong Kong.) From 1978 to 1983, he was engaged in two entrepreneurial businesses that entailed extensive market research and development and product distribution. From 1970 to 1978, he was district manager of a major retail grocery store operation having 18 retail outlets.

D. Bruce Horton   Mr. Horton was appointed to his present position in June of 1986. In late 1984 and 1985, he was a partner with D.L. Mason in Continental Consulting. In 1984, Mr. Horton was consultant in connection with the reorganization, refinancing, and the ultimate sale of California Cooperage U.S.A. to the Coleman Company of Wichita, Kansas. From 1972 to 1984, he was a partner of Horton, Butler and Schneider, Certified General Accountants of Kelowna, British Columbia.

Glen D. Foreman   Mr. Foreman joined the company in October of 1988 as director of marketing. In July of 1989, he was appointed vice-president of sales and marketing. Prior to joining the company, Mr. Foreman had been with the Coca-Cola Company for 15 years.

Stuart R. Ross   Mr. Ross joined the company in September of 1986. From 1981 to 1986, he was controller for a medium-sized automobile dealership. Prior to that, he held positions as accountant and controller with corporations within British Columbia.

The Product

Clearly Canadian has attained a "must carry" status in most major U.S. supermarkets and grocery outlets. Sold primarily in the United States and Canada and positioned as a premium brand, the product is an unflavored, natural carbonated mineral water and a sparkling water beverage which comes in six natural flavors—wild cherry, orchard peach, western loganberry, mountain blackberry, country raspberry, and coastal cranberry. The unflavored water competes in the $2 billion bottled water industry, which is predicted to grow 10 percent annually over the next several years. The flavored products compete in the soft drink market, which is estimated to grow 2.5 percent–3.0 percent annually in unit volumes.

The products consist of natural fruit flavors, Canadian water, fructose, malic acid, citric acid, sodium benzoate, tartaric acid, and contain two-thirds of the calories of general carbonated soft drinks, or about 100–110 calories per 11-ounce bottle. Retail prices range from $0.70 to $1.30 per 11-ounce bottle and from $2.50 to $4.00 for four-packs at retail. A 23-ounce family-size bottle is also available from $1.50 to $2.00

Marketing

The company initially introduced its product into new markets through convenience stores and "on-premise" accounts (stores that sell cold, single bottles such as delis, liquor stores, and restaurants), which created the perception that the product was everywhere. When the company felt the product had sufficient brand recognition, it introduced four packs and 23-ounce bottles to supermarkets. Consumer awareness of the product allowed the distributors to reduce the high cost of supermarket plotting allowances from the start. It is estimated that supermarkets account for only 20 percent of the company's revenues. About 60 percent of the company's sales are single-serve bottles or sold through convenience stores, and the remaining 20 percent is sold through restaurants, hotels, and institutional accounts.

Beverage Marketing Corporation (New York) published an annual report on the category entitled "New Age and Isotonic Beverages in the U.S. 1990." According to this report, 176.1 million gallons of New Age beverages were consumed in the United States in 1989, of which 34.7 percent were flavored waters (as compared with 12.7 billion gallons of soft drinks and 2.7 billion of fruit beverages). Clearly Canadian has been a strong beneficiary of the growth trends in New Age beverages, being deemed by Beverage Marketing as one of the hottest brands in the all-natural soda category. According to the A. C. Nielsen studies, Clearly Canadian has been able to secure a 5 percent to 25 percent market share (averaging 10 percent) in markets where it has been established for one year. In fact, 60 percent of sales occur in on-premise outlets and convenience stores—A. C. Nielsen reflects sales data only for major supermarket chains. In more mature markets, Clearly Canadian is still achieving 15 percent–20 percent growth, which is not surprising considering its award-winning packaging and the quality of the product, made with pure Canadian water and natural fruit flavors.

The award-winning, blue-tinted bottles with attractive silkscreen graphics have contributed to the strong initial trial trends for the product; the product's quality and taste have led to repeat purchases and the success of the brand. Although this packaging is more expensive, it has distinguished Clearly Canadian from competitors' products, which often are in clear bottles with paper labels, and has even served as its own form of advertising. However, another New Age beverage called "Mystic" has pirated the unique design of Clearly Canadian's packaging to the extent that at first glance it is difficult to discern the two brands.

Clearly Canadian is available in all 50 states in the United States, as well as in Canada, Japan, the United Kingdom, and the Caribbean Islands. The company distributes and sells its products through a network of distributors. Master Distributors is contractually responsible for bottling and distributing the product in a given area after purchasing the water and the concentrates from Clearly Canadian. U.S. distribution is primarily done through these partnerships, in which the spread between the end-user price and the production cost (in 1991, around $2/case for purchases of primarily concentrate and water) is divided. Master Distributors is contractually required to pay for various marketplace costs, including local promotion. Many of these distributors have an equity investment in the company and are required to spend a minimum of $0.50 per case sold on advertising. Distributors often subcontract distribution of their product within their regions. Exhibit 1A shows the company's nine Master Distributors in the United States.

On March 3, 1992, Clearly Canadian announced that, through Nippack Co. Ltd, the company's Japanese Master Distributor, it entered into an exclusive distribution agreement with Asahi Breweries Limited (see Exhibit 1B). Asahi will distribute the company's line of sparkling beverages to the Japanese market, which has a population of 150 million. Asahi's opening order was 500,000 cases, which translates into approximately US $10 million at wholesale. Asahi has committed to launching a multimillion dollar aggressive advertising campaign using television, radio, and print.

Headquartered in Tokyo, Asahi is one of the largest beer companies in Japan, with annual sales in excess of US $6 billion. Clearly Canadian will be sold by the nonalcoholic division of Asahi, which also handles the distribution of Schweppes and other premium juices and soft drinks.

Clearly Canadian currently seeks a European partner, one who could take up to a 20 percent stake in the company. To date, the largest single owner of stock is its Japanese Master Distributor, Nippack Co. Ltd, of Tokyo, which has about a 7 percent equity ownership. Currently, Japanese distribution and marketing methods are being reviewed and improved. One such improvement is the planned introduction of a smaller lower-priced 200 ml bottle solely for this market, a redesign expected to do much to revive sagging sales.

All of the Master Distributors must meet minimum sales requirements in their territories to maintain distribution rights. These distributors have experience in marketing premium brands. The head count behind these distributors constitutes a sales force of about 14,000 people.

Clearly's flexible distribution system plays a pivotal role in its accomplishments. Strong partnerships with its suppliers, bottlers, and distributors, coupled with Clearly Canadian's experienced management team, are the driving forces behind its success. The distribution system has been and will continue to be an extremely important factor in facilitating market penetration.

Production

Clearly Canadian owns land and water rights at two well sites in Canada. One site, located about 300 miles north of Vancouver in Okanagan Valley, B.C., is situated on about 150 acres. It has five wells and the capacity to produce 18 million cases

Exhibit 1A   Clearly Canadian Master Distributors by Territory

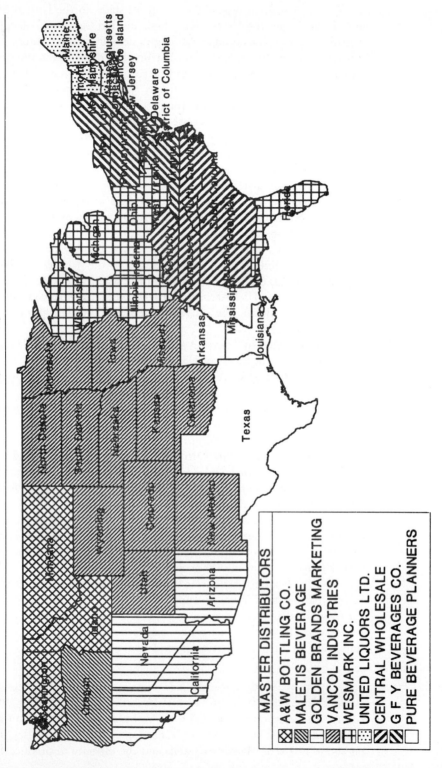

MASTER DISTRIBUTORS
A&W BOTTLING CO.
MALETIS BEVERAGE
GOLDEN BRANDS MARKETING
VANCOL INDUSTRIES
WESMARK INC.
UNITED LIQUORS LTD.
CENTRAL WHOLESALE
G F Y BEVERAGES CO.
PURE BEVERAGE PLANNERS

Source: Company data, 1992.

Exhibit 1B   **Clearly Canadian Japanese Master Distributor**

Source: Company data, 1992.

of product per year. Water drawn from this source is used to produce the company's natural mineral water. The excess is used to produce flavored water products for the western United States, western Canada, and Japanese markets. The second well site, located on five acres in Thornton, Ontario, can produce 23 million cases and is used to supply the eastern United States, eastern Canada, and Europe with the company's flavored water products. Combined, these well sites can produce about 41 million cases. As more water supplies are needed, additional wells could be drilled. Water is shipped to the bottlers in stainless steel tankers specifically dedicated to Clearly Canadian. The cost of transporting the water from the well site to the bottler is borne by Clearly Canadian. In turn, the transportation cost is included in the price paid by bottlers. Also, the company is reviewing the acquisition of other Canadian land and water sources in strategic locations to serve international markets in the longer term.

The company contracts out its bottling requirements to nine carefully selected, strategically located bottling facilities in North America, seven in the United States and two in Canada. Exhibit 2A shows Clearly Canadian U.S. bottler production facility locations. Exhibit 2B shows Canadian bottler production facility locations and well sites. Additional facilities will begin operation in late 1992, which will bring total bottling capacity to 50 million cases per year. Negotiations are continuing to further increase production capacity.

Other raw materials include the bottles and flavoring. The company contracts with four glass manufacturers: Vitro Packaging of Monterrey, Mexico; Owens-Brockway of Oakland, California; Consumer Glass Ltd. of Lavington, B.C.; and Consumers Glass of Bramalea, Ontario. For flavorings Clearly Canadian owns the recipes that are produced by two suppliers. Each supplier has the technology to produce all the flavors. New flavors are under development and being tested.

Clearly Canadian's capital expenditure requirements are low, since it does not own any manufacturing plants, bottling facilities, or trucks, nor does it need to pay a large sales force. Instead, it enters into long-term contracts with the industry's leading bottlers, distributors, and transportation companies.

Quality Control

The company's quality control system is state-of-the-art and second to none in the beverage industry. The quality of the company's products exceeds the most stringent requirements of any regulatory agency in the United States or Canada. The water is pumped through stainless steel pipes from a number of wells which are 250–300 feet below the surface, with quality continuously monitored. It is then stored in stainless steel storage tanks and shipped in dedicated stainless steel tankers to the bottlers' dedicated stainless steel tanks. The tankers are sealed and returned empty to the well sites. The water is tested a second time at the bottling facility and then once again as a finished product. A quality control team randomly inspects the quality control systems at each bottling facility. Every production run is tested to insure that product specifications are met. Water samples are sent to two independent testing labs as well. Clearly Canadian's quality control process also measures torque on bottle caps, sugar, PH level, and microbiological content.

Management Information Systems

Clearly Canadian has not devoted a lot of time or manpower towards the development of an information system to report on its overall operations. This is typical of most entrepreneurial companies whose main focus is to develop a desirable product for an industry, market it, and become profitable immediately. Management at Clearly Canadian has been exhausting their time creating an entrepreneurial success story. Douglas Mason, for the most part, has been reluctant to budget money for an

Clearly Canadian United States Bottler Production Facilities

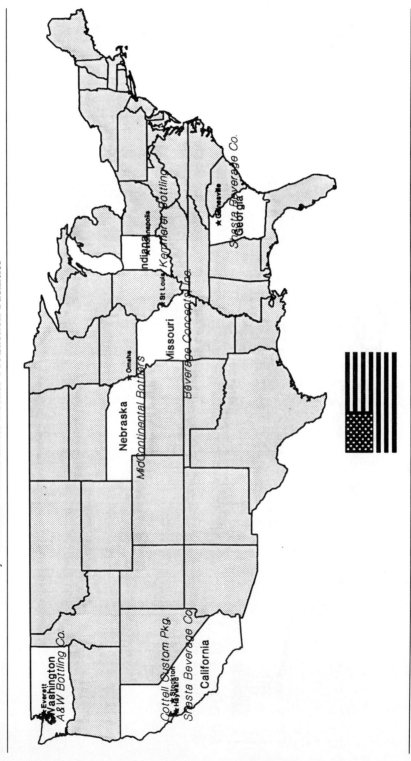

Annual U.S. Production Capacity = 30 million cases.
Source: Company data, 1992.

Canadian Bottler Production Facilities and Well Sites

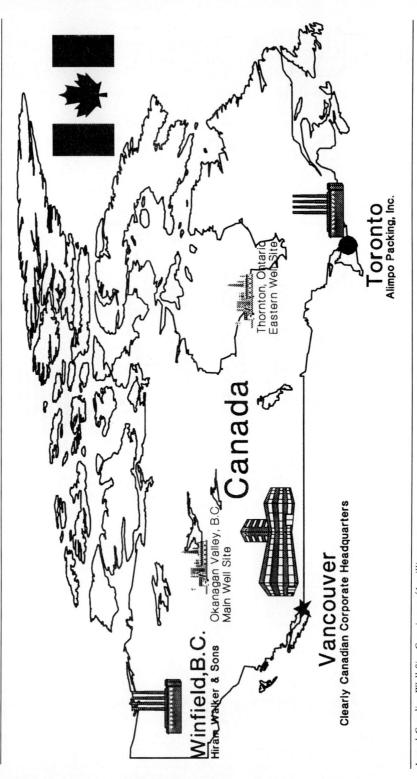

Annual Canadian Well Site Capacity = 41 million cases.
Annual Canadian Bottler Production Capacity = 11 million cases.
Source: Company data, 1992.

MIS system because of the costs associated with hardware, software, development, and training.

The executives at Clearly Canadian require a system to monitor operations and report on operational data. Specifically, they need to report on their current markets: retail markets, supermarkets, and international markets. They have no formalized method of measuring performance of distributors, bottlers, forecasting of inventory levels, or tracking the performance of their portfolio of beverage products. They require a process to streamline the reporting of their operational data results, i.e., volumes of cases sold, capacity versus demand, and revenue segmented by markets.

Financial Situation

Clearly Canadian's financial position is strong, with $15.5 million in cash on the balance sheet at the end of the June quarter and no long-term debt. The balance sheet status is remarkable given the routinely high introduction and promotion costs associated with a consumer success of this nature and the appetite for working capital typical of such a growth pattern.

Exhibit 3 presents the balance sheet, Exhibit 4 presents the income statements, and Exhibit 5 presents the geographic sales segmentation for the years 1990 to 1992. The company follows Canadian accounting principles. All figures are reported in Canadian dollars. Monetary assets and liabilities are translated into Canadian dollars at the balance sheet date rate of exchange and nonmonetary assets and liabilities at historical rates. Revenues and expenses are translated at appropriate transaction date rates except for depreciation, which is translated at historical rates. Inventories are stated at the lower of cost and net realizable value. Cost is generally determined on a first-in, first-out basis. Investments represent marketable securities and are valued at the lower of cost and quoted market value. Property, Plant, and Equipment are recorded at cost. Depreciation is provided as follows: Water Storage Facilities—10 percent on a straight-line basis; Equipment—20 percent–30 percent, on a diminishing balance basis; Leasehold Improvements—straight-line basis over a term of the lease. The company has available a $3 million line of credit with a chartered bank. A mortgage charge against certain real property of Clearly Canadian and a security interest upon all of the present and future property of the company is pledged as security for the line of credit. No borrowing against this line of credit was outstanding as of October 31, 1992.

Clearly Canadian recorded equivalent case sales of 14,451,954 for the first six months of 1992 compared with 6,164,496 for the same period last year. Clearly Canadian was able to improve on gross profit dollars per case for the six months ended June 30, 1992 to $1.57 per case compared with $1.19 for the same period in 1991.

On August 4, 1992, Clearly Canadian announced plans to raise US $35 million to US $45 million through a common-share issue to investors outside North America. The beverage production and marketing concern said it retained investment dealer Deacon Barclays de Zoete Wedd Ltd. to manage the offering in Europe. The shares will be offered at a price to be determined by the company and Deacon Barclays, an executive of Clearly Canadian said. The issue is subject to regulatory approval. Proceeds of the issue, which is expected to close in September 1992, will be used to finance future capital spending and for working capital.

Exhibit 3

Clearly Canadian Beverage Corp. Consolidated Balance Sheet
As of June 30, 1992, 1991 and 1990
(in Canadian Dollars)

	1990	1991	1992
Assets			
Current			
Cash	$ 140,895	$ 479,001	$15,507,002
Accounts receivable	4,499,569	16,263,794	31,870,531
Inventories	1,821,083	11,785,232	14,913,178
Prepaid expenses and deposits	218,966	465,460	593,824
Investments	104,412	—	—
	6,784,925	28,993,787	62,884,535
Property, Plant, and Equipment	1,210,594	3,201,208	3,858,589
	$ 7,995,519	$32,194,995	$66,743,124
Liabilities			
Current			
Accounts payable and accrued liabilities	$ 3,515,025	$15,161,437	$14,288,100
Current portion of investments	—	23,335	17,738
	3,515,025	15,184,772	14,305,838
Capital Leases	—	84,058	41,390
	$ 3,515,025	$15,268,830	$14,347,228
Shareholders' Equity			
Share Capital			
Issued and outstanding			
14,852,035 common shares without			
par value			
(1991 — 12,400,889)	22,978,765	28,528,448	39,058,928
(1990 — 10,895,884)			
Retained Earnings (Deficit)	(18,498,271)	(11,602,283)	5,760,854
	4,480,494	16,926,165	44,819,782
	$ 7,995,519	$32,194,995	$68,136,010

New Age Beverage Industry

Even bottled water cannot match the phenomenal growth being racked up by the fledgling New Age beverage category.

Underscoring the importance of New Age beverages, New York-based Beverage Marketing Corp. this fall published its second annual report on the category *New Age & Isotonic Beverages in the U.S. 1991*. The Beverage Marketing report establishes three basic criteria for New Age beverages. They must be:

1. Relatively new to the marketplace—the report tracks sales back to 1985.
2. Perceived by consumers as healthy, "riding a wave of goodwill," and allowing consumers to feel good about the products and themselves for drinking them.
3. Natural products free of artificial ingredients, preservatives, or flavors.

Exhibit 4

Clearly Canadian Beverage Corp. Consolidated Statements of Operations and Retained Earnings
For the Years Ended June 30, 1992, 1991, and 1990
(in Canadian Dollars)

	1990	1991	1992
Sales	$ 20,373,885	$ 71,408,918	$85,438,026
Cost of sales	16,449,786	57,556,490	66,193,226
Gross profit	3,924,099	13,842,428	19,244,800
Selling, administrative, and general expenses	4,971,196	6,869,242	6,184,048
Other (income) expenses	(247,894)	(93,866)	(456,138)
Net income (loss) for the year before income taxes	(1,416,962)	6,895,988	13,353,017
Income taxes			
Current	—	2,988,000	5,765,077
Utilization of prior year's income tax losses, Note 10	—	(2,988,000)	—
Net income (loss) for the year	(1,416,962)	6,895,988	7,587,940
Rated earnings (deficit), beginning of year	$(17,081,309)	$(18,498,271)	$ (1,827,086)
Retained earnings (deficit), end of year	$(18,498,271)	$(11,602,283)	$ 5,760,854
Basic earnings (loss) per share	$ (.16)	$ .59	$ .49

Exhibit 5
Geographic Sales Segmentation
For the years ended June 30, 1992, 1991, 1990

The company oeprates principally in the beverage industry and exports to various countries in the world. Export sales relative to these geographic segments are presented below:

	1990	1991	1992
U.S.A.	$13,654,107	$61,402,321	$73,464,741
Canada	6,279,626	8,733,097	10,440,526
Japan	347,731	572,600	695,467
Europe	92,421	700,900	837,292
Total	20,373,885	71,408,918	85,438,026

According to Beverage Marketing, three types of beverages meet these standards: sparkling juices, flavored waters, and natural sodas. Club sodas, unflavored seltzers, and sparkling and noncarbonated bottled waters are not included in the New Age grouping. None of these is classified as "new age" beverages because, like 100 percent juices, they are not new.

However, New Age drinks are expected to have an increasingly important impact on beverage consumption in years to come. Consumers are increasingly aware of artificial ingredients and preservatives in their beverage choices, and New Age beverages offer a healthy, yet satisfying, alternative. The likely entry of new major players capable of offering national distribution and advertising campaigns will also cultivate growth for this evolving market.

Several trends will contribute to popularizing flavored and unflavored bottled water in the coming years. Growing concern about tap water purity will spur domestic demand for bottled water. So too will greater health consciousness. Particularly in the U.S. market, as consumers continue to cut alcohol and sugar from their diets, reduced-calorie beverages and naturally flavored water will benefit.

Exhibit 6   **Demographics of the New Age Beverage Consumer 1992**

| | Flavored Sparkling Water/Seltzer, and Natural Soda | | | |
Classification	Total U.S. (millions)	Number of Users (millions)	User Incidence*	User Profile**
Total Adults	182.5	14.2	7.8%	100.0%
Males	87.1	6.4	7.4	45.3
Females	95.4	7.8	8.1	54.7
Age				
18–24	25.5	2.5	9.9	17.8
25–34	44.1	4.7	10.7	33.3
35–44	37.5	3.3	8.9	23.5
45–54	25.3	1.6	6.4	11.4
55–64	21.0	1.2	5.6	8.3
65 or older	28.9	0.8	2.8	5.8
Education				
Graduated college	35.3	3.5	9.8	24.4
Attended college	35.2	3.8	10.7	26.6
Graduated high school	70.9	4.8	6.8	34.0
Did not graduate high school	41.1	2.1	5.2	15.0
Employment				
Professional/manager	31.8	3.3	10.3	23.2
Technical/clerical/sales	39.6	3.6	9.1	25.5
Precision/craft	14.8	0.9	6.2	6.5
Other employed	39.0	2.7	7.0	19.4
Marital Status				
Single	40.2	4.1	10.3	29.1
Married	108.8	7.7	7.1	54.2

Noteworthy is the attempt of several alcoholic beverage companies to revive their moribund earnings by diversifying into bottled water.

Demand will also increase as domestic consumers become more accustomed to bottled water, perhaps viewing it one day as a staple, much as the French do who drink 26 gallons a year of it compared to Americans' six. Exhibit 6 provides a demographic analysis of the New Age beverage consumer.

Competition

The introduction of a similar beverage product by a larger international beverage company represents an unquantifiable risk to Clearly Canadian. Many companies have already introduced similar beverages without much success. Examples include Pepsi with $H_2OH!$, Coca-Cola with Clarte, McKesson with WallaRoo, and Seagrams with Soho. Many large companies spend $30–$40 million to roll out a product nationally; Clearly Canadian has been able to achieve its current success without any major television or ad campaigns.

Exhibit 6   *continued*

| | Flavored Sparkling Water/Seltzer, and Natural Soda | | | |
Classification	Total U.S. (millions)	Number of Users (millions)	User Incidence*	User Profile**
Divorced/separated/widowed	33.5	2.4	7.0%	16.6%
Parents	60.9	5.8	9.5	40.9
Ethnic Groups				
White	156.5	11.4	7.3	80.6
Black	20.5	2.0	9.8	14.2
Other	5.5	0.7	13.5	5.2
Geographical Area				
Northeast	38.6	2.8	7.3	19.9
Midwest	44.3	3.0	6.8	21.3
South	62.6	3.4	5.4	24.0
West	37.0	4.9	13.3	34.8
Income				
$60,000 or more	36.8	3.8	10.5	27.3
$50,000 or more	53.2	4.8	9.0	33.7
$40,000 or more	75.3	6.7	9.0	47.6
$30,000 or more	102.4	8.9	8.6	62.5
$30,000–$39,999	27.1	2.1	7.8	14.9
$20,000–$29,999	30.3	2.5	8.3	17.8
$10,000–$19,999	29.9	1.5	5.1	10.7
Under $10,000	19.9	1.3	6.4	9.0

Note: The demographics include both sparkling water flavored with 100 percent juices and essences.
* Usage in the last seven days.
**Some of the categories do not add up to 100 percent because of no responses or duplicate answers.
Source: Simmons Market Research Bureau: 1992 Study Media and Markets.

Overall, approximately 15 beverage companies worldwide produce and distribute "new age" beverages. Some of these major players include: New Era Beverage Co. (Sundance); Perrier Groups (Perrier, Poland Spring, Calistoga); Cadbury Schweppes (Canada Dry, Schweppes); Snapple Natural Beverage (Snapple); and Clearly Canadian Beverage Corp. (Clearly Canadian).

Coca-Cola Company

The Coca-Cola Bottling Co. of Philadelphia is adding Clearly Canadian to its distribution line of beverages. Joe Casey, the vice-president of marketing for Coca-Cola, indicated that the decision to add Clearly Canadian to its distribution system was based on Clearly's three-year sales performance in the United States. Unlike competitors Snapple, Mystic, and Best of Health, Casey said, "Clearly Canadian has the potential to be a category leader among light soft drinks," the main reason Coca-Cola Bottling chose to distribute the line. Coca-Cola Corporation says it has no current plans to come out with a similar product; but the company has repositioned FRESCA, a diet grapefruit soda, in new green bottles.

Recently a new marketing innovation gave the company a competitive edge with the introduction of talking vending machines, each costing over $3,000 and equipped with computerized voice synthesizers to converse with consumers. Other new designs included energy-efficient machines and vendors equipped with electronic games for play after purchase.

Perrier Group

The Perrier Group was the first company to introduce a sparkling water with an essence of fruit flavor into the American market on a national level. In 1985 a flavored Perrier brand was introduced and was immediately successful. Since that time many of its other regional domestic water brands have added line extensions with natural essence of fruit or have further extended selected lines to include sparkling or still flavored water products.

The Perrier Group has been on the cutting edge of several movements in the beverage industry, starting with its pioneering work in promoting an imported sparkling water into a much-sought-after symbol of urban vogue in the late 1970s and well into the 1980s. The group also added flavored essence, first to its flagship brand, and later to the Poland Spring and Calistoga lines. Arrowhead and Ozarka also appeared with flavored essences as line extensions. In early 1992 Calistoga introduced into northern California Calistoga, Country Orchard, a line of flavored noncarbonated juice-based products.

Perrier is slowly regaining the national distribution that it had before the 1990 product recall. Perrier's flavored line did not recover its vibrancy in 1991. In 1991 there continued to be distribution voids in the off-premise trade. The flavored products were the last to be reintroduced in late 1990 and early 1991. Wholesale dollar sales dropped to $10.6 million from 1990's $14.4 million. The overall Calistoga flavored line had relatively flat volume in 1991 at $34.8 million, down by 2.2 percent from 1990's $35.6 million (see Exhibit 7). In the case of Poland Spring, the flavored sparkling juice line is being phased out. Consumers have a mental picture of Poland Spring as a flat water, and the sparkling line has not

Exhibit 7
Top Ten New Age Brands Estimated Dollar Sales, 1986–1991
(Millions of Dollars)

Brand	Rank	Parent Company	Estimated Wholesale Volume[a]					
			1986	1987	1988	1989	1990	1991
Clearly Canadian	1	Clearly Canadian	—	—	$ 7.1	$ 16.2	$ 20.3	$ 71.4
Sundance	2	EverFresh Beverages, Inc.	$ 14.0	$ 35.0	75.0	80.0	66.5	55.0
Original NY Seltzer	3	Original NY Seltzer	60.0	100.0	95.0	85.0	55.0	44.0
Crystal Geyser	4	Crystal Geyser	3.0	5.0	12.2	18.7	34.0	39.0
Canada Dry	5	Cadbury Schweppes	10.0	24.0	29.5	34.5	35.6	36.7
Koala Springs	6	Koala Springs International	1.0	8.0	14.5	30.4	32.0	36.0
Snapple	7	Snapple Natural Beverages	3.5	6.0	9.5	16.0	20.8	35.0
Calistoga	8	Perrier Group	9.4	21.5	32.2	33.3	35.6	34.8
Tropicana Sparklers	9	Seagrams	—	—	—	—	15.0	30.0
Quibell	10	Quibell	—	—	—	—	12.4	19.0
Subtotal			$100.9	$199.5	$275.0	$314.1	$344.4	$456.9
All others			145.1	227.5	268.0	305.9	295.6	300.3
Total			$246.0	$427.0	$543.0	$620.0	$640.0	$757.2

[a]Sales volume includes *only* New Age beverage sales. Excluded are each brand's sales for unflavored sparkling and nonsparkling waters, regular sodas, iced teas, juices, juice drinks, etc.
Source: Beverage Marketing Annual Industry Survey.

proven to be a winner for the brand. The Arrowhead brand is strong in southern California and appears to be gaining market share at the expense of Evian in that area. Ozarka is strong in Texas and has continued to build its flavored water franchise in that state.

Each of the company's New Age flavored products has very different distribution patterns. The flavored products of Poland Spring are limited to New England and some distribution in New York, New Jersey, and Pennsylvania, plus the District of Columbia and Baltimore. Calistoga and Arrowhead are strong in northern and southern California, respectively, and Ozarka has its strength in Texas.

The Perrier New Age beverages have the resources of The Perrier Group and its French parent strongly behind these new ventures. With the recent acquisition of Source Perrier by Switzerland's Nestle, it is expected that the new owners will continue to support the New Age products that the American subsidiary has so successfully introduced. The Perrier Group has an extremely able group at its Greenwich, CT, U.S. headquarters. Ron Davis, president and CEO, and Kim Jeffrey, EVP and COO, have both had wide experience in the soft drink industry, and are seasoned executives of the bottled water industry.

EverFresh Beverages, Inc.

In February 1992 it was announced that EverFresh Beverages, Inc. had been formed, with James T. Pomroy as president and chief executive officer. The new company combines the former EverFresh USA and EverFresh Canada, previously owned by

John LaBatt Ltd. of Canada, and the New Era Beverage Company, whose prior owners were Guinness and Stroh Brewery. The new company will feature flavored sparkling juices and fruit-based drinks in both the United States and Canada. The New Age products marketed by EverFresh Beverages are Sundance Sparkling Juice and the EverFresh sparkling juice line.

EverFresh Sparkling Juice, introduced into the U.S. market in 1990, is a combination of slightly more than 70 percent fruit juice and the remainder sparkling mineral water. The brand contains no added sugar, fructose, artificial sweeteners, caffeine, preservatives, added color, or sodium. The flavors are: Summer Peach, Wild Blackberry, Pink Grapefruit, Orange Passion Fruit, Red Raspberry, Cranberry Raspberry, and Strawberry Kiwi.

Sundance was introduced in California in 1986, and expanded into additional markets in 1987 before going national in 1988. In 1991 it had wholesale sales of $55.0 million, down from $66.5 million in 1990, a 17.3 percent drop (see Exhibit 7). The product contains no added sugar or preservatives and is low in sodium. The last two years have witnessed steady sales declines for this brand. Several reasons have been given for these declines. The main reason was that the company elected to concentrate advertising, marketing, and promotional dollars in the major, most profitable markets and to allow distribution in secondary markets and low-priced warehouse outlets to be phased out.

Sundance was a target for all New Age beverages flooding the market in 1989 and thereafter. Whatever the New Age category, all natural sodas, sparkling juices, or flavored waters, Sundance was the brand to beat.

The 1990–1991 recession caused growth of the total category to slow. Additionally, there appeared to be some customer resistance to the higher cost of the sparkling juice category. In March of 1991 the company introduced two new flavors: Passion Fruit/Pineapple and Concord Twist.

The new company has complete national distribution with its New Age beverages. For Sundance, the distribution is concentrated in major markets across the country, with special emphasis on the large metropolitan areas of New York, Los Angeles, and Dallas. Sundance has its greatest concentration of sales in the retail trade. The EverFresh sparkling juice line has its greatest distribution strength in the Midwest. Leading states include Minnesota, Wisconsin, and Iowa, plus the Washington D.C./Baltimore areas. This product line relies heavily on cold-box distribution in quick-stop stores, as well as upscale supermarkets and gourmet food stores in urban and suburban stores and malls.

Cadbury Schweppes, Ltd.

Cadbury Schweppes has two entries in the flavored water segment of the New Age beverage market. These are line extensions under its Canada Dry and Schweppes lines. Canada Dry introduced its all-natural flavored water on the West Coast in 1986. The brand, as sparkling water, has less carbonation than does the seltzer product. This is also true for the Schweppes product. The Canada Dry flavored sparkling line had sales of $36.7 million in 1991. (See Exhibit 7.) Canada Dry Seltzer/Sparkling Water comes in nine flavors distributed throughout the country, but not all flavors in all markets. The flavors include: Original, Lemon/Lime,

Mandarin Orange, Raspberry, Black Cherry, Strawberry, Peach, Grapefruit, and Cranberry/Lime. The Schweppes Sparkling Water is also marketed as a seltzer in certain markets, such as New York. The brand has eight flavors in various stages of distribution. These flavors are: Original, Lemon, Lime, Lemon/Lime, Orange, Black Cherry, Wild Raspberry, and Peaches and Creme.

Cadbury Schweppes established separate distribution networks for its flavored sparkling water brands. Each brand's existing soft drink bottler network was beveraged for each flavored line extension.

Cadbury Schweppes has very strong financial resources. The company has made several acquisitions in the U.S. market, solidifying its place as a niche marketer. Through its U.K. parent company, it has sufficient monies to back its American ventures. John Carson is president of Cadbury Schweppes North America. He has a very knowledgeable staff, and the company has been making steady progress in its markets.

Snapple Natural Beverages Company

This regional company is based in the New York metropolitan area and until recently was privately owned. The company was founded by two brothers-in-law and a mutual friend. In 1990 it moved its headquarters to Valley Stream, Long Island, from Ridgewood, New York, a development that added considerable space to the headquarters operation. In its embryonic years, the company had fairly slow growth. All the growth was funded internally. However, in recent years its growth had accelerated and it has become a healthy business with strong consumer franchises in its base areas of the Northeast and the mid-Atlantic states, as well as a growing franchise in new areas as it rapidly expands distribution.

In 1991 Snapple's line of New Age products reached an estimated sales volume of $35.0 million, excluding the iced tea line. The company has products in all-natural sodas, sparkling flavored waters, and juice added to nonsparkling waters. In April 1992 Snapple brand's owners, the Unadulterated Food Corporation, was acquired by a newly formed corporate entity, Snapple Beverage Corporation, for an estimated $140.0 million. Thomas H. Lee Company, a successful investment firm, obtained 70 percent of the new entity, and Snapple's three founders control the remaining 30 percent.

In the New Age market, Snapple's all-natural soda line had seven flavors in 1991. These flavors were Lemon/Lime, Cherry/Lime, Orange, French Cherry, Passion Supreme, Raspberry, and Peach Melba. Cola, a flavor that was deleted from the line in 1990, was brought back in 1992 because the distributors (and presumably their customers) demanded it. Flavors added in 1992 were Jamaican Ginger Beer and Strawberry. In addition, the Orange flavor was reformulated.

Included in the all-natural soda category are the company's 100 percent natural seltzers, which have four regular and four diet flavors. These products are flavored with all-natural essences, no caffeine, and the diet products contain Nutrasweet. The nonsparkling juice line has 10 percent pure fruit juice and 90 percent nonsparkling water. In 1991, Pink Lemonade was added to a line that included Fruit Punch, Grapeade, Lemonade Orangeade, and Kiwi Strawberry. The company is planning on adding a few more tropical flavors to this line.

Snapple's flavored seltzer line is distributed only in the Northeast, where there is both recognition of seltzers and appreciation of their value. The brand continued to be strongest in the Boston, New York, and Washington, D.C., corridor, with some sales spilling over into the suburbs of these cities. The rest of the product lines have reached distribution in all 50 states.

Seagram Beverage Company, Inc.

Just out from Seagram is the New Age product, 2 Calorie Quest, a two-calorie flavored mineral water that contains Nutrasweet. Seagram has had the brand in testing for two years. The brand was introduced in four test markets: Sacramento, CA; Atlanta, GA; Columbus, OH; and Portland, ME. 2 Calorie Quest is sold in four flavors: Black Cherry, Raspberry, and two proprietary flavors—Peach Citrus and Tangerine Line. It is packaged in a unique spiral-shaped bottle of clear glass and has an attractive pear-shaped label. It also has grooves near the base to make it easier to hold. It is priced competitively to Clearly Canadian, with a four pack of ten-ounce bottles retailing for about $2.99 and a 23-ounce bottle for approximately $1.49. Advertising features Howie Mandel with the theme "Amazing Taste." Both radio and television were used in the four test markets.

In September 1990 Seagram's Tropicana Products, Inc. launched Tropicana Juice Sparklers nationally, after a successful test market in Maine. The brand is a blend of juices with "just a touch of carbonation" and was Tropicana's first entry into the New Age category. The Tropicana Juice Sparklers' introduction was backed by a reported $13.5 million advertising campaign. The product is marketed in four flavors: Tropical Orange, Golden Grapefruit, Cranberry Orchard, and Wild Berries.

The product is packaged in 10-ounce and 23-ounce glass containers and is priced at $2.59 per four pack of 10-ounce bottles or $1.29 for the 23-ounce bottle. In January 1991 Seagram's experienced a recall of this brand after it was found that pressure was building up in some glass bottles and causing them to explode on grocery or pantry shelves. The pressure was thought to have been caused by a suspected contaminant from a chemical cleaning fluid. The company took immediate steps to remove all existing stock from the nation's grocery shelves and to alert consumers to bring back any bottles that they might have in their homes. By February 1991 most of the distribution network was reestablished and the product was once again selling well. The brand is natural and follows the distribution of its sister brands. Tropicana moved all of its brands into food service, convenience stores, and military food stores in 1991.

With Seagram's backing, Tropicana is part of a well-financed multinational corporation that gives its brands strong support. Seagram has invested heavily in R&D functions. Tropicana sparklers have been backed by strong advertising budgets since they were introduced.

In September 1991 Tropicana announced the resignations of Robert Soran, president, and George Sulanas, executive vice-president, finance and procurement. In January 1992 William G. Pietersen, president of the Seagram Beverage Group based in Montreal, who had been temporarily filling the job, was formally named as president.

PepsiCo Inc.

PepsiCo Inc. has introduced a clear, colorless cola called "Crystal Pepsi" in three test markets. The new cola is sold alongside traditional Pepsi in Dallas; Providence, RI; and throughout Colorado.

Crystal Pepsi is priced at regular cola prices. That is often less than two-thirds the cost of current new age drinks, which cost from 89 cents to more than $1. The new product made its debut in both clear bottles and silver cans and has 130 calories in a 12-ounce serving, compared with the 150 calories in the usual Pepsi. It touts having low sodium, all-natural flavorings, and no preservatives, which is not different from the regular Pepsi. The new product's main appeal is image, according to beverage analysts. With the can and bottle label tinted blue, the product is designed to convey "good health, purity, and icy cold water," says Tom Pirko, president of Bevmark Inc., a consulting firm.

Pepsi hopes Crystal will boost sales among less-frequent cola drinkers, or those who might now be trying new age products in addition to drinking cola. Clear sodas tend to appeal to an older crowd, 21 to 25 years old, compared with regular colas, which are most popular among 14- to 21-year-olds, says Michael Bellar, president of Beverage Marketing Corp.

Crystal and similar entries into the market by other big companies are expected to steamroll the current new age category and may turn the niche into a mainline brand. Pepsi, in its new venture with Ocean Spray, is also working on a sparkling fruit juice called "Splash," and the beverage maker is expected to come out with a line of fruit flavored clear beverages patterned after Crystal.

Pepsi has been tenacious in its crusade to dominate market share in the fast-food and vending machine markets. In 1990 Pepsi entered into a joint venture nondisclosure agreement with American Business Computers, a NASDAQ listed company, to develop a state-of-the-art beverage dispensing machine for its fast-food markets. The objective of the joint venture was to increase the dispensing speed of its current fast-food configurations, as well as the quality. Pepsi also worked closely with Dixie Narco, a premier vending machine manufacturer from West Virginia, in developing a vending machine for its 12-ounce can beverage line.

References

Michael E. Porter. *Competitive Advantage.* New York: The Free Press, 1985.

Beverage World, 150 Great Neck Road, Great Neck, NY 11021.

Beverage Industry, 1 East First Street, Duluth, MN 55802.

Beverage Marketing Corp., 850 Third Avenue, New York, NY 10022.

Clearly Canadian Beverage Corp., 1700–355 Burrared Street, Vancouver, B.C., Canada V6C 268. Phone: (604) 683–0312.

John F. Rockart, David W. DeLong. *Executive Support Systems.* Homewood, Illinois: Business One Irwin, 1988.

J. Fred Weston, Kwang S. Chung, Susan E. Hoag. *Mergers, Restructuring and Corporate Control.* Englewood Cliffs, NJ: Prentice-Hall, 1990.

Gretchen Morgensen. "Clearly Fuzzy." *Forbes,* November 11, 1991, 132.

C A S E • *Bulldog Pizza and Spirits*

Ken Gardner, University of South Carolina
John Leslie, University of South Carolina
James J. Chrisman, University of Calgary

"I really don't know what I'm going to do Jim," said Stan Hanson, owner and general manager of Bulldog Pizza and Spirits, a popular student bar and restaurant in Athens, Georgia. "I opened this place four years ago and it's finally beginning to show a profit. But when the drinking age goes up to 20 this September, I stand to lose a lot of business which I may not be able to replace."

"I don't know what to tell you Stan," commented the customer. "Maybe you should just sell out now before everyone starts to panic and the value of your business drops."

"I know, I know. I've thought of that," Hanson responded. "I hate to give up without a fight though. There just has to be some other alternative."

Hanson turned away and filled a pitcher of beer for some customers. It was the night of May 8, 1985, and through the local news on the bar's TV, Hanson had been reminded that the Georgia State Legislature had recently passed a bill that would raise the legal drinking age in the state from 19 to 21. This change was going to occur in two stages. The drinking age would first be raised to 20 in September 1985, and then to 21 in September 1986. Although Hanson had known this for several months, hearing the news again disturbed him.

Nearly 50 percent of Hanson's business came from the sale of alcoholic beverages, and of this amount, approximately 60 percent was to individuals under the age of 21. Most of these customers were students at the University of Georgia which was located within walking distance of the restaurant. The potential 30 percent drop in overall revenue was an obvious concern for Hanson. However, he was also worried that the change in the legal drinking age would cause a loss of food revenue; if students under 21 could not drink, they might stop eating at his restaurant too. Although the full impact of the change in the drinking age would not be felt for 18 months, Hanson knew he had to start considering alternative plans. Bulldog Pizza and Spirits had recorded a small profit in both 1983 and 1984 and Hanson had thought that it was "turning the corner" profit-wise (see Exhibits 1 and 2 for financial information). A 30 percent drop in sales, however, could be too much to take. Hanson knew that he had to find a way to replace the anticipated loss of revenue, or else risk losing his business.

Background

Bulldog Pizza and Spirits began operation in April 1981 under the ownership of Stan Hanson. Hanson had considerable experience in the restaurant and bar business dating back to 1974 when he underwent an extensive nine-month training program for a large national chain of family-style restaurants. Upon completion of the training program, Hanson operated one of the chain's franchised restaurants for two years.

Exhibit 1	**Bulldog Pizza and Spirits: Income Statements (1983–1984)**

		1984		1983
Sales		$415,784		$344,000
Food	$220,332			
Alcohol	186,354			
Machines	9,009			
Other	89			
Cost of Goods Sold		150,529		127,000
Food	$ 75,270			
Alcohol	68,225			
Machines	4,719			
Other	2,315			
Gross Margin		$265,255		$217,000
Operating Expenses		$256,239		$212,700
Hourly wages			58,800	
Administrative salaries			28,000	
Payroll taxes			8,100	
Rent			13,000	
Advertising and promotion			14,700	
Supplies			12,700	
Utilities			21,000	
Telephone			5,000	
Automobile			1,800	
Repairs and maintenance			2,100	
Spoilage			1,600	
Insurance			6,000	
Taxes and licenses			7,500	
Legal			2,200	
Bank			4,700	
Interest			11,300	
Depreciation (equipment)			10,300	
Miscellaneous			3,900	
Net Income (before taxes)		$ 9,016		$ 4,300

This experience, and his desire to own his own restaurant, led Hanson to become a partner in two distinctly different restaurant operations: a French restaurant and a pizza operation. After two years, disagreements among the partners caused Hanson to sell out of the businesses, although both had been profitable. With a new partner, Hanson launched another venture in Florida called Sunshine Pizza. Although the restaurant was successful, after a year and a half Hanson began looking for a suitable location to start his own restaurant.

After conducting demographic studies on several southern cities, Hanson selected Athens, Georgia, as a prime location in which to open a restaurant. Hanson and his wife Elise soon moved to Athens and purchased an existing establishment.

Exhibit 2
Bulldog Pizza and Spirits: Balance Sheet,
February 28, 1985

Assets:			Liabilities:		
Current:			Current:		
Cash on hand	$ 250.00		Accounts payable	$ 8,011.00	
Petty cash	200.00		FICA payable	1,282.00	
Bank	(5,175.00)		Federal withholding	309.00	
Returned checks	661.00		State withholding	65.00	
Accounts receivable	100.00		Sales tax payable	1,308.00	
Inventory	6,896.00		Taxes payable	237.00	
Deposits (utilities)	1,460.00		Accumulated state tax	380.00	
Prepaid interest	697.00		Notes payable	10,880.00	
		$ 5,089.00			$22,472.00
Fixed:			Long-Term:		
Furniture and equipment	93,414.00		Notes payable	160,000.00	
Less accumulated			Loan	(110,056.00)	$49,944.00
depreciation	(71,164.00)				
Building	56,253.00		Equity:		
Less accumulated			Common stock	500.00	
depreciation	(22,032.00)		Paid-in capital	(444.00)	
Signs	1,526.00		Retained earnings	(3,451.00)	
Less accumulated					(3,395.00)
depreciation	(1,258.00)				$69,021.00
Leasehold improvements	11,686.00				
Less accumulated					
depreciation	(4,493.00)				
		63,932.00			
		$69,021.00			

It had been a popular student bar, located just off the main campus of the University of Georgia (UGA). Hanson renovated the old building extensively and in April 1981, Bulldog Pizza and Spirits opened for business.

Bulldog Pizza and Spirits was directly across the street from three of the school's main dormitories, which together housed over 3,000 students. Hanson thought that the students would find the combination of good pizza and spirits attractive, and since its opening the business had developed a reputation as a student hangout. Hanson also believed that the restaurant had built a reputation for quality pizza. Bulldog's sales had increased moderately each year, and until threatened by the change in the drinking age, Hanson had been confident that the future of the business was bright.

Athens, Georgia

Located in northeast Georgia, about 65 miles to the east of Atlanta, Athens was the principal city of Clarke County (see Exhibits 3 and 4 for a demographic profile of Clarke County). In 1983 the median household income in Athens was over

Exhibit 3
Population by Age and Sex, Clarke County, 1984

Age Group	Male	Female	Total	Percentage of Total
0–5	3,014	2,970	5,984	7.8
6–11	2,440	2,433	4,873	6.4
12–17	2,687	2,611	5,298	6.9
18–24	10,180	10,507	20,687	27.0
25–34	7,513	7,086	14,599	19.1
35–44	3,757	4,257	8,014	10.5
45–54	2,518	2,824	5,342	7.0
55–64	2,250	2,865	5,115	6.7
Over 65	2,224	4,364	6,588	8.6
Total	36,583	39,917	76,500	100.0

Exhibit 4
Households by Effective Buying Incomes, Clarke County, 1984

EBI Dollars	Number of Households	Percentage of Total
Under 5,000	3,469	12.2
5,000–9,999	4,232	14.8
10,000–14,999	4,188	14.7
15,000–19,999	3,736	13.1
20,000–24,999	2,927	10.3
25,000–34,999	4,184	14.7
35,000–49,999	3,686	12.9
Over 50,000	2,078	7.3
	28,500	100.0%

Median EBI = $18,068.

$18,000. Residents of Athens spent over $45 million eating and drinking out in 1983.

One of the reasons Hanson had chosen Athens was the presence of the University of Georgia's main campus. The campus was an important part of life in Athens. The UGA student population was over 25,000, while the population of the entire city was only about 45,000. Due to the large student body, the 18- to 24-year-old age group was the largest population subgroup in the city.

The population of Clarke County was expected to increase 7.6 percent by 1988. On the other hand, the student population at UGA was expected to remain relatively stable for the next three years. The student population was tightly controlled by the University's admissions policy and the change in enrollment was expected to be small from year to year. Exhibit 5 provides the 1980–1984 enrollment by class at UGA.

Exhibit 5   Enrollment at the University of Georgia, 1980–1984

Class	1980	1981	1982	1983	1984	Historical Percentage Male
Freshman	3,298	4,393	3,904	3,662	4,028	44.9
Sophomore	3,771	4,067	4,552	4,559	4,352	47.1
Junior	3,775	4,325	4,190	4,183	4,108	50.0
Senior	4,469	4,357	4,663	4,443	4,786	51.8
Graduate	4,163	4,319	4,504	4,671	4,568	49.8
Professional	1,603	1,577	1,570	2,102	2,172	47.0
Other	2,391	2,603	2,526	1,422	1,171	NA
Total	23,470	25,641	25,909	25,402	25,185	

NA = Information not available.

The economy of Athens was heavily dependent upon the student population. Virtually every business in the city was affected to some extent by the seasonality of the academic year. The student population dropped considerably during the summer months and in December. The holiday sales that stores in other areas traditionally relied upon during December were severely reduced in Athens because of the number of students who returned home for the holidays.

Industry Trends

The short-term outlook for eating and drinking establishments was positive. Americans spent 37 percent of their food dollars at restaurants in 1984, and industry sales had increased 55 percent since 1979 (*U.S. Industrial Outlook*). Furthermore, sales were projected to increase by another 10 percent in 1985 as restaurants continued to expand and diversify their menus. Salad bars and dishes with chicken and fish were the most popular menu additions.

Exhibits 6 and 7 provide common size income statements and balance sheets, respectively, for restaurants and drinking places with assets of less than $1 million in 1984. Exhibit 8 shows selected 1985 financial ratios for these businesses.

Despite favorable sales trends, increasing legal pressure had been placed on owners of establishments which sold alcoholic beverages. Georgia state law held the owner of an establishment liable for damages caused by a patron (e.g., drunk driving accidents) if it was shown that the patron had become intoxicated at the owner's establishment. The enforcement of such laws was becoming more strict, largely due to the influence of groups such as Mothers Against Drunk Driving (MADD), and Students Against Drunk Driving (SADD). An establishment found guilty in a case involving an intoxicated driver could be fined, lose its license to sell alcohol, and even face a civil lawsuit. Furthermore, the number of these actions was increasing.

There were, however, steps that could be taken to reduce the likelihood of involvement in legal actions. The most common precaution was the purchase of a

---

Exhibit 6
Average Common Size Income Statements for Restaurants and Drinking Places in the U.S. with Assets of Less Than $1 Million in 1985

	Restaurants (N = 500)	Drinking Places (N = 38)
Sales	100.0%	100.0%
Cost of goods sold	44.4%	39.8%
Gross profit	55.5%	60.2%
Operating expenses	50.6%	55.1%
Other expenses	2.2%	2.5%
Net profit before taxes	2.7%	2.6%

Source: Robert Morris Associates, *1985 Annual Statement Studies.*

Exhibit 7
Average Common Size Income Statements for Restaurants and Drinking Places in the U.S. with Assets of Less Than $1 Million in 1985

	Restaurants (N = 500)	Drinking Places (N = 38)
Assets:		
Cash and equivalents	11.1%	10.7%
Trade receivables (net)	4.1%	2.0%
Inventory	7.4%	11.4%
All other current assets	2.7%	4.2%
Total current assets	25.3%	28.3%
Fixed assets (net)	58.6%	54.9%
Intangibles (net)	4.5%	6.4%
All other noncurrent assets	11.6%	10.4%
Total assets	100.0%	100.0%
Liabilities and Owners' Equity:		
Current liabilities	39.6%	35.5%
Long-term debt	32.6%	32.7%
All other noncurrent liabilities	2.5%	1.1%
Total liabilities	74.7%	69.3%
Owners' equity (net worth)	25.3%	30.7%
Total liabilities + owners' equity	100.0%	100.0%

Source: Robert Morris Associates, *1985 Annual Statement Studies.*

Exhibit 8
Financial Ratios for Restaurants and Drinking Places in the U.S. with Assets of Less Than $1 Million in 1985

Ratios	Restaurants			Drinking Places		
	Upper Quartile	Median	Lower Quartile	Upper Quartile	Median	Lower Quartile
Current	1.3	0.6	0.3	1.7	0.8	0.3
Quick	0.8	0.4	0.1	0.7	0.3	0.2
Cost of sales/inventory	46.9	27.4	17.5	37.3	19.3	12.0
Sales/working capital	62.8	−30.3	−10.4	18.6	−60.8	−10.1
Asset turnover	4.9	3.4	2.1	3.8	2.2	1.5
Return on equity (%)	66.0	24.4	3.0	43.7	22.5	0.7
Return on assets (%)	17.8	6.7	−0.7	15.7	4.9	−1.5

Source: Robert Morris Associates, *1985 Annual Statement Studies.*

liquor liability insurance policy which protected the owner from civil suits. The cost of such policies was rising dramatically, however, because of the increase in the number of cases. In many instances the cost of the policy was so high that the establishment chose to operate without any insurance. This practice was risky though, because one lawsuit could potentially bankrupt a small restaurant as well as ruin its owner.

Local Competition

Competition in the restaurant and bar business in Athens was intense in early 1985. There were over 130 eating and drinking establishments in the city, all of which competed with Bulldog Pizza and Spirits to varying degrees. Bulldog Pizza and Spirits had a bar upstairs, a restaurant downstairs, and offered pizza delivery. Therefore, it competed with area restaurants, bars, and food delivery operations. Exhibit 9 shows a breakdown of the restaurants and bars in Athens by number of employees. Exhibit 10 provides pizza and alcohol prices for selected competitors in 1984.

Competing Pizza Restaurants—Eat-In

Although Bulldog Pizza and Spirits offered chicken, sandwiches, and a variety of snacks, most of its food revenue came from pizza sales. Its primary food competitors, therefore, were the eight pizza restaurants (not including their satellite stores) in the city. These included national chain stores like Pizza Hut and Pizza Inn, and local establishments such as Bianca's, Enterprise, Georgieo's, and Hill's.

Located only a block away, Enterprise Pizza was perhaps Bulldog's closest pizza competitor. Enterprise catered to an older crowd, offered a wide variety of food, and served inexpensive draft beer. It did not have a liquor license, although it had recently applied for one. Enterprise was also planning to remodel its facility slightly in anticipation of the changes in the drinking age to further appeal to the older crowd.

Competing Pizza Restaurants—Delivery

In addition to the more traditional, sit-down establishments there were two major pizza delivery operations, Domino's and Pizza Perfect. Although most pizza restaurants in Athens offered delivery, these two operations were unique because delivery was their specialty; neither competitor provided space for in-store dining.

Exhibit 9   Number of Establishments by Employment Size Class

		Number of Employees						
	Total	1–4	5–9	10–19	20–49	50–99	100–249	250–499
Eating and drinking places	134	33	20	29	45	6	1	0
Eating places	121	27	16	27	44	6	1	0
Drinking places	13	6	4	2	1	0	0	0

Source: *County Business Patterns,* Georgia, 1982, Department of Commerce.

Exhibit 10
Pizza and Beer Prices of Competing
Restaurants and Bars

	Small Cheese Pizza	Large Cheese Pizza	Pitchers of Beer
Bulldog Pizza and Spirits	$4.50	$8.40	$3.00–3.50
Bianca's	4.75	8.00	3.50
Enterprise	4.85	6.95	2.25
Carter's	4.20	8.20	2.25–3.00
Domino's	5.25	7.75	3.25
Pizza Perfect	5.90	8.45	3.75

Domino's was a nationally franchised operation which had established the trend towards faster delivery service with its guarantee that customers would get "hot pizza in less than 30 minutes" or the pizza would be free. With its reputation for fast service, Domino's had become the leader in pizza delivery nationwide, although the quality of its pizza was generally considered average. The Domino's store in Athens took advantage of the chain's strong national advertising and kept its costs low by using centrally purchased materials.

Competing Bars

Since many people went to Bulldog Pizza and Spirits primarily to drink, it also competed with other local bars and nightclub operations, such as Uncle John's, MacDougall's, the White Rabbit, the Downtown Bar and Grill, and Harley D's. These operations served alcohol and light snack food, rather than full meals. MacDougall's, White Rabbit, Downtown, and Harley D's also provided live musical entertainment on the weekends to attract customers.

Although all of these bars would be affected by the change in the drinking age, few had formulated definite plans for the future. The managers of MacDougall's and Uncle John's, for instance, were "just sitting back and waiting to see what happens," and "didn't intend to change anything." On the other hand, nightclubs such as the White Rabbit had toyed with various ideas, including starting an "all ages" club which would not serve alcohol, and changing the entertainment format to attract an older crowd.

Bulldog's closest bar competitor was Uncle John's. Located two blocks up the street from Bulldog, Uncle John's employed 13 part-time employees, including 12 bartenders and a janitor. Uncle John's catered to the campus's "Greek" crowd; 85 percent of its business came from fraternities and sororities. Approximately 60 percent of its customers were under 21, and about 90 percent of its revenues came from the sale of beer and liquor. Beside alcohol, Uncle John's offered its customers a limited menu of "snack" foods, a jukebox, and a large variety of video games.

According to its owners, the bar had enjoyed its most profitable year in 1984. Although Uncle John's sales were still somewhat lower than Bulldog's, they had doubled over the previous year. Its before-tax profits were also considerably greater than Bulldog's. Low overhead, a strong regular clientele, an expanded product line, and daily drink specials were among the factors to which the owners attributed their success.

Restaurant and Bar Operations

In addition to the pizza, Bulldog Pizza and Spirits offered chicken fingers (also very popular), a variety of sandwiches, french fries, and snacks such as nachos, fried vegetables, and potato skins. Hanson had also considered adding hamburgers to the menu. Exhibit 11 shows Bulldog's menu items and prices.

In late 1984 the restaurant began offering a lunchtime buffet featuring "all-you-can-eat" pizza for a single price. Hanson believed that the buffet had been successful in increasing lunch business. He wanted to try the same idea to attract dinner business, and had recently started an all-you-can-eat pizza and salad special between 5:30 p.m. and 7:30 p.m. Since it had been offered for only one month it was too early to determine if the dinner buffet would increase sales as the lunch buffet had.

The bar offered a large selection of alcoholic beverages. Draft and bottled beer were available, as well as wine, liqueurs, a wide variety of spirits, and specialty

---

Exhibit 11 **Bulldog Pizza and Spirits: Menu Items and Prices**

Salad Bar $2.75 ($1.25 with meal)
Lunch Pizza Buffet $3.25

Snacks

Nachos	2.75	Chicken Fingers	3.50
Bean Nachos	2.95	Sandwiches:	3.25
Mucho Nachos	3.25	Smoked Ham	
Fried Veggies	2.25	Chicken	
Potato Skins	3.50	Meatball	
French Fries	.85		

Pizza	Cheese	Extra Toppings	Bulldog Special*	Vegetarian Special**
Thick Crust:				
Small (9")	4.50	0.85	7.05	6.20
Medium (12")	6.40	0.95	9.25	8.30
Large (14")	8.40	1.05	11.55	10.50
Thin Crust:				
Small (12")	4.75	0.85	8.15	6.45
Large (16")	7.70	1.05	11.90	9.80

Soft Drinks, Coffee, Tea, and Milk   0.45

*Includes six toppings.
**Includes four toppings.

Exhibit 12
Bulldog Pizza and Spirits: Alcohol Prices for the
Upstairs Bar

Wine	$1.25/Glass
Draft Beer (16 oz.)	1.00/Glass
	3.00–3.50/Pitcher
Bottle Beer:	
Budweiser	1.35
Miller Lite	1.35
Michelob/Light	1.60
Imports	1.85
Special Drinks:	
Frozen Margarita	2.50
Daquiri	2.50
Pina Colada	2.50
Long Island Tea	3.00
Shooters	1.75–2.50
Bar Brand Highballs	1.75
Bar Brand Cocktails	2.00
Canadian Club, Seagrams, etc.	2.25
Jack Daniels, Crown Royal, etc.	2.50
Chivas, Grand Marnier	2.75

---

drinks, such as Long Island tea and shooters. Exhibit 12 shows Bulldog's alcohol
items and prices.

Facilities

Bulldog Pizza and Spirits had a seating capacity of approximately 250. This capacity
was divided among the three sections of the restaurant; the downstairs restaurant,
the upstairs bar, and the outdoor deck.

The restaurant was located on the first floor and could seat approximately 100
people. The second floor housed the main bar and had a capacity of 80. Food items
ordered upstairs were prepared in the downstairs kitchen and transported to the
second floor via a dumbwaiter. The outdoor deck, which could accommodate about
70 people, was a popular addition to the business. It was used frequently by
customers from late April through early October.

Delivery

Bulldog Pizza and Spirits also delivered its pizza, chicken fingers, and sandwiches
to the immediate area. The primary customers for this service were the students
who lived on or very near campus. Hanson felt it was necessary to offer delivery
in order to compete with the other delivery stores. He had advertised the delivery
service in local student papers and through flyers to generate more delivery business.
Although he felt the delivery service was doing all right, he had never separated
the sales and costs of the delivery operation from the overall restaurant's.

Food Sales and Costs

Pizza was Bulldog's most popular item, accounting for around 55 percent of total food sales. Exhibit 13 provides average pizza sales breakdowns between January and April 1982–1985.

Although Bulldog's pizza prices had risen twice since 1981 (see Exhibit 14), they were competitive with other Athens restaurants. In 1985 a small cheese pizza cost $4.50, while a large cheese pizza was $8.40. These prices put Bulldog in the medium to high bracket among competing pizza restaurants. Hanson justified the higher prices because he felt the quality of his pizza was superior to his competitors'. Since pizza was Bulldog's most popular food item, Hanson had worked hard to develop and maintain the quality of his pizza. After four years in business, Hanson felt that Bulldog's reputation for quality had begun to spread.

The cost of goods sold for pizza was approximately 28 percent of sales. The cost of goods sold for food overall was usually about 35 percent of sales. Food costs had been relatively stable and Hanson believed they would remain so for at least

Exhibit 13

Bulldog Pizza and Spirits: Pizza Sales Breakdowns, January through April (1982–1985 Average)

Percentage of Unit Sales Volume

	Total	Bulldog Special*	Vegetarian**	Cheese	Average Number of Toppings per Cheese Pizza
Small	51.28	7.02	0.46	43.80	1.346
Medium	34.14	6.04	0.26	27.84	1.255
Large	14.58	2.56	0.20	11.82	1.656
Total	100.00%				

*Includes six toppings.
**Includes four toppings.

	1982	1983	1984	1985
Dollar sales	$51,834	$51,561	$51,023	$36,826
Average price	$6.52	$6.68	$6.68	$7.20

Exhibit 14

Bulldog Pizza and Spirits: Pizza Price Changes, September 1981–April 1985

	Cheese			Bulldog Special			Vegetarian			Toppings		
	9/81	8/82	6/84	9/81	8/82	6/84	9/81	8/82	6/84	9/81	8/82	6/84
Small	$4.10	4.10	4.50	6.35	6.65	7.05	5.61	5.81	6.20	.75	.85	.85
Medium	5.81	5.81	6.40	8.35	8.65	9.25	7.51	7.71	8.30	.85	.95	.95
Large	7.61	7.61	8.40	10.46	10.76	11.56	9.51	9.71	10.50	.95	1.05	1.05

the next year. Exhibit 15 gives a breakdown of sales and cost of goods sold by food item for the last 15 months of business.

Alcohol Sales and Costs

Hanson felt that Bulldog's alcohol prices were competitive with other bars catering largely to students, such as MacDougall's and Uncle John's. The cost of goods sold for alcohol was slightly less than 40 percent of sales (see Exhibit 16). Hanson did not foresee any dramatic increases in prices from his alcohol distributors.

Hanson held a liquor liability policy that was due to expire in July 1985. He was currently paying about $750 per year for the policy and was concerned that the premium would rise at renewal. He had heard of other restaurants of similar size having to pay three to four times this amount.

Sales Fluctuations

Exhibit 17 provides monthly sales figures for Bulldog Pizza and Spirits from April 1981 through March 1985. Sales were the lowest in June, July, August, and

---

Exhibit 15   Bulldog Pizza and Spirits: Sales and Cost of Goods Sold by Food Item, January 1984–March 1985

| | Sales | | | | Cost of Goods Sold | |
	Pizza	Finger Food	Sandwiches	Other Food, Beverages*	Total Food	Total COGS
January, 84	$ 12,918	NA	NA	NA	$ 21,984	$ 8,284
February, 84	13,163	NA	NA	NA	22,785	7,473
March, 84	13,398	NA	NA	NA	22,311	8,133
April, 84	11,543	NA	NA	NA	21,435	7,420
May, 84	12,191	6,818	1,136	1,940	22,085	7,466
June, 84	8,298	3,475	928	1,169	13,870	4,758
July, 84	6,678	1,755	447	651	9,531	3,369
August, 84	7,215	2,093	506	760	10,574	3,814
September, 84	14,272	6,999	2,040	2,452	25,763	7,240
October, 84	12,293	6,822	1,729	2,056	22,900	8,159
November, 84	10,710	5,575	1,309	1,587	19,181	6,551
December, 84	3,953	2,598	693	669	7,913	2,603
Total 1984	$126,632	NA	NA	NA	$220,332	$75,270
January, 85	$ 10,884	$ 6,005	$1,436	NA	NA	$ 7,546
February, 85	9,022	5,627	1,207	NA	NA	6,200
March, 85	8,860	5,493	1,208	NA	NA	5,759
Total first quarter 1985	$28,766	$17,125	$3,851	NA	NA	$19,505

*Does not include alcohol.
NA = Information not available.

Exhibit 16
Bulldog Pizza and Spirits: Alcohol Sales and Cost of Goods Sold, January 1984–March 1985

	Sales	Cost of Goods Sold
January, 84	$ 12,451	$ 4,462
February, 84	13,323	4,605
March, 84	16,489	6,021
April, 84	19,332	6,526
May, 84	22,806	7,977
June, 84	10,325	4,507
July, 84	9,981	4,101
August, 84	10,564	4,511
September, 84	21,351	7,517
October, 84	25,090	8,893
November, 84	19,372	6,869
December, 84	5,270	2,236
Total 1984	$186,354	$68,225
January, 85	$ 21,786	$ 8,637
February, 85	18,247	6,928
March, 85	18,241	7,064
Total first quarter 1985	$ 58,274	$22,629

Exhibit 17
Bulldog Pizza and Spirits: Monthly Sales (Dollars in Thousands)

	1981	1982	1983	1984	1985
January		42.0	42.5	34.0	40.0
February		34.0	30.0	35.0	34.0
March		31.5	32.5	38.0	34.0
April	25.0	33.0	34.0	41.0	
May	27.0	33.0	33.0	43.0	
June	21.0	22.0	19.0	23.0	
July	15.0	14.0	11.0	19.0	
August	15.0	16.0	14.0	20.5	
September	33.0	40.0	34.0	44.5	
October	37.0	48.0	41.0	46.0	
November	25.0	30.0	32.0	37.0	
December	18.0	16.0	15.0	13.0	
Average	21.0	29.9	28.0	32.8	36.0

December, when there were few students on campus. In 1984 summer sales accounted for only 16 percent of total annual sales and were about evenly split between food and alcohol. Hanson had considered closing the restaurant during the summer, but was not sure if this was a good idea.

Sales were highest from September to November. High sales during this period were due to the return of the students and to the college football season. The University of Georgia football team was very successful and attracted crowds of over 70,000 when they played in Athens. Therefore, football weekends were always extremely busy at Bulldog.

Advertising and Promotion

Bulldog's advertising and promotion was handled by Hanson's wife, Elise. Because of its reputation for quality pizza, pizza was emphasized in advertising and promotions. Advertisements were placed in the University newspaper—*The Red and Black*—and other small circulars in Athens. These ads often included money-off coupons for pizza. Hanson had also distributed fliers with pizza coupons throughout the UGA residence halls. Hanson, however, was not sure if any of this advertising was effective or not.

In addition to advertising food items, the bar offered drink specials for each night of the week except Sunday (alcohol sales were prohibited on Sundays). These specials were intended to attract students to the bar on less popular nights such as Monday and Tuesday. For example, on Tuesday nights the bar offered tequila at $1.00 per shot and margaritas for $1.50.

Bulldog Pizza and Spirits offered a 15 percent group discount with the purchase of four or more pizzas, if 24-hour notice was given. It also offered a 10 percent discount for law and graduate students, and a 10 percent discount to all softball teams in uniform. This softball team discount was featured in an ad that the restaurant had run on local TV the previous summer.

Personnel

Bulldog Pizza and Spirits employed 22 people including Hanson and his wife, Elise, two managers, five waitresses, four bartenders, three cooks, two drivers, two doormen, and two clean-up people. Hanson was the only full-time salaried employee. All employees were paid on an hourly basis. Managers earned $5.00 per hour, cooks were paid $3.75 per hour, and clean-up people made $3.35. The bartenders, doormen, and drivers made $3.35 plus tips. The food servers were paid $2.05 per hour plus tips. The number of employees fluctuated during the year according to sales volume. Less labor was required during the summer months than in the spring and fall.

Bulldog Pizza and Spirits suffered from high employee turnover. Hanson had difficulty maintaining a stable workforce for any period of time. Many students lasted only a few weeks, and even some of the more reliable students quit in December when final exams were being held. The average length of service for employees during 1984 was about six months. Hanson felt the constant training of new personnel was costing the restaurant money, both in terms of actual training time and lost sales due to inexperienced serving personnel.

The problem was further complicated by the fact that Bulldog's busy season coincided with the time when the most new employees had to be trained. Students rarely returned to work after the summer vacation, and therefore Hanson had to deal with the problems of large fall crowds and inexperienced employees at the same time. Football games were especially bad, because employees often did not show up for their assigned shifts, leaving the restaurant short-staffed during the busiest days of the year.

Alternatives for the Future

The increasing legal risks involved in operating a bar had prompted Hanson to consider concentrating on food sales, even before the drinking age change was announced. Most of his experience was in the restaurant side of the business, and he admitted that he was more interested in the restaurant than the bar. He felt confident that his restaurant had a good reputation for pizza, but was unsure how to capitalize on this strength.

One idea Hanson had considered was opening other Bulldog restaurants. These other locations would be smaller, satellite stores with limited dining space and would be used primarily for takeout orders. In order to cut down on the expense of opening and operating the new locations, Hanson had considered preparing the food at the current location and transporting it to the satellite operations. The food would be kept warm, and reheated if necessary, at the outlets. Hanson recognized that preparing food at one location and transporting it to another might compromise the quality, but felt future competition would be based more on speed of delivery than quality. Furthermore, this approach would eliminate the need for expensive cooking equipment in the new stores. The only equipment that would be required

---

Exhibit 18   Customer Survey Results (N = 100)

Food and Alcohol Consumption Away from Home

Frequency	Percentage Eating Out	Percentage Drinking Out
Never	2	13
Less than once per week	5	10
Once per week	19	17
Twice per week	29	27
More than twice per week	45	33

Age Distribution

Age	Overall Percent	Bar Only Percent
18	32	—
19	35	28
20	19	27
21	5	27
22–25	8	17
Over 25	1	1

Favorite Restaurant/Bar

	Percentage
Bennigans	33
Bulldog	17
Carter's	14
Enerprise	9
Hill's	9
Georgieo's	3
Other	15

Frequency of Visits to Bulldog's

Frequency	Restaurant Percent	Bar Percent
Never	32	42
Seldom	32	37
Once/Month	20	6
Twice/Month	11	9
Once/Week	3	1
More than once/week	2	5

If the Upstairs Bar Was Renovated, What Would You Like to See it Turned into?

	Percentage
Oyster Bar	46
Wine and Cheese Shop	17
Deli	21
Dessert Bar	10
Game Room	4
Dancing	1
Wide Screen TV	1

What Do You Like Most about Bulldog's?

	Percentage
Atmosphere	47
Food	44
Drinks	9

would be two or three food warmers and one or two microwave ovens. Hanson was fairly sure he could obtain foodwarmers for about $600 each (half the price of a new foodwarmer), and microwaves for less than $350 each.

Hanson had also considered renovating the upstairs bar and opening some other type of restaurant. A customer survey conducted the previous year by some UGA business students (see Exhibit 18) had indicated that an oyster bar would be popular, and there was only one other oyster bar in the area. An oyster bar would require the purchase of coolers, steamers, and shuckers. Hanson figured that $5,000–10,000 would cover all the equipment and the renovation costs. However, he was concerned that having an oyster bar upstairs might have a bad effect on pizza sales downstairs.

A third possibility that Hanson had considered was to try to change Bulldog's current image as a student bar and try to attract the 21–30 crowd. Such customers would include Athens locals, professionals, UGA faculty, and graduate students. Hanson knew that one reason why his business was popular with students was its high visibility and proximity to the campus. He knew, however, that he couldn't necessarily rely on his location if he was going after the older crowd, which would be spread out over the city. Some sort of extra advertising and promotion would likely be required.

Hanson was aware that Bulldog's reputation as a student hangout had hurt his sales to local residents, and that reacquiring their business would be difficult. On the other hand, Hanson reasoned, his business might be better-off in the long run catering to such customers. Furthermore, because area families had at one time accounted for a substantial proportion of Bulldog's food sales, Hanson believed that changing the image of the bar might have a positive carryover effect on his food business.

Hanson had also considered going after the local sports teams to increase his bar business. Summer sports, especially softball, were very popular in Athens, and many teams went to a bar to relax after the game. The people who played on these teams were generally in the 21–30 age range, and attracting their business would also help increase summer sales.

Conclusions

Stan Hanson topped off the pitcher of beer and looked over at the table of students who had ordered it. None looked 21 to him. There was little question that something had to be done to change the image and customer base of his business. Hanson enjoyed living in Athens, and had put a lot of effort into building the business over the past four years. He still felt that Bulldog Pizza and Spirits could have a good future, and was resolved to come up with a plan to ensure it.

5

Valuation and Succession of Entrepreneurial Ventures

Key Topics

- Valuation of a Venture
- Methods of Valuation
- Succession and Continuity of a Venture
- Key Factors in Succession
- Developing a Succession Strategy

Comprehensive Entrepreneurial Cases

- Bay Cast, Inc.: A Two-Year Buy Out
- Reversal of Fortune
- Johnson Products Co., Inc.

Introduction

It is important that entrepreneurs know how to value a business for purchase or succession reasons. Either way, a number of things should be kept in mind.

1. Get a lawyer involved at the beginning. The purchase of assets often involves tax questions, unknown risks, and, in some cases, the assumption of liabilities. A lawyer can help the entrepreneur be aware of these issues before they become problems.

2. Be aware of hidden risks that could surface in 12 to 18 months. For example, a customer who was injured by a company-made product before the firm was sold may decide to sue the new owner.

3. The owner should sign a noncompete clause whereby he or she promises not to re-enter the business for a certain number of years (at least not in the immediate area). Be sure that this clause is reasonable in terms of what is being promised, otherwise the courts may set it aside.

4. Have a certified public accountant or some outside financial expert confirm all income and expenses as well as asset accounts. In this way, you know what you are selling.

5. Before closing the deal, investigate the buyer. Is the individual honest in business dealings? If not, the person might try to walk away from the deal before the purchase has been finalized.[1]

---

[1]"Buying a Business: What to Watch Out For," *Financial Enterprise* (Summer 1987): 13–14.

After understanding certain purchase factors, the entrepreneur can begin to examine various methods used to value a business. It should be noted that determining an actual value is more of an art than a science. Estimations, assumptions, and projections are all part of the process. The quantified figures are calculated, based in part on such hidden values and costs as goodwill, personal expenses, family members on the payroll, planned losses, and the like.

Several traditional valuation methods are presented in this chapter, each using a particular approach that recognizes these hidden values and costs. Employing these methods will help the entrepreneur understand how the financial analysis of a firm works. Remember also that many of these methods are used concurrently and that the final value determination will be the actual price agreed on by the buyer and the seller.

Valuation of A Venture

Table 5.1 lists various methods that may be used to make a **business valuation**. Each of the methods listed is described and key points are presented. Specific attention is given to three methods that are considered to be the principal measures used in current business valuations: (1) adjusted tangible assets (balance sheet values), (2) price/earnings (multiple earnings value), and (3) discounted future earnings.

Adjusted Tangible Book Value   A common method of valuing a business is to compute its net worth as the difference between total assets and total liabilities. However, it is important to adjust for certain assets in order to assess true economic worth, since inflation and depreciation affect the value of some assets.

In computing the adjusted tangible book value, goodwill, patents, deferred financing costs, and other intangible assets are considered with the other assets and deducted from or added to net worth. This upward or downward adjustment reflects the excess of the fair market value of each asset above or below the value reported on the balance sheet. Here is an example:

	Book Value	Fair Market Value
Inventory	$100,000	$125,000
Plant and equipment	400,000	600,000
Other intangibles		(50,000)
	$500,000	$675,000

Excess = $175,000

Remember that in industry comparisons of adjusted values only assets used in the actual operation of the business are included.

There could be other significant balance sheet and income statement adjustments such as (1) bad debt reserves; (2) low-interest, long-term debt securities; (3) investments in affiliates; and (4) loans and advances of officers, employees, or other companies. Additionally, earnings should be adjusted. Only true earnings derived from the operations of the business should be considered; one-time items (from the sale of a company division or asset, for example) should be excluded. Also, if the company has been using a net operation loss carryforward so that its pretax income has not been fully taxed, this also should be considered.

Table 5.1   Methods for Valuation of a Venture

Method	Description/Explanation	Notes/Key Points
Fixed price	Two or more owners set initial value.	Inaccuracies exist due to personal estimates.
	Based upon what owners "think" business is worth.	Should allow periodic update.
	Uses figures from any one or combination of methods.	
	Common for buy/sell agreements.	
Book value (known as balance sheet method) 1. Tangible 2. Adjusted tangible	1. *Tangible book value:* Set by the business's balance sheet.	Some assets also appreciate or depreciate substantially, thus not an accurate valuation.
	Reflects net worth of the firm.	
	Total assets less total liabilities (adjusted for intangible assets).	
	2. *Adjusted tangible book value:* Uses book value approach.	Adjustments in assets eliminate some of the inaccuracies and reflect a fair market value of each asset.
	Reflects fair market value for certain assets.	
	Upward/downward adjustments in plant and equipment, inventory, and bad debt reserves.	
Multiple of earnings	Net income is capitalized using a price/earnings ratio (net income multiplied by P/E number).	Capitalization rates vary as to firm's growth, thus estimates or P/E used must be taken from similar publicly traded corporation.
	15% capitalization rate is often used (equivalent to a P/E multiple of 6.7, which is 1 divided by 0.15).	
	High-growth businesses use lower capitalization rate (e.g., 5%, which is a multiple of 20).	
	Stable businesses use higher capitalization rate (e.g., 10%, which is a multiple of 10).	
	Derived value is divided by number of outstanding shares to obtain per-share value.	
Price/earnings ratio (P/E)	Similar to a return on investment approach.	More common with public corporations.
	Determined by price of common stock divided by after-tax earnings.	Market conditions (stock prices) affect this ratio.
	Closely held firms must multiply net income by an appropriate multiple, usually derived from similar publicly traded corporations.	
	Sensitive to market conditions (prices of stocks).	
Discounted future earnings (discounted cash flow)	Attempts to establish future earning power in current dollars.	Based on premise that cash flow is most important factor.
	Projects future earnings (5 years), then calculates present value using a discounted rate.	Effective method if: (1) business being valued needs to generate a return greater than investment, and (2) only cash receipts can provide the money for reinvesting in growth.
	Based on "timing" of future income that is projected.	

Table 5.1 *continued*

Method	Description/Explanation	Notes/Key Points
Return on investment (ROI)	Net profit divided by investment. Provides an earnings ratio. Need to calculate probabilities of future earnings. Combination of return ratio, present value tables, and weighted probabilities.	Will *not* establish a value for the business. Does not provide projected future earnings.
Replacement value	Based on value of each asset if it had to be *replaced* at current cost. Firm's worth calculated as if building from "scratch." Inflation and annual depreciation of assets are considered in raising the value above reported book value. Does *not* reflect earning power or intangible assets.	Useful in selling a company that's seeking to break into a new line of business. Fails to consider earnings potential. Does not include intangible assets (goodwill, patents, etc.).
Liquidation value	Assumes business ceases operation. Sells assets and pays off liabilities. Net amount after payment of all liabilities is distributed to shareholders. Reflects "bottom value" of a firm. Indicates amount of money that could be borrowed on a secured basis. Tends to favor seller since all assets are valued as if converted to cash.	Assumes each division of assets sold separately at auction. Effective in giving absolute bottom value below which a firm should liquidate rather than sell.
Excess earnings	Developed by the U.S. Treasury to determine a firm's intangible assets (for income tax purposes). Intent is for use only when there is no better method available. Internal Revenue Service refers to this method as a last resort. Method does not include intangibles with estimated useful lives (i.e., patents, copyrights).	Method of last resort (if no other method is available). Very seldom used.
Market value	Needs a "known" price paid for a similar business. Difficult to find recent comparisons. Methods of sale may differ—installment vs. cash. Should be used only as a reference point.	Valuable only as a reference point. Difficult to find recent, similar firms that have been sold.

Source: Donald F. Kuratko and Richard M. Hodgetts, *Entrepreneurship: A Contemporary Approach,* 2nd ed. (Fort Worth, TX: Dryden/HBJ Publishers, 1992): 526–528.

Upward (or downward) income and balance sheet adjustments should be made for any unusually large bad-debt or inventory write-offs and for certain accounting practices such as accelerated versus straight-line depreciation.

Price/Earnings Ratio (Multiple of Earnings) Method   The price/earnings ratio is a common method used to value publicly held corporations. Valuation is determined by dividing the market price of the common stock by the earnings per share. In the case of a company with 100,000 shares of common stock and net income of $100,000, the earnings per share should be $1. If the stock price rose to $5 per share, the P/E would be 5 ($5 divided by $1). Additionally, since the company has 100,000 shares of common stock, the valuation of the enterprise would now be $500,000 (100,000 shares × $5).

The primary advantage of a price/earnings approach is its simplicity. However, this advantage applies only to publicly traded corporations. **Closely held companies** do not have prices for their stock in the open market and so must rely on the use of a multiple derived by comparing the firm with similar public corporations. Four major **drawbacks** to this approach are listed below.[2]

1.   The stock of a private company is not publicly traded. It is illiquid and may actually be restricted from sale (i.e., not registered with the Securities and Exchange Commission). Thus, any P/E multiple usually must, by definition, be subjective and lower than the multiple commanded by comparable publicly traded stocks.

2.   A private company's stated net income may not truly reflect its actual earning power. To avoid or defer paying taxes, most business owners prefer to keep pretax income low. In addition, a closely held business may be overspending on fringe benefits that are instituted primarily for the owner's benefit.

3.   Common stock that is bought and sold in the public market normally reflects only a small portion of the total ownership position of the business. The sale of a large, controlling block of stock (typical of closely held businesses) demands a premium.

4.   It is very difficult to find a truly comparable publicly held company, even in the same industry. Growth rates, competition, payments of dividends, and financial profiles (liquidity and leverage) are rarely the same. When allied to a closely held firm, here is an example of how the multiple-of-earnings method could be used:

Shares of common stock	= 100,000
1993 net income	= $100,000
15% capitalization rate assumed	= 6.7 price/earnings multiple (derived by dividing 1 into 15)
Price per share	= $6.70
Value of company = 100,000 × $6.70 = $670,000	

---

[2]Adapted from Thomas J. Martin, *Valuation Reference Manual* (Hicksville, NY: Thomar Publications, 1987), 7.

Discounted Earnings Method   Most analysts agree that the real value of any venture is its potential earning power. This method, more than any other, determines the firm's true value. One example of a pricing formula using earning power as well as adjusted tangible book value is illustrated in Table 5.2.

The idea behind discounting the firm's cash flows is that dollars earned in the future (based on projections) are worth less than dollars earned today (due to the loss of purchasing power). With this in mind, the "timing" of projected income or cash flows is a critical factor.

The following business acquisition example provides a step-by-step example of the discounting cash flow process. Basically, this method uses a four-step process.

1.   Expected cash flow is estimated. For long-established firms, historical data are effective indicators, although adjustments should be made when available data indicate that future cash flows will change.
2.   An appropriate discount rate is determined. When establishing this rate, the buyer's viewpoint has to be considered. The buyer and seller often disagree because each requires a particular rate of return and will view the risks differently. Another point often overlooked by the seller is that the buyer will have other investment opportunities to consider. The appropriate rate, therefore, must be weighed against these factors.
3.   A reasonable life expectancy of the business must be determined. All firms have a life cycle that depends on such factors as whether the business is one-product/one-market, or multiproduct/multimarket.
4.   The firm's value is then determined by discounting the estimated cash flow by the appropriate discount rate over the expected life of the business.

What is a Business Worth?

Let's assume you wish to acquire a business.

1.   Present the *net* cash flow projections for this business for five years (1993 through 1997).
2.   Change the format for presenting the data. (You may find it easier to use.)
3.   Use a present value rate of 24 percent.

You have an opportunity to buy a small division of a large company. Because you intimately know the business, you can accurately forecast the company's growth. Right now it is not profitable, but with your expertise and plans you expect it can generate $380,000 net cash flow over five years and have a value (net worth) of $400,000 at the end of Year five. (The $380,000 net cash flow is *after* all cash outlays.)

Question: Since you want to earn a minimum annual return of 24 percent on your investment (i.e., the purchase price), how much should you pay for the division?

Here are the facts: Assume the acquisition will occur on December 31, 1992, and the projected annual net cash flow (the excess of all cash inflow over all cash outflow) is as follows:

	1993	1994	1995	1996	1997
Net cash flow (thousands)	$0	$40	$80	$110	$150

Table 5.2	**The Pricing Formula**

Step 1. Determine the adjusted tangible net worth of the business. (The total market value of all current and long-term assets less liabilities).

Step 2. Estimate how much the buyer could earn annually with an amount equal to the value of the tangible net worth invested elsewhere.

Step 3. Add to this a salary normal for an owner–operator of the business. This combined figure provides a reasonable estimate of the income the buyer can earn elsewhere with the investment and effort involved in working in the business.

Step 4. Determine the average annual net earnings of the business (net profit before subtracting owner's salary) over the past few years.

This is before income taxes, to make it comparable with earnings from other sources or by individuals in different tax brackets. (The tax implications of alternate investments should be carefully considered.)

The trend of earnings is a key factor. Have they been rising steadily, falling steadily, remaining constant, or fluctuating widely? The earnings figure should be adjusted to reflect these trends.

Step 5. Subtract the total of earning power (2) and reasonable salary (3) from this average net earnings figure (4). This gives the extra earning power of the business.

Step 6. Use this extra earnings figure to estimate the value of the intangibles. This is done by multiplying the extra earnings by what is termed the "years-of-profit" figure.

This "years-of-profit" multiplier pivots on these points. How unique are the intangibles offered by the firm? How long would it take to set up a similar business and bring it to this stage of development? What expenses and risks would be involved? What is the price of goodwill in similar firms? Will the seller be signing an agreement with a covenant not to compete?

If the business is well established, a factor of five or more might be used, especially if the firm has a valuable name, patent, or location. A multiplier of three might be reasonable for a moderately seasoned firm. A younger but profitable firm might merely have a one-year profit figure.

Answer: Since you want an annual return of 24 percent on your money, simply compute the present value of the projected net cash flow stream. You must also compute the value of the $400,000 net worth position (projected assets less liabilities) at the end of Year five.

Referring to present value tables in financial handbooks (or using a calculator) you can obtain the following data:

Year	Present Value Factor for 24 Percent Rate of Return
Today	1.000
1	0.806
2	0.650
3	0.524
4	0.423
5	0.341

All that is needed now is to prepare a table showing the net cash flows for the five-year period. You then multiply the present value factor (for a 24 percent return) by the net cash flow for each year.

Table 5.2   *continued*

Step 7. Final Price equals Adjusted Tangible Net Worth plus Value of Intangibles (Extra Earnings times "Years of Profit").

Example	Business A	Business B
1. Adjusted value of tangible net worth (assets less liabilities).	$100,000	$100,000
2. Earning power at 10%[a] of an amount equal to the adjusted tangible net worth, if invested in a comparable risk business.	10,000	10,000
3. Reasonable salary for owner–operator in the business.	18,000	18,000
4. Net earnings of the business over recent years (net profit before subtracting owner's salary).	30,000	23,350
5. Extra earning power of the business (line 4 minus lines 2 and 3).	2,000	(4,650)
6. Value of intangibles—using three-year profit figure for moderately well-established firm (3 times line 5).	6,000	None
7. Final price (lines 1 and 6).		$100,000
	$106,000	(or less)

In example **A** the seller receives a value for goodwill because the business is moderately well established and earning more than the buyer could earn elsewhere with similar risks and effort. Within three years, the buyer should have recovered the amount paid for goodwill in this example.

In example **B** the seller receives no value for goodwill because the business, even though it may have existed for a considerable time, is not earning as much as the buyer could through outside investment and effort. In fact, the buyer may feel that even an investment of $100,000— the current appraised value of net assets—is too much because it cannot earn sufficient return.

[a]This is an arbitrary figure, used for illustration. A reasonable figure depends on the stability and relative risks of the business and the investment picture generally. The rate of return should be similar to that which could be earned elsewhere with the same approximate risk.

Source: Reprinted with permission from Bank of America NT&SA, "How to Buy and Sell a Business or Franchise," *Small Business Reporter*®, copyright 1987, p. 17.

Year	Net Cash Flow	Present Value Factor	Today's Value
1993	$ 0	0.806	$ 0
1994	40,000	0.650	26,000
1995	8,000	0.524	41,920
1996	110,000	0.423	46,530
1997	550,000*	0.341	187,550*
	$780,000		$302,000

*Includes $150,000 net cash flow and $400,000 net worth of division at end of fifth year.

As computed, the total value of the projected net cash flow stream is $302,000 today—and this includes the projected $400,000 net worth at the end of Year five. In other words, if the division were purchased *today* for its net cash flow value of $302,000, and if the projected cash flows for the next five years were generated (including the projected net worth value of $400,000), you would realize a 24 percent annual rate of return on your $302,000 investment over the five-year period.[3]

[3]Adapted from Thomas J. Martin, *Valuation Reference Manual* (Hicksville, NY: Thomar Publications, 1987), 7.

Succession and Continuity of a Business Venture

Management succession is the transition of managerial decision making in a firm, and is considered one of the greatest challenges confronting owners and entrepreneurs in family businesses. At first glance, succession would not seem to be a major problem; all an owner has to do is designate which heir will inherit the operation or, better yet, train one (or more) of them to take over the business during the founder's lifetime. Unfortunately, this is easier said than done. A number of problems exist with one of the major ones being the owner. The individual's personality and talents make the operation what it is, and if this person is removed from the picture, the company might be unable to continue. Additionally, this individual may not want to be removed. So even if the owner–manager has health problems or is unable to manage effectively, he or she may still hang on. The family's attempts to get the person to step aside are often viewed by the owner as efforts by greedy family members to plunder the operation for personal gain. (A detailed family business is presented in Chapter 9.) Successor problems are not insurmountable, however. In our consideration of these problems, the best place to begin is by identifying key factors in succession.

Key Factors in Succession

Forcing Events

Forcing events, those happenings that cause the replacement of the owner–manager, are events that require the entrepreneur to step aside and let someone else direct the operation. Following are typical examples:

- **Death,** which forces the heirs to immediately find a successor to run the operation.
- **Illness** or some other form of nonterminal physical incapacitation.
- **Mental** or **psychological breakdown** that forces the individual to withdraw from the business.
- **Abrupt departure,** as in the case of an entrepreneur who decides, with no advance warning, to retire.
- **Legal problems,** such as being incarcerated for violation of a law. (If this period of confinement is for more than a few weeks, succession usually becomes necessary, if in name only.)
- **Severe business decline** causing the owner–manager to leave the helm.
- **Financial difficulties** that cause lenders to demand the removal of the owner–manager before they will lend necessary funds to the enterprise.

These types of events are often unforeseen and contingency plans seldom exist for dealing with them. As a result, when they occur they often create major problems for the business. These considerations influence the environment within which the successor will operate. Unless the individual and the environment are compatible, the successor will be less than maximally effective.

Sources of Succession

An **entrepreneurial successor** is someone who is ingenious, creative, and driven. This person often provides ideas for new-product development and future ventures. The **managerial successor** is interested in efficiency, internal control, and the effective use of resources. This individual often provides the stability and day-to-day direction needed to keep the enterprise going.

When the entrepreneur is looking for an insider as a successor, he or she usually considers a son, daughter, nephew, or niece with the intention of gradually giving this individual operational responsibilities at first followed by strategic power and ownership later. An important factor in the success or failure of the venture is whether the founder and the heir can get along. The entrepreneur must be able to change from being a leader to being a coach, from being a doer to being an advisor. The heir must respect the founder's attachment to the venture and be sensitive to this person's possessive feelings. At the same time, the heir must be able to use his or her entrepreneurial flair and initiate necessary changes.[4]

When looking ahead to choosing a successor from inside the organization, the founder often trains a team of executive managers consisting of both family and nonfamily members. This enables the individual to build an experienced management team from which a capable successor will be chosen. The founder assumes that, in time, a natural leader will emerge from the group.

One key strategy in the succession process centers around the entry of the inside, younger generation and when ownership actually changes hands. Table 5.3 illustrates the advantages and disadvantages of **early entry** versus **delayed entry** of the younger generation. The question centers around the successor's ability to gain credibility with the firm's employees. The actual transfer of power is a critical issue in the implementation of any succession plan.[5]

If the founder seeks a family member outside the firm to take control, he or she usually prefers to have the heir first work for someone else. The hope is that the individual will make his or her initial mistakes before assuming the family business reins.

Sometimes the founder prefers a nonfamily outsider to be the successor, if only temporarily. The entrepreneur may not see an immediate successor inside the firm and may decide to hire a professional manager, at least on an interim basis, while waiting for an heir to mature and take over.

Another temporary measure is to hire a nonfamily, outside specialist who is experienced in getting ventures out of financial difficulty. In this case the founder usually gives the specialist total control until the firm is in a better position and then this person hands the rejuvenated venture to another leader.

Still another nonfamily approach is for the founder to bring an individual with the right talents into the venture as an assistant, with the understanding that he or she will eventually become president and owner.

---

[4]For an interesting perspective, see Sue Birley, "Succession in the Family Firm: The Inheritor's View," *Journal of Small Business Management* (July 1986): 36–43.

[5]T. Roger Peay and W. Gibb Dyer, "Power Orientations of Entrepreneurs and Succession Planning," *Journal of Small Business Management* (January 1989): 47–52. *See also* Wendy C. Handler, "The Succession Experience of the Next Generation," *Family Business Review* (Fall 1992): 283–307.

Table 5.3

Comparison of Entry Strategies for Succession in Family Business

	Advantages	Disadvantages
Early Entry Strategy	Intimate familiarity with the nature of the business and employees is acquired.	Conflict results when owner has difficulty in teaching or relinquishing control to successor.
	Skills specifically required by the business are developed.	Normal mistakes tend to be viewed as incompetence in the successor.
	Exposure to others in the business facilitates acceptance and the achievement of credibility.	Knowledge of the environment is limited and risks of inbreeding are incurred.
	Strong relationships with constituents are readily established.	
Delayed Entry Strategy	Successor's skills are judged with greater objectivity.	Specific expertise and understanding of organization's key success factors and culture may be lacking.
	Development of self-confidence and growth independent of familial influence are achieved.	Set patterns of outside activity may conflict with those prevailing in the family firm.
	Outside success establishes credibility and serves as a basis for accepting the successor as a competent executive.	Resentment may result when successors are advanced ahead of long-term employees.
	Perspective of the business environment is broadened.	

Source: Jeffrey A. Barach, Joseph Gantisky, James A. Carlson, and Benjamin A. Doochin, "Entry of the Next Generation: Strategic Challenge for Family Business," *Journal of Small Business Management* (April 1988): 53.

Developing a Succession Strategy

Several important steps should be taken to develop a successful succession strategy: (1) understand the contextual aspects, (2) identify successor qualities, (3) understand influencing forces, and (4) carry out the succession plan.[6]

Understanding the Contextual Aspects

The five key aspects that must be considered for an effective succession are discussed next.

Time   The earlier the entrepreneur begins to plan for a successor, the better are his or her chances of finding the right person. The biggest problem the owner faces is events that force immediate action and result in inadequate time to find the best replacement.

---

[6]Donald F. Kuratko and Richard M. Hodgetts, "Succession Strategies for Family Businesses," *Management Advisor* (Spring 1989): 22–30.

Type of Venture   Some entrepreneurs are easy to replace; some cannot be replaced. This is determined to a large degree by the type of venture. An entrepreneur who is the idea person in a high-tech operation is going to be difficult to replace. The same is true for an entrepreneur whose personal business contacts throughout the industry are the key factors for the venture's success. On the other hand, a person running an operation that requires a minimum of knowledge or expertise can usually be replaced without much trouble.

Capabilities of Managers   The replacement's skills, desires, and abilities will dictate the future potential and direction of the enterprise. As the industry matures, the demands made on the entrepreneur may also change. Industries in which high technology is the name of the game often go through a phase in which marketing becomes increasingly important. A technologically skilled entrepreneur with an understanding of marketing, or with the ability to develop an orientation in this direction, will be more valuable to the enterprise than will a technologically skilled entrepreneur with no marketing understanding.

Entrepreneur's Vision   Most entrepreneurs have expectations, hopes, and desires for their organization. A successor, it is hoped, will share this vision, except, of course, in those cases where the entrepreneur's plans have jeopardized the organization and a new vision is needed. For example Apple Computer co-founder, Steven Jobs, was replaced by John Sculley because Apple's board of directors felt that a more managerial, day-to-day operations entrepreneur was needed to replace the highly conceptual, analytical Jobs.

Environmental Factors   Sometimes a successor is needed because the business environment changes and a parallel change is needed at the top. The Sculley–Jobs example is one case in point. Another is Edwin Land of Polaroid. Although his technological creativity made the venture successful, Land eventually had to step aside for someone with more marketing skills. In some cases owners have allowed financial types to assume control of the venture because internal efficiency was more critical to short-run survival than was market effectiveness.[7]

Identifying Successor Qualities

There are many qualities or characteristics that successors should possess, and depending on the situation, some will be more important than others. Some of the most desirable of these successor qualities are sufficient knowledge of the business or a good position from which to acquire this knowledge within an acceptable time (especially marketing or finance); fundamental honesty and capability; good health; energy, alertness, and perception; enthusiasm about the enterprise; a personality that is compatible with the business; a high degree of perseverance; stability and maturity; a reasonable amount of aggressiveness; thoroughness and a proper respect

---

[7]Irving L. Blackman, "A Financial Guide to Turning Over the Helm," *Nation's Business,* January 1986, 40–42.

for detail; problem-solving ability; resourcefulness; the ability to plan and organize; a talent to develop people; the personality of a starter and a finisher; and an appropriate agreement with the owner's philosophy about the business.

Understanding Influencing Forces

Locating an individual with the desired traits can be difficult. If the ideal cannot be achieved, the emphasis should be placed on selecting a successor with the potential to develop the attributes mentioned previously within an appropriate time frame. This choice must take into account (1) family and business culture issues, (2) the owner's concerns, and (3) family member concerns. Specific areas within each of these influencing forces follow:

- **Family and business culture issues**
    Business environment
    Stage of the firm's development
    Business's traditions and norms
    Family culture, strength, and influence
    Owner's personal motivations and values
- **Owner's concerns**
    Relinquishing power and leadership
    Keeping the family functioning as a unit
    Defining family members' future roles in the business
    Assuring competent future leadership in the firm
    Educating family and nonfamily members about key roles
    Keeping nonfamily resources in the firm
- **Family member concerns**
    Gaining and losing control of family assets
    Having control over business decisions
    Protecting interest when ownership is dispersed among family members
    Getting money out of the business, if necessary
    Assurance that the business will continue[8]

Carrying out the Succession Plan

These forces and concerns prepare the entrepreneur for establishing a management continuity strategy or policy. A **written policy** can be established with one of the following strategies:

1. The owner entirely controls the **management continuity strategy.** This is very common, yet legal advice is still needed and recommended.
2. The owner consults with selected family members. Here the owner may want to establish a **liaison** between family and owner to construct the succession mechanism.

---

[8]Richard Beckhard and W. Gibb Dyer, Jr., "Managing Continuity in the Family-Owned Business," *Organizational Dynamics* (Summer 1983): 7–8.

3. The owner works with **professional advisors.** This is an actual board of advisors from various professional disciplines and industries that works with the owner to establish the mechanism for succession. (Sometimes referred to as a "Quasi-Board.")

4. The owner works with **family involvement.** This alternative allows the core family (blood members and spouses) to actively participate in and influence the decisions regarding succession.

If the owner is still reasonably healthy and the firm is in a viable condition, the following additional actions should be considered:

5. Formulate **buy-sell agreements** at the very outset of the company, or soon thereafter, and whenever a major change occurs. This is also the time to consider an appropriate insurance policy for key individuals that would provide the cash needed to acquire the equity of the deceased.

6. Consider **employee stock ownership plans (ESOPs).** If the owner has no immediate successor in mind and respects the loyalty and competence of his employees, then an ESOP might be the best solution for passing on control of the enterprise. After the owner's death, employees could decide on the management hierarchy.

7. Sell or liquidate the business when the owner loses enthusiasm for it but is still physically able to run it. This could provide capital needed to launch another business. Whatever the owner's plans, the firm would be sold before it failed due to disinterest.

8. Sell or liquidate when the owner discovers a terminal illness but still has time for the orderly transfer of management or ownership.[9]

With any of these strategies legal advice is beneficial, but of greater benefit is having advisors (legal or otherwise) who understand the succession issues and are able to recommend a course of action.

Entrepreneurial founders often reject the thought of succession, yet neither ignorance nor denial will change the inevitable. It is therefore crucial for entrepreneurs to carefully design plans for succession because it is these plans that can prevent today's flourishing businesses from becoming a statistic of failed family dynasties.

---

[9]Adapted from Harold W. Fox, "Quasi-Boards—Useful Small Business Confidants," *Harvard Business Review* (January–February 1982): 64–72; Kenneth W. Olm and George G. Eddy, *Entrepreneurship and Venture Management* (Columbus, OH: Merrill, 1985), 282; "CEO Profile: The Case for Succession Planning," *Small Business Report* (February 1985): 79–85; Glenn R. Ayres, "Rough Family Justice: Equity in Family Business Succession Planning," *Family Business Review* (Spring 1990): 3–22; and Ronald E. Berenbeim, "How Business Families Manage the Transition from Owner to Professional Management," *Family Business Review* (Spring 1990): 69–110.

C A S E • *Bay Cast, Inc.: A Two-Year Buy Out**

Brian G. Gnauck, Northern Michigan University
Irvin Zaenglein, Northern Michigan University

In November of 1990 Mr. Scott Holman, president and owner of Bay Cast, Inc., was in Scottsdale, Arizona, along with 15 other finalists in *INC Magazine* and Ernst and Young's entrepreneur of the year activities. The excitement in the room was high since all of the participants were here to find out who would become the entrepreneur of the year in various categories.

In the January 1991 issue of *INC Magazine,* Mr. Holman was recognized as the National Turnaround Entrepreneur of the year. He had taken a company which had operated at a loss and brought it to a profitable position with sales of over $12 million. Under Holman's direction, the company had been profitable every year since he assumed ownership and control. The tasks and challenges that faced Mr. Holman in 1991 were significantly different than those which confronted him when he bought the Bay City Foundry from Forstmann Little in 1987.

Background Material

Bay Cast Inc. was started in 1895 as the Bay City Foundry. Mr. Jack Bean purchased the Foundry in 1957. The Midland Ross Corporation bought the Bay City Foundry from Mr. Bean in 1978. Bean had converted the foundry from iron to steel in 1967. The Bay City Foundry was then transferred to the ownership of Forstmann Little in an acquisition of Midland Ross Corporation by Forstmann Little. Mr. Holman finally acquired the assets of Bay City Foundry, currently Bay Cast Inc., in April of 1987.

The foundry business has always been rather difficult because of its cyclical nature. It required a significant demand for products to force the industry to buy new castings especially where they were part of complex machinery or dies for large production runs. An economic upturn had to be substantially underway for orders to occur. In addition, the foundry business has some negative connotations associated with it since it's a basic industry and can be perceived as being rather dirty in nature. A foundry has a great deal of emissions in the smoke from its furnaces. As a result, buildings nearby the foundry will have "dust" from the foundry operations. Profitability of foundry businesses in the late '70s and early '80s was low. Over 25 major foundries across the United States disappeared due to bankruptcies and plant closings.

---

*The authors wish to gratefully acknowledge Mr. Scott Holman whose cooperation made the writing of this case possible. This case was prepared by Dr. Brian G. Gnauck and Dr. Irvin Zaenglein of Northern Michigan University. All rights reserved to the author and to the Midwest Society for Case Research. Copyright © 1991 by Dr. Brian G. Gnauck.

Mr. Holman had joined Bay City Foundry when it was owned by Mr. Bean prior to 1978. Midland Ross Corporation acquired the foundry that year. Mr. Holman was appointed General Manager at the end of Mr. Bean's employment contract three years later in 1981. The foundry was one of 17 divisions of Midland Ross Corporation, a Fortune 500 company.

Bay City Foundry's production facilities were split into two geographical locations within the limits of Bay City, Michigan. Pouring took place at a facility located on the Saginaw River and the finishing took place in a facility on the east side of town approximately three miles away. Both of the facilities were old, having been constructed in various stages over a period of time from 1885 to the present.

The finishing work could be accomplished by mostly unskilled labor since the process was primarily grinding metal, chipping, sanding, and cutting work. The finishing work required workers to rid the casting of excess metal. This was accomplished by use of grinders and sanders.

Conversely, the coremaking, molding, and pouring activity required much greater skill. Coremaking and molding require skills of a cabinet or tool and die maker, while pouring required knowledge of metal and the behavior of metal in the molten state. Coremakers are like cabinetmakers or sculptors. That is, they have to structure out of wood and metal a form, which, when filled with molten steel, will make the final product desired. This form requires one to think in reverse. For example, when a sculptor makes a mold of a human face, the nose of the face is a depression in the mold. The metal fills the depression and becomes the nose which protrudes from the face. Many cores have complex surfaces, planes, and cavities which must be planned for. The designer must be able to read blueprints, think in three dimensions, and reverse the dimensions.

The pouring process is equally as complex. Knowledge of when metal is at the exact temperature and ready for pouring requires skill gained through experience and practice. An error in this part of the process can cause part of the mold to not fill properly, therefore converting a potentially valuable casting into scrap.

Foundry Profitability

Mr. Holman, in the early 1980s, was faced with a depressed market for foundry business. Condensed balance sheets and income statements for Midland Ross Corp. are presented in Exhibit 1. Even though there was some improvement in overall losses in the company over this period of time, it failed to generate a profit for the parent corporation in 1986. The decade of the '80s was not a bright spot in the history of Bay City Foundry. The company had focused primarily on the auto market, and the sales of domestic automobiles had taken a downturn. Capital was not available for the purchase of new technology. There were a number of technical problems which were causing the business to incur excessive costs. For example, the company used pouring ladles which emptied from the top versus the bottom. This reduced the quality of the castings. On many jobs, this increased the product rejection rate and also increased finishing costs in terms of man hours. Midland Ross's Bay City Foundry was averaging 55 man hours per ton of final castings. Mr. Holman estimated that with the appropriate equipment in place this could be reduced to 45 hours or less.

Exhibit 1   **Midland Ross Bay City Foundry**

| | Profit and Loss Statement, 1982–1986 | | | | |
	1982	1983	1984	1985	1986
Income	$5,002,510	$3,711,584	$6,423,618	$8,789,385	$5,992,067
Cost of sales	6,056,313	4,237,202	6,296,063	7,410,564	5,917,745
Gross profit	(1,053,803)	(525,618)	127,555	1,378,821	74,322
Expenses	1,248,988	1,110,295	1,151,720	1,464,082	1,247,205
Profit (loss)	(2,302,792)	(1,635,913)	(1,024,165)	(85,261)	(1,172,883)
Other income	413,275	394,196	600,983	588,656	357,904
Other expenses	347,132	255,875	115,452	415,919	192,783
Total	66,143	138,321	485,532	172,737	165,121
Net profit/(loss)	(2,236,648)	(1,497,592)	(538,633)	87,476	(1,007,762)
	Balance Sheet				
Assets					
Current assets	$1,676,531	$1,564,730	$1,783,309	$2,062,231	$1,221,847
Fixed assets	5,155,426	4,806,161	4,617,720	4,535,079	4,116,613
Other assets		62,245	45,281	294,112	
Total assets	6,831,957	6,370,891	6,463,274	6,642,591	5,632,572
Liabilities					
Current	512,260	250,605	429,222	447,258	104,646
Long-term	379,468	302,428	318,411	392,216	357,006
Total liabilities	891,728	553,033	747,633	839,474	461,652
Capital					
Stock	500	500	500	500	500
Additional paid in	8,176,377	8,137,024	8,137,024	8,137,024	8,127,024
Retained earnings	(2,236,648)	(2,319,666)	(2,421,883)	(2,334,407)	(2,956,604)
Total L&SE	$6,831,957	$6,370,891	$6,463,274	$6,642,591	$5,632,572

Capital was also not available to purchase microcomputers. As Holman said. "Corporate computer types believed that micros were incompatible with the mainframes of the Cleveland operation."

The Bay City Foundry Division of Midland Ross Corporation was organized under the United Steel Workers Local 5014. There was an average of 124 unionized workers employed by the foundry during the 1978–1986 time frame. Some of the productivity problems associated with the foundry related to the lack of modern capital and some were the result of complex work rules which had evolved over the years.

The combination of depressed markets, a high wage scale, work rules, a lack of modern equipment, and basic bureaucratic structures of a Fortune 500 company contributed to the red ink of Bay City Foundry.

In the early 1980s there was a change in the senior corporate personnel at Midland Ross Corporation. As a result, Bay City Foundry made a number of improvements. For example, modern pour ladles were acquired. This improved the overall quality of the castings. A wood and poly patterned shop was built. This made for better-built cores which improved quality. The company acquired spectrograph and metallograph capability which allowed it to check for air bubbles in the casting and the uniformity of the pour. Bay City Foundry installed a 15 $\times$ 30 foot carbottom annealing furnace and an automatic shot blast system for cleaning. This made the final product look cleaner on the exterior and helped lessen the amount of hand labor required in the finishing of the casting. In addition, the company acquired in-house testing for quality control.

The First Offer

While it was managed by Midland Ross, Bay City Foundry lost money. However, Mr. Holman believed that there were a number of things that could be done which would allow this operation to succeed. By January 1985, Mr. Holman had carefully analyzed the situation and made a formal inquiry regarding Midland Ross's corporate interest in selling the Bay City Foundry operation. Mr. Holman's first offer for the foundry's operation was $2.8 million. Midland Ross was far more interested in an offer which approximated $3.2 million.

In light of the inability of the two parties to come to terms, Midland Ross decided to shop for other potential buyers. One year was spent in the process of trying to improve on the $2.8 million offer. The result of this activity was that no successful buyers could be found.

Consequently, in January of 1986, Midland Ross reapproached Mr. Holman regarding his interest in the Bay City Foundry. Mr. Holman realized that even though the loss rates had been improved from earlier in the decade, the future of the foundry business was somewhat bleak, especially given the current configurations of the collective bargaining agreement. Consequently, he offered $1.8 million for the Bay City Foundry. Midland Ross considered this insufficient. However, in the intervening six-month period, through a series of negotiations, a final agreement for the purchase of the Midland Ross Bay City Foundry by Mr. Scott Holman was consummated. The two parties agreed on a transaction price of $2.4 million. This transaction was financed through $100,000 of Mr. Holman's money and a series of other sources.

Midland Ross Is Acquired

Two weeks prior to closing the deal, Mr. Holman learned that Midland Ross Corporation had been acquired by Forstmann Little. Midland Ross Corporation was a $1 billion company. Forstmann Little was much larger. For example, it had recently purchased Lear-Siegler for $2.1 billion. At first Mr. Holman was informed that the sale of the Bay City Foundry would be allowed to be completed. However, he later found out that senior executives within Forstmann Little objected to the low price deal and, consequently, the deal was terminated. In the following three months, a series of discussions took place and finally Forstmann Little agreed to a sale, but wanted a strictly cash deal. Given this occurrence, Mr. Holman approached Forstmann Little with a proposal to negotiate concessions from the United Steel Workers in order that an acquisition of this type could make the transaction not only feasible but also profitable.

Mr. Holman approached the union with the suggestion that there would have to be some reduction in hourly compensation and some work rule changes if he was actually to buy the foundry. During a four-month period, six votes were taken on the issue and all of them voted down any changes. Forstmann Little was becoming impatient with Mr. Holman as well as the union and, consequently, told Mr. Holman that they were going to close Bay City Foundry. In light of this, one last vote was taken regarding concessions. Eighty-five members voted no concessions, 12 said yes to concessions, and 20 did not vote. Mr. Holman met with the unions and after some negotiation they agreed to settle for $300 per member severance pay and to dissolve the Local. Each individual signed a Hold Harmless Agreement as did the International Union. The local newspaper's heading "Workers reject cuts; means foundry will close," spoke to the demise of the Bay City Foundry.

Mr. Holman was informed that he should develop a plan for the closing of the Bay City Foundry. This plan-to-be was a three-month phase out, and was to include a detail of activities which needed to be accomplished. Mr. Holman talked with executives at Forstmann Little in New Jersey and presented his plan. The plan was immediately rejected with the statement that their intent was to "crash the foundry." Mr. Holman soon understood that "crash it" meant to sell all of the work in process as scrap (see Exhibit 2).

Mr. Holman expressed a great deal of concern at this approach since scrapping the castings which had been promised to important customers would reflect negatively on his character. He indicated to Forstmann Little that many of those castings were going to organizations such as the U.S. Navy, Ford, Chrysler and A.O. Smith, and that these organizations were relying on receiving those castings within the coming weeks. Local inquiry indicated a scrap sales value of those castings (work in process) of $148,000.

Holman's Last Attempt to Buy

Since it was the last hour, Mr. Holman brought together some of the consortium of financial sources associated with his previous offer. He explained to them that they had one last opportunity to buy the foundry, but they would have to move quickly so as to consummate the transaction on the following Monday. He did not, however, receive a warm reception from his potential investors. Instead, they wanted to further discuss the actual potential of the new corporation. Most of the participants indicated they would need two to three weeks in order to make a decision.

Mr. Holman realized that he was in a last-minute situation. Consequently, he drew up a letter of intent to buy (even though he did not have the funds) the Bay City Foundry assets less the receivables for $500,000. Mr. Drew of Forstmann Little received this offer via FAX and was extremely upset at the price. Drew phoned Holman and indicated to him that he would be going to Paris. He would call him later, and expected Holman to increase his offer significantly. In the following phone conversation, Mr. Holman raised his offer by $50,000. This further infuriated Mr. Drew. He indicated that he would call back in a half-hour and expected the offer to be increased. Mr. Holman consequently agreed that he would absorb $100,000 worth of payables, but that they would be payables of his choice. Mr. Holman's net offer for the business was $650,000.

Exhibit 2

Customer	Purchase Number	Status Hours Completed[a]	Cast Date	Weight	Total Retail Value
A.O. Smith	1-12111	20	1/29/87	1,250	$ 1,250
Abby Etna	1-12112	50	1/29/87	2,470	2,470
Acme Steel	1-12116	30	1/26/87	15,670	15,670
Acutus	1-12107	70	12/28/86	38,002	38,002
AEMCO Steel	1-12101	RFS[b]	12/28/86	21,001	21,001
American Dred	1-12110	30	12/24/86	15,011	15,011
Atols Tools	1-12096	75	12/22/86	17,000	17,000
BOC	1-11101	RFS	12/20/86	28,000	28,000
Bailey Hoogovens	1-11100	30	12/19/86	1,700	1,700
Budd Co.	1-11009	50	12/19/86	26,020	26,020
Carthage Machine	1-11096	25	12/18/86	20,010	20,010
Chrysler	1-11000	20	12/17/86	7,069	7,069
Chrysler	1-11001	15	12/17/86	17,000	17,000
Chrysler	1-11002	25	12/15/86	27,185	27,185
Chrysler	1-11006	10	12/12/86	17,060	17,060
Diamond Crysl Salt	1-11027	RFS	12/11/86	39,000	39,000
Ford	1-11025	125	12/11/86	38,117	38,117
Fisher Body	1-11010	100	12/9/86	27,001	27,001
Fisher Body	1-110196	60	12/9/86	21,079	21,079
Fisher Body	1-110187	50	12/5/86	12,188	12,188
Heyl Patterson	1-110165	45	12/5/86	13,760	13,760
Keystone Steel	1-110111	30	12/1/86	47,210	47,210
Keystone Steel	1-110137	70	12/1/86	16,000	16,000
Lerhardt Tools	1-110162	80	11/28/86	17,000	17,000
Navy	1-110127	100	11/28/86	26,017	26,017
Swan Engineering	1-110172	27	11/27/86	13,011	13,011
All others	—	2,247	—	675,169	675,169
TOTAL		3,384			$1,200,000

[a] Hours to completion

[b] Ready for shipment

While Forstmann Little was considering this offer, Mr. Holman described the environment at Bay Cast as like, "canoeing the Niagara River with everyone fully aware of what lie ahead." He was uncertain from day to day as to whether the deal would go through and asked his employees to take on good faith that he was doing the best he could to negotiate a transaction. Mr. Holman knew time was important. In late January 1987, Holman persuaded Forstmann Little to release to him the work in process, $400,000 worth of raw materials and about $200,000 worth of equipment including trucks, grinders, air compressors, and general portable tools, for $148,000. However, it was agreed that payment in total would be due on the first of April 1987. This gave Holman some breathing room. He needed extra time to raise money since he only had $100,000 of his own money. The remainder of the deal was to be worked out and put in place by that date. With this much of the transaction in place, Mr. Holman sat back and wondered about how he could complete this deal. He carefully studied all aspects of the business, including the work in process, as he formulated a plan.

C
A
S
E

C A S E • *Reversal of Fortune*

Frederick T. Stein, Kent State University
Kendra Earley, Kent State University

History of Petrie Stores Inc.

The history of the Petrie Stores Corporation so closely follows that of its founder and chairman, that to present an accurate overview of the company one must start in 1902 with the birth of Milton Petrovitzky, which was later shortened to Petrie. The son of a Russian immigrant, Milton Petrie spent his early years in Salt Lake City, Utah. In 1904, when his father's retail business collapsed, the family moved to Indianapolis, Indiana. The father took a job as a policeman, and the family slipped into poverty. In 1973, in an article in *Fortune,* Petrie recalls: "I can remember my mother claiming she wasn't hungry and giving me her food. . . .When our shoes wore out, we would put cardboard in them" (Louis, 230).

After graduating from high school, Petrie held a variety of jobs including a four-year stint at J. L. Hudson, a large department store in Detroit, Michigan; he also worked in his father-in-law's cigar business (But We Never Make a Deal, 39). By 1927, Petrie had accumulated enough capital to set up a small hosiery store in Cleveland, Ohio.

The hosiery business prospered, and with the backing of four silent partners, Petrie was soon able to open several more stores, and began to expand his product line to include women's apparel (Louis, 230). After several years, the chain had reached a sales volume of $7 million, but in 1937 the Depression forced him into bankruptcy. It took Petrie three years and $37,500 to repay his partners and creditors (Louis, 230). With the creditors appeased, Petrie soon began to reestablish his chain of stores.

Business was good, and by 1960, Petrie had not only recovered from his financial problems, but was strong enough to risk $2.5 million, half of his capital, to acquire stock in Lerner Stores, a major competitor (Rudnitsky, 55). Petrie claims he bought the stock to try to lessen the competition by forcing Lerner Stores to merge with his company. A 1981 article in *Forbes* quotes Petrie as saying, "They [Lerner Stores] were squeezing me. . .telling the underwear guys if you sell to him you can't sell to us, so I became their biggest outside shareholder to try to get a merger" (Rudnitsky, 55). But the merger attempt was unsuccessful. With Rapid-America Co. tendering for Lerner's stock, the value of Petrie's investment doubled, and Petrie chose to sell his share of Lerner's (Rudnitsky, 55). The profits from this sale enabled him to expand his own business still further, and eight years later he took his stores public, personally retaining over 50 percent of the stock.

In 1978, Petrie began to acquire a large stock position in Toys Я Us. Petrie had hoped that a merger would lure Charles Lazarus, founder and chairman of Toys Я Us, into running the Petrie Stores. However, Lazarus, who owned 7.5 percent of Toys Я Us stock at the time, was not interested in merging with or managing the Petrie Stores.

Undaunted, Petrie concentrated on expanding his stores during the remainder of the 1970s and the early 1980s by taking over smaller chains. The companies he acquired were:

Davids Specialty Shops, Joseph R. Harris Company, G&G Shops, Franklin Stores, Hartfield Stores, Ranch Shops, Whitney Stores, Miller-Wohl, and Winkelman Stores. These acquisitions proved to be a good strategy for Petrie. By taking over already established stores, Petrie was able to utilize the long-term, low-rent leases that already existed with mall owners. Not all of Petrie's investments were successful, however. Petrie Stores took smaller stock investments in Paul Harris, which was written off due to a Chapter 11 bankruptcy, and in the Deb Shops which have yet to show a gain.

Not satisfied with merely perpetuating corporate takeovers for the rest of his life, Petrie again tried to secure a successor by appointing Michael J. Boyle, former president of the Lazarus division of Federated Department Stores, to the position of president and chief executive officer of Petrie's. This attempt, like the previous attempt with Charles Lazarus of Toys Я Us, failed when Boyle resigned after only three months as president.

The latest potential heir, Matthew Miller, Milton Petrie's grandson, joined the Petrie Stores in June 1986 after graduating from Columbia Law School. After quickly rising to the position of senior vice president, Miller resigned in 1988 without any comment as to why he left the company. The investment community, already disturbed by Petrie Stores' decline in profitability, grew wary of what would happen when Petrie was no longer able to run the company.

Financial Analysis

Major causes of concern among investment analysts were Petries' increasing operating expenses, falling return on assets, and the virtual collapse of Petries' profit margins. For the purpose of analysis, financial ratios for Petrie Stores will be compared to those of Charming Shoppes, a Petrie competitor whose stores operate under the Fashion Bug name.

Charming Shoppes was chosen for a number of reasons. First, its corporate history is similar to that of Petrie Stores'. Both companies began as a single store: Milton Petrie's Petrie Stores in 1927, in Cleveland, Ohio; and Moe and Artie Sidewater's Charming Shoppes in 1940, in Philadelphia, Pennsylvania. The businesses prospered in their early years, and both eventually expanded with the financial backing of outsiders. Milton Petrie chose to raise capital through four silent partners. The Sidewaters elected to merge with David and Ellis Wachs to fund their store's expansion. The similarity between the two companies continues even today. Milton Petrie, chairman and chief executive officer of Petrie Stores, continues to run his chain, as do David and Ellis Wachs, who serve as chairman/chief executive officer and senior vice president of Charming Shoppes.

Another reason Charming Shoppes was chosen for comparison is because the company targets the same customer as Petrie Stores. The target market for both is a young, budget-conscious junior customer who is aware of current style trends. In an article in *Forbes* (1976), Milton Petrie talked about his target market: "Those girls. . .they'll live on hotdogs so they can spend their money on clothes. You can't beat a market like that" (But We Never Make a Deal, 39).

The reason for comparing Petries' to Charming Shoppes is that the chains carry comparable merchandise at similar price points. Jeans, a staple at both stores, sell in the $25-to-$35 range at Petrie, and from $20 to $40 at the Fashion Bug, the name that Charming Shoppes uses for its stores. Sweaters are at both stores. Petries' sells them for $23–$30 and Fashion Bug $25–$35.

Other companies were considered for comparison, but those that were similar in size or sales volume tended to have somewhat different target markets and price points. The similarities in history, target market, and merchandise between Charming Shoppes and Petrie Stores outweigh any small differences. Therefore, Charming Shoppes will be used for purposes of comparison. The chains will be evaluated in three areas: ability to control operating expenses, return on assets, and net profit margins.

As can be seen in Exhibit 1, operating expenses for Petrie Stores and Charming Shoppes were 15 percent and 21 percent of net sales, respectively, in the first year of comparison. Both stores' expenses fell for the next five years. In 1977, however, the trend reversed and costs climbed, peaking in 1983, Petrie's at 18.19 percent,

---

Exhibit 1   **Operating Expense Margin**

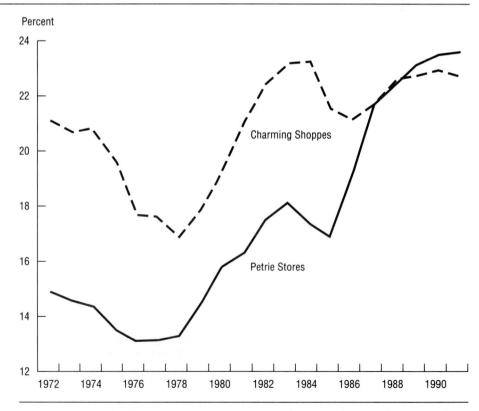

Charming Shoppes' at 23.29 percent. After a slight decrease, Petrie Stores' expenses soared to new highs of 23.50 percent in the 1990s. However, Charming Shoppes kept costs from following a similar pattern, and currently maintain cost ratios of roughly 22.50 percent.

Returns on assets for both companies have been very erratic over the past 20 years (see Exhibit 2). In 1972, Petrie Stores had returns of 19 percent. Charming Shoppes, however, had only 15 percent. A small decrease for both companies was followed by an upward trend that ended in the late 1970s. Petries' leveled in the 23 percent range, while Charming Shoppes' fluctuated between 18 percent and 19 percent. In 1980, Charming Shoppes' returns exceeded those of Petrie Stores' for the first time. A rather sizable decrease in margins for Charming Shoppes in 1982 allowed Petries' briefly to surpass Charming Shoppes. The following year, however, Petries' returns slipped to 10.50 percent, while Charming Shoppes' increased to 15 percent. Petries' returns continued to slide, except for a brief jump in 1988, and reached a low of 0.34 percent in 1990. Although Charming Shoppes' returns have also suffered, they have never fallen below 7.50 percent.

Profit margins for Petrie Stores grew from 8.4 percent in 1972 to a remarkable 11.5 percent in 1979 (see Exhibit 3). During the same time period, Charming

Exhibit 2	Return on Assets

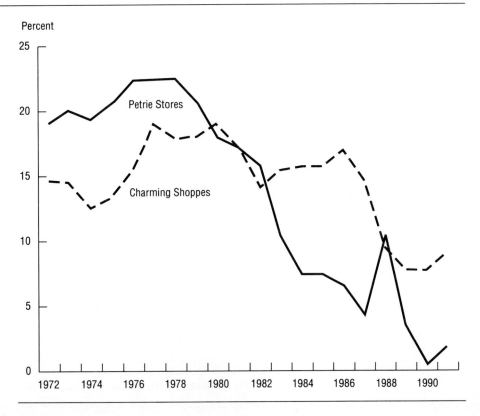

Shoppes' margins fluctuated between 5 percent and 8 percent. Profit margins for Petries' fell steadily for the next five years, reaching a 1984 low of 5.7 percent. At this time, Charming Shoppes' profit margin slightly exceeded Petries'. Except for an unusually high margin in 1988, Petries' has been unable to regain its former levels of profitability.

Petrie Stores' Management

Corporate Officers

When looking at a record of Petrie Stores' top corporate officers, two things are immediately apparent. The first is that Petrie Stores' executives have been predominantly women. The most notable of these women are Hilda Kirschbaum Gerstein, vice chairman of the company, and Dorothy Fink Stern, executive vice president. Hilda Kirschbaum Gerstein, now age 81, has been with Petrie Stores since its inception in 1927. She got her start in the Petrie company by sneaking past a line of applicants directly into Milton Petrie's office (Berman, 130). During most of the past 65 years Hilda Kirschbaum and Dorothy Fink Stern have been in

Exhibit 3	Net Profit Margin

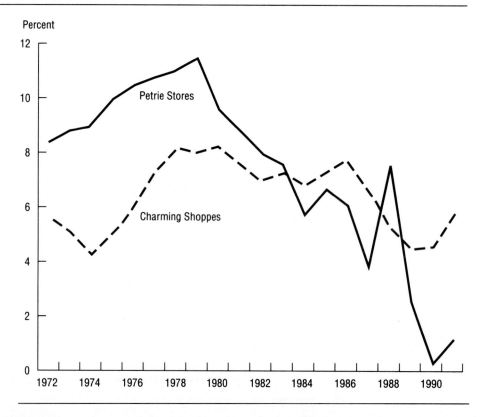

charge of the day-to-day operations of the company such as merchandising and store operations in order to leave Milton Petrie free to concentrate on real estate negotiations (But We Never Make a Deal, 39). An article in *Fortune* (1973) quotes Milton Petrie:

> They [Kirschbaum Gerstein and Fink Stern] are tremendously regarded in the market. The manufacturers, some of them, will not start their season or start their lines without consulting them. I really think these two women are the top two women in America in any field, retail or anything (Louis 230).

Although this statement may have been valid in 1973, is it valid in 1992? Recent losses in Petrie Stores' profitability suggest the possibility that Kirschbaum Gerstein and Fink Stern are currently not able to accurately predict the wants of Petrie's target market.

The second thing that one would notice from the ranks of Petrie executives is that they are considerably older than most executives in companies catering to the teenage market. For example, David Wachs, chairman and chief executive officer of Charming Shoppes, is 65; Donald Fisher, chairman and chief executive officer of the Gap, is 62; and Les Wexner, chairman and president of The Limited, is only 53. Of the 12 members of the Petrie board of directors, 8 are over the age of 60. Milton Petrie and Hilda Kirschbaum Gerstein, who still controls the day-to-day running of the company, are in their 80s. How do these older executives keep up on what's happening in the junior market? Judging by recent performance, one might guess that the executives are no longer able to track the market with the accuracy they once did. At the age of 89 and 81, respectively, Milton Petrie and Hilda Kirschbaum Gerstein might have difficulty interacting with today's junior market. By allowing someone younger to exert more influence in the company, a better understanding of what today's youth is looking for could possibly be gained.

This need for new management is especially pressing due to the age of Milton Petrie. At 89, Petrie continues to oversee company operations, but what will become of Petrie Stores when he is no longer able to run the business? It is a problem that surfaced as far back as 1973, but to date has not been resolved.

Successor Management

In 1978 Milton Petrie began to buy large quantities of Toys Я Us stock. His intent was clear; a merger with Toys Я Us would mean a successor for his chain of stores. Charles Lazarus, founder and chairman of Toys Я Us, was to be this chosen successor. However, Lazarus, who owned 7.5 percent of the Toys Я Us stock at the time, was not willing to merge with Petrie. In fact, at a meeting between the two executives, Charles Lazarus showed up wearing boxing gloves (Rudnitsky, 57). Milton Petrie eventually gave up his hope for a merger. In a 1981 *Forbes* article he explained why: "If we [Petrie Stores and Lerner Stores] merged he [Lazarus] would own too small a piece of the business. We're both very opinionated, so we would probably fight" (Rudnitsky, 57). Charles Lazarus's stock ownership, if the companies merged, would place him in a minority position in comparison to Milton Petrie's. Although Lazarus would in theory run both operations, his subservient stock position would leave Milton Petrie dominant. In reaction to Lazarus's rejection, Petrie now treats his Toys Я Us stock strictly as a good investment in a thriving company.

Another potential heir was lost when Robert Mandel resigned as senior vice president of Petrie Stores in 1981. A Petrie employee for 27 years, Mandel knew the business and was considered to be the logical replacement should Milton Petrie decide to step down. It seems Milton Petrie often subjected his employees to irritating and rather humiliating experiences. As an example of Milton Petrie's extreme behavior, a story is told in which Milton Petrie called the state highway patrol to search for Robert Mandel, even though he only needed some minor information (Ricci, 23).

The next possible successor, Michael J. Boyle, joined Petrie Stores on September 21, 1982. Originally from New Jersey, Boyle started his career in 1964 at Bambergers, a division of Macy's. By 1973 Boyle was executive vice president of two apparel divisions of the Melville Corporation. From there, he had a short stint at Abraham & Strauss, and was eventually promoted to president of the Lazarus division of Federated Department Stores. It was from this position that he resigned to assume control of Petrie Stores. In an interview in *The Wall Street Journal,* Milton Petrie stated, "He'll ask the questions and I'll answer them, that's all" (Petrie Stores Names..., 16). This statement was supposed to indicate that Petrie was willing to delegate control of the company.

The question-and-answer session that Petrie proposed was rather short-lived. Michael Boyle resigned on January 14, 1983, four months after he started. At the time, Milton Petrie stated that Boyle's departure was due to a "policy difference regarding the way the company should be run" (Petrie Stores' Boyle..., 32). In a *New York Times* article, analyst Fred Kopf agreed, saying "There was a big difference in management styles of big companies like Federated and operations such as such as Petrie's" (Founder of Petrie . . ., D2).

There are, however, other speculations as to why Michael Boyle left. Security analyst Robert Roth (quoted in the same *New York Times* article) said it was a question of "the passion Milton Petrie has for the company, of not being able to let go in the sense of having somebody come in as chief executive officer" (Founder of Petrie..., D2). One area of disagreement between the two men included a conference room that Michael Boyle ordered built in the Petrie Stores' headquarters in New Jersey. Evidently Petrie thought the expense was needless due to the fact that "all decisions are made in Milton's office" (Ricci, 1). Another area in which the two executives had a disagreement concerned the location of the company headquarters. Shortly after the new year, Boyle sent Milton Petrie a note requesting the company headquarters be moved from New Jersey to New York City (Ricci, 1). In response to these differences, Michael Boyle was asked to leave the company.

Shortly after Michael Boyle's resignation, Milton Petrie uncharacteristically acknowledged in a *Wall Street Journal* article that there was "a weakness in the business due to a lack of successor management" (Ricci, 23). Of course, Petrie declined to elaborate on his comment. But when his employees were asked, they felt differently about the need for successor management:

> Once Mr. Petrie passes away, his presence will still be felt [one executive says]. People will still react as if he's in the front office. We will still run through the halls. We do when he's around and we do when he's not around. It's just ingrained in us (Ricci, 23).

This employee's statement shows how Milton Petrie has conditioned his employees to quickly respond to his orders. It is questionable that this behavior will continue when Petrie dies.

Another attempt to secure a successor was made in 1986 when Matthew Miller, the only son of Milton Petrie's daughter, Marrianne, joined the company. He quickly moved up the Petrie Stores' career ladder, and after only 15 months became a senior vice president. Miller came to the company with many innovative ideas. A 1987 *Forbes* article quotes Matthew Miller: "There are no strokes of genius in the kind of changes I'm thinking about. . . .I only want us to be great" (King, 376). The changes Miller proposed included introducing information systems and controls (Berman, 132). Petrie resisted having Miller tamper with his company, and after his plans were thwarted by Petrie, Matthew Miller resigned in July 1988.

These examples of failed attempts to bring new management to the company are reasons for us to ask a number of questions. Is there a resistance to change? Is there a corporate atmosphere that encourages and identifies successor management? What type of corporate culture should prevail that promotes the concept of delegation of authority and spurs empowerment to lower level employees?

Corporate Culture

To describe the corporate atmosphere at Petrie Stores is to describe an atmosphere where fear and admiration are inevitably linked. Known for his attention to detail, quick temper, and at times his generosity, Milton Petrie runs the business with supreme authority.

All details of the business are painstakingly scrutinized. With Milton Petrie running the show even routine expenses are examined and eliminated if possible. For example, in the early 1980s it came to his attention that no one looked up his stores' phone numbers in the Yellow Pages. So at a savings of $200,000 a year, Milton Petrie canceled all paid listings (Barmash, F16). Also eliminated were advertising expenses. Instead of advertising, Milton Petrie decided to rely on impulse shoppers who come to the mall in response to the Sears or J. C. Penney circular. A *Forbes* article quotes Milton Petrie: "We're sort of a parasite on the department stores' advertising" (But We Never Make a Deal, 38). It may be the department stores that attract women to the malls, but once they are there, Milton Petrie feels his bargains will convince them to purchase from his store, rather than the higher-priced department stores.

His attention to detail carries over to dealings with suppliers as well. Milton Petrie has a habit of paying in advance for his merchandise, and in today's rough economy, manufacturers are eager to become his supplier. But in exchange for prepayment, the manufacturer must be willing to accept returns or reorders with little notice (Rudnitsky, 55).

His temper also flares with little warning. In "A Special Case" (*Forbes* 1988), a former employee recalls a particularly volatile meeting:

> I remember the day Petrie lost his temper and picked up a file—now you've got to understand it's a 2-inch pack of paper—and throws it at Hilda Kirschbaum. He hits her in the chest and almost knocks her out of her chair. She gets angry, picks up the file and throws it at another employee (Berman and Murray, 130).

At the time of the incident, Petrie was in his 80s and Kirschbaum Gerstein in her late 70s. Might there have been a better method of communicating displeasure, without displaying hostility? Would consensus building have enhanced employee support and resulted in a sound solution?

A novel by former Petrie buyer, Jack Martin Oppenhiem, called *The Buyers,* is rumored to be based on Petrie Stores. The novel "portrays an entrepreneur's employees treated with an explosive mixture of abuse and generosity" (Berman and Murray, 130). While Oppenhiem denies that he based the novel on his experiences at Petries', reports of the atmosphere at Petrie Stores closely resemble descriptions in the novel.

If the fear has become routine for Milton Petrie's employees, his generosity still takes them by surprise. Employees chastised for mistakes one minute will be the subject of Milton Petrie's fatherly concern the next. After reprimanding an employee for poor performance, it is not unusual for Petrie to inquire about his or her health. Moreover, "employees fired without explanation may wind up getting shares of stock months later for their years of loyal service" (Ricci, 23). Milton Petrie operates his company based on old-fashioned personal values. He continues to look out for his employees. He has paid rent and medical expenses for employees that were in need.

This philanthropy extends much farther than his own company. In a *New York times* article, Milton Petrie stated: "I love my business. . . .The nice thing is the harder I work the more I make. The more I make, the more I can give away" (The Tireless Milton Petrie, C16). Judging from the size of his contributions, Milton Petrie has indeed worked very hard. Each year Milton Petrie donates to 100 organizations and individuals, including museums, churches, schools, and hospitals (Suro, B4). In Israel there is a museum room and plaza named for him in honor of his humanitarianism (The Tireless Milton Petrie, C16). Furthermore, New York City's Cathedral Church of Saint John the Divine was so honored by his contribution that a limestone corbel was carved in his likeness (Upon This Rock. . ., 202). In addition to donating to organizations, Petrie also gives his money to individuals. Most of the money donated to individuals outside the Petrie Corporation is targeted to families of police officers killed in the line of duty. It is not unusual for Milton Petrie, upon hearing of such a tragedy, to establish rather sizable trust funds for college for the children of the police officers (Milton Petrie. . ., 171).

Conclusion

Although Petrie's generosity is very honorable, it is far from his typical behavior. More common are displays of egotistical power. Recall, for example, Petrie's firing of Michael Boyle in 1983. Areas of disagreement between the men included the building of new facilities and the movement of company headquarters. Instead of compromising, Milton Petrie chose to fire Boyle. Was the firing the result of Petrie's fear of change, not a reflection of Boyle's abilities? Did Petrie fear that changes in the company would diminish his power?

Petrie's reluctance to change was exhibited again in 1988 when Matthew Miller's plans for computerization were canceled by Milton Petrie. As senior vice president, Miller should have had the power to implement changes. But he did not, nor has anyone else. Petrie expects, and receives, final approval of every proposed change in the company. Petrie's need for control and fear of change have been the reasons why no successor has been found.

The lack of successor is an especially pressing problem due to Milton Petrie's age. At 89, it is undeniable that Petries' will soon be needing a replacement for Milton Petrie. Rising operating expenses, declines in return on assets, and a falling profit margin point to the fact that Petrie is not able to run his company as profitably as he once did. This decline is due partially to the economy, but Milton Petrie's age has substantially influenced his ability to effectively control his company. If Petrie was more tolerant of change and was willing to delegate more power, a successor could possibly have been found that was better able to run the company.

Works Cited

Barmash, Isadore. "The Petrie Way to Success." *New York Times*, June 20, 1971, 6:16.

Berman, Phyllis, and Kathy Murray. "A Special Case." *Forbes*, Oct. 24, 1988, 128+.

"But We Never Make a Deal." *Forbes*, Dec. 1, 1976, 38–39.

"Founder of Petrie Replaces New Chief." *New York Times*, Jan. 14, 1983, 4:2.

King, Ralph, Jr. "Grandson Power." *Forbes*, Oct. 26, 1987, 376.

Louis, Arthur M. "The New Rich of the Seventies." *Fortune*, Sept. 1973, 170+.

"Milton Petrie: the Gift of Money." *Ladies' Home Journal*, Dec. 1986, 168+.

"Petrie Stores' Boyle Leaves as President After 2½ Months." *The Wall Street Journal*, Jan. 14, 1983, 1:32.

"Petrie Stores Names M. J. Boyle as Chief to Succeed Founder." *The Wall Street Journal*, Sept. 21, 1982, 1:16.

Ricci, Claudia. "Apparel Empire: At Petrie Stores Corp., Key to Future Success May Be the Succession." *The Wall Street Journal*, Sept. 16, 1983, 1:1+.

Rudnitsky, Howard. "Retailing through Intimidation." *Forbes*, Nov. 9, 1981, 50+.

Suro, Roberto. "Inner-City Fund Hails Philanthropist." *New York Times*, Dec. 10, 1985, 2:4.

"The Tireless Milton Petrie." *New York Times*, Mar. 15, 1984, 3:16.

"Upon This Rock. . . ." *Fortune*, Nov. 7, 1988, 202.

Works Consulted

Barmash, Isadore. "The Acquisition Kings of Women's Wear." *New York Times*, Mar. 31, 1985, 6:6.

Barmash, Isadore. "Milton Petrie's Latest Surprise." *New York Times*, Sept. 16, 1988, 4:6.

Hicks, Jonathan. "Petrie Stores Chief Considering Buyout." *New York Times*, Sept. 14, 1988, 4:5.

"Lazarus Chairman Is New Petrie Chief." *New York Times*, Sept. 21, 1982, 4:2.

McCoy, Frank. "Is Petrie's Tight Grip Strangling His Stores?" *Business Week*, Aug. 8, 1988, 28+.

"Petrie May Be Ready for Privacy." *Business Week*, Aug. 11, 1986, 54.

Savitz, Eric J. "Storing Up Value: Why Bargain Hunters Are Attracted to Petrie Stores." *Barron's*, Oct. 9, 1989, 13.

Troxell, Thomas N. "Hemline Watchers." *Barron's*, Jan. 28, 1980, 35.

C A S E • *Johnson Products Co., Inc.: Son's Resignation, or Machiavellian Family Coup?**

Thomas L. Wheelen, University of South Florida
J. David Hunger, Iowa State University
Patricia A. Roberts-Grandoff, University of South Florida

On March 9, 1992, a company representative of Johnson Products Company, Inc. announced that Eric G. Johnson had quit as President and CEO "to pursue personal business interests." Eric Johnson (age 40), President, had been appointed CEO on October 28, 1989.[1] This appointment was the result of his mother, Joan B. Johnson, Treasurer and co-founder, receiving the company as part of a divorce settlement from her husband, George E. Johnson, Chairman, CEO, and co-founder. George transferred his 49.5 percent of the company's stock ownership to his former wife, Joan. Joan's stock ownership then comprised approximately 61 percent of the outstanding common stock. The estimated value of Mr. Johnson's stock was $5.5 million. The Johnsons had co-founded the company with a $500 loan in 1954. She served as Treasurer and Director beginning in 1957. On October 2, 1989, she was elected Chairman of the Board of Directors with the resignation of George, who remained affiliated with the company as a consultant.[2]

Family Machiavellianism, or Resignation?

Eric G. Johnson had overseen the turnaround strategy of the company for the past two and one-half years. During the decade of the 1980s the company had sustained losses of $14,012,000 on sales of $344,698,000 under the direction of George E. Johnson (see Exhibit 1).

In 1991, Joan M. Johnson (age 27), Eric's sister, had joined the family business as Director of Marketing Research. She had earned an MBA from Northwestern University. Joanie (Joan M.) deemed the title too lowly. She supposedly retaliated by engineering her mother's ousting of her brother, Eric. George's explanation— "He [Eric] underestimated the rancor of his sister and how far she would go to get revenge."[3]

On April 1, 1992, Thomas P. Polke, Vice-President, Finance, announced that the company's operations committee, formed over three years before, will function as the "office of the president," and will consist of four executives. The committee, of which one member will be Joanie (Joan M.) Johnson, will be responsible for the day-to-day activities of the company.[4] George characterized the four-person office of the president as "a joke."[5] Comer Cottrell, Chairman of a major competitor, Pro-Line Corp., said, "Frankly, I think the timing may have been bad."[6] Concerning Eric, Cottrell said, "I've seen him definitely increase his self [display] and market share, but he has been very profitable in so doing."[7]

---

*This case was prepared by Professor Thomas L. Wheelen of the University of South Florida, Professor J. David Hunger of Iowa State University, and Patricia A. Roberts-Grandoff, doctoral student at the University of South Florida. Copyright © 1992 by Thomas L. Wheelen.

Exhibit 1

Financial Performance by CEOs Eric G. Johnson (1990–1992) and George E. Johnson (1980–1989): Johnson Products Co., Inc.

(Dollar amounts in thousands, except per share data, employees, and stock prices)

A. Eric G. Johnson Tenure as CEO (1990–1992)

Year[1]	Net sales	Cost of Sales	Selling, General and Administrative Costs	Advertising and Promotion	Research and Development	Income (Loss)	Working Capital	Shareholders' Equity	Dividends per share	Net Income per Share[3]	Number of Employees	Stock Price Range High	Stock Price Range Low
1992[2]	$17,907	$8,213	$7,941	NA	NA	$978[4]	NA	NA	$0.28	$0.82[4]	NA	$21½	$15¼[5]
1991	38,406	18,167	12,166	$3,999	$332	1,894	$7,450	$15,905	None	2.67	224	23¾	6
1990	33,497	15,909	11,190	4,080	322	1,448	5,248	12,645	None	1.78	232	11⅝	4½

Notes:
[1] Fiscal year ends August 31st.
[2] 1992 is for six months ending February 29, 1992.
[3] Net Income per Share restated to reflect the two stock splits in December 1990. The 1990–1980 net incomes were factored by 3.36.
[4] Includes a one-time write-off of $480,000 to cover Eric's separation package. It was equivalent to $.40 per share.
[5] The price range for first two months of 1992.

Source: Johnson Products Co., Inc., 1992, 1991, and 1990.

B. George E. Johnson Tenure as CEO (1980–1989)

Year	Net sales	Cost of Sales	Selling, General and Administrative Costs	Advertising and Promotion	Research and Development	Income (Loss)	Working Capital	Shareholders' Equity	Dividends per share	Net Income per Share[1]	Number of Employees	Stock Price Range High	Stock Price Range Low[2]
1989	$29,368	$13,515	$10,564	$4,736	$362	$1,255	$4,883	$106,221	None	$1.18	190	$12½	$5⁷⁄₁₆
1988	29,104	13,292	11,657	6,496	542	(2,474)	3,987	8,612	None	(3.16)	246	10	4⁹⁄₁₆
1987	31,641	12,999	11,066	5,518	540	580	7,725	12,378	None	1.04	285	16¹¹⁄₁₆	7¹⁄₁₆
1986	29,811	13,178	12,134	5,384	693	(1,730)	6,327	11,150	None	(1.18)	325	11¾	5¹³⁄₁₆
1985	33,580	14,986	15,185	5,986	840	(3,571)	4,809	13,118	None	(3.80)	405	21¹¹⁄₁₆	8⁵⁄₁₆
1984	35,589	15,419	21,055	10,031	818	(4,083)	7,711	17,646	None	(3.46)	540	33⁵⁄₁₆	9⁹⁄₁₆
1983	40,937	16,649	18,490	7,226	799	1,628	12,708	21,715	None	1.38	550	37⁵⁄₁₆	10⅞
1982	39,177	18,191	19,122	7,467	868	(3,623)	11,060	20,062	None	(3.06)	540	11¹¹⁄₁₆	6¹¹⁄₁₆
1981	43,197	19,528	17,866	8,067	870	385	13,429	23,660	None	.34	568	17⅛	8¾
1980	32,294	15,250	16,773	7,243	782	(2,379)	13,177	23,257	0.18	2.02	563	NA	NA

Notes:
[1] Net Income per Share restated to reflect the two stock splits in December 1990. The 1989–1990 net incomes were factored by 3.36.
[2] These figures are from Standard ASE stock reports—January 9, 1992, p. 8259.
NA = not available

Source: Johnson Products Co., Inc., 1991, 1990, 1987, 1984, 1983, 1982, 1981, and 1980.

Mrs. Johnson said, "Eric Johnson has made a significant contribution at Johnson Products."[8] She went on to say, "I understand his decision and wish him well in his future endeavors." When asked if Eric resigned or was ousted, Mrs. Johnson said, "Whatever you're looking at is the will of the Chairman."[9]

Mr. Polke's announcement also included the appointment of Joan B. Johnson, Chairman, to the additional position of CEO. Mrs. Johnson said, "Internally, it's back to business as usual at the company. This team has proven over the last three years that they can produce solid results. Having seen them operate in the past, I am confident they will continue to prove this to the business community and to our stockholders."[10]

Timothy Elbright, a portfolio manager for Eagle Asset Management, who holds a 3.5 percent stake in the company, said about the events, "I will keep a very wary eye on the company for the next six months."[11]

Comer Cottrell came to the heart of the issue when he said, "Even if the company prospers after this latest management shakeup, the Johnson family may have 'fractured for good.' "[12]

Highlights of Eric's Management Tenure

In June 1988, Eric had been appointed Vice-President, Chief Operating Officer, and elected as Director. Eric's charge was ". . .to take whatever operating measures necessary to put the company on a consistent profitability footing."[13] Under his direction, a massive organizational renewal was implemented. He reduced the company's payroll by almost 50 percent, including seven of the company's ten officers, in order to reduce the firm's breakeven point. He also overhauled the marketing and sales departments, which he felt had been providing inadequate customer service.[14] He restructured the company's vendor relationships, so that these managers dealt with 50 suppliers rather than 140 vendors.[15] In October 1989, Eric was appointed CEO, replacing his father, George E. Johnson, who left the company.

On February 2, 1990, under Eric's direction, the company acquired four brands (Curly Perm, Sof-N-Free, Sta-Sof-Fro, and Moxie) and their inventories for $5 million from a competitor, M & M Products Co., Inc. of Atlanta. These four brands were estimated to have $12.5 million in sales in 1989. The $5 million purchase consisted of $1.5 million in cash and two promissory notes of $2.4 million and $1.1 million. The notes are interest free, unless the company defaults.[16] In event of default the notes then become interest bearing at the prime lending rate. After the sale, M & M Products announced it was ceasing its operations. It ranked 36th on the *1989 BE* (Black Enterprise) *Industrial Services 100* with sales of approximately $20 million. According to analyst Sheila Poole, ". . .the business [ethnic hair-care companies] was perhaps damaged the most when mainstream companies began to make inroads into the ethnic hair-care market."[17]

In 1990, Johnson Products became the main sponsor of the Grambling Football Radio Network, which covered 40 markets nationwide. The company management felt the sponsorship had been a ". . .very successful promotion."[18] They renewed their sponsorship for 1991.

In September 1990, it was announced that the company management was considering moving its headquarters from 8522 South Lafayette Avenue (South Side), where it had been since 1954, to the suburbs. This was to be another step in the company's ongoing cost-cutting efforts. The company had about 232 employees. The new site would offer the company lower taxes, and the space required to expand or modernize its facility, which would lower operating costs. Eric said, "The advantage of a new facility is that we can get better efficiencies and upgrade the equipment."[19] Eric noted that he was not committed to leaving the city or even its existing South Side site. He had been holding talks with Chicago's Department of Economic Development, which had offered the company several city sites and some tax incentives. Eric explored economic development incentives offered by other local municipalities. Finally, in April 1991, management announced they would remain at the present South Side location because of the city's better access to the firm's 232 employees, a downturn in the real estate values, and management's continued focus on restructuring its operations.[20]

On May 29, 1991, a special committee, comprising Eric Johnson and two outside directors—James H. Lowry, President of James H. Lowry and Associates (a consulting firm) and William G. Giles, Chairman of E.P.C. International, Inc., proposed a $20.6 million leveraged buyout (LBO) of the company, thereby taking the company private. The group proposed to purchase the 39 percent of the company stock not owned by Mrs. Johnson for $17.25 a share, or $8 million. The stock closed on the previous day at $15.37, up ⅛. Initially, Mrs. Johnson would own all the company, with senior management acquiring a "substantial stake" over time.[21] Mrs. Johnson favored any transaction that provided a fair price to shareholders and "satisfied my financial requirements."[22] She withheld any final determination until her advisers and the special committee (the takeover group) could fully review the offer. The LBO offer was made pending the procurement of financing, the negotiation of a definitive agreement, and, of course, the Board and shareholder approval.

Cornelia Stanek, hair-care consultant, said about taking the company private that "they won't have to answer to stockholders or wait for them to vote," thereby allowing the company to make strategic decisions faster.[23] She went on to say, "Things like launching a new product can happen quickly." So, the company can make strategic decisions faster. Eric Johnson said, "We haven't talked about changing directions but rather. . .what we have talked about is going from a public public company to a private one."[24]

Two months after the initial LBO proposal on June 25, 1991, the offer was withdrawn. The two principal reasons cited were (1) the debt terms were too tough, and (2) Mrs. Johnson's personal risk was too great. The lenders were requiring the company to pledge the majority of its assets as collateral. This would choke off any access to future capital to sustain and expand the business. The proposed LBO also would hamper new product development (the lifeblood of this business) and advertising spending. Eric said, "More [LBOs] have done poorly in meeting their plans than have done well. So, it was better not to do it."[25] The other factor was that Mrs. Johnson was the sole shareholder, so she would be extremely vulnerable if the company were to suffer a downturn in performance and the lenders were to gain control from management. Additionally, a class action lawsuit had been filed in a Delaware court charging that the offer was a "grossly inadequate and unfair price."[26] The stock had closed at $14.50 on June 26, 1991.

In 1991, the company management became a co-sponsor with Wrigley's Spearmint Gum of the Singsation Gospel Competition, which was held in Atlanta, Greensboro, and New York. This allowed the company to reach an audience of at least 4,000 at each competition, thereby boosting the public's awareness of Johnson products.

During the same year, the company management entered into a promotional agreement with *Upscale* magazine. Although in circulation only for one year, *Upscale* was the third largest African–American magazine, with 600,000 readers. The agreement consisted of Johnson Products flagging a subscription offer to *Upscale* on its hair relaxer (Ultra Sheen, Supreme Gentle-Treatment, and Sof-N-Free) cartons. Additionally, management bartered for a full-page monthly exposure for the company's brands, and prime magazine positioning of its advertisements next to much-read articles or features.[27]

In early 1992, Eric decided to implement a strategic marketing shift from price promotions to emphasizing brand advertising. The company produced (in-house) three television commercials.

Financial Performance

Under Eric's direction as CEO, the company had sales of $71,903,000 and profits of $5,313,000 for 1990 and 1991 (see Exhibits 2 and 3). The sales and profits for the first months of 1992 were $17,907,000 and $978,000,000, respectively. There was a one-time charge of $480,000 the second quarter of 1992 for part of Eric's severance package. In each of the ten quarters under Eric, the company earned a profit, and each quarter on a yearly comparison had shown progressive increases (see Exhibit 4). Eric's performance was a direct turnaround from the 1980s. During that decade, under the direction of George as CEO, the company sustained losses in 21 out of 40 quarters, which totaled $14,012,000 on sales of $344,698,000 (see Exhibit 1).

On December 12, 1990, the shareholders had approved a one-for-ten reverse stock split for the company's issued and outstanding stock. So, for every 100 shares under this reverse stock split, the shareholder would have 10 shares. Immediately following this reverse stock split, a three-for-one forward stock split was implemented. The reverse stock split was initiated to attract more interest in the company's stock. The two splits reduced the number of outstanding shares to about 1.2 million from nearly 4 million. The investor with 100 shares before the two splits ended up with 30 shares. The stock price increased from $4⅝ to $6¼ (adjusted for the split) in the week following the announcement, an increase of 135.1 percent.[28]

As a result of the rapid financial turnaround, in December 1991, the company declared a dividend of $.28 per share, payable in January 1991. The company had not paid a dividend since 1980. Management's stated intention was to pay $.07 regular quarterly dividend thereafter.

During Eric's tenure, the stock price had appreciated from a low of $1.63 at the end of 1989 to a high of $23.75. The stock closed at $19.50 the day after Eric

Exhibit 2
Consolidated Statement of Operations: Johnson Products Co., Inc.
(Dollar amounts in thousands, except per share data)

Years Ending August 31	1991	1990
Net sales[1]	$38,406	$33,497
Cost and expenses		
Cost of sales	18,167	15,909
Selling, general and administrative expenses	16,165	15,270
Total costs and expenses	34,332	31,179
Income from operations	4,074	2,318
Other income (expense)		
Interest expense, net	(810)	(797)
Gain on sale of land	—	—
Gain on sale of investment	—	369
Other income	—	269
Income before income taxes and extraordinary item	3,264	2,159
Income taxes	1,370	711
Income before extraordinary item	1,894	1,448
Extraordinary item		
Utilization of tax loss carryforward	1,294	677
Net income	$ 3,188	$ 2,125
Net income per common and common equivalent share		
Income before extraordinary item	$ 1.59	$ 1.21
Extraordinary item	1.08	.57
Net income per common and common equivalent share	$ 2.67	$ 1.78

[1]All notes were deleted.

Source: Johnson Products Co., Inc., *1991 Annual Report,* p. 12.

Exhibit 3
Balance Sheet: Johnson Products Co., Inc.
(Dollar amounts in thousands, except per share data)

Years Ending August 31	1991	1990
Assets[1]		
Current assets		
Cash	$ 426	$ 149
Receivables		
Trade, less allowance for doubtful accounts of $472 in 1991 and $464 in 1990	8,439	9,348
Other	340	238
Inventories	5,494	6,347
Prepaid expenses	534	581
Total current assets	15,233	16,663
Property, plant and equipment	16,679	16,065
Less accumulated depreciation	11,096	10,579
	5,583	5,486
Intangibles, net	3,415	3,605
Other assets	557	306
Total assets	$24,788	$26,060
Liabilities and Shareholders' Equity		
Current liabilities		
Short-term loans	$ 3,042	$ 4,630
Current maturities of long-term debt	879	1,230
Accounts payable	3,193	4,917
Accrued expenses	669	638
Total current liabilities	7,783	11,415
Long-term debt	1,100	2,000
Shareholder's equity		
Capital stock		
Preferred stock, no par; authorized 300,000 shares; none issued		
Common stock, $.50 par; authorized 7,504,400 shares; issued 1,215,979 shares	608	608
Additional paid-in capital	2,040	2,040
Retained earnings	13,638	10,450
Cumulative translation adjustment	(29)	(101)
Treasury stock, 19,578 shares in 1991 and 1990, at cost	(352)	(352)
	15,905	12,645
Total liabilities and shareholders' equity	$24,788	$26,060

[1]All notes were deleted.

Source: Johnson Products Co., Inc., *1991 Annual Report,* p. 13.

Exhibit 4

Quarterly Financial Statement for 1991, 1990, and 1989: Johnson Products Co., Inc.
(Dollar amounts in thousands, except per share data)

Quarters Ending	November 30 (First)	February 28 (Second)	May 31 (Third)	August 31 (Fourth)	Totals for Year
1991					
Net sales	$7,223	$9,075	$11,375	$10,733	$38,406
Gross profit	4,069	4,669	5,988	5,513	20,239
Income before extraordinary item	386	413	717	378	1,894
Extraordinary item	174	184	310	626	1,294
Net income	560	597	1,027	1,004	3,188
Net income per share					
Before extraordinary item	.32	.35	.60	.32	1.59
Extraordinary item	.15	.15	.26	.52	1.08
Net income	.47	.50	.86	.84	2.67
1990					
Net sales	$6,146	$8,166	$ 9,652	$ 9,533	$33,497
Gross profit	3,187	4,423	5,209	4,769	17,588
Income before extraordinary item	259	136	482	571	1,448
Extraordinary item	161	72	277	167	677
Net income	420	208	759	738	2,125
Net income per share					
Before extraordinary item	.22	.11	.40	.48	1.21
Extraordinary item	.14	.06	.23	.14	.57
Net income	.36	.17	.63	.62	1.78
1989					
Net sales	$ 5,976	$7,238	$ 7,680	$ 8,474	$29,368
Gross profit	3,107	3,775	4,311	4,660	15,853
Income from continuing operations	1,152	14	80	9	1,255
Extraordinary item	606	8	41	99	754
Net income	1,758	22	121	108	2,009
Net income per share					
Continuing operations	.29	—	.02	—	.31
Extraordinary item	.15	—	.01	.03	.19
Net income	.44	—	.03	.03	.50

Source: Johnson Products Co., Inc., *1991, 1990,* and *1989 Annual Reports.*

resigned, off $.875 from the closing of the previous day. On February 27, the stock closed at $15.25, which was a decrease of $5.125 or 25.2 percent.

Notes

1. Jeff Bailey, "Chief of Johnson Products Quits; Row Is Reported," *The Wall Street Journal,* March 10, 1992, B–8.

2. "Johnson Products Co., Inc., Announces Resignation of George E. Johnson," October 2, 1989, 1–2.

3. Karen Springen and Larry Reibstein, "So Much for Family Ties," *Newsweek,* March 23, 1992, 49.

4. Johnson Products Co., Inc. *Announcement,* April 1, 1992, 1.

5. Lois Therrien, "Brawl in the Family at Johnson Products," *Business Week,* March 22, 1992, 34.

6. *Ibid.*

7. *Ibid.*

8. Frank McCoy, "Johnson Products Regroups After Family Row," *Black Enterprise,* May 1992, 17.

9. Therrien, "Brawl in the Family at Johnson Products," 34.

10. Johnson Products Co., Inc., *Announcement,* April 1, 1992, 11.

11. Therrien, "Brawl in the Family at Johnson Products," 34.

12. *Ibid.*

13. Johnson Products Co., Inc., *1988 Annual Report,* 1.

14. *Ibid.*

15. Leslie Brokaw, "Putting the House in Order," *INC.,* March 1991, 102.

16. Johnson Products Co., Inc., *Form 10-Q,* February 28, 1990, 7.

17. Sheila M. Poole, "M & M Products to Close Atlanta Operations After Selling Brands," *Atlanta Journal,* February 3, 1990.

18. Johnson Products Co., Inc., *1991 Annual Report,* 7.

19. *Crain's Chicago Business,* September 17, 1990, 4.

20. "Johnson Products Opts to Stay In City," *Crain's Chicago Business,* April 29, 1991, 70.

21. Charles Storch, "Johnson Family Sets Buyout Bid," *Chicago Tribune,* May 29, 1991, 3.

22. *Ibid.*

23. Jerry Thomas, "JPC Seeks Stock Buy-Back," *Black Enterprise,* September 1991, 18.

24. *Ibid.*

25. Judith Crown, "Why Johnson Deal Failed," *Crain's Chicago Business,* July 1, 1991, 80.

26. *Ibid.*

27. Johnson Products Co., Inc., *1991 Annual Report,* 8.

28. *Crain's Chicago Business,* December 24, 1990, 30.

6

Women Entrepreneurs

Key Topics

- The Growth of Women Entrepreneurs
- Generations of Women Entrepreneurs
- Barriers Confronting Women Entrepreneurs
- Operating Problems Encountered by Women Entrepreneurs
- Information Gathering and Networking
- Prescriptions

Comprehensive Entrepreneurial Cases

- Carol Jerrell: Suburban Realty Services
- Dainty Designs
- High Self-Esteem Toys Corporation

Introduction

Women-owned businesses are no longer a new phenomenon. An increasing number of women are able to juggle their career, children, and marriage. Before 1970 women owned only 5 percent of all U.S. businesses, but today they own approximately 30 percent of all businesses.[1] Cognetics reports that more than 40 percent of women-owned businesses have been in business 12 years or longer and that they operate in all industries and represent all businesses with a concentration in retail trade and services. They provide as many jobs as do all of the Fortune 500 firms combined, and are as likely as other firms to provide employment in construction, wholesale trade, and agribusiness. The National Foundation of Women Business Owners reports that women-owned businesses are somewhat more likely to be stable and a little less likely to demonstrate high growth. These women entrepreneurs have changed history by undertaking great risk, facing great personal difficulties, legal barriers, discrimination, ridicule, and danger in order to pursue their dreams of entrepreneurship and self-employment.[2]

---

[1]L. Pinson and J. Jinnett (Justin, CA: Out of Your Mind. . . and Into the Marketplace, 1992).

[2]National Foundation for Women Business Owners, "Women-Owned Business: The New Economic Force: 1992 Data Report" (Washington, D.C.: National Foundation for Women Business Owners, 1992).

The Growth of Women Entrepreneurs

In 1972 the Bureau of the Census indicated that women-owned businesses accounted for only 4.6 percent of all businesses and only .03 percent of sales in the United States. Since that time there has been a dramatic increase in the number of women business owners due to the fact that more women are choosing entrepreneurship as a career choice (see Table 6.1). However, this increase may also be due to faulty counting and documentation of women business owners. Varying figures are now being quoted as the interest in women entrepreneurship grows. Bowen and Hisrich report that the female self-employment growth rate between 1972 and 1979 was five times faster than that of men's.[3] The Wisconsin Women's Business Council reports that three out of every five women entering the labor force are starting their own business.[4] There are now about 1.3 million more women-owned businesses in the United States than previously reported. The 1987 census counted 4.1 million female entrepreneurs, a 57 percent increase from 1982. The National Foundation of Women Business Owners financed a study that raises the total to 5.37 million by identifying additional companies missed by the census or started since 1987.[5] In other words, women entrepreneurs are undercounted. "The consequences of not being counted properly are continued invisibility, ongoing trivialization, dismissal and stereotyping, which enjoys an unwarranted life span."[6] There is some question

---

Table 6.1
Increasing Business Ownership by Women

Year	Number of Self-Employed Females	Source
1972	1,475,000	Census Bureau
1979	2,102,000	Census Bureau
1982	3,500,000	*Chicago Tribune*
1987	4,100,000 ($278.1 billion in receipts)	Joline Godfrey
	184,000 Corporations	
	4,284,000	
1990	5,400,000	National Foundation for Women Business Owners, 1992

---

[3]Donald D. Bowen and Robert D. Hisrich, "The Female Entrepreneur: A Career Development Perspective," *Academy of Management Review* 11, No. 2 (1986).

[4]Joline Godfrey, *Our Wildest Dreams: Women Entrepreneurs Making Money, Having Fun, Doing Good* (New York: Harper Business, 1992).

[5]"The New Economic Force: Women-Owned Businesses, 1992 Data Report" (Washington, D.C.: National Foundation for Women Business Owners, 1992).

[6]Ibid.

why it takes three to five years to produce reliable figures on women's business participation and ownership. "This lack of timeliness leads to fragmented knowledge." Lack of accurate and timely information inhibits progressive policy making. "Informed decisions about policy related to businesses owned by women, minorities and veterans are often constrained by lack of timely and accurate information."[7]

Generations of Women Entrepreneurs

Despite the fact that there is a critical gap in the modern history of women entrepreneurs, author Joline Godfrey believes we have enough documentation to categorize women into three generations:

1. **First generation,** which goes back to the turn of the century and included many service activities that catered to the personal needs of customers. These businesses included seamstress shops, laundries, teashops, and bakeries. Many of these businesses did not require capital.
2. **Second generation,** which included those businesses taken over by the daughters of their founding parents as well as those businesses that were started by women with education and training who left high-level jobs in corporate America to start their own businesses.
3. **Third generation,** which represents women who have more than one business, have sold one or more businesses, invest in other businesses, and have sufficient capital (or access to it) to move into other business opportunities. These women may be board members, leaders of major advocacy and policy-making bodies, and are in a position to influence the next generation of owners.[8]

Women of the future will be more venturesome in spirit as they model themselves after and read about the success stories of today. They will have the protection of the law to lessen the probability and impact of discrimination and more opportunities will be open to them in construction, medicine, high-tech, and engineering fields as well as in service and retail industries. As our dependence on physical labor and manufacturing declines, more opportunities that utilize the brain rather than brawn will be emerging. The knowledge and service industries that require research, communication and human resource capabilities will favor women and as education becomes a prerequisite for innovative activity, women's investment in learning and personal development will be an advantage.

Women will become more confident in traditionally male-dominated areas as they receive more support and encouragement from their spouses and families. Postponement of marriage and children, surrogate parenting, day-care centers, and an increasing number of successful role models will pave the way for a larger number of successful women entrepreneurs.

It is projected that by the end of the decade, 40 to 50 percent of all businesses will be owned by women. "Like a great wave—we are coming. Like the effluence

---

[7]Status Report to Congress, *Statistical Information on Women in Business* (Washington, D.C.: U.S. Government Printing Office, December 1990).

[8]Godfrey, *Our Wildest Dreams*.

of the great rivers we are altering the landscape and enriching the economy. Flowing through your lives, we are changing the very nature of business."[9]

Barriers Confronting Women Entrepreneurs

Discrimination

Women entrepreneurs have long felt that they have been victims of **discrimination.** Various studies have examined the types of discrimination and some have even attempted to document them. In 1988 the Subcommittee on Exports, Tax Policy, and Special Problems examined credit issues related to women-owned businesses and identified four obstacles: (1) the need for management and technical training; (2) inequity of access to credit; (3) virtual exclusion of women from government procurement activities; and (4) the inadequacy of information and data on women-owned businesses.

Researchers Sexton and Bowman-Upton suggest that female business owners are subject to gender-related discrimination, especially by financial institutions.[10] They further report that Myers found a "lingering but potentially potent bias in people's beliefs, feelings, and actions regarding women."[11] Buttner and Rosen also found that women are viewed as less entrepreneurial than men and are judged to be significantly less effective in terms of leadership, autonomy, risk-taking, readiness for change, energy level, and support. They are also perceived as being more emotional.[12]

Survival and success in business are difficult for everyone, but women may face additional barriers that men do not face. Gassman identified the following eight additional barriers that women entrepreneurs must overcome.

1. *Difficulty in obtaining credit*—Women might not have a business track record, credit history, or banking relationship and are less likely to own their own home or car. They are subject to myths that women are not good at managing money and are viewed as hobbyists instead of serious business operators.
2. *Limited exposure to math and finance*—Traditional socialization of women has led to a lifetime of negative messages regarding math, technology, and financial matters. The pattern of math and technology avoidance continues as males receive more positive reinforcement from parents and teachers in areas that are perceived as "unfeminine."
3. *Societal biases*—Women entrepreneurs are often not taken seriously, being viewed as "hobbyists," "dabblers," or "part-timers" and set up by their husbands so they can have fun or keep busy. They may be viewed as overemotional or unable to understand the inner workings of business.

---

[9]Ibid.

[10]Donald L. Sexton and Nancy Bowman-Upton, "Female and Male Entrepreneurs: Psychological Characteristics and Their Role in Gender-Related Discrimination," *Journal of Business Venturing* 5, No. 1 (1990): 29–36.

[11]D. G. Myers, *Psychology* (New York: Worth Publishers, Inc., 1986).

[12]E. H. Buttner and B. Rosen, "Bank Loan Officers' Perceptions of the Characteristics of Men, Women and Successful Entrepreneurs," *Journal of Business Venturing* 3, No. 3 (1988): 249–261.

4. *Not thinking big enough*—Women are found to have a greater fear of failure than men. They have been socialized to be cautious, avoiding risks and danger, and as a result they are susceptible to setting their business sights too low. Sometimes they are afraid to travel, relate to strange people, hire subordinates, or borrow large sums of money. They may start their business small and very often keep it small.

5. *Ambivalence about being a competitive, profit-oriented deal-maker*—Women may be averse to being perceived as a "hustler," "money-grubber" or "competitor" because they have been socialized into nurturing, mothering, and serving others. They are sensitive to rejection and are hesitant to ask something to close a deal.

6. *Isolation from business networks*—Since most young women are not expected to someday operate a business, they are not taught the ropes of the system or encouraged to join business-oriented organizations. In fact, until recently some professional/community organizations were actually closed to women. This lack of contacts has led to feelings of isolation, especially among minority women.

7. *Balancing home and work roles*—Having the major responsibility for managing home and family tasks as well as working full time places a double burden on women entrepreneurs. Because it takes an abundance of time to do both jobs, women face exhaustion and stress as they try to balance these responsibilities. This is especially true for women operating home-based businesses.

8. *Developing a management style*—Because of socialization and relative lack of experience, women entrepreneurs may be unsure about their leadership ability and assertiveness potential. They may be more comfortable tackling smaller, technical problems than with the big picture of the total business.[13]

A study recently completed by the Alberta (Canada) Department of Economic Development and Trade identified several additional barriers:

9. *Negative self-perceptions*—Women view themselves as having personal characteristics that negatively affect their business activities. There is some indication that rural, native, and immigrant women may be more affected by their perceived personal deficiencies than the population as a whole.

10. *Hostile environment*—This barrier includes such factors as lack of respect from the male business community, overt societal discrimination, social conditioning, and sexual stereotyping.

11. *Lack of business/management training and experience*—Most women entrepreneurs have not been in business before and many have little management experience. While women entrepreneurs generally have a higher level of education than their male counterparts, their programs of study tend to be less business related than those of male entrepreneurs. Specific management areas of greatest concern include employee relations (recruiting and retaining staff and delegating responsibilities), financial management, marketing, and planning.

12. *Lack of female role models*—While this problem seems to be dissipating with the exposure of success stories and publicity surrounding female entrepreneurs,

---

[13]Roberta Gassman, "Women in Business Curriculum Materials: Overcoming Barriers and Building Upon Strengths," University of Wisconsin—Extension and Small Business Development Center, 1988.

there is nevertheless a shortage of successful women who take others under their wing to train and protect them as they develop in their own right.[14]

Finally, Taylor identified three additional barriers to entrepreneurship:

13. *Virtual exclusion of women-owned businesses from government procurement activities*— Women rarely are the recipients of government contracts.
14. *Inadequate management and technical training to "fast-track" women into the market-place*—High-quality, sustained management training and technical assistance to improve women's entrepreneurial skills are lacking.
15. *Inadequate information and data on women-owned businesses*—Policymakers are not fully informed about the contributions that women business owners are making.[15]

Congressional hearings conducted by Rep. John LaFalce in 1988 indicated that little, if any, progress had been made to break down the barriers Taylor identified,[16] and empirical research validates that women entrepreneurs are still struggling with these obstacles. One hundred twenty-nine women were surveyed to empirically verify the existence and extent of these barriers based on actual experience. In order of frequency, the barriers encountered are listed in Table 6.2.

Women entrepreneurs suffer some **unique circumstances** not encountered by their male counterparts (see Table 6.3). For example, a woman feels it is her obligation to raise the children, tend the house, and run her business successfully; the male entrepreneur often focuses only on the last responsibility. Additionally, while both males and females are routinely rejected for loans, there appears to be some evidence that women are rejected more frequently and are often asked to have their spouse or other male family member cosign the loan application. Also, women are not exposed to business training as often as are men and usually start their businesses later because they have taken time out to have children. Lacking guidance, counsel, and knowledge of information sources is often the result of not being in the "old boy network" or being in any network that supplies this needed informal support function or information. Customers' lack of confidence, finding a good location, and lack of support from family members appear to occur less frequently.

Operating Problems Encountered by Women Entrepreneurs

Women in business often encounter **operating problems** similar to those of their male counterparts, that is, they frequently suffer from lack of capital and inadequate time for managerial functions (Table 6.2). In addition to cash flow and marketing problems, entrepreneurs must also manage information search, retrieval, and correct

---

[14]Gassman, "Women in Business Curriculum Materials."

[15]C. Taylor, *Women and the Business Grade: Strategies for Successful Ownership* (Washington, D.C.: Venture Concepts Press, 1980).

[16]Congressional hearings conducted by Rep. John LaFalce in Small Business Committee, 1988.

Table 6.2
Frequency of Barriers Encountered by Women Entrepreneurs

1. Lack of working capital
2. Lack of total capital
3. Inadequate time for managerial functions
4. Seasonal fluctuations in cash flow
5. Inadequate sales
6. Promotion and advertising
7. Fierce competition
8. Slow collection of accounts receivables
9. Heavy operating expenses and overhead
10. Coordination of activities
11. Training and developing new employees
12. Inadequate information for planning
13. Need for market research
14. Recordkeeping and control
15. Lack of financial information and financial ratios
16. Selection of supervision of personnel
17. Lack of operating experience in product buying, pricing, and handling finances
18. Inadequate knowledge of competition
19. Credit practices and overextension of credit
20. Lack of complete product line or range of service

Table 6.3
Unique Circumstances of Women Entrepreneurs

1. Bearing the entire risk of start-up
2. Fatigue from long hours
3. Scheduling business and family activities
4. Narrow attitude toward women in business
5. Lack of knowledge of relevant information sources
6. Lack of guidance and counsel
7. Obtaining a loan
8. Finding enough time to spend with children
9. Extension of credit from suppliers
10. Lack of confidence from customers because of gender
11. Finding a good location
12. Initially being taken seriously by family members
13. Lack of encouragement from family members

direction of the communication flow process. Financial information, recordkeeping, and control, as well as information for planning, are often critical to the successful operation of the business.

The empirical results of the frequency of occurrence of the operating problems encountered by women as shown in Table 6.2 are not meant to show how unique the day-to-day problems are, but to reinforce the need for basic training in the functional fields of business. Women want to be given a chance, on an even playing field, to show that they can solve problems "in the trenches" as competently as other entrepreneurs.

Information Gathering and Networking

Gathering **quality information** for decision making is critical to the operation and survival of a business. Where to find the appropriate information and counsel is perhaps as high on the priority list as is maintaining cash flow. Information flow is the lifeline of a business, especially in changing markets, evolving economic conditions, and when combating aggressive competitors' strategies.

Where do women entrepreneurs look for their information? In a survey conducted by Welsch and Young, 129 women entrepreneurs ranked the importance

Table 6.4
Ranking of Information Sources

1. Customers	25. Local government
2. Employees	26. SBA
3. CPA	27. State government
4. Business associates	28. Agents
5. Lawyers	29. Management consultants
6. Professional journals	30. Business neighbor
7. Competitors	31. *Sun-Times*
8. Suppliers	32. *Business Week*
9. Trade journals	33. Universities
10. Reference books	34. *Money*
11. Professional societies	35. *INC*
12. Vendors	36. Middleman
13. Manuals	37. *Time*
14. Yellow Pages	38. *Fortune*
15. Business club/Civic organization	39. Commerce Department
	40. *Forbes*
16. Bankers	41. *New York Times*
17. Handbooks	42. *Newsweek*
18. *Crains*	43. *Barrons*
19. Catalogs	44. *Nations Business*
20. Family members	45. *US News*
21. *Wall Street Journal*	46. OSHA
22. IRS	47. Personal neighbors
23. *Chicago Tribune*	48. EPA
24. Market consultants	49. Engineers

(N = 129)   (Range = 1 to 5)

Source: H. P. Welsch and E. C. Young, "Profiling the Information Search Activity of Women Entrepreneurs," submitted to the Academy of Management Women's Division, 1990.

and utilization of various information sources.[17] Table 6.4 shows that customers and employees were clearly ranked at the top of the list as sources that are very close to the heart of the business, its market, and operations. A variety of professional advisors, such as CPAs, lawyers, and bankers, were also ranked near the top of the list. In addition to reading a variety of journals, books, and newspapers, there was strong evidence that these women entrepreneurs engaged in extensive networking, or external communication.

Networking is defined by Welch as "the process of developing and using your contacts for information, advice, and moral support as you pursue your career." Male entrepreneurs have long used both formal and informal networks to help promote their business. Their "old boy" networking occurs often as a by-product of membership in social clubs, civic organizations, and participation in athletic events.[18]

[17]Harold P. Welsch and Earl C. Young, "Profiling the Information Search Activity of Women Entrepreneurs," submitted to Academy of Management Women's Division, 1990.

[18]M. S. Welch, *Networking: The Great New Way for Women to Get Ahead*, S. Duck and D. Perlman, eds. (Beverly Hills, CA: Sage Publications, 1987), 28–41.

Prescriptions

In addition to networking, women can prepare themselves through education, seminars and workshops, planned experiences, role-playing, professional mentors, internships, and forcing themselves out of their "comfort zones." Hisrich has suggested six ways to help women entrepreneurs successfully develop and manage new enterprises.[19]

1. *Acquire some experience in dealing with money*—Apply for a loan and pay it off even if it is not needed; complete the family tax return; manage the family finances; obtain bookkeeping experience in a voluntary or professional trade association.

2. *Conduct honest self-appraisals*—Compensate for weaknesses or gaps in education by attending seminars and minicourses; hire experts in those areas where deficiencies have been identified.

3. *Gain occupational experience*—Rotate positions to various middle management or technical areas to gain experience in managing and to obtain exposure to planning, marketing, and financial matters.

4. *Prioritize responsibilities*—Identify and delegate household and business responsibilities if necessary; work out the role conflict and manage time efficiently.

5. *Establish a support system*—A strong network of family, friends, clients, and business associates should be established, as well as an "old girl network" with mentors and professional groups.

6. *Be determined and professional*—Perseverance through thick and thin and a strong motivation to succeed are reflected by entrepreneurs to their customers. It is also important for women to be professional in order to be taken seriously in business and to gain respect and establish business contacts. An appearance that employs a straightforward, down-to-earth approach that confidently conveys knowledge is recommended.

---

[19]Robert Hisrich, "Women Entrepreneurs: Problems and Prescriptions for Success in the Future," in *Women-Owned Businesses* (New York: Praeger, 1989), 3–32.

C A S E • *Carol Jerrell: Suburban Realty Services**

Cynthia Iannarelli, Seton Hill College
G. R. Patton, Seton Hill College

The Early Years

Carol Jerrell sat behind the desk in her fifth floor Chevy Chase, Maryland, office. The Connecticut Avenue traffic was just subsiding from the morning rush hour. About to complete her twentieth year in real estate, she had agreed to discuss her start in the real estate business, issues she had encountered as a woman business owner and impending issues facing the industry, company and her personally.

> There are times that I look back and wonder about the turns and twists my life has taken. I was born in the late 1930s and grew up in what was then typical fashion. I was married in 1960. I had started college; but after marriage, I had to quit in order to support my husband while he completed law school. Our first child, Joe, was born two years later and our daughter, Lisa, was born the following year.
>
> About ten years later, when the children were in elementary school, I became very concerned about what would happen to the family if my husband were incapacitated or died and I had to support the family. My husband, Bill, suggested that I take the exam for a real estate agent's license. It made sense to me; I like working with people, I'm outgoing, hardworking and energetic. I thought real estate would be a great field for me and I passed the exam with no trouble.
>
> I also liked the fact that I would have some flexibility in my schedule and hours so I could still give the kids the attention they needed. I've always felt a little guilty about abandoning the children. I used to get up extra early in the morning to bake chocolate cakes for the kids before I went to work so I wouldn't feel so guilty. Concern for family is always a problem that working women and business owners have. It seems like men don't have to give up the traditional family role for careers. Women shouldn't have to either.

The real estate bug bit Carol hard. There was a lot of variety, it was a dynamic industry, a chance to meet people and make good friends and to be involved in what for most people is the biggest purchase decision they make. Like almost all real estate sales agents, Carol was an independent contractor to an owner/broker. While she loved the industry, she soon saw room for improvements and innovation. She was also troubled that there were so many talented women selling agents whose

---

skills were not being fully utilized and rewarded, and that there were so few women broker/owners.

Within a year, Carol tried to convince the owner of her agency to set up a second Maryland location with Carol as the manager. When she couldn't convince the owner, Carol left the agency and formed Jerrell Realty. Her first two employees were her mother and father.

To establish the company, Carol needed a $25,000 bank loan. The bank would only agree to the loan if her husband Bill would cosign the note, a requirement which really made Carol mad. She did finally agree to the terms when she learned that she would have been required to cosign any loan that her husband took out.

To succeed in the real estate business, a broker must belong to the regional multiple listing service. Multilist is a service that allows brokers to share house-for-sale information with other brokers in return for splitting sales commissions. With no access to multilist information, a broker/owner has a very small inventory of homes to show prospective buyers. When Carol applied to the regional service, she was turned down.

> It was clearly illegal. It was restraint of trade. In some part it was discrimination because I was a woman in a male-dominated business but mostly it was because the existing brokers didn't want any new competition. Bill, my husband, offered to take a leave of absence from his law firm to fight it in the courts. He was convinced that we would eventually win, but how long is eventually?
>
> We had no access to for sale listings, no advertising in "HOME" for sale books. I became very creative in marketing. I would "sweet talk" my way into a lot of information. Eventually, people recognized what was being done to me. Multilist listings started showing up under my office door.
>
> I had to negotiate each deal with the listing agency separately on a deal-by-deal basis. One agent told me that I could show a house he was listing as long as he came along and we split the commission 90%–10%, and he got the 90%! Some agents would refuse to take my clients' purchase offers to the owner. I got very good at calling the owners and telling them that I had an offer on their house but couldn't locate their sales agent. That always got the agents to respond!
>
> Other than a lot of dedication and hard work, I'm not sure how we survived. I'm sure you have heard this before, but if I knew what I was getting myself into, I never would have gone out on my own. Things are much better now. In the late 1970s antitrust laws in real estate were tightened up. Contracts became standardized and more regulated. What happened to me probably couldn't happen today.

About a year later, Bill Jerrell had a client who was a broker/owner and a multilist member. The client offered to sell the business to Carol, which would have made her a member of multilist. Carol sought the advise of a well-known real estate "mover and shaker" friend.

> He said it was simple. If my ego wanted to see the "Jerrell" name on a few for sale signs, then I should remain independent. But, if I was interested in building a substantial business, gaining access to the multilist was the only reasonable alternative.

The two businesses were merged into Crossroads Realty and Carol gained a partner—and access to the multilist system.

The Franchise Period

The late 1970s were the time of the franchise agency—Century 21, ERA, Caldwell Banker, Prudential, etc. We became the first Century 21 agency in the D.C. area, known as Century 21/Crossgate in 1977.

> Joining Century 21 was probably the smartest thing I ever did. We gained national exposure, instant name recognition and credibility, and assistance building a sales force. This is what really got us moving along the growth path.

Also in 1977 Carol split with her merger partner. Her partner was more interested in the home development business while Carol's interest remained in sales. Carol stayed with the company, changing the name to Century 21/Suburban Realty.

> All together, I stayed with the Century 21 franchise for fourteen years—about twelve years too long in hindsight. While they were very valuable in the beginning, there was very little value added beyond that point. The franchiser was collecting substantial fees for providing us very little. The innovations that were occurring came from us. In 1991 we became Suburban Realty Services.

Other franchise operations also began to run into hard times, primarily because the franchisers lacked the ability to control the activities of sales agents who were all independent contractors. Merrill Lynch sold its business to Prudential Realty. Several key Merrill Lynch agents and managers in the Washington area joined Suburban to form a "super office" in the Bethesda/Chevy Chase area.

> This was very important. It moved us into the much higher-priced homes, the new construction area and really added to our management depth. Our company has doubled in size in the last two years. We have eight locations, all organized as profit centers and all making money. We may not be the largest but we are the best! Our sales per agent are the highest in the area. All of our agents are "producers." I want my agents making a very good living, not just selling one or two homes a year on a part-time basis.

Women in Business

Over the years, Carol has found that her women sales agents have been substantial contributors to her success.

> I've gone out of my way to include women as a big part of my business. It's an exciting field, one where a woman can make just as much money as a man, doing exactly the same work. We have had problems; for example, some women can't seem to learn to handle success, particularly financial success. At times husbands are jealous and want control. I have had to intervene when the husband of one of my agents has tried to take over the sales process, negotiating with the client. Commercial real estate is still a "man's world," but we have done just great in residential.
>
> I mentioned the guilt issue before. Because of that I go out of my way to include children in the process here at Suburban. We have installed special phone lines just for the kids. If a child calls and mom is out on a sales call and can't come home and fix lunch or take the child to the swimming meet, someone else in the office will do it. Children get a commission on every sale. It goes into a special bank account for each of them. We provide office tours to see where mom

works. We really get them involved. . . and they can be a great source of referrals! We also provide training to our agents on dealing with spouses, working long and weird hours, etc. It can put pressure on home life.

Moving into the Future

Like any business, the environment is becoming increasingly complex. There are a number of issues facing Carol. Some impact the industry in general. Some are specific to Suburban Realty. Some deal with women/family businesses.

Regulation and Litigation

Increasing regulation and litigation potential means we need to provide more training and supervision in the company. Environmental regulations currently cover asbestos, radon, lead paint. In the future what about overhead electrical wires or other concerns?

There is proposed legislation covering mandatory home inspection that requires disclosure of any significant structural deficiencies. Is a small roof leak five years ago significant?

Who is our client? Historically we have had a fiduciary responsibility to the home seller, not buyer. But two years ago we were the first agency to offer "Buyer Brokers."

How do we implement programs or policies to comply with these kind of laws? How do we keep from getting sued given all of the changes that are occurring?

Succession Planning

I've made up my mind that I want to be out of the business, at least day-to-day operations, within the next five years. It's funny that women don't seem to have the power concerns that men have. I have no problem passing on the business to the next generation. They have more energy, education and creativity. I've talked a little bit to the managers about this issue, but I'm not totally sure how I should proceed.

Both my son and son-in-law are employees of Suburban. Bill still provides the legal advice, along with our daughter, Lisa, who is an attorney. And Dad, at 82, is still in the office every day!

Family Issues

This has always been critical to me. From the very beginning I made a decision that family comes first. When the kids were growing up, I would always take their phone calls. There was no such thing as an interruption when it came to the family. There have always been minor problems. What do you do when your son—employee calls you "mom" during a significant contract closing? Is it worth making an issue about that?

The Board of Directors is made up of all family members. . . the same people I have dinner with on Sunday night. We really have to be careful about bringing the business "home" with us. Discussing business with the family is a normal release for most people but we can't do that. Occasionally I run into situations where our son, Joe, complains to Bill who complains to me. Or our son-in-law, Jim, complains to Lisa who gets upset with me. Who do I go to talk to?

Son-in-Law

My son-in-law, Jim, is a wonderful man. However, he has an acquaintance that married into a family business and eventually divorced his wife. The next day he was out of a job. Jim wants to know what kind of security he has. What are his rights. . . he has invested seven years in the business. How do I answer him?

What about Jim and my son, Joe? Joe feels he should be the heir apparent, after all, "I'm your son and he's your son-in-law." How do I divide up the responsibilities, ownership, etc.?

I have a lot of faith in my family. So far we have avoided any abuses of power. But, how do I assure the future?

Office Conduct

I've started a commercial realty division and staffed it initially with two retired senior executives, both former CEOs and long-time family friends. They are great workers, but every time I walk into their office they insist on a hug and little peck on the cheek. Every request of mine is answered with, "OK, honey, I'll take care of that." Should I put up with that? After all, they are 70 years old.

Putting Something Back

I fell like I have an obligation to assist other women as they come along. I do a fair amount of public speaking and as much charitable work as possible, but I really want to see more women business owners. Some women have the image that they couldn't work for other women. I find just the opposite. . . competent women excel when they work together. How do I find ways to promote this? I've had help over the years. How can I best help others?

C A S E • *Dainty Designs*

Candida G. Brush, School of Management, Boston University

Senorita, my best price for you is 20 percent, and this is a very good price! I will be your exclusive representative and sell your little baby dresses only in the finest stores. Our buying season will start very soon, and I need to have your cute little dresses very soon to do the best job I can for you. When will you be shipping your dresses?

Barbara was thinking quickly as she listened to the voice on the other end of the telephone. The commission rate suggested by this foreign manufacturer's representative was 5 percent less than the rate offered by the export management company. On the other hand, Manuel Hernandez of Groupa Estrella sounded quite sincere and eager for her business.

Manuel, I need some time to think about this; I will give you a call in two weeks. Thank you.

As she put the telephone down, she looked at the piles and piles of satin and silk hand-smocked baby dresses all around the living room of her condominium.

How was she going to figure out the costs, distribution, and transportation requirements and marketing arrangements within two weeks? She was anxious to begin selling her special occasion baby dresses in Mexico ever since she had read about the opportunities in retailing children's wear to upscale Mexican consumers. It was hard to believe she had come this far with her business.

Dainty Designs' Early Years

Barbara Walker had started her business in 1986 as a hobby. As a single flight attendant for a major airline, she used to buy expensive fabrics in foreign ports and hand-smock designs on the dresses and pinafores as something to do on layovers. She customized each dress with ornate ribbons, hand-made flowers, and touches of antique lace. At first Barbara gave the dresses away to her friends and family as special occasion gifts for christenings or holidays. Soon friends of friends asked to buy them, so she sold them for $25 a dress. After a year-and-a-half of part-time sales effort, she decided to try selling the dresses retail. Because she had 10 years seniority with the airline, she was able to arrange her schedule to fly on weekends so she could run her new business during the week. She called her fledgling enterprise, "Dainty Designs."

At first, she did most of the smocking and sewing herself at night and spent the mornings visiting upscale small shops in Michigan, Wisconsin, and Minnesota to see if they would sell her dresses on consignment. The response was so overwhelming, she found she couldn't keep up with the demand. Barbara placed an ad for "smockers and sewers" and found local housewives who could sew and decorate dresses for her at $7/hour. January 1987 marked her first complete year of sales and she had sold $52,300 worth of dresses at an average price of $25 each. Barbara decided it was time to try to expand her markets.

Realizing that in order to substantially increase her sales, she needed to get into a major department store. This would be no easy task. How could a company with one full-time employee possibly persuade a major department store to accept her dresses? As she thought about it, she came up with a plan. In March of that year, she put her plan into action.

Taking New York by Storm

It was March 3rd and raining outside her condominium. "Where was the taxi?" she wondered. At 5:05 the yellow taxi showed up and Barbara anxiously adjusted her stylish rain hat, picked up her leather briefcase and new raincoat. The flight from Minneapolis to New York City went smoothly, and she thought again about her sales pitch: "unique stitching patterns, high-quality imported fabrics, special gifts for the special occasions."

Upon arrival in New York, she was dismayed to see it was still raining steadily, but at least the limousine had arrived. She carefully got into the limo and told the driver to take her directly to Bonwit Tellers. As the limo pulled out of LaGuardia

Airport into rush hour traffic, Barbara picked up the car phone and called Cecilia Thorpe, her contact at Bonwits. Reaching only Cecilia's answering machine, she left this message:

> Good Morning, Cecilia. This is Barbara Walker and I am just leaving the airport and my limousine will be at your store about 10:15. I have made luncheon arrangements at the Four Seasons for three, you, me, and your assistant. I look forward to seeing you soon.

After what seemed like an eternity in the drizzling rain, the limousine pulled up to Bonwit Tellers, and Barbara asked the limo driver to assist her upstairs to the offices with the parcels of baby dresses. As she took off her coat and prepared to wait for Cecilia, she instructed the driver to be ready at 12:00 to take them to lunch. Barbara was not the least bit nervous. She was confident she had a good product and she knew she was dressed appropriately for the situation. The fact that this entire sales visit would cost more than $1,000 didn't bother her at all.

As expected, Cecilia Thorpe adored the dresses. She took Barbara to meet the salespeople in the Infants Department and they reacted similarly. Everything went as planned, the sales meeting, the lunch, the flight home, and all. Barbara ended the day with an order for 8,000 dresses to be delivered in September.

Expansion Difficulties

Barbara had been so elated with her success in selling the dresses to Bonwits, she had failed to consider how difficult it might be to manage the operations associated with producing these dresses. The next few months were so hectic, Barbara had to take a leave of absence from flying to sew dresses herself and design patterns for the housewives who were smocking. The fabric was late arriving, some of the ribbons were frayed, one of her best smockers moved, and the other one had a new baby. Moreover, she was running out of space in her condominium to keep things. Trying to keep a handle on everything, Barbara stayed up many nights paying bills and packing her products. The worst part was that she was so short on cash. She had to pay for supplies and labor as she went, and wouldn't see any payments from Bonwits until the end of September, thirty days after the first shipment arrived. To make ends meet, she financed most of her expenses on her Mastercard, even though the interest rate was 18%.

By October, somehow Barbara had completed her order to Bonwit, paid off her charge card, her seamstresses and smockers, and her other bills. She had just recovered from two weeks in bed with exhaustion and was happy she was going to be back flying soon. Best of all, she had hired an assistant to help out with the business while she was out of town. The business was going to make it and so would Barbara.

Dresses por Ninas

Barbara had been reading about opportunities in Mexico for small businesses. With trade policies encouraging U.S. businesses to sell products in Mexico, she had decided this might be a great opportunity to expand her sales. Her annual sales in

1991 were $231,000 which translated into 9,240 dresses which she wholesaled at an average price of $25 each. The dresses sold in the stores for $60 to $80 each. She had 6 standard smocking patterns, 12 different decorating styles, 4 different fabric choices, and 10 color combinations. Each dress took about 1 hour to sew. Only sleeveless pinafores or short-sleeved dresses were offered in sizes 6 months to 4 toddler. All dresses had round necks, no collar, and were gathered below the shoulders. Smocking and decorating took about 1.5 to 2 hours. She had a staff of 5 seamstresses and 8 smockers who worked an average of 30 hours per week. Because she did not have a separate place of business, she simply deducted a portion of her home maintenance expenses as overhead (i.e., light, heat, and office space). She typically sold her dresses for a 50 percent markup over her costs. Her average costs were:

Materials*	$ 2.15
Labor/hour	7.00
Overhead	1.00
Sales expense	.09
Advertising	.07
Shipping and storage	.08
Miscellaneous	.06
Total	$10.77

*Includes fabric, thread, lace, and ribbons

In considering her options for selling abroad, she had to consider the different services that would be provided. For example, if she signed a 3-year contract with the Coronado Export Management Company, it would contact the major upscale retailers throughout Mexico, negotiate the terms, arrange for the payment and the shipping, freight, delivery, and incremental expense, in addition to creating a brochure and display piece to promote the product. Coronado was a Texas-based company, but it had representatives in New York. It did require a $1,200 fee to start and then a 25 percent commission. Maria Delgado, her contact there, had explained that they would not carry competing products, and would provide personal service and any market and sales information about Mexico that she needed.

On the other hand, she had thought why not sell the product directly herself? She could fly to Mexico using her airline discount, and by making 4 trips a year she could get to know the buyers personally. Furthermore, she could see and talk to customers and have a better idea of how to decorate her dresses to suit their tastes. In addition, she had taken college Spanish and thought this might help. She estimated she could put together a Spanish language point-of-purchase poster for the 4 major stores in Mexico City for about $200, and secure Spanish labels for about $50 for the 5,000 dresses she hoped to sell the first year.

Finally, there was Manuel from Groupa Estrella in Mexico. He was willing to help with displays and placement of the dresses in the stores, and promised he would not carry any competing lines. Because he represented many lines of children's products, there would be only a small charge to include Barbara's dresses in his Spanish/English language brochure. Besides, if she did business with him, either one of them could discontinue the arrangement with just 30 days' notice.

Barbara had estimated her expenses to sell her product in Mexico as follows:

Packaging	$ .11
Ship to port	.05
Ship from port	.05
Freight (air)	1.25
Banking	.04
Insurance	.01
Import duties	1.45
Delivery	.10
Incremental expenses	.03
	$3.09/dress

As she considered the costs and the three options, she wondered: "What if my goods are damaged in shipment? When will I get paid? What if my dresses aren't displayed properly and don't sell?" She pulled out her legal pad and began to analyze the situation.

CASE • *High Self-Esteem Toys Corporation**

Ann Walsh, Iowa State University
Charles B. Shrader, Iowa State University

The "Happy to Be Me" Doll

The "Happy to Be Me" doll is the first of what Cathy Meredig hopes to be one of many toys designed to promote children's self-esteem. Meredig is the founder and owner of High Self-Esteem Toys. Her story is that of the reluctant entrepreneur who realized that if children were to have more realistic dolls, she had to be the one to market them. The toy companies were not interested.

Cathy Meredig's story begins with a discussion with her friends about why they were displeased with their bodies.[1] Even the women who were well within what is considered normal body ranges expressed discontentment with their figures; their hips were too wide, their feet were too big, their stomachs protruded, their waists were not curvy enough, and they needed to lose 10 to 15 pounds. Meredig said they wanted to have the bodies of models, not necessarily real models, but ones that resembled Barbie dolls.

Following this disturbing conversation, Meredig wondered when we develop our self-images. Assuming that most people probably form self-images during

*The authors would like to thank Cathy Meredig for providing helpful information in assembling this case. Support was also provided by the Murray G. Bacon Center for Business Ethics, College of Business, Iowa State University. Address correspondence to: C. B. Shrader, College of Business, 300 Carver Hall, Iowa State University, Ames, IA 50011.

adolescence, she decided to research the topic at the University of Minnesota's biomedical library and the St. Paul children's library. Much to her amazement, she discovered that by the age of six children have well-defined notions of adult body images.[2] She noted that women, in particular, were dissatisfied with the way they look; 70 percent thought that all or part of their bodies were too fat. In addition, she found that eating disorders among young women were prevalent: approximately 2 percent of girls grow up with anorexia and 15 percent suffer from bulimia.[3] Some girls start dieting as young as 8 or 9 years old.[4]

Based on these findings and further discussions with other women, Meredig thought about childhood activities which influence the development of self-image. She noted that young girls three to five years of age spend hundreds of hours playing with fashion dolls. They dress/undress dolls and engage in endless role-playing with them. Yet, girls and parents have no choices when it comes to selecting fashion dolls. Virtually all fashion dolls have distorted, unrealistic physical proportions. Take, for example, Barbie—the doll has a more-than-ample bosom, narrow rib cage, miniscule waist, and slim hips which do not compare to even top fashion models' measurements. Meredig questioned the fantasy messages instilled by these dolls: Does one have to be thin and sexy with expensive clothes and cars to be happy? She could not help but conclude that the hours spent playing with these kinds of dolls affect children's concept of beauty.[5,6] Inevitably, unrealistic models of beauty must trigger negative self-images in little girls. To prevent the erosion of these fledglings' self-images, Meredig saw a relatively simple solution: Change the shape of the plastic to reflect more realistic body proportions. Give children role-model dolls rather than fashion-model dolls.

But, when Meredig offered her research findings and her suggestions to major toy companies, she was turned down flat. She was advised that dolls had to be very high-fashion and "fantasylike" in order to sell. In one case she was also informed that women, indeed, could be shaped like a fashion doll. The secretary to the president of the company had a figure like a Barbie doll.[7,8] To add insult to injury, one toy company executive told her that the average American wouldn't get the idea that body image is important to young children.[9] This rude awakening to the toy industry made for one "steamed woman" more determined than ever to find a way to get realistic dolls into the hands of children.[10] In reaction, Meredig was quoted as saying, "I thought something had to be done. I couldn't stomach another 10 to 20 years of children seeing fashion dolls and believing that's the way adult women look."[11] Thus, the reluctant entrepreneur who knew little about dolls or the toy industry set out on her own.

Cathy Meredig

Cathy Meredig is not only the founder and developer of High Self-Esteem Toys Corp., she is also the operations manager, marketing strategist, public relations officer, and salesforce for her company. For these many roles, Meredig draws upon her education and work experience. She graduated from the University of Wisconsin, Madison, with a degree in industrial engineering. She has since worked for Formica, Procter & Gamble, and the 3M Company. In 1985 she started Practical Software

Inc., a software development services company.[12] Like the toy company, it was based in her home. Meredig has used the profits from her software company to fund her "Happy to Be Me" venture.

Meredig is 40 years old and married to Brian Leininger. She resides with her husband and seven-year-old son in Woodbury, a suburb of St. Paul, Minnesota.

When asked about her motivation for starting this business, she makes it clear that it was not to make large sums of money or to break away from a large bureaucracy. She started the company as a result of her deep belief that a realistic doll is better and healthier for children.[13] In fact, Meredig, who was content with the progress of her software company, had no intentions of producing and marketing the dolls herself. She tried unsuccessfully to get established toy companies to adopt her ideas. If the motivation for starting this company had been to make lots of money, she would have given up a long time ago. Many times the obstacles and setbacks have seemed insurmountable. What drives her is the absolute conviction that she is right. She must pursue this challenge because no one else has come forward to take up the cause.

How Does Happy Compare with Fashion Dolls?

Meredig describes Happy as a role model doll, *not* a fashion doll like Barbie.[14] "Happy has been designed with realistic body proportions of a young woman, unlike fashion dolls which project an impossibly distorted figure supposedly representing female beauty."[15] Meredig insists that Happy does not represent a "best" weight or body shape, just typical proportions. Exhibit 1 shows the comparisons between Happy and a fashion doll.[16,17,18,19]

Do consumers like the new doll? If Meredig's mail is any indication, the answer is "yes." One man wrote, "It's about time a doll is created that looks like a real woman! As a father, I think it's important to teach our children that the fashion doll figure is not only mystique—it's unreal and unattractive." What about the experts—children? Do they like the doll? Of all the children who have played with the doll, one little girl summed up the overwhelming response, "I love the Happy to Be Me Doll. She's much more fun. She is my favorite doll. She looks more real."[20] Although Meredig has been told that children make the decisions when it comes to buying toys, she believes that parents have significant influence. Therefore, she markets Happy more toward parents than children.[21]

Meredig doesn't plan to stop with one version of Happy. Prototypes for Black, Hispanic, and Asian,[22,23] as well as grandparent dolls, have been developed. In contrast with the ethnic versions of fashion dolls, Meredig's designs go beyond skin tones. Her new dolls emphasize head-to-toe racial features. For instance, the Asian Happy has smaller breasts, hips, and waist, deep brown, almost black slightly wavy hair, brown eyes, and skin color that is close to the Asian skin tone.[24] Each doll is developed from descriptions provided by focus groups and anatomical illustrations of women of that ethnicity.[25] For the grandparent dolls, facial and body features more accurately reflect older people. The grandfather doll will be the first doll in the marketplace with wrinkles.

Exhibit 1	Comparison Between Happy and a Fashion Doll	
	"Happy to Be Me"	Fashion Doll
	36–27–38	36–18–33
	5'1"	6'1"
	Average legs, neck, feet	Abnormally long legs, long neck, tiny feet
	Has butt	No butt
	Straight rib cage	Sharply indented rib cage
	Flexible arms	Rigid arms
	Slightly protruding tummy	Flat tummy
	Flat feet	Flexed feet in high-heeled position
	Green eyes in normal proportion to the head	Large eyes with dilated pupils
	Some make-up	Lavish make-up
	Straight head position	Tilted head
	Long reddish-brown hair	Usually long blond hair
	Limited wardrobe; normal clothes worn by women in everyday activities	Extensive wardrobe; extravagant clothes for rock stars and entertainers

Development and Competition

The one word that accurately describes the development of her new toy company is "setbacks." Her first setback came with her attempts to raise badly needed capital. Most banks were not even willing to help with small loans. They told her that she did not have anything they wanted to take. The Small Business Administration and other supposedly helpful government programs only added to Meredig's frustrations. Finally, she put up approximately $100,000 of her own money to start the new business.[26] She continued to borrow from her successful software business to fund her doll business. A journalist quoted Meredig, "It's taken over my life, my husband's life, my son's life."[27]

Meredig also found the creative aspects of a new business to be equally uncertain. Finding an artist's conception of a normal female body image proved to be much more difficult than she ever imagined. Numerous artists and fashion industry personnel could not provide her with a concept of the normal female form. Even a library search failed to generate pictures of average females. She eventually settled on Michelangelo's "Venus de Milo" as the prototype.[28] A model-maker and a face-painter were contacted.

Working on the prototypes was an iterative process. Meredig sent the model-makers an idea only to have it returned and revised. All correspondence with the model-makers had to take place by FAX and by telephone because Meredig simply could not afford to fly to meet with them. After much give and take, a consensus was reached and work on the first dolls began. To keep costs down all manufacturing operations were sent to Hong Kong. Also, only one version of the doll with a limited wardrobe was produced. When the doll went into production, Meredig first saw them being made on a videotape she received from the manufacturing plant in Hong Kong.

Issues of how and where to package the dolls surfaced. If the doll could not be manufactured in the United States, perhaps it could be packaged here. Again, Meredig encountered obstacles. Employing Americans would create additional costs. Workmen's compensation insurance for packaging 4½-ounce dolls and unemployment benefits based on seasonal fluctuations would add so much to the production costs that the selling price would be much higher than that of fashion dolls. Thus, the dilemma Meredig faced was how to keep the selling price competitive, yet provide employment for Americans. She ultimately decided that until she had the time and capital to explore other possibilities here at home, she would have all the work done overseas.

During the spring of 1991 Meredig developed a promotional strategy with Kerker & Associates, a Bloomington advertising and public relations firm. Due to the lack of money for a major advertising campaign, a public relations strategy was adopted. The response to the first public releases was overwhelming. Apparently, Happy had touched a nerve with parents, doctors, and counselors worldwide. International news services picked up the story and Meredig was asked to be a guest on radio and television talk shows and a speaker for numerous organizations.[29,30] Chuck Wanous, president of Kerker & Associates, claimed that the publicity generated a 80 to 90 percent exposure to the U.S. market, an astronomical feat.[31] The following year the TV program "48 Hours" carried a segment about Meredig and the doll.[32]

In late November of 1991, Happy made her debut in Byerly's, an upscale grocery store, which ordinarily does not carry toys. Happy's debut was announced in a small 2×4 inch column. Buoyed, no doubt, by the international publicity, 1,500 dolls were sold within 36 hours.[33]

After what appeared to be an entrepreneur's dream start-up, more setbacks followed. Major retailers such as SHOPKO, Target, Daytons, and Toys Я Us agreed to carry the doll. However, two of them decided that for Happy's trial run they would stock the doll but not the clothes. As Meredig knew, children would not play with just the doll, they needed the clothes. The third company unexpectedly canceled its order without giving an explanation. Without a good trial run, how could Meredig show the retailers that Happy could turn a profit?[34]

Although large and highly competitive, the fashion doll market is almost totally dominated by Mattel with Barbie. Of the $1.8 billion overall doll market, Barbie share makes up approximately $800 million of it. Furthermore, Barbie accounts for about half of Mattel's business.[35] Obviously, Barbie is not about to share her many retail aisles with a new cousin.

As one journalist describes the situation, "She [Meredig] is David taking on Goliath."[36] Faced with the reality that Mattel had a stranglehold on the fashion-doll market,[37] Meredig ponders over what other avenues might be available to her. How can she avoid going head-to-head with Barbie?

Criticism

Happy has not been welcomed in all circles with open arms. Critics charge that children are bombarded with distorted images of how they should look.[38] Mattel argues that girls know that Barbie is only a doll in a fantasy world, not a human being.[39] So what's the big deal? In response, Meredig admits that she has no solid medical evidence that fashion dolls harm girls' self-images. She also concedes that other sources such as the fashion industry itself probably contribute to the development of negative self-images.[40,41] However, she still believes that Happy is a step in the right direction.[42]

Other critics take the opposite view that Happy does not go far enough. With 47 percent of adult women wearing size 14 and larger,[43] Happy reflects only thinner women. Meredig agrees, but humorously chides, "One has to be elected president before one can make changes." In other words, Meredig realizes that a smaller Happy has to gain acceptance in young consumers' doll collections before a "heavier" Happy will be welcomed.

The Future

In addition to the current prototypes, Meredig's crusade includes a "chubby" Happy and other ethnic dolls.[44] She wants to give every girl a doll which reflects an accurate adult woman of the child's heritage.[45] She also has a designer and a children's author developing clothes and stories for Happy. In addition to the doll lines, Meredig has other toys in various stages of development. While not at liberty to discuss her ideas before their introduction, she affirms that all of her toys are designed with high self-esteem as the primary goal.

Notes

1. Karin Winegar, "Happy to Be Her," *Minnesota Monthly,* March 1992, 36–37.

2. Ibid.

3. Joyce Vanaman, "Guy and Doll," *The Press of Atlantic City,* December 29, 1991, F1, F2.

4. "New Doll Line May Be Shape of Things to Come," *Waco Tribune Herald,* August 25, 1991.

5. Jim McCartney, "Jousting with Giants," *Saint Paul Pioneer Press,* September 30, 1991, 1E, 6.

6. "Throwing Barbie a Curve," *Woodbury News,* December, 1991, 1, 19.

7. Julie Hinds, "Valley of the Dolls," *Detroit News,* August 19, 1991, 1D, 5D.

8. "New Doll Has Shape Like Venus," *Denver Post,* August 19, 1991.

9. Winegar, "Happy to Be Her."

10. Hinds, "Valley of the Dolls."

11. Cindy Richards, "Go Figure—Barbie's Rival Dolly Says Hello to Reality," *Chicago Sun-Times,* August 13, 1991, 1, 20.

12. McCartney, "Jousting with Giants."

13. Ibid.

14. Ibid.

15. "Happy to Be Me," High Self-Esteem Toys Corp., P.O. Box 25208, Woodbury, MN 55125.

16. Cathy Madison, "Minneapolis' Kerker Is Happy to Be Doll Agency, Even without Dollars," *Adweek/Midwest,* August 19, 1991, 1, 7.

17. "Happy to Be Me Creations Provide Doll Market with Reality Measure," *The Salt Lake Tribune,* February 14, 1992, 28.

18. Hinds, "Valley of the Dolls."

19. "Happy To Be Me," High Self-Esteem Toys Corp., P.O. Box 25208, Woodbury, MN 55125.

20. Ibid.

21. McCartney, "Jousting with Giants."

22. Lois Blinkhorn, "Barbie Faces Some Competition from a More Realistic New Doll," *Milwaukee Journal,* October 20, 1991, 1, 4.

23. McCartney, "Jousting with Giants."

24. "Happy to Be Me Creations Provide Doll Market with Reality Measure."

25. Winegar, "Happy to Be Her."

26. Blinkhorn, "Barbie Faces Some Competition. . . ."

27. Ibid.

28. "New Doll Has Shape Like Venus."

29. McCartney, "Jousting with Giants."

30. "New Doll Line May Be Shape of Things to Come," *Waco Tribune Herald,* August 25, 1991.

31. Madison, "Minneapolis' Kerker Is Happy to Be Doll Agency, Even without Dollars."

32. Ibid.

33. Ibid.

34. Richards, "Go figure—Barbie's Rival Dolly Says Hello to Reality."

35. McCartney, "Jousting with Giants."

36. Ibid.

37. Ibid.

38. "Happy to Be Me Creations Provide Doll Market with Reality Measure."

39. McCartney, "Jousting with Giants."

40. Ibid.

41. "Happy to Be Me Creations Provide Doll Market with Reality Measure."

42. McCartney, "Jousting with Giants."

43. Chris Bynum, "Just No Comparison," *Huntsville Times,* December 23, 1991.

44. Blinkhorn, "Barbie Faces Some Competition. . . ."

45. Vanaman, "Guy and Doll."

Case Appendix A

Minneapolis' Kerker Is Happy to Be Doll Agency, Even Without Dollars

MINNEAPOLIS—This is not an advertising story. Yet.

It's a guerilla story, proof that today's agencies are hardly novices when it comes to integrated selling. All it takes is a good idea.

Source: Karin Winegar, "Happy to Be Her," *Minnesota Monthly,* (March 1992): 36–37.

That came two years ago, when industrial engineer and computer software developer Cathy Meredig first met with Kerker & Associates, a smallish Minneapolis shop. She explained to president Chuck Wanous her mission, a "Happy To Be Me" doll patterned after Mattel's Barbie but without the fashion doll icon's inimitable proportions; not 36-18-33, but 36-27-38 with comfortable clothes to boot.

"It touched our emotional hot button," Wanous recalls.

That ad dollars didn't exist didn't matter. The agency, then in the process of adopting the positioning line, "in the business of creating customers," figured it could circumvent traditional channels and still create customers aplenty.

The channels were familiar enough. Kerker was named Tonka's first agency when that company was headquartered in a two-car garage and continued with the toy maker for 23 years. Ertl, Lakeside, and Schaper were among other toy names once gracing the client list.

But entrepreneur Meredig's funds were "near and dear," says Wanous; she'd invested her time and $90,000 of her own money to launch High Self-Esteem Toys Corp. That meant restricting agency activities to packaging, point-of-purchase, PR and strategic counsel.

"Like it or not, buyers will not stock a product unless they envision some demand. We had to be efficient in our communications and, from a strategic standpoint, create demand so that it can be demonstrated to buyers," he said.

Thus the strong PR component. A news release went on the wire last Tuesday afternoon; by Wednesday the agency's phone lines were so jammed the phone company had to intervene. Erma Bombeck called. So did *The New York Times, London Daily Times, Washington Post, Los Angeles Times,* CBS, NBC, ABC, *Glamour, Seventeen, Newsweek, Harper's, People,* French magazine *Le Pointe* and others, plus "consumers by the zillions," Wanous said.

He figures it's the right idea at the right time, an alternative for parents who want their daughters to play with a doll that won't create false expectations and negative body images, which are said to contribute to adolescent eating disorders. Barbie has a solid hold on the market, he points out, but a certain segment of the population may not want to buy what she represents. If media interest is any indication, he may be right.

"I've spent 27 years in marketing, and this is the most incredible thing I've seen in my entire life, bar none. I can't exaggerate it enough...We've been exposed to 80–90% of the U.S. market in two days. That's astronomical."

Now, however, response must be converted to sales; the product will hit shelves mid-fall. But will there be ad dollars? Says the seasoned ad guy: "That depends on what happens from here on out."

Case Appendix B Mailing Piece Used to Market The Doll

SPECIAL OFFER #1

"Happy" can be purchased in her Sparkling Pink Evening Dress and white pumps, beautifully gift boxed for $19.95.

Fashion Doll

Happy To Be Me Doll

YOURS ABSOLUTELY FREE!

Dear Parents and Grandparents,

The "Happy To Be Me" doll was developed when I uncovered some startling research about the development of body image and its relationship to self-esteem.

Research indicates that little girls form a mental image of what a woman's body should look like to be attractive and lovable by the time they are SIX YEARS OLD! This surprising fact becomes distressing if girls are forming this mental image based upon the unrealistic and distorted proportions of fashion dolls.

Even more startling is the fact that 70% of all girls grow up to believe they are fat. 2% of all girls develop anorexia nervosa and 15% will battle the eating disorder bulimia.

The "Happy To Be Me" doll is designed with a waist that barely indents, a rounded tummy, normal sized feet and hips, normally proportioned legs and neck, a rib cage that doesn't indent, and intelligent, focused eyes to teach children about realistic body proportions and to promote self-acceptance.

Psychologists, pediatricians, educators, and counselors have called and written to say, "It's about time!" Just what caring parents and grandparents have told me.

Good News! After your first order, you will receive a color brochure of Happy To Be Me dolls and outfits every four months. **More News!** If you like to sew, you'll enjoy the McCall Pattern Company's new patterns for Happy. Because she has realistic proportions, she's easier and more fun to sew for.

While "Happy" was designed with realistic body proportions...she was also designed for fun! Her long beautiful Italian doll hair is easy to comb and style. She has bendable arms which not only make her easier to dress — but she can be posed in many active stances. Her knees bend and her shoes actually stay on!

Rather than allowing little girls' thoughts, hopes, and dreams, to be shrunken down to 18 inch waists and size 2 feet, let's teach girls to love and accept their bodies just the way they are.

We at High Self-Esteem Toys Corp. truly believe that if young girls are to grow up feeling good about themselves and their bodies... they must be given the tools to learn healthy, happy body images for women.

"Happy" together with a caring adult explaining that realistic body proportions are attractive and lovable represents a remarkably easy way to promote high self-esteem.

Sincerely,

Cathy Meredig

Cathy Meredig
President & Founder

P.S. By giving a lucky little girl the "Happy To Be Me" doll, especially in those formative years of 3 - 6...you're sending a positive and powerful message of love and acceptance. A message that promotes...High Self-Esteem!

Purchase **Happy's Collection** which includes Special Offers #1, #2, and #3 for $64.00...and receive this romantic, beautifully detailed Wedding Dress (a $22 value) absolutely FREE as a special welcome gift to the "Happy To Be Me" Collection of Dolls! Limited time offer. The Wedding Dress comes beautifully gift boxed complete with pearly beaded veil, bouquet, and white wedding slippers.

Absolute Guarantee Of Satisfaction

If for any reason you are not completely delighted with your purchase, please return it to High Self-Esteem Toys for a prompt credit, refund or exchange. We desire your complete satisfaction.

HIGH SELF-ESTEEM TOYS CORP.

Intrapreneurship: The Process of Corporate Entrepreneurship

Key Topics

- Specific Elements for a Corporate Intrapreneuring Strategy
- Revolutionary Results of an Intrapreneurial Approach
- A Continuum of Intrapreneurial Activity
- Models of Corporate Entrepreneurship (Intrapreneurship)

Comprehensive Entrepreneurial Cases

- The Douglas Call Company, 1989: Power Spray Technologies Division
- Wal-Mart Stores, Inc.: Strategies for Market Dominance
- Medicap Pharmacies, Inc.: A Balanced Strategy for the Nineties

Introduction

Progress in understanding the process of corporate entrepreneurship may help the development of new managerial approaches and innovative administrative arrangements to facilitate the collaboration between entrepreneurial individuals and the organizations in which they are willing to exert their entrepreneurship.[1]

The last two decades have seen corporate strategies focused more heavily on innovation. This new emphasis on entrepreneurial thinking developed during the **entrepreneurial economy** of the 1980s. Peter Drucker (1984), the renowned management expert, described four major developments that explain the emergence of this economy. First, the rapid evolution of knowledge and technology promoted the use of high-tech entrepreneurial start-ups. Second, demographic trends such as double-income families, continuing education of adults, and the aging population added fuel to the proliferation of newly developing ventures. Third, the venture capital market became an effective funding mechanism for entrepreneurial ventures. Fourth, American industry began to learn how to manage entrepreneurship.

This contemporary thrust in entrepreneurship as the major force in American business has led to a desire for this type of activity inside enterprises. While some researchers have concluded that entrepreneurship and bureaucracies are mutually exclusive and cannot coexist, others have described entrepreneurial ventures within

---

[1]Robert A. Burgelman, "Designs for Corporate Entrepreneurship," *California Management Review* 26 (1984): 154–166.

the enterprise framework. Successful corporate ventures have been used in many different companies, including 3M, IBM, Hewlett-Packard, AT&T, General Electric, and Polaroid. Today there is a wealth of popular business literature describing a new "corporate revolution" taking place thanks to the infusion of entrepreneurial thinking into larger bureaucratic structures. This infusion is referred to as **corporate entrepreneurship** or **intrapreneurship**.[2]

In 1985 Gifford Pinchott coined the term *intrapreneurship* as entrepreneurial activity inside the corporation where individuals (intrapreneurs) will "champion" new ideas from development to complete profitable reality.[3] Other authors have expanded this definition to include sanctions and resource commitments for the purpose of innovative results. While on the surface this concept may appear straightforward, a number of authors have concluded that intrapreneurship may take several forms. One researcher, Hans Schollhammer, proposed five broad types of internal entrepreneurship that he labeled administrative, opportunistic, imitative, acquisitive, and incubative.[4] Incubative entrepreneurship appears to resemble the intrapreneurial model the closest because it refers to the creation of semiautonomous units within the existing organization for the purposes of sensing external and internal innovative developments; screening and assessing new-venture opportunities; and initiating and nurturing new-venture developments.

Researcher Karl Vesper developed three major types of corporate venturing that he identified as (1) new strategic direction; (2) initiative from below; and (3) autonomous business creation.[5] Vesper believed that corporate venturing could be any one of these individual types, as well as any or all possible combinations. Similar to Schollhammer's incubative form, the "initiative from below" approach, where an employee undertakes something new (i.e., an innovation), best represents the type of corporate entrepreneuring activity that has become recognized as intrapreneurship. While all of these forms of intrapreneuring are considered important, the factors that are essential in developing an entrepreneurial environment are the focus of this chapter. If an organization's atmosphere does not support innovative efforts, then intrapreneuring will probably not occur.

Over the last few years there has been a growing interest in using intrapreneurship (corporate entrepreneurship) as a way for corporations to enhance employees' innovative abilities and, at the same time, increase corporate success through the potential creation of new corporate ventures. However, the creation of corporate entrepreneurial activity can be difficult because it involves radically changing traditional forms of internal organizational behavior and structure.

The desire to pursue corporate entrepreneurship has arisen from a variety of pressing problems including: (1) required changes, innovations, and improvements in the marketplace to avoid stagnation and decline; (2) perceived weaknesses in the traditional methods of corporate management; and (3) the turnover of innovative-

---

[2]Peter F. Drucker, "Our Entrepreneurial Economy," *Harvard Business Review* (January–February 1984): 59–64. See also Donald F. Kuratko and Richard M. Hodgetts, *Entrepreneurship: A Contemporary Approach,* 2d. ed. (Fort Worth, TX: Dryden Press/Harcourt Brace, Inc., 1992).

[3]Gifford Pinchott, *Intrapreneuring* (New York: Harper & Row, 1985).

[4]Hans Schollhammer, "Internal Corporate Entrepreneurship" in *Encyclopedia of Entrepreneurship,* C. Kent, D. Sexton, and K. Vesper, eds. (Englewood Cliffs, NJ: Prentice-Hall, 1982).

[5]K. H. Vesper, "Three Faces of Corporate Entrepreneurship: A Pilot Study" in *Frontiers of Entrepreneurship Research* (Wellesley, MA: Babson College, 1984), 294–320.

minded employees who are disenchanted with bureaucratic organizations. This loss of talented employees is intensified by entrepreneurship's new appeal as a legitimate career and the increased ability of the venture capital industry (as well as informal capitalists) to finance more new ventures.

However, the pursuit of corporate entrepreneuring as a strategy to counter these problems creates a newer and potentially more complex set of challenges on both a practical and theoretical level. On a practical level, organizations need guidelines to direct or redirect resources toward establishing effective intrapreneuring strategies. On a theoretical level, researchers need to continually reassess the components or dimension that predict, explain, and shape the environment in which corporate entrepreneuring flourishes. Recently there have been studies focusing on factors contributing to or enhancing the establishment of corporate venturing. The purpose of this chapter is to present an overview of the concept of intrapreneurship from an organizational perspective by outlining recommended steps for a strategy in corporate entrepreneurship based on organizational factors that would encourage the development of innovative-minded employees.

Specific Elements for a Corporate Intrapreneuring Strategy

What conditions or steps must be followed in order for a corporate intrapreneuring program to succeed? Figure 7.1 describes a flowchart that outlines the prescribed steps. These steps are described in the following sections.

Figure 7.1   Flowchart of the Key Steps in Developing an Intrapreneurial Strategy

---

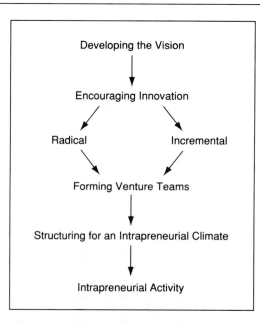

Developing the Vision

Encouraging Innovation

Radical   Incremental

Forming Venture Teams

Structuring for an Intrapreneurial Climate

Intrapreneurial Activity

Developing the Vision

The first step in planning an intrapreneurship strategy for the enterprise is sharing the vision of innovation that the corporate leaders wish to achieve. Since it is suggested that corporate entrepreneuring results from the creative talents of people within the organization, employees need to know about and understand this vision. The importance of shared vision is a critical element for a strategy that seeks high achievement. This shared vision requires identification of specific objectives for corporate entrepreneuring strategies and the programs needed to achieve those objectives. Author and researcher Rosabeth Moss Kanter has described three major objectives and their respective programs designed for venture development within companies.[6] These are outlined in the following table.

Objectives and Programs for Internal Venture Development

Objectives	Programs
Make sure that current system, structures, and practices do not present insurmountable roadblocks to the flexibility and fast action needed for innovation.	Reduce unnecessary bureaucracy and encourage communication across departments and functions.
Provide the incentives and tools for entrepreneurial projects.	Use internal "venture capital" and special project budgets. (This has been termed *intracapital* to signify a special fund for intrapreneurial projects.) Allow discretionary time for projects (sometimes referred to as "bootlegging" time).
Seek synergies across business areas so that new opportunities are discovered in new combinations.	Encourage joint projects and ventures among divisions, departments, and companies. Allow and encourage employees to discuss and brainstorm new ideas.

Source: Adapted by permission of the publisher from "Supporting Innovation and Venture Development in Established Companies," by Rosabeth Moss Kanter, *Journal of Business Venturing,* Winter 1985, pp. 56–59. Copyright 1985 by Elsevier Science Publishing Co., Inc.

Encouraging Innovation

The next step for a corporation seeking to establish an intrapreneurial strategy is to encourage innovation among employees as the key element in their strategy. The importance of developing innovation within the corporate environment is a critical component of contemporary competitive strategies. Innovation has been described as chaotic and unplanned by some authors, while other researchers insist it is a systematic discipline. Both positions can be true depending on the nature of the innovation. One way to understand this concept is to recognize two types of innovation—radical and incremental.[7]

---

[6]Rosabeth M. Kanter, "Supporting Innovation and Venture Development in Established Companies," *Journal of Business Venturing* (Winter 1985): Vol. 1, No. 1, 47–60.

[7]Harry S. Dent, Jr., "Reinventing Corporate Innovation," *Small Business Reports* (June 1990): 31–42.

Radical innovation represents inaugural breakthroughs that have been launched (e.g., personal computers, Post-it Notes, disposable diapers, and overnight mail delivery). These innovations take experimentation and determined vision that are not necessarily managed but *must* be recognized and nurtured. **Incremental innovation,** however, refers to the systematic evolution of a product or service into newer or larger markets. Examples include microwave popcorn, popcorn used for packaging (to replace styrofoam), and frozen yogurt. Many times incremental innovation will take over after radical innovation introduces a breakthrough. A corporation's traditional functional areas such as marketing, financing, and so forth as well as its formal systems can help implement incremental innovation. (See the following table.)

Characteristics of Radical vs. Incremental Innovation

Radical	Incremental
Stimulate through challenges and puzzles	Set systematic goals and deadlines
Remove budgetary and deadline constraints when possible	Stimulate through competitive pressures
Encourage technical education and exposure to customers	Encourage technical education and exposure to customers
Allow technical sharing and brainstorming sessions	Hold weekly meetings that include key management and marketing staff
Give personal attention—develop relationships of trust	Delegate more responsibility
Encourage praise from outside parties	Set clear financial rewards for meeting goals and deadlines
Have flexible funds for opportunities that arise	
Reward with freedom and capital for new projects and interests	

Source: Adapted from Harry S. Dent, Jr., "Growth Through New Product Development," *Small Business Reports* (November 1990): 36.

Both types of innovation require vision and support.[8] This support requires different steps for effective development. For example, it has been widely recognized that entrepreneurial activity needs a **champion**—a person with a vision and the ability to share it. In addition, both types of innovation require that an effort be made by top management to educate employees about innovation and entrepreneurship—a concept known as **top management support.**

Encouraging innovation requires a willingness to not only tolerate failure but also to learn from it. For example, one of the early founders of 3M, Francis G. Oakie, had an idea to replace razor blades with sandpaper. He believed that men could rub sandpaper on their face rather than use a sharp razor. He was wrong and the idea failed, but his ideas evolved until he developed a waterproof sandpaper for the auto industry, a blockbuster success!

---

[8]Dean M. Schroeder, "A Dynamic Perspective on the Impact of Process Innovation Upon Competitive Strategies," *Strategic Management Journal* 2 (1990): 25–41.

Thus, 3M's philosophy was born. Innovation is a numbers game; the more ideas you have, the better the chances for a successful innovation. In other words, to master innovation there must be a toleration for failure. This philosophy has paid off for 3M. Antistatic videotape, translucent dental braces, synthetic ligaments for knee surgery, heavy-duty reflective sheeting for construction signs, and, of course, Post-it Notes are just some of the great innovations developed at 3M. Overall, the company has a catalog of 60,000 products that contributed to more than $10.6 billion in sales.[9]

Today 3M follows a set of innovative rules that encourage employees to foster ideas. The key rules include:

- **Don't kill a project**—If an idea can't find a home in one of 3M's divisions, a staffer can devote 15 percent of his or her time to prove it is workable. For those who need seed money, as many as 90 Genesis grants of $50,000 are awarded each year.
- **Tolerate failure**—By encouraging plenty of experimentation and risk-taking, there are more chances for a new-product hit. The goal: Divisions must derive 25 percent of sales from products introduced in the past five years. The target may be boosted to 30 percent.
- **Keep divisions small**—Division managers must know each staffer's first name. When a division gets too big, perhaps reaching $250 to $300 million in sales, it is split up.
- **Motivate the champions**—When a 3M employee comes up with a product idea, he or she recruits an action team to develop it. Salaries and promotions are tied to the product's progress. The champion has a chance to someday run his or her own product group or division.
- **Stay close to the customer**—Researchers, marketers, and managers visit with customers and routinely invite them to help brainstorm product ideas.
- **Share the wealth**—Technology, wherever it is developed, belongs to everyone.

Formation of Venture Teams

A third step in developing an intrapreneurial strategy is to focus on **venture teams.** Venture teams and the potential they hold for producing innovative results are being increasingly recognized as the productivity breakthrough of the nineties. There is certainly little doubt that their popularity is on the rise. Companies that have committed to a venture team approach often label the change a "transformation" or "revolution." This breed of work team is a new direction for many firms. The teams are often referred to as self-directed, self-managing, or high-performance, but usually a venture team includes all of these descriptions.

By examining many of the successful entrepreneurial developments within established corporations, it can be shown that entrepreneurship is not the sole province of the company's founder or its top managers. Rather, it is diffused throughout the company where experimentation and development go on all the time, as the company searches for new ways to build on the knowledge already

---

[9]See Russell Mitchell, "Masters of Innovation," *Business Week,* April 10, 1989, 58–63.

accumulated by its workers. U.S. Labor Secretary Robert B. Reich has referred to the term, **collective entrepreneurship,** where individual skills are integrated into a group and their collective capacity to innovate becomes something greater than the sum of its parts.[10] Over time, as group members work through various problems and approaches, they learn about each other's abilities. Specifically, they learn how they can help one another perform better, what each can contribute to a particular project, and how they can best take advantage of one another's experience. Each participant is constantly on the lookout for small adjustments that will speed and smooth the evolution of the whole.

The net result of many such small-scale adaptations, effected throughout the organization, is to propel the enterprise forward. In keeping with this focus on collective entrepreneurship, venture teams offer corporations the opportunity to utilize the talents of individuals but with a sense of teamwork. An excellent example of project team development is Signode Industries, Inc., a $750-million-a-year manufacturer of plastic and steel strapping for packaging and materials handling, located in Glenview, Illinois. The corporate leaders wanted to chart new directions to become a $1 billion-plus firm. In pursuit of this goal, Signode set out to devise an aggressive strategy for growth by developing "new legs" for the company to stand on. According to Robert F. Hettinger, a venture manager with Signode, it formed a corporate development group to pursue markets outside the company's core businesses but within the framework of its corporate strengths.

Before launching the first of its venture teams, Signode's top management identified the firm's global business strengths and broad areas with potential for new product lines: warehousing/shipping; packaging; plastics for nonpackaging, fastening, and joining systems; and product identification and control systems. The goal of each new business opportunity suggested by a venture team was to generate $50 million in business within five years. In addition, each opportunity had to build on one of Signode's strengths: industrial customer base and marketing expertise, systems sales and service capabilities, containment and reinforcement technology, steel and plastic process technology, machine and design capabilities, and productivity and distribution know-how.

The criteria were based on business-to-business selling only because Signode did not want to market directly to retailers or consumers. The basic technology to be employed in the new business had to already exist and there had to be a strong likelihood of attaining a major market share within a niche. Finally, the initial investment in the new opportunity had to be $30 million or less. Based on these criteria, Signode began to build its "**V-Team**" (venture team) approach to intrapreneurship. It took three months to select the first team members. The six initial teams had three common traits: high risk-taking ability, creativity, and the ability to deal with ambiguity. All were multidisciplinary volunteers who would work full time developing new consumer product packaging businesses. The team members came from such backgrounds as design engineering, marketing, sales, and product development. They set up shop in rented office space five miles from the firm's headquarters. All six teams were not able to develop remarkable new ventures;

---

[10]Robert B. Reich, "The Team as Hero," *Harvard Business Review* (May–June 1987): 81.

however, the efforts did pay off for Signode as one venture team developed a b̲ ̲_̲_̲_̲_̲
plan to manufacture plastic trays for frozen entrees that could be used in either
regular or microwave ovens. The business potential for this product was estimated
to be in excess of $50 million a year within five years. Thus, the V-Team experience
rekindled enthusiasm and affected morale throughout the organization. Most important, the V-Team approach became Signode's strategy to invent its future rather
than waiting for things to happen.[11]

Structuring for an Intrapreneurial Climate

In reestablishing the drive to innovate in today's corporations the final, and possibly
most critical, step is to invest heavily in an **entrepreneurial structure** that allows
new ideas to flourish in an innovative environment. This concept, when coupled
with the other elements of a strategy for innovation, can enhance the potential for
employees to become venture developers. In fact, in developing employees as a
source of innovations for corporations, it has been found that companies need to
provide more nurturing and information-sharing activities. In addition to establishing entrepreneurial ways and nurturing intrapreneurs, there is a need to develop a
climate that will help innovative-minded people reach their full potential. The
perception of an innovative climate is critical for stressing the importance of management's commitment to not only the organization's people but also to the innovative projects.

As a way for organizations to develop key structural factors for intrapreneurial
activity, one group of researchers developed an **Intrapreneurship Training Program** (ITP) as a facilitation to induce the change needed in the work atmosphere.
It is not our intent to elaborate completely on the content of the training program
here; however, a brief summary of the actual program is presented to provide a
general understanding of this training program designed to introduce an intrapreneurial environment in a company. This award-winning program was intended to
create an awareness of intrapreneurial opportunities in an organization. The program
consisted of six four-hour modules, each designed to train participants to be able
to support intrapreneurship in their own work area.[12] The modules and a brief
summary of their contents are as follows:

1. *Introduction*—This consisted of a review of management and organizational
   behavior concepts, definitions of intrapreneurship and related concepts, and a
   review of several intrapreneurship cases.
2. *Personal creativity*—This module attempted to define and stimulate personal
   creativity. It involved a number of creativity exercises and had participants
   develop a personal creative enrichment program.
3. *Intrapreneuring*—A review of the current literature on the topic was presented
   here, as well as in-depth analyses of several intrapreneuring organizations.

---

[11]Interviews with Robert F. Hettinger of Signode Industries and Brian S. Moskal, "Inventing the
Future," *Industry Week*, Sept. 30, 1985, 45–46.

[12]Donald F. Kuratko and Ray V. Montagno, "The Intrapreneurial Spirit," *Training and Development
Journal* (October 1989): 83–87.

4. *Assessment of current culture*—A climate survey was administered to the training group for the purpose of generating discussion about the current facilitators and barriers to change in the organization.

5. *Business planning*—The intrapreneurial business planning process was outlined and explained. The specific elements of a business plan were identified and illustrated and an example of an entire business plan was presented.

6. *Action planning*—In this module participants worked in teams and created action plans designed to bring about change to foster intrapreneurship in their own workplaces.

To validate the training program's effectiveness a questionnaire entitled the **"Intrapreneurship Assessment Instrument (IAI)"** was developed to provide for a psychometrically sound instrument that represented key entrepreneurial climate factors. The responses to the IAI were statistically analyzed and resulted in five identified factors: Management Support for Intrapreneurship, Risk-Taking Activity, Rewards, Resource Availability, and Organizational Boundaries.[13]

The results demonstrated support for an underlying set of internal environmental factors that need to be focused on by organizations seeking to introduce an intrapreneurial strategy. The research revealed factors that were consistently mentioned in the literature: top management support, risk-taking activity, organizational structure, rewards, and resource availability. These factors, as well as the previous research mentioned, are the foundation for the critical steps involved in introducing an intrapreneurial strategy.

After reviewing these elements, it becomes apparent that *change* in the corporate structure is inevitable if entrepreneurial activity is going to exist and prosper. The change process consists of a series of emerging constructions of people, corporate goals, and existing needs. In short, the organization can encourage innovation by relinquishing controls and changing the traditional bureaucratic structure.[14]

Revolutionary Results of an Intrapreneurial Approach

The results of an intrapreneurial strategy are best illustrated by changes at **The Associated Group.** Under the vision and direction of L. Ben Lytle, chairman and CEO of The Associated Group, a startling restructuring plan was put into effect during 1986 to facilitate the intrapreneurial process. In 1983 the company was operating as Blue Cross/Blue Shield of Indiana and was literally bogged down in its own bureaucracy. Because of this bureaucratic pyramidal structure common to many large corporations, The Associated Group (the new name taken by the company rather than Blue Cross/Blue Shield of Indiana) was losing ground in a fast-

---

[13]Donald F. Kuratko, Ray V. Montagno, and Jeffrey S. Hornsby, "Developing an Intrapreneurial Assessment Instrument for an Effective Corporate Entrepreneurial Environment," *Strategic Management Journal* 11 (1990): 49–58.

[14]See Donald F. Kuratko, Jeffrey S. Hornsby, Douglas W. Naffziger, and Ray V. Montagno, "Implementing Entrepreneurial Thinking in Established Organizations," *Advanced Management Journal* (Winter 1993): 28–33.

paced, changing insurance industry. However, by 1986 Lytle had divided the company legally, emotionally, physically, geographically, and culturally into operating companies named Acordia Companies, ranging in size from 42 to 200 employees.

The opportunities for entrepreneurial individuals within the organization began to expand with the development of the Acordia companies. These "mini-corporations" were designed to capture market niches and innovatively develop new ones. Each separate Acordia company has an individual CEO, vice president, and *outside* board of directors that is delegated full authority to run the business. In 1986 The Associated Group was one large corporation with 2,800 employees serving only the state of Indiana with all revenue generated from health insurance. By the end of 1991, 1,800 days had gone by, culminating a five-year strategic plan to restructure and infuse entrepreneurial thinking into the organization. The results were that the company now employed 7,000 people in 50 different companies, serving 49 states, and generating more than 25 percent of its $2 billion in revenue in lines of business outside health insurance. The results, according to Lytle, point to the effectiveness of an intrapreneurial strategy that captured the imagination of the entire company. The decentralized structure appealed to the "builder types" in the company seeking challenge and accountability for their innovative ideas and abilities.

There are currently 23 Acordia Companies where corporate clients can obtain all types of insurance-related services including commercial property and casualty coverage, group life and health insurance, third-party claims administration for self-insured benefit plans, and employee benefits consulting. In order to institute self-perpetuating change in the Acordia network the mini-corporation CEOs are encouraged (and rewarded through stock options) to expand business and then spin off certain parts of the business either geographically or by specialty when there are more than 200 employees or there are too many management layers. In addition, Acordia CEOs are also evaluated on their ability to identify and nurture additional potential CEOs within their own organization. Thus, the Acordia strategy is to "concentrate and divide," which leads to continuous innovation, growth, and entrepreneurial development. Acordia now ranks fourteenth in *Business Insurance*'s worldwide broker rankings.[15]

A Continuum of Intrapreneurial Activity

Overall, the major elements of an intrapreneurial strategy point to a proactive change in the existing corporate status quo that leads to a newer, more flexible organization. However, it should be recognized that an intrapreneurial strategy cannot be effected all at once. There must be a progression of activity when using the steps that have been identified. Figure 7.2 provides an illustrative look at the dimensions of intrapreneurial activity.

The continuum presents ventures that may be considered corporate-assigned projects, characterized by a great deal of corporate control and commitment, and then

---

[15]*See* The Associated Group: *Annual Report*, 1991; Tom Peters, *Liberation Management* (New York: Alfred Knopf, 1992) pp. 274–282; and "Business Insurance's World's 20 Largest Brokers," *Business Insurance,* June 29, 1992, 48–50.

Figure 7.2   **The Intrapreneuring–Venturing Continuum**

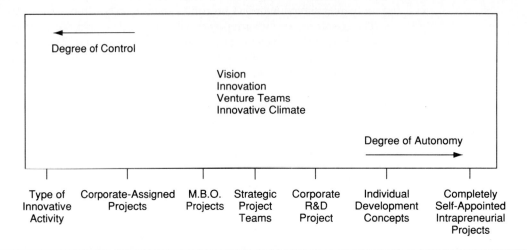

progresses through Management by Objectives projects, Strategic Team projects, and Corporate R&D projects, based on increased individual autonomy and decreased corporate control. The degree of project control and corporate commitment pushes certain projects toward greater corporate control and, thus, assignment and supervision. The need for autonomy and freedom to run a project will push other projects toward the ideal intrapreneurship—completely self-appointed champions of new-venture development.

Various forms of intrapreneurial activity can exist between the two extremes. Projects that seem semi-intrapreneurial (due to corporate control) or semicorporate research (due to freedom given to an individual project leader) are all within the scope of entrepreneurial behavior. Intrapreneurship is a risk and it has to start somewhere even if it starts small and is kept under corporate control. But once initiated, there is a good chance that it will progress through the steps of the continuum. People become more comfortable with the idea, confidence builds, results occur, and soon the first corporate-assigned projects evolve into more autonomous ventures that involve the innovative abilities of all the team members. The key steps of vision, innovation, venture teams, and innovative climate need to develop and progress within an organization, and this is a realistic approach of which managers should be aware.

The major thrust behind intrapreneurship is a revitalization of innovation, creativity, and managerial development in our corporations. The strategies and insights presented here can serve as a foundation to understand the current increase in entrepreneurial interests inside corporations. It appears that intrapreneurship may possess the critical components needed for the future productivity of our organizations. If so, then managers need to recognize the objectives, requisites, and range of potential activities required to establish an intrapreneurship program strategy.

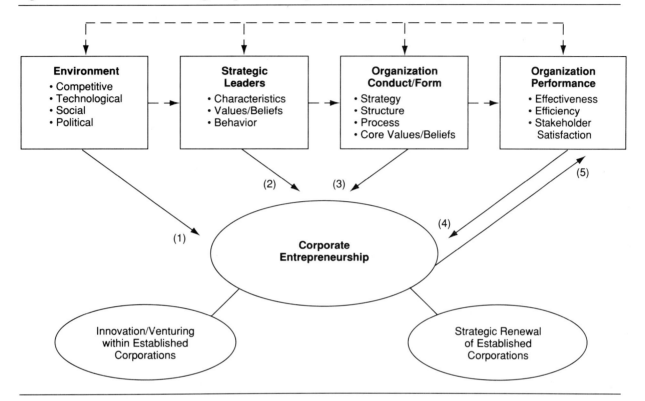

Figure 7.3   **Fitting Corporate Entrepreneurship into Strategic Management**

Models of Corporate Entrepreneurship (Intrapreneurship)

Research concerning corporate entrepreneurship has been rapidly increasing over the last few years. A number of leading research journals have published articles that present exploratory work in this emerging field. A variety of models have been developed from this new research that attempt to provide a better framework for future understanding and study of intrapreneurial activity.

A Domain Model for Corporate Entrepreneurship

One model developed by William D. Guth and Ari Ginsberg attempted to provide a framework for tracking the research in corporate entrepreneurship.[16] According to these researchers, the domain of corporate entrepreneurship encompasses two types of processes: **internal innovation,** or venturing through the creation of new businesses within existing organizations, and the **strategic renewal** of key corporate ideas that transform organizations. Figure 7.3 provides an illustration of this model.

---

[16]William D. Guth and Ari Ginsberg, "Introduction: Corporate Entrepreneurship," *Strategic Management Journal* 11 (Summer 1990): 5–15.

Key components in this model include the environment, strategic leaders, organization form, and organization performance. Each of these components is an important element within the domain of corporate entrepreneurship.

A Conceptual Model of Firm Behavior

In examining the behaviors of entrepreneurs and thus their impact on the firm's actions, researchers Jeffrey G. Covin and Dennis P. Slevin developed an organization level model.[17] They contend that entrepreneurial behavior at the firm level is affected by the firm's particular strategies, structures, systems, and cultures. Figure 7.4

Figure 7.4   A Conceptual Model of Entrepreneurship as Firm Behavior

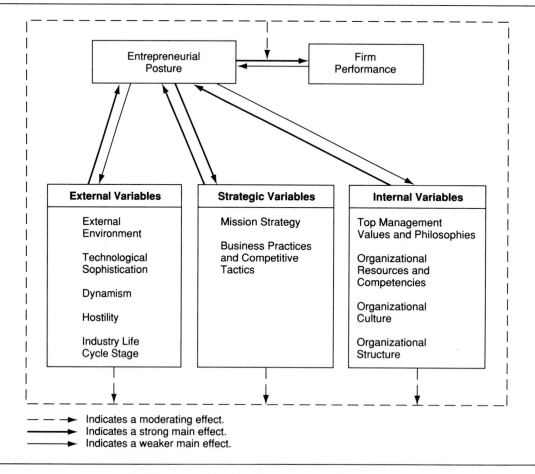

- - - → Indicates a moderating effect.
——→ Indicates a strong main effect.
——→ Indicates a weaker main effect.

---

[17]Jeffrey G. Covin and Dennis P. Slevin, "A Conceptual Model of Entrepreneurship as Firm Behavior," *Entrepreneurship Theory and Practice* (Fall 1991): 7–25.

depicts the key elements of this model. The major purpose of this behavioral model is to allow for considerable managerial intervention and thus reduce the view of corporate entrepreneurship as serendipitous or mysterious.

An Organizational Model for Internally Developed Ventures

In defining corporate venturing as "an internal process that embraces the ultimate goal of growth through the development of innovative products, processes, and technologies" that should be institutionalized as a process geared toward long-term prosperity, researcher Deborah V. Brazeal created a framework model to explain this concept.[18] Figure 7.5 illustrates this model. The focus of this approach is a *joint function* between innovative-minded individuals and organizational factors. Thus, in order for organizations to promote innovation among its employees careful attention must be given to the melding of an individual's attitudes, values, and behavioral orientations with the organizational factors of structure and reward. Ultimately the key objective is to enhance a firm's innovative abilities through an organizational environment supportive of these individuals.

Figure 7.5   **The Joint Function of Individual and Organizational Factors for Internal Ventures**

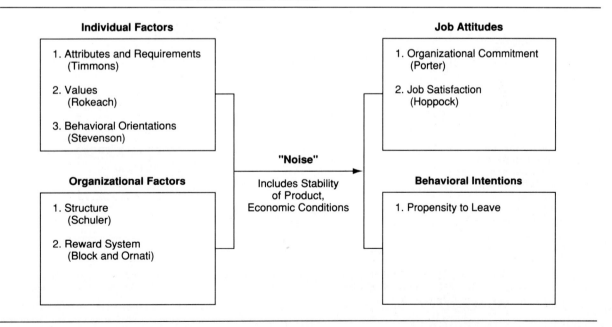

---

[18]Deborah V. Brazeal, "Organizing for Internally Developed Corporate Ventures," *Journal of Business Venturing* 8 (1993): 75–90.

An Interactive Model of the Intrapreneurial Process

The last model presented in this section is based on the same concepts of the previous model developed by Professor Brazeal; however, researchers Jeffrey S. Hornsby, Douglas W. Naffziger, Donald F. Kuratko, and Ray V. Montagno have attempted to describe the **interaction** of organizational factors and individual characteristics that is ignited by a **precipitating event** that leads to successful intrapreneurship. Figure 7.6 illustrates this interactive model.[19] This precipitating event could be a change in company management, a merger or acquisition, development of a new technology, or an event that acts as the impetus for the interaction between individual characteristics and organizational factors.

Figure 7.6   An Interactive Model of Corporate Entrepreneuring

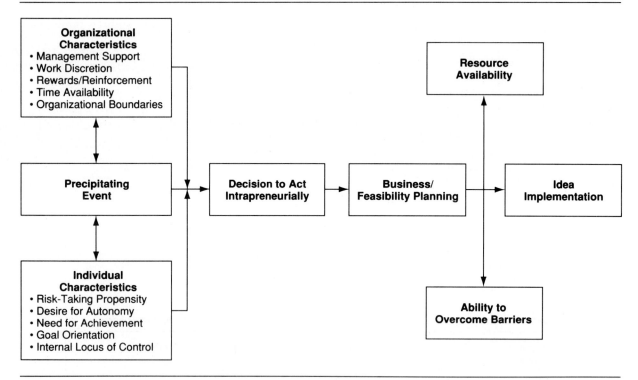

---

[19]Jeffrey S. Hornsby, Douglas W. Naffziger, Donald F. Kuratko, and Ray V. Montagno, "An Interactive Model of the Corporate Entrepreneurship Process," *Entrepreneurship Theory and Practice* (Spring 1993): 29–37.

C A S E • *The Douglas Call Company, 1989:*
Power Spray Technologies Division*

Vernon A. Quarstein, Old Dominion University
Claire J. Anderson, Old Dominion University

In Spring 1989, the Douglas Call Company of Virginia Beach, Virginia, faced a decision about its newly developed Powerarc 1500 Metal Spray System. The new technology offered a low-cost means to metal coat structural surfaces to prevent water and environmental damage. According to Doug Call, owner and president of the firm, the innovation had excellent potential given its technological advantage and almost assured proprietary rights. His major concern was "how to exploit the technology."

Although the Powerarc 1500 had tremendous potential, Doug Call was painfully aware that one major barrier to launching the product was the shaky financial condition of his firm. Since its founding in 1976, the company was a local sole provider for Department of Defense metal abrasive blasting contracts. Loss of government contracts, combined with sunk costs of developing the Powerarc 1500, placed the firm on a precarious financial footing, posting losses of over $700,000 in two years.

Doug Call needed to find the best means of ensuring long-range returns on this innovation and, to do this, needed to place the present operations on a firm footing.

Background

The Douglas Call Company

The Douglas Call Company was founded in 1976 in Newport News, Virginia. Expansions resulted in moves, first to Norfolk, Virginia, and later to its present location in Virginia Beach.

Historically, the Call Company performed maintenance and repair for the Department of Defense. The firm's original technological base was a portable deck blasting machine that provided maintenance for Navy ship decks in Hampton Roads, home of the largest naval base in the world. In 1978, the firm became the first to acquire equipment and facilities to accommodate the Navy's requirements for metallized coatings in the Hampton Roads area. In 1986, the Call Company

---

set up an automated reconditioning facility for Marine Corps landing mats. These landing mats were used for temporary airfields and to stabilize beaches to support heavy traffic during amphibious operations. The Douglas Call reconditioning facility was the first of its kind in the United States and by 1989 was still considered state-of-the-art in comparison to competitors.

In 1987, the Douglas Call Company expanded into the highly technical field of metal coatings for industrial and government use. R&D expenditures were focused on several ventures, one of which produced a better means of applying metal coatings. This gave rise to development of the Powerarc 1500.

The firm had a reputation for quality work and enjoyed healthy profit margins from its inception in 1976 to 1986. In 1987 revenues dropped drastically from $2.3 to $1.4 million and profits fell drastically, posting a two-year cumulative pre-tax loss of over $700,000 by the end of 1988. The losses resulted from two major setbacks for the firm. As the result of a change in government procedures, the Call Company lost a major government ship deck renovation contract to a lower bidder in 1987. This loss was compounded when, over a year later, another major contract (for the AM2 Mats) was tied up in litigation by the Navy. A competitor had underbid the Call Company and the competitor subsequently defaulted. The contract was to be awarded to the Call Company pending resolution of legal matters. By Spring 1989, the matter was still in the courts. During these hard times, the

Exhibit 1   **Organization Chart: The Douglas Call Company**

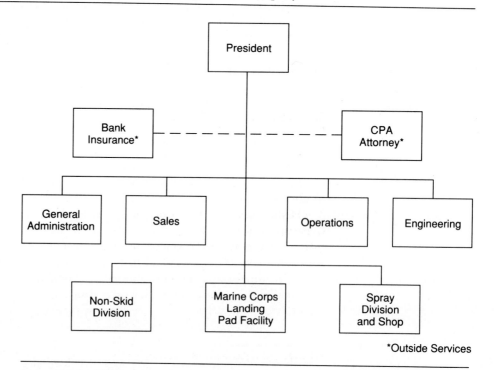

*Outside Services

Source: Douglas Call Company.

| Exhibit 2 | Income Statement: Douglas Call Company |

	1985	1986	1987	1988
Revenue	$2,134,000	$2,337,000	$1,449,000	$1,159,000
Cost of goods sold	(821,260)	(1,038,956)	(1,009,661)	(832,074)
Gross margin	1,312,740	1,298,044	439,339	326,926
Operating expenses				
General and administration	650,000	717,064	423,700	327,894
Research and development	107,201	117,399	72,790	58,222
Sales	96,000	105,132	65,185	52,139
Depreciation	222,000	182,000	162,000	122,002
Total operating expenses	1,075,201	1,121,595	723,675	560,257
Operating income	237,539	176,449	(284,336)	(233,331)
Interest income	15,466	17,587	33,361	28,016
Interest expense	(127,927)	(132,827)	(132,827)	(132,827)
Pre-tax income	125,078	61,209	(383,802)	(338,142)
Tax	37,286	11,613		
Income after taxes	$ 87,792	$ 49,596	$ (383,802)	$ (338,142)

Financial data are disguised.
Source: Douglas Call Company.

company continued to operate through funds generated from the remainder of its major contract commitments, other smaller contracts, and the support of its creditors.

The Douglas Call Company was a closely held corporation, headed up by the founder and majority owner, Douglas Call. At the end of 1988, the firm employed 15 workers and reported sales of $1.2 million. The company operated out of leased office and shop space in Virginia Beach.

Power Spray Technologies Division

In 1988, Power Spray Technologies became a division of the Douglas Call Company (Exhibit 1). Dr. Thomas Fox, director of the division, invented the Powerarc 1500 system in 1987. Sunk research and development costs were nearly $800,000 in equipment and salaries of those involved in the system's development. The product did not generate any revenues until September 1988 and these revenues were limited. Development costs were absorbed within the Douglas Call Company by current income and borrowing.

The Douglas Call Company, 1988

By the end of 1988, the firm had experienced a second consecutive year of losses in excess of $300,000. Exhibits 2 and 3 contain financial statements for 1985 through 1988.

Exhibit 3   **Balance Sheet: Douglas Call Company**

	1985	1986	1987	1988
Assets				
Current assets				
Cash	$ 219,837	$ 421,928	$ 355,117	$ 121,600
Accounts receivable	355,667	389,500	241,500	193,167
Inventory	25,608	28,044	17,388	13,908
Vendor deposits	135	330	270	323
Total current assets	601,247	839,802	614,275	328,998
Noncurrent assets				
Vehicles	63,038	63,038	63,038	63,038
Equipment	1,828,461	1,828,461	1,828,461	1,828,461
Other	7,311	7,311	7,311	7,311
Less depreciation	(422,000)	(604,000)	(766,000)	(888,002)
Total noncurrent assets	1,476,810	1,294,810	1,132,810	1,010,808
Total assets	$2,078,057	$2,134,612	$1,747,085	$1,339,806
Liabilities and stockholders' equity				
Liabilities				
Accounts payable	$ 181,108	$ 197,523	$ 125,718	$ 102,268
Notes payable	913,764	868,076	822,388	776,699
Credit line used	35,000	35,000	35,000	35,000
Total liabilities	1,129,872	1,100,599	983,106	913,967
Equity				
Contributed capital	200,000	236,232	350,000	350,000
Retained earnings	748,185	797,781	413,979	75,839
Total owner equity	948,185	1,034,013	763,979	425,839
Total liabilities and equity	$2,078,057	$2,134,612	$1,747,085	$1,339,806

Financial data are disguised.
Source: Douglas Call Company.

Financial statements reflect the following practices. Contract income was recognized using a percentage of completion method of accounting based on proportion of square footage completed relative to contract estimated square footage. Inventory was valued on a first-in, first-out basis. Property and equipment were recorded at cost and depreciation computed on a straight-line base using the following estimated useful lives.

Asset	Projected Life
Machinery and equipment	5 to 7 years
Vehicles	3 to 8 years
Office furniture and fixtures	5 to 7 years
Leasehold improvements	7 to 31.5 years

All property and equipment were pledged as security on a note. As of the end of 1988, notes payable consisted of:

Demand note to individual, guaranteed by a major stockholder; interest at 11.5%	$ 50,000
Demand notes to finance company, secured by machinery, equipment, accounts and inventory; interest at prime plus 3%	700,000
Other notes payable	26,699

The New Product

Metal coating provided long-term protection to steel and other materials against environmental damage. Three technological processes were available: plasma, combustion, and electric arc (thermal),[1] in order of rate of application, with electric arc being the fastest. Plasma was a very expensive, slow process used mostly for coating small parts. Combustion had been the workhorse of the metallizing industry for 90 years. Both plasma and combustion technologies were prohibitively expensive for any large-scale use. Electric arc application (used in the Powerarc 1500) was developed in the 1940s to increase production rates.

Although the fastest, use of electric arc spray technology was limited to low-volume jobs due to low production rates (until the advent of the Powerarc 1500). Most common applications in the United States were on small areas such as exterior railings, guard rails, exterior stairways, highway light poles and signs, and ship deck fixtures. Applications for very large structures were common in England, France, Norway, and Canada. But domestically, such applications were generally considered cost prohibitive compared to painting. Some industry analysts claimed that this view was the result of the short-term focus of U.S. management.

Since introduction in the 1940s, electric arc application rates had remained stable; however, the Powerarc 1500 promised far better performance. The Powerarc 1500, was the first in a new generation of high-speed electric arc spray equipment. It provided an efficient, economical means of rapidly applying metal coatings to base metals to prevent environmental damage. A drive mechanism fed two wires into a gun where the tips were melted with an electric arc. Jets of compressed air atomized the melted material that was sprayed onto the base metal resulting in a coating of high quality.

The system could produce high-grade coatings at a speed many times faster than previously available (Exhibit 4). The new technology consisted of a "gun," a console/wire stand, and power supply. For good adhesion, the surface had to be grit blasted to white metal with a good consistent pattern. For most steel products,

---

[1]Plasma uses a high-melting temperature powder and high-pressure inert gases to apply coatings with a handheld electric arc torch. Combustion uses oxygen and acetylene burning at medium-high melting temperatures applied with a handheld gun. The electric arc method uses a continuous wire that is melted by an electric arc and sprayed onto the surface under pressure as the wire passes through a handheld electric arc gun.

Exhibit 4
Coats Large Areas Fast With High Productivity

The unique design of the Power Arc 1500 provides the highest spray rates available in the industry. This results in very fast coverage rates—see table below.

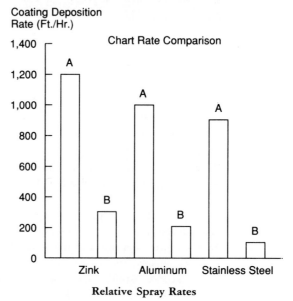

Powerarc 1500(a) and Conventional 200 Amp Arc System (B) represented in square feet per hour for a coating .005″ thick.

Source: Douglas Call Company.

metal coatings approximately .005″ thick were adequate for normal protection. The gun weighed approximately four pounds. Although the cables added some drag, the gun was still easy to maneuver by human hands and was also suitable for use by a robot. When in use, the gun produced high noise, very bright light, and much dust requiring environmental and personal protection. Operators were provided ear, eye, and breathing protection. The total system was light enough for easy transport. Operating costs were at a minimum as the system required only electrical power and compressed air. The effect was to reduce the cost of metal applications by 40 percent. (See Exhibit 5.)

Dr. Fox maintained that the system was revolutionary for two reasons. First, metal spray could be applied seven to eight times faster than other technologies. Second, when coupled with automatic application at steel fabrication plants, the system could reduce the cost to a level close to multiple coatings of paint, making long-term protection economically feasible.

The Call Company produced only two guns in 1988. Both guns were retained by the firm and were used on small local contracts. Although the gun worked well

---

Exhibit 5
The Powerarc 1500 Spray System

Features

High Speed Spray: High Power 1500 Amp power supply rated at 100 percent duty cycle. Water cooled high power spray head. Unique high efficiency high speed spray gun. (330 lbs./hr. of zinc wire)

Spray Quality Coatings: Permanently aligned contact tips for optimum atomization. Accurately focused air jets. Separate control of atomizing and pattern shaping air.

Easy to Operate: Simple on-off operation. Safety switch to disarm gun when not in use. Easy initial wire feeding. Light weight gun (4 lbs.). Very maneuverable.

Easy to Service: Designed for fast easy service. All ball bearing construction. Permanently lubricated motors.

Push-Pull Wire Feed: Assures reliable stable wire feeding even around bends. Optional 50' cables available.

Applies Wide Variety of Coatings: Sprays all currently used spray metals. Takes wire sizes $\frac{1}{16}$–$\frac{1}{8}$" diameter. Controllable coating thickness, bonds strength and texture.

Source: Douglas Call Company.

---

on small jobs, it had yet to be tested on large high-arch bridges or under rugged field conditions over an extended time.

The Metal Coatings Industry

As of 1988, the metal coatings industry was fragmented primarily due to low demand associated with cost and small scale usage. Yet, the Douglas Call Company's technical analyst reported high growth expectations for the industry particularly with a more economical means to apply coatings to metal surfaces. Structural design engineers in the United States, although generally dissatisfied with the short protective lives of non-metallic coatings, were not prepared to recommend high-cost metallic coatings. Further, the service was not readily available. Despite all this, the industry was growing, implying pent-up demand.

As environmental concerns grew, some coatings, such as lead paint, were no longer used because of their toxic qualities. Many states did not allow the use of urethanes because of carcinogenic effects. All paint applications were subject to regulation concerning release of volatile organic compounds into the atmosphere. The outcome of these constraints was that the cost of painting was increasing—sometimes, approaching the cost of thermal metal spray coatings.

Bridges and other metal structures, due to corrosion and water intrusion, often deteriorated to a point that urgent measures needed to be taken to ensure their safety. The technology of thermally sprayed zinc and aluminum coatings was widely used in Europe where bridges sprayed as long as 50 years ago were still well protected against corrosion with minimal maintenance. Major bridges throughout the world that had been protected against corrosion with sprayed coatings were the Forth River bridge, a one and one-half mile long structure in Great Britain; the Pierre LaPorte bridge over the St. Lawrence River; and Istanbul's Bosphorus bridge that connects Europe to Asia. Metal spraying of bridges was rare in the United States. The Ridge Avenue bridge in Philadelphia was an exception. It was coated with zinc in 1937. In 1985, an area of the bridge was cleaned to determine the condition of the coating. After almost 50 years, the zinc coating was still intact and continuing to protect the structure.[2]

Other potential applications for the Powerarc 1500 existed. In utility power generating plants and in paper and pulp mills, boiler interiors needed frequent metal coating to extend the life of the equipment and to ensure safety. Additionally, both government and industry used zinc or aluminum coated ferrous materials for structures subjected to corrosion, particularly when exposed to salt spray in marine environments.

Markets and Competition

If the Powerarc 1500 proved successful, the market for metal coatings was expected to change considerably because high-speed coating of bridge steel with zinc and aluminum at the steel manufacturing plants would be economically feasible. Also, metals used in the process such as zinc and aluminum were in abundant supply.

Major industrial segments included the construction, steel, pulp and paper, power, marine, and chemical industries. The construction and steel segment posed a new, lucrative market. Demand for metal coatings in the United States was weak because of cost. Bridge failure due to corrosion or structural failure was a matter of public concern. In 1987, a study by the Federal Highway Administration (FHWA) concluded that some 27,000 bridges qualifying for federal aid and 108,000 others had deteriorated to a point that they needed replacement. Another 85,000 bridges were in better condition but needed rehabilitation The time of rehabilitation provided an excellent opportunity to refurbish the underside with electric arc metal coating or to replace girders with sprayed ones. In 1988, the FHWA authorized $3.4 billion for bridge construction and rehabilitation. The Chief of the Bridge Management branch of the FHWA stated that 20 percent of these federal funds was earmarked for rehabilitation. He estimated that total government expenditure (federal, state, and local) was between $5 and $6 billion annually for bridge rehabilitation alone.[3] Projections for 1988 new-bridge construction in the United States were $400 million for coatings only.

Additionally, the rise in air pollution, particularly acid rain, and the banning of red lead in paints contributed to the need for better coatings. Thermally applied zinc or aluminum coatings were nonpolluting, required infrequent maintenance for up to 30 years (15–20 years for surfaces exposed to environmental pollution and

---

[2]*Roads and Bridges,* August, 1988, NY: The Zinc Institute.

[3]*Engineering News Review,* March 14, 1988.

50 years otherwise), and provided superior binding surfaces for additional paint coatings.

In the electrical utilities and pulp and paper boiler markets, plant down time was critical. The speed of the Powerarc 1500 was a major factor in making this segment lucrative.

Several likely markets existed. The U.S. Navy was a potential major customer as metal spray coating was used for protection of ship deck fixtures. In 1988, the Navy was the largest user of these coatings in the United States. Routine application of zinc or aluminum coatings to structural steel at fabricating plants and in-place bridges was also a new market. Still other markets included cathodic[4] protection for concrete bridge spans and structural members, bulk holding tanks in the petroleum industry, boilers and incinerators in the waste disposal industry, distillation plants in the petrochemical and desalinization industries, and railroad cars and containers in the transportation industry.

Seven distinct market segments could be identified. These included (1) bridge steel fabricators (large girder), (2) other steel used in new construction (small girder), (3) internal coating of utility company and paper and pulp mill boilers, (4) U.S. Navy anticorrosion programs, (5) cathodic protection of concrete structures to prevent intrusion of moisture and rusting of reinforcing bars, (6) general use for a variety of structures to reduce maintenance costs, and (7) new-steel fabrication.

The cyclical and countercyclical nature of the business was also attractive to the firm. Historically, government funding for structures such as bridges increased during economic downturns while industrial applications fell with the economy.

The long-range outlook for the industry was promising even without faster technologies. Hugh Morrow, executive director of the Zinc Institute, estimated that the metal coatings industry would grow at a rate of 23 percent through 1997.[5]

The Market Approach

While questions existed over the exact means to take advantage of the Powerarc 1500, both Doug Call and Tom Fox agreed that the best route was to provide spraying services rather than selling the guns. The two felt that this tactic would assure proprietary rights. But, given the firm's financial condition, they might have to settle for less desirable options.

By 1989, several possibilities appeared favorable to Doug Call. If the firm were to undertake applications, he believed that, given proprietary rights and adequate financial backing, he could expect revenues reaching $12 million by 1993. On the other hand, if the firm were to sell the Powerarc 1500, sales might reach $2 million within the first five years.

Separate approaches would be required to meet the needs of three distinct industrial applications: temporary and permanent factory setups and mobile units. Temporary robotic setups at steel fabrication plants would facilitate low-cost applica-

---

[4]Cathodic protection consists of arc-sprayed zinc coating to concrete surfaces. The coating is then exposed to low-voltage direct current to draw negatively charged chloride ions from the steel to stop future corrosion.

[5]*Journal of Protective Coatings and Linings,* January 4, 1987.

tion of long-lasting coatings for steel before it was used in bridges and other structures. A temporary setup could be easily dismantled, moved, and erected at another site at least once during its useful lifetime. Alternatively, permanent installations used construction methods and designs that assumed the installation would remain at the original location throughout its useful lifetime. Permanent installations at steel plants would afford automatic application of zinc or aluminum coatings to steel before it was sent to fabrication plants for cutting and drilling. The Douglas Call Company was to retain ownership of the equipment and provide technical personnel to operate both permanent and temporary setups. Mobile facilities, mounted on a truck or having wheeled or tracked mounts, could be used at work sites to coat existing structures such as bridges, towers, and boiler interiors.

Management favored the temporary setups at fabrication plants for the initial introduction of the services. Tom Fox felt more confident with this approach as he had already used the Powerarc 1500 to coat steel at a fabrication plant. Doug Call agreed. He also favored bridge coating because he was most familiar with this application. Fox also expressed interest in the coating of boilers. This market was attractive because Call's technology could provide the speed needed in this market. Further, they both agreed permanent installations of the Powerarc 1500 at steel plants would most likely be the big money-maker due to expected demand.

Competition

The Douglas Call Company was one of several hundred similar firms scattered throughout the United States that held only a very small part of the metal coating market. Competition existed on two different levels: firms that supplied equipment and materials and firms that applied coating to structures.

Suppliers consisted of two manufacturers of spray guns: METCO in Westbury, New York, and TAFA Incorporated in Concord, New Hampshire. According to Doug Call, both could potentially be serious competitors. METCO posted $150 million in sales and $13 million in profits in 1988. Further, METCO was a subsidiary of financially strong Perkins-Elmer, which posted a net increase of 14 percent in revenues to $683.8 million primarily due to the strength of its Instruments Division that grew 16 percent. TAFA, which was almost exclusively engaged in metals coating, reported $8.1 million in revenue. This privately held firm did not disclose its profitability.

METCO offered a complete line of thermal spray equipment. Although slow in comparison to the Powerarc 1500, METCO's product had several valuable features including (1) a simple handheld gun with flow meter and controls; (2) an automated system consisting of a heavy-duty gun, standard work and gun handling equipment and an electronic control unit; (3) a computer-controlled system consisting of a heavy-duty gun, an articulated arm robot, a computer-controlled tilting turntable, a microprocessor-based gun control, and a robot controller that could hold up to 40 programs in its 128K permanent bubble memory; and, (4) a custom-designed turn-key system consisting of a thermal spray gun or guns, gun- and-workpiece-handling equipment, computer control, and a special spray room. Similar to METCO, TAFA supplied individual spray guns, controls and power units, and a wide range of spray materials. The firm also designed and installed complete manual and automated systems. Spray application rates for the TAFA product were similar to METCO's. The Powerarc 1500 gave the Call Company an advantage over both competitive products in rates of application by 7 to 10 times.

Zinc, aluminum, and special alloys used in the process were supplied by firms such as Platt Brothers of Waterbury, Connecticut. Platt Brothers was a primary source in the Western Hemisphere for zinc and zinc-based alloys that were sold as strips, rods, and wire products.

Competitors in primary metal spray applications included many firms such as Metal Spray Company of Richmond, Virginia; Flame Spray Incorporated, San Diego, California; Akron Sand Blast, Akron, Ohio; Racine Metal Spray, Inc., Racine, Wisconsin; and C.W.S. Corporation of Portland, Oregon. Call's competitors bid for metal spray contracts on a local and regional basis.

Early Introduction of the Powerarc 1500

Tom Fox wanted to exploit local and regional markets in North Carolina, Virginia, Maryland, and New Jersey. His initial approaches to potential users in three states outside Virginia generated a good deal of interest, but prospective buyers wanted evidence of the capabilities of the system. The Powerarc 1500 had been successfully used for small local projects. These early contracts upheld the technological capability of the Powerarc 1500 system. However, the work consisted of small jobs done under controlled conditions.

Production and Operations

Initial plans called for an investment of $1.6 million. A good part of this initial investment was to set up temporary metal spray facilities and to put two mobile, truck-mounted units into operation. In the first year of operation, a few Powerarc 1500s could be produced by hand at the Douglas Call Company using existing leased shop facilities in Virginia Beach.

A metal spray facility was to be set up at a steel fabrication plant using robot-controlled articulated arms to hold the Powerarc 1500 and to apply the metallic coatings as the fabricated steel members rolled off the lines. The mobile units, which could go to construction or application sites, consisted of a crew and a truck equipped with the Powerarc 1500, electrical generators, and abrasive blasting machines. These mobile units could apply metal coatings economically either at fabrication plants or directly to existing structures such as small bridges, boilers and other on-site jobs.

Alternatively, the Powerarc 1500 could be produced by licensing other manufacturers. Detailed drawings were available for licensing.

Early in the development of the Powerarc 1500, a thorough search of patent and engineering literature established that the ideas embodied in the new spray gun were novel and could be patented. The firm had applied for a patent and Tom Fox expected that the U.S. Patent Office would most likely uphold the request.

At the outset, both Doug Call and Tom Fox agreed that they should start with applications Should this prove unsuccessful, other possibilities existed such as production and sale of the Powerarc 1500 or outright sale of the technology.

Sales Promotion

As of early 1989, the firm had no sales force and no marketing function capable of introducing a sales campaign for a brand-new product as the firm's primary business was providing services unique to the U.S. military market. The company had not launched an intensive marketing campaign for the Powerarc 1500 due to lack of resources. The cost of bidding jobs was substantial particularly for government contracts that required extensive paperwork. Initial promotion consisted of brochures and a few responses to government invitations. Some of the $1.6 million initial investment was earmarked for marketing of the Powerarc 1500.

Whether the firm decided to sell the services or to sell the product in industrial markets, a sales force of technical representatives was needed. The sales force would work on a salary plus commission basis. Training for the technical sales force would take place at the Virginia Beach location to insure control. A demonstration facility would be established at the home location. The sales force would be equipped with VCR tapes to demonstrate equipment to potential customers. As sales mounted, regional offices were to be established to provide a base for the sales force and act as a demonstration facility. Advertising would use direct mail and technical publications.

Target markets were large-scale users both in government and industry. If the Powerarc 1500 lived up to expectations, cost effectiveness would be the major selling point. At the same time, Call could enjoy comfortable margins.

Financing

If Doug Call were to retain the technology and provide services, the new venture required an outlay of $1.6 million to be raised in loans and venture capital in the first year after start-up. The bulk of the investment would provide installed equipment for a new metal coating facility, to produce a few Powerarc 1500s, and to develop a small sales force.

Two plans were considered. One called for equal amounts to be raised by venture capital and bank loans. The bank loans were to be over two years. A second plan provided for 75 percent of the needed funds to be raised by venture capital in 1989 and the remainder to be financed by a bank loan in 1990. Varying combinations of the two were acceptable. A local venture capital firm expressed interest and was willing to provide $1.6 million in capital despite the faltering financial status of Call's other undertakings. The only negative aspect of the venture capitalist's interest was the insistence on a controlling interest in the enterprise. This demand was a major barrier as Doug Call, from the inception of the endeavor, firmly held to the demand that equity to outside investors be limited to 49 percent and that he (Doug Call) personally would retain the majority share.

Management set performance objectives of $2.1 million in revenue for 1990. By 1993, revenues were forecasted to exceed $12 million with a return on equity of 35 percent. Pro forma statements in Exhibits 6, 7, and 8 were predicated on the assumption that the Call Company would retain proprietary rights to the technology and deliver the service.

Exhibit 6	**Pro Forma Income Statement: Douglas Call Company**			
	1989	1990	1991	1992
Revenue	$345,000	$2,134,000	$3,657,000	$7,275,000
Cost of goods sold	(188,876)	(1,025,356)	(1,821,114)	(3,500,179)
Gross margin	156,124	1,108,644	1,835,886	3,774,821
Operating expenses				
General and administration	80,371	632,857	1,195,136	2,128,874
Research and development	17,331	107,201	183,708	365,457
Sales	15,520	96,001	164,515	327,275
Depreciation	292,000	303,123	234,222	125,444
Total operating expenses	405,222	1,139,182	1,777,581	2,947,050
Operating income	(249,098)	(30,538)	58,305	827,771
Interest income	9,335	36,826	20,789	18,727
Interest expense	(103,158)	(88,420)	(11,900)	(32,900)
Pre-tax income	(342,921)	(82,132)	67,194	813,598
Taxes (including loss carryforward)				
Income after taxes	$(342,921)	$ (82,132)	$ 67,194	$ 813,598

Financial data are disguised.
Source: Douglas Call Company.

Capital to be contributed by the venture firm was $1.081 million in 1989 and $539,000 in 1990. Projected 1989 expenditures include $500,000 for production of five Powerarc 1500s and other equipment for the metallizing facility. Major projected expenditures included $500,000 in 1989 for blast machines and spray equipment and $600,000 in 1990 to complete the metal spray facility and procure equipment.

Management

The principal organization members who participated in the Powerarc 1500 development were Douglas Call, Tom Fox, Dave Hubert, and Ted Call.

Douglas Call, founder of the Douglas Call Company, was a graduate of the University of Virginia. He served as a Marine Corps pilot in World War II and in the Korean conflict. Before forming the Douglas Call Company he worked for Wheelabrator, a pollution control and blast cleaning company. He was acknowledged as a pioneer in the (Norfolk) market for his firm's nonskid coatings technology. He was completely committed to exploiting the Powerarc 1500 and was equally committed to paying off the company's debts.

Tom Fox, Ph.D. (in physics) invented the Powerarc 1500. Before joining the Call Company in October 1985, he was employed by METCO where he had developed other spray systems. Fox left METCO for a smaller, entrepreneurial firm

Exhibit 7	Pro Forma Balance Sheet: Douglas Call Company			
	1989	1990	1991	1992
Assets				
Current assets				
Cash	$ 460,331	$ 259,869	$ 234,086	$ 530,416
Accounts receivable	58,650	362,780	621,690	1,236,750
Inventory	4,140	25,608	43,884	87,300
Vendor deposits	255	244	135	212
Total current assets	523,376	648,501	899,795	1,854,678
Noncurrent assets				
Vehicles	63,038	63,038	63,038	63,038
Equipment	2,328,461	2,928,461	3,193,461	3,273,461
Other	12,311	12,311	17,311	22,311
Less depreciation	(1,180,002)	(1,483,126)	(1,717,349)	(1,842,794)
Total noncurrent assets	1,223,808	1,520,684	1,556,461	1,516,016
Total assets	$1,747,184	$2,169,185	$2,456,256	$3,370,694
Liabilities and owners' equity				
Liabilities				
Accounts payable	$ 121,567	$ 341,755	$ 533,275	$884,115
Notes payable	426,699	121,643	0	
Credit line	35,000	85,000	235,000	(15,000)
Total liabilities	583,266	548,398	768,275	869,115
Owner equity				
Contributed capital	1,431,000	1,970,000	1,970,000	1,970,000
Retained earnings	(267,082)	(349,213)	(282,019)	531,579
Total owner equity	1,163,918	1,620,787	1,687,981	2,501,579
Total liabilities and equity	$1,747,184	$2,169,185	$2,456,256	$3,370,694

Financial data are disguised.
Source: Douglas Call Company.

believing that he would have greater freedom to build a better metal coating system and reap higher financial rewards. Although he was the inventor of the new technology, the proprietary rights (once granted) were to be retained by Douglas Call. Fox and Call had excellent working relationships and shared common views on the future of the Powerarc 1500. In 1989, Dr. Fox headed up the Power Spray Division.

Mr. Dave Hubert, general manager of the Douglas Call Co., provided the expertise to develop good relations and maintain needed quality demanded by the U.S. Navy. In 1989, the Navy was the mainstay of the Call Company.

Mr. Ted Call, the owner's son, grew up with the company. He had eight years' experience with jobs in the field and as shop superintendent. He had set up the Marine landing pad plant for the company. Initially, he would fill the position of Manager of the Spray Facility and Mobile Units.

Exhibit 8	Pro Forma Cash Flow Statement: Douglas Call Company			
	1989	1990	1991	1992
Beginning cash	$ 121,600	$460,332	$259,870	$234,087
Cash inflows				
Capital contributed	1,081,000	539,000		
Pre-tax income	(342,921)	(82,131)	67,194	813,598
Plus depreciation	292,001	303,124	234,223	125,445
Accounts payable funding	19,299	220,188	191,520	350,841
Credit line used	50,000	150,000	(250,000)	
Cash outflows				
Accounts receivable financing	(134,517)	304,130	258,910	615,060
Equipment expenditures	500,000	600,000	265,000	80,000
Other expenditures	5,000		5,000	5,000
Principal paid on loan	350,000	305,056	121,643	
Inventory	(9,768)	21,468	18,276	43,416
Vendor deposits made	(68)	(11)	(109)	77
Net increase (decrease)	338,732	(200,462)	(25,783)	296,331
Ending cash	$ 460,332	$259,870	$234,087	$530,418

Financial data are disguised.
Source: Douglas Call Company.

The Decision

Management at the Call Company faced two major related issues. One focused on how to exploit their new technology. The other centered on the dire financial situation of the firm. As the primary business of the firm was tied to government contracts, serious effort was needed to recapture this business to keep the company afloat. Doug Call had one edge. He had 27 years' experience in the field and was considered a pioneer in the Norfolk market for nonskid coatings.

The Powerarc 1500 promised a means of strengthening the firm through a broader customer base. Time was important if Call was to be the prime mover in introducing the new technology. A good probability existed that other firms were attempting to develop an equal, if not better, product. The immediate decision focused on developing a viable business plan.

The Call Company's management team was working under several disadvantages. However, they had some experience in bridge spraying. In 1987, the company provided cathodic protection on a 27-year-old concrete overpass in Virginia. At the time, they used METCO and TAFA machines that allowed coating speeds of 150 to 200 square feet per day. Nevertheless, the Call Company was a virtual unknown in the metal spray business with a technology yet to be tested under field conditions.

Given the firm's present financial condition, what was the best way to fund the project? Should the firm not be able to raise the needed capital, what alternatives might Doug Call pursue?

CASE • *Wal-Mart Stores, Inc.: Strategies for Market Dominance**

James W. Camerius, Northern Michigan University

It's dusk in the foothills of the Ozark Mountains in north central Arkansas. One of the most successful retailing entrepreneurs in modern history is driving a battered red 1980 Ford pickup truck minus two hubcaps down a rural road. A hunting dog named Buck is seated next to him, inside the cab. Coffee and conversation with friends await at Fred's Hickory Inn in Bentonville.

As noted in an interview with a reporter of the *Arkansas Gazette,* Sam Walton was down-to-earth and old-fashioned in his views of the past, the present, and the future:

> I didn't sit down one day and decide that I was going to put a bunch of discount stores in small towns and set a goal to have a billion-dollar company some day. I started out with one store and it did well, so it was a challenge to see if I could do well with a few more. We're still going and we'll keep going as long as we're successful.

From this beginning Wal-Mart Stores, Inc. has emerged as a modern retail success story.

An Emerging Organization

At the end of 1992, Wal-Mart Stores, Inc. completed its 28th consecutive year of growth in both sales and earnings. The firm operated stores under a variety of names and retail formats including Wal-Mart (discount department stores); Sam's Wholesale Clubs (wholesale/retail membership warehouses); Hypermarket*USA (combination grocery and general merchandise stores in excess of 200,000 square feet); and Wal-Mart Supercenters (scaled-down versions of hypermarkets). It also owned Dot Discount Drugstores, a super discount drug chain, and Bud's, off-price outlet stores. In 1991, it passed both K mart Corporation and the retail division of Sears, Roebuck & Co. to become the nation's top-volume retailer. The firm's corporate offices were located in Bentonville, Arkansas.

The Sam Walton Spirit

Much of the initial and continuing success of Wal-Mart was attributed to the entrepreneurial spirit of its founder and Chairman of the Board, Samuel Moore Walton. Sam Walton, or "Mr. Sam" as some referred to him, had traced his down-to-earth, old-fashioned, homespun, evangelical ways to growing up in rural Oklahoma, Missouri, and Arkansas. Some suggested that it was a simple belief in hard work and ambition that had "unlocked countless doors and showered upon him, his customers, and his employees . . . , the fruits of . . . years of labor in

---

building [this] highly successful company." As noted in a Wal-Mart corporate interview, Sam Walton said:

> Our goal has always been in our business to be the very best. And, along with that, we believe that in order to do that, you've got to make a good situation and put the interests of your associates first. If we really do that consistently, they in turn will cause . . . our business to be successful, which is what we've talked about and espoused and practiced. The reason for our success is our people and the way that they're treated and the way they feel about their company.

Many suggested that it was this "people first" philosophy, which guided the company through the challenges and setbacks of its early years, and allowed the company to maintain its consistent record of growth and expansion in later years. "Walton does a remarkable job of instilling near-religious fervor in his people," said analyst Robert Buchanan of A.G. Edwards. "I think that speaks to the heart of his success."

There was little about Sam Walton's background that reflected his success. He was born in Kingfisher, Oklahoma, on March 29, 1918, to Thomas and Nancy Walton. He grew up in rural Missouri in the depths of the Great Depression. He discovered early that he "had a fair amount of ambition and enjoyed working" as he noted later in a Wal-Mart corporate interview. He completed high school at Columbia, Missouri, and received a Bachelor of Arts degree in economics from the University of Missouri in 1940. "I really had no idea what I would be," he said, adding as an afterthought, "at one point in time, I thought I wanted to become president of the United States." He married Helen Alice Robson on February 14, 1942. They would eventually have four children: sons, S. Robson, James C., and John, and a daughter, Alice.

Most industry analysts conceded that Sam Walton was not a fabrication of the Wal-Mart Stores' public relations department. *Business Week* magazine called him "just your basic homespun billionaire." One source suggested that ". . . Mr. Sam is a lifelong small-town resident who didn't change much as he got richer than his neighbors." He had tremendous energy, enjoyed bird hunting with his dogs and flew a corporate plane. When the company was much smaller he could boast that he personally visited every Wal-Mart store at least once a year. A store visit usually included Walton leading Wal-Mart cheers that began "Give me a W, give me an A . . ." To many employees, he had the air of a fiery Baptist preacher. Paul R. Carter, a Wal-Mart executive vice president, said "Mr. Walton has a calling." He became the richest man in America, and by 1991 had created a personal fortune for his family in excess of $21 billion.

Sam Walton's success has been widely chronicled. He was selected by the investment publication, *Financial World,* as the 1989 "CEO of the Decade." The University of the Ozarks, the University of Arkansas, and the University of Missouri granted him honorary degrees. He also received many of the most distinguished professional awards of the retail industry like "Man of the Year," "Discounter of the Year," "Chief Executive Officer of the Year," and was the second retailer to be inducted into the Discounting Hall of Fame. He was recipient of the Horatio Alger Award in 1984 and acknowledged by *Discount Stores News* as "Retailer of the Decade" in December of 1989.

In late 1989 Sam Walton was diagnosed as having multiple myeloma, or cancer of the bone marrow. He planned to remain active in Wal-Mart as chairman of the board.

The Marketing Concept

Genesis of an Idea

Sam Walton started his retail career in 1940 as a management trainee with the J. C. Penney Co. in Des Moines, Iowa. He was impressed with the Penney method of doing business and later was said to have modeled the Wal-Mart chain on "The Penney Idea" as reviewed in Exhibit 1. Founded in Kemerer, Wyoming, in 1902, J. C. Penney followed a strategy of locating stores on the main streets of small towns and small cities throughout the United States. The Penney Company also found strength in calling employees "associates" rather than clerks, another concept Wal-Mart would later embrace.

Following service in the U.S. Army during World War II, Sam Walton acquired a Ben Franklin variety store franchise in Newport, Arkansas. He operated this store successfully until losing the lease in 1950. He opened another store under the name of Walton's 5 & 10 in Bentonville, Arkansas, the following year. By 1962, he was operating a chain of 15 variety stores.

The early retail stores were relatively small operations of 6,000 square feet, were located on "main street," and displayed merchandise on plain wooden tables and counters. Operated under the Ben Franklin name and supplied by Butler Brothers, a Chicago wholesaler, they were also characterized by a limited price line, low gross margins, high merchandise turnover, and concentration on return on investment. The firm was the largest Ben Franklin franchisee in the country in

---

Exhibit 1
The Penney Idea, 1913

---

1. To serve the public, as nearly as we can, to its complete satisfaction.
2. To expect for the service we render a fair remuneration and not all the profit the traffic will bear.
3. To do all in our power to pack the customer's dollar full of value, quality, and satisfaction.
4. To continue to train ourselves and our associates so that the service we give will be more and more intelligently performed.
5. To improve constantly the human factor in our business.
6. To reward men and women in our organization through participation in what the business produces.
7. To test our every policy, method, and act in this wise: "Does it square with what is right and just?"

Source: Vance H. Trimble, *Sam Walton: The Inside Story of America's Richest Man* (New York: Dutton, 1990).

1962. Units operating as variety stores were phased out by 1976 to allow the company to concentrate on the growth of Wal-Mart discount department stores.

Foundations of Growth

The original Wal-Mart discount concept was not a unique idea. Sam Walton became convinced in the late 1950s that discounting would transform retailing. He traveled extensively in New England, the cradle of "off-pricing." "He visited just about every discounter in the United States," suggested William F. Kenney, the retired president of the now-defunct Kings Department Stores. Later, he tried to interest Butler Brothers executives in Chicago in the discount store in a small community, and in that setting he would offer name-brand merchandise at low prices and would add friendly service. Butler Brothers executives rejected the idea. The first K mart, as a "conveniently located one-stop shopping unit where customers could buy a wide variety of quality merchandise at discount prices," opened in 1962 in Garden City, Michigan. The first "Wal-Mart Discount City," a 16,000-square-foot store, opened in late 1962 in Rogers, Arkansas.

Wal-Mart stores sold nationally advertised, well-known brand merchandise at low prices in austere surroundings. As corporate policy, they cheerfully gave refunds, credits, and rain checks. Management conceived the firm as a "discount department store chain offering a wide variety of general merchandise to the customer." Every emphasis was placed upon opportunistic purchases of merchandise from whatever sources were available. Heavy emphasis was placed upon health and beauty aids (H&BA) in the product line.

Wal-Mart developed an aggressive expansion strategy as the firm grew larger. New stores were located primarily in towns of 5,000 to 25,000 population. The stores' sizes ranged from 30,000 to 60,000 square feet compared to a discount industry average of 80,000 square feet. It also expanded by locating stores in contiguous areas, town by town, state by state. When its discount operations came to dominate a market area, the firm chose to develop an adjoining geographic area. While other retailers built warehouses to serve existing outlets, Wal-Mart built the distribution center first and then spotted stores all around it, pooling advertising and distribution overhead. Most stores were less than a six-hour drive from one of the company's warehouses. The first major distribution center, a 390,000-square-foot facility, opened in Searcy, Arkansas, outside Bentonville in 1978.

National Perspectives

At the beginning of 1991, the firm had 1,573 Wal-Mart stores in 35 states. Each store offered a wide variety of general merchandise to the customer. The stores were designed to offer one-stop shopping in 36 departments which included family apparel, health and beauty aids, household needs, electronics, toys, fabric and crafts, automotive supplies, lawn and patio, jewelry, and shoes. At certain store locations, a pharmacy, automotive supply and service center, garden center, and snack bar were also operated. Management emphasized an "everyday low price" as opposed to special promotions, which called for multiple newspaper advertising circulars.

Stores were expected, according to company policy, to "provide the customer with a clean, pleasant, and friendly shopping experience."

Although Wal-Mart carried much the same merchandise, offered similar prices, and operated stores which looked much like K mart or Target, there were many differences. In the typical Wal-Mart store, employees wore blue vests to identify themselves, aisles were wide, apparel departments were carpeted in warm colors, a store employee followed customers to their cars to pick up their shopping carts, and the customer was welcomed at the door by a "people greeter" who gave directions and struck up conversations. In some cases, merchandise was bagged in brown paper sacks rather than plastic bags because customers seemed to prefer them. A simple Wal-Mart logo in white letters on a brown background on the front of the store served to identify the firm. In consumer studies it was determined that the chain was particularly adept at striking the delicate balance needed to convince customers its prices were low without making people feel that its stores were too cheap. In many ways, competitors like K mart sought to emulate Wal-Mart by introducing people greeters, by upgrading interiors, by developing new logos and signage, and by introducing new inventory response systems. In 1990, sales per square of retail space at Wal-Mart were $263. K mart, in contrast, sold only $189 per square foot worth of goods annually.

A "Satisfaction Guaranteed" refund and exchange policy was introduced to allow customers to be confident of Wal-Mart's merchandise and quality. Technological advancements like scanner cash registers, handheld computers for ordering of merchandise, and computer linkages of stores with the general office and distribution centers improved communications and merchandise replenishment. Each store was encouraged to initiate programs which would make it an integral part of the community in which it operated. Employees were encouraged to "maintain the highest standards of honesty, morality, and business ethics in dealing with the public."

In the decade of the 1980s, Wal-Mart developed a number of new retail formats. The first Sam's Wholesale Club opened in Oklahoma City, Oklahoma, in 1983. The wholesale club was an idea which had been developed by other firms earlier but which found its greatest success and growth in acceptability at Wal-Mart. Sam's Wholesale Clubs featured a vast array of product categories with limited selection of brand and model, cash-and-carry business with limited hours, large (100,000 square foot) bare-bone facilities, rock-bottom wholesale prices, and minimal promotion. The limited membership plan included wholesale members who bought membership and others who usually paid a percentage above the ticket price of the merchandise. At the beginning of 1991, there were 148 Sam's Wholesale Clubs open in 28 states. Effective February 2, 1991, Sam's Clubs merged the 28 units of The Wholesale Club, Inc. of Indianapolis, Indiana, into the organization.

Wal-Mart opened its first superstore, called Hypermarket*USA, in 1988 in the Dallas suburb of Garland, Texas. The 222,000-square-foot unit combined a discount store with a large grocery store, a food court of restaurants, and other service businesses such as a bank and a videotape rental store. A scaled-down version of Hypermarket*USA was called the Wal-Mart Super Center. It was similar in merchandise offerings to the hypermarket, but had about half the square footage. These expanded store concepts also included convenience stores and gasoline distribution outlets to "enhance shopping convenience." The company proceeded slowly with expansion plans in these areas. It later suspended its plans for building any more hypermarkets in favor of the super-center concept.

Wal-Mart acquired the McLane Company, Inc., a provider of grocery distribution services for retail stores, in 1991. In October of 1991, management announced that it was starting a chain of stores called Bud's, which would sell damaged, outdated, and overstocked goods at discounts even deeper than regular Wal-Mart stores.

The External Environment

Industry analysts had labeled the 1980s as an era of economic uncertainty for retailers. Some first faced difficulty upon merger or acquisition. After acquiring U.S.-based Allied Department Stores in 1986 and Federated Department Stores in 1988, Canadian developer Robert Campeau was declared bankrupt with over $6 billion in debt. Several divisions and units of the organization were either sold or closed. The flagship downtown Atlanta store of Rich's, a division of Federated, was closed soon after completing a multimillion-dollar remodeling program. Specific merchandise programs in divisions like Bloomingdale's were reevaluated to lower inventory and to raise cash. The notion of servicing existing debt became a significant factor in the success or failure of a retailing organization in the latter half of the decade. Selected acquisitions of U.S. retailers by foreign firms over the past decade are reviewed in Exhibit 2.

Other retailers experienced changes in ownership. The British B.A.T. Industries PLC sold the Chicago-based Marshall Field department store division to the Dayton Hudson Corporation. L. J. Hooker Corporation, the U.S. arm of Australia's Hooker Corporation, sold its Bonwit Teller and Sakowitz stores; it liquidated its B. Altman chain after fruitless sale efforts. The R. H. Macy Company saddled itself with $4.5

Exhibit 2   **Selected Acquisitions of U.S. Retailers by Foreign Firms, 1980–1990**

U.S. Retailer	Foreign Acquirer	Country of Acquirer
Allied Stores (general merchandise)	Campeau	Canada
Alterman Foods (supermarkets)	Delhaie-Le Leon	Belgium
Bonwit Teller (general merchandise)	Hooker Corp.	Australia
Brooks Brothers (apparel)	Marks & Spencer	Great Britain
Federated Department Stores (diversified)	Campeau	Canada
Great Atlantic & Pacific (supermarkets)	Tengelmann	West Germany
Herman's (sporting goods)	Dee Corp.	Great Britain
International House of Pancakes (restaurants)	Wienerwald	Switzerland
Talabots (apparel)	Jusco Ltd.	Japan
Zale (jewelry)	PS Associates	Netherlands

Source: Barry Berman and Joel R. Evans, *Retail Management: A Strategic Approach,* 4th ed. (New York: Macmillan Publishing Company, 1989).

billion in debt as a result of acquiring Bullock's and I. Magnin specialty department stores. Chicago-based Carson, Pirie, Scott & Company was sold to P. A. Bergner & Company, operator of the Milwaukee Boston Store and Bergner Department Stores. Bergner declared a Chapter 11 bankruptcy in 1991.

Many retail enterprises confronted heavy competitive pressure by lowering prices or changing merchandise strategies. Sears, Roebuck & Company, in an effort to reverse sagging sales and less-than-defensible earnings, unsuccessfully introduced a new policy of "everyday low pricing" (ELP) in 1989. It later introduced name-brand items such as Whirlpool alongside its traditional private label merchandise like Kenmore and introduced the "store within a store" concept to feature the name-brand goods. Montgomery Ward and, to a lesser extent, K mart and Ames Department Stores, Inc., an eastern discount chain based in Rocky Hill, Connecticut, followed similar strategies. The J. C. Penney Company, despite repositioning itself as a more upscale retailer, expressed concerns that an impending recession and the Persian Gulf War would combine to erode consumer confidence. The Penney Company noted in its 1990 Annual Report, "As a result, sales and profits within the industry were more negatively impacted than at any time since the last major recession of 1980–82."

The discount department store industry by the early 1990s had changed in a number of ways and was thought to have reached maturity by many analysts. Several formerly successful firms like E. J. Korvette, W. T. Grant, Atlantic Mills, Arlans, Federals, Zayre, Heck's, and Ames Department Stores, Inc., which had found strength in the urban and suburban markets of the East and Midwest, had declared bankruptcy and, as a result, either liquidated or reorganized. Regional firms like Target Stores and Shopko Stores began carrying more fashionable merchandise in more attractive facilities and shifted their emphasis to more national markets. Specialty retailers such as Toys "Я" Us, Pier 1 Imports, and Oshmans were making big inroads in toys, home furnishings, and sporting goods. The "superstores" of drug and food chains were rapidly discounting increasing amounts of general merchandise. Some firms like May Department Stores Company with Caldor and Venture and the F. W. Woolworth Co. with Woolco had withdrawn from the field by either selling their discount divisions or closing them down entirely.

Several new retail formats emerged in the marketplace to challenge the traditional discount department store format. The superstore, a 100,000- to 300,000-square-foot operation, combined a large supermarket with a discount general merchandise store. Originally a European retailing concept, these outlets were known as "malls without walls." K mart's Super K mart, American Fare, and Wal-Mart's Super Center Store and Hypermarket*USA were examples of this trend toward large operations. Warehouse retailing, which involved some combination of warehouse and showroom facilities, used warehouse principles to reduce operating expenses, thereby offering discount prices as a primary customer appeal. Home Depot combined the traditional hardware store and lumberyard with a self-service home improvement center to become the largest home center operator in the nation.

Some retailers responded to changes in the marketplace by selling goods at price levels (20 to 60 percent) below regular retail prices. These off-price operations appeared as two general types: (1) factory outlet stores like Burlington Coat Factory Warehouse, Bass Shoes, and Manhattan's Brand Name Fashion Outlet, and (2) independents like Loehmann's, T. J. Maxx, Marshall's, and Clothestime which bought seconds, overages, closeouts, or leftover goods from manufacturers and other retailers. Other retailers chose to dominate a product classification. Some super-specialists like Sock Appeal, Little Piggie, Ltd., and Sock Market offered a single narrowly defined classification of merchandise with an extensive assortment of brands, colors, and sizes. Others, as niche specialists, like Kids Mart, a division of F. W. Woolworth, and McKids, a division of Sears, targeted an identified market with carefully selected merchandise and appropriately designed stores. Some retailers like Silk Greenhouse (silk plants and flowers), Office Club (office supplies and equipment), and Toys "Я" Us (toys) were called "category killers" because they had achieved merchandise dominance in their respective product categories. Firms like The Limited, Victoria's Secret, and The Banana Republic became mini-department specialists by showcasing new lines and accessories alongside traditional merchandise lines.

Others, like K mart, felt that many existing firms would grow by putting some competitors out of business. As noted by K mart Executive Vice President Richard Miller in a 1991 interview with *Forbes* magazine,

> The largest opportunity is in consolidation. About 25% of the discount industry comes from regional discounters. There is a big market share opportunity with undersized and undercapitalized regional discounters. You don't necessarily have to take it from your biggest competitors.

Wal-Mart became the nation's largest retailer and discount department store chain in sales volume in 1991. K mart Corporation, the industry's second-largest retailer and discount department store chain with over 2,300 stores and more than $32 million in sales in 1990, was perceived by many industry analysts and consumers in several independent studies as a laggard, even though it had been the industry sales leader for a number of years. In the same studies, Wal-Mart was perceived as the industry leader even though, according to *The Wall Street Journal,* "they carry much the same merchandise, offer prices that are pennies apart and operate stores that look almost exactly alike." "Even their names are similar," noted the newspaper. The original K mart concept of a "conveniently located, one-stop shopping unit where customers could buy a wide variety of quality merchandise at discount prices" was thought to have lost its competitive edge in a changing market. As one analyst noted in an industry newsletter, "They had done so well for the past 20 years without paying attention to market changes. Now they have to."

Wal-Mart and K mart sales growth in the ten-year period from 1980 to 1990 is reviewed in Exhibit 3. A competitive analysis is shown of four major retail firms in Exhibit 4. The financial performance of Wal-Mart Stores, Inc., 1982–1990, is covered in Exhibit A at the end of this case.

Some retailers like K mart had initially focused on appealing to professional, middle-class consumers who lived in suburban areas and who were likely to be price-sensitive. Other firms like Target, which had adopted the discount concept early, generally attempted to go after an upscale consumer who had an annual household income of $25,000 to $44,000. Fleet Farm and Menard's served the rural consumer, while firms like Chicago's Goldblatt's Department Stores returned to their immigrant heritage to serve blacks and Hispanics in the innercity.

Exhibit 3	Competitive Sales and Store Comparison, 1980–1990

	K mart			Wal-Mart[1]	
Year	Sales	Stores		Sales	Stores
	(000)			(000)	
1990	$32,070,000	2,350		$32,601,594	1,573
1989	29,533,000	2,361		25,810,656	1,402
1988	27,301,000	2,307		20,649,001	1,259
1987	25,627,000	2,273		15,959,255	1,114
1986	23,035,000	2,342		11,909,076	980
1985	22,035,000	2,332		8,451,489	859
1984	20,762,000	2,173		6,400,861	745
1983	18,597,000	2,160		4,666,909	642
1982	16,772,166	2,117		3,376,252	551
1981	16,527,012	2,055		2,444,997	491
1980	14,204,381	1,772		1,643,199	330

[1]Wal-Mart fiscal year ends January 31. Figures are assigned to previous year.

In rural communities Wal-Mart's success often came at the expense of established local merchants and units of regional discount store chains. Hardware stores, family department stores, building supply outlets, and stores featuring fabrics, sporting goods, and shoes were among the first to either close or relocate elsewhere. Regional discount retailers in the Sunbelt states like Roses, Howard's, T. G. & Y, and Duckwall-ALCO, which once enjoyed solid sales and earnings, were forced to reposition themselves by renovating stores, opening bigger and more modern units, remerchandising assortments, and offering lower prices. In many cases, stores like Coast-to-Coast, Pamida, and Ben Franklin closed upon a Wal-Mart announcement to build in a specific community. "Just the word that Wal-Mart was coming made some stores close up," noted one newspaper editor.

Corporate Strategies

The corporate and marketing strategies that emerged at Wal-Mart to challenge the turbulent and volatile external environment of the late 1980s and early 1990s were based upon a set of two main objectives. In the first objective, management featured the customer. The objective read, "customers will be provided what they want, when they want it, all at a value." In the second objective, the firm emphasized the team spirit. The objective said, "treating each other as we would hope to be treated, acknowledging our total dependency on our Associate-partners to sustain our success." The approach included aggressive plans for new-store openings; expansion to additional states; upgrading, relocation, refurbishing, and remodeling of existing stores; and opening new distribution centers. The plan was to not have a single operating unit that had not been updated in the past seven years. In the 1991 Annual Report to stockholders, the 1990s were considered "a new era for

Exhibit 4   **An Industry Competitive Analysis, 1990**

	Wal-Mart	Sears, Roebuck	Kmart	J. C. Penney
Sales (thousands)	$32,601,584	$55,972,000*	$32,070,000	$17,410,000
Net income (thousands)	$ 1,291,024	$ 902,000	$ 756,000	$ 577,000
Net income per share	$ 1.14	$ 2.63	$ 3.78	$ 4.33
Dividends per share	$ .14	$ 2.00	$ 1.72	$ 2.64
Number stores (see note)	1,724	1,765	4,180	3,889
Percent sales change	26.0%	1.2%	.6%	2.1%

Note: Wal-Mart and subsidiaries (number of outlets)
   Wal-Mart stores—1,573
   Sam's Wholesale Club—148
   Hypermart* USA—3

  Sears, Roebuck & Company
   *Merchandise Group sales, $25,093,200 (000)
  Merchandise Group (number of outlets)
   Department stores—863
   Paint and Hardware Stores—98
   Catalog Outlet Stores—101
   Western Auto—504
   Eye Care Centers of America—94
   Business Systems Centers—65
   Pinstripes Petites—40

  K mart Corporation (number of outlets)
  General Merchandise—2,350
  Specialty Retail Stores—1,830
   PACE Membership Warehouse
   Builders Square
   Payless Drug Stores
   Waldenbooks
   The Sports Authority

  J. C. Penney Company, Inc. (number of outlets)
  Stores—1,312
   Metropolitan Market Stores—697
   Geographic Market Stores—615
  Catalog Units—2,090
   J. C. Penney Stores—1,312
   Freestanding Sales Centers—626
   Drug Stores—136
   Other, Principally Outlet Stores—16
  Drug Stores (Thrift Drug or Treasury Drug)—487

Source: Company Annual Reports.

Wal-Mart; an era in which we plan to grow to a truly nationwide retailer, and should we continue to perform, our sales and earnings will also grow beyond where most could have envisioned at the dawn of the 80s."

  Several programs were launched to "highlight" popular social causes. Wal-Mart initiated the "Buy American" program in 1985. The theme was "Bring It

Home To The USA" and its purpose was to communicate Wal-Mart's support for American manufacturing. In the program, the firm encouraged manufacturers to produce goods in the United States rather than import them from other countries. It also encouraged vendors indirectly to participate in the program by contacting manufacturers directly with proposals to sell only goods which were made in the United States. Wal-Mart buyers also targeted specific import items in their assortments on a state-by-state basis to encourage domestic manufacturing. According to Haim Dabah, president of Gitano Group, Inc., a maker of fashion discount clothing which imported 95 percent of its clothing and during the late 1980s made about 20 percent of its products in the United States, "Wal-Mart let it be known loud and clear that if you're going to grow with them, you sure better have some products made in the U.S.A." Farris Fashion, Inc. (flannel shirts), Roadmaster Corporation (exercise bicycles), Landers Industries, Inc. (lawn chairs), and Magic Chef (microwave ovens) were examples of vendors that chose to participate in the program.

From the Wal-Mart standpoint, the "Buy American" program centered around value—producing and selling quality merchandise at a competitive price. The promotion included television advertisements featuring factory workers, a soaring American eagle, and the slogan, "We buy American whenever we can, so you can too." Prominent in-store signage and store circulars were also included. One store poster read, "Success Stories—These items formerly imported, are now being purchased by Wal-Mart in the U.S.A."

Wal-Mart was one of the first retailers to embrace the concept of "green" marketing. The program offered shoppers the option of purchasing products that were better for the environment in three respects: manufacturing, use, and disposal. The program was introduced through full-page advertisements in *The Wall Street Journal* and *USA Today*. In-store signage identified those products which were environmentally safe. As Wal-Mart executives saw it, "customers are concerned about the quality of land, air, and water, and would like the opportunity to do something positive." To initiate the program, 7,000 vendors were notified that Wal-Mart had a corporate concern for the environment and asked for their support in a variety of ways. Wal-Mart television advertising showed children on swings, fields of grain blowing in the wind, and roses. Green and white store signs, printed on recycled paper, marked products or packaging that had been developed or redesigned to be more environmentally sound.

As the nation's largest retailer and in many geographic areas the dominant distributor, Wal-Mart exerted considerable influence in negotiation for the best price, delivery terms, promotion allowances, and continuity of supply of many name-brand items. Many of these benefits were passed on to consumers in the form of name-brand items available at lower-than-competitive prices. As a matter of corporate policy, management often insisted on doing business only with a producer's top sales executives rather than going through a manufacturer's representative. As a result of this activity, some industry critics accused Wal-Mart of threatening to buy from other producers if firms refused to sell directly to it. In the ensuing power struggle, Wal-Mart executives refused to talk about the controversial policy or admit that it existed. One sales agency representative suggested, "In the Southwest,

Wal-Mart's the only show in town." An industry analyst added, "They're extremely aggressive. Their approach has always been to give the customer the benefit of a corporate saving. That builds up customer loyalty and market share."

Another key factor in the mix was an inventory control system that was recognized as the most sophisticated in retailing. A high-speed computer system linked virtually all the stores to headquarters and the company's distribution centers. It electronically logged every item sold at the checkout counter, automatically kept the warehouses informed of merchandise to be ordered, and directed the flow of goods to the stores and even to the proper shelves. Most important for management, it helped detect sales trends quickly and speeded up market reaction time substantially.

Decision Making in a Market-Oriented Firm

One principle that distinguished Wal-Mart was the unusual depth of employee involvement in company affairs. Corporate strategies put emphasis on human resource management. Employees of Wal-Mart became "Associates," a name borrowed from Sam Walton's early association with the J. C. Penney Co. Input was encouraged at meetings at the store and corporate level. The firm hired employees locally, provided training programs, and through a "Letter to the President" program, management encouraged employees to ask questions, and made words like "we," "us," and "our" a part of the corporate language. A number of special award programs recognized individual, department, and division achievement. Stock ownership and profit-sharing programs were introduced as part of a "partnership concept."

The corporate culture was recognized by the editors of the trade publication, *Mass Market Retailers,* when it recognized all 275,000 Associates collectively as the 1989 "Mass Market Retailers of the Year." "The [term] Wal-Mart Associate," the editors noted, "in this decade has come to symbolize all that is right with the American worker, particularly in the retailing environment and most particularly at Wal-Mart. . . ." The "store within a store" concept, as a Wal-Mart corporate policy, trained individuals to be merchants by being responsible for the performance of their own departments as if they were running their own businesses. Seminars and training programs afforded them opportunities to grow within the company. "People development, not just a good 'program' for any growing company but a must to secure out future," is how Suzanne Allford, vice president of the Wal-Mart People Division, explained the firm's decentralized approach to retail management development in a *Wall Street Journal* interview.

"The Wal-Mart Way," was a phrase that was used by management to summarize the firm's approach to business and the development of its corporate culture. As noted in the 1991 Annual Report when referring to this development program: "We stepped outside our retailing world to examine the best managed companies in the United States in an effort to determine the fundamentals of their success and to 'bench mark' our own performances." The name "Total Quality Management" (TQM) was used to identify this "vehicle for proliferating the very best things we do while incorporating the new ideas our people have that will assure our future."

The Growth Challenge

David Glass, 53 years old, has assumed the role of president and chief executive officer at Wal-Mart in 1988, the position previously held by Sam Walton. Known for his hard-driving managerial style, Glass gained his experience in retailing at a small supermarket chain in Springfield, Missouri. He joined Wal-Mart as executive vice president for finance in 1976. He was named president and chief operating officer in 1984.

And what of Wal-Mart without Mr. Sam? "There's no transition to make," said Glass in a *Fortune* interview in early 1989, "because the principles and the basic values he used in founding this company were so sound and so universally accepted." "As for the future," he suggested, "there's more opportunity ahead of us than behind us. We're good students of retailing and we've studied the mistakes that others have made. We'll make our own mistakes, but we won't repeat theirs. The only thing constant at Wal-Mart is change. We'll be fine as long as we never lose our responsiveness to the customer."

Exhibit A   **Wal-Mart Stores, Inc.: Financial Performance, 1990–1981**

Ten-Year Financial Summary	1990	1989	1988	1987
(Dollar amounts in thousands except per-share data)				
Earnings				
Net sales	$32,601,594	$25,810,656	$20,649,001	$15,959,255
Licensed department rentals and other income—net	261,814	174,644	136,867	104,783
Cost of sales	25,499,834	20,070,034	16,056,856	12,281,744
Operating, selling, and general and administrative expenses	5,152,178	4,069,695	3,267,864	2,599,367
Interest costs				
Debt	42,716	20,346	36,286	25,262
Capital leases	125,920	117,725	99,395	88,995
Taxes on income	751,736	631,600	488,246	441,027
Net income	1,291,024	1,075,900	837,221	627,643
Per share of common stock				
Net income	1.14	.95	.74	.55
Dividends	.14	.11	.08	.06
Stores in operation at the end of the period				
Wal-Mart Stores	1,573	1,402	1,259	1,114
Sams Wholesale Clubs	148	123	105	84
Financial position				
Current assets	6,414,775	4,712,616	3,630,987	2,905,145
Net property, plant, equipment, and capital leases	4,712,039	3,430,059	2,661,954	2,144,852
Total assets	11,388,915	8,198,484	6,359,668	5,131,809
Current liabilities	3,990,414	2,845,315	2,065,909	1,743,763
Long-term debt	740,254	185,152	184,439	185,672
Long-term obligations under capital leases	1,158,621	1,087,403	1,009,046	866,972
Preferred stock with mandatory redemption provisions				
Shareholders' equity	5,365,524	3,965,561	3,007,909	2,257,267

Wal-Mart Stores, Inc. had for over 25 years experienced tremendous growth and, as one analyst suggested, "been consistently on the cutting edge of low markup mass merchandising." Much of the forward momentum had come from the entrepreneurial spirit of Samuel Moore Walton. Mr. Sam remained chairman of the board of directors and corporate representative for the immediate future. A new management team was in place. As the largest retailer in the country, the firm had positioned itself to meet the challenges of the next decade as an industry leader. The question now was: Could the firm maintain its blistering growth pace—outmaneuvering the competition with the innovative retailing concepts that it had continued to develop better than anyone else?

Epilogue

Samuel Moore Walton, founder of Wal-Mart Stores, Inc. and one of the most influential retailers of this century, died April 5, 1992. He was 74 years old.

Exhibit A   *continued*

1986	1985	1984	1983	1982	1981
$11,909,076	$8,451,489	$6,400,861	$4,666,909	$3,376,252	$2,444,997
84,623	55,127	52,167	36,031	22,435	17,650
9,053,219	6,361,271	4,722,440	3,418,025	2,458,235	1,787,496
2,007,645	1,485,210	1,181,455	892,887	677,029	495,010
10,442	1,903	5,207	4,935	20,297	16,053
76,367	54,640	42,506	29,946	18,570	15,351
395,940	276,119	230,653	160,903	110,416	65,943
450,086	327,473	270,767	196,244	124,140	82,794
.40	0.29	0.24	0.17	0.11	0.08
.0425	0.035	0.0263	0.0175	0.113	0.0082
980	859	745	642	551	491
49	23	11	3		
2,353,271	1,784,275	1,303,254	1,005,567	720,537	589,161
1,676,282	1,303,450	870,309	628,151	457,509	333,026
4,049,092	3,103,645	2,205,229	1,652,254	1,187,448	937,513
1,340,291	992,683	688,968	502,763	347,318	339,961
179,234	180,682	41,237	40,866	106,465	104,581
764,128	595,205	449,886	339,930	222,610	154,196
	4,902	5,874	6,411	6,861	7,438
1,690,493	1,277,659	984,672	737,503	488,109	323,942

Figures are taken from beginning-of-year balances.
Source: Wal-Mart Annual Report, January 31, 1991.

The company announced on Monday, April 6, 1992, that his son, S. Robson Walton, vice chairman of Wal-Mart, would succeed his father as chairman of the board. David Glass would remain president and CEO.

References

Barrier, Michael. "Walton's Mountain." *Nation's Business,* April 1988, 18–20+.

Bergman, Joan. "Saga of Sam Walton." *Stores,* January 1988, 129–130+.

Blumenthal, Karen. "Marketing with Emotion: Wal-Mart Shows the Way." *The Wall Street Journal,* November 20, 1989, B3.

Bragg, Arthur. "Wal-Mart's War on Reps." *Sales & Marketing Management,* March 1987, 41–43.

Caminiti, Susan. "What Ails Retailing." *Fortune,* January 30, 1989, 63–64.

Castro, Janice. "Mr. Sam Stuns Goliath." *Time,* February 25, 1991, 62–63.

Corwin, Pat, Jay L. Johnson, and Renee M. Rouland. "Made in U.S.A." *Discount Merchandiser,* November 1989, 48–52.

"David Glass's Biggest Job Is Filling Sam's Shoes." *Business Month,* December 1988, 42.

"Facts about Wal-Mart Stores, Inc." Press Release, Corporate and Public Affairs, Wal-Mart Stores, Inc.

"Glass Is CEO at Wal-Mart." *Discount Merchandiser,* March 1988, 6+.

Helliker, Kevin. "Wall-Mart's Store of the Future Blends Discount Prices, Department-Store Feel." *The Wall Street Journal,* May 17, 1991, B1, B8.

Higgins, Kevin T. "Wal-Mart: A Pillar in a Thousand Communities." *Building Supply Home Centers,* February 1988, 100–102.

Huey, John. "America's Most Successful Merchant." *Fortune,* September 23, 1991, 46–48+.

Huey, John. "Wal-Mart, Will It Take Over the World?" *Fortune,* January 30, 1989, 52–56+.

"Jack Shewmaker, Vice Chairman, Wal-Mart Stores, Inc." *Discount Merchandiser,* November 1987, 26+.

Jacober, Steve. "Wal-Mart: A Boon to U.S. Vendors." *Discount Merchandiser,* November 1989, 41–46.

Levering, Robert, Milton Moskowitz, and Michael Katz. *The 100 Best Companies to Work for in America.* Reading, Mass.: Addison-Wesley, 1984, 351–354.

"Management Style: Sam Moore Walton." *Business Month,* May 1989, 38.

Marsch, Barbara. "The Challenge: Merchants Mobilize to Battle Wal-Mart in a Small Community." *The Wall Street Journal,* June 5, 1991, A1, A4.

Mason, Todd. "Sam Walton of Wal-Mart: Just Your Basic Homespun Billionaire." *Business Week,* October 14, 1985, 142–143+.

"Perspectives on Discount Retailing." *Discount Merchandiser,* April 1987, 44+.

Peters, Tom J., and Nancy Austin. *A Passion For Excellence.* New York: Random House, 266–267.

Rudnitsky, Howard. "How Sam Walton Does It." *Forbes,* August 16, 1982, 42–44.

Rudnitsky, Howard. "Play It Again, Sam." *Forbes,* August 10, 1987, 48.

"Sam's Wholesale Club Racks Up $1.6 Billion Sales in 1986." *Discount Merchandiser,* February 1987, 26.

"Sam Walton, the Retail Giant: Where Does He Go from Here?" *Drug Topics,* July 17, 1989, 6.

"Sam Moore Walton." *Business Month,* May 1989, 38.

"Samuel Moore Walton: Biographical Data." Press Release, January 1990, Corporate and Public Affairs, Wal-Mart Stores, Inc.

Schwadel, Francine. "Little Touches Spur Wal-Mart's Rise." *The Wall Street Journal,* September 22, 1989, B1.

Sheets, Kenneth R. "How Wal-Mart Hits Main St." *U.S. News & World Report,* March 13, 1989, 53–55.

Smith, Sarah. "America's Most Admired Corporations." *Fortune,* January 29, 1990, 56+.

"The Early Days: Walton Kept Adding 'a Few More' Stores." *Discount Store News,* December 9, 1985, 61.

Trimble, Vance H. *Sam Walton: The Inside Story of America's Richest Man.* New York: Dutton, 1990.

Wal-Mart Stores, Inc., *Annual Report*(s). Bentonville, Arkansas, 1990, 1991, 1992.

"Wal-Mart to Acquire McLane, Distributor to Retail Industry." *The Wall Street Journal,* October 2, 1990, A8.

Walton, Sam, with John Huey. *Sam Walton: Made in America.* New York: Doubleday, 1992.

Weiner, Steve. "Golf Balls, Motor Oil and Tomatoes." *Forbes,* October 30, 1989, 130–131+.

Weiner, Steve. "Pssst! Wanna Buy a Watch? A Suit? How About a Whole Department Store?" *Forbes,* January 8, 1990, 192+.

"Work, Ambition—Sam Walton." Press Release, Corporate and Public Affairs, Wal-Mart Stores, Inc.

C A S E • *Medicap Pharmacies, Inc.: A Balanced Strategy for the Nineties* *

John K. Wong, Iowa State University
Charles B. Shrader, Iowa State University
Keith R. Hausman, Iowa State University

Bill Kimball, chief operating officer, could not figure out why it happened! As he pulled his Jaguar X16 into the Medicap Pharmacies, Inc. corporate headquarters parking lot in West Des Moines, Iowa, he searched his mind for answers. How could Medicap have lost the bid for "Share," the largest HMO contract for filling prescriptions for which the company had ever submitted a bid? Walgreen's had won the bid which would amount to an estimated $1 million in annual sales.

However, Kimball reasoned that "Share" probably had some fatal flaws. First of all, the bid had gone so low that it was difficult for him to see how Walgreen's could make it profitable. Additionally, he felt the contract probably did not match the strong corporate philosophy that had developed at Medicap, namely, high-quality personal service and value to customers. The contract would force margins so low that Medicap franchises probably could not offer the service that had become a tradition within the company.

*The authors thank William C. Kimball, President of Medicap Pharmacies for the information he provided in developing this case. Copyright © 1992, John Wong and Charles B. Shrader.

Kimball realized that perhaps the "Share" deal was better off lost, and he turned his thoughts to Medicap's current challenges. How could Medicap continue to grow in an era of increasing medical costs and increasing medical supply competition? In what states would expansion be most likely, and most profitable? Medicap is basically a Midwestern company, but now that it is so successful expansion to the east and west seems likely. Yet Kimball knew growth had to be cautious.

The company's growth strategy is careful, deliberate, and superb. Environmental/market feasibility studies have been perfected by Medicap and have contributed greatly to the company's ability to facilitate growth. The number of franchises or stores has grown twenty-fold since 1974, sales are increasing, and the company is continually adding new employees.

Bill Kimball twisted a key that stopped the low purr of the Jag's engine and entered the corporate offices. He knew he had a successful strategy and energetic employees and he looked forward to the challenges that the future would bring to Medicap.

Company History[1]

Medicap Pharmacies was founded by Russell Johnson, Jr. in 1971. Johnson, who had been a pharmacist in his father's store for years, learned that the major drawback to the small independently owned drug store was the lack of the ability to compete on price. Large chain stores could sell drugs much more cheaply than could the smaller stores because of their large purchasing power.

Yet the drawback to the large stores was their lack of customer service, their impersonal approach to doing business. One of the lessons Johnson learned from his father's business was that drug usage had to be patiently explained to customers. The large stores did not do a good job of this. Nor did the large stores give pharmacists the opportunity to be their own bosses.

Therefore, the small stores attracted a limited, but loyal, clientele, while the large stores grabbed the lion's share of the market. Johnson, however, figured that he could maximize the strengths of both the large and small stores. He came up with a brilliant idea: Sell drug store franchises to independent pharmacists, and allow the franchisees to have access to the strength of a centralized purchasing organization. This idea captured the benefits of the small store (personal service and attention) while also reaping the benefits of the large ones (lower prices due to large purchasing power).

Johnson was able to convince a group of investors of the merit of his idea and his first store was opened in 1971 in Des Moines, Iowa.[2] It was called the Medicine Store. Johnson hired a marketing expert, William Kimball, and a newly trained pharmacist, Charles Porter, who helped make out a plan for accomplishing Johnson's objectives. The first three years were profitable, and in 1974 Johnson sold his first franchise to Byrl Blackmer of Ames, Iowa, who is still in business today. The company changed its name to Medicap Pharmacies. In 1975, three more franchises were sold, and by 1991 the company had grown to a total of 78 stores in 14 states.[3] Most of the stores (48) are in Iowa, with the others being in the neighboring states of Nebraska, Missouri, South Dakota, Minnesota, Illinois, and Wisconsin. The expansion outside of Iowa did not begin until 1985, so growth had been rapid.

There also have been store openings in states as far away as Alabama, New Mexico, Pennsylvania, and North Carolina. Each new franchise requires an approximate $110,000 as an initial investment.

Annual sales in 1973 were $150,000 compared to $20.1 million in 1987. Growth continued in 1991 with sales of approximately $50 million and 1992 sales were projected to reach $60 million. By 1992 the company employed 240 people.[4] Medicap competes with other drug chains such as Walgreen's, Revco, and Wal-Mart and has successfully positioned itself as a discount pharmacy offering personal face-to-face service with a trained pharmacist, and the convenience and savings of a large chain store.

Company Philosophy

Medicap's business is a blend of excellent customer service and very competitive prices. The corporate mission is as follows:

> As the franchisor, we at MEDICAP blend the positive elements of the traditional independent who knows and serves the customer, with the power of the chain and its cost-advantage situation.
>
> We believe that the future, the vigor, and the independence of the practice of pharmacy can best be guaranteed by supporting pharmacists . . . with professional business services, that foster the independent practice of the profession.
>
> We believe . . . competitive edge is strengthened by this decentralized free enterprise approach.
>
> We believe in the synergistic effect of strong group buying power, of negotiated contracts with third-party providers, of name recognition through targeted advertising and promotion, convenience with the image of low price, of positive mental attitude, and the cooperation of the franchisee and franchisor.
>
> We believe that our professional services should be extended . . . through a clear comprehensive agreement that outlines what we do for [our franchises]. . . .
>
> We believe that . . . we must commit our staff to share all of their knowledge and insights . . . to help anticipate problems and solve, to search out and develop the best of the new ideas and techniques available in the marketplace. . . .
>
> We believe in the rights of the individual. Independent pharmacists to practice the profession as they know it. Our mission is to continue to help our franchisees toward independence with the system, to build a profitable practice in the community of their choice, with hours of a professional, and lifestyle that enriches themselves and their families.[5]

Russ Johnson was once quoted as saying, "I see Medicap as a big extended family, and I enjoy being on a first name basis with everyone."[6] These corporate values have provided the framework from which Medicap's success has been built.

Corporate Structure

Russell Johnson, chief executive officer of Medicap, is a native of West Des Moines, Iowa. He has a degree in pharmacy from Drake University and provides leadership to the company in that area.

Bill Kimball was raised on a farm in western Iowa. He earned a bachelor's degree in economics from William Penn College in 1970. He provides expertise in the basic management functions for the company; things such as planning, promotion, and environmental analysis.

Together with a small board of directors, this constitutes the top management of Medicap Pharmacies, Inc. The company is privately held between Johnson and Kimball.

Medicap operates with a modified "functional" form of organizational structure. The major departments are operations, marketing, franchise development, and the controller. Under operations there is an operations coordinator, a personnel director, and a director of purchasing.

The Medicap structure is graphically portrayed in Exhibit 1. The structure as drawn has some very interesting and innovative features. First, the names of the employees are listed on the structure, indicating an appreciation that the person is in that position. Another innovation is that there is a provision for growth built in. For example, when the company grows to 75 stores, it will add an operations supervisor. At 80 stores it will add an operations secretary, and so forth.

This combines the traditional strength of stability of the functional structure with the flexibility of planning for growth. The emphasis on operations indicates the company's concern for the day-to-day operations of each outlet. The company never forgets the importance of each store to its customers. The contingency plans for growth that are built into the structure also fit well with the franchise concept and allow the company to be very flexible.

The structure offers Medicap some other advantages as well. For example, Medicap has centralized purchasing as well as both operational and accounting services. This means the corporation can provide franchises with a corporate operations advisor who is also a pharmacist. The advisor acts as a liaison between the corporate office and the franchise, providing expert technical advice on store layout and inventory. Meanwhile, Medicap encourages the individual store owner to ultimately make all final decisions.

Accounting services are also provided by the corporate office. These include preparing payroll programs, formal monthly financial statements, and a range of other accounting services as requested by the individual franchise owner.

Consequently, there are strong links between the franchises and the corporate offices. These links allow the corporation tight control over some important functions and at the same time allow individual owners flexibility in running their operations.

Purchasing[7]

Kimball decided early on in the company that Medicap would go it alone when it came to purchasing. As the volume from suppliers increased, the buying power of Medicap became greater.

Kimball set up programs whereby Medicap representatives go to suppliers and negotiate for the best price. Suppliers who offer the best prices are referred to the individual pharmacists. The pharmacists order from "preferred" suppliers and get the prices that were negotiated by the central office.

This purchasing arrangement allows Medicap to deal like a very large chain, and pass the savings on to the retail outlets and eventually to customers.

Exhibit 1

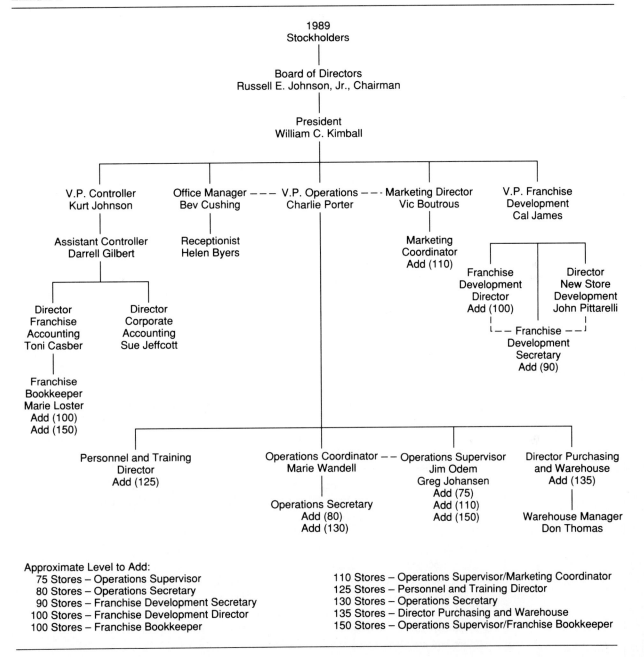

1989
Stockholders

Board of Directors
Russell E. Johnson, Jr., Chairman

President
William C. Kimball

V.P. Controller
Kurt Johnson

Office Manager – – – V.P. Operations – – - Marketing Director
Bev Cushing   Charlie Porter   Vic Boutrous

V.P. Franchise
Development
Cal James

Assistant Controller
Darrell Gilbert

Receptionist
Helen Byers

Marketing
Coordinator
Add (110)

Franchise
Development
Director
Add (100)

Director
New Store
Development
John Pittarelli

Director
Franchise
Accounting
Toni Casber

Director
Corporate
Accounting
Sue Jeffcott

└ – – Franchise – – ┘
Development
Secretary
Add (90)

Franchise
Bookkeeper
Marie Loster
Add (100)
Add (150)

Personnel and Training
Director
Add (125)

Operations Coordinator – – Operations Supervisor
Marie Wandell   Jim Odem
Greg Johansen
Add (75)
Add (110)
Add (150)

Director Purchasing
and Warehouse
Add (135)

Operations Secretary
Add (80)
Add (130)

Warehouse Manager
Don Thomas

Approximate Level to Add:
  75 Stores – Operations Supervisor
  80 Stores – Operations Secretary
  90 Stores – Franchise Development Secretary
  100 Stores – Franchise Development Director
  100 Stores – Franchise Bookkeeper

110 Stores – Operations Supervisor/Marketing Coordinator
125 Stores – Personnel and Training Director
130 Stores – Operations Secretary
135 Stores – Director Purchasing and Warehouse
150 Stores – Operations Supervisor/Franchise Bookkeeper

Promotion and Customer Service[8]

Medicap management is concerned that the communities in which it operates perceive it to be more than a drug store. Medicap wants to be perceived as involved in the prevention of illness.

The company offers several wellness programs. There are free cholesterol screenings and blood pressure tests set up in malls and at first aid stations at the state fair. The company wants to convey the message of "being there" and "caring."

Medicap is also the corporate sponsor for the Iowa Association for the Prevention of Blindness. Medicap also co-sponsors the Blood Center of Central Iowa's annual Blood Donor Day Drive.[9]

At each Medicap store, every month there is a specific focus on a special health issue. These range from the prevention of heart disease to personal and home safety. The goals are prevention and awareness. In line with the social focus, the stores provide free brochures, counseling, and special bargains. Customers may confer with the pharmacist about any questions they may have in private consultation areas.

At individual stores, customer records are kept in a computer-generated medical profile containing diagnoses, prescriptions, drug interactions, and tax records. On request, the pharmacies will file insurance claims for their customers. After-hours telephone calls, prescription delivery, and mail orders are offered as well.[10]

The company also wants to promote the basic strengths of the company, namely, competitive prices, convenience, professional and personal service. Bill Kimball states, "We call it 'customer care' instead of 'customer service' because we feel our biggest strength is the one-on-one contact our customers receive. The word 'care' imparts a meaning of attention to detail and concern for the health of our customers."[11]

Medicap spends about 2 percent of profits on advertising. Corporate headquarters control 1 percent of a $400,000 ad budget which is spent on television advertising and ads in large newspapers. The individual franchises spend the other 1 percent on local radio advertising, small newspaper ads, and printed fliers. Bill Kimball handles advertising himself, explaining, "I haven't delegated it. I feel it's that important."[12]

None of the Medicap stores is located in a major retail center or shopping mall. Kimball feels that locating away from major retail centers fits the overall corporate strategy better. "We have built our company with a well-defined service strategy in mind," says Kimball. "Our stores are designed as intimate, professional settings as opposed to a mass merchandising atmosphere."[13]

Medicap is serious about customer service. It was one of the first pharmacies in the country to offer a "drive-thru" prescription pickup service. The drive-thru windows have proven to be very popular with customers. "Mothers with small children love them," says Kimball, "as well as the rest of us who have ten other things to do." Company research finds that at some stores as many as 40 percent of the customers use the drive-thru windows.[14]

Company Performance[15]

Sales have been steadily increasing since the company was founded in 1971.[16] Over the past ten years, Medicap has experienced sales increases averaging 28 percent per year. For the fiscal year ending June 30, 1990, sales increased 25 percent over the previous year and retail sales for stores open longer than two years increased almost 17 percent. In 1973, annual sales amounted to $150,000, in 1987 sales grew to $20.1 million, and sales for 1991 were approximately $50 million.[17]

Medicap stores carry an inventory of healthcare items only. About 90 percent of annual revenue is from the sale of prescription drugs. The remainder is from the sale of health-related, over-the-counter remedies. The stores do not sell cosmetics or shampoo. "We believe that adding cosmetics or gifts would dilute our identity as a medication provider and educator," says Kimball. "The pharmacist is running a pharmacy, not worrying about whether the motor oil is stocked on the shelves."[18]

Feasibility Study[19]

Medicap undertakes an extensive environmental analysis of each potential new store location to reduce uncertainty and to help ensure the success of the franchise. These market feasibility studies are developed under the direction of John Pittarelli, director of New Store Development at Medicap's corporate headquarters in Des Moines.

The purpose of these studies is to assist the potential franchise owner in securing funding, or venture capital, from a bank or other financial institution, and to give the potential franchise owner all the information and support possible in starting a new store. Medicap representatives armed with the feasibility study accompany the new applicant to the bank in an attempt to secure a loan. Total costs for establishing a franchise are between $100,000 and $120,000, of which $15,000 is for the franchise fee. The franchise owner also has to pay a royalty of 4 percent of gross sales plus a 1 percent advertising fee. The franchisee is required to own at least 25 percent of the franchise.[20] The typical new franchise applicant has previously worked for another pharmacy and is 30 to 35 years of age.

Factor Conditions   The environmental factors considered in the feasibility study are as follows. Demographic information is obtained from the potential area's chamber of commerce. A wide array of demographic and economic factors are taken into account when considering a potential store location.

Regional information such as population and number of households is considered along with economic factors such as labor force, employment, construction, personal income, retail sales, and new businesses. Population density and employment density of the region are considered. Traffic maps and patterns are utilized as well when assessing a region.

Specific population statistics are obtained from census tracts. Age characteristics, employment characteristics, housing characteristics, household, family, and per capita income, education, and other factors are taken into account.

The area's climate is even considered. Precipitation amounts for the year, average temperature, and even wind speeds are examined.

The region's infrastructure is examined in the studies. The number of colleges and universities in the area, as well as the primary and secondary education system are included in the study. The number of hospitals, clinics, and, if the area is large enough to support it, medical schools, pharmacy colleges, and even schools of nursing are included. Transportation services in the area such as airports, major highways, local trucking companies, rail terminals, and waterways are given attention. The area's water supply and sewage facilities are factors as well. The region's energy resources, such as supplies of electricity, natural gas, and oil are considered. Regional telephone service is also examined.

The business climate of the area is examined. Tax rates, financing, and incentives are taken into account when assessing the region's business environment. Corporate income tax rates, sales and use tax rates, and property tax rates are just a few that are examined. Financial incentives such as investment tax credits, community and urban development block grants, and property/sales tax exemptions are other facets of the attractiveness of the business climate. Large companies and manufacturers which are based in the area are considered as well.

Competitive Climate   This is perhaps the most salient feature of the feasibility study. A map of the area under consideration is plotted with hospitals, clinics, and, most important, other competing drug stores. Medicap also includes its desired location on the map.

In order to gain a competitive feel of the competing drug stores, Medicap rates each individual store on a competitive profile. These profiles include store name, address, sales area, and approximate annual volume. Medicap then examines five key store factors. The first is general, which includes store access, parking, and store hours. The second is merchandise, which includes selection and availability. The third is price, which includes value. The fourth is appearance, which includes store exterior, interior, and general appearance. The fifth is personnel, which includes courtesy and product knowledge. All of these factors are rated on a Likert scale from zero to ten, meaning zero as poor and ten as excellent. Each store is rated in terms of these store factors. For example, a rating for appearance in terms of the store's interior would appear as a six on the zero to ten scale from poor interior to excellent interior. All of these factor ratings are added and a total is obtained. A total which falls in the 111–95 range is considered excellent. A total which falls in the 94–80 range is considered good, while a total which falls in the 79–65 range is considered average, and anything below 65 is considered poor. Comments concerning the individual store, such as how well established the store is, the area it draws from, and if it is computerized or not, are just a few that are included in the profile as well.

A study of consumer buying habits pertaining to healthcare products for the desired area is undertaken. Dollars spent on prescriptions in one year is examined for each competing drug store. Consumers are asked where they now buy their prescription drugs and percentages are listed for each competing drug store. Consumers are asked why they shop at the pharmacy where they shop currently, and are given choices of low prices, convenience, liking the service or people, or for other reasons. The results are listed for each individual drug store. Finally, consumers are asked if they would consider changing pharmacies if price is competitive and location convenient, and they are given the choices of yes, no, or not sure. Again, the results are listed for each competing drug store.

A competitive price survey is conducted of all the competing drug stores in the area. Medicap is included in the survey twice, meaning the price of a prescription drug at the regular Medicap price and the price at the new Medicap store are listed. Various prescription drugs from Naprosyn to Zantac are included in the price survey.

Investment Potential   The final part of the feasibility study includes various projected financial statements pertaining to the new store.

An estimated projection and forecast of three years' earnings is listed. Gross receipts, merchandise cost, expenses, and net profit are listed for three consecutive years. A projected cash flow statement for the first three years of operation is drawn up for the new store.

A pro forma balance sheet is drawn up for the proposed new store. Besides the usual components of the balance sheet, the assets, liabilities, and owner's equity, Medicap includes the base bank loan, and the interest rate, number of payments, monthly payment, and lender security.

Finally, a worksheet to determine capital requirements for the new store is drawn up. Five areas are considered: merchandise inventory, store fixtures/equipment and betterments, leasehold improvements, cash, and other capital needs. The end result of this worksheet is a total dollar amount needed for the new store.

A feasibility study was done for the first Medicap franchise ever sold and for every one since. The company feels that these studies play a major role in its success. CEO Johnson told of how in one case the pharmacist did not like the location proposed by the study. The pharmacist was allowed to locate where he thought best; however, the store soon proved to be unprofitable and eventually closed. Consequently, Medicap has learned not to compromise on the location recommended by the feasibility study.

Pharmacy Conversions

In addition to being a franchising corporation, Medicap will also aid an entrepreneur in changing his or her existing pharmacy over to a Medicap store. The company is so confident in its competitive strategy and in its ability to successfully accomplish the changeover that it guarantees improved profit performance in the first 12 months of the changeover or the individual entrepreneur is free to "walk away" from the deal without any further obligation.[21]

The Future

As Bill Kimball and the other company officers look to the future, many problems and questions enter their minds. Will their attention to planned, sustained growth be able to be balanced with their trademark of strong customer service and reasonable prices as time moves on? What will happen as expansion occurs outside the Midwest into other areas of the United States?

How will Medicap continue to compete in an industry which is dominated by large discount retail stores, while it remains a relatively small, differentiated firm? How will the entrance of the combination stores into the industry impact Medicap's position? How will these large competitors affect the future growth and profits of Medicap? Should future feasibility studies give more consideration to these large competitors? Kimball pondered these and other pertinent questions that will need to be dealt with as Medicap moves ahead into the 1990s.

A Note on the Chain Drug Store Industry[22]

Drug store retailing is attractive due to the makeup of the industry, but that industry makeup has drawn many competitors. Recently drug store chains have had to compete against independents as well as supermarkets, discount retail chains like Wal-Mart and K mart, deep discount drug store chains like Phar-Mor and Drug Emporium, mail order businesses, and health maintenance organizations (HMOs). A factor keeping retail pharmacy margins down is third-party prescription programs through unions, corporations, HMOs, and government medical plans.

A favorable trend in the drug store industry is the aging of the American populous. Americans aged 65 and over, as a group, are growing at more than twice the rate of the general population, and along with this increase will come an increased demand for pharmaceuticals. Another trend is the increasing number of working women who have a need for convenient shopping. The greater use of generic drugs provides retailers with higher margins than they would achieve with brand-name drugs. The trend toward preventive measures and self-medication has benefited drug stores. This new health awareness will boost demand, but will also allow pharmacists to regain that one-on-one personal service with those customers who seek advice about pharmaceutical products.

Chain drug retailers have tried to gain market share by emphasizing their image as healthcare specialists, and have assumed a more aggressive stance on pricing their products than they had previously. Increased investment in technology should result in cost savings which should help the industry succeed in the more challenging environment.

Competitive conditions will most likely toughen in the years ahead, but new entrants will be attracted by the stability and growth of the market. Discount store retailers and supermarket operators have found that adding pharmacies along with health and beauty aids provides extra revenues.

Mergers and Buyouts

In the 1980s one of the quickest ways to extend and strengthen a chain was through mergers, but in 1989 buyout activity in the industry slowed down.

In the 1980s drug store chains were withdrawing from unprofitable markets in order to increase their presence in more lucrative ones. The decline of independent drug stores, as well as the selling off of unprofitable stores, helped increase the pool of store locations. Market entry through the purchase of an existing store is much cheaper than the large investment necessary when entering a new market. Many large drug chains acquire stores and smaller regional chains to increase their market size.

Drug stores will continue to change hands in the 1990s. Since market share is an indicator of chain store strength, the major chains will undoubtedly be buying for it in the years ahead.

Market Share

Twenty-five years ago chain drug stores had less than 30 percent of industry volume, while today they have about 60 percent. The top five chains account for about 44 percent of total chain drug sales, while the top ten chains account for 63 percent.

Independent drug store operators will continue to lose market share to drug store chains. Large chains have the advantage of volume purchasing, large, centralized warehouses, and advanced information technology, all of which give the chains a distinct advantage over the independents.

The drug store chain merchandising strategy focuses on core departments in order to differentiate them from their rivals, supermarkets and mass merchandisers. Four of these departments or categories are prescription drugs, over-the-counter (OTC) drugs, cosmetics, and toiletries.

Prescription drug sales in chain drug stores marked a 19.3 percent increase in 1989 to $10.4 billion. Prescriptions accounted for 24.2 percent of the chain drug business in 1989, up from 22.5 percent in 1988. Part of the reason for the increase in this category is a higher "script" count, prescriptions written, which has increased because of the growing number of elderly Americans. Third-party payment plans, which now account for 40 percent of overall drug-pharmacy store sales, also boosted pharmacy revenues, along with new-product introductions.

Over-the-counter sales reached a high of $19.8 billion in 1989, which was 7.8 percent above that in 1988. Retail drug chains made 29 percent of these sales, which helped gain ground over the supermarket and food/drug combination stores whose share was 24 percent.

Beauty aids marked a 6.9 percent sales gain in 1989, which brought the total sales volume to $9.1 billion. In 1989 the chains recorded $2.8 billion in toiletries sales, which gave them 31 percent of all toiletries volume at retail. Chain drug sales of cosmetics and fragrances increased 7.3 percent in 1989 to a record $3.23 billion. Drug chains' market share was at 28.6 percent of this $11.3 billion market, while department stores had 37.5 percent share, discounters had 12.3 percent share, and food/drug combination stores had 9.0 percent share.

Combination The supermarket industry opted to offset declining margins on basic grocery items by housing nonfood and a variety of higher-margin specialty food departments. The addition of a pharmacy created the combination food/drug store which, according to Towne-Oller & Associates, number about 4,000 in the United States, and the trend is growing.

Supermarkets have a competitive advantage over drug chains in terms of their convenience and customer exposure. When a pharmacy is added, sales of health and beauty aids and over-the-counter drugs can increase anywhere from 20 percent to 40 percent. Customers are more willing to purchase pharmaceuticals, over-the-counter drugs, and health and beauty aids when a professional pharmacist is on hand.

In 1989 combination stores accounted for over 15 percent of overall prescription volume, and it is projected that percentage could increase to 20 percent by 1992. According to Towne-Oller & Associates, combination stores generate twice the health and beauty aids volume than that of normal discount stores or drug stores. Combination stores devote more space to health and beauty aids and pricing is highly competitive.

Drug stores, over the past decade, have seen an attrition of their share of the health and beauty aids and over-the-counter business, while supermarkets and mass merchandisers have gained share in these areas. The prescription area is not safe for drug stores anymore. The combination store has presented itself as a definite threat and a challenger in the competitive environment of the chain drug store.

Deep Discounters

Deep discount drug stores have added competitive pressure to the chain drug industry. In 1984 there were 225 units with an estimated market share of 3 percent to 4 percent, while in 1988 the number of units increased to 600 with over $3 billion in sales and market share of almost 8 percent. The top three deep discounters are Drug Emporium, Phar-More, and F & M Distributors, which account for more than half of that $3 billion in sales.

Deep discounters are experts at keeping costs down, and they operate on paper-thin margins. Deep discounters match prices only in the prescription area. Many deep discount drug outlets don't feature pharmacies because prescription drugs can be handled better by conventional drug chains. Conventional drug chains normally consider the pharmacy the backbone of their business, as in Walgreens which has pharmacies in 96 percent of its stores. Drug Emporium, on the other hand, has pharmacies in only 46 percent of its stores. A higher percentage of sales volume for deep discounters is derived from health and beauty aids rather than from pharmaceuticals.

Certain conventional chains have tried deep discounting to cut into the large sales volume that their discount chain competitors require for profitability. Others have tried deep discounting in order to gain competitive experience and new merchandising skills. Yet others operate deep discount stores as growth-oriented profit centers.

Mass Merchandisers

Mass merchandisers such as K mart, Wal-Mart, and Woolworth are increasing their commitment to health and beauty aids and pharmacies. Over half of Wal-Mart and K mart stores now have pharmacies, and Woolworth has eight deep discount pharmacies. The number of pharmacies, according to *Chain Drug Review,* at six leading discount chains which include K mart and Target, rose 47 percent to 870 stores in 1988. According to *Chain Drug Review,* health and beauty aids volume rose 20 percent to $1.82 billion, and over-the-counter drug volume rose 14 percent to $2.78 billion for all discount stores.

Adding to the competitive arena of drug stores are warehouse clubs, which are large, high-volume, low-price outlets located generally in markets with high population density. At the other end of the spectrum are convenience stores, which carry basic health and beauty aids at fairly high prices.

Mail

Mail-order pharmaceuticals are a growing threat to retail drug store chains. Prices are lower due to bulk discounts. Mail order benefits from the rising cost of prescriptions and from elderly Americans' medical needs. The majority of bulk-order prescriptions are for maintenance drugs which are meant to treat such diseases as diabetes, arthritis, and high blood pressure, and cost 25 percent less than they do in drug stores.

Approximately 3.6 million members of the American Association of Retired Persons (AARP) purchase 9 million prescriptions yearly from AARP's pharmacy. The AARP and the Veteran's Administration accounted for about one-fourth of the $1.9 billion mail-order drug market. Medco Containment Services is the largest publicly traded company in the mail-order business. Medco has nine mail-order pharmacies that fill 430,000 prescriptions a week, and has annual sales of $1.1 billion. A number of employee health benefit plans now offer mail-order services.

Third-Party Payments

A nationwide study by the Purdue University School of Pharmacy found that, on average, it costs $6.72 to dispense a third-party prescription, as opposed to $5.60 for a prescription that is paid with cash, leaving out the product cost. Also, stores had to wait approximately 42.8 days to receive reimbursement on the third-party plans which hurt their cash position. It was also found that labor costs increased because one in twelve claims required a resubmission.

It is expected, according to the study, that third-party prescriptions will increase to 60 percent to 75 percent of all prescriptions by 1995, from 39 percent in 1988. Insurance companies and large employers insist that they are entitled to lower prices since they are volume buyers. Operators of chain drug stores don't agree because third-party prescriptions hurt their margins, caused by additional labor, computer, and administrative costs.

Demographics

The greying of America is a boon for pharmacy operators. Older households spend more on healthcare than the national average. For people between the ages of 30 and 60, prescription use nearly doubles to 10.5 prescriptions a year, and for those more than 70 years of age, the number of prescriptions increases to 13 a year. In 1990, 12.7 percent of the U.S. population was at least 65 years of age, but by the year 2000 that percentage will increase to 13 percent, which is indicative of the continued growth of pharmaceutical sales. Industry studies have shown that older age groups tend to be cautious, avoid risk, and prefer shopping at traditional drug stores. This is another positive note for chain drug stores.

On the other end of the demographic profile is the large number of baby boomers now in the child-bearing age group. The sale of baby care products is expected to increase in the next few years, which is good for drug stores.

The trend toward self-medication and fitness programs has benefited drug chains. These trends are very apparent in the baby-boom generation. Almost three out of four baby boomers try to take care of medical problems themselves before visiting a doctor, according to *Drug Topics*. This has been reinforced by the availability of proprietary drugs, such as analgesics and cold remedies, which have been turned into over-the-counter status from prescription products. Increased consumer interest in self-medication will boost over-the-counter sales, and with this more brand-name manufacturers will seek over-the-counter status for prescription drugs.

The rising cost of hospital stays is forcing patients to opt for home healthcare. The home healthcare market is growing yearly which provides chain drug stores with yet another area of promising growth. Consumers like home diagnostic testing because of its convenience, confidentiality, and cost savings. Home diagnostic kits, such as pregnancy, ovulation, and glucose tests have created a new niche for drug stores.

Future Trends

Chain drug stores want the pharmacist to be seen as a solver of healthcare problems, rather than someone who merely fills prescriptions. The pharmacist can play an important role in providing valuable information pertaining to the disease process and self-monitoring. An attentive pharmacist can develop a number of strategies and materials to aid patients in complying with their prescriptions. At the time of dispensing, the pharmacist may study the patient's drug profile to spot possible interactions or overuse of medications. The pharmacist may even send out reminders that prescriptions are about to run out. An attentive pharmacist can do a lot to ensure compliance, patient loyalty, and refill revenues.

In the next few years a number of brand-name drugs will be coming off patent, and this will lead to expanded offerings of generic drugs. Industrywide profit margins on brand-name drugs are about 20 percent, while margins on generics can be as high as 80 percent. The bad news for drug retailers is that generic drugs are priced well below brand-name drugs. Due to high inflation rates for prescription drugs and increased cost-consciousness in the healthcare industry, the government and other third-party payers are attempting to cut costs through generic substitution. Programs that make it mandatory to substitute generic drugs for brand-name drugs should be a boon to drug chains.

Diversification is out, and back to basics is in. Some drug retailers have cultivated a more exclusive identity by sticking to the basics of healthcare products and services.

Drug retailers still cater to working women who opt for convenience, rather than price, when making shopping decisions. Many stores will carry a wide variety of household items, ranging from pet foods, dry groceries, and alcoholic beverages.

The nation's drug chains are seeing the need for computers in managing store operations. The rapid growth of third-party payments pushed the industry to implement the computer in the pharmacy. By keeping records in computer files, pharmacists can track payments and prices quickly and efficiently.

The next area targeted for computerization is point-of-sale scanning in the front of the store. Chains like Rite Aid and Walgreens are on their way toward this goal. Some benefits of point-of-sale scanning are firm control of prices at the register and better tracking of inventory and reorders.

Some retailers are moving into networking and data communications. More chain drug stores are beginning to see the need to move information electronically between stores, between stores and headquarters, between stores and chain warehouses, and between warehouses and product vendors.

Case Appendix

Breakdown of Chain Drug Sales—1989

Department	Percent of total sales
Prescription drugs	24.2
O-T-C drugs	17.2
Toiletries	12.1
Tobacco products	7.8
Cosmetics/fragrances	7.6
Groceries	5.0
Housewares	4.8
Sundries/seasonals/promotionals	4.4
Stationery/greeting cards	3.8
Photography	3.6
Candy	3.5
Electronics	3.1
Toys	2.9
Total	100.0

Source: Standard and Poor's Industry Surveys, April 19, 1990, R91.

Top 15 Chain Drug Stores, 1989

	Headquarters	Volume (mil.$)	Number of Stores
1. Walgreens	Deerfield, IL	5,560	1,525
2. Osco Drug	Chicago, IL	3,520	672
3. Eckerd	Clearwater, FL	3,230	1,632
4. Rite Aid	Shiremanstown, PA	3,140	2,352
5. Thrifty	Los Angeles, Ca	3,100	1,065
6. Revco D.S.	Twinsburg, OH	2,760	1,870
7. Shoppers Drug	Willowdale, Ontario	2,200	635
8. Longs Drug	Walnut Creek, CA	2,110	248
9. CVS	Woonsocket, RI	1,950	801
10. Pay Less NW	Wilsonville, OR	1,510	301
11. Hook-SupeRx	Cincinnati, OH	1,480	1,110
12. Phar-Mor	Youngstown, OH	1,300	170
13. Thrift Drug	Pittsburgh, PA	1,090	471
14. Drug Emporium	Worthington, OH	1,090	193
15. Peoples Drug	Alexandria, VA	1,000	499

Source: Standard and Poor's Industry Surveys, April 19, 1990, R92.

Sales Growth and Market Share Drug Chains and Independents

Year	Chain Sales (bil.$)	Independent Sales (bil.$)	Total Sales (bil.$)	Chain Drug Gain (percent)	Chain Drug Share of Market (percent)
1979	14.2	13.0	27.2	17.4	52.2
1980	16.4	13.9	30.3	15.5	54.1
1981	18.5	14.9	33.4	12.8	55.4
1982	20.5	15.7	36.2	10.8	56.6
1983	22.8	16.9	39.7	11.2	57.4
1984	25.5	17.7	43.2	11.8	59.0
1985	28.2	18.8	47.0	10.6	60.0
1986	30.2	20.0	50.2	7.1	60.2
1987	32.7	20.8	53.5	8.3	61.1
1988	36.0	21.9	57.9	10.1	62.2

Source: Standard and Poor's Industry Surveys, April 19, 1990, R94.

Endnotes

1. "Large Doses of Expansion Give Medicap Healthy Growth in Sales," *Des Moines Register,* February 22, 1988, 1B, 4B.

2. Ibid.

3. Medicap Pharmacies press release, March 14, 1991.

4. InfoTrac, General Business File, 1992.

5. Medicap Pharmacies, Inc., 1988.

6. Medicap Pharmacies, Inc., Long-Range Planning Report, September 14, 1988.

7. Authors' interview with Bill Kimball, 1989.

8. Ibid.

9. "Annual Blood Donor Drive to Be Held Today," *Des Moines Register,* July 12, 1989.

10. Medicap Pharmacies press release, March 14, 1991.

11. Ibid.

12. "Medicap Locates the Right Advertising Prescription," *Des Moines Register,* September 22, 1986, 5B.

13. Medicap Pharmacies press release, March 14, 1991.

14. Ibid.

15. Authors' interview with Bill Kimball, 1989.

16. "Large Doses of Expansion Give Medicap Healthy Growth in Sales," *Des Moines Register,* February 22, 1988, 1B, 4B.

17. Medicap Pharmacies press release, March 14, 1991.

18. Ibid.

19. Authors' interview with Bill Kimball, 1989.

20. Medicap Pharmacies press release, March 14, 1991.

21. The Conversion Factor, Medicap Pharmacy, April 1991.

22. Standard & Poor's Industry Surveys, April 19, 1990, 91–97.

CHAPTER 8

Entrepreneurship Career Strategy

Key Topics

- The Dynamic Entrepreneur
- Career Choices
- Self-Employment As a Career Option
- Advantages of Self-Employment
- Characteristics Associated with Entrepreneurship
- Entrepreneurial Intentions
- Entrepreneurship As a Second Career

Comprehensive Entrepreneurial Cases

- China Rose Gifts, Inc.
- A Licence to Print Money?

The Dynamic Entrepreneur

The image of robber baron villains of the nineteenth century has given way to an image of successful entrepreneurial heroes of the 1990s. The values and concerns of the **entrepreneurship professional** are based on the concepts of creativity, innovation, and opportunity development within a dynamic environment. Today it is widely accepted that entrepreneurial activity is the key to innovation, improved productivity, and more effective competition in the marketplace.

The modern entrepreneurial "hero" is expected to lead economic recovery and create the majority of new jobs in the coming decade. The spirit of opportunity abounds in the United States, as well as in the privatizing countries of Europe, the Far East, and Central and South America. Wiesen states, "This dynamism seems to be irrepressible. Today's generation believes that any kind of positive change is attainable."[1]

In the United States, the "hero" image of the successful entrepreneur was established by the popular media as early as the 1920s. Henry Ford embodied the entrepreneurial "Zeitgeist" that permeated the culture with his revolutionary concept of providing people with what they needed. A generation ago Apple Computer

---

[1]Jeremy Wiesen, "Dynamism: The Belief in Forward Movement," *Entrepreneurship Forum* (New York University: Center for Entrepreneurial Studies, Spring 1990), 2.

and Microsoft did not exist, and neither did the broad array of computer firms now challenging IBM's leadership. They all began as small, entrepreneurial companies and rode technology to the top. Entrepreneurs like Thomas Watson, William Hewlett and David Packard, Ray Kroc, Walt Disney, and Steve Jobs embodied a new set of values that included creating value where none existed before, legitimatizing the opportunity to acquire wealth, and being free to succeed or fail. Risk taking, leadership, achievement, and action in pursuit of opportunities were also recognized as important cultural components of entrepreneurship.

A measure of the maturation of a field is whether it leads to an occupational position and career. Although several efforts are currently being made to establish entrepreneurship awareness programs, that is, to communicate entrepreneurship as a career possibility, many individuals and students deciding on a career still seek a position that provides a "security blanket" for life. In the past secure job opportunities were sought in such "stable" industries as banking, automobile, insurance, steel, aviation, and the government. However, recent changes in government deficits, basic industries, mergers and acquisitions, and globalization have served to overturn many of the expectations of stability, continuity, and career programs. It appears that "womb-to-tomb" positions are vanishing faster than the myth on which they were based.

Career Choices

Facing uncertainty has become an underlying reality in all career choices. Therefore, a **career choice** approach should be one based on creativity, vision, innovation, and identification of new opportunities. Unfortunately, not all individuals perceive entrepreneurship that exploits these uncertainties to its advantage as a possible career alternative. Starting a new venture, however, is only one possibility among entrepreneurial career choices; several career options exist within entrepreneurship. One can seek employment in a newly established firm where the individual can experience and see the vision and zeal of the entrepreneur and where the structure and activities are evolving and fluid. The individual is able to design concepts, in concert with the vision, zeal, and personal expression of the entrepreneur, to help structure the uncertainty and ambiguity into something meaningful.

Another option exists within established firms where institutional slack, flexibility, and freedom to fail do not exist. Such a fossilized situation may need an infusion of entrepreneurial activity to mobilize forces for renewal and change. As a change agent in an executive role, the entrepreneurial individual may choose to assume a career risk when pursuing a new idea within an established setting (Intrapreneurship). He may share in the reward if the project he sponsors is successful, or he may lose his job and reputation if the project is unsuccessful.

A third option is to serve as an entrepreneurial executive in an established firm where there is enough freedom to create vision, a new product or service, and implement an idea fashioned in the entrepreneur's own style. Thus, this entrepreneurial executive must be in a position to work within existing structures, as well as form new frameworks to help implement the innovation (also intrapreneurship). Often board members and other stakeholders provide general approval and support while the entrepreneurial executive retains operational and financial responsibility. These options are only some of the career alternatives open to individuals.

Self-Employment As a Career Option

Individuals become self-employed in a variety of ways, some of which are listed below:

1. By providing goods or services as a lone operation, e.g., self-employed salesmen, physicians, attorneys
2. By creating a business as a start-up, perhaps hiring employees and serving as owner–manager
3. By purchasing an existing enterprise
4. By inheriting a family business
5. By purchasing a franchise

Do entrepreneurs exhibit different characteristics than do nonentrepreneurs? Is it possible to distinguish students with entrepreneurial intentions from others with traditional career paths in mind? What factors predict entrepreneurial intentions?

These questions are on the minds of many career counselors, university educators, researchers, and company recruiters, as well as students planning their careers, and they remain largely unanswered. One research study claimed that there is little or no research on the process of becoming an entrepreneur through self-employment. Furthermore, the current paucity of knowledge of self-employment implies that "researchers working in these areas often either neglect the phenomenon or rely on impressionistic evidence."[2]

Attempts to determine the characteristics of successful entrepreneurs have resulted in numerous studies over the past 25 years. Yet very little research has focused on entrepreneurship intentions prior to the actual start-up decision. In reviewing some studies, Sexton and Bowman reported the preexisting psychological factors play a significant role in the selection of an occupation and that it is possible to accurately predict an individual's career selection.[3]

If business ownership seems a less promising road to enormous riches than it did several years ago, many young adults are not complaining about it. In the recent past many young people had the romantic view that entrepreneurship was a way to obtain great wealth. Today, however, there is a growing trend among the younger generation to choose entrepreneurship as a way to maintain autonomy.

Surveys of students' intentions to choose self-employment as a career option generally include some element of independence. The nation's 48 million "baby busters," generally defined as those people 18 to 29 years old who grew up in the shadow of the 77 million baby boomers, also say that getting ahead means more than finding work in a shrinking job market or making a lot of money. They also

---

[2]G. R. Carroll and E. Mosakowski, "The Career Dynamics of Self-Employment," *Administrative Science Quarterly* 32 (1987): 570–589.

[3]Nancy B. Bowman and Donald L. Sexton, "The Effects of Preexisting Psychological Characteristics on New Venture Initiations." Presented at the Academy of Management Meeting, Boston, 1984.

are looking for greater job satisfaction and independence.[4] It is assumed that entrepreneurship intentions are related to behavior. This chapter will help provide a deeper understanding of the motivation to be self-employed and also offer career guidance for students and individuals considering becoming entrepreneurs. We will also discuss the image an entrepreneur projects. It may be possible that the image is negative and counselors may want to steer individuals away from self-employment career choices.

At the environmental level, there has been a strong impetus to create new business. It must be recognized that the **entrepreneurial spirit** "is now a significant force in the U.S. economy . . . there has been a gigantic boom in the economy, with 40 million new jobs created in smaller organizations since the late 1960s and more than 600,000 start-ups occurring each year."[5] "The industries of tomorrow will spring from the nearly 8 million small businesses in the fields of biotechnology, computer software, advanced materials, environmental testing and control, health care and a broad range of individual services."[6] In Figure 8.1. Selz reports that a large portion of America's youth still feels the pull of the entrepreneurial life. According to a long-running survey by the Higher Education Research Institute at the University of California at Los Angeles, 42 percent of college freshmen in 1991 said succeeding in their own business was essential or very important to them. This is less than the 49 percent to 52 percent reported in the mid-1980s, but about at the same level as in the 1970s.[7]

Although high levels of career interest in entrepreneurship are widely reported, there is little data to confirm this phenomenon. Innovation, productivity, and our future well-being hinge, in large part, on the best minds entering the relatively unfettered environment of new and growing ventures.

As researchers in entrepreneurship know, more studies concerning the **characteristics** of entrepreneurs have been done than on any other topic in this emerging discipline. Yet many studies produced conflicting results and there is a continued need for research. Although extensive literature is available today, only some of it is briefly highlighted here. The literature, although focusing on entrepreneurs, is also assumed to be of value in identifying variables worthy of study in the context of intentions to start a business. Numerous studies have focused on successful entrepreneurs with and without comparative groups of unsuccessful entrepreneurs or managers.

An earlier review of this literature was presented by Brockhaus.[8] Although acknowledging the absence of full scientific proof, he closes the review with a scenario that represents, in effect, a set of viable, partially supported hypotheses. He concludes that entrepreneurs are better educated than the general population (although a large majority do not have college degrees); the values held by entrepre-

---

[4]Michael Selz, "Young America Still Fosters Entrepreneurial Ambitions," *The Wall Street Journal*, April 6, 1992: B2.

[5]T. Jackson and A. Vitberg, "Career Development, Part I: Careers and Entrepreneurship," *Personnel* (February 1987): 12–17.

[6]W. Neikirk, "Entrepreneurial Energies Power Small Businesses," *Chicago Tribune*, February 24, 1993: 1, 1.

[7]Selz, "Young America Still Fosters Entrepreneurial Ambitions."

[8]Robert H. Brockhaus, Sr., "The Psychology of the Entrepreneur," in C. Kent, D. Sexton, and K. Vespers, eds., *Encyclopedia of Entrepreneurship* (Prentice-Hall, Inc., Englewood Cliffs, NJ, 1982): 39–56.

Figure 8.1   Tomorrow's Entrepreneur

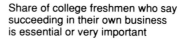

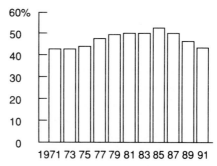

Share of college freshmen who say
succeeding in their own business
is essential or very important

Source: Michael Selz, "Young America Still Fosters Entrepreneurial Ambitions," *The Wall Street Journal,*
April 6, 1992.

neurs include the **need for achievement, independence,** and **effective leadership**; entrepreneurs' values and expectations tend to generate dissatisfaction with their jobs; and entrepreneurial acquaintances and family members serve as role models to help make a business start-up a plausible act. One of the most supported characteristics found in the reviewed literature, an **internal locus of control,** tends to counteract entrepreneurs' naiveté about the low probability of success and the consequences of failure. Several studies also found that entrepreneurs have a high need for autonomy and endurance, and a low need for support, conformity, and orderliness.

The growth of interest in entrepreneurship is evidenced by the recent continuous surge in the number of small business start-ups. U.S. new-business incorporations totaled nearly 647,675 in 1990, after a decade of yearly incorporation exceeding the 500,000 mark.[9] In an opening letter to Congress on the state of small business in 1988, former President Reagan stated: "A wider appreciation of the innovation, the competitive strength, and the quality of life that small firms bring to our economy is an important goal for all who are interested in the long-term economic health of our nation."[10]

Advantages of Self-Employment

The advantages and disadvantages of a self-employment career are described in glowing, positive accounts in the popular press and in reserved, cautious tones in more balanced publications.[11] Even though the actual rate of failure and termination

[9]Personal correspondence, Office of Advocacy.

[10]Joline Godfrey, *Our Wildest Dreams: Women Entrepreneurs Making Money, Having Fun, Doing Good* (New York: Harper-Collins, 1992): 39–47.

[11]D. P. Boyd and D. E. Gumpert, "The Loneliness of the Small-Business Owner," *Harvard Business Review* (November–December, 1984): 18–24.

of small businesses is quite high, the self-employed person is often glamorized as a winner, folk hero, role model, cultural icon, source of job creation, and economic developer. The role of the entrepreneur is no longer one of a "dull purveyor of car parts or groceries," and instead was transformed during the 1980s into the "courageous risk taker."[12] Galante reports that "popular culture has made heroes of entrepreneurs. They're the rock stars of the 80's."[13] Osborne stated "Today it is acceptable to join an unknown company, to take risks and perhaps fail; indeed it is acceptable to dare to be rich."[14]

It is now acceptable to be an entrepreneur. In fact, millions of men and women of all ages and ethnic backgrounds are starting their own businesses, buying failing businesses, reinvigorating family businesses, inventing and innovating. The label of "entrepreneur" used to connote someone undesirable, like a snake oil promoter, a con artist, or a manipulator. But today's entrepreneurs are not only socially accepted, they can be modern heroes.

In Duffy and Stevenson's survey of Harvard MBA graduates, a substantial portion of graduates did not conform to the image of "the prototypical administrator or 'big business' creature that the school has a reputation for producing."[15] In response to the question, "Do you consider yourself an entrepreneur?" the following percentages answered "yes":

Class	Percentage
1978	40.7
1973	47.5
1968	48.2
1963	55.7
1958	45.4
1953	56.4
1948	50.7
1943	50.0

Why is self-employment seen as an attractive career choice? At a personal level, self-employment is often viewed as the road to success, wealth, and self-fulfillment. It is the dream of many individuals to own a business. *Nation's Business* reports that when they were asked to identify their dream job, both men and women overwhelmingly put **business ownership** as their number one choice, ahead of even president of a large corporation.[16] This survey of 59,500 households is indicative of motivation and career choices of a large segment of the population. More and more Americans are realizing that only by controlling their own destiny and starting their own business can they achieve the quality of life they envision for themselves

---

[12]B. Wysocki, "Digging for Dollars," *The Wall Street Journal Reports*, February 24, 1989, R1–R2.

[13]S. P. Galante, "Hot Classes on Campus Teach Students How to Be Owners," *The Wall Street Journal*, October 12, 1987, 21.

[14]A. E. Osborne, Jr., "Understanding Entrepreneurship," *Business Forum* (Fall 1987): 12–13.

[15]P. B. Duffy and H. H. Stevenson, "Entrepreneurship and Self-Employment: Understanding the Distinctions," *Frontiers of Entrepreneurship Research* (1984): 461–477.

[16]*Nation's Business*, "How We Work, Jobs We Want—Top 7 Dream Jobs," November 1986, 11.

and their families. In other "dream" jobs selected by respondents, **independence** emerged as a common denominator and the passion to "do your own thing" was in full bloom.

Indeed, these realizations have been fueled by breaches of implied contracts of performance based on job security. Many employers rush to cut costs by large lay-offs with little or no finesse, "irresponsibly casting aside generations of employee commitment, loyalty and pride."[17] The resulting opportunism, desertion, sellouts, and selloffs are replacing traditional values of loyalty, security, ownership of results, and quality of work. The career development perspective of Bowen and Hisrich[18] and the displaced, uncomfortable entrepreneur amid difficult circumstances and/or life stages[19] suggest that self-employment is often the only advantageous choice.

What is the nature or form of the initial thought processes of potential entrepreneurs? At a childhood or adolescent stage young people are often influenced by role models and mentors who plant seeds in their impressionable minds as they move from desiring careers as firemen or astronauts to more realistic ones. Later, as self-employment possibilities are considered, the entrepreneur image becomes a dream that may be reinforced by scores of books, talk shows, seminars, lectures, courses at prestigious schools, and even corporate slogans espousing the **entrepreneurial approach.** This dream or vision has been identified in a recent work by Frank, et al., who found "strategic vision" to be an important component of entrepreneurs of recent start-up firms.[20] This vision has also been identified by Rockey in his study of more than 50 entrepreneurs who utilized **visualization** when starting a business. His interviews yielded insight into how visual imagery helps keep the challenge and excitement alive, clarify the business activity, develop the business plan, and project oneself into an aggressively growing business. He reported on one entrepreneur who pictured himself as the owner of a number of companies. "I envisioned my staff, various business opportunities and, of course, financial rewards." Another entrepreneur reported visualizing an event as a learning experience: "It's as if I've been there and I've got it in my head permanently. In fact, I can vividly recall visualizations I had years ago, including some I had as a teen-ager."[21]

Characteristics Associated with Entrepreneurship

Studies that surveyed journalistic articles and academic treatises attempt to dissect the entrepreneurial motivation and spirit. Some of the research concludes that entrepreneurs are aggressive, achievement oriented, have an internal locus of control (i.e., are not "victims" of the environment), are independent, and have tenacity,

---

[17]T. Jackson and A. Vitberg, "Career Development, Part I: Careers and Entrepreneurship."

[18]Donald D. Bowen and Robert D. Hisrich, "The Female Entrepreneur: A Career Development Perspective," *Academy of Management Review* 11 (1986): 393–407.

[19]Albert Shapero, "The Displaced, Uncomfortable Entrepreneur," *Psychology Today,* November 1975, 83–88.

[20]H. Frank, G. R. Plaschka, D. Roessl, and H. P. Welsch, "Planning Behavior in New Ventures: A Comparison between Chicago and Vienna Entrepreneurs." Paper presented at the Babson Entrepreneurship Research Conference, St. Louis, MO., April 18, 1989.

[21]E. H. Rockey, "Envisioning New Business: How Entrepreneurs Perceive the Benefits of Visualization," *Frontiers of Entrepreneurship Research* (1986): 344–360.

persistence, and perseverance. However, the great variety among types of entrepreneurs and the methods they have used to achieve their successes defy notions of any single psychological profile that can predict future success. Osborne believes that the modern entrepreneur cannot be characterized simply by a set of psychological traits or single-minded beliefs.[22] The following list identifies many elements that have been associated with entrepreneurship and entrepreneurial intentions according to various authors.

- **Hornaday and Aboud**[23]
  Achievement
  Self-Reliance
  Competitiveness
  Initiative
  Confidence
  Versatility
  Perseverance
  Resilience
  Innovation
  Good Physical Health
- **Considine, MacMillan, and Tsai**[24]
  Potential for Self-Development and Status
  Creating a Support System for Community and Building Status in Society
  Quality of Life—the Route to Increased Wealth and Increased Material Well-Being Is to Start a New Business
- **Sexton and Bowman**[25]
  High Need for Achievement, Autonomy, Endurance, and Independence
  Low Need for Support and Conformity
  Internal Locus of Control
  Tolerance of Ambiguity
  Poor Interpersonal Skills
  Need to Control and Direct Emotional Stability
  High Energy Level
  Creativity
  Self-Confidence and Self-Esteem
  Perseverance
  Risk-Taking Propensity
- **Shapero**[26]
  A Magic Number

---

[22]A. E. Osborne, "Understanding Entrepreneurs," *Business Forum* (Fall 1987): 12–13.

[23]J. Aboud and J. Hornaday, "Characteristics of Successful Entrepreneurs," *Personnel Psychology* 24 (1971): 141–153.

[24]M. Considine, I. C. MacMillan, and W. Tsai, "Geo-Ethnic Differences between Entrepreneurs' Motivations to Start a Firm." Paper presented at the Babson Entrepreneurship Research Conference, 1988.

[25]Nancy B. Bowman and Donald L. Sexton, "The Effects of Preexisting Psychological Characteristics on New Venture Initiations." Presented at the Academy of Management Meeting, Boston, 1984.

[26]Albert Shapero, "The Displaced, Uncomfortable Entrepreneur," *Psychology Today,* November 1975, 83–88.

       External Business Students
       Imaginable Acts
       Familiarity Breeds Confidence
       Ethnics
       Adventuresome Loan Officers

- **Schollhammer and Kuriloff**[27]
       Need for Achievement
       Independence and Mastery
       Supportive Family Climate
       Innovative Ability
       Tolerance for Ambiguity
       Realistic Planning Ability
       Goal-Oriented Leadership
       Objectivity
       Personal Responsibility
       Adaptability
       Ability As Organizer and Administrator

- **Welch and White**[28]
       Need to Control and Direct
       Drive and Energy
       Challenge Taker, Not Risk Taker
       Taking Initiative and Personal Responsibility
       Internal Locus of Control
       Long-Term Involvement
       Competing against Self-Improved Standards
       Superior Conceptual Ability
       Perspective of a Generalist
       Realistic
       Tolerance of Ambiguity
       Persistent Problem Solving
       Goal Setting—Use of Feedback
       Willingness to Seek Assistance
       Successfully Dealing with Failure
       Sufficient Emotional Stability
       Low Need for Status
       Objective Interpersonal Relationships
       Good Health

- **Chamard, Catano, and Howell**[29]
       (Based on McClelland, 1961)
       Presence of a Father

---

[27]A. Kuriloff and H. Schollhammer, "The Nature of Entrepreneurship" in *Entrepreneurship and Small Business Management* (New York: Wiley, 1979), 7–27.

[28]J. A. Welch and J. F. White, "Converging on Characteristics of Entrepreneurs," *Frontiers of Entrepreneurship Research* (Spring 1981): 504–515.

[29]V. M. Catano, J. Chamard and C. Howell, "Entrepreneurial Motivation: Some Evidence to Contradict McClelland," *Journal of Small Business* 1, No. 1 (Summer 1983): 18–23.

Low Authoritarian Behavior on His Part

High Standards of Excellence

Rewards for Achievement

- **Ronstadt**[30]

Greater Financial Rewards

Desire to Be Own Boss

Personal Challenge

Desire to Build Something of Your Own

Frustrated with Corporate Life

Bored with Job

Other

- **Ronstadt**[31]

Entrepreneur

"The Right Stuff"

Educational Incubation

Familial Incubation

Displacement

Situation

Venture Opportunity

Necessary Factors

Proper Sequencing

Size Factors

Environment

Macro Factors

Cultural Factors and Displacement

Industry Incubation

Entrepreneurial Environments

MacMillan, Siegel and Narasimha[32]

Capability of Sustained Intense Effort

Articulation in Discussing the Venture

Attention to Detail

Familiarity with Target Market

Ability to Evaluate and React to Risk Well

Track Record Relevant to the Venture

- **Drucker**[33]

Behavior Rather than Personality Trait

Enormously Risky

The Unexpected—the Unexpected Success, the Unexpected Failure, the Unexpected Outside Event

[30]Robert C. Ronstadt, "The Decision Not to Become an Entrepreneur," *Frontiers of Entrepreneurship Research* (1983): 192–211.

[31]Robert C. Ronstadt, "Entrepreneurial Careers and Research on Entrepreneurs," *Frontiers of Entrepreneurship Research* (1981): 591–600.

[32]I. MacMillan, P. Narasimha, and R. Siegel, "Criteria Used by Venture Capitalists to Evaluate New Venture Proposals," *Journal of Business Venturing* 1 (1985): 119–128.

[33]Peter F. Drucker, *Innovation and Entrepreneurship* (New York: Harper & Row, 1985).

The Incongruity—between Reality As It Actually Is and Reality As It Is
Assumed to Be or As It "Ought to Be"
Innovation Based on Process Need
Changes in Industry Structure or Market
Structure that Catches Everyone Unawares
Demographics
Changes in Perception, Mood, and Meaning
New Knowledge, Both Scientific and Nonscientific

- Herzberg[34]

Qualities Associated with Innovation Are:
Intelligence Focused on Clients and Products
Expertise Developed on the Job
Unconventionality
Effectiveness in Ambiguity
Feeling of Self
Separation of Motivation from Hygiene Values
Active Control of Anxiety
Control of Career
Intuition
Passionate Enjoyment of Life

- Timmons[35]

Motivation
   Drive and Energy
   Initiative
   Money As a Measure
   Moderate Risk Taking
   Seek and Use Feedback
   Self-Imposed Standards

Goals, Attitudes, and Values
   Ethics
   Professional and Economic Values
   Commitment
   Responsibility
   Goal Oriented
   Have Vision
   Tolerance of Uncertainty and Ambiguity

Expectations
   Internal Locus of Control
   Integrity
   Reliability
   Self-Confidence
   Belief in Self
   Self-Awareness

---

[34]Frederick Herzberg, "Innovation: Where Is the Relish," *Journal of Creative Behavior* 21, No. 3, 3rd Quarter (1987).

[35]Jeffry Timmons, *New Venture Creation,* 2d ed. (Homewood, IL: Irwin, 1985).

Sense of Humor
Decisiveness
Patience
Creativity and Innovation
Health and Emotional Stability
Ability to Cope with Stress
Skills and Competencies
Team Building
Capacity to Inspire
Learn from Mistakes
Problem Solving
Conceptual Ability
Business Acumen
Dealing with Failure

- **Cromie**[36]
Autonomy
Achievement
Job Dissatisfaction
Money
Career Dissatisfaction
Child Rearing
Outlet for Skills
Offer Employment
Market Opportunity
Job Insecurity
Entrepreneurship
Inheritance
Status
Others

- **Scott and Twomey**[37]
Role Models
Work Experience
Hobby
Perception of Self As Entrepreneur
Looking for Work
Career Advice Received
Prospect of Unemployment
Possession of Business Idea

- **Bird and Jelinek**[38]
Focusing Attention through Vision
Providing Meaning to Others through Communication

---

[36]S. Cromie, "Motivations of Aspiring Male and Female Entrepreneurs," *Journal of Occupational Behavior* 8 (1987): 251–261.

[37]M. G. Scott and D. F. Twomey, "The Long-Term Supply of Entrepreneurs: Students' Career Aspirations in Relation to Entrepreneurship," *Journal of Small Business Management* (October 1988).

[38]B. Bird and M. Jelinek, "The Operation of Entrepreneurial Intentions," *Entrepreneurship: Theory and Practice* (Winter 1988): 21–27.

Positioning through Communication
Maintaining Trust through Positioning
Positive Self-Regard
Structuring Resources
Flexible Focus on Business Issues
Temporal Agility
Behavioral Flexibility
Influencing Others to Commit Resources

- **Herron, Robinson, and McDougall**[39]
Ability to Learn (Intelligence)
Risk-Taking Propensity
Need for Achievement
Locus of Control
Stamina
Tolerance for Ambiguity
Experience
Eight Managerial Skills of Mintzberg (1983)
Functional and Technical Skills of Katz (1974)
Five Entrepreneurial Proclivities of Stevenson and Gumpert (1985)

- **Feeser and Dugan**[40]
Absence of Challenge
Felt Victimized
Advancement Restricted
Inadequate Reward for Superior Performance
General Feeling of Frustration
Belief that Employer Doing the Wrong Thing
Offended by Having to Justify Ideas
Rejection of New-Product/Market Ideas
Doing the Kind of Work You Want
Avoiding Working for Others
Making More Money Than You Would Otherwise

- **Hartman**[41]
Control Own Life
Be Own Boss
Large Company Frustration
Make Money

- **Carland, Hoy, Boulton, and Carland**[42]
Achievement

---

[39]L. Herron, R. B. Robinson, Jr., and P. McDougall, "Evaluating Potential Entrepreneurs: The Role of Entrepreneurial Characteristics and Their Effect on New Venture Performance." Paper submitted to the Entrepreneurship Division of the Academy of Management, 1988.

[40]K. W. Dugan and H. R. Feeser, "Entrepreneurial Motivation: A Comparison of High and Low Growth High Tech Founders." Paper presented at the Babson Entrepreneurship Research Conference, April 27–29, 1989.

[41]C. Hartman, "Main Street," *INC,* June 1986, 49–58.

[42]W. R. Bolton, J. A. Carland, J. W. Carland, and F. Hoy, "Differentiating Entrepreneurs from Small Business Owners: A Conceptualization," *Academy of Management Review* 9, No. 2 (1984): 354–359.

Independence
Responsibility
Power
- **Casale**[43]
Lack of Organizational Fit
Lack of Reward
Trouble Getting Ideas Advanced
Lack of Advancement
- **Smith and Miner**[44]
Self-Achievement
Avoiding Risk
Seeking Feedback
Personal Innovation
Positive Orientation to the Future
- **Frankel**[45]
Autonomy
Creativity
Adventure
- **Kahl**[46]
Primacy of Business—the Extent to which the Business Dominates One's Life
Independence—the Extent to which a Person Stands on His Own Feet
Planning—the Extent to which a Person Plans His Affairs Rather than Leaving
    Things to Chance
Trust—the Extent to which a Person Has Faith in His Fellow Man
- **Blais, Blatt, Kyle, and Szoni**[47]
Achieve a Personal Sense of Accomplishment
Be My Own Boss; Work for Myself
Have Considerable Freedom to Adapt My Own Approach to My Work
Be Challenged by the Problems and Opportunities of Starting and Growing
    a New Business
Have Opportunity to Lead, Rather than Be Led by Others
Make a Direct Contribution to the Success of a Company
Be Able to Develop an Idea for a Product or a Business
Keep Learning
It Was a Time in My Life When It Made Sense
Control My Own Life
Make Better Use of My Training or Skills

[43]A. M. Casale, *Tracking Tomorrow's Trend* (Kansas City: Andrews, McNeel & Parker, 1986).

[44]J. Miner and N. Smith, "Type of Entrepreneur, Type of Firm and Managerial Motivation: Implications for Organizational Life Cycle Theory," *Strategic Management Journal* (October–December 1984): 325–340.

[45]G. Frankel, "Nordic Female Entrepreneur," *Equal Opportunities International* 3 (1984): 24–29.

[46]J. A. Kahl, "Some Measures of Achievement Orientation," *American Journal of Sociology* 70 (1965): 669–681.

[47]R. A. Blais, R. Blatt, J. D. Kyle, and A. J. Szoni, "Motivations Underlying Canadian Entrepreneurship in a Cross-Cultural and Cross-Occupational Perspective," *Journal of Small Business and Entrepreneurship* 6, No. 3 (Spring 1989): 7–21.

Be Able to Work with People I Choose
Desire to Have High Earnings
Be Innovative and Be in the Forefront of Technological Development
To Have Fun
Have Greater Flexibility for My Personal and Family Life
Work with People I Like
Give Myself, My Husband/Wife, and Children Security
Achieve Something and Get Recognition for It
To Be Respected by Friends
Frustrated in Previous Job
Be Able to Work in the Location that Is Desirable for Me and My Family
Achieve Higher Position for Myself in Society
Contribute to the Welfare of My Relatives
Not to Work for an Unreasonable Boss
Have Access to Fringe Benefits
Need More Money to Survive
To Become Part of a Network of Entrepreneurs
Contribute to the Welfare of My Community
Increase the Status and Prestige of My Family
Have More Influence in My Community
Escape Unsafe Working Conditions
It Was the Only Thing I Could Do
Follow the Example of a Person I Admire
Continue Family Tradition
Contribute to the Welfare of My Ethnic Group

- **Welsch, Young, and Triana**[48]
  Financial Independence
  A Hobby that "Just Grew"
  To Supplement the Family Income
  To Resume My Business Career
  To Give Me Something Challenging to Do
  Family Encouragement
  Because I Saw My Friends Establishing Successful Businesses

Thus, it appears that a multidimensional set of predictors is required to explain the tendency toward entrepreneurship as a career choice. The preliminary model shown in Figure 8.2 identifies four categories of predictors—personality, demographic, educational, and situational—to help explain this phenomenon.

Entrepreneurial Intentions

Studies with specific relevance to students' behavioral intentions are few. In surveying 659 business students, Hills and Barnaby found that 59 percent were "very likely" or "somewhat likely" to someday own and/or operate a business of their

---

[48]A. R. Triana, H. P. Welsch, and E. C. Young, "Differences between U.S. Hispanic and Non-Hispanic Entrepreneurs," *International Small Business Journal* 5, No. 2 (Winter 1986/1987): 8–16.

Figure 8.2   **Four Factors Showing Tendency Toward Entrepreneurship**

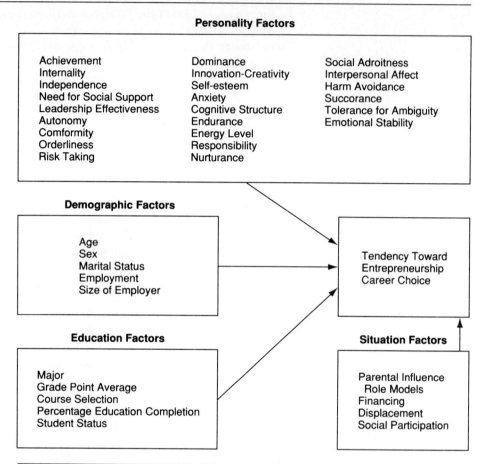

Personality Factors

Achievement	Dominance	Social Adroitness
Internality	Innovation-Creativity	Interpersonal Affect
Independence	Self-esteem	Harm Avoidance
Need for Social Support	Anxiety	Succorance
Leadership Effectiveness	Cognitive Structure	Tolerance for Ambiguity
Autonomy	Endurance	Emotional Stability
Comformity	Energy Level	
Orderliness	Responsibility	
Risk Taking	Nurturance	

Demographic Factors

Age
Sex
Marital Status
Employment
Size of Employer

Tendency Toward Entrepreneurship Career Choice

Education Factors

Major
Grade Point Average
Course Selection
Percentage Education Completion
Student Status

Situation Factors

Parental Influence
Role Models
Financing
Displacement
Social Participation

own.[49] Eighty-seven percent of the students indicated they would be "interested" in taking an entrepreneurship course. The following characteristics (predictors) were statistically related to high entrepreneurial intentions: undergraduates (higher than graduate students); juniors (versus seniors); under a 3.0 GPA (versus over); and single (versus married). No statistical differences were found regarding age, parents' occupation, or family size.

In a survey of 1,133 undergraduate women students, Brannen found that 29 percent "planned a career in small-business management."[50] Thus, women were

[49]D. J. Barnaby and G. E. Hills, "Future Entrepreneurs from the Business Schools: Innovation Is Not Dead." *Proceedings, International Council for Small Business* (1977).

[50]W. H. Brannen, "College Women As Future Small Business Managers: What Do They Think about Small Business and Marketing." Proceedings, 24th Annual Conference, International Council for Small Business, 1979.

found to be less likely than men to consider managing a small business in their career plan.

Sexton and Bowman conducted the most extensive analysis of student intentions and psychological characteristics to determine **entrepreneurial potential**. In comparing entrepreneurship majors with other students (n = 401), they found entrepreneurial-minded students to score higher in areas of autonomy, dominance, endurance, energy level, innovation, and self-esteem; and lower in areas of anxiety, cognitive structure, and conformity. In a later study (n = 218), they reported no significant differences in psychological characteristics across business majors (excluding entrepreneurship). Potential entrepreneurs (entrepreneurship majors) scored higher than nonbusiness majors in self-esteem, dominance, endurance, innovation, and breadth of interests. They scored lower in anxiety, responsibility, social participation, nurturance, affiliation, and tolerance of ambiguity. Entrepreneurship majors scored higher than both business and nonbusiness majors in areas of energy level, risk taking, social adroitness, change, and autonomy; and scored lower in areas of conformity, interpersonal affect, harm avoidance, and succorance. Entrepreneurship majors had much in common with successful entrepreneurs, including a high need for autonomy and endurance, a low need for support and conformity, an internal locus of control, high tolerance for ambiguity, poor interpersonal skills, a need to control and direct, emotional stability, creativity, self-confidence, self-esteem, perseverance, and risk-taking propensity.[51]

Small-Firm Employment Opportunity

Both small and large companies can offer exciting, yet different, **career opportunities**. The individual who is stimulated and challenged in a small company is likely to be motivated by different factors than a person working in a large corporation. The entrepreneurship environment demands flexibility and the ability to deal with ambiguity, while large corporations challenge the employee's ability to implement programs in a structured and potentially bureaucratic environment.[52]

In comparing careers in large and small companies, career satisfaction depends on whether one has a generalist's or a specialist's orientation toward business. Although large corporations need to develop general managers to guide their businesses in the future, many business and career consultants believe smaller companies offer a broader exposure to various business activities at low levels in the organization.

Large companies tend to create specialists, while small organizations demand that their employees wear a variety of hats. Because jobs in small organizations are less defined, employees may work in areas that they did not originally anticipate. This tends to appeal to workers with broad business interests who can adapt to the flexible nature of small companies. Conversely, workers with specialized interests

---

[51]Nancy B. Bowman and Donald L. Sexton, "Determining Entrepreneurial Potential of Students: Comparative Psychological Characteristics Analysis." Presented at the Academy of Management Meeting, Dallas, 1983.

[52]Mark Satterfield, "Company's Size Can Be a Factor," *Atlanta Constitution*, October 21, 1990, 17.

may find requests to work in areas outside of their expertise to be a source of frustration.

Small companies may be directed by charismatic leaders or industry experts. While in large organizations these industry leaders may be viewed only from afar, small companies offer individuals greater opportunity to interact with these leaders on a day-to-day basis.

Management training programs are often offered by large companies. This training establishes a baseline of management competency. If one believes the premise that management skills can be taught, then large companies, with their well-established training programs, have a considerable advantage.

While limited financial resources of small companies may indicate a potential lack of security, recent restructurings and layoffs in Fortune 500 firms and in virtually all sectors of business indicate that job security is an antiquated concept. Although small businesses may not have extensive financial resources, this ensures that only the projects that are directed to building the business will be implemented. Small-company employees are less likely to work on assignments that do not directly impact the bottom line. Thus, the value of one's day-to-day activities may be more visible in small, rather than large, companies.

Entrepreneurship As a Second Career

Some people have realized that their current job has no future and that they are frustrated or mistreated. Shapero reported as early as 1975 on comments he heard over and over again: "I was fired"; "I was going to be transferred to Hoboken by my company and I just didn't want to go"; "I worked for the company for ten years, day and night, and then they brought in their idiot son as my boss"; "My boss sold the company."[53]

Brenner and Singer reported earlier that a person who chose to switch careers in mid-stream was an outlaw or an oddity.[54] But times are changing as large corporations downsize, merge, and squeeze employees out. Today an increasing number of successful individuals are leaving their careers and entering entirely different types of work such as opening their own businesses. Studies show that between one-third and 35 percent of executives are likely to make extreme career changes. Nearly one-third of the entire U.S. work force has changed occupations during a five-year period. The trend continues.

This notion of changing careers may be related to the "total life" concept, which suggests that once people have achieved initial career success, they experience a change in the extrinsic and intrinsic job rewards that they value. This reevaluation leads to the decision to **change careers.** Several reasons are reported for changing careers, as listed in the table below: to obtain more meaningful work; to accomplish more; to take risks; and to create harmony between work and personal values. Only a small majority change jobs for a higher salary or for greater job security.

---

[53]A. Shapero, "The Displaced, Uncomfortable Entrepreneur," *Psychology Today,* November 1975, 83–88.

[54]O. Brenner and M. Singer, "Career Repotters," *Personnel* (November 1988): 54–60.

Reasons for Making a Career Change

Reason	Percentage of Repotters
More meaningful work	74
Better fit between values and work	71
Changed values	64
Chance for greater achievement	42
More leisure time	31
Less stress on job	22
More variety	16
Health	16
Less travel	15
Freedom to pursue hobby	11
Boredom	8
Different geographic location	5
More money	4
Escape from company politics	3

As the trend "love what you do" continues, a growing body of evidence indicates that successful managers are becoming increasingly dissatisfied with their chosen careers as they approach middle age. More and more frequently disenchantment with their current vocations is causing both successful and unsuccessful managers to seek fulfillment through new careers that are totally unrelated to their former professions. Individuals' value systems can change radically so they seek careers that fit with their new values. Merging vocation with avocation is often the alternative of choice.

Work Values of Repotters versus Stayers

More Important to Repotters
Leisure time
Working independently
Risk taking

More Important to Stayers
Many fringe benefits
Job security
High income
Advancement opportunity

A survey of nearly 2,000 students at two urban universities currently in progress provides a rich database for studying entrepreneurship behavioral intentions, attitudes, and preferences.[55] A very high intentions level of 52 percent is found among the students overall. Eighty percent indicate an interest in entrepreneurship courses and 67 percent indicate they may declare their major in this field.

---

[55]H. Welsch and G. Hills, "Entrepreneurial Behavior Intentions," in progress.

Analysis reveals a statistically significant relationship between high levels of preferences/intentions and student characteristics such as being full-time, day students, being male, working for a small (or large) employer, and being a lower class rank (e.g., sophomore). Also, having entrepreneurs in the family or personal experience with owning/operating one's own business contributed to higher entrepreneurial intentions. Entrepreneurship intentions are also positively related to a composite measure of independence and interest in entrepreneurship course work, as well as perceptions of entrepreneurs. Not significantly related are degree versus nondegree status, employed versus not employed, grade point average, and business major.[56]

Conclusion

Small is beautiful, small is in, and small is necessary as large industries downsize and become less profitable and nimble in the new economy. These corporations are decentralizing, and putting many talented and "hungry" people into opportunities to create their own businesses. Even the government recognizes that entrepreneurs are creating most of the new jobs and that they can be the spark that ignites new economic growth. Many believe a **new age** of the **entrepreneur** is dawning.

---

[56]Ibid.

C A S E • *China Rose Gifts, Inc. (A)**

Julie Schmidt, Babson College
John W. Newman, Babson College

Cynthia Wong sat staring out the window of the jet. Deep in thought, she didn't notice the ocean far below. As she traveled back to the U.S. after a hurried visit home, Cynthia wrestled with a desire she had to start her own business.

"China Rose Gifts," Cynthia muttered. She loved the way that sounded.

For years, Cynthia had dreamed of opening a small shop to sell gifts and other novelties native to her home in China. For years, she had pondered the idea, churning it over and over in her mind, constantly changing and adding detail to it until she was convinced it had merit.

Now, only weeks after her graduation from an American business school, Cynthia was forced to make a decision: should she open an Oriental Gift Shop as she had always dreamed or should she accept an attractive job offer she had received from a prestigious investment firm?

"The time has come to decide," she thought. The investment firm had been unusually patient in allowing Cynthia several weeks to make up her mind. She had promised them an answer by the end of the upcoming week.

"This is it," Cynthia thought, "it's now or never. The investment firm is a wonderful opportunity but I'm afraid I'll get trapped in the job. Importing into my own shop might be difficult at first," Cynthia continued, "but I'm certain it can work."

Still, there was a nagging doubt in Cynthia's mind. The consequences of a wrong decision seemed so harsh at this point in her life. Was she about to make the right decision?

Background

Cynthia Wong was born in Beijing, China, the eldest of four children. Her family belonged to a privileged class. Both of her parents worked at a manufacturing company her father owned. While their lives weren't material by U.S. standards, their family was quite comfortable and never lacked the necessities of life.

Cynthia's early years had been uneventful. A quiet child, she was nonetheless popular with her playmates and frequently organized field trips with her closest friends.

As she grew up, Cynthia was exposed to two different worlds, In school, she studied Chinese history and was fascinated by the traditions of her ancestors. She felt a responsibility to her heritage: a strong desire to dedicate her life to the culture

---

*This case was written by Research Assistant, Julie Schmidt, under the supervision of Assistant Professor John W. Newman, Babson College, Family Business Institute.

she so loved and respected. At home, most of the family's energies were devoted to her father's factory, a small company which made lacquer vases and other gift pieces.

The passion with which her father devoted himself to his work made a powerful impression on Cynthia. Through her father, she came to appreciate business and the way in which a fulfilling career could enhance the quality of one's life.

Cynthia studied hard at school and was a very good student. Her teachers were impressed by her devotion to her work and her unshakable sense of discipline. By the time she graduated from secondary school, her determination had paid off: Cynthia won several awards and a state scholarship to continue her studies abroad if she chose.

Cynthia was excited about the prospect of going to school overseas but was nervous about how her family would react. At first, her family expressed disappointment that she would consider leaving home, but eventually her parents were supportive. They wanted what was best for their daughter and knew that Cynthia was mature enough to make her own decisions. They had confidence that, someday or other, their daughter would return to them, stronger for the experience.

Cynthia applied to many schools in Europe and the United States. Her strong academic record and thoughtful application essays helped her get accepted to most of the schools to which she'd applied. After a great deal of deliberation and consultation with her family, Cynthia decided to continue her studies in the United States, at business school in Seattle, Washington. Before she knew it, Cynthia was on a plane to America and was starting her first semester classes.

The adjustment to a foreign country was difficult. Cynthia had studied English in China and considered herself to be bilingual. But, as she soon discovered, the work vocabulary of college students was not part of what she had learned at home.

Of more concern to her than her language problem, however, was the extreme difference between the two cultures. Cynthia was surprised by how important money and prestige seemed in this new country and by how relatively less important personal values and ethics seemed to be. She had numerous debates on these subjects with her classmates but never felt that they understood her views. Cynthia simply accepted these differences and adapted well to them. Her language problems, too, diminished over time.

International Trade

During the summer between Cynthia's sophomore and junior years, she had an idea. While at home for the summer, Cynthia spoke with her father about the possibility of exporting some of her father's products overseas. Cynthia proposed a test: she would bring some unique vases back to school with her the next semester and try to sell them to other students. If the test was successful on a small scale, they could consider exporting the products in larger quantities. To Cynthia's delight, her father agreed to the idea.

When she returned to school, Cynthia set out to sell the vases she had brought back with her. She showed them to her schoolmates and even to some of her professors and charged $24 for each vase. Her original supply of 25 vases sold out within three days.

Encouraged by this response, Cynthia called her father and asked him to send more vases. Much to her surprise, he refused, stating that she was in the U.S. to go to school, not to be a merchant. When she was all done with her studies, he would discuss the idea further. Cynthia was disappointed by his decision but sensed that he was right.

Graduation Nears

Cynthia's junior and senior years passed quickly. As at home, she applied herself to her studies and did very well in school, becoming a favorite of many of her professors. As her senior year progressed, she thought more and more of her plans after graduation. By this time, she had grown fond of Seattle and was beginning to think about settling there after school if she could get a work visa.

Meanwhile, another idea was evolving in her mind. She was growing increasingly excited about the possibility of opening a shop to sell Oriental gifts which she would import from China. She had been convinced by her vase experience that Oriental gifts would be very popular in the Seattle area. So, she decided not to participate in the job search process with her fellow students and would, instead, discuss her ideas with her family when she went home after graduation.

Opportunity Abounds

About a month before graduation, one of Cynthia's professors approached her with the name of a large, prominent investment firm which was looking for creative, young, business students. The company was eager to hire students for a new management training program but would only consider students who were referred by faculty members known to the firm. The professor suggested to Cynthia that she would be highly appropriate for the position and encouraged her to contact the company. Cynthia thanked the professor for thinking about her and for his support.

The professor's remarks created a dilemma for Cynthia. Although she had previously decided not to interview for jobs, she felt that there was no harm in exploring the opportunity further. Cynthia sent a letter to the company. About ten days later, she received a call from Lisa Turin, an officer of the firm. They arranged a meeting at the company's headquarters.

Several days later, Cynthia was sitting in Lisa Turin's office. The two women hit it off immediately and spoke nonstop for two-and-a-half hours. Originally, Cynthia was sure that she would not be interested in a job with the company, but there was something about Lisa's enthusiasm that was contagious.

Lisa spoke in detail about the company, its history, her relationship with the firm, and finally about the new management training program that was being instituted for college students. Cynthia would assist one of the account managers but not in a clerical function. She would have her own secretary and would train as she worked with the manager. The job would require a lot of traveling, mostly by car, around the state. For the first year, she would receive quarterly reviews to make sure that everyone's expectations were realized. After that, there would be substantial opportunity for advancement based upon performance.

"Cynthia, your professor speaks very highly of you," Lisa finished. "After meeting you, I'm sure that you'd fit in right away. I'd like you to say you'll join us. What do you say?"

Cynthia was stunned. She had researched the company briefly and knew that the company had an outstanding reputation in the financial community. Her research had shown a lower-than-average turnover rate at the firm. In all, the company would be an excellent one for which to work.

Cynthia paused, not knowing quite how to respond. She explained to Lisa that, while she greatly appreciated Lisa's interest, she had been considering another opportunity for some time. She asked Lisa if she could have some time to make up her mind. Lisa agreed.

As a parting gesture, Lisa reached for her briefcase and took from it a single sheet of paper and handed it to Cynthia. On company letterhead, it was a detailed job description.

"Maybe this will help you over the next few weeks," Lisa added.

As she got up to go, Cynthia graciously thanked Lisa for her offer and her patience.

Going Home

After graduation, Cynthia flew home to Beijing. During the first few days of her visit, Cynthia did nothing but spend time with her family. Her father hosted a big celebration in her honor.

After several days of relaxation and revelry, Cynthia decided to discuss her dilemma with her father. Her father tried to be supportive and listened intently. He felt that the investment firm opportunity sounded very attractive but had a hard time understanding why Cynthia would want to stay in the United States in the first place. Despite his good intentions, Cynthia found his support not to be particularly helpful.

Cynthia decided that it would be a good idea to research the types of gift items available and the vendors of those products while she was in China. Cynthia began her research by walking through several of the gift shops in the city. As she went on her rounds, she made a list of all the items she liked and wrote down the name of the manufacturer. She also made a brief description of each item and noted the price. By the end of the day, Cynthia's list was almost four pages long. By noting in the margins which items on the list belonged to which gift shops, Cynthia began to see similarities in the stock of the shops. Certain manufacturers' names kept showing up over and over again. In this way, she compiled a list of what she believed were the major suppliers.

Next, Cynthia contacted the major suppliers and requested catalogs and dealer price lists. In a few instances, she managed to speak with the company's representatives and got a lot of information about credit terms, export requirements, and minimum order sizes.

About a week later, it was time for Cynthia to bid farewell to her family and return to the U.S. She went out of her way to express to her parents that she would return to visit them soon and often. Nevertheless, it was a tearful goodbye.

The Day of Reckoning

Cynthia's daydream was interrupted by the gentle prodding of a cabin steward.

"Miss, I'm sorry to disturb you but the captain has turned on the seat belt sign. We'll be landing in just a few moments."

Cynthia gathered her belongings together. Several minutes later, the jet landed smoothly and taxied into the hangar. After picking up her luggage, Cynthia walked outside to hail a cab. Once in the cab, Cynthia's mood turned very somber.

The cab pulled up in front of Cynthia's apartment, she paid the driver, and he helped her take her bags from the trunk. Once inside her apartment, she set her bags down and walked to the window to let a little fresh air in. It was Sunday night, and before the end of the week she would have to decide on her new job. She still didn't know which path to follow.

Cynthia wondered if there was anything she could do in the few days remaining that would help her make up her mind.

CASE • *China Rose Gifts, Inc. (B)**

Julie Schmidt, Babson College
John W. Newman, Babson College

Cynthia had one week to decide whether to open China Rose Gifts or accept the position offered by Lisa Turin. She knew that the position in the investment firm was an outstanding opportunity, but the gift shop was an idea Cynthia was reluctant to discard; it was something she had always wanted to do.

She decided to spend her one week grace period doing more research on China Rose Gifts. Maybe, she thought, additional information could provide a better picture on whether or not China Rose Gifts was a feasible idea.

Her visit to the Orient had proven very productive. Cynthia returned with an excellent idea of the products she would carry and of the importing costs involved in getting those items into the United States. She had collected wholesale price sheets from several leading Chinese gift suppliers and had researched approximate shipping, insurance, and duty costs. She also understood the credit terms and financing vehicles (primarily letters of credit) that would be involved.

In order to make the best decisions possible regarding China Rose Gifts, Cynthia began researching those areas that were the cloudiest in her mind. Studying the market and determining demand were her first priorities. Then, she would research and estimate the cost of renting space.

The week went by very quickly. Using reference materials in the City Hall, Cynthia found that the 1980 U.S. Census listed Seattle's population at 493,000,

---

*This case was written by Research Assistant, Julie Schmidt, under the supervision of Assistant Professor John W. Newman, Babson College, Family Business Institute.

Exhibit 1   Seattle Gift Shops

	Anne's Hallmark	Clever Hand	Peacock Shop	Christmas Shop
Sales	$174,600	$198,600	$125,700	$166,650
Square feet	2,200	2,700	1,900	2,050
Dollars/square feet	79	74	66	81

up 11 percent from the 1970 survey. The local economy, it appeared, was recovering nicely from the massive round of layoffs by the Boeing Corp., one of Seattle's largest employers. Disposable income per capita for the state ranked high in the nation.

Cynthia also spent some time visiting the existing gift shops in the area. She identified four and, through conversations with the managers and a little outside research, she estimated the sales for each store (Exhibit 1). Some of the drug stores and most of the hotels in the area carried a small selection of gift items (usually 15 pieces or less), but she didn't see them as her competition. Cynthia estimated that combined these secondary channels probably accounted for $100–200,000 in annual gift and souvenir sales. In general, the gift industry worked on 50 percent margins—or what was called a keystone markup in the business. Whatever the cost was of a product, the retail would simply be double.

After long hours in the library, Cynthia assembled information on the demand for her product category. The National Association of Gift and Novelty Item Retailers (NAGNIR) had surveyed thousands of gift shops throughout the country. Excerpts from the 1987 NAGNIR report are provided in Exhibit 2. Cynthia recognized that this information was an annual average and would vary depending on the season.

About midweek, Cynthia contacted several real estate brokers in Seattle to check on retail space. Two locations were immediately available. The first was a street-level shell in downtown Seattle. It was within a two-block area comprised mostly of retail shops with a few professional offices intermingled. There were no other gift shops in the area. The 1,600-square-foot space was being offered for $19 per square foot. Since the space was unimproved, Cynthia would be responsible for the interior work necessary to obtain an occupancy permit. The broker estimated that this work would probably cost $20,000 to $30,000.

The other location was in a strip mall several miles outside the city. The property consisted of a 1,500-square-foot storefront with an additional 500 square feet of basement storage. The landlord was asking $14 per square foot plus a 3 percent override on gross sales over $600,000 annually. The road on which the mall was located drew a great deal of weekend shoppers. Two of Cynthia's prospective competitors, Anne's Hallmark and The Peacock Shop, were located within one-half mile of the empty store. This store already had a glass front—perfect for gift merchandising—and a small stockroom already partitioned in the back.

Armed with this information, Cynthia sat down to reconsider her options.

"The investment firm is a wonderful opportunity," Cynthia mused, "but I'm afraid I'll get bored."

Like it or not, the time to decide was almost at hand.

Exhibit 2
Excerpts from the National Association of Gift and Novelty Item Retailers Study
(as of 1987)

City	Population	Sales/100 People
Anchorage	173,017	90–110
Atlanta	425,022	130–145
Boston	562,994	160–185
Chicago	3,005,072	180–210
Dallas	904,078	132–150
Denver	491,396	155–175
Detroit	1,203,339	177–195
Houston	1,594,086	180–200
Jacksonville	540,898	140–165
Los Angeles	2,966,763	250–275
New York	7,071,030	325–350
Philadelphia	1,688,210	150–180
Portland	366,383	115–130
San Diego	875,504	140–160
San Francisco	678,974	140–165
Seattle	493,864	135–165
Spokane	171,300	100–120
Washington, D.C.	637,651	165–180

C A S E • *China Rose Gifts, Inc. (C)**

Julie Schmidt, Babson College
John W. Newman, Babson College

Cynthia became increasingly convinced that Seattle could support a gift shop which specialized in Oriental items. As her enthusiasm grew, she decided that her next task would be to determine her monthly operating expenses and how much she'd need to open the store.

First, Cynthia considered the store's staffing requirements. She figured that she would have to hire someone to help run the store. Cynthia estimated that a competent assistant manager could be hired full time for about $18,000 annually. Cynthia decided to defer her own salary for at least six months until the store was profitable.

Based on information real estate brokers had given her, Cynthia knew that her rent would be about $2,400 per month. A security deposit of $5,000 would be required along with prepayment of the first three months' rent. Rent would be the company's largest monthly expense.

*This case was written by Research Assistant, Julie Schmidt, under the direction of Assistant Professor John W. Newman, Babson College, Family Business Institute.

Before she could begin to move inventory into the shop, there were some improvements that would be necessary to display the merchandise and to create the proper Oriental environment. Wiring was already in place but additional track lighting would have to be added to highlight the store displays. New carpeting was needed as the previous tenant ripped the carpet out when they left. Including the interior and the storefront, Cynthia estimated that the shop would need about $35,000 in capital improvements.

While the store renovations were being completed, Cynthia would have to begin ordering stock. Cynthia figured that she would need about $30,000 in inventory (at retail prices) to open her store. Her foreign suppliers had insisted that she pay for all goods COD. After she developed an operating history, Cynthia felt confident that her suppliers would offer her more liberal credit terms.

Equipment for the store included a cash register, a small safe, metal shelving units for the stockroom, and display fixtures for the selling floor. Cynthia estimated that these items would cost approximately $5,000. Costs amounting to about $1,000 for letterhead, purchase orders, and office supplies also had to be considered. Eventually, Cynthia wanted to invest in a personal computer for the business, but she did not think it would fit in the "budget" right now.

The cost of the utilities for the space would not be substantial. There was a deposit of $500 that would have to be paid three weeks before the power would be turned on. From then on, utilities of about $150 per month could be expected. Virtually all of her suppliers were in the Far East and phone expenses might be quite high. She estimated that her monthly phone bill would be about $350. The phone company also required $115 to install the phone and a $250 deposit.

Cynthia discussed her idea with a local attorney who suggested that she incorporate China Rose Gifts for protection. In addition to the incorporation papers, the attorney would also prepare the necessary documents to allow Cynthia to import goods wholesale. Initial legal fees would be approximately $1,600.

Insurance was also a must. Cynthia could not operate her business without proper coverage. She would need a standard retailing policy which would include fire, theft, and vandalism. The estimated annual cost would be $3,600. Premiums would be due at the beginning of each quarter with a requirement that the first installment be prepaid.

Cynthia now had the difficult task of projecting her annual sales. She based her sales estimates on the market research she had done which indicated that no other gift shop in the area imported or carried Oriental wares. She decided to follow the standard industry practice of pricing her goods based on a 100 percent markup (i.e., doubling her cost of goods).

Monthly Sales Estimates
(Year One)

January	2,500	May	12,500	September	10,000
February	5,000	June	15,000	October	10,000
March	7,500	July	12,500	November	12,500
April	10,000	August	12,000	December	20,000

Cynthia wasn't quite sure what to do with the figures she'd collected. How could this financial information help with her career decision?

C A S E • *A License to Print Money? (Part A)**

David Molian, INSEAD
Michael Ullman, INSEAD

> *Chance favours the prepared mind.*
> Louis Pasteur

A Change of Plan

"I'm sorry, sir, but you've missed the flight."

John Pryke set down his suitcase, and gave himself a few seconds to catch his breath. He'd been tearing through the terminal building ever since he got off the underground, hoping for once that the plane had been delayed. Having managed to get a stand-by ticket at short notice, he felt particularly galled that a delay on the train system should prevent him from getting away.

"When's the next flight to Barbados?" he asked in a resigned tone. It was the week before Easter and the airlines were heavily booked, but finally he succeeded in getting himself on a flight in three days' time, on Good Friday. In the meantime, it was back to Ipswich. At least the delay would give him some extra time to work on the business plan.

The Past Week

It had been one of the more eventful weeks in Pryke's life. Six days previously, he had had the latest in a series of disagreements with his fellow directors, and had resigned from the typesetting company that he helped to found nearly five years before. He had walked out of the building and, with nowhere else to go, he went home. He did not know what he was going to do, not even what his next move should be. He simply knew that he had had enough. From now on, he would be working for himself.

Yet by the evening of that same day, he was swept up and heading in a completely unforeseen direction, thanks to a chance telephone call. Out of the blue he had been offered the opportunity of pitching for the European licence for a North American board game. It was novel, exciting, and doing well in the US— the only drawback was that no one on this side of the Atlantic had ever heard of it. Yet when he'd been asked if he would fly out to Barbados the following week to present his ideas, there was only one answer he could give. Pryke loved a challenge. If someone said something was impossible, he would move hell and high water to prove them wrong. He had just better be sure that this time he hadn't bitten off more than he could chew.

---

*This case was prepared for INSEAD by David Molian MBA, of David Molian Associates, in collaboration with Michael Ullmann MBA, Entrepreneur in residence, INSEAD. The authors gratefully acknowledge the assistance of the management of Serif Cowells PLC, and in particular that of John Pryke.

"After all," he reflected, "all I need to take is a water-tight business plan and a pair of swimming trunks. . . ."

John Pryke

John Pryke left school in his native Ipswich at sixteen, with some mediocre exam results and a string of school reports that had a consistent theme: he had ability, but would not use it. At school he had found little that motivated him to work, although he discovered an aptitude for art and craft. Photography was his main interest, and after school he looked for an opportunity to train as a professional photographer, first locally, and then in London. Nothing turned up and so, very much as a second choice, he approached a number of local printers for an apprenticeship. Two options were open—to become a machine operator, or to train as a compositor and typesetter. The latter seemed to offer more scope, so Pryke began a three-year apprenticeship with the Ipswich firm of Ancient House Press in the autumn of 1970.

At Ancient House, Pryke received a good all-round training, supplemented by a course in printing at nearby North East Essex Technical College. He was intrigued by the technical processes of printing, and rapidly found the incentive to learn that had been lacking at school. He also developed the knack of cramming for examinations and distinguished himself by scoring the highest marks ever recorded by a student in his course. Within two years, Pryke was running the typesetting section of the Press and enjoyed considerable responsibility and autonomy. Then circumstances changed. Shortly after he had joined, Ancient House was acquired by another local company, Orwell Press. Just when Pryke was settling into his new position as head of his section, Orwell Press itself was bought up, and Pryke learned that his department was to be reorganized and staff made redundant. Prospects looked distinctly bleak, and he began to hunt for another job.

Moving On

Signing off his apprenticeship one year early, Pryke joined World Media, a printing and publishing group based in Diss, some thirty miles away. The company specialised in newspaper and magazine production, and was in the process of introducing computerised photocomposition. In the early 1970s the use of computers in printing was still fairly novel. This was John Pryke's introduction to the processes involved, and he was fascinated by what he saw. Over the months that followed he mastered whatever he could until he was as expert in the technology as anybody else in the company. As the department's competence increased, Pryke started to analyse the pattern of work and consider ways of improving or modifying it. It struck him that by "front-loading" the start of the week, five days' work could be compressed into four, giving everyone the opportunity to take on other work or to leave early for the week-end.

The trick was to re-organise to create an atmosphere of urgency. Pryke's suggestions were taken up and, within a few weeks, the week's work was finishing regularly by late on Thursday night. The majority of the department then spent Friday unwinding, or left early. Pryke used the time to involve himself in other aspects of magazine production, particularly design and lay-out, and to undertake extra work on his own account.

After some two years the operation was running without a hitch and Pryke was acquiring a growing list of clients for whom he worked out of hours on a variety of typesetting and production work. Then a re-structuring of the group was announced. Pryke's unit was to be hived off to join another company in Diss, in his eyes a retrograde step. They would be working with inferior technology, and to a lower standard of quality. For the second time, he started to look through the situations vacant columns.

Now aged twenty, John Pryke joined a Colchester firm, ET Heron, and knew from day one that he had made a mistake. The atmosphere and style of the company were completely out of sympathy with his own approach to work. Heron was a long-established printer with a tradition of paternalism and an entrenched hierarchy of management. On the shop-floor, the union representatives exercised tight control over work practices. The scope of innovation or re-organisation—especially by someone of Pryke's age—was minimal. Anyone stepping out of line was liable to find himself becoming rapidly unpopular and with little prospect of promotion. It was particularly frustrating for Pryke, since Heron was computerising its typesetting operations and his experience made him an obvious choice for a leading role in the department. The situation dictated otherwise. After one year, one month and one day, Pryke finally left to take a job with Essex Counties Newspapers.

Continuing Education

John Pryke was some seven years out of school, and starting his fourth job. The more he reflected on the fact, the less he liked it. By the conventional wisdom of the job market, this was not a good track record. His time at Heron, however, had not been entirely wasted. Two evenings a week Pryke had attended night-school, taking courses in print estimating, book-keeping and accountancy. His tutor, a man named Bill Smurthwaite, was co-incidentally the Chief Estimator at Heron, and took considerable interest in him, encouraging him to enlarge his knowledge and range of skills. In his new job with Essex Counties, Pryke had the opportunity to employ them.

Essex Counties was a progressive East Anglian company that was expanding its workforce to launch a new evening paper in the Colchester area. Pryke was recruited to work on this project and, from the outset, was able to involve himself in the production activities outside the compositing room, which encompassed paste-up, design, copy preparation and lay-out. The Managing Director of the firm was experimenting with new approaches to production and distribution. Observing and questioning, Pryke began to take an interest in the broader issues of running a business, in particular sales and marketing.

The First Business

Ever since his time at World Media, Pryke had taken on freelance work out of hours. Most of it came through personal referral and recommendation from contacts in the local printing industry, and Pryke took each job as it was offered. Now, as his work for Essex Counties settled into a regular pattern of eight-hour shifts, it seemed that there was an opportunity to build something more substantial than irregular "moonlighting." With an old friend from the Printing College, Pryke set up Avenue Press; the name was chosen originally because of Pryke's address, but he also noted the advantage of appearing under the "A" listing in the telephone directory.

In the months that followed, Avenue Press steadily increased its client base and turnover until Pryke's partner, Tony Grimsey, entered the business full time. Pryke was spending a large part of his out-of-office hours with Avenue, and the two founders managed the flow of work by enlisting freelance help from friends and colleagues in the printing trade. In July 1979, Avenue suddenly had the opportunity to acquire its own photocomposition equipment at a good price. By coincidence, the company was also offered its first substantial, long-term contract to print the East Anglian Farmers' Guide. Pryke weighed the potential of the business against the risks, and made his decision. He handed in his notice at Essex Counties. He was now twenty-four.

Monarch Origination

Avenue Press was a partnership. Pryke and Grimsey decided that the venture should become a limited company, which they christened Monarch Origination. They were joined in this by two of Pryke's former employers from his days at Ancient House, who were keen to expand their existing business base. Monarch's equity ownership was split 49 percent to 51 percent between Pryke and Grimsey and the two others, shareholdings being proportional to the capital invested by each individual. Pryke, who was by some years the youngest of the four, was the smallest shareholder, with 24.5 percent.

Pryke's chief task was that of getting new business. When he and Grimsey had first set up Avenue Press, there had been a loose understanding between them that Grimsey would be mainly responsible for selling, while Pryke concentrated on production. In fact, it rapidly transpired that Grimsey was disinclined to spend time cold-calling and drumming up business, and within a few weeks Pryke found himself handling virtually all contact with new and prospective clients. He was the obvious choice, therefore, to continue in this role as Monarch got underway. None of the founding directors had been allotted actual titles, but when Pryke printed the first set of business stationery he described himself on his own business card as Managing Director. When this came to the notice of the others, it excited a certain amount of friction. No one, however, was prepared to argue openly about it, and so Pryke remained Managing Director.

By the third year of operation, Monarch's turnover exceeded the £500,000 mark. The directors worked very successfully as a team, and the business established a strong base of loyal clients. Pryke's philosophy, which was shared by the others, was to find the work first, and then worry about how it was going to be done. From the start it was agreed that the business should expand through its retained earnings, and not seek external funding. As a result, the company's limited resources were constantly struggling to cope with the volume of work. Frequently the directors worked through the night, and were continually calling on their network of contacts in the industry to help out or subcontract in their spare time. From the original base of typesetting, Monarch diversified into producing camera-ready copy, graphic design and print broking (negotiating with printers on a client's behalf). Business grew at a frenetic pace and, in the words of Pryke, they "broke every business rule in the book—except three."

The three sacred rules were these:

- never to work at a loss
- never to work for late payers
- and never to take on anything they could not do themselves

There were two reasons for the third rule: first, the company's insistence on quality, and the ability to control it; and second, to ensure that the business was never at the mercy of someone else's exclusive technical expertise. When Monarch acquired a second-hand camera, for example, Pryke brought in one of his former College tutors to teach the directors how to use it, before they employed a qualified camera operator.

Upheaval

By the latter part of 1984, the existing premises were bursting at the seams, and it was clear that the company would have to move. The directors agreed among themselves that Monarch should gamble on a large jump forward at one go— bigger premises, more staff and improved equipment. All the signs were that the business was "out there for the taking," the company having recently acquired a number of prestigious clients, including the dictionaries division of the publisher, Longmans. By now everyone's eyes were set firmly on the target of £1 million turnover.

Monarch geared up for expansion and moved into new premises on the outskirts of Ipswich. Then, with no prior warning, one of the founding directors announced that he wanted to quit the business, and promptly did so. He was not replaced. From that point on, relations between the directors deteriorated. The sense of team spirit disappeared, and disagreements became more frequent and protracted. Policies would be agreed, and subsequently ignored or repudiated by one of the parties. Opinion was especially sharply divided on the question of Monarch's forward strategy.

Pryke had been convinced for some time that there was a significant opportunity for the company to get into desk-top publishing (DTP). Already Monarch was typesetting for Longmans directly from computer disc and Pryke had been looking closely into the state of the technology and its likely development over several months. His interest was largely the result of a chance telephone call, asking whether Monarch had the facility to typeset from a disc prepared on an Apple II. Pryke had dealt with the call, and had had to reply that Monarch was not set up to communicating with Apple hardware, but if a disc were sent to him he would see if he could rig something up. The disc arrived, and Pryke came into the office at the week-end to "play around with it." He succeeded in reading the data, and contacted the author, Steve Birch, to tell him that Monarch would be able to take on the job.

Birch was preparing a UK edition of a board game developed in North America, which had specific and fairly exacting typesetting requirements. He and Pryke worked closely together, and within a few weeks Monarch was asked if it could also typeset various European versions of the game. By now Pryke was talking directly with the North American proprietors, and advising them on print and production problems as well as handling their typesetting and artwork. He got on well with the company at the personal level, and the value of the business to the company was considerable. Pryke felt strongly that the expertise which Monarch was acquiring as a result should be capitalised on quickly, while the field was still open and the costs of entry comparatively low.

His fellow directors were luke-warm in their support, with the consequence that some investment in new equipment was forthcoming, but insufficient to allow Pryke to make a whole-hearted pitch for new DTP business. The company made an interim agreement with the print union, but the pace of development was agonisingly slow from Pryke's point of view. Frustrated and demoralised, Pryke was reaching the end of his tether. A particularly acrimonious dispute proved the final straw, and on the afternoon of 11th March, 1985, Pryke walked out of the building.

What Next?

Pryke was thirty. His personal wealth was largely tied up in Monarch, and it would clearly take some time to disentangle himself from his old firm. On the other hand, he was unmarried and free from major personal commitments. He might not know what he was going to do, but he was certain that he had sufficient experience and contacts to start again. This time, however, it was going to be his business, and his alone.

He went home, and immediately telephoned Ray Deeks, the senior partner in the Ipswich accountancy firm of Deeks and King. Pryke's association with Deeks stretched back to the early days of Avenue Press, when Pryke had consulted him on setting up book-keeping and accounting systems. They had stayed in close touch, and Deeks had been involved with the financial planning at Monarch, as well as advising Pryke on his personal finances. Despite an age gap of nearly twenty years, the two men were close personal friends.

Deeks listened to Pryke's account of what had happened, and agreed with his assessment of the situation: there was nothing to stop him going out on his own, and indeed the sooner the better. Deeks would help him put together a business plan, and advise him on the financial side. Pryke's immediate priority, in Deek's opinion, was to find suitable premises.

An Unexpected Offer

Feeling greatly reassured, Pryke replaced the receiver and started to think about the right estate agents to contact. The phone rang, and he found himself talking to the UK office of the North American games company. They had run across a production problem, and wanted to take Pryke's advice over it. When they called

Monarch Origination, they had been told that Pryke was at home, and so it fell to Pryke to break the news of his resignation. He chatted for a few minutes, made some suggestions, and the conversation ended with both parties agreeing to stay in touch. Faced with rather more pressing concerns, Pryke thought no more about it.

At about 7 pm that evening, Pryke was telephoned by the company's head office in Barbados. They had been informed of what had happened, and were calling to offer him a permanent position with the company as their print and production consultant. Much as he was tempted by the prospect of life in the Caribbean, Pryke replied that he was committed to setting up his own business. Both sides were eager, however, to continue the association, and Pryke assured them that he would stay in close touch, and the conversation ended on a friendly note.

Half an hour later, the phone rang for the third time. The firm's MD was phoning personally to ask whether Pryke in his new capacity would be prepared to take over the manufacture of the game for the European market, with the volumes, prices, and payment terms specified by Horn Abbot, and deliver the product to Kenner Parker, the present licencee. Right away, he agreed. There was a pause at the other end. Would he consider taking over as licencee, as well as producer, for the European market?

Pryke stopped to think for a moment. He knew that the game was doing well in the US and Canada. Indeed, he had obtained a copy for himself, played it with friends and enjoyed it. He also knew that the proprietors were disenchanted with the current European licencee. Soon to be launched, the game seemed to have a good chance of taking off in the UK if it was properly handled. But acting as licencee, with overall responsibility for production, marketing, distribution and achieving sales targets, was on a different scale from simply manufacturing the product. And, apart from anything else, there was the little matter of funding the business.

Cash would not be a problem, he was told. If he could put together a realistic business plan, fully costed and with all the angles covered, the company was confident that the money would be available. Could he present his business plan in Barbados within a week?

"Yes," said John Pryke.

The Preparations

Within 72 hours, Pryke was ready to call Barbados. He had spent the intervening three days mainly in London having samples made up to confirm that the game could be produced to the specifications he had in mind. Working through the night, Pryke had persuaded his key potential suppliers, board and box manufacturers, to produce a mock-up of the game complete apart from the questions. They provided estimates for monthly production runs ranging between 10,000 and 40,000 units, and a confirmed price per unit once the specification was agreed. The spread between minimum and maximum volumes was a considerable one, but in advance of launching the product Pryke could only estimate the likely sales range. The existing success in North America gave him grounds for confidence that they would be more likely to hit the upper limit, although beyond 40,000 units a month Pryke would have to find additional resources to supply the demand.

Pryke paid particular attention to the question of specification, because he was aware that Horn Abbot were concerned about the discrepancies in the existing product range: the thickness of the playing board, for instance, varied from 180 grams to 250 grams, and the exact colours of the printing inks differed substantially from one edition to another. Taking control of the European operation would also mean standardising the product by preparing a full specification.

The quotations he obtained gave Pryke the basis for detailed production costings. He then sat down with Ray Deeks to work out the business plan for producing the game (Appendix A). Assuming that the company could ship 40,000 units a month to UK retailers during the first year, they would need funding of around £190,000 to get the business up and running. Would the boys in Barbados still be so keen when they heard that? And, in any case, what exactly did they have in mind?

Appendix A: San Serif Ltd. Business Plan

San Serif International Ltd.
Trading and Profit and Loss Account
Year Ended 28-2-86

Sales		1,114,000
Cost of Sales		914,000
Gross Profit		200,000
Interest Received		22,400
		222,400
Overheads		
Tooling Costs Written Off	9,000	
Other Costs	8,000	
		(17,000)
Net Profit for the Year		205,400

Balance Sheet At 28-2-86

Cash at Bank and in Hand	205,400
Represented by:	
Profit and Loss Account	205,400

San Serif International Ltd.

Cash Flow 1985–86

Beginning Month	Opening Balance	Cash Received Deposit	Cash Received Income	Manufacturing Costs	Other Costs	Closing Balance	End Month
1	—	—	—	—	—	—	1
2	—	40,000	—	—	—	40,000	2
3	40,000	80,000	—	—	—	120,000	3
4	120,000	71,800	—	—	—	191,800	4
5	191,800	191,800	—	(9,000)	(1,000)	181,800	5
6	81,800	(40,000)	222,800	—	(1,000)	363,600	6
7	363,600	(40,000)	222,800	(182,800)	(1,000)	362,600	7
8	362,600	(40,000)	222,800	(182,800)	(1,000)	361,600	8
9	361,600	(40,000)	222,800	(182,800)	(1,000)	360,600	9
10	360,600	(31,800)	222,800	(182,800)	(1,000)	367,800	10
11	367,800			(182,800)	(1,000)	184,000	11
12	184,000	—	22,400	—	(1,000)	205,400	12
		—	1,136,400	(923,000)	(8,000)		
After		—	—	—	—		
		—	1,136,400	(123,000)	8,000		

San Serif International Limited

Assumptions re:	Cash Flow 1985–86

1) Games will be manufactured in batches of 40,000.

2) Each game will cost $4.57 to make and will be sold for $5.57.

3) Other incidental costs of $1,000 a month will be incurred on the prospect from month 5.

4) Tooling costs will be $9,000.

5) A deposit of $191,800 will be received in months 2, 3 and 4 as follows:

2	40,000
3	80,000
4	71,800
	191,800

6) First manufacture is in month 5. Payment from company will be one month after manufacture. Payment to suppliers

will be one month later. Will deduct $40,000 from first to fourth payment and $31,800 from fifth.

7) Tooling costs will be paid month 5.

8) There will be manufacturing runs in the following months:

5
6
7
8
9

9) The company will be separated vat Registred to obtain monthly refunds as refunds will be received in the month of payment of liabilities or before vat may be ignored in the cash flow.

10) Interest on cash balances is received in month 12 at 10% on average balance.

11) Combined cash balances schedule uses figures from the san serif cash flow which assumes no new leasing.

CASE • *A License to Print Money? (Part B)**

David Molian, INSEAD
Michael Ullmann, INSEAD

In business, you go on the person above all else.

John Pryke

Flight to Barbados

On the flight to Barbados, Pryke had plenty of time to reflect on his last conversation with the games company. When he had called them back, they'd re-iterated that the money he would need was not an issue. Pryke, however, was still unhappy. Whatever they said, he knew he would need a sizeable six-figure sum. From his experience, in a situation like this the obvious route for the other party was to take a substantial stake in the new venture in exchange for a cash injection. He could see himself all too easily ending up as a minority shareholder in his own business. That was not a position he would accept, no matter how good the offer. He made his views clear, and was delighted, not to say surprised, to hear that that was not the company's intention. They had a problem that needed solving. Pryke had helped them solve their production problems in the past, and they had every reason to think that he was the person to turn to in this case—provided they could agree between them the business plan. Now, how soon could he be in Barbados?

He finally arrived in Barbados in the late afternoon of Good Friday. He was met at the airport and taken, not, as he expected, to a hotel, but to the house of the managing director, Blake LeBlanc. LeBlanc handed him a pair of shorts, and invited him to return to the swimming pool when he had unpacked and felt rested.

For the next 72 hours, Pryke stayed as LeBlanc's house guest. The first night, he talked with LeBlanc and other board members until 4 am, while the company's accountants systematically dissected the business plan. The talks continued through-out most of the following day, until the whole group went out to dinner. In the restaurant, the conversation turned to social topics, and Pryke started to feel distinctly uneasy. By the end of the meal, he was convinced that his hosts were simply looking for a way to let him down gently. He'd given it his best try, and it looked like that wasn't good enough. Tomorrow he would move into a hotel while he waited for the next flight to the UK.

Back at LeBlanc's house, the two of them sat by the pool drinking beer, and the conversation reverted to business. They talked once again into the small hours, until LeBlanc suddenly posed a direct question: "No bullshit, with your hand on your heart, can you do it?"

*This case was prepared for INSEAD by David Molian MBA, of David Molian Associates, in collaboration with Michael Ullmann MBA, Entrepreneur in residence, INSEAD. The authors gratefully acknowledge the assistance of the management of Serif Cowells PLC, and in particular that of John Pryke.

"If I've got the money, I can do it."

"You've got the licence."

The Company and the Game

The business is mostly run by space cadets . . . It's still the Jimmy Buffett school of capitalism. Most corporations have five-year plans; we're lucky if we think five minutes ahead.
                                        Founding Director, Horn Abbot International

The name of the company was Horn Abbot, and the name of the game, Trivial Pursuit. Although by 1985 Trivial Pursuit was North America's top-selling new game, it had experienced a long and difficult birth. In January 1980, four Canadians, all in their early thirties, incorporated Horn Abbot to produce and market an idea thought up by two of the founders, Chris Haney and Scott Abbott. Haney, a newspaper picture editor, and Abbott, a sports writer, had been playing Scrabble one evening, and began to talk about inventing another board game with the same sort of universal appeal. Haney had a passion for sports trivia, and gradually the idea evolved of a game based on questions and answers covering all sorts of fields.

Between the initial concept and the trial marketing of the first version in Toronto and Vancouver was a year's unremitting hard grind. Chris Haney and his brother, John, held 22 percent and 18 percent of the company, respectively; Abbott and a lawyer friend, Ed Werner, also held 22 percent and 18 percent, respectively. To raise the $40,000 extra which they estimated was needed to get the game to market, the four sold the remaining equity for $200 per share to a total of 34 investors. The Haney brothers and Abbott spent much of the winter in Spain, composing thousands of questions, and returned to Canada in February to attend the Canadian Toy Fair and address the problems of actually producing the game.

Over the Christmas period in 1981, Horn Abbot sold all 1,100 trial sets at a trading loss of $44,000. It was not until September 1982, however, that the founders persuaded Selchow and Righter, the US producers of Scrabble and Parcheesi, to manufacture and distribute Trivial Pursuit under licence. The game at last took off in 1983, selling 2.3 million units in Canada alone, but not before Chris Haney and Scott Abbott had suffered breakdowns from nervous exhaustion. Both men recovered, and the company turned the corner in spectacular fashion. In 1984, 22 million copies of Trivial Pursuit were sold just in the US, worth more than $50 million to Horn Abbot in royalties. The company shifted its headquarters to the Caribbean, and Blake LeBlanc, a legal associate of Werner's, was appointed managing director. LeBlanc's chief responsibility was to handle international licensing; he had been recruited not just for his experience in corporate legal work, but because he fitted in with the ethos of Horn Abbot. Chris Haney described him as "another one of us; he's right out of a Jimmy Buffett song."

By the end of that year, Horn Abbot had recruited a network of friends and contacts to start preparing editions for sale in more than a dozen different countries. Since the founders were determined to restrict themselves to co-ordinating the development of each new edition and language variant, they were obliged to find licencees for each territory. For the UK and western Europe, they planned to use the subsidiary of the US games company, Kenner Parker (itself part of the giant General Mills).

By the spring of 1985, Horn Abbot were unhappy with Kenner Parker's plans for the UK launch, which was to be the game's entry into the European market. Although Kenner Parker was a large company of long standing, Horn Abbot were far from convinced that they were the right people to be in overall control of the operation. What LeBlanc had in mind was that Kenner Parker's role should be reduced to that of a sub-licencee, responsible basically for distribution, with Pryke taking over the licence itself, initially for the UK and subsequently for other European territories if things went well.

San Serif

The financial arrangement proposed by LeBlanc was a straightforward loan, advanced as Pryke required, and repayable interest-free in November 1986. Nothing was signed, and the deal was concluded with a hand-shake. The two men also agreed that in the first instance Pryke should be responsible solely for manufacture, with Kenner Parker continuing as licencee until both Horn Abbot and Pryke were satisfied that he was in a position to take the licence over. Pryke then departed for the cooler climes of Ipswich.

Initially, Pryke had envisaged that Horn Abbot would be his customer. During his conversations with LeBlanc, however, it emerged that while Horn Abbot might be prepared to advance Pryke the money, they did not want to be involved in the actual trading chain.

Instead, Pryke's immediate customers would be three North American games companies, Selchow and Reichter, Gessler and American Eagle, who would themselves be selling the games on for distribution through Europe. Assuming that their terms of payment were 60 days from the end of the month following the invoice (i.e., up to a maximum of 90 days theoretically), Pryke reckoned that he could manage the buyer-supplier position in such a way that funding of £180,000 should take care of all eventualities. LeBlanc agreed to provide this in three installments of £60,000 drawn down as required.

Back home, Pryke moved into a corner of the offices of Deeks and King, and got to work. He chose San Serif[1] as the name of the new company and, by the end of April, one month later, it was clear to both Pryke and Deeks that their complimentary skills worked well together. Pryke offered Deeks the post of Managing Director (he himself was Executive Chairman), and 10 percent of the new company. Deeks accepted, and for the next four months both of them worked frantically in anticipation of selling the product into the trade for a 1985 Christmas launch. To refine the product, Pryke spent considerable time with the two English question writers, Steve Birch and Ray Loude, who were supervising a panel of European writers as well as preparing 6,000 questions for the UK edition.

By the beginning of August, orders reached the target level of 40,000 units. Pryke had managed to solve the major problems of manufacturing in the UK to

---

[1]"San serif" is a type style commonly used in printing.

the required standards by putting together a number of suppliers who, between them, could source and sub-assemble the various components of the game. However, the arrangement left him unconvinced that he had adequate control over quality. In particular, he was finding that sourcing the boards and the outer boxes in sufficient quantities was a constant headache.

Dash to America

San Serif by now had moved to premises of its own, in nearby Martlesham. Pryke and Deeks had recruited their first full-time employee, Steve Packard, an old colleague of Pryke's, whom he regarded as the best print and production manager he knew. Just when Pryke and Packard felt that they were on top of the situation, the UK retail trade came alive to the potential of Trivial Pursuit as a leading Christmas item. In four weeks the order book jumped over 40,000 units to 1,400,000[2], all confirmed.

The three men were staggered. The scale of demand was completely unanticipated. Pryke had always felt confident about the product, but this was something else. It also posed a very real threat to the survival of the company. For one thing, where were they going to find suppliers who could produce that sort of volume? There was certainly no one in Britain. For another, how could the company fund activities of that order? As yet San Serif had no overdraft facility with its bank, and Pryke refused on principle to approach Horn Abbot for additional funds. And, third, if the company failed to deliver because of the first two reasons, its own credibility and that of Trivial Pursuit would be sunk forever. It was now the end of August. San Serif had under three months in which to meet the shipment dates.

Deeks thought it might be possible to structure terms in such a way that receipts would come into the company before payments to the main sub-contractor—the producer of the boards and boxes—for the completed products were made. But would they be able to strike a deal with a suitable manufacturer without putting substantial sums of money upfront? Pryke knew of only one company that could supply on the scale required—Western Publishing of the US, the largest printing business in the world. Without more ado, he rang and made an appointment at Western's head office in New York.

Pryke and Deeks arrived in New York on the first available flight, and presented their case. Yes, Western could fulfill the order, but with the dollar at 1.32 to the pound, the unit cost was high. Pryke was prepared to sacrifice a little margin, and agreed. Western were looking for more than a favourable price, however. San Serif was unknown to them, and Pryke sensed that Western's negotiators were unwilling to conclude an agreement without something else on the table. In the absence of cash, which was out of the question, he suspected that Western was looking for a substantial slice of San Serif equity. That, too, was out of the question. He and Deeks conferred privately, and Deeks then asked whether Western would be happy to deal with San Serif if the company had an American bank account. The answer, in principle, was yes.

---

[2]For the UK and European territories combined.

Pryke and Deeks arranged to return within a few days to complete the deal, and the meeting was adjourned. The two men went at once to a branch of Chemical Bank, where Deeks opened two accounts for a dollar apiece, and they then caught the next flight to London.

When they returned to New York, Pryke felt confident that the deal would go through. Apart from anything else, Western had provided him and Deeks with a private plane which they could use to tour various manufacturing plants up and down the country, discussing San Serif's production requirements. They returned to New York to sign the final agreement, and left once more for the UK.

Time of Trial

Pryke had taken what he considered to be the biggest calculated risk of his life. San Serif was now completely in the hands of Western Publishing, and the weeks that followed were the most anxious that he had ever spent. He, Deeks and Packard were even busier than before, desperately trying to ensure that the risks on their side of the Atlantic were kept to a minimum. September became October, and the news from the States was good. It looked as though the November shipment dates would be met.

San Serif took delivery of Western's goods in November, and was able to pay immediately (assisted by a dollar:pound exchange rate of 1.48). Through Kenner Parker the finished games were shipped to stockists in the latter part of the month and, by the end of November, copies of Trivial Pursuit filled the shelves of shops all over the UK. At the start of December, Pryke returned to Barbados and wrote Blake LeBlanc a cheque covering all of San Serif's borrowing, repaying Horn Abbot twelve months early. (Although the loan was interest-free, Horn Abbot made money on the exchange rate.) Pryke also asked for, and received, the licence to market Trivial Pursuit in the UK and a number of other European countries.

The Results

Trivial Pursuit took the UK games market by storm. Sales over the Christmas period in 1985 exceeded 1,000,000 units, overtaking the perennial favourites Monopoly and Scrabble. It looked set to remain Britain's top-selling game, in both volume and value terms, for some time to come. The relationship between San Serif and Horn Abbot was strengthened and developed, with the two parties holding regular quarterly planning and review meetings, in Ipswich and Barbados, alternately.

Into Europe

Pryke and Deeks had decided that they were in business for the long haul. Pryke had carefully observed the fate of the game in the United States, where it enjoyed dramatic success and then steady decline until the issue of the next edition. He had determined to avoid a similar pattern with European sales. Properly handled, Trivial Pursuit could be taken from a whirlwind phenomenon and turned into a perennial like Monopoly. It required, however, correct marketing, short supply to the trade, and a planned programme of updated editions.

San Serif was by now licencee for the UK, France and West Germany. In the spring of 1986, Pryke busied himself recruiting an experienced marketing team to open up other territories. Tony Prior joined on the marketing side along with Rae Potter, a former Kenner Parker employee. Their first priority was to standardise the marketing approach across the various European markets. Pryke felt that under Kenner's stewardship Trivial Pursuit had drifted: the marketing was as uncoordinated as the product specification. It was sold under different names, packaged in a variety of ways, and promoted by a host of national advertising agencies and PR companies. The result, in Pryke's view, was a serious dilution of the brand and a set of disparate marketing policies. It was, frankly, "a dog's breakfast." The game was at once re-branded as Trivial Pursuit, the number of promotional agencies was drastically cut and a strategy was developed to segment the consumer market, aiming at specific target groups in a series of carefully orchestrated campaigns. At the same time, sales and distribution remained largely the province of Kenner Parker as sub-licencee, who had the infrastructure to handle the product in the volumes required.

First Results

San Serif was set firmly on the path of becoming the first pan-European games company which was not a subsidiary of a North American corporation. It produced its first set of accounts for the period ended 30th June 1986, covering fifteen months. The company had been actively trading for the last twelve months of that time, and recorded a turnover of £18.5 million, with profits before tax of £1.7 million (Exhibits 1 and 2). Of the company's ordinary share capital of 1,000 shares of £1 each, John Pryke held 800, Ray Deeks 100, and Pryke's father, Victor, a further 100. Pryke senior had joined the board, and the directors proposed a dividend to shareholders of £350,000.

Acquisitions

The first set of accounts also revealed that San Serif Ltd, increasingly referred to as "the Serif group," controlled seven subsidiary companies, as seen in Figure 1.

Pryke had embarked on the acquisition trail in early 1986 with the purchase of Crayston, a locally based firm which provided the packaging for Trivial Pursuit. Shortly afterwards, San Serif acquired TND Associates, a graphic design company, and Pryke's old firm of Monarch Origination. Pryke now controlled directly the typesetting, design and packaging of Trivial Pursuit.

The philosophy was simple. Integrate vertically to gain control of the quality of the product, and add value to the acquired business in the process. The value that San Serif brought was twofold: systems and management. In each business they looked at, Pryke and Deeks concluded that the fundamentals were sound, but there was room for improvement. The plant and equipment were adequate, if not good, and the workforce was skilled and competent. Yet the incumbent management had failed to make the best use of both. The fact that the acquisitions were local companies with whom Serif had been trading closely meant that Pryke and Deeks had a fair idea from the outset of what needed to be done.

Exhibit 1
San Serif Ltd, Accounts, Period Ended 30 June 1986

San Serif Limited Consolidated Profit and Loss Account for the Period Ended 30 June 1986

	Note	£
Turnover	2 and 3	18,519,196
Other operating income		46,984
		18,566,180
Operating Costs	4	16,978,187
Group Operating Profit	5	1,587,993
Other income	8	182,494
		1,770,487
Interest payable and similar charges	9	81,948
Profit on Ordinary Activities before Taxation		1,688,539
Taxation	10	776,127
Profit on Ordinary Activities after Taxation	11	912,412
Minority interest		—
Dividends	12	350,000
Retained Profit for the Period	13	£562,412

Figure 1
San Serif Subsidiary Companies at 30th June 1986

Company	Nature of Business
San Serif Print Ltd	Printing
San Serif Print Promotions Ltd	Wholesaling
Crayston Packaging Ltd	Packaging
TND Serif Ltd	Graphic Design
Monarch Origination Ltd	Typesetting
Serif Marketing Ltd	Marketing
Serif Soft Toys Ltd	Dormant

Source: The Serif Group, Report & Accounts, 30th June 1986

Exhibit 2
San Serif Ltd, Accounts, Period Ended 30 June 1986

San Serif Limited Consolidated Balance Sheet for the Period Ended 30 June 1986

	Note	£
Fixed Assets		
Tangible assets	14	676,546
Current Assets		
Stocks	16	2,001,525
Debtors	17 and 21	2,773,978
Investments	18	600
Cash at bank and in hand		1,721,117
		6,497,220
Creditors—amounts falling due within one year		
Bank loans and overdrafts	19	66,507
Trade and other creditors	20	6,253,185
Proposed dividend	12	350,000
		6,669,692
Net Current Liabilities		(172,472)
Total Assets Less Current Liabilities		504,074
Creditors—amounts due after more than one year	20	81,394
Total Assets Less Liabilities		£422,680
Capital and Reserves		
Called-up share capital	22	1,000
Retained profits	13	391,680
		392,680
Minority interest		30,000
On behalf of the Board		
J M Pryke ⎞ Directors		
R Deeks ⎠		£422,680

To each acquisition, they brought a two-pronged attack. First, on the financial side, Ray Deeks would head a team that overhauled internal reporting procedures to bring performance monitoring into line with the practices which he and Pryke had established. Eventually, the system would enable group management to have provisional trading figures for the month by the 14th of the following month, and final trading figures by the 23rd.

Second, there would be changes in management style and structure. One of the first of Deeks' tasks was to produce an updated balance sheet showing exactly where the acquired company stood. This would be scrutinised by San Serif senior management, and form the basis for an open discussion with the acquired company's staff, where they would be told the current state of affairs and given a clear idea of the new objectives for the year ahead. They would also be introduced to their new managing director, a senior member of San Serif.

Diversification

The Serif Group was unquestionably a stronger, more broadly based entity as a result of this first wave of acquisitions. What it had still to achieve, however, was to break out of being essentially a one-product company.

Ever since he had turned his thoughts to expansion, Pryke had intended to go into publishing as a logical extension of his business activities. In May, he learnt that Britain's biggest publisher of local business directories, Kemps, was coming up for sale. He knew that the owner, Tom Proctor, would have three basic options: (i) to sell to the company's management; (ii) to float the company on the stock market; or (iii) to sell to a third party. Through further enquiries Pryke found out that ill health would prevent Proctor from making the institutional presentations necessary for a flotation. He also learnt that the management were interested in a buy-out, and that Proctor was looking for a price of £1.4 million for Kemps and its associated company, Halesworth Press, a Suffolk-based printer. The price was acceptable. Kemps was an established company with a strong management, well placed to benefit from an injection of the Serif philosophy. Halesworth was a less attractive proposition, but could only be improved by a dose of hands-on Serif management.

So far San Serif had no long-term borrowing on its books. All acquisitions to date had been funded from internal cashflow, and Pryke wanted to keep it that way. If the sale could be delayed for three months, San Serif would be in a position to finance the purchase from its own funds. Pryke began informal discussions with the Kemps management to establish what they were looking for. Both parties agreed that their ambitions both for the business and for the management themselves could be achieved under Serif ownership, and together they produced a business plan to that end. When Pryke made his formal offer to Proctor, he had the full support of the Kemps management, and the deal was completed on July 1st 1986.

Fifteen months ago, he had walked out of his job with nowhere to go. Now, Pryke was chief executive of a group of nearly a dozen companies, turning over between them several million pounds a month. What next?

Onwards and Upwards

The Serif Group made no further acquisitions until the very end of 1986, but Pryke and his team had plenty to occupy them. Over the year, their sales of Trivial Pursuit approached the 3,000,000 unit mark, divided more or less equally between the

UK and the rest of Europe. From then on, the UK market reached a peak, and expansion was greater in the three principal western Europe markets of France, Germany and Spain. The complexity of the licensing arrangements was by now considerable, with Serif producing fourteen language variants for sale in eighteen countries. Relations with Horn Abbot continued to strengthen, and Pryke began to talk about licensing the game for territories outside Europe, chiefly the Gulf states and, eventually, the communist bloc. It was also agreed that Serif should take on the European licence for Horn Abbott's follow-up to Trivial Pursuit, UBI, to be launched in the US for the 1987 Christmas market.

As far as the core games business was concerned, Pryke could see two main strands of development. One was the international licencing of products developed in other markets, most likely North America, and fitted into Serif's pattern of production, marketing and distribution through sub-licencees. The second was the origination of games for the domestic UK market, developed in-house and remaining throughout under Serif control. Already the marketing department were working on two ideas, based on popular television series.

Serif's one further acquisition in 1986 was Grigsmore Ltd, an Ipswich advertising and publicity agency which the company used extensively. In December, Serif acquired 76 percent of the share capital. The venture was not a success. The two companies' philosophies rapidly proved to be incompatible, and within months Grigsmore's management were negotiating to buy the business back. Pryke was happy to sell, and did so at a profit.

Consolidation

For 1987, the emphasis at Serif was on consolidation. Kemps moved into new, larger premises and its systems were fully computerised. Halesworth invested substantially in new equipment, and extended its customer base under an enlarged salesforce. The group filled the one remaining gap in its range of printing and production facilities with the acquisition of Hilo Offset, a local reproduction and plate-making firm. Pryke also formed Serif Travel Ltd, specifically for the acquisition of an Ipswich travel agency.

A three-part divisional structure was beginning to take shape: Publishing, in the form of Kemps, Printing and Production, and Leisure, embracing games and the newly created travel business. At the heart of the company, however, remained Trivial Pursuit. Serif had also finished the development of the two home-grown, TV-based games, Antiques Roadshow and Sporting Triangles. To reflect the dependence of the group on games, and to give a fair picture of the company's performance in an industry with a trading cycle corresponding to the calendar year, Pryke and Deeks decided to defer the second reporting period to 31st December. This resulted in the second set of accounts covering eighteen months. The results spoke for themselves (Exhibit 3): the Serif group had achieved sales of £91 million, and a profit before tax figure of £6.5 million. The combined remuneration of the three directors was in excess of £1 million while, as shareholders, the trio participated in an interim dividend of some £650,000. And the company was still less than three years old.

Exhibit 3   San Serif Ltd, Accounts, 1986–1988

Consolidated Profit and Loss Accounts	Note	15 Months to 30th June, 1986 (£'000)	18 Months to 31st December, 1987 (£'000)	3 Months to 31st March, 1988 (£'000)
Turnover	1	18,519	91,106	12,547
Other operating income				
Royalties and commissions		47	704	118
		18,566	91,810	12,665
Operating costs	2	16,978	85,629	11,780
Group operating profit	3	1,588	6,181	885
Other income	4	182	509	62
		1,770	6,690	947
Interest payable and similar charges	5	82	180	38
Profit on ordinary activities before taxation		1,688	6,510	909
Taxation	6	776	2,433	369
Profit on ordinary activities after taxation		912	4,077	540
Extraordinary items	7	—	(68)	—
		912	4,009	540
Minority interest		—	10	—
		912	3,999	540
Dividends	8	350	650	—
Retained profit for the period	9	562	3,349	540
Earnings per share	10	£1.82	£8.13	£1.08

Consolidated Balance Sheets	Note	As at 30th June, 1986 (£'000)	As at 31st December, 1987 (£'000)	As at 31st March, 1988 (£'000)
Fixed assets				
Tangible assets	11	677	2,811	2,780
Current assets				
Stocks	12	2,001	2,451	1,960
Debtors	13	2,774	8,508	7,843
Deposits	14	1	1,720	2,167
Cash at bank		1,721	2,476	498
		6,497	15,155	12,468
Creditors: amounts falling due within one year				
Bank loans and overdrafts		67	—	—
Trade and other creditors	15	6,253	15,187	12,047
Proposed dividend		350	—	—
		6,670	15,187	12,047
Net current (liabilities)/assets		(173)	(32)	421
Total assets less current liabilities		504	2,779	3,201
Creditors: amounts falling due after more than one year	16	81	342	374
Provisions for liabilities and charges		—	15	—
Total assets less liabilities		423	2,422	2,827

(continued)

Exhibit 3   *continued*

Consolidated Profit and Loss Accounts	Note	15 Months to 30th June, 1986 (£'000)	18 Months to 31st December, 1987 (£'000)	3 Months to 31st March, 1988 (£'000)
Capital and reserves				
Called-up share capital	18	1	500	500
Retained profit	9	392	1,878	2,327
		393	2,378	2,827
		30	44	—
Minority interest		423	2,422	2,827

Where Next?

Pryke was not yet thirty-four. He was Chief Executive and majority shareholder in an enormously successful, cash-rich young company. All avenues appeared to be open. The only problem was, which one to choose? There was no question of his cashing in and retiring to a tax haven in the sun (although if he did, it was likely to be Barbados). He was a self-confessed workaholic, usually in the building for twelve hours a day, who found it very, very difficult to go home at night. At the week-end, he would frequently drop into one of the group's local subsidiaries and work on the shop-floor, and he retained the old habit of looking through telexes and faxes late at night or first thing, to maintain a grasp of what was happening in the different parts of the business.

If selling out was out of the question, then the most promising long-term route for Serif to take was that of a stock exchange listing. There were many approaches, however, to this. Towards the end of 1987 Pryke and Deeks began to discuss the idea with each other, when a turn of events made the idea suddenly much more of a tangible reality.

WS Cowell Ltd

One lunchtime, Steve Packard (now Managing Director of Crayston) was having a drink in an Ipswich wine bar where a celebration was taking place. The party was being given by Gerry Barnes, a local businessman, to mark his retirement from the board of WS Cowell, one of the town's largest printing companies. Packard was invited to join in, and struck up conversation with one of Barnes' ex-colleagues, Douglas Kemp. Kemp and Barnes were two members of a three-man team which had led a management buy-out of Cowells, as it was known, from its parent company, Grampian Holdings, in 1982. Three years later, the same team had taken Cowells to the Unlisted Securities Market[3] through a share placement. Now that Barnes was retiring, there was a gap in the senior management of the business, and Kemp was looking for help in taking the business forward.

[3]The London Stock Exchange's second-tier market.

Kemp and Packard talked in general terms for a while, and it was clear there was interest on both sides in further discussion. When Packard reported the conversation to Pryke later that day, the immediate response was a wry smile. WS Cowell was one of the firms that Pryke had approached sixteen years ago, when he was looking for an apprenticeship. They had turned him down. Life, Pryke reflected, could take some strange turns.

Go for It?

Some weeks later, Pryke settled down in his office for an afternoon's heavy reading. On the desk in front of him lay the last five years' figures for WS Cowell (Exhibit 4). Since Packard's chance meeting in the wine bar, the two companies had been meeting regularly, and it looked increasingly that a deal of some sort would soon be on the table. Pryke was by now well briefed on Cowell's activities. They fell into the three divisions that follow.

Exhibit 4   Cowells Plc, Accounts, 1983–1987

		Years ended 31st December,				
Consolidated Profit and Loss Accounts	Notes	1983 (£'000)	1984 (£'000)	1985 (£'000)	1986 (£'000)	1987 (£'000)
Turnover	1	6,786	7,278	8,774	9,042	9,762
Cost of sales		5,780	6,118	7,334	7,557	8,132
Gross profit		1,006	1,160	1,440	1,485	1,630
Distribution costs		133	147	173	182	199
Administrative expenses		352	410	375	367	389
		485	557	548	549	588
Operating profit	2	521	603	892	936	1,042
Interest receivable		1	4	—	12	46
Interest payable	4	(182)	(67)	(66)	(67)	(66)
		(181)	(63)	(66)	(55)	(20)
Profit on ordinary activities before taxation		340	540	826	881	1,022
Taxation	5	54	218	278	293	230
Profit on ordinary activities after taxation		286	322	548	588	792
Extraordinary items	6	(127)	(20)	(7)	2,486	69
		159	302	541	3,074	861
Dividends	7	57	143	182	221	257
		102	159	359	2,853	604
Amortisation of revaluation surplus		2	3	2	2	2
Goodwill acquired during the year		—	—	.(30)	—	—
Retained profit brought forward		115	219	381	712	3,567
Retained profit carried forward		219	381	712	3,567	4,173
Earnings per share	8	$3.9p	$4.4p	$7.5p	$8.0p	$10.8p

(continued)

Exhibit 4   *continued*

		At 31st December,				
Consolidated Balance Sheets	Notes	1983 (£'000)	1984 (£'000)	1985 (£'000)	1986 (£'000)	1987 (£'000)
Fixed assets						
Tangible assets	9	1,454	1,519	1,780	1,834	4,483
Current assets						
Stocks	10	997	1,370	1,444	1,816	1,845
Debtors	11	2,324	2,094	2,974	5,480	3,780
Cash at bank		2	3	2	451	1,473
		3,323	3,467	4,420	7,747	7,098
Creditors: amounts falling due within one year	12	1,793	1,881	2,592	2,329	3,164
Net current assets		1,530	1,586	1,828	5,418	3,934
Total assets less current liabilities		2,984	3,105	3,608	7,252	8,417
Creditors: amounts falling due after more than one year	13	380	372	377	840	1,085
Provision for liabilities and charges:						
Deferred taxation	15	71	40	1	338	654
		451	412	378	1,178	1,739
Total assets less liabilities		2,533	2,693	3,230	6,074	6,678
Capital and reserves						
Called-up share capital	16	1,375	1,375	1,838	1,838	1,838
Share premium account	17	—	—	53	53	53
Revaluation reserve	17	289	287	189	178	176
Other reserves	17	650	650	438	438	438
Profit and loss account	17	219	381	712	3,567	4,173
		2,533	2,693	3,230	6,074	6,678

Security and Financial Planning, which had grown from one major post office contract in the late 1970s to a leading position in the field of magnetic strip application on printed documents for retaining encoded information. Building societies were major customers, with a continuing requirement for encoded passbooks. This business had led Cowells into production of plastic "smart" cards, plus credit and charge cards. The company was also an important supplier of passports and examination papers, and had recently entered the financial publications market, producing company reports and related documents.

Colour Printing and Books, which covered three main types of quality illustrated books, general interest, medical and children's, as well as fine art reproduction. During 1986 and 1987, the company had invested in new presses which could deliver significantly better resolutions, and would enhance Cowells' reputation as a quality printer.

Bingo Tickets, which Cowells had been producing since the late 1930s. Here too the company had invested heavily in new technology, and had just been awarded a five-year contract with Mecca Leisure, Britain's biggest operator of Bingo clubs.

Pryke had noted a number of items from Cowells' latest accounts that struck him as significant. Of the company's 7.35 million ordinary shares, the board held about 1.7 million in beneficial ownership, and a further 1.1. million in non-beneficial ownership. Three large institutional investors held between them a further 2.6 million shares. With a nominal value of 25 pence each, Cowell shares had been trading at around the 140 pence mark. For the most recent trading year Cowells had paid a dividend of £257,000, and recorded an earnings per share of 10.8 pence. Directors' remuneration for the same period was £170,000.

Pryke also knew that the majority of Cowells' senior managers were in their fifties, and would be coming up to retirement in the next five to ten years. There was no doubt, therefore, that the management opportunities for his own senior staff in a merged business could be very attractive.

This afternoon, Pryke wanted to find answers to several questions. What benefits, for example, should Serif be looking to derive from a deal? What was the proper basis on which to value Cowells? And, if they were to do a deal, what form should it take?

He began to work his way through the figures.

CHAPTER

Family Business Strategies

Key Topics

- Family-Owned Businesses
- Advantages and Disadvantages of a Family Business
- Problems in Family Businesses
- The Succession Issue
- Prescriptions

Comprehensive Entrepreneurial Cases

- The Outstanding Outsider and the Fumbling Family
- Is Kohler Company Bathing in Paternalism?
- Emge Packing Company, Incorporated

In many cultures male–female distinctions have been dichotomized into wage-earner, warrior, external interfacer (male) and housekeeper, child-bearer, internally focused (female) roles. These traditional stereotypic conceptions are reinforced through accepted norms and behaviors that define individuals and their tasks. The family is the social unit that helps blend these tasks together and smooths over the rough edges when conflicts arise concerning individuals' roles.

A unique combination arises in **family businesses** that blends economic considerations with the traditional roles of the family social unit. Fathers, mothers, and children take on additional or modified responsibilities in family businesses as they seek to integrate employer, employee, owner, supervisor, with their family member roles.

Family businesses are usually defined by whether the company is closely held and controlled by the family, the existence and extent of family investors, and by the number of family members employed in the business.

Family-Owned Businesses

Sixty to seventy percent of U.S. small businesses define themselves as family owned, according to a recent survey by Arthur Andersen Enterprise Group and National Small Business United.[1] The survey found that family owned also means family operated.

---

[1] Arthur Andersen Enterprise Group and National Small Business United, Survey Results of Small and Middle Market Businesses, July 1992, 19.

Nearly 40 percent of small-business owners hire a spouse, while 37 percent have children on the payroll. A smaller percentage—17 percent—employs parents. But it appears that these owners are less anxious to have a sibling around: Only 12 percent hire brothers or sisters (see Figure 9.1).

The real cold shoulder, however, is reserved for in-laws. Those hoping to get ahead by marrying the boss's son or daughter should know that only 3 percent of the nation's family-owned businesses employ in-laws. Family business experts say that many in-laws stay out of family businesses because they fear that the strain of working with their in-laws will hurt their marriage. Another reason is that the possibility of divorce discourages some business owners from bringing in-laws into the corporate fold. Marriages may end, but the business must go on.

The next generation to take over a family business can assume a variety of roles. Which role is played depends on needs, interests, and personal qualities. The decision to join a family venture is both subtle and dynamic and can take many years and several periods in and out of the business to solidify. Three categories of roles can be identified:

1. **Helper or faithful apprentice**—Learning from the "bottom up," the helper sometimes stays on as the dutiful apprentice, sometimes not having a formal title or position but expected to perform all kinds of tasks.
2. **Stepping stone**—Allows an individual to gain job experience by using the family firm as a stepping stone on a career path. It provides an opportunity for personal growth and development of business skills necessary to move into the next stage of a career. It also fulfills the sense of personal obligation members of the younger generation are likely to feel toward the family business.
3. **Socialized successor**—When younger-generation individuals join the family business they become socialized with the strong likelihood of becoming the next-generation president. Thus, they have an opportunity to be creative, innovative, and goal oriented.[2]

Figure 9.1   **The Employees of Family-Owned Businesses**

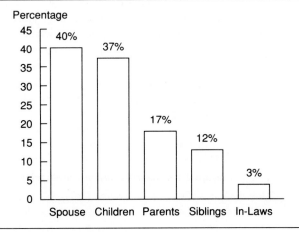

---

[2]Wendy C. Handler, "The Family Venture," in William A. Sahlman and Howard H. Stevenson *The Entrepreneurial Venture* (Harvard Business School Publications, 1992), 311–321.

Several complications can arise as a younger-generation person enters the family business. Sometimes it is difficult to establish boundaries between the business and family life, resulting in tensions that spill over into both domains. This person also runs the risk of becoming a permanent person-in-waiting as owners–founders unconsciously may prefer not to let go or may want to prove that no one can fill their shoes. A related issue is establishing credibility, a slow and gradual process between parent and child. Founding parents have difficulty believing the children ever grow up. They expect their offspring to enter the business but fail to give them authority or encouragement. Family business owners often have higher expectations of family members thereby implying that because they are family, praise is not necessary.[3]

Advantages and Disadvantages of a Family Business

Some economic development economists believe that the family is a major barrier to entrepreneurial activity. They contend that instead of encouraging and supporting entrepreneurial endeavors, the family dampens incentives to achieve, discourages risk taking, and impedes the mobilization of capital. The obligation to share the wealth with family members or elders in order to provide support and security may deter the potential entrepreneur from building a nest egg large enough to invest in a business. The fruits of an investment may also be subject to family sharing, so the child of a family business owner may not view the benefits of entrepreneurship as positively as does a nonfamily member.

The counterargument is based on a **resource dependency model,** which contends that the family may be instrumental in helping the entrepreneur establish a business. It may be that an entrepreneur is dependent on the family for initial capital, room and board, building space, tools, encouragement, and moral support to help start the business. "The family may also help the fledgling entrepreneur obtain access to suppliers, merchants, creditors, market authorities, local officials, and persons with economic power and influence" (e.g., extension of credit when the family guarantees payment).[4] Table 9.1 provides an overview of some key advantages and disadvantages of family controlled firms.

Conflicts sometimes arise when relatives look at the business from differing perspectives. Those who are engaged in daily operations may choose to conserve their salary in order to retain capital for future investment and growth in the company. Other relatives not involved in operations, such as silent partners, directors, or stockholders, may prefer to receive higher levels of payout in the form of dividends.

Other conflicts are generated when "favorite" children are promoted to executive positions ahead of others. The problem is aggravated when those family members who are promoted are viewed as less competent than others. Weak offspring of founders of companies or those relatives who must be "taken care of" eventually

---

[3]Ibid.

[4]Wayne E. Nafziger, "The Effect of the Nigerian Extended Family on Entrepreneurial Activity," *Economic Development and Cultural Change* (1968): 19–24.

Table 9.1	Advantages and Disadvantages of Family Controlled Firms

Advantages	Disadvantages
• Long-term orientation	• Less access to capital markets may curtail growth
• Greater independence of action —less (or no) pressure from stock market —less (or no) takeover risk	• Confusing organization —messy structure —no clear division of tasks
• Family culture as a source of pride —stability —strong identification/commitment/motivation —continuity in leadership	• Nepotism —tolerance of inept family members as managers —inequitable reward systems —greater difficulties in attracting professional management
• Greater resilience in hard times —willing to plow back profits	• Spoiled kid syndrome
• Less bureaucratic and impersonal —greater flexibility —quicker decision making	• Internecine strife —family disputes overflow into business
• Financial benefits —possibility of great success	• Paternalistic/autocratic rule —resistance to change —secrecy —attraction of dependent personalities
• Knowing the business —early training for family members	• Financial strain —family members milking the business —disequilibrium between contribution and compensation
	• Succession dramas

Source: Manfred F. R. Kets de Vries, "The Dynamics of Family-Controlled Firms: The Good and The Bad News," *Organizational Dynamics* (Winter, 1993): 61.

lead to more serious problems later. In some cases a nonrelative enters the firm who becomes a spectacular superstar in terms of management talent, becomes indispensable, and then demands a portion of the business.

Figure 9.2 illustrates the normal overlap of family and business systems, as well as a situation in which the overlap leads to excessive, destructive conflict.

Common Cultural Patterns in Family Firms

Similar patterns occur over and over again across a wide variety of circumstances and demographic changes. These patterns are related to different methods of dealing with authority, goal attainment, decision making, and coping with conflict. Three patterns have been discovered in the research:

1. **The patriarchal or matriarchal family** is characterized by a dominant authority figure and family life revolves around the needs and wishes of that person. All major decisions about the family are made by this person and family

Figure 9.2   **Normal and Excessive Family–Business Overlaps**

In a "normal" situation the overlap is within reasonable limits and thus manageable.

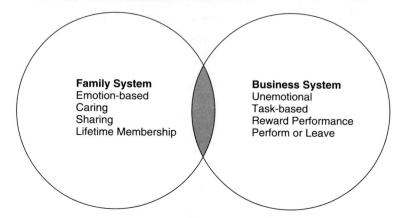

When the overlap is excessive conflict can be destructive.

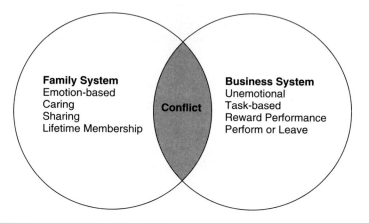

Source: Adapted from Paul Rosenblatt, Leni de Mik, Roxanne Marie Anderson, and Patricia A. Johnson, *The Family in Business* (San Francisco, CA: Jossey-Bass, Inc. 1985), 131–135.

members are expected to follow obediently. The family leader sets the goals for the entire family, with the spouse and children playing subservient roles. In setting goals for the family, the leader is often secretive about activities, rarely taking children or even the spouse into his or her confidence.

2. **The collaborative family** shares the power. The head of the family often takes the spouse and children into his or her confidence and relies on them for information and ideas when making decisions. The family creates and shares goals and values and places a high priority on maintaining family solidarity. Family members see the interdependencies in their relationship and make every effort to work cooperatively. Difficult situations such as death, retirement,

choosing a successor, and estate planning are discussed and debated. Collaborating on these kinds of problems can lead to increased understanding within the family and increased family solidarity.

3. **The conflicted family** does not share goals, with individual/personal motives and desires guiding everyone's action. Family members are distrustful of each other and seem to be constantly defending themselves against the designs of others. Relationships are counterdependent in nature and are always in conflict. Family members rarely communicate with each other, avoid each other, or rely on lawsuits to establish their position. This type of family is characterized by mistrust, alienation, and conflict. Members are unable to develop problem-solving mechanisms to resolve their differences.[5]

A similar set of cultural patterns can be outlined according to the family's philosophy about business decisions, as described in Table 9.2. Three basic philosophical orientations can be identified:

1. Some families choose **business first,** supporting what is best for the company, including its customers, employees, and shareholders. They select sound business principles and policies to administer such matters as compensation, hiring, and titles. They believe that these principles are sound and constitute excellent criteria by which they will be able to make tough decisions even if they lead to unequal treatment of family members.

2. Those families that choose the **family first** believe that the family's happiness and cohesiveness should come before anything else. Their decisions favor family equality and unity, even if they come at some expense to the company's future. Such families will allow every family member to enter the business, pay everyone equally, and guarantee their jobs for life. Differences in quality of decision making and contributions generally are not recognized.

3. The third philosophy seeks a **balance** between the two previous orientations and posits that any decision must provide for both the satisfaction of the family and the economic growth of the business. This **family enterprise** approach implies a long-term commitment to the future of the business and the family and requires the family to creatively resolve conflicts between the two interests.

Competitive Advantages of Family Firms

Individuals are attracted to work in family firms as opposed to careers in corporations for many reasons. Individuals work with and report to a family member in whom they can confide. By growing with the firm, they viscerally understand what makes their colleagues and the business tick. The best family businesses convert this understanding into an efficiency that breeds more effective management. Also, compared with a large corporation, family firms afford more flexibility, control, compatibility, trust, and opportunity.

Externally, in a world of images and perceptions, the experience of dealing with a family member can reassure a customer as much as speaking to a firm's

---

[5]W. Gibb Dyer, Jr., *Cultural Change in Family Firms* (San Francisco: Jossey-Bass, 1986).

Table 9.2
Family Philosophy's Impact on Business Decisions

Business Decision	Business First	Family First	Family Enterprise First
Entry Rules	For specific job, if qualified	All welcome	Opportunities will be developed for all individuals in or out of the business, depending on family business needs
Compensation	As job description warrants	Equal pay for all members of same generation	Acceptable family standard of living assured for everyone
Stock Ownership	According to business philosophy (that is, all to chief executive or distributed according to contribution or possibly among nonfamily employees)	Equal to branch of family	Equal values of all—some in business stock, others in passive investments or entrepreneurial opportunities
Dividends	None	Stable, fair return to capital	Variable, modest return of capital
Titles and authority	Based on merit in a business hierarchy honoring the principle of each person having only one boss	Equal titles for all members of same generation and role in decision making for all shareholders	Equal roles for all those with high degree of competence
Governance	Board of outside directors	Broad family consensus	Representative family council
Role in community	Leadership	Voluntary	Active according to family needs and individual interests

John Ward, *Keeping the Family Business Healthy* (San Francisco: Jossey-Bass, 1987).

president. Internally, few people in business with family members have cause to second-guess their partners' motives. A sense of trust has the potential to make family partners more secure, more open, and more informed than any team of unrelated persons could be. Presenting themselves as a family operation, owners can convey an image of stability that the company is in business for the long haul and will provide continuity for customers and employees alike.[6]

Family values and influences can make a positive impact on the operation of a business. According to researcher Peter Davis, three advantages may be forthcoming:[7]

1. **Preserving the humanity of the workplace.** A family business can easily demonstrate higher levels of concern and caring for individuals than are found in the typical corporation.
2. **Focusing on the long run.** A family business can take the long-run view more easily than corporate managers who are being judged on year-to-year results.
3. **Emphasizing quality.** Family businesses have long maintained a tradition of providing quality and value to the consumer.

---

[6]Leslie Brokaw, "Why Family Businesses Are Best," *Inc,* March 1992, 20–22.
[7]Peter Davis, "Realizing the Potential of the Family Business," *Organizational Dynamics* (Summer 1983): 53–54.

Problems in Family Businesses

Problems in family businesses are often different from the problems that confront nonfamily-owned businesses. When close relatives work together, social and emotional variables often interfere with business decisions. Over time, many problems may be acknowledged, but others may lurk in the background without recognition, sometimes ultimately causing serious, or even fatal, consequences for the family business.

Narrow or Outdated Viewpoints

Originators of family businesses view their creation as their "baby." Those relatives who are silent partners, stockholders, or directors often see only dollar signs when judging capital expenditures, growth, and other major matters. Relatives who are engaged in daily operations judge major matters from the viewpoint of production, sales, and personnel necessary to make the company successful. Often viewpoints conflict. Because the family business owner is usually the boss, his or her decisions are largely unquestioned by other family members. But what will happen after the death of the owner, when the ownership is diffused among members of the family? Sons, daughters, grandchildren, and spouse may be in conflict and will perhaps be constantly competing for financial advantage. Conflicts that were latent during the life of the original owner can materialize after his or her death.

Not Matching Rewards with Contributions

A typical unrecognized problem in a family business is the proliferation of family members within the company, particularly after the firm's profitability has been established. Members of the owner's family frequently hold positions and draw salaries that are not commensurate with their contributions to the company. Sometimes key personnel are added long before they are needed. In other cases, an owner might be inclined to hold down expenses and not hire needed personnel. The family business owner often is subject to the "I'd rather do it myself" syndrome, failing to delegate adequately.

The Sky Is the Limit

Setting realistic goals and objectives is a process generally ignored within the small business, particularly in terms of long-run opportunities. The family business owner usually is involved in day-to-day operations and finds it difficult to plan for the long-term future. Often action is not taken today to adjust for almost-certain changes in business conditions that could have substantial impact on the business tomorrow. The family business owner sometimes neglects to set realistic goals and objectives in the intermediate or short term.

Brother-in-Law Needs a Job

One of the most common problems in a family business is the hiring of relatives who do not have talent. When a close relative says, "Bob needs a job badly," the emotional aspect of such a family relationship is hard to fight. It will be hard to fire Bob if he turns out to cost more money than his presence is worth.

The major concern is not necessarily the relative but how he or she affects other employees. In some cases a relative can demoralize the organization by his or her dealings with other employees. For example, he or she may loaf on the job, avoid unpleasant tasks, take special privileges, or make snide remarks about family members.

My Family Is the Greatest

Every parent has a natural tendency to favor his or her children over others. The family business owner often believes that his or her child will naturally succeed to the ownership and management of the business and that the child has the competence and ability to operate a successful enterprise. It is difficult to recognize that a son, daughter, son-in-law, or daughter-in-law might have other needs and interests that preclude his or her entry into the family business. In addition, some family members may not have the ability to successfully operate the small business. What, then, does the family business owner do about the management succession problem? Should professional management be hired?

High Nonfamily Turnover

Some family-owned companies are plagued with a high turnover among their nonfamily employees. Sometimes relatives are responsible. They resent outside talent and, at best, make things unpleasant for nonfamily executives. In other cases top-notch managers and workers leave because promotions are closed to them. They see relatives being promoted to executive positions and their own career advancement at a dead end.

The Aging Entrepreneur

When relatives in a family-owned business grow older, they may develop an attitude of status quo. They do not want things to change and are afraid of risk. With this attitude they can, and often do, block growth in their family's business.

After years of effort in building a successful enterprise an aging owner may become tired and knows that he or she cannot continue indefinitely as the head of the family business. Should the owner retain the business for his or her family or should the business be sold or merged? The owner probably feels a lifelong sentimental attachment to the enterprise and would be gratified to have the family continue the business as an external monument in memory of its founder. The family business owner is apt to be quite emotional on this subject, and may not fully appreciate the fact that monuments do not pay for food, clothing, and shelter for the surviving family.

The same personal traits that made a family business owner successful can impede the growth and profitability of the business. The drive for accomplishment, ego involvement, willingness to make decisions, and dedication to hard work sometimes limit the owner's perspective as to when he or she needs assistance.

The Inflated Ego Problem

The egotistical and confident family business owner believes that he or she is indispensable to the success of the business and must have a say in every phase of the business, often denying well-educated, well-trained children or key employees the opportunity to demonstrate their competence. It is difficult for this owner to recognize the need for successor management. Yet, the owner is aging, and his or her decision-making competence is diminishing.

The Key Personnel Problem

The family business owner who is getting on in years decides not to sell or merge the business, and recognizes the value and contributions of key employees—the persons who often provide continuity of management during the owner's lifetime and after his or her demise. The owner must determine how best to keep these key employees within the business. What type of compensation package might be suitable and attractive to them?

The Key Personnel–Absentee Ownership Problem

A unique problem occurs when ownership of the business passes to family members who are not active in it. Key personnel might be quite competent to provide continuity of good management, but also might be resentful of absentee owners receiving what seems to them to be a disproportionate share of earnings through dividends. The problem can be accentuated if a family member succeeds to the presidency of the business without first having been active in the business and having gained the respect of key personnel. Without a respected member of the family active in the business at the helm, will the key personnel exert their best efforts on behalf of the business? What can be done to motivate key personnel?

Role Reversal and Sibling Rivalry

A family business owner can find himself or herself in an awkward position when employing a parent. This role reversal may be a difficult adjustment given the history of relating as a son or daughter. The parent may experience resentment, especially if the work is tedious, unrewarding, or difficult. Sibling rivalry problems of jealousy, power, and competitiveness, perhaps existing since childhood, are now exacerbated in a more stressful functional setting.

Many times when members of a family are active in the business, it is difficult to make objective decisions about the skills and abilities of each other. For example, one says about another relative, "He was lazy when we were kids, and he's still lazy." Or a distinguished wife says about an aunt, "What does she know about the business? She's only here because of her father's money."[8]

---

[8]Adapted from R. Levinson, "Problems in Managing a Family-Owned Business," U.S. Small Business Administration, Management Aid #2.004, 1987; and Benjamin M. Becker and Fred Tillman, "Family Owned Business," 2d ed. (Chicago: Commerce Clearinghouse, Inc., 1978).

The Succession Issue

One problem that most family businesses experience is planning how to pass control of the business on to the next generation. Chapter 5 has examined some of the key strategic issues in **succession planning;** however, it is important to review some of the family business concerns (see Table 9.3). The cruel, hard fact is that one generation succeeds the other with biological inevitability. Yet most family-owned businesses never formulate succession plans.

There are a number of reasons for this failure to plan for an orderly transfer of family businesses. In some cases the owner/founder is the roadblock due to his/her **anxiety** over **death.** Psychologist Manfred Kets de Vries states: "Some presidents of family firms act as if death were something that happens to everyone except themselves. Talking about death is taboo. Raising the topic is viewed as a hostile act, and may be interpreted as a wish to have the person in question dead."[9] Owners may also fear losing their identity by turning over the company or they simply hate losing their powerbase.

In other cases it may be the family that represents the roadblock. Not only can the family members be hampered by the death anxiety already mentioned but they may also suffer from the fear of **sibling rivalry** or a change in their position or status.

Whatever the reason, Leon Danco, founder of the Center for Family Business, states: "It is a daily miracle that there are any owner-managed businesses left in the world with so few making plans for their own continuity. The toughest thing for the business owner to realize is that time is running out on him."[10]

Death and retirement are facts of life, and a well-conceived succession plan has to take them both into consideration. Inevitably, transferring a family business is always difficult and often emotional; it affects family members, bankers, employees, managers, competitors, lawyers, spouses, and friends. The only sure thing is that *failing* to plan will make the transfer more difficult and painful.

The Next Generation

One generation's failure to successfully pass ownership of a business to the next generation is well documented. Many small businesses go out of existence after ten years, and only three out of ten survive into the second generation.[11] More significantly, only 16 percent of all family enterprises make it to the third generation.[12] The average **life expectancy** for a family business is 24 years, which, ironically, is the average tenure for the founders of a business.[13]

---

[9]Manfred F. R. Kets de Vries, "The Dynamics of Family Controlled Firms: The Good News and the Bad News," *Organizational Dynamics,* Winter 1993, p. 68.

[10]Leon A. Danco, *Inside the Family Business* (Cleveland, Ohio: Center for Family Business, University Press, 1985).

[11]Donald F. Kuratko and Richard M. Hodgetts, "Succession Strategies for Family Businesses," *Management Advisor,* Spring 1989, pp. 22–30.

[12]John L. Ward, *Keeping the Family Business Healthy* (San Francisco, CA: Jossey-Bass Publishers, 1987).

[13]Richard Beckhard and W. Gibb Dyer, "Managing Continuity in the Family-Owned Business," *Organizational Dynamics* 7–8 (Summer 1983).

Table 9.3
Barriers to Succession Planning in Family Firms

Founder/Owner	Family
• Death anxiety	• Death as taboo 　—Discussion is a hostile 　　act 　—Fear of loss/aban- 　　donment
• Company as symbol 　—Loss of identity 　—Concern about legacy	
• Dilemma of choice 　—Fiction of equality	• Fear of sibling rivalry
• Generational envy 　—Loss of power	• Change of spouse's position

Source: Manfred F. R. Kets de Vries, "The Dynamic of Family Controlled Firms: The Good News and the Bad News," *Organizational
Dynamics* (Winter, 1993), 68.

At first, succession planning seems to be no big problem: All the older generation has to do is designate which heirs will inherit the business. Ideally, the older
generation trains one or more heirs and then lets the younger generation take over
while the founder is still alive. Unfortunately, this is often easier said than done.

One researcher, Wendy C. Handler, has examined the importance of the **next
generation** in family business and contends that the quality of the succession
experience is based upon individual as well as relational influences. Figure 9.3
illustrates the description framework of these factors.[14] **Individual influences** are
within the individual and impact his/her personal experience of the succession
process. They include personal needs fulfillment (career, psychosocial, and life stage)
as well as the ability to personally influence the fulfillment of those needs in the
context of a family business. **Relational influences** involve the next generation's
relation to a group or other individuals. Two of the influences—mutual respect
between generations and sibling accommodation—are interpersonal. The remaining
two issues—commitment to family business perpetuation and separation strains
due to family involvement—are intergroup. That is, they are a function of the
overlap between family and business systems.

As research continues on these influences for the next generation, we will
learn more about the quality of succession and hopefully, better understand the
succession process.

Effective management succession can reduce the legal problems associated not
only with ownership, but with taxes and inheritance as well. As with many of the
challenges confronting family business, professional advice is useful in effectuating

[14]Wendy C. Handler, "The Succession Experience of the Next Generation," *Family Business Review* (Fall
1992): 283–308.

Figure 9.3   A Descriptive Framework of the Succession Experience

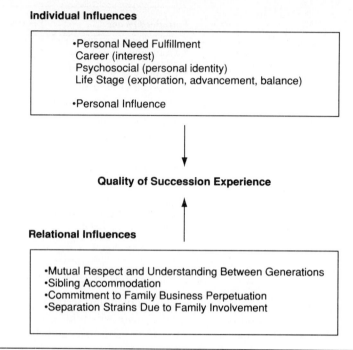

Source: Wendy C. Handler, "The Succession Experience of the Next Generation," *Family Business Review* (Fall 1992): 288.

proper succession plans.[15] Yet, despite all of the recommendations to properly plan, finance, and manage a family firm, many business owners watch their firms self-destruct because they have not confronted the challenge of succession. In attempting to avoid problems and prepare for succession there are four critical steps to remember.[16]

Identify a Successor   Difficult as it is, every owner-manager should identify a successor or at least the characteristics and experience needed in such an individual. The basic question that must be answered is: Who can do the best job in keeping the firm going? Survival and growth should be the primary areas of concern. The greatest hurdle is getting the key manager(s) to select someone. If one relative is designated as the heir apparent, how will the other relatives take it? Some founders,

[15]Glenn R. Ayres, "Rough Family Justice: Equity in Family Business Succession Planning," *Family Business Review* (Spring 1990): 3–22; and Ronald E. Berenbeim, "How Business Families Manage the Transition from Owner to Professional Management," *Family Business Review* (Spring 1990): 69–110.

[16]Donald F. Kuratko and Richard M. Hodgetts, *Entrepreneurship: A Contemporary Approach,* 2d ed. (Fort Worth, TX: The Dryden Press/Harcourt Brace & Co., 1992), 615–621. *See also:* Ivan Lansberg, "Twelve Tasks in Succession," *Family Business* (Summer 1993): 18–24.

not wishing to hurt anyone, never make a decision. If there is no identification of a successor, the next two steps are also ignored.

Groom an Heir   In some firms the entrepreneur will pick a successor and let it be known. However, many owners waiver when it comes to actually announcing a choice. There may be one person who appears to have the inside track or a small number from whom the successor will be chosen, but no one knows for sure who will get the job and no formal grooming takes place. Regardless of who eventually heads the firm, precious time is lost learning the job. Even if the heir is designated, the founder finds it difficult to relinquish the authority necessary for effective grooming. The ego factor proves to be a major stumbling block.

Agree on a Plan   Effective succession requires a plan. There usually is a need for a detailed person-to-person discussion of how responsibilities will be transferred to the successor. No owner wants to step aside for a person who will change things dramatically; no entrepreneur wants to see a lifetime of effort unraveled. If the person leaving the position has any power to influence future decision making, now is the time to use it, if only by spelling out a philosophy or general course of action.

Attention should be given to day-to-day operations. Such consideration helps eliminate (or at least reduce) feuding. At this point, it can be helpful to bring into the plan those who will be most affected by it. This participatory approach will often co-opt some critics and alleviate the fears of others. In any event, it is a useful management tactic for helping to create unity behind the new person.

Consider Outside Help   Promotion from within the family can be a mistake. When the top person does a poor job, does promoting the next individual in line solve the problem? The latter may be the owner clone. Or consider family-owned businesses that start to outgrow the managerial ability of the top person. Does anyone in the family really have the requisite skills for managing the operation? The question that must be answered is: How can the business be effectively run and who has the ability to do it? Sometimes this calls for an outside person. In family businesses, there is the ever-present ego factor. Does the owner have the wisdom to step aside and the courage to let someone else make strategic decisions? Or is the desire for control so great that the owner prefers to run the risks associated with personally managing the operation?[17]

Prescriptions

The term *family business* connotes and projects positive images based on values held in high esteem by many different peoples. One reason for this image is the entrepreneurial culture and management practices that allow continuity from one generation to the next. It is important to create a **cross-generational** culture and

---

[17]Johannes H. M. Welsch, "The Impact of Family Ownership and Involvement on the Process of Management Succession," *Family Business Review* (Spring 1993): 31–54.

continuously reinforce these values and practices over various stages in the life cycle of the firm. Table 9.4 attempts to integrate the requirements of strategy and culture in easing the firm through its intergenerational stages.

By means of strategic exploration, organizational development, financial restructuring, and behavioral modification the stage can be set for renewal and growth. Innovations in reward or information systems, diversification, or specialization where in-house expertise already exists or other creative changes can stimulate necessary regeneration throughout the organization stages.

In an early-stage operation several questions may be asked:

- What, exactly, is the area of responsibility of each family member, and to whom is he or she responsible?
- What is the compensation: salary, bonus, equity shares, or some mixture?
- What will be done in the event of a disagreement or if one family member is not pulling his or her weight?
- What is the ante—can it be redeemed if the joining family member changes his or her mind?

Table 9.4
Integrating Strategies for Cross-Generational Success

	Requirements	Strategy
Strategy	Knowledge of product and manufacturing process technology	Specialization
	Knowledge of market	Diversification
	Overcoming absence of growth vision	Entrepreneurial approximations
Organization	Role differentiation and separation between family and business and between owners and managers	Task and business terms
	Focused structures	Reward systems
	Communication and problem solving	Rationalize duties and responsibilities
	Overcoming distance from customers and employees	
Finance	Creating an information-rich decision-making environment	Information systems
	Funding of new ventures	Family venture capital company
	Overcoming obsession with data and the "nervous money" syndrome	
Family	Equity structures that support "focused" organization structure and a distinction between active and inactive owners	Ownership equity structures
	Commitment and sense of ownership by nonfamily employees	Programmed training for family members
	Overcoming inappropriate roles and boundaries between founder, family, and business	Human resource policies and practices
	Overcoming perception of high social risk	Competence based job opportunities

Source: Adapted from Ernesto J. Poza, "Managerial Practices that Support Entrepreneurship and Continued Growth," *Family Business Review* 1, No. 4 (Winter 1988).

The regeneration process requires new blood and fresh initiatives to maintain and grow the business. Individuals planning to enter an early-stage family business should ask themselves:

- What are my strengths and what do I need to work on?
- What other aspects of the business do I need to learn?
- Do I have the qualities to be a leader?
- Am I happy working in the business?
- Is there anything else I should do to meet my goals?[18]

In addition, researcher Wendy Handler suggests that family member applicants are more likely to achieve success for themselves and the business when they are clear about their needs and communicate them directly to the owner in charge. Learning as much as they can about the business, followed by a specialization stage to acquire specific skills, is part of the strategy. Then they must become a generalist to learn how to manage. By developing a relationship with a **mentor** or several people who can act as coach, protector, moderator, role model, counselor, or even friend, the applicant has support on several fronts. They should also look to respected individuals outside the family for counseling and long-term development because parents may have difficulty accepting the reality that their children are grown up. Acquiring practical **business experience** outside of the family business helps increase their knowledge, experience, and confidence and is also likely to enhance their credibility with employees who may be skeptical about qualifications of family members.

Other strategies such as establishing various communication mechanisms (both informal sessions for sharing and formal sessions for planning and exchange) have been suggested. For example, the creation of a **family council,** one composed of all family members critical to the future of the business such as founder, spouse, and children, as well as other relatives who have significant interest in the business, could be one significant solution. A council can help establish open communication, understanding, and trust and serve as a planning forum for the family and the business. It can also allow the airing of problems or differences that might otherwise be ignored.

Family members should take responsibility for the development of both the business and their own personal goals by asking themselves:

- Am I cultivating an "entrepreneurial mind" (i.e., attitudes and behaviors)?
- What are the critical skills and know-how required in the business now and in the immediate future?
- In what ways will my personal needs be satisfied through the family venture?
- If we plan to double the size of the business in the next three, five, or ten years, what are the likely requirements?
- What do I bring to the team now, and later?
- What are my strengths and what do I need to work on?
- What additional relevant "chunks" of experience do I need and how can I get them?

---

[18]Wendy C. Handler, "The Family Venture," in Sahlman and Stevenson *The Entrepreneural Venture* (Harvard Business School Publications, 1992), p. 320.

- What other aspects of the business do I need to learn?
- Do I have the qualities to be a leader?
- Am I happy working in the business and does it "give me energy"?
- Is there anything else I need to be doing to meet my goals?[19]

Conclusion

Family businesses have been in existence for many centuries and there are strong indications that they will continue to survive, split, merge, or continue in a new vein in the future. Government has discovered the economic development, job creation, and taxation advantages of family businesses and is currently designing legislation to help keep businesses within the family. John L. Ward concludes that family business is an old idea whose time has come.[20]

Family businesses are unique combinations of rationality and emotion. Family business members claim that family businesses are special because they are a labor of love. Building a company with people you care about can be more fulfilling than building a firm with people who do not share so fundamental a connection. Common sacrifices and success enable individuals to achieve a real sense of pride in accomplishing the dual goals of business growth and family happiness.

---

[19]Jeffry Timmons, *New Venture Creation,* 3rd ed. (Homewood, IL: Irwin, 1990).

[20]John L. Ward, "What is a Family Business and How Can We Help?" *Small Business Forum* (Winter 1990/1991): 63–71.

CASE • *The Outstanding Outsider and the Fumbling Family*

Thomas A. Teal and Geraldine E. Willigan*

> Sooner or later, every family business has to choose between professional and family managers.

In 1945, after four years in the navy, Paul Ballisarian came home to a suburb of Chicago, married his childhood sweetheart, and joined his father in the family butcher shop. Paul was an energetic young man, and when his father retired several years later, he transformed the business from a retail shop into a meat wholesaler.

The wholesaling business grew steadily as Paul developed personal relationships with a growing list of fine restaurants that counted on Ballisarian Beef for a dependable supply of superior meats. Paul was in his element. He liked doing business on the basis of friendship and quality, and he enjoyed his role as a local church, community, and business leader. He made an excellent income, and he and his wife, Jeanette, were happily married and had two children, Gregory and Katherine.

Paul hoped that one day Gregory would help him run the company and eventually take over. Then in 1965, when Katherine was 16 and Gregory still only 12, Paul hired Mike Post, with a B.S. in business administration, as his second-in-command. The business had become too much for one person to handle, though with Mike's drive and energy, it was not enough for two. Mike began looking for new ways to expand.

He started by selling meat to hotels and fast-food chains, markets Paul had always avoided. Then he began to wholesale frozen Argentine beef, and gradually he moved into other food products—prepared foods, cheese, and fish. By the mid-1970s, he had established Ballisarian Beef in areas far beyond the scope of Paul's original expansion, and by 1980, his ventures accounted for more than half of company revenues.

Paul, who did business with his friends and made friends of all his customers, saw Mike's aggressive acquisition of new markets as peripheral to the core business of restaurant meat supply, but despite their differences in age and outlook, Paul and Mike worked together well. They handled customer relations separately but shared the important investment and personnel decisions.

Paul paid Mike a handsome salary and, at Mike's urging, incorporated Ballisarian Beef and allowed Mike to acquire 20 percent of the stock. At the same time, Paul gave 10 percent of the stock to each of his children.

Mike was a friend of the family. Gregory saw him almost as an older brother, and Katherine and Bonnie, Mike's wife, only two years apart in age, were like sisters.

In 1975, fresh out of college, Gregory came into the business as expected. Gregory learned everything from meat cutting to accounting and showed himself to be his father's son—hardworking, affable, a good friend to his customers, and

---

*Thomas A. Teal and Geraldine E. Willigan are both associate editors at Harvard Business Review. Reprinted by permission of *Harvard Business Review*, "The Outstanding Outsider and the Fumbling Family" by Thomas A. Teal and Geraldine E. Welligan September–October, 1989 pp. 14–30. © 1989 by the President and Fellows of Harvard College. All Rights Reserved.

a light in the community. He took over some of his father's accounts and landed a number of his own, but he spent most of his time in the office or the warehouse, where he knew nearly everyone by name. If the meat cutters or the accountants had a problem, they went to Gregory instead of his father.

Mike continued the expansion of wholesale food supply. Supermarkets were his latest target, first the independents and then a couple of chains not yet big enough to cut all their own meat and supply their own delicatessen departments. By the late 1980s, Ballisarian Beef had a staff of 47, a modern processing facility, revenues of $23 million, a profit margin of 4 percent—and a life-threatening problem of succession and control.

Scene: The Ballisarian dining room. Jeanette Ballisarian, her white-blond hair pinned back, sits at the head of the table with her two children on either side. Gregory is now in his mid-thirties, slightly balding but athletic, fashionably dressed, and handsome. Katherine, his older sister, is an independent, cheerful, 40-year-old divorceé with strong opinions about almost everything. Dinner is over.

Katherine (putting down her coffee cup): You know, Greg, I can't believe you didn't see this coming.

Gregory: Oh come on, Katherine, he's been with the company 24 years! He owns 20 percent of the business and manages a bigger piece than that. He's never seemed dissatisfied. Why should I have seen it coming?

Katherine: Because we're all getting older, that's why. He may have been willing to work for Dad all these years while he was young, but he's smart and aggressive and experienced and, most of all, he's 46. And he's ready for something more. I understand it all too well.

Jeanette: Understand what, Katherine? What has Mike done?

Gregory: Well, Mother, Mike's been having delusions of grandeur. On Monday he presented Dad with a formal business proposal that amounts to lunacy. He wants us to spin off his side of the business and form a separate company—and give him half.

Jeanette: Why ever would he do such a thing?

Gregory: It's a mystery to me. He's not a Ballisarian. And surprise, surprise, this is a family business.

Jeanette: Gregory dear, it's still your father's business, and if Mike is having any kind of problem, your father will handle it.

Katherine: No, Mother, I'm afraid the problem is more serious than that. I don't think Dad *will* handle it. Dad wants everything to stay the way it is, the way it's been. At least I think he does. You know he won't talk about the future. But if he doesn't take Mike seriously, we're going to lose half of what we've got. Half? Two-thirds is more like it. Mother, like it or not, the truth is that Ballisarian Beef is Mike Post's business.

Jeanette: Katherine, I'm really amazed! Mike is your father's employee.

Gregory: For heaven's sake, Katherine, you're letting your friendship with Bonnie get the better of your common sense.

Katherine: And you're kidding yourself, Greg. How much of your profit comes from restaurants? 30 percent?

Gregory: More like 60 percent. And growing.

Katherine (wagging her finger at him): Careful, Greggie, I can see your nose getting longer. Look, Greg, I'm sorry if it hurts your feelings, but you forget that I've seen the books. Half of that 60 percent from restaurants is all the products—and all the hotels and the restaurant chains—that Mike is responsible for. He's a go-getter, Greg. Meat alone to the restaurants you handle isn't more than a third of the business. You know that's true.

Gregory: What I know is that we've been incredibly generous with Mike, and we've given him opportunities he wouldn't have had anywhere else—and suddenly he wants us to hand him half the business. It makes me mad.

Katherine: Of course it does, Greg. You've been jealous of Mike ever since you went to work for Dad. But the fact is, Mike made his own success. His proposal isn't the least bit lunatic. He's earned it, and he'd make us all a lot of money. And if he doesn't get it—or something like it—he's going to leave. Why shouldn't he? And who'll run the company then?

Gregory: Katherine, Mike doesn't run the company. He does some seat-of-the-pants managing, but he doesn't make strategy. I do the thinking and planning. But most important, I'm the one who's been making sure we fill the orders and pay the bills and maintain our reputation.

People buy from us because they know we're dependable and we have the highest possible quality at excellent prices and on terms that none of those people could match anywhere else. We're a family doing business with other families. They'd cut off their arms before they'd buy from someone else, and with good reason. We've helped them through crises, we've carried them in bad times, we've never compromised on quality or held their feet to the fire on price or let them down on a holiday weekend or any other time. Why do you think Mike does so well? You think he has some special magic with his big-time customers? He doesn't even know half their names! We make him look good because we have a reputation and we live up to it. We, Katherine. The Ballisarians. Dad and then me and then maybe my sons.

Katherine: I hate to break it to you, Greg, but if you take over, Mike's going to leave for sure. He couldn't work for you. You're like his little brother. And if Dad doesn't do something for Mike now, Mike's going to leave in a matter of months. And we can't afford it.

Gregory: Do something for him? Dad gives him more freedom than anyone else in the company—including me—and we've made him a part owner. Katherine, you've always got a lot to say about what we're doing wrong, but where have *you* been for the last 14 years? I didn't see you at the office every day.

Katherine: Oh come on, Greg, you wouldn't give me an office if I wanted it. All *your* precious Ballisarians are males.

Gregory: Really, Katherine, what do you know about the way this business is run?

Katherine: How much do I need to know? You say Mike doesn't make strategy. But I'll tell you what he does make—money. And if that's not more important than strategy, I'll eat my hat. You say we make him look good, but you read the financials; he makes us look good too.

Gregory: Now you're just talking dividends.

Katherine: You bet I am.

Jeanette: Gregory and Katherine, you're forgetting yourselves. Your father owns this company and runs it, and he doesn't need your help. Not yet. Not for a long time. To hear you talk, you'd think he was already in his grave. He's only in Omaha.

Katherine: I'm sorry, Mother, but Dad doesn't run the company the way he used to. He doesn't have the energy for it. He isn't in Omaha trying to land some big account. He's socializing with his friends.

Jeanette: Sometimes I think he has more energy than he ever did. And you know what he says? He says that going to work every morning is what keeps him young. Leaving the business would kill him.

Katherine: Mother, believe me, Greg and I love and respect Dad. But the business is facing a crisis, and Dad simply won't talk about it. We have got to talk plain English if we're going to survive.

Gregory: What do you mean, survive? Don't be melodramatic.

Katherine: Greg, I happen to know that an investment group—including two customers—has offered to back Mike in his own wholesaling operation. They want him to have total control of the business, and they're talking about structuring the deal so he can eventually buy them out.

Now I'm not sure Mike wants us to know that, but we do. Bonnie told me. All Mike wants us to know is in the proposal he gave Dad. And you know what that proposal tells us?

Gregory: It tells us he wants half the company. . .

Katherine: It tells us he doesn't want to leave. He wants to stay with Ballisarian Beef. But he's 46 years old, and he doesn't want to end his days as some kind of junior clerk. The question is, why do we want to *force* him to leave?

Gregory: You mean we should give him what he wants?

Katherine: I never said that. I said it was a reasonable request. It would keep him and his customers inside the company. It would give him a bigger share of the profits, of course, but the way he expands he'd make that up in a couple of years.

Gregory: And by then he'll have us in soft drinks and ski clothes.

Katherine: Well, I've got a better way out—for everybody. There are only three points that matter.

Number one: Unless we're willing to give Mike some measure of control—a bigger share of the company, autonomy in his own area of the business, control of some kind—he's going to leave us. And he's going to take his customers with him.

Number two: Unless Dad steps down or gives up a good part of his control, we can't accommodate Mike, and you, Greg, will perish of frustration, and the business is going to get set in its ways and die of paralysis. We must have been the last company east of the Rockies to get computers.

Number three. . .

Gregory (sarcastically): Yes, I can hardly wait for number three.

Katherine: Number three: I think the time has come to professionalize this company. I think we should make Mike CEO.

Gregory (rising involuntarily to his feet): You've lost your mind!

Katherine: Oh, sit down and listen to me. It makes sense. What Mike really *wants* is to be CEO. He'll settle for being head of his own separate division, he'd probably settle for more stock, but making him CEO is better for all of us. I mean it. We've given away too much stock already. And making him head of his own division is a setup. It carves out a unit that Mike can walk away with anytime he wants.

As for booting him out the door, well, that would be completely idiotic. No. The way to hold on to this company *and* its profits is to make Mike CEO. You can be president, Greg, and chairman of the board after Dad retires. It makes perfect sense.

Gregory: Dad didn't build this company so his grandchildren could work for Mike's kids.

Jeanette: If Michael is making the demands you say he is, we should ask him to leave. I can't believe he could be so ungrateful.

Katherine: Mother, Mike is the one who puts the food on this table. And pays for the house in Florida and the condo in Hawaii and the trips to Europe and the furs and the jewelry. Mother, Mike brings in 70 cents of every dollar you and Dad spend. Dad knows that. Maybe that's why he won't even discuss the question of who's going to take over.

Gregory: Katherine, those hotels and supermarkets that Mike went out and got are doing business with Ballisarian Beef, not just with Mike. It makes me mad that you think Mike can walk away with any customer he wants. Sure, I'd prefer that Mike stayed on. I'd be terribly sorry to see him go. But if Mike's departure cost us even 20 percent of our profits, I'd be surprised.

Katherine: Aren't you forgetting that if Mike leaves, we have to buy back his stock? At 20 percent over book—isn't that what the agreement says? Borrow that much money, and the debt service alone is going to eat so far into profits you'll have to give up the country club. So you're right. You'll be terribly sorry to see him go. Dad may not want to give up control, but he's not foolish enough to let Mike get away.

Gregory: If the stock is all you're worried about, you just leave that to me. With the kind of slow, steady growth our business and our name depend on, the worst that can happen is a couple of lean years. But we can certainly survive—and prosper—without Mike. I'm a professional manager too, you know. I'm conservative, I stick to a core business, and I cultivate my customers the way Dad always has. But I also understand money, I understand risk, and I understand Ballisarian Beef.

As for Dad, well, we'll see just how far he's willing to go for Mike.

Jeanette: Indeed we will. I'm just glad your father isn't here now. This conversation would break his heart.

Who Should Do What?

We asked five experts on family business to write a letter giving advice to any one of the characters involved.

John A. Welsh *is retired director of Southern Methodist University's Caruth Institute of Owner-Managed Business, which he started in 1970, and the founder of Flow Laboratories, Inc.*

Dear Katherine,

The situation at Ballisarian Beef is a tragic drama that has been reenacted thousands of times in every culture since before the Babylonian camel traders built their city into a commercial center.

The final scene, with only rare exception, is predictable. Paul Ballisarian, old, bitter, and broke, is unable to comprehend the motives of the bright young man he trained, trusted, and brought into his family—and gave an even bigger share of the company than he gave his own son. Neither can be fathom the bitter quarrel between his children.

Ironically, Katherine, you are simultaneously a principal in the drama, a part of the audience, and one of the victims of the tragedy. From that unique position, you may be the only person who can alter the course of events and make the final curtain one of those rare exceptions.

Your father is faced with the most intractable dilemma of his lifetime. It is not the business decision but the emotional one that seems so insurmountable. If he accepts Mike's proposal, what can he offer his son Gregory that will be comparable or better? How will he explain to his cronies that he gave away 50% of such an important part of his life's work? How can he convince your mother and Gregory that Mike is not just greedy and ungrateful?

Perhaps your father could find a commendable reason for agreeing with Mike's proposal. Suppose he saw the possibility of avoiding a major tax burden on his son and daughter by making gifts to them each year starting right now. I don't know what the net worth of Ballisarian Beef is, nor the fair market value as a going business. But breaking it into two pieces and selling half of one piece to Mike Post at the low price Mike would find attractive might justify your father's giving his children a large part of the remaining half at a low valuation for tax purposes.

It seems unwise to make Gregory a large minority stockholder in Mike's company since Gregory will someday become the manager of Ballisarian Beef. He and Mike will likely disagree on the management of Mike's company. Your father could claim to foresee this possible conflict and resolve it by giving you an interest in Mike's company while giving Gregory proportionately more interest in Ballisarian Beef. Mr. Ballisarian could tell his cronies that he trained and guided Mike and successfully launched him in his own business. Now he is doing the same thing for his son.

There is one thing I would ask of you, Katherine. Do not ever again mention where the profits of Ballisarian Beef come from. Just think what your father and brother are hearing when you say Mike generates most of the business and the profits. You impugn your father's success. He is a proud man and has every right to be. He took over his father's butcher shop and built it into a $27 million a year wholesaler. Of course, he had help—and maybe more help than he can ever admit—but he is Mr. Ballisarian of Ballisarian Beef, the successful son of a humble butcher.

The numbers you want to present to your father are the inheritance tax numbers. If anything should happen to him, heaven forbid, it's his family who will have to pay the big taxes. Mike won't have that problem, because he is only a stockholder. With the company making 4% on the bottom line from $27 million in sales, that puts earnings at more than a million dollars. If a price-earnings ratio of five to ten can be applied to Ballisarian stock, your father's 60% ownership could imply inheritance taxes on $3 million to $6 million.

The company probably has a lawyer or accountant your father likes and trusts. That person is the most likely to succeed in getting your father to listen to the facts and to at least consider the suggested solution. Perhaps you could talk to that person to initiate the discussion. You should then step back and allow your father to display his wisdom.

These suggestions will not be easy to execute, but you have to try something. You must do it right away and without emotion. Let the IRS and your father's love for you take care of the emotion.

Katherine, I must tell you that had Mike Post asked for my advice, I would tell him that his proposal to your father displays his great respect and affection for Paul Ballisarian. In my opinion, however, Mike should end the relationship as quickly as possible and get on with starting his own business. Mike has no future with Ballisarian Beef.

I cannot help but wonder if Mike knows his proposal will be rejected and offers it only to salve his conscience when doing what he really wants to do—own and manage his own business. In my opinion, making Mike CEO of Ballisarian Beef will not satisfy him, and it will make Gregory's position untenable.

With that in mind and assuming your father agrees to divide the company, you might make an agreement with Mike that he can buy the stock you will receive from your father on terms equal to those available from Mike's new investors. That would make the Ballisarian deal as good as the one available from the new investors while giving Mike an existing customer base.

No doubt Mike will take some Ballisarian customers with him when he opens his business. Beyond that, he will find that Gregory was correct. Customers deal with Ballisarian Beef, not Mike Post.

If you find yourself the proud owner of stock in Mike's company with an agreement for Mike to purchase your stock over time, find yourself an investment adviser you can trust. You will want to reinvest the proceeds from stock sales in a diversified portfolio that provides current income and growth in principal over the long term. In years to come, you will want to be financially independent of the family.

The part of the company that Gregory receives may never grow to $27 million in sales. Gregory seems to be a chip off the old block who will manage much like his father did. But he too may find a bright young person to help him run the business. We may all be pleasantly surprised when Gregory gets to be his own boss.

Sincerely,
John

Joseph A. Baute *is the chairman and CEO of the Markem Corporation in Keene, New Hampshire*

Dear Mike,

Thanks for describing your proposal to Paul Ballisarian. As a nonfamily CEO in a family business, I had many strong reactions, and I'd like to offer you some fairly blunt but, believe me, heartfelt advice.

In a nutshell, Mike, I suggest you withdraw that proposal as quickly as you can and then—putting yourself in the Ballisarians' shoes—rethink it step-by-step.

The proposal you've given them is essentially a loss for them and a loss for you as well. It threatens their control and their future prosperity. It does nothing to promote Paul's dream of seeing his son eventually run Ballisarian Beef. It ignores Gregory's present frustration and his need for broader experience and helpful coaching. It weakens your own position by undermining the commitment you've demonstrated so well in 24 years of outstanding performance. Mike, even if they agreed to your proposal, my guess is that the tensions created by the new business would ultimately cause a break between you and the Ballisarians, bring about your departure, and lead to a period of economic difficulty for all of you. I can't believe this is how you'd want to end the productive relationship you've had with this family all these years.

I'm convinced there is a win-win proposal you can make instead by picking up the leadership opportunity posed by Paul's succession dilemma. Obviously, he doesn't want to retire completely. He founded the business and loves what he does.

In his heart of hearts, Paul probably knows Gregory is not yet ready for the top management job. But Paul needs help to chart a course that gives Gregory the breadth and experience he needs without diminishing your responsibilities, interest, and performance. My guess is that he doesn't know how to make the critical decisions affecting the business and the lives of those important to it.

You hold the key, Mike. Paul must see you almost as a son, must feel great pride in what you and he have accomplished together. With his 60% interest, he could always have done whatever he wanted, but he has focused his efforts on his restaurant niche and left the newer growth segments and the overall performance responsibility to you. Why not talk to Paul? Sit down with him, reaffirm your commitment by telling him you mean to invest yourself fully in the continuing success of Ballisarian Beef, and offer the following suggestions:

Begin by recognizing Gregory's need for more experience and responsibility. Suggest that he assume some of your accounts and, if Paul is willing, some of his. This would give you an opportunity to play a greater coaching role with Gregory and to spend more of your time on other ventures that further build the business. You and Paul can agree on whom to promote from within the organization to fill Gregory's current job.

The next logical step in this discussion should be to clarify Ballisarian Beef's organizational structure in a way that faces the succession question and considers your qualifications for the top job you've earned. Encourage Paul to think about assuming the chairmanship and appointing you president and CEO and Gregory executive vice president and chief operating officer. This would send a clear signal that a succession plan exists, and it would formalize the mentoring responsibilities so important to you and to Gregory.

By taking a leadership role in helping Gregory develop his potential, you are relieving Paul of a very difficult training task and ensuring the eventual family succession. Paul is certain to welcome your efforts to help Gregory prepare himself to run the business after you retire. In terms of age, experience, and performance, this is after all the logical sequence—Paul, then you, then Gregory. Point out to Paul that it also gives Gregory the challenge he needs right now and eliminates the frustration that comes through in so many of his statements and actions. (Just between you and me, it's hard to work for one's father without feeling inadequate and losing a sense of self.)

As this new structure evolves, suggest to Paul that he create a small Ballisarian board of directors. This board might consist of you, Paul, Gregory, several capable outsiders, and, if Paul is willing, his daughter Katherine as well. She is clearly able and interested.

Mike, I see this as a winning scenario for everyone. Ballisarian Beef continues without external or internal threat. Company leadership develops a logical succession plan. Paul continues to do as he likes with his own restaurant niche, and you get a chance to follow him as CEO as you work to develop Gregory as your own successor.

Instead of throwing down a challenge, you offer a solution that preserves the best in the Ballisarians' family business and that gives you room for your own business potential. But it all depends on you, Mike, and on your leadership and sales ability. Paul has been more than fair with you in the past. If you can make your case convincingly, he'll be fair with you now. Good luck.

Sincerely,
Joe

Charles E. "Gus" Whalen, Jr. *is president of the Warren Featherbone Company of Gainesville, Georgia, which his great-grandfather founded in 1883.*

Dear Greg,

I well understand your difficult position as a family member leading your company from what it was to what it will become. The situation you've described concerning Mike Post is symptomatic of a larger organizational issue that has not been resolved: Where is Ballisarian Beef headed?

As a family business, Ballisarian Beef can grow only so far. You recognize Mike Post's special contribution, but his existence in the company really runs counter to the family environment as you define it: a business run by Ballisarians. If that's the type of family business you want, Mike Post probably will leave, as will others, not because of earnings or ownership but because he won't really fit in. You will be able to maintain such a narrowly defined family business only as long as you can find competent family members to fill the organizational slots. Once you're out of family, you're out of business.

If you'd like Ballisarian Beef to really grow, you need to reconsider the nature of your family business. You will have to enlarge the "family" to encompass all of your 47 employees. These people need the respect, dignity, and sense of control that you want for yourself. They have hopes and dreams and probably can make a tremendous contribution to "their" business so long as they are given genuine recognition, compensation, and a chance to control their destinies.

In short, you need to find and help develop new heroes for your business. There are all sorts of ways to build this into your corporate culture without substantially changing the ownership. Ownership in small companies really has limited value—it's valuable only when you sell, and only if you can find a qualified buyer. Most people want recognition, compensation, and a chance to develop and contribute their talents *now* as opposed to the possibility of selling their piece of the rock later.

Greg, I offer three suggestions as you work through this period of transition:

1. Discuss the situation with your Dad and work out transition of ownership. Do it now, while he's still in good health.
2. Discuss Mike's situation with Mike. Your knowledge of his intentions and desires is secondhand. Perception and reality may be different.
3. Decide which road you want to see Ballisarian Beef travel in the years ahead. Do you see your company as a family business dominated in fact and concept by Ballisarians? Or do you see your company as a larger, more professionally run organization where "family" is open to competent professionals like Mike who are recognized and paid to see their collective dreams become reality?

Chances are your industry, like most, is going through consolidation; the big customers and suppliers are becoming much larger. Ballisarian Beef's ability to survive over the long run may depend on continued expansion. In that case, you will need a larger, professional family to take care of the business. Your job, then, is to grow the family.

Sincerely,
Gus

Wendy C. Handler *teaches family business management at Babson College in Welles-ley, Massachusetts, and has participated in her own family's businesses.*

Dear Katherine,

Haven't you been on the sidelines long enough?

It's natural for family members to be concerned when the family business is threatened by a powerful outsider, a potential takeover, or intensified competition. But for you, the situation must be not only worrisome but also frustrating. You care deeply about the business and have some valuable information, but you don't have much credibility with your father and brother for a number of reasons.

For one thing, you're not actively involved in the company. Second, as you mentioned, the family business has employed only male Ballisarians fo: three generations. Third, your advice is threatening to your brother because it implies change from the status quo. He believes that Ballisarian Beef will live forever and that he'll succeed your father; your recognition of Mike's capabilities tells him there may be someone more qualified to take over the company. Fourth, you seem to be accusing your father and brother of mishandling the whole situation, which is of course insulting and makes them discount whatever you say.

Your strong feelings about Mike's proposal to spin off part of the company may stem from your frustration at having information but no credibility—or it may be more deeply rooted than that. Maybe one of the reasons you're reacting so strongly is that you have some underlying resentment about being excluded from the business. At Ballisarian Beef, as in most family businesses, the men run the business and the women are on the sidelines. Maybe you're more dissatisfied with that than you've been willing to admit. If you are really interested in the company, it may be time to break the generational pattern and stand up for yourself. You have a right to participate. You certainly seem to have the commitment, and you have a lot to offer, like your ability to see things clearly and your willingness to raise difficult issues.

Getting involved in the business would go a long way in giving you the credibility you need to be heard. But it might also give you some insight into what actually goes on at the company. You seem to be pretty impressed by Mike Post, but you may be surprised to learn how much your father and brother contribute and how hard they work, and you might come to respect Gregory more. Also, many people who go to work for a family business discover just how special it is to be part of the team. If you make a similar discovery, you may be more empathetic with Greg and much less willing to turn things over to Mike.

But joining the business doesn't mean your father and Gregory should follow your advice. It's not for you to be the sole decision maker. Their opinions are also very important, so any course of action should be discussed among the three of you and, ultimately, with Mike.

You can be a catalyst to stimulate that kind of conversation. So far, you've been trying to act as an objective adviser. You shouldn't. Because you're a family member, you have your own biases. But you can take your father aside and encourage him to talk to Gregory, and you can take your brother aside and urge him to approach your father. And when the family has decided what to do with the business, you should encourage your father to have a frank conversation with Mike to clarify Mike's goals and whether he can achieve them at Ballisarian Beef. Performance reviews are one good way to determine how personal and career aspirations align with organizational goals and to monitor competence.

A professional manager can be very valuable—if the culture is conducive. Your company seems to be strongly oriented toward family. It could be, then, that Mike will have to leave if he can't get along with Greg. On the other hand, it may be possible to divide responsibilities between Mike and Greg along product or market lines. Each could be a vice president of operations, Mike for wholesale products and Greg for beef.

One good thing about the crisis at Ballisarian Beef is that it is forcing your family to confront things that have been there right along. Now it has to deal with them. Please understand how extremely threatening this is, especially to your father, and be careful not to criticize him. Succession planning is a disturbing topic. Think of your mother's remark at the dinner table; to her, the conversation suggested your father was "already in his grave."

For your father and your brother, the crisis is an opportunity to plan. For you, it's an opportunity to encourage family members to interact openly and to rethink your feelings about the business and the role you want to have in it. Bear in mind that even if you do join the business, your father and your brother will have a hard time accepting you because you don't conform to the role women have traditionally had in your family. You must be prepared to work very hard—even harder than Gregory—in order to be taken seriously. And as unfair as that is, the satisfaction and credibility you gain may well be worth it.

Sincerely,
Wendy

Harry Levinson *is president of the Levinson Institute. He has published more than a dozen articles in* HBR, *including "Conflicts That Plague Family Businesses" (March–April 1971).*

Dear Paul,

Now it's your turn to face the most difficult problem that the head of a family business has to deal with—the problem of succession. Clearly, you are proud of the business you have built and of the immense contributions Mike and Gregory have made.

Since Gregory is a competent executive, you naturally want to keep the company in the family and see him as president and CEO. And since Mike is not a family member, it's easy to think of him as an employee. But the fact is that he has taken both the family and the company to heart. He has acted as if he *were* a member of the family. And for all practical purposes, he has worked just as hard, just as imaginatively, and just as successfully as any member of the family could have.

In many ways, Mike is like you. He took the business into areas where it had never been before. He did such a good job of it that all of you profited handsomely. No doubt he even taught Greg a significant part of what Greg knows. As Katherine points out, it is with considerable justification that he feels entitled to succeed you as chief executive officer, even if he doesn't say so. Like most men his age and with his record, he is ready to be at the top of an organization—if not yours, his own. He knows that, and so do you. (It's surprising nobody has yet recruited him away from you.) But his wish to be his own man makes life very difficult for you because, after all, this company is your child. You don't want to become a nothing, which is what so often happens to chief executives when they give up their organizations.

But give it up you must. Not to do so, as Katherine points out, means that you will likely lose a significant portion of it anyway. Giving it up means several things.

First, you must face the anguish you feel and talk it over with a psychologist who can help you explore your feelings about the company, about Mike and Gregory, and about yourself and the prospect of role "on the shelf." If you should choose this course, then you cannot interfere with Mike and his right to run the business. That will be hard for you to do and is another reason you should be involved in continuing discussions with a psychologist.

Next you have to deal with Gregory. Greg is entitled to his place in the sun, and he will have it. In the meantime, both you and Mike will have to support him as he learns to develop new dimensions of the business to prepare himself for the chief executive role. In fact, Mike can be a mentor for Greg and teach him those aspects of the business he knows best, but you will have to help Greg accept this subsidiary position until his own turn comes. You will have to help him understand the difference between his contribution and Mike's. He needs to understand his naturally rivalrous feelings and his reluctance to see the family business in anyone's hands but his own. Greg, too, will need to talk with someone outside the company who can help him explore his feelings.

Once you have come to understand what you must do if you're to hold on to Mike and keep the company growing, then it will be time to work out an agreement that guarantees each of you a unique niche in the organization without intruding on Mike's capacity to provide leadership for the company as a whole.

The process I have described here will mean a good deal of pain and discomfort for you. All entrepreneurs are reluctant to pass the baton. Most also fail to resolve family tensions that can interfere with an orderly succession of leadership and control. They become defensive, resistant, and rigid. Sometimes even when they do relinquish ostensible authority, they go on trying to run the organization as if they were still CEO, and that, of course, exacerbates internal conflicts and makes it difficult for the organization to follow a single leader and a clear course of action.

You must not lose sight of what matters most. The fundamental issue is the survival of the company. This is no time for self-centered thinking or for failing to understand the deeply held wishes and aspirations of the people you work with.

I offer you one more word of caution. Beware of the complaints of your peers who have passed on their businesses, or sold them off, and now feel deserted and angry. There is no need for you to abandon the business or turn your back on it. Both Mike and your son will profit from your wisdom, from your help in resolving disputes, and from their shared desire to please you by making your company more successful. Give them your attention and your affection. Take pride in what you have wrought. You have given life to an organization that, if you properly manage this stumbling block of succession, will become an evergrowing monument to your creativity.

Sincerely,
Harry

CASE • *Is Kohler Company Bathing in Paternalism?*

Barbara B. Buchholz, Margaret Crane*

> Third-generation head Herbert V. Kohler, Jr., contends the company is a facilitator: it offers opportunities and amenities to attract and keep employees, but it does so for a price rather than for free, which makes for smarter business and a surer way for employees to appreciate benefits.

Kohler Company, founded 118 years ago, is the nation's leading manufacturer of plumbing products, generating $1.5 billion a year in sales and employing 14,000 worldwide. It is a diversified family company, whose culture has long reflected benevolence toward employees and residents of Kohler, Wisconsin, a Camelot-like woodland with a population of 1,800 one hour north of Milwaukee.

Is the village a paradigm of the benevolent side of capitalism? Many would say yes as they survey the riches: cultural and recreational amenities ranging from a sleek design center to a formidable Scottish-mound golf course, clean air, sparkling lake and wildlife preserve, excellent schools, and curving streets lined with steeple-topped churches, village hall, and colonial-style homes. Even factory buildings are neatly clustered behind the imposing executive headquarters.

A model community is what second-generation head Walter Kohler had in mind in the early 1900s and what his successors forged with help from master planners, first the Olmsted brothers and later the Frank Lloyd Wright Foundation. More recently, corporate executives have boasted that no one lives "across the tracks" here. Kohler remains a place where all turn out for high school graduations and Fourth of July band concerts.

But ask Herbert V. Kohler, Jr., 52, current chairman, president, and grandson of the founder, if he thinks his company is paternalistic, and you do not get a simple response. Sitting in his company's boardroom overlooking the factories and

---

*Barbara B. Buchholz and Margaret Crane are partners in Family Industry Resource Management. They are coauthors of *Corporate Bloodlines: The Future of the Family Firm.* This case was reprinted from *The Family Business Review* Vol. IV, #3 (Fall 1991) with permission of the publisher. © Jossey-Bass Publishers, 1991. All rights reserved.

the firm's world-class resort that Kohler helped transform from a dormitory for immigrant workers nine years ago, Kohler spoke in a wide-ranging, two-hour interview. The handsome bearded leader, who came to work full-time 25 years ago, talked in his low, mellifluous voice about paternalism and company towns, the vicissitudes of running a successful enterprise stalked by eager buyers, and the need to diversify into related businesses in order to keep pace with changes in homes of the 1990s and beyond.

Kohler expresses his views about why scions should determine their own destinies, but he is adamant about keeping the business in the family. The family currently owns 98 percent of the stock, which resides in the hands of family members, the Kohler Foundation, and various trusts. Kohler's branch, one of two, controls 70 percent. He works with his wife of two years, Natalie A. Black, general counsel, vice-president of the Interiors Group, and a board member; a cousin, J. Michael Kohler, who manages a plant in Spartanburg, South Carolina, and sits on the board; and his sister, Ruth DeYoung Kohler, who runs the John Michael Kohler Arts Center in nearby Sheboygan, Wisconsin.

As to a fourth generation, it is a possibility that he relishes but not one that he counts on. His three grown children are actively pursuing graduate business studies, acting, and management consulting careers.

FBR: Tell us about the company's history of paternalism, of developing a town with workers in mind.

Herbert V. Kohler, Jr.: How do you define *paternalism?*

FBR: According to Webster's Dictionary, it's a system under which an authority treats those under its control in a fatherly way, especially in regulating conduct and supplying their needs.

Kohler: In that context, we don't offer paternalism. In fact, that's so far off the mark of what we're doing and of what we have done. At Kohler, it's a combination of self-interest and good citizenship. The rich living environment of this area of Wisconsin makes it easier to attract executives. Our real estate and hospitality businesses are growing enterprises for the company, enabling us to offer a variety of opportunities to both blue- and white-collar workers. For example, the company set up a construction subsidiary. We did not want to create a typical company town that builds houses for employees and rents them. That way employees tend up owning nothing. My predecessor and uncle, Walter Kohler, Sr., encouraged employees to create a building and loan, which they owned, akin to a latter-day mutual savings and loan. Any worker could go to that building and loan and borrow money, buy a plot, and build a house at cost from the construction end of the company. The house was theirs.

FBR: Do you give employees anything for free?

Kohler: We don't give anything outright. Many amenities are offered at cost. It's been our experience that people over time simply don't appreciate something for nothing. Rather, if they've paid at least 50 percent of the cost, they take a degree of ownership. We consider ourselves a facilitator. We create opportunities, options. It makes for smarter business, a better and more equal partnership between both sides.

FBR: Along that line, what does the company get from this philosophy?

Kohler: Little turnover. Healthier, more productive employees. We've had generations of families who work at Kohler.

FBR: Give us an example of opportunities.

Kohler: Many companies build an athletic facility that's offered free to employees. We didn't. We built one that operates as the centerpiece of a development north of the village. The Sports Core is open to all of Sheboygan County's 100,000 residents. It acts as an attractive amenity for the hotel guests. Blue- and white-collar employees of Kohler Company get to use it at a 20 percent discount on the membership fee. They don't pay an initiation. They get another 30 percent discount if they exercise at least 13 times a month for 30 minutes, but not during work. This keeps employees healthier, cuts health costs, and reduces insurance rates.

FBR: How about another example?

Kohler: We've got a day care center on site, open to employees and residents of the area. Kohler built the building and leased it to an independent operator with expertise in providing quality care. The center is licensed to take in 104 children from 6 weeks to 12 years of age. Everyone who uses it pays.

We haven't planned elder care, though we'll consider it in the future. The nature of Kohler is intergenerational, young and old. It's also moderate and high income, a healthy mix.

FBR: How about flexible work arrangements—staggered shifts, compressed work weeks, working from home?

Kohler: We have flexible work schedules in certain cases. We give the opportunity to work from home if the work permits it, like computer work, or after a pregnancy, or in other unusual circumstances. We have summer hours, where employees toil nine hours a day four days a week and then four hours on Fridays. There's also some flexibility in certain departments. Some take 30 minutes instead of 60 for lunch, then close up earlier.

FBR: Tell us about health and pension benefits, cultural amenities.

Kohler: When it comes to health and pension benefits, I don't think we necessarily offer more than other companies. But we insist on getting good value for the dollars we spend. We attempt to hold down the costs of benefits, keep them in line with inflation or just a little bit more. (The company has cut costs by switching to processing its own health claims and having an ongoing utilization review.)

We also create good work opportunities in other locations. They're all removed from expensive metropolitan centers, whether in Texas, South Carolina, or France. The life-styles are safe, relaxed, clean, and comfortable. Boring? Never in Wisconsin. Cultural opportunities abound. For more than 50 years, the Kohler Foundation has brought distinguished guest artists here. I sometimes wish it was more boring, less to choose from.

The costs here and elsewhere are also a lot, lot less than on the coasts and in large cities. A house in San Francisco, for example, would be four times more. And yet the salary differential probably would only be 20 to 25 percent higher.

FBR: Are there negative effects from the philosophy you've described?

Kohler: I can't think of any other than when we began our investments in hospitality and real estate, a lot of doubting Thomases in our executive ranks resented the flow of capital into those activities from our manufacturing operations.

FBR: Are employees still appreciative of your philosophy now?

Kohler: We don't have problems hiring people. We usually employ whom we target. We're not the highest wage rate in the county. When we set out to build the hospitality business, our attitude was that the business had to stand on its own financially at most four years after it began. At this point, it has succeeded.

FBR: Let's get back to our original question about the beginnings of Kohler's philosophy of taking care of employees.

Kohler: There's been a long history of entrepreneurship and social concern in our family and the company. Uncle Walter, who built the dormitory for workers, did so because European immigrants coming to the shores of America found few places to stay other than next to a flop house. Imagine a young husband coming alone to this country and trying to find a place to work and live. Not only where his moral values attacked but his work ethic as well. Chances were that he wouldn't call for his family back home. So, we would have lost all the way around.

FBR: What did Kohler do?

Kohler: After the factory was moved from Sheboygan to this site in 1900, workers resented commuting the four miles by streetcar. They began to put up little shacks around the periphery of the plant. So Uncle Walter went to England, met with a wild-eyed socialist by the name of Sir Ebenezer Howard, the architect of the English garden city. They toured Europe, came back to Boston, and sat down with the Olmsted brothers, who laid out Harvard University's campus and Central Park in New York, and created a plan for the village of Kohler, one of the earliest planned communities in the country. Part of the plan included a place for employees to live, a pub, bowling alleys, and barbershop, all called The American Club. The creation of this was a little bit to my thinking paternalistic—that a worker deserves not only wages but roses.

FBR: Was there any concern that the village and company would become a single entity?

Kohler: No. We forbade executives of the company to run in an election for the village government, which is still in effect. Uncle Walter did not want the company dominating or controlling the community. He wanted the town to be a healthy, growing environment. Today, a little less than 40 percent of the households actually work at Kohler, which altogether has an employment of 6,000 here. But we think that's healthy. We do a strong job in promoting land lots to the outside community, though we give employees a slight discount.

FBR: Your company has a second 50-year plan in place for development of the community by the Frank Lloyd Wright Foundation?

Kohler: We had purchased this huge piece of land in 1910 and in the 1920s for $25 an acre. Inflation has taken care of the high values, so we're not pushed to rapidly develop it. As a result, we use our development plan, which is constantly changing, as a general guide. Plans are subject to approval by the village planning commission. Where we deviate, we have to show good cause. Remember, the middle and upper management at Kohler can't serve in government or run it.

FBR: Have you looked at other planned communities to get ideas or see what they've done with this concept?

Kohler: I haven't seen one that's similar to ours. Columbus, Indiana, home of Cummins Engine Company, has focused on selecting preeminent architects to erect individual architectural structures. That's the only thing that's cohesive there. Cummins used to be our largest vendor and customer. They sold us engines for our generators, and we sold them power units and generator sets. In the mid-1980s, Cummins purchased our largest competitor, so we severed ties. Also, in creating our second master plan in 1977, we looked at Reston, Virginia, and Columbia, Maryland. We also toured Hershey, Pennsylvania, to study hospitality before we converted The American Club into a resort in the late 1970s.

FBR: Could anyone establish a company town today?

Kohler: It's probably impossible. People wouldn't tolerate it. The only way it might work is where a company has an operation in such a remote region that it would be hard to get to. People wouldn't want to invest long term in such an isolated area.

FBR: Tell us about your decision to come to work at Kohler. We heard the corporate mantle wasn't easy to bear and that you rebelled as a teenager.

Kohler: The company went through an eight-year strike from 1954 to 1962 that got incredible notoriety. Here I was with the name Herbert V. Kohler, Jr.

To please my father, I went to Exeter but was kicked out. I got myself into Choate (another proper school) and did fairly well. And then, like my father, I went to Yale University. To get my military obligation out of the way and then come back, I entered a six-month Army Reserve program. When I finished, I went to Europe for six months, lived with a Swiss family, and attended the University of Zurich, where I took courses in German. I then decided not to go back to Yale but to apply to a small Midwestern school, Knox College, in Galesburg, Illinois.

FBR: How did your parents react?

Kohler: At that point, I had become a complete rebel. My mother had died in the 1950s, and my father and I weren't really communicating. I wrote poetry, started a magazine, and fell in love with the theater. There was a student director whom I despised. She was the apple of the dean's eye and got straight A's. After she graduated, I ran off with that director, and we married four months later! Prior to my marriage, I met my father at Union Station in Chicago and told him I was going to marry and was not taking money from him henceforth.

Later, unbeknownst to my father, I went back to Yale University and finished with a degree in business administration.

FBR: When did you start work in the company?

Kohler: We have to talk about part-time versus full-time work. I worked on the farms when I was 16. Then in the spring of my eighteenth year, I asked my father to give me the toughest job he had in the factory for the summer. He put me in the foundry as a dumper of a molding line. I'll never forget my first day.

I had to take about 200 engine blocks, each weighing about 90 pounds, out of a mold when they were red hot, clean the flask, clean the block, knock off the sand, and put them on a pallet. I was on the wrestling team at Choate, but this was as much as I could physically take. On my first day, we cleaned up the area at the end of the work shift and were a little ahead of schedule. I meandered out to the scrap yard. It was a brilliant, sunlit afternoon. I found this huge, marvelous piece of scrap, flat, circular in circumference, and I lay down on it and fell asleep. The whistle blew, and all employees on that shift rushed past me. I lay there until 9 P.M. It was dark, and all of a sudden someone was poking me and saying, "Do you think he's dead?" It was a guard. That was my first day at work in Kohler Company proper.

FBR: Did you go back the next day?

Kohler: Absolutely.

FBR: Did it get easier?

Kohler: It always gets easier once you're there and involved.

FBR: When did you start full-time work?

Kohler: In 1965, as a research technician and from there became a schedule coordinator, then a general supervisor. Although my father asked me into the company, I never worked with him. I told him I'd come in on one condition—that there would be absolutely no protection or special treatment of me. I told him that I'd have to be allowed to make whatever mistakes in the normal course of things. He couldn't cover for me. He complied.

FBR: Isn't that hard to do when your name is Kohler?

Kohler: At first it was very hard for people to speak up to me. But if I challenged them hard enough on avant-garde issues, they'd get back and question me.

FBR: Did anyone show you what to do, train you?

Kohler: The job was explained as it is for any employee. Any Kohlers were welcome at the company, but to receive a promotion, they had to prove themselves about twice as much. This was a marvelous weeding process. Hence, the reason that only four Kohlers are in the company today.

FBR: How and when did you inherit your leadership position?

Kohler: In 1968, our president, formerly a plant manager who came up through the ranks, was 56. My father, chairman, was 76. Both died in the same week, and the company had a major crisis. My father had thought carefully about succession and acted by promoting within, never expecting this to happen. I'll never forget the week after the funerals. The treasurer, senior vice-president of industrial relations and general counsel, and I sat around the room across the hall from the boardroom. I was manager of factory systems. We decided who'd be senior vice-president and president. Who would be chairman. What I would be. I became vice-president of operations. The treasurer became president. I became chairman and chief executive in 1972 and president in 1974 through normal succession.

FBR: What did your experience of growing up in a community with the same name as the village do?

Kohler: As soon as you stop worrying about what people say, then you can be at peace with yourself. It's hard to teach that to children. I told mine that people would say incredibly nasty things about them, and if they took those things seriously, that they'd be in a lot of trouble and neurotic. I decided long ago you have to ask yourself whether you're doing what you have to do and want to do to the best of your ability. If you keep on that track, you'll be a wonderful human being, no matter what anyone says.

FBR: How have the business and village of Kohler changed under your leadership?

Kohler: We acquired about 12 companies in the 1980s, and there were several reasons. We wanted to create a second-tier plumbing company with direct access to the rapidly growing retail markets of the home centers and hardware chains that are expanding in some markets. We did not have that access with Kohler brand plumbing products, because they were sold only to plumbing distributors. Our major thrust in that effort was to acquire private companies. We bought Sterling Faucet Company, Ownes Corning Bathing Products, Polar Stainless Sinks, Kinkead Shower Doors, and Bathroom Jewelry, a small faucet company on the West Coast. We took five profitable companies and brought them together under Sterling Plumbing Group, Schaumburg, Illinois. It's a successful, cohesive, growing retail company.

FBR: Why furniture now?

Kohler: Furniture was another thrust. We decided in the eighties that the home of the future was changing. Walls of conventional rooms were changing and disappearing. We saw a growing commonality between the bathroom and bedroom, between the kitchen and great room. To remain a leader in this decade, we knew it would behoove us to have as one of our resources a major furniture line with a reputation and philosophy much like ours. We bought Baker for that reason, a high-end premier company.

FBR: Where did you get the money for the acquisition, and does your board have to okay expenditures?

Kohler: It was acquired in 1986 and very well thought out after some healthy discussions with the board. We've never been a highly leveraged firm. We did bet the company on a foundry molding machine in the early 1970s and had to go out for a public debenture at that time, but we paid it off in the early 1980s. Our debt beyond that was minimal, so it was just an internal generation of funds and extending some long-term lines.

FBR: And the decision to acquire McGuire furniture?

Kohler: We created a new group called the Interiors Group, which my wife heads. It is headquartered in Grand Rapids. We bought McGuire in January 1990 as part of this group. It was a company I knew would make a wonderful marriage. It had been sold to Chicago Pacific. In 1989, Maytag bought Chicago Pacific and sold the furniture group to Ladd, a mid-sector company in the home furnishings area that didn't know how to deal with high-end companies such as McGuire. McGuire, based in San Francisco, was founded by John McGuire, who started the rattan boom both in the United States and the Philippines. But John McGuire confined himself to an interior design niche. As part of Kohler, McGuire will remain with interior designers, but we'll take rattan and move it into retail under the Baker name.

FBR: Do you have other plans to take over companies, including parts of Interco in St. Louis?

Kohler: I can't comment. We're always looking. Interco's Ethan Allen and Lane are excellent companies. It's a good time to buy other companies, but our plate is full for now.

FBR: With your plate full, wouldn't you love to have any, or all, of your children in the business?

Kohler: Of course, but I vowed I wouldn't push them in any direction. I tried to teach them to be independent. You don't protect children. You create opportunities, and let them get into trouble, and get burned and wiggle their way out. You don't come to their rescue. You try to see they're prepared, but once in it, they're on their own. We offered them Outward Bound when each was 16. My goal was to persuade them toward more risk, with significant personal growth if they got through it. We've been successful with all three. Sure, it's hard, but today I have three beautiful, aggressive children.

FBR: To avoid another crisis, wouldn't you encourage your children to come into the firm or put into operation a good plan of succession?

Kohler: We have nothing in writing. I never talked with my children about the business at dinner. What I tried instead was to create opportunities. All three children could come in at some point, but I wouldn't bet they would. My older daughter, Laura, is 28; her acting career has taken off. My second daughter, Rachel, is 25; her consulting career is booming. My son, David, 24, has developed some incredible relations with the union and blue-collar workforce here and has been accepted as one of the crew. He attends Northwestern University's Graduate Business School. I don't know what's going to happen. They own a little stock, and I'm trying to get more out of my estate. We have two classes: voting common and restricted. Our branch owns about 70 percent.

FBR: But who would take over if something happened to you?

Kohler: The board would decide. I've tried to have some pretty strong executives in each of the major businesses, people who really run those businesses, not puppets on a short leash. They're fairly independent.

FBR: What have you done to avoid another labor strike?

Kohler: It taught us you don't get blocked into a philosophical corner from which you can't extricate yourselves with any degree of integrity. My father and Walter Reuther, the former president of the United Auto Workers, got locked into two positions and couldn't budge. It wasn't economic; it was philosophical. My father believed in the right of every worker to make a decision about his job and joining an organization without being concerned about losing his job. Reuther believed fiercely that workers had to join the union to be protected. You avoid that, but you still take a strong stand. We were unionized in 1952. Before that it was an independent union, which later voted to affiliate with the U.A.W. for just the factory workers. My uncle, who was governor of Wisconsin beginning in 1929, also fought for workers to be able to make choices without union threats.

FBR: Are you involved in family business groups?

Kohler: I went to a few sessions with Harris Bank in Chicago. I've also sent an executive. I don't have a lot of friends in family businesses. We try to run this company, management-wise, like a public company, without short-term constraints. We even go so far as to produce our own 10K, which costs $50,000 a year, and give it to board members. It's a discipline that we've done for 15 years.

FBR: You must have had some attractive offers.

Kohler: Yes. Our sales are healthy. Raiders look at us all the time, but most know they'd have a hell of a fight. I've been offered a P/E ratio of 50 and turned it down. That's phenomenal, since most companies would take it in an instant, I think. But you have to understand that money is not our main interest. We have a mission—to create a higher level of gracious living for most levels of income. That propels everything we do, whether making a Baker chair or Kohler toilet or operating our hotel.

FBR: Is that your way to pay back others for the riches and opportunity you've been given?

Kohler: Yes. We love to create. It's worth a hell of a lot more than money.

FBR: What would you like your legacy to be?

Kohler: My mission has been consistent with the company's. Not to copy anyone. To do something a little bit better. Not just to create more clutter, but to improve that level of gracious living.

Epilogue

Company towns may seem a modern equivalent of feudalism. Workers gain jobs and homes, but they have little chance to alter their circumstances.

In the contemporary version, there is still another problem. When the company mill, mine, or automotive plant hits rough economic times, everyone may be out of work. The town may shut down.

George M. Pullman's dream of solving Chicago's social ills by building a showplace for his workers had to be abandoned after riots followed a strike in 1894. Workers resented not being able to own homes and have a say in local government.

The modern day company town mentality is less intrusive, a greater separation of state and company. Some firms have gone further and literally given employees the town. Kennecott Corporation sold its mining town of Hayden, Arizona, to workers years ago. "In the early days of the West and later the South, many company towns were established in remote locations, and a company had to build an entire infrastructure," says Kennecott spokesman Frank Fisher. "But with better transportation, there was less reason for everyone to work and live in one place. It also got too costly for a company to ride to the rescue of its tenants and fix every leaky faucet."

Still other companies no longer want their city dependent on a single business or even a handful of businesses. Columbus, Indiana, home at one time to five significant family firms, including Cummins Engine Company, a diesel engine maker that has been threatened with a hostile takeover, took aggressive measures when it saw manufacturing start to dry up in the 1970s, mirroring a national trend. City leaders knew that they could not replace all 5,400 lost manufacturing jobs with service sector jobs. Yet, they feared that if they failed to do so, they would not be able to maintain their quality of life. The solution in 1976 was to hire an economic director with the mandate to bring in new companies.

To date, 22 businesses have set up shop in Columbus, including nine Japanese companies. The number of new jobs totals 3,700, which includes some expansion at existing businesses. Most of the new firms have added between 100 and 300 jobs. "Not a big footprint," according to Brooke Tuttle, president of the Economic Development Board. "Our goal is to keep hitting lots of singles and doubles and grow steadily and not worry about home runs." Adds Tuttle, who formerly was director of manufacturing logistics at Cummins, the company is known for bestowing a rich panoply of modern architecture on its town.

At the same time, the city is not resting on its laurels. "We haven't won the battle yet," Tuttle says. "We lost a lot of jobs paying $12 to $15 an hour and saw them replaced with new jobs paying $6 to $8 an hour. We still are—and have to be—aggressive."

C A S E • *Emge Packing Company, Incorporated*

Michael E. Busing, Clemson University*

In the late nineteenth century, Peter and Barbara Emge opened a small butcher shop in Fort Branch, Indiana, a small southern Indiana rural community. The shop provided an adequate existence for Peter and Barbara who had four children— Oscar, Ralph, Christina, and Alma. Oscar and his father dedicated their lives to the meat shop and built a reputation of providing quality meat at fair prices to the community.

In 1919, it was apparent that Emge could no longer serve the growing community with the small one-room shop. Oscar acquired a parcel of land in the town and began construction of a full slaughtering operation for beef and pork. The company was named Emge and Sons. Emge served the southern Indiana area through

---

truck route distribution. A truck would be stocked early in the morning with a variety of fresh beef and pork as well as a few processed items (i.e., sausages) and would make several stops throughout the community during the day. The name Emge began to catch on in the southern part of the state and the firm began to supply grocery stores and restaurant accounts. Oscar and his brother Ralph became very active in running the company as their father began to age. The company was built up slowly, always funding capital purchases with income from operations. Emge did not believe in doing business with borrowed money and therefore never incurred debt financing.

Over the next twenty years, the company continued to grow and expand its territory. The business became successful mainly from the "mom-and-pop" grocery store accounts which it had worked hard to gain the support of. In 1948, it was decided that the company could easily serve the entire state of Indiana if it had another plant in the northern part of the state. Oscar found a small operation in Anderson, Indiana, and acquired the business. It was at this time that the business became Emge Packing Company, Incorporated. Oscar became the President and C.E.O., while Ralph helped manage the operations. The rest of Peter and Barbara's descendants continued to work for the company in both the Fort Branch and Anderson operations. The company continued to grow which necessitated expansion and modernization of both plants. By 1960, Emge became a well-known name to grocers in Indiana, Illinois, Ohio, Michigan, and Kentucky. The Emge name continued to be associated with fresh, high-quality beef and pork at fair prices with good customer service. Emge's slogan, "Just Like a Family," was symbolic of the association of customers with their own family.

In 1978, Walter Emge, son of Oscar Emge, became president while his father remained C.E.O. until 1980. Oscar Emge passed away in 1986.

Through the years, Emge continued to grow until today it employs 1,000 people at the two plants. Both plants are represented by the United Food and Commercial Workers Union. Annual sales are approximately $170 million.

Mission and Objectives

Emge's business mission is to become a major wholesale meat packing/processing company serving the midwest retail, hotel, and institutional market with fresh beef and pork as well as processed items such as hams, bacon, luncheon meats, sausage, and hot dogs. Emge attracts and maintains customers by offering fresh, high-quality products at low prices with excellent customer service.

The objectives of the firm are as follows:

1. Protect Emge's market share in the Midwest by becoming a major force in the warehouse distribution system;
2. Begin to offer more value-added, higher-margin processed items;
3. Cut low-margin fresh pork production;
4. Purchase modern packaging equipment to increase efficiency, quality, and appearance of packaging;
5. Continue buying top quality raw materials (hogs and cattle) for operations. Pay for quality.

General Environment

Although meat and meat products shipments grew 1 percent in 1988, per capita consumption of *beef* declined 3.4 percent (*U.S. Industrial Outlook*, 1988). Poultry consumption rose due mainly to consumers' concerns about health and diet. Poultry is also cheaper per pound on average than red meat which tends to weaken red meat sales (Standard & Poor's, 1989).

The industry itself consists of three major companies who slaughter more than 70 percent of grain fed cattle used for steaks and roasts (*U.S. Industrial Outlook*, 1988).

More red meat producers are beginning to expand into poultry production and are closing inefficient plants.

Imports of red meat are increasing. Australia, New Zealand, Canada, and Denmark supply about 80 percent of all U.S. meat imports. Fifty-nine percent of U.S. meat imports are beef while 31 percent are pork (*U.S. Industrial Outlook*, 1988).

At the same time, however, U.S. exports of red meat increased 23 percent in 1988. The main share of this is to Japan (Bjerklie, 1989).

Per capita poultry consumption rose from 53.2 pounds in 1977 to 82.5 pounds in 1988 (*U.S. Industrial Outlook*, 1988).

It is estimated that when adjusted for inflation, shipment of red meat grew less than 1 percent in 1989 (*U.S. Industrial Outlook*, 1989). Beef production will continue to decline, while pork production will reach a plateau. Poultry consumption per capita will be at an all-time high by the end of this year.

Long-term trends are calling for leaner meat. Research suggests that by redirecting substances in animal hormones, fat content could be decreased fifty percent (*U.S. Industrial Outlook*, 1988).

While the consumption of red meat continues to fall, it is suggested that continued profitability is achievable by introducing new products which are more value added, convenient, and nutritious (Duewer, 1989).

Industry Environment

Key Success Factors in Industry

In the meat packing industry (beef, pork, and poultry), ultimate success of course depends on a firm's ability to offer high quality at competitive prices. However, it seems to go much beyond this.

Distribution is extremely important. Since meat is a perishable product, the customer expects products to be delivered when they need them in the store—not before, and not after. This requires a firm to establish a distribution system which is not only agreeable to each customer, but which is economical to the firm. For example, a firm in Illinois cannot profitably send a truck to Ohio which is half-full five days per week. However, there is a fine line of customer service and economies of scale in distribution.

Since meat products are perishable, it is impossible for firms to have extensive inventories. Therefore, it is difficult to stock up for peak periods such as Easter and Christmas (when ham demand is greatest). It is likely, then, that the firm would need somewhat greater capacity than utilized on average throughout the year for satisfying demand during these peak periods. Also, when part of the animal is being demanded at a high rate, the other, less desirable, parts must be able to be sold in the marketplace quickly (before they perish) at prices which still allow the producer to profit or at least break even. There are three or four big names such as Kahns, Eckrich, Swift, and Oscar Mayer whose marketing campaigns have gained them extensive amounts of brand loyalty. The smaller players rely on their past track record for customer support. The name brand recognition is much more crucial in processed (packaged) items than in fresh beef and pork.

Driving Forces Causing Change in Meat Packing Industry

Recently, there have been several changes occurring in the meat packing industry which affect its structure and attractiveness. The health concerns of many Americans are causing changes in the type of meat products being purchased (Duewer, 1989). The focus by many consumers has been on the amount of fat present in the various meat products. This is leading to closer trimming of beef and pork by the meat packaging plants which, in turn, leads to fewer pounds of meat being shipped to the retailers. Hog producers are being forced to produce leaner animals (see Figure 1). Consumers are also demanding innovative ways in which the product can be

Figure 1   **Hogs are Getting Leaner**

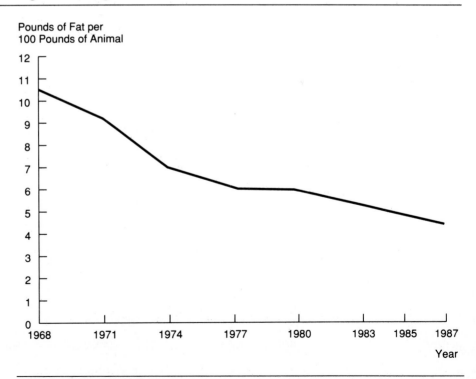

Source: *Livestock Slaughter,* National Agriculture Statistics Services USDA Summary, 1988.

prepared as well as preparations which take less time. This causes packing plants to become more consumer and product conscious.

Cost saving operations have recently been implemented in the meat industry. The major trend related to cost savings is the cutting of beef carcasses into smaller, more packagable pieces. This change to "boxed beef" has caused a shift in the way beef is leaving the packing plant (Duewer, 1989). Boxed beef refers to beef which is cut, vacuum packaged, and shipped in boxes. This trend in the industry is causing a movement away from the traditional hanging carcasses (see Figure 2). Boxed beef reduces the overall system cost, yet increases the meat packer's costs many times as their plants are not geared toward boxed beef.

Boxed beef reduces overall cost in several ways. The labor rates are usually lower in the packing firm than in the retail stores. In addition, the equipment in the packaging plants allows faster and more efficient cutting. Because beef is boxed, transportation costs are decreased as heavy carcasses are no longer being transported due to the fact that scrap and bones are removed prior to distribution. The main problem this presents to the meat packer is that margins are decreased as more actual labor is going into the product and more scrap is removed before sale (i.e., less weight actually purchased by the retailer). Therefore, meat packing firms must find other innovative ways to command a high price for the product.

Retailers are also to eliminate costs associated with selling all the cuts of the carcass. Because the cuts available are most customized, the retailers do not need to lower prices on the less popular items. This again presents a new challenge to

Figure 2   **Trend toward Boxed Beef**

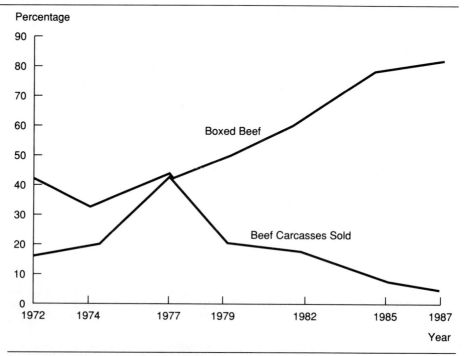

the meat packer in that it must smooth demand for all the various cuts without accepting a loss due to lack of demand for certain cuts and excess demand for others.

Strong marketing innovation is very important in order to persuade retailers to carry a particular producer's brand. The trend for leaner meats which have simpler preparations must be responded to quickly by firms who wish to have their products on the shelves.

Financial Characteristics of Participation in Industry

The financial characteristics of participation in the meat packing industry have remained fairly stable over the six-year period between 1983 and 1988 (see Table 1). The profit margin of meat packing is lower than other industries in general. It is a business in which profits depend on volume.

Total industry sales have been steadily decreasing over the past five years (see Figure 3). The 1988 dollar sales have increased substantially, however. The main reason for the increase in sales dollars is due to a drought which weakened supply and bid prices up (Standard & Poor's, 1989).

Fixed assets and long-term debt have been steadily increasing over the six-year period. This would suggest that perhaps investment in newer, automated equipment is being made.

Intangibles are low relative to other industries. This indicates that a lack of research and development dollars are being invested which is crucial for patents and trademarks.

The increase in long-term debt requires firms in the meat packing industry to generate more revenues to meet these obligations. In an industry such as this with total sales stabilized, lowering operating cost is the best way to generate higher profit margin.

Current assets are 1.5 times current debt in the meat packing industry. This is fairly consistent with other industry groups. Average collection time is low relative to other industries. Normally 30 days is considered good. However, this industry requires quick collection due to the narrow margins available on sales and obligations of the sellers to their suppliers and employees.

Fixed assets turnover has been decreasing over the past six-year period. Between 1987 and 1988, the ratio decreased substantially. With higher sales dollars in 1988, it seems logical to believe that this is a result of higher increases in automation relative to sales.

Overall, no great changes are observed in the financial characteristics of the industry for the past six years. This is generally a low profit margin business with high capital requirements and a need for close control over collection of accounts receivable and manufacturing cost. Profitability is generally a function of volume.

Strategic Group Structure of Industry Competitors

The main way in which rival firms in the meat packing industry compete is through product line breadth and geographical market coverage (see Figure 4).

There are competitive advantages associated with being a small independent wholesaler with local market coverage as well as from being a large multinational

Table 1		Financial Characteristics of Meat Packing Industry					
		1983	1984	1985	1986	1987	1988

Assets (percentage of total assets)

	1983	1984	1985	1986	1987	1988
Cash and equiv.	7.9	7.3	6.0	6.8	5.5	7.3
Acct. recv.	30.6	30.3	32.0	29.9	30.9	28.2
Inventory	22.3	22.6	23.0	22.8	22.3	21.6
All other curr.	2.3	1.1	1.3	1.5	1.6	1.8
Total current	63.1	61.3	62.3	61.0	60.1	58.9
Fixed assets	29.1	29.9	29.0	31.0	31.5	32.1
Intangibles	1.0	0.6	0.7	0.7	0.8	0.7
Other n-curr.	6.7	8.2	8.0	7.3	7.6	8.3

Liabilities and net worth (percentage of total liabilities and net worth)

	1983	1984	1985	1986	1987	1988
Accounts pay.	14.3	14.1	13.5	13.5	14.1	12.9
Notes payable	14.4	14.4	17.4	14.7	14.7	15.3
Income tax pay.	0.0	0.9	0.7	0.9	0.6	0.6
All other curr.	12.7	11.8	10.3	11.1	11.3	10.6
Total current	41.4	41.2	41.9	40.2	40.7	39.4
Long-term debt	16.3	16.8	14.3	16.7	16.3	17.5
Deferred tax	0.0	0.9	0.8	1.1	0.8	0.9
Other n-curr.	1.9	1.8	3.7	2.2	3.2	1.1
Net worth	40.4	39.4	39.3	39.8	39.1	41.1

Ratios
Profitability

	1983	1984	1985	1986	1987	1988
Net prof. marg.	0.7	0.7	0.9	0.7	1.0	0.9
Return on assets	5.7	5.4	6.0	6.1	7.5	5.3
Ret. on s.h. eqy.	8.8	8.4	9.3	9.5	11.6	8.2

Liquidity

	1983	1984	1985	1986	1987	1988
Curr. ratio	1.7	1.6	1.5	1.5	1.4	1.5
Quick ratio	0.9	0.9	0.9	0.9	0.9	0.8

Leverage

	1983	1984	1985	1986	1987	1988
Debt/equity	1.5	1.6	1.5	1.7	1.9	1.7

Activity

	1983	1984	1985	1986	1987	1988
Inv. turnover (no. of times)	35.0	29.6	32.0	31.1	40.2	33.9
Fixed assets turnover (no. of times)	23.9	20.8	26.2	22.2	24.9	18.8
Total assets turnover (no. of times)	6.8	6.2	6.9	6.6	7.2	5.6
Avg. coll. period (days)	14.5	13.9	14.2	15.1	14.5	13.7

Sources: *Industry Norms and Key Business Ratios,* 1988, 1989; and *RMA Annual Statement Studies,* 1989.

full-line producer. Smaller, local companies have the advantage of being able to respond quickly to customer needs (Thompson, 1989). By being small and local, they are able to customize products for individual customer needs. Also, since firms covering a national or global market are unable to provide this level of customer service, the local competitor can demand a higher price for its product.

Larger companies who compete in a broader geographic area, while having fewer customer service capabilities, enjoy the economics of scale associated with raw material quantity discounts and efficient utilization of plant and production

Figure 3   **Total Sales**

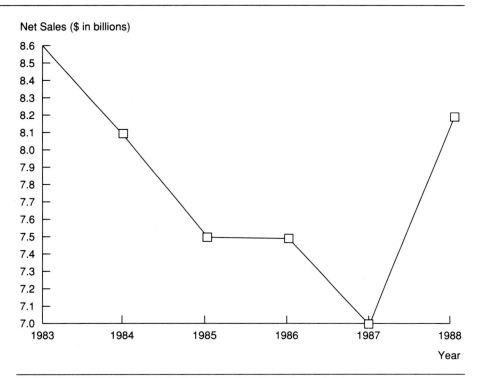

Net Sales ($ in billions)

Source: RMA Annual Statement Studies, 1989.

equipment, distribution systems, and marketing efforts from which smaller firms do not benefit (Thompson, 1989).

Competitive advantages are also associated with product-line scope. Firms with broad product lines are able to divide risk of uncertain conditions adversely affecting each product over a much broader range than firms specializing in one or two products. Narrow scope firms are able to concentrate on quality and product/process innovations for their specialized products. This allows them to respond better to specific customer needs than firms producing a wide array of products.

Description of Major Competitors

The major competitors can be classified into six basic groups. These are: small independent wholesalers, hotel/restaurant/institutional suppliers, regional full-time producers, national limited-line producers, single-line producers, and full-line multinationals.

Small Independent Wholesalers   Al Peat Meats, Delaware Foods, and Croxin Wholesale Meats are firms which can only serve a limited geographic market. These firms serve mainly "mom-and-pop" grocery store accounts. The main reason for

Figure 4   Strategic Group Map

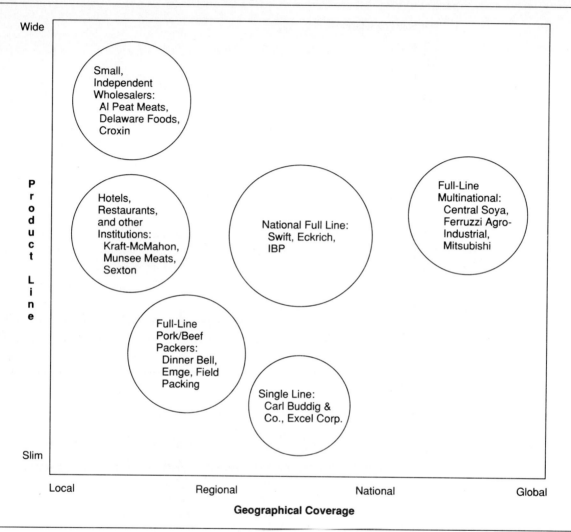

Wide

P
r
o
d
u
c
t

L
i
n
e

Slim

Small, Independent Wholesalers: Al Peat Meats, Delaware Foods, Croxin

Hotels, Restaurants, and other Institutions: Kraft-McMahon, Munsee Meats, Sexton

Full-Line Pork/Beef Packers: Dinner Bell, Emge, Field Packing

National Full Line: Swift, Eckrich, IBP

Single Line: Carl Buddig & Co., Excel Corp.

Full-Line Multinational: Central Soya, Ferruzzi Agro-Industrial, Mitsubishi

Local   Regional   National   Global

Geographical Coverage

success here is their high level of customer service and high-quality, specialty product approach. "Mom-and-pop" stores are generally not able to buy in volume and therefore rely on these producers for a limited volume distribution to their business. These competitors normally do not have extensive distribution systems, therefore, customers oftentimes must actually go to the plant to receive the product.

Hotel/Restaurant/Institutional Suppliers   Kraft-McMahon, Munsee Meats, and Sexton are key firms which service restaurant accounts with portion-controlled products. These are ready-to-prepare steaks, hamburger patties, pork chops, and often times, entrees which only need to be heated before serving. The distribution system is more extensive here than with the small independents. Since portion control requires more extensive labor input, a premium price is commanded.

Full-Line Pork/Beef Producers (Regional)   Dinner Bell Foods, Emge, and Field Packing are the main full-line pork/beef producers competing in the Midwest. They all provide basically the same line of products (fresh beef and pork as well as bacon, sausage, luncheon meats, and hot dogs) and compete on the basis of price and brand name recognition. Dinner Bell has a good reputation in the Ohio area for their ham and ham-related products. Emge is well known in a tri-state area (Indiana, Kentucky, and Ohio), but also serves Illinois and Tennessee for fresh pork, hams, and bacon products. Field Packing is based in Kentucky, but competes with Emge and Dinner Bell in their home states.

These three firms have typically relied on grocery chains and warehouse distributors as their main customers. Emge and Dinner Bell jointly supply a majority of the meat to ScotLad foods, a warehouse distributor in Defiance, Ohio. Marsh Supermarkets based in Yorktown, Indiana, with over 100 stores purchases more than 25 percent of their fresh beef and pork from Emge.

Limited-Line National Firms   Swift-Eckrich, Louis Rich (Oscar Mayer), Iowa Beef Producers, and Wilson Foods are the name brand nationals who have broad geographic coverage throughout the United States. They are currently the innovators in product offerings. For example, Wilson Foods has recently developed a deli-type ham which is 95 percent fat-free. This boosts its brand name recognition as an innovative, quality producer. These firms traditionally set the industry pace.

Single-Line Nationals   Carl Buddig and Excel Corporation are national firms who provide one single product line. For example, Buddig is the leader in slender-sliced luncheon meats. Excel, on the other hand, only sells fresh boxed beef and is quickly becoming a major competitor in boxed beef with its "brand name" beef (Kay, 1989).

Full-Line Multinational   Mitsubishi, a Japanese firm, and Central Soya, a U.S. based manufacturer, process hogs into a full line of consumer-ready products such as boneless pork, ham, bacon, and sausage, as well as by-products such as pharmaceutical commodities and feed ingredients. They provide top-quality products and focus on buying lean, high-quality animals. They are known to buy value and pay accordingly (Central Soya, 1989).

Competitive Forces (Porter)

Rivalry   Rivalry in the meat packing industry is intense. Although there are three very large competitors who dominate 70 percent of the market (*U.S. Industrial Outlook,* 1989), there are many firms of approximately equal size competing for the other 30 percent. While demand is expected to increase over the next 10 years for meat in general (Thompson, 1989), there are plenty of competitors who are competing for the business.

Demand for the product is growing very slowly. Many firms have merged in the past few years which makes the overall group of firms smaller but stronger. The existence of the conglomerate interest in the meat packing industry has meant lower costs for these firms and decreasing market share for the independents.

The structure of the industry as low volume-based combined with the product being perishable means that rival firms oftentimes resort to price concessions in order to gain sales. This is evidenced by Excel Corporation supplying its products in two midwest K mart Stores in order to give its beef program a much needed boost (Kay, 1989).

Customers do not have a high switching cost between suppliers due to the fact that the products are not highly differentiated—pork is basically pork. Also, the processed items on the market are all basically the same. Every company in the processed luncheon meat business, for example, offers bologna, salami, and summer sausage. For all practical purposes, these products are not highly differentiated. Therefore, an incentive on the part of rival firms to induce customers to switch from one brand to another exists.

In the past, payoffs for successful strategic moves were not great in the meat packing industry. However, there has been a recent move toward fat content reduction in raw materials which packing firms have invested a lot of money in. At the same time, automation can help reduce production costs greatly. These two moves are not easily copied. First, the genetic engineering involved in raising livestock can take years, and automation requires serious consideration due to high capital requirements.

Threat of Entry   The threat of entry is weak due to the requirement of new firms to enter on a large scale basis with state-of-the-art equipment. Combine this with a shortage of raw materials due to a small number of raw material suppliers and a new entrant suddenly realizes a lack of capacity utilization.

Brand preference and consumer loyalty are most present in the packaged or branded products such as lunch meats, hot dogs, and the newly branded beef which Excel Corporation pioneered. This causes new, unknown firms to have difficulty in gaining business required for survival. The only areas in which they could be successful in gaining share quickly are in fresh, unbranded beef and pork.

The requirement of firms to enter with state-of-the-art equipment means a high capital dollar investment. In order to establish a clientele, a new firm must usually meet or beat the prices at which existing firms are offering identical products. This may involve taking a loss for a period of time until a reputation for the product itself can be built.

The main advantage available to existing firms, independent of size, is the fact that their plants and equipment are generally very old and thus were purchased at preinflation prices. Potential entrants could possibly acquire equipment of existing firms who are liquidating or modernizing their plants. However, timing is a key factor and automation is the road to a successful future.

Governmental actions actually encourage entry into the meat packing industry. The Indiana Department of Commerce recently offered a $2.5 million grant from state taxpayers to Mitsubishi of Japan and Central Soya Corporation to place a new highly automated packing plant in Delphi, Indiana. The plant would be a major force in the United States in that it would process approximately three thousand hogs per day (Juday, 1989).

Substitute Products   Substitutes for meat are fish, seafood, soybean products, and certain vegetables. While seafood consumption per capita is growing, it does not represent a significant threat to the meat packing industry.

Economic Power of Suppliers   The input, live animals, is definitely a vital part of the production process. There are other input suppliers in the meat packing industry as well—labor, packaging suppliers, and equipment suppliers being the main players.

The live animal production is beginning to be dominated by a few large producers who are forming exclusive contracts with meat packers who are willing to invest money in genetic engineering of their feed-lots. There is beginning to be more and more differentiation across supplying firms with respect to animal fat contents as well. This results in suppliers having more power over the customers.

The buying firms do represent important customers to farmers, but currently there is much more production capacity than raw material availability (Thompson, 1989). This allows suppliers the ability to command a premium price for their quality products.

The future may see a backward integration on the part of meat packers into livestock development. The big producers are currently investing large amounts of capital into research and development for lean animal development. The next step is to see large firms begin feed-lots of their own. This is the only way to lessen the power of the suppliers.

Economic Power of Buyers   Customers in this industry are mainly grocery stores, restaurants, and other smaller restaurant/hotel/institutional suppliers. As there is a move toward central warehousing, customers become larger in size, smaller in number, and generally more powerful.

With the standardized product, brand switching is easy. However, there is a resistance to do so because of high brand loyalty on the part of the ultimate buyer, the consumer. The threat of switching can give the retail buyer a certain amount of power. Also, buyers are not locked in to just one brand at a time. It is not feasible for buyers to rely on just one producer. Competing brands can be carried simultaneously, which allows a buyer to pick and choose among the various brands, carrying only products which allow the best margin from each producer.

Sellers have been known to forward integrate such as Bob Evans did with its restaurant chain. However, this does not really affect the economic power of most buyers due to its small scale.

In conclusion, rivalry among competing firms in the meat packing industry is high. There is a limited amount of market share available and growth is slow. Thus, firms must work to gain share at the expense of competitors.

Entry barriers are relatively high. In order to enter, a firm must invest a great amount in plant, equipment, and promotion efforts. This often involves taking a loss until the product gains brand recognition and is able to compete at prices comparable to other brands.

Substitutes exist but are not really a significant threat to meat packers.

Supplier power is increasing. This is mainly due to the fact that the capacity of plants is greater than supply of hogs and cattle. This gives the supplying firm economic power to demand a higher price for its product.

Buyer power is high because buyers are generally becoming smaller in number and larger in size. Also, there are plenty of producers available to choose from and switching cost is low.

The industry is not particularly attractive due to the extent in which environmental factors affect meat packing firms.

Conclusions about Major Problems Emge Faces from Environment

The major environmental problems which Emge faces are:

1. Trend toward chicken (poultry) consumption;
2. Warehousing distribution and buyer power;
3. Automation of major competitor firms;
4. More competitors having backing of larger conglomerate;
5. Buyouts/mergers;
6. Competitors from foreign shores.

Emge is solely in the business of providing beef and pork products. It does not have the facilities to process poultry products. It would be difficult, if not impossible, for it to become well established in poultry since there are many existing well-known brands. If the trend toward poultry continues, Emge could face serious problems in future scales.

Emge was built on its ability to serve the "mom-and-pop" grocery store and restaurant accounts. With the trend toward centralized warehousing, Emge must be able to remain competitive on the basis of price in order to compete with larger firms who have the advantage of lower costs as a result of automation and lower labor costs.

Larger firms have been employing automation in order to gain competitive advantage through lower cost, more consistent quality of products, and increased daily production. With automation of other firms, Emge is in a position to lose its competitive edge.

The existence of a market niche which Emge may be able to serve is seriously affected by firms equal in size who have backing of a large conglomerate. The deep pockets of parent firms combined with their marketing experience pose a threat to Emge's competitive position.

Diversified food giants are taking over meat packing firms and driving smaller companies out of business through their knowledge of marketing and pre-established distribution channels.

Japanese firms such as Mitsubishi are entering the midwest region and competing head-to-head with smaller firms like Emge through new high technology plants which allow them lower costs and higher consistency of quality.

Emge Organization Analysis

Current Strategy

Emge's business level strategy focuses on maintaining its current market share. It has continued to focus on the midwest market with little effort to expand its geographic coverage. Its main competitive approach is low-cost/low-price. This is how it is able to compete with well-known national brands. Product differentiation is based mainly on customer service. Since Emge is physically closer to customers than its national brand competitors, it can respond to customer needs in a more timely manner.

Emge does not have any specific strategic plans in response to changing industry conditions and other emerging developments in the external environment, even though the management does realize the importance of the environment.

Functional Area Strategy

Human Resources/Labor Relations   Emge realizes that automation is the key to future success. Along with the automation comes a reduction in labor force. The company is not expanding its labor base and is actually allowing it to decrease by means of attrition. This supports its overall strategy of being a low-cost producer while not causing union retaliation.

Marketing, Promotion, and Distribution   Emge's strategy of serving its customer base is supported by marketing, promotion, and distribution. It is not uncommon for the firm to do custom packaging for various large accounts. For example, Emge vacuum packages hot dogs with the special Marsh Supermarket "Val-U" logo.

Distribution is efficient in delivering products to the customers. This is mainly due to the firm's insistence on serving only the midwest market.

Manufacturing and Operations   Emge does not invest extensively in its operations. Equipment is normally replaced when it is fully depreciated and obsolete to the point that it cannot be repaired any longer. The firm concentrates on a simple, low-cost package with a quality product inside. This has traditionally kept manufacturing cost low.

Finance   Capital investment has always been financed through retained earnings from operations. Emge's financial strategy has been to build capital reserves while incurring no debt and keeping operating costs low.

Like many corporations, Emge's functional areas do not support one another. Finance and production, having a conservative approach, do not make it feasible for marketing and production to serve changing customer needs in the long run.

Qualitative Resources

Personnel   Emge's top-level managers have a willingness for the corporation to prosper mainly because they have a personal financial interest in the company. The C.E.O. is aging, however, and no plan for succession has been made. In fact, there is a power struggle for his position. The older generation of managers are all near retirement age and it is questionable whether or not the younger family members will be able to meet the challenges which the competitive environment of the future is expected to present. Few middle-level managers exist. This is a lean organization.

Production workers have strong union support. The union presents a barrier between the company and its employees in that management feels the union places many unnecessary restrictions on management's reign of the company.

The sales force is dedicated to the success of the company. It is apparent that they take pride in the company name and the products it produces.

Image   Emge has a good image among suppliers as well as with its customers. Suppliers are always paid for raw materials on time and Emge is willing to pay the extra price for quality products. Customers feel that they receive quality products at reasonable prices. If problems with quality arise, the company is always willing to compensate the customer.

Facilities   The facilities are becoming older and there is a need for newer, more advanced technology equipment to remain competitive with other producers. Capacity utilization is nearing 100 percent for much of the plants' equipment. This could cause the company problems in serving customers' future demands.

Willingness to Compete   The company's objective has been to remain conservative and not compete in areas in which it does not have a sure competitive advantage. This may have resulted in lost opportunity for gaining competitive edge many times.

As far as challenges in the future, management succession and aging plant and equipment are most prevalent.

Financial Resources and Performance

Emge's 1988 financial performance at first glance appears to be satisfactory compared to the industry averages (see Tables 2, 3, and 4).

Table 2
Financial Characteristics: Emge versus Industry

	1988			1988	
	Industry	Emge		Industry	Emge
Assets (percentage of total assets)			Other n-curr.	1.1	0
Cash and equiv.	7.3	14.9	Net worth	41.1	92.2
Acct. Recv.	28.2	15.8			
Inventory	21.6	12.2	**Ratios**		
All other curr.	1.8	36.6	Profitability		
Total current	58.9	79.5	Net prof. marg.	0.9	2.7
Fixed assets	32.1	8.2	Return on assets	5.3	10.1
Intangibles	0.7	0	Ret. on s.h. eqy.	8.2	10.9
Other n-curr.	8.3	12.3	Liquidity		
			Curr. ratio	1.5	12.8
Liabilities and net worth			Quick ratio	0.8	10.8
(percentage of total liabilities and net worth)			Leverage		
Accounts pay.	12.9	2.0	Debt/equity	1.7	0
Notes payable	15.3	0	Activity		
Income tax pay.	0.6	0.4	Inv. turnover (no. of times)	33.9	77.8
All other curr.	10.6	3.8	Fixed assets turnover (no. of times)	18.8	45.1
Total current	39.4	6.2	Total assets turnover (no. of times)	5.6	3.67
Long-term debt	17.5	0	Avg. coll. period (days)	13.7	15.7
Deferred tax	0.9	1.5			

Sources: *Industry Norms and Key Business Ratios,* 1988, 1989; *RMA Annual Statement Studies,* 1989; and Geo. S. Olive Audited Financial Statement of Emge as of Dec. 31, 1988.

Table 3
Emge Packing Company, Inc.: Statement of Income (Year Ended December 31, 1988)

Net sales	$175,954,700	Gain on sale of assets	7,707
Cost of sales	161,327,381	Increase in cash surrender value and proceeds received,	
Gross profits	14,627,319	net of premiums paid	49,781
Selling and administrative expenses	8,999,393	Other miscellaneous income	80
Operating income	5,627,926		$ 2,033,787
		Income before income taxes	$ 7,661,713
Other income		Income taxes	2,848,705
Sale of scrap	$ 30,625	Net income	$ 4,813,008
Rental income	7,571		
Interest income	1,938,023		

Table 4
Emge Packing Company, Inc.: Balance Sheet at December 31, 1988

Assets			Liabilities and stockholders' equity		
Current assets			Current liabilities		
Cash and cash equivalents	$ 7,118,754		Accounts payable	$ 970,678	
Investments at cost			Salaries and wages	1,086,001	
(approximates market)	16,846,843		Accrued expenses	687,879	
Accounts receivable	7,572,636		Federal and state income		
Inventory	5,822,309		taxes	185,815	
Deferred income tax benefit	356,964		Deferred farm income	50,000	
Prepaid expenses	327,029		Total current liabilities		$ 2,980,373
Total current assets		$38,044,535	Deferred income taxes		$ 734,876
Property and equipment			Stockholders' equity		
Land	$ 555,323		Common stock: no par value		
Buildings	3,686,186		Authorized: 50,000 shares		
Machinery and equipment	5,116,665		Issued and outstanding:		
	9,358,174		10,003 shares	$ 1,914,200	
Less accumulated			Additional paid-in cpaital	44,353	
depreciation	5,456,343	$ 3,901,831	Retained earnings	42,178,898	
Other assets					$44,137,451
Cash surrender value of life					$47,852,700
insurance	$ 893,777				
Trust account	1,254,913				
Investments at cost	1,946,312				
Prepaid pension	1,811,332				
		$ 5,906,334			
		$47,852,700			

Assets   Emge's high liquidity ratios exemplify its ability to meet its obligations to short-term creditors. Cash is a high percentage of total assets compared to the industry which allows Emge to easily meet short-term obligations. Accounts receivable, inventory, and fixed assets are all low as a percentage of total assets due to the high percentage of cash. The large portion of cash assets is good in that it gives Emge protection against environmental uncertainties. High levels of cash and marketable securities can represent a lost opportunity if these could be better utilized for operations. The firm has no intangible assets.

Liabilities   Emge has no long-term liabilities. Greater than 92 percent of the liabilities and net worth are stockholders' equity. Stockholders in this corporation have great control. They are small in number (less than 100) and all of the senior-level managers are major stockholders. This forces management to have a strong commitment to the company.

Profitability   Emge's profitability level has out-performed the industry average. Its net profit margin is three times the industry average for 1988. This is mainly due to the fact that Emge's revenues contain a large percentage of non-operational interest income (see Table 3). Its high return on assets demonstrates that Emge is gaining more return on its investments relative to the industry. This is again due to the high amount of cash which earns interest at a higher rate than the industry profit margin from operation (see Table 4).

Activity   Emge has more inventory turns than does the industry. This suggests that they may not keep enough inventory on hand to adequately serve their customer base. This may result in a loss of accounts over time.

Fixed assets turnover is higher than the industry average. This shows that Emge is utilizing its plants and equipment efficiently relative to the industry as a whole. Total assets turnover, however, is low relative to the industry. This is due to the large percentage of total assets in cash and equivalents.

In summary, Emge has very high amounts of cash and equivalents and low investment in plant and equipment. The cash surplus of the firm could probably be better utilized.

Competitive Position

Emge's short-term competitive position seems strong in the Midwest as it is the only full-line meat packer in the state of Indiana and competes very well in this market on the basis of price and customer service.

The long-term competitive position may be hindered due to the environmental changes taking place such as the decreasing per capita consumption of beef and pork. Rival firm conglomerate financial backing as well as the internal challenges the firm is confronted with in areas of strategic direction, managerial succession, and facilities present problems. Emge's financial resources may assist its future competitive efforts only if management is willing to make the commitment.

Problems as a Result of Resources and Past Strategy

Emge's main problems are a result of not using resources to prepare for future competitiveness and a strategy which doesn't develop the company for long-term survival. The strategy combined with Emge's limited resources has posed the following problems:

1. Plant and equipment are not consistent with industry norms. The conservative strategy of management has neglected to implement new technology necessary for competing with a new industry of high automation. For example, Emge's plants are more compatible with hanging beef which has been replaced by boxed beef.

2. Emge has not invested R&D dollars into consumer health concerns which are changing demand patterns for meat. For example, many beef and pork producers are investing in poultry plants. Emge has made the same products for years. They have not moved forward with lowering fat contents of processed items in order to address health concerns.

3. Managerial succession problems are inevitable. Emge has not planned for replacement of the current chief executive. The power struggle suggests that any family member who takes over this position will be challenged in gaining control and following of other managers. This will affect the direction of the firm and its ability to move forward or even hold its own in the market. Internal problems will surely cause Emge to lose sight of the environment.

4. Emge is sure to find its competitive future challenging with the decrease of independent firms and the increase of large conglomerate and international parent company financial backing. This will no doubt give competitors cost as well as distribution advantages which Emge does not have.

5. With respect to the strategic structure of the industry (Figure 4), Emge is more or less caught in the middle. It is not able to concentrate as well on customer service as are small firms, but also doesn't enjoy the economies of scale which larger national and multinational firms experience.

Date: Saturday,
March 31, 1990
Time: 9:00 A.M. (C.S.T.)
Event: 44th Annual Meeting of Stockholders

The directors of the corporation of Emge Packing Company gathered at the Fort Branch, Indiana, office for what was planned to be an average, unexciting annual meeting. This was unfortunately not the case. This year, many more non-management shareholders were present for the meeting and were ready with questions for the board of directors.

Specifically, they were very concerned that the net income after taxes fell from nearly $5.5 million in 1988 to just over $2 million in 1989. Also, of concern was that for the first time in many years, the operating portion of income was negative. This sent a red flag to many stockholders that their investment was at great risk.

Walter Emge, the C.E.O., seemed to be the target of much criticism. One of the founder's grandchildren was very much against Mr. Emge and let it be known that she does not believe he has any motion of a long- or short-term strategic plan for Emge. A very hectic, out of control meeting with many personal insults followed. The stockholders were concerned that their investments would be lost if the firm continued in the direction it was headed. They additionally felt that Mr. Emge did not have confidence in the Emge family managers.

It was pointed out that the industry is becoming increasingly more difficult to compete in as more months go by.

Many stockholders are becoming money hungry and have a great desire to liquidate the stock of the company—either by sale of the company to an outside investor or by a discontinuation of operations. They feel strongly that Emge's current dividend policy is much too conservative. Mr. Emge as well as other board members do not wish to see this happen on the basis that they feel an obligation to the employees of the company for as long as the firm can turn a profit. Walter also feels an obligation on behalf of his deceased father to carry on the family business.

Walter, now 67 years old, sat in his chair at the head table looking very grim and fatigued. It was obvious that he knew something had to be done—but what?

Emge Problem

Properly determining the root cause of business problems is the key to the success of proper strategy formulation and implementation (McNichols, 1983).

Emge has one main problem caused by two factors. One is industry environment changes and the other is Emge resources and past strategy.

Environment

Automation of Major Competitor Firms   In this relatively mature industry there are many firms leaving the business of meat packing/processing. The firms who choose to remain and compete have found it necessary to emphasize automation on the production floor—as well as in procurement of live animal raw material.

More Competitors Receiving Backing from Large Conglomerate Firms   The expense of automation has caused most remaining firms to seek financial backing as well as distribution channels from the deep pocketed conglomerate companies.

Foreign Competition   Foreign companies, especially the Japanese, have found the U.S. market attractive and have decided to enter the meat packing industry. The foreign firms generally have substantial financial resources as well as technological know-how. This has provided them lower costs as well as a higher consistency of quality. In short, foreign competition is presenting firms such as Emge with competitive pressures.

Poultry Consumption Trend   The consumer trend toward leaner meats—especially poultry—could cause Emge serious problems since it currently focuses on beef and pork exclusively, and current production facilities cannot be easily adapted for poultry processing. Also, the problem of government inspection arises as it may be difficult, if not impossible, to persuade the U.S.D.A. to grant inspection for poultry as well as for beef and pork in the same facility.

Problems as a Result of Emge Resources and Past Strategy

Outdated Plant and Equipment   The plant and equipment at both the Fort Branch and Anderson plants are not consistent with industry norms. The conservative strategy of current management has neglected to allow for implementation of new technology necessary for competing in an industry of highly automated production.

R&D Investment   Emge has not directed R&D dollars toward consumer health concerns which are changing demand patterns for meat. For example, many beef and pork producers are investing in poultry plants. Emge has been producing the same line of products for years. They have not moved forward by investing in procurement of leaner animals and thereby lowering fat contents of processed items. Actions such as this will address consumers' health concerns.

Managerial Succession   Managerial succession problems are inevitable. Emge has not planned for replacement of the current chief executive. The power struggle which exists would suggest that any family member taking over will be challenged in gaining control and following of other managers.

Main Problem Resulting from Emge

Emge's main problem is that they are simply not able to compete effectively in today's market. This is a result of management's conservative nature and lack of response to the environment in a timely manner. A factor which is out of Emge's direct control is the conglomerate backing and foreign competitor entry. Emge is a small force in a relatively over-crowded, mature industry.

The future does not currently look bright for Emge. Many of its problems are not a result of the environment, but rather internal in origin. Non-management stockholders want larger dividends—perhaps even liquidation of the cash surplus. Management, on the other hand, is divided as to what should be the fate of the company and the strategic plan necessary to carry the corporation to this goal.

Strategic Alternatives

Emge can take one of two routes in making a strategy decision.

1. Exit: Hofer (1978) addresses appropriate strategies for firms with weak competitive position in mature or saturated markets. It is pointed out that even when bankruptcy is not imminent, exiting may be a viable alternative.

    Emge would discontinue operations in the meat packing business. This can be carried out in one of two ways.
    a. Liquidation of cash and other assets after locating an existing packing firm to purchase plants, equipment, Emge trademark, etc.
    b. Liquidate completely; discontinue operations. This involves selling the plants and equipment in a piecemeal fashion as quickly as possible, as they would become a liability under this plan.
2. Option to Stay in Business: One common approach to formulating strategy is to seek competitive advantage in the form of cost leadership or differentiation (Stringer, 1986). If Emge is to stay in business, an appropriate strategy would need to facilitate achievement of these advantages. The extent to which Emge

would be able to gain a competitive advantage is directly related to its financial constraints (Hamermesh, 1986).

Emge could restructure and continue operations in the meat packing industry. They could follow one of two alternate plans.

a. Modernize current operations with highly automated computer-integrated equipment. Recently, Hatfield, a regional meat processor, invested $19 million in modernization of its plant (Murphy, 1989). Emge could duplicate this automation effort for approximately the same cost. Cash surplus from past operations can be used to fund this project. This may include any combination of the following:

    i. Build highly automated plant at a location found to be strategically advantageous with respect to raw materials procurement, distribution, labor rates, tax rates, etc.

    ii. Close Fort Branch plant, Anderson plant, or both.

    iii. Refurbish Fort Branch plant, Anderson plant or both, adding state of the art computer-integrated equipment.

b. Pay out as dividend to shareholders cash and other assets not needed for day-to-day operations (approximately $19 million). If current/future management can operate successfully without interest income from these non-operating assets, then continue operations.

The option to stay in business would require restructuring in order to combat problems of managerial succession and to reduce fixed overhead expenses resulting from the current high degree of labor intensity.

Bibliography

Bjerklie, Steve, "Technology: Solutions from Problems," *Meat & Poultry,* 35 (September, 1989), 19.

Central Soya, "Central Soya Selects Delphi, Indiana, for Pork Processing Plant," News Release, September 20, 1989.

Duewer, Lawrence A., "Changes in the Beef and Pork Industries," *National Food Review,* 12 (1989), 5–9.

Emge Packing Company, Inc., Audited Financial Statements, December 31, 1988.

Galbraith, Jay R. and Daniel Nathanson, *Strategy Implementation: The Role of Structure and Process,* West: St. Paul, (1978) 19–25.

Hamermesh, Richard G., *Making Strategy Work,* Wiley: New York, (1986), 56–63.

Hofer, Charles W. and Dan Schendel, *Strategy Formulation: Analytical Concepts,* West: St. Paul, (1978) 104–106.

Industry Norms and Key Business Ratios. New York: Dun & Bradstreet, 1989, 36.

Juday, Paul, "Really necessary?" *Anderson Herald Bulletin,* 121, November 22, 1989, Editorial.

Kay, Steve, "Big 3 Plans" *Meat & Poultry,* 35 (September, 1989), 16.

Livestock Slaughter, National Agriculture Statistics Services, U.S.D.A. Annual Summary, 1988.

McNichols, Thomas J., *Executive Policy and Strategic Planning,* McGraw-Hill: New York, (1977) 74–78.

McNichols, Thomas J., *Executive Policy and Strategic Planning,* McGraw-Hill: New York, (1983), 90–95.

Murphy, Dan, "Phenomenal Family, Futuristic Facility," *Meat Processing,* 28 (June, 1989), 28–34.

Pearce, Johan A. and Richard B. Robinson, *Strategic Management,* Irwin: Homewood, (1982), 240–253.

RMA Annual Statement Studies, Philadelphia: Robert Morris Associates, 1989, 76.

Standard & Poor's *Industry Surveys.* New York: Standard & Poor's Corp., February 2, 1989, 15–21.

Stringer, Robert A., *Strategy Traps,* Lexington Books: Lexington (1986), 25–28.

Thompson, Kevin, "Business: It could be a joy ride." *Meat & Poultry,* 35 (September 1989), 14–16.

U.S. Industrial Outlook. Washington, D.C.: U.S. Department of Commerce, (1988), 39: 1–5.

U.S. Industrial Outlook. Washington, D.C.: U.S. Department of Commerce, (1989), 40: 1–5.

10

CHAPTER

International Entrepreneurship

Key Topics

- Venturing Abroad
- Why Internationalize?
- International Threats and Risks
- North American Free Trade Agreement (NAFTA)

Comprehensive Entrepreneurial Cases

- Pizza Hut in Moscow: The Pre-coup Vision
- Encyclopaedia Britannica International: Exploring Emerging Market Opportunities
- Acer Computers

Venturing Abroad

For many years U.S. entrepreneurs shuddered at the thought of "going international" because it was just too big a step, too risky, and too uncertain. On the other side of the ocean, Lenin wrote that foreign investment represented the final stage of capitalism. It is therefore ironic that the world's greatest boom in foreign investment took place in the dying years of Lenin's communism. From 1983 to 1990 foreign investment grew four times faster than world output and three times faster than world trade. Entrepreneurs rushed enthusiastically to those countries that were blighted by communism, state socialism, or authoritarian, isolationist governments. Prime targets included China, India, other parts of Asia, Latin America, and Eastern Europe.

Historically, the United States was a major exporter, especially after World War II when goods were in short supply and the worldwide market was insatiable. After production of more goods began in other countries, U.S. exporters found themselves being squeezed out of markets by European and Japanese producers who took the initiative away from them. Japanese businesses have learned that they have to export or die while American businesspeople have grown up saying "I'd rather die than export." For many entrepreneurs exporting is the biggest hurdle.

Marx and Lenin taught others to fear business initiatives from abroad. They believed foreign entrepreneurs were ruthless and greedy and would exploit the poor, manipulate governments, and flout popular opinion.

Why Internationalize?

Countries vary with respect to the quantity and proportion of resources they possess, which forms the basis for a competitive advantage of nations. **Resource-rich countries** (those having extractive assets) include the OPEC block nations and many parts of Africa. Labor-rich, rapidly developing countries include Brazil, Sri-Lanka, India, the Philippines, and South and Central America. **Market-rich countries** such as Europe, Brazil, Mexico, and the United States have purchasing power, in contrast to India or China, which possess large populations but suffer from lack of purchasing power. Each country has something that others need, thus forming the basis of an interdependent international trade system.

Internationalization can be viewed as the outcome of a sequential process of **incremental adjustments** to changing conditions of the firm and its environment. This process progresses step-by-step as risk and commitment increase and entrepreneurs acquire more knowledge through experience. The entrepreneur's impression of the risks and rewards of internationalizing can be determined by feasibility studies of the potential gains to be won.

An entrepreneur's willingness to move into international markets is also affected by whether he or she has studied a foreign language, has lived abroad long enough to have experienced culture shock, and is internationally oriented. Another factor is the **entrepreneur's confidence** in the company's competitive advantage in the form of price, technology, marketing, or financial superiority. This advantage might include an efficient distribution network, an innovative or patented product, or possession of exclusive information about the foreign market.

> Decentralization is the key to Nebraska-based American Tool Company's international marketing strategy. Gunnar Birnum, director of marketing for the firm's international division, says "We delegate responsibility for running the local operations in foreign countries to our resident managers. They are, almost exclusively, natives of the country. They know the subtleties and peculiarities of their homeland the way no outsider can. The point is to bring as much responsibility to our local managers as possible. This is really the same approach most Japanese manufacturers use to market here in the United States. They hire Americans to move their products through our distribution chain—as we know, that's worked rather well for them."[1]

Deteriorating market conditions at home may propel entrepreneurs to seek foreign markets to help offset declining business, or a countercyclical market may be sought to balance the fluctuations of a single market subject to one set of local economic conditions.[2]

Some small businesses internationalize immediately and do not wait to expand their horizons. Multinational from inception, these companies break the traditional expectation that a business must enter the international arena incrementally, becoming global only as it grows older and wiser.

According to Oviatt and McDougal, seven characteristics of successful global start-ups are: (1) global vision from inception; (2) internationally experienced management; (3) a strong international business network; (4) preemptive technology

---

[1] William A. Delphos, ed., *The World is Your Market: An Export Guide for Small Business* (Washington, D.C.: Braddock Communications) 1990.

[2] A. Kuriloff, J. Hemphill, and D. Cloud, "Managing International Trade," in *Starting and Managing the Small Business*, 3d ed. (New York: McGraw-Hill, 1993), 273–308.

or marketing; (5) a unique intangible asset; (6) a linked product or service; and (7) tight organizational coordination worldwide.[3]

Top 10 Reasons to Invest in Hungary

1. The political process is stable and democratic.
2. Foreign companies have been able to acquire 100 percent of a formerly state-owned business since 1991.
3. There is no double taxation.
4. There is a 100 percent tax holiday for joint ventures during their first five years.
5. U.S. businesses have invested $1.8 billion in Hungary—more than half of all the country's foreign direct investment and more than U.S. investment in Poland and in the former Czechoslovakia combined.
6. The Foreign Investment Act protects foreign investors against losses resulting from nationalization, expropriation, and joint-venture liquidation.
7. Since 1990 legislation has allowed, through the National Bank of Hungary, full repatriation of capital invested, capital gains, profits, and dividends in hard currencies.
8. Hungary is geographically the gateway to Western and Eastern European markets.
9. The labor force is low-cost (wages average less than $200 per month) and highly skilled.
10. Foreign companies are eligible for subsidies from the $20.5 million Investment Promotion Fund if they have equity capital of at least $685,000 and a 30 percent interest in the project.[4]

As global opportunities expand, entrepreneurs are becoming more open-minded about internationalizing. The primary advantage of trading internationally is that a company's market is expanded significantly and growth prospects are greatly enhanced. Other advantages include utilizing idle capacity; minimizing cyclical or seasonal slumps; getting acquainted with manufacturing technology used in other countries; learning about products not sold in the United States; learning about other cultures; acquiring growth capital more easily in other countries; and having the opportunity to travel for business and pleasure.[5]

Before entering a foreign market, it is important to study the **unique culture** of the potential customers. Different concepts of how the product is used, demographics, psychographics, and legal and political norms are usually different from those in the United States. Therefore, it is necessary to conduct market research to identify these important parameters.

- **Government regulations:** Must you conform to import regulations or patent, copyright, or trademark laws that would affect your product?
- **Political climate:** Will the relationship between government and business or political events and public attitudes in a given country affect foreign business transactions, particularly with the United States?

---

[3]B. Oviatt and P. McDougal, "Global Start-ups," *Inc,* June 1993, 23.

[4]A. Warson, "Exploring Hungarian Opportunities," *Inc,* June 1993, 96.

[5]R. Anderson and J. Dunkelberg, *Managing Small Business* (Minneapolis: West, 1993), 510.

- **Local customs:** Is your product in violation of cultural taboos?
- **Infrastructure:** How will the packaging, shipping, and distribution system of your export product be affected by the local transportation system, for example, air, land, or water?
- **Distribution channels:** What are the generally accepted trade terms at both wholesale and retail levels? What are the normal commissions and service charges? What laws pertain to agency and distribution agreements?
- **Competition:** How many competitors do you have and in what countries are they located? On a country-by-country basis, how much market share does each of your competitors have, and what prices do they charge? How do they promote their products? What distribution systems do they use?[6]
- **Market size:** How big is the market for your product? Is it stable? What is its size individually, country by country? In what countries are markets opening, expanding, maturing, or declining?

> Although Domino's Pizza executives in Ann Arbor, Michigan, believed they could sell a pizza anywhere, it took a few modifications to succeed in selling their pizzas in certain foreign markets. After all, everyone might like pizza, but not the same kind.
>
> In Germany, where pizzas are smaller and eaten individually, Domino's delivered personal-size pizzas. In Japan, pizzas were also reduced in size because the people will not buy bigger portions, according to David M. Board, Jr., Domino's vice president for international operations. Modifications were also made to suit regional tastes. For example, popular toppings in Japan are tuna and sweet corn, while in Australia, prawns and pineapple are favorites.
>
> The basic recipe and menu choices, however, have remained primarily standard Domino's fare—two sizes, 12 topping choices, and a cola beverage.
>
> In some instances, Domino's promotional themes also needed slight alterations. In England, the "One call does it all," slogan could hardly be used since the king's English considers a call the same thing as a personal visit. In Germany, where pizza is seen as a snack food, the company advertisements were designed to emphasize the nutritional value of pizza and its appeal as a full meal in order to expand market potential.
>
> For a company that prides itself on consistency, the diversity of international markets has posed some interesting challenges—challenges that have been met only with flexibility and minor modifications.[7]

By making use of market research done for its Russian restaurants, McDonald's has managed to create a gleaming island of quality, service, and satisfaction where indifferent waiters, filthy surroundings, and ghastly food were commonplace. Opening just three years ago, serving 40,000 customers a day, and selling more food in three weeks than the average McDonald's restaurant sells in a year, the Moscow McDonald's is the busiest one in the world.

Journalists predicted in 1990 that the Moscow McDonald's would fail: Within a few months the restrooms would be trashed, employees would grow nasty, and

---

[6]Kuriloff et al., "Managing International Trade."

[7]William A. Delphos, ed., *The World is Your Market: An Export Guide for Small Business* (Washington, D.C.: Braddock Communications) 1990.

the food would turn rancid. Not only has this not happened, but three years later two other smaller restaurants in downtown Moscow have been opened. McDonald's accomplished its foreign objectives with liberal doses of clout and savvy and huge amounts of patience.

The Global Manager/Entrepreneur

Individuals who internationalize and carry out a coordinated strategy are characterized as being **integrators;** that is, they work across country boundaries to ensure the dissemination and development of core competence. "They create personal relationships to increase the speed and effectiveness of programs being implemented. They understand and mediate conflicts between divisions and worldwide product and country operations, with a decidedly overall local focus. Their travels and contacts make them useful for the collection and dissemination of information that is vital to the establishment of feedback and control systems."[8]

Global entrepreneurs are opportunity-minded and open-minded, able to see different points of view and weld them into a unified focus. They rise above nationalistic differences to see the big picture of global competition without abdicating their own nationalities. They have a core language plus working knowledge of others. They confront the learning difficulties of language barriers head-on, recognizing the barriers such ignorance can generate. The global entrepreneur is required to wear many hats, taking on various assignments, gaining experience in various countries, and seizing the opportunity to interact with people of different nationalities and cultural heritages.[9]

International Threats and Risks

Capturing foreign markets is not as simple as picking fruit from a vine. Instead, a series of dangers must be monitored carefully. **Ignorance** and **uncertainty,** combined with **lack of experience** in problem solving in a foreign country, top the list. **Lack of information** about resources to help solve problems contributes to the unfamiliarity. **Restrictions** imposed by the host country often contribute to the risk. Many host countries demand development of their exports and insist on training and development of their nationals. They can also demand that certain positions in management and technological areas be held by nationals. Many seek technologically based industry rather than extractive industry. In other instances, the host country may require that it own controlling interest and/or limit the amount of profits or fees entrepreneurs are allowed to take out of the country.

Political risks include unstable governments, disruptions caused by territorial conflicts, wars, regionalism, illegal occupation, and political ideological differences. **Economic risks** that need to be monitored include changes in tax laws, rapid rises in costs, strikes, sudden increases in raw materials, and cyclical/dramatic shifts in GNP. Social risks include antagonism among classes, religious conflict, unequal

---

[8]L. Hrebiniak, "Implementing Global Strategies," *European Management Journal* (December 1992): 399.
[9]Ibid.

income distribution, union militancy, civil war, and riots. **Financial risks** incorporate fluctuating exchange rates, repatriation of profits and capital, and seasonal cash flows.[10]

> The costs and penalties for not complying with export regulations can be substantial. For example, an Irvine, California, company was recently fined $100,000 for violating the Export Administration Act by failing to obtain a "Swiss Blue" import certificate, which would have protected the company's product from unauthorized re-export.
>
> In another instance, a New York electronics company executive was given a three-year suspended prison sentence for failing to notify the Department of Commerce of changes in his license application to export a high-tech integrated circuit test system. Penalties for other export violations can reach into the millions of dollars.[11]

Foreign government import regulations can affect a company's ability to export successfully. These regulations represent an attempt by foreign governments to control their markets—to protect a domestic industry from excessive foreign competition; to limit health and environmental damage; or to restrict what they consider excessive or inappropriate cultural influences.

Most countries have import regulations that are potential barriers to export products. Exporters need to be aware of import tariffs and consider them when pricing their product. While most countries have reduced their tariffs on imported goods, there are still other major restrictions to global trades, such as nontariff barriers (NTB). These include prohibitions, restrictions, conditions or specific requirements that can make exporting products difficult and sometimes costly. An example of a NTB is when a country requires all labels and markings to be in a specified language.

> In France all labels, instructions, and other printed material for imported goods must be in French. In addition, certain products must now be labeled with their country of origin when foreign merchandise has a trademark or name that suggests that the product may have originated in France.
>
> In Sweden, sanitary certificates of origin testifying to the good condition of a product and its packaging at the time of export are required for meat, meat products, and other items of animal origin, margarine, vegetables, fresh fruits, and plants.[12]

Most entrepreneurs avoid international trade because they believe it is too complicated and fraught with bureaucratic red tape. They also believe that international trade is only profitable for large companies that have more resources than smaller businesses. Some other perceived drawbacks of international trade include becoming too dependent on foreign markets; foreign government instability that could cause problems for domestic companies; tariffs and import duties that make it too expensive to trade in other countries; products manufactured in the United States that may need significant modification before they are accepted by people in other countries; and foreign cultures, customs, and languages that make it

---

[10]John Burch, *Entrepreneurship* (New York: Wiley, 1986).

[11]William A. Delphos, ed., *The World is Your Market: An Export Guide for Small Business* (Washington, D.C.: Braddock Communications) 1990.

[12]Ibid.

Table 10.1
Comparing U.S. and International Operations

Factor	U.S. Operations	International Operations
Language	English used almost universally	Domestic language must be used in many situations
Culture	Relatively homogeneous	Varies between countries and within a country
Politics	Stable and of varying importance	Often volatile and of decisive importance
Economy	Relatively stable	Wide variations among countries and between regions within countries
Government interference	Minimal and reasonably predictable	Extensive and subject to arbitrary interventions
Labor	Skilled labor available	Skilled labor often scarce, requiring training or redesign of production methods
Financing	Well-developed financial markets	Poorly developed financial markets; capital flows subject to government interference
Market research	Data easy to collect	Data difficult and expensive to collect
Advertising	Many media available; few restrictions	Media limited; many restrictions; low literacy rates rule out print media in some countries
Currency	U.S. dollar used without restriction	Must change from one currency to another; changing exchange rates and government restrictions are problems
Transportation/communication	Among the best in the world	Often difficult and sporadic
Control	Ability to define when centralized control will be effective	A worse problem; must walk a tightrope between over-centralizing and losing control through too much decentralizing
Contracts	Once signed, are binding on both parties, even if one party makes a bad deal	Can be voided and renegotiated if one party becomes dissatisfied
Labor relations	Collective bargaining; can lay off workers easily	Often cannot lay off workers; may have mandatory worker participation in management; workers may seek change through political process rather than collective bargaining
Trade barriers	Nonexistent	Extensive and complicated

Adapted form R. G. Murdick, R. C. Moor, R. H. Eckhouse, and T. W. Simmerer, *Business Policy: A Framework for Analysis,* 4th ed. (Columbus, Ohio: Grid, 1984).

difficult for Americans to do business in some countries.[13] Table 10.1 identifies some additional **complications** of international operations.

International sales were not a problem for Thermal Bags by Ingrid of Des Plaines, Illinois. A single trade show in England led to the sale of $160,000 worth of insulated bags.

[13]Anderson and Dunkelberg, *Managing Small Business.*

Yet the company ran into difficulty financing the sale. President Ingrid Skamser thought they might have to pass on the large English orders because she lacked the capital to produce enough bags. "Up to this point, we thought we had no choice but to get full payment in advance—a policy that lost us a lot of orders," she said.

When Skamser contacted the Illinois District Export Council, she was pleasantly surprised to learn that financial assistance was available to her from the Foreign Credit Insurance Association and the Illinois Export Authority. As a result, Thermal Bags by Ingrid was able to fulfill the international orders it received at the trade show.[14]

McDonald's Corporation also has some difficulties with its overseas operations. In Russia, employee theft is a problem even though company-issued uniforms have only a single small pocket. There is also rising worker discontent over salaries that are not keeping pace with Russia's runaway inflation. Employees who press their case for labor unions are threatened with dismissal. Employees also claim they can earn faster promotions if they are willing to act as informers against their fellow workers. The entrepreneur claims that his 51 percent partner, the city of Moscow, is not pulling its share of the weight, yet it is getting half of the profits.

Some of the raw materials McDonald's needs, such as iceberg lettuce, grows outside Russia in an independent country where an ethnic group is fighting for its own independence. Other factors must also be dealt with, such as a shabby man who hawks pornography just outside the front door, and young toughs packing handguns that protrude from beneath their leather jackets who barge to the front of the entrance line.

However, by withdrawing from Russia, McDonald's would be abandoning its $77 million investment and the tantalizing prospect of huge future earnings. Russia would lose fresh tax revenues and thousands of new jobs. Neither side can afford to withdraw.[15]

North American Free Trade Agreement (NAFTA)

The United States is the **world's largest exporter,** selling more than $422 billion in industrial and agricultural products and more than $164 billion in services overseas in 1991. Since 1986 the United States has been successful in increasing exports by 90 percent. Being able to compete internationally through the competitiveness of American industries has led to sharp increases in global trade and investment flows and, in turn, to enhanced economic growth and job creation. Approximately 7.5 million jobs are tied to merchandise exports, up from 5 million in 1986. Of these jobs, 2.1 million are created by exports to Canada and Mexico. As **NAFTA** phases out barriers to trade in goods and services, a massive open market will be created with more than 360 million people and more than $6 trillion in annual output. It is estimated that NAFTA will create an additional 300,000 U.S. jobs, although critics claim that jobs will be lost to lower-paid international employees.

---

[14]William A. Delphos, ed., *The World is Your Market: An Export Guide for Small Business* (Washington, D.C.: Braddock Communications) 1990.

[15]H. Witt, "The Big Mac Revolution," *Chicago Tribune Magazine,* July 25, 1993, 11–15.

Mexico joined the General Agreement on Tariffs and Trade (GATT) and began reducing its tariffs and trade barriers in 1986. Earlier, Mexico had used high tariffs and licensing restrictions to encourage import substitution and industrial development. Both Presidents de la Madrid and Salinas encouraged the Mexican government to open its markets and implement sweeping economic reforms. The inflation rate dropped from over 100 percent in 1986 to currently under 20 percent while the economy has grown at an average annual rate of 3.1 percent.

Canada joined NAFTA talks in February 1991, leading to a three-way negotiation. After formal negotiations began in June 1991, Congress approved the "fast-track" procedures that authorized the Administration to submit the agreement with implementing legislation for a yes–no vote.

Highlights of NAFTA include the following:

1. **Land transportation**—While 90 percent of U.S. trade with Mexico is shipped by land, U.S. truckers are currently forced to return home empty-handed. By 1995 NAFTA assures that U.S. trucking companies will be allowed to carry cargo to U.S.-contiguous Mexican states and it will give them access to all of Mexico by 1992. Bilateral investments will be allowed, permitting a combination of rail, truck, and sea transport breakthroughs to help create an efficient, intermodal North American transport system.

2. **Increased investment**—U.S. firms operating in Mexico will be treated the same as Mexican-owned firms. Mexico will drop export performance requirements and domestic content rules will be eliminated, permitting additional U.S.-originated inputs.

3. **Tariff elimination**—Within five years 65 percent of U.S. agricultural and industrial goods will be eligible for duty-free treatment.

4. **Financial services**—By the year 2000 Mexico's closed financial services market will be opened and U.S. securities firms and banks will be allowed to open wholly owned subsidiaries.

5. **Telecommunications**—By July 1995, NAFTA will provide nondiscriminatory access to Mexico's $6 billion market for telecommunications equipment and services.

6. **Agriculture**—All remaining tariffs on agricultural goods will be phased out within 15 years, while Mexican input licenses (covering 25 percent of U.S. agricultural exports) will be phased out immediately.

7. **Apparel**—All trade restrictions will be eliminated within ten years and barriers to 20 percent of U.S. exports will be lifted immediately.

8. **Insurance**—Existing joint ventures will be permitted to obtain 100 percent ownership by 1996 and all equity and market share restrictions will be eliminated by the year 2000. New opportunities in Mexico represent a $3.5 billion market.

9. **Intellectual property rights protection**—NAFTA will provide a higher level of protection in this field than does any other bilateral or multilateral agreement.

10. **Auto rule of origin**—NAFTA will require an auto to contain a minimum of 62.5 percent content from North America with strict rules of origin so that individual parts can be identified.

---

[16]"White House Fact Sheet on NAFTA," *Business America*, August 24, 1992, 22–25.

11. **Motor vehicle and parts tariffs**—Under NAFTA, Mexican vehicle and light truck tariffs will be immediately cut in half and within five years duties on 3/4 of U.S. parts exported to Mexico will be eliminated. Mexican "trade balancing" and "local content requirements" will be phased out over ten years.[16]

The historic NAFTA trade agreement will further open markets in Mexico, Canada, and the United States. It is projected to create jobs and generate economic growth in all three countries. NAFTA represents an ambitious effort to eliminate barriers to agricultural, manufacturing, and services trade to protect intellectual property rights and to remove investment restrictions. While everyone is not in agreement about the beneficial aspects of the NAFTA accord, their voices will generate some heated rhetoric in the next few years.

CASE • *Pizza Hut in Moscow: The Pre-coup Vision**

Sandra Honig-Haftel, Wichita State University
Ronald L. Christy, Wichita State University

Introduction

Pizza Hut opened two restaurants in Moscow in what was then the USSR in September of 1990. This was the outcome of a joint venture agreement with the Moscow City Council. Today, the venture is profitable despite operating in a volatile environment where political, monetary, social, and economic infrastructures are continuously changing en route to free markets. Since the introduction of *perestroika* (the policies designed to adopt more market-oriented approaches toward production and distribution of products and services), change has been progressing exponentially. The attempted political coup which failed in 1991 ultimately resulted in the resignation of Mikhail Gorbachev and the rise of Boris Yeltsin as leader.

Marked by hyperinflation, movement toward privatization, an inconvertible currency, and volatile political and governmental systems, the infrastructure of Communism collapsed. A commonwealth of independent states has become the transitional form of economic cooperation among the republics. Most of the former republics have now moved toward independent status. These republics lack political stability, have no legal precedents or laws to effect legal transfer of ownership of property, have little protection for intellectual property, and have a work force that has little work experience in the context of free market incentive systems. Protection of intellectual property is difficult, the tax system is undergoing dramatic revisions, and risk is further compounded by the threat of potential repatriation in a highly volatile governmental system with competing political forces vying for positions of power. Against this historical past and future scenarios, the current outlook is highly uncertain and unpredictable.

PepsiCo Background

Pizza Hut, which had gained the number one leadership position in the pizza food service market, was acquired by PepsiCo in 1977. PepsiCo had developed early formal business ties to the Soviet Union which dated back to 1972. At that time, an agreement was reached to trade Pepsi for Stolichnaya vodka which would be sold by PepsiCo in the West as a means of generating hard currency. Pepsi-Cola has become the major consumer product in the former USSR and is ranked as Pepsi-Cola's fourth largest national market worldwide.

---

*Some of the data for the writing of this case was adapted and edited by the case writers from "Pizza Moscow," a study commissioned by Pizza Hut International from the London Business School in June of 1991 and co-authored by Assheton Don, Claire Don, Amy Stoner, and Andy Rafalat. Additionally, data were collected through personal interviews, surveys, and observations of company documents and archival records.

PepsiCo's substantial interests in the USSR, and the company's contacts made at high levels within the Soviet political system, reflected the drive and commitment to the development of the Soviet market from the very top of the company. According to company reports, PepsiCo's Chairman, Donald Kendall, "was himself pushing hard for the opportunity to open restaurants in the USSR in the mid-1980's."

Kendall made some of his first visits to the USSR in the early 50's, introducing the concept of Pepsi-Cola to Khruschev and initiating negotiations. The 20 or so years of negotiation and preparation that followed ultimately culminated in Pepsi-Cola becoming the widest spread foreign product trademark in the USSR. This history was invaluable in helping the firm establish a full operating business and laid the groundwork for the Pizza Hut venture in Moscow (Exhibit 1).

The Early Vision

The restaurant business as it is known in the West and in Europe was culturally alien to the USSR. Kendall had no rules and no recognizable ways of proceeding. There was only a vision and an intention that this thing had to be done. According to Steve Bishop, vice president of finance for Pizza Hut, Kendall really was the one who sparked the idea. "Don has always been involved with the Soviet Union in business, and saw opportunity to develop business with them, because Pizza Hut was one of the businesses in his corporation when he was Chairman."

An early letter from the Polit Bureau in the Kremlin suggested that the Soviet Union of the mid-1980s did not cater to families. Alcoholism was focused upon as a serious problem and officials were looking for ways to provide a family environment where families could be fed and entertained. Pizza Hut was determined to

---

Exhibit 1
Chronology of Events for Start-up Joint Venture

1972	Agreement reached to trade Pepsi for vodka
September 1987	Letter of intent signed with Moscow City Council
1988	Feasibility studies conducted
February 1989	Contracts signed
1989	Moscow general manager (Alex Antoniadi) employed
January 1990	Building work began
April 1990	$3 billion trade deal signed
June 1990	Staff fully employed; training began
September 1990	First two restaurants opened
April 1991	Andy Rafalat returned to London

Adapted from Pizza Hut, "Pizza Moscow," 1991.

provide a wholesome nonalcoholic setting, one that could contribute to solving this social problem. The missionary work by Kendall was followed by invitations to Pizza Hut managers to see for themselves what was possible.

In 1985, a team was sent by PepsiCo to evaluate pizzerias in Moscow. A team member observed, "From that very first moment when we got on the plane, we recognized that the conventional rules of business had to be put to one side. We had to look at what we saw with objectivity and common sense to be able to react to it in an unbiased way."

According to Andy Rafalat, then director of technical services for PepsiCo's Eurafme (Europe, Africa, and the Middle East) catering operation, "We all knew that potential customers were there, but we also recognized that the system really didn't allow free enterprise to take place. On that November day (in 1985) it really was the start of an adventure into the unknown, an unknown where there were no points of reference."

With the Pizza Hut team reporting a familiarity with and ready acceptance for pizza, particularly among young people in Moscow, PepsiCo choose Pizza Hut as the vanguard of the push into the USSR. According to a company document, "Its major attraction was the relatively simple, cheap and widely available nature of most of the ingredients." Flour, tomato paste, oil, and many items for the salad bar could all be purchased from Soviet sources.

By early 1987, when joint ventures were permitted in the USSR, Kendall visited the mayor of Moscow. In September of that year, a letter of intent was signed with *Mosobschepit,* the catering arm of the city council. This was the first joint venture agreement signed between the Soviets and a U.S. company.

Much of the foundation for the eventual success of the negotiations, which were concluded in 1989, is attributed to the single-minded way that Kendall developed his contacts in the United States, and with Soviet and Eastern European politicians. A company executive observed, "He was a unique man, and the Chairman of a big international company. Yet he always found the time to regularly visit these market places, to make it his business not only to know the leaders, but also to gain an understanding of how those systems were actually working. He had a strong opinion, his own opinion, because he actually saw what was taking place. That was a unique perspective, a chief executive who actually spent time in those markets and understood the problems and really was able to lead his team from the front."

Skilled at networking and making business contacts, Kendall met the former Soviet Ambassador in Washington. "Don was able to meet the man, not only the Ambassador but the man who had a family with him, the man who enjoyed sidling down to the Pizza Hut on a Sunday morning and who was able to share his thoughts and deep perspective of the Russian psyche and mentality."

Contacts were essential and Kendall ensured that invitations were forthcoming from a number of organizations. In the early and mid-1980s few Western business-people knew how to establish business contacts in the Soviet Union, then the world's largest government bureaucracy. Kendall secured those contacts and re-minded PepsiCo and Pizza Hut executives that they should visit these countries. Kendall's persistence, demonstrated through meetings, extensive contacts, and letters to organizations, resulted in the creation of a plan of action for how to do business with the Soviets.

Plan of Action

By 1987, the laws had changed and joint ventures were now permitted. According to Rafalat, "It was now feasible for an organization to work with a Soviet organization and develop something resembling a private enterprise. We started to recognize the importance of having locally driven businesses. . . . We also recognized the importance of 'living off the land,' which meant using local facilities and resources to maximum effect."

In 1987, a letter of intent was signed delineating each partner's objectives and expectations for the new joint venture. Early in the planning process, two Moscow restaurants were conceptualized, one taking rubles and the other hard currency. It was planned that the joint venture would maximize local sourcing and would possibly be expanded at a later date.

The operation would generate both a positive ruble and hard currency cash flow. Although rubles could not be converted into the firm's home currency for the benefit of shareholders in the short term but hard currency could, it was thought that the first restaurants would give the company a toehold in a potentially huge market and that "rubles could well become convertible in the longer term." Furthermore, opening the two restaurants was seen as a valuable learning experience of how things actually work in the USSR. The company would be building contacts with Soviet authorities and training a core force of local employees. According to company reports, the media coverage was also an added benefit to Pizza Hut's worldwide operations. PepsiCo's primary motivations were to initiate actions towards "the long-term goal of a significant restaurant presence in this potentially huge market."

Negotiating the Contract

Negotiations begun in 1987 took almost two years to complete. The partners were eager to explore the new opportunities offered by the joint venture, which they regarded at the time as "almost a fashionable thing to do." They were content to be led by Pizza Hut and had little desire to control the business. Yet culture and language became a barrier toward completing negotiations in a timely manner.

"We were talking two different languages whose words conveyed different meanings because we were from different systems where everything was incomparable . . . even dictionaries became to an odd extent useless. . . . Negotiation took close to two years, eighteen months. I think we recognized that they were going to take a long time . . . How we progressed, how we learned, how once we were negotiating {with} Moscow was changing around the thinking, the laws, the gradual acceptance of pizza *Perestroika* and the market forces."

After the letter of intent was signed in 1987, things did not go smoothly. The partners failed to keep the many time tables set, delayed their planned visit to the UK, neglected to arrange supplier visits for Pizza Hut representatives, failed to arrange translations of many necessary documents, and even told the firm that previously confirmed restaurant sites were now unavailable. There seemed to be a complete lack of willingness or knowledge of how to overcome obstacles. This was viewed as symptomatic of a lack of understanding of how a market-based business worked.

"We had a small, flexible negotiating team. There was Scott, a lawyer who was able to detail the structure of an agreement, presenting options and scenarios for both us and the Soviets. There was David Williams, our Vice President who was able to bring in his tremendous experience in negotiating joint ventures in different countries. I was very much the local element, spending time in Moscow looking at various sites, learning how Russian operations work, trying to understand the supply structures and what we needed to do. We also brought in our Finance Director when required to produce numbers and calculations. Between us, we had a good balance.

"We found, however, that the Russians approached negotiations very differently. There seemed to be no real seriousness attached to the operation. The negotiating team was frequently being changed. This was so new to them that they really didn't know how to handle a structured negotiation. One of our biggest problems was always negotiating through an interpreter. It really was only through the many days and weeks that we were spending on these negotiations that we really started to appreciate the huge differences and gaps which we would have to recognize and overcome.

"We spent weeks and months negotiating details which in hindsight proved to be totally useless. For example, we negotiated for the number of telephone lines we ought to have for days. When we actually moved to Moscow, these efforts proved useless because there was no power to get a telephone line. None of us really knew how to get these things done. That's just part of doing business in that part of the world. We were all learning."

Restating Problems As Opportunities

Problems were not considered insurmountable by the Pizza Hut team. According to Andy Rafalat, "Failure is not a word used with us. Problems may occur if management in a given venture is weak or inexperienced." Generally, new-business opportunities were viewed as arising from technological or market changes. The company viewed itself as more oriented toward developing existing resources than toward the pursuit of new opportunities.

After the Pizza Hut team learned more about the Moscow market, team members felt that success was assured. What may have been perceived as problems by others were constantly restated as an opportunity by Pizza Hut. This consistent philosophy propelled the venture forward. Eventually, the Soviets fulfilled all of the required commitments and the two parties moved toward signing a legal contract. Contracts were concluded in February of 1989. The first two restaurants were planned to open at the end of 1989. The joint venture was to have a board of six members, three nominated by each partner, and a Soviet citizen as director general. The director general and a deputy director general would jointly decide all major issues.

The contracts detailed the partners' roles. Pizza Hut would provide personnel and training and the partners would deal with negotiating local matters such as visas, customs, utilities, and supplies. By-laws were also drawn up stating how the partnership would resolve disputes and how the chain of command would operate. A standard franchise agreement was also signed between Pizza Hut and the new joint venture detailing the initial franchise fee at $25,000 and the monthly service fee (royalty) at 4 percent of gross sales.

Two feasibility studies ran in parallel with the joint venture negotiations. Although many of the early assumptions turned out to be false, these studies succeeded in formulating the basic operating conditions for the venture.

"Pizza Hut was to provide experienced personnel and training, their partners would deal with the local matters such as utilities, visas, customs, and suppliers. The contract also stipulated in what order claims could be made on any hard currency earned in the business. Royalties to Pizza Hut come first, followed by other payments . . . to PepsiCo before the Soviet party could make claims."

Financing the Venture

The foundation for financing the initial joint venture between Pizza Hut and the Moscow City Council relied upon earlier agreements made by PepsiCo. In 1990, a $3 billion countertrade arrangement (see Chronology of Events) between PepsiCo and Soviet authorities was finalized. This extended the trade of vodka and Pepsi to the year 2000, called for 25 additional Pepsi plants for a total of 50, and introduced a new component—the building of ten Soviet commercial ships for sale and lease internationally. This barter arrangement set the scene for financing the first two Pizza Hut restaurants.

At market exchange rates, the upfront cost of the project was very low. Pizza Hut was able to pay for the hard currency costs in rubles, acquiring them through a Soviet bank loan and converting them into hard currency at the official exchange rate. The new business was capitalized at $2.96 million, contributed by the partners as follows:

Soviet Party	$000	Pizza Hut	$000
Land/building	1,200	Equipment	856
		Plans and drawings	184
Start-up expenses	120	Start-up expenses	200
Reconstruction	200	Reconstruction	200
Total	1,520 (51%)		1,440 (49%)

Strategy and Organization

Andy Rafalat was assigned to Moscow in 1988 as a full-time chief executive. As stated by Rafalat, "By now, I had been with this project three and a half years. Once the realization came that it was going to happen, I think the truth dawned on me that a project has to have a person behind it. Somebody has to lead it, and it was also an automatic that for it to be transformed to reality, I would have to lead it and really own it. Then the realization came that . . . relocation to the Soviet Union would be required.

"We then gave thought to the hiring of key people, how they would be trained both in London and the Soviet Union, and how systems would have to be developed. We would have to tackle supplies and logistics in an area where there was a total lack of any infrastructure that made sense in any commercial way of thinking. There was no business structure in Moscow.

"I told my family that we would be moving to Moscow in the wintertime. The kids had to change schools, we had to find living quarters and learn how to adapt to an environment where shopping and services were unavailable. Finally in February 1990 the actual move to Moscow took place."

The management strategy was to staff the venture with Soviet personnel. As their abilities strengthened, Rafalat would withdraw and return to London where he was based, focusing more on the potential expansion of the business rather than overseeing day-to-day operations.

A management team was recruited, with Alex Antoniadi as general manager, to instill Pizza Hut's management theory into the system with hands-on responsibility of daily business management. (See Exhibit 2.)

Alex Antoniadi formerly ran five restaurants in Moscow and brought this experience into the new venture along with his industry contacts and high food and staff quality standards. His mission was to convey the Pizza Hut culture of high standards for cleanliness, quality, staff performance, and service.

Exhibit 2   **Pizza Hut Moscow**

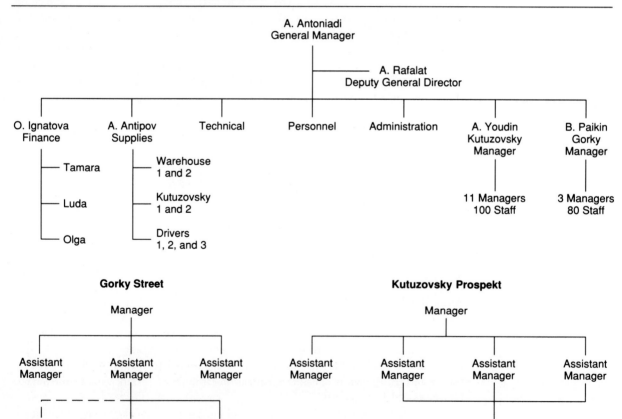

Antoniadi accepted a proposal to come to London for training only after he was assured the general manager's position and allowed to select his own restaurant managers—Boris Paiken and Sacha Youdin.

Antoniadi's high personal work standards helped to permeate Pizza Hut's management standards throughout the venture. A hard worker, Antoniadi quickly became a local celebrity.

His long-term associations and Rafalat's persistence in pursuing the venture in combination with ongoing open communications with the partners provided the strategic foundation for effectively managing the partnership relationship.

Antoniadi's contacts were also invaluable in helping to obtain approval documents from various state agencies and authorities.

Pizza Hut pursued a *laissez faire* strategy with Rafalat, empowering him with full entrepreneurial operating responsibility. This seemed to be the general style of the firm. As stated by one executive, "While the company tends to carry out as much homework as realistic on new ideas and markets, once they are established, these projects are handed over to small teams or to individuals to guarantee ownership and provide freedom of action for the relevant individual in charge. This ensures that projects have definite sponsors on whom success or failure rests."

Consistent with *laissez faire* philosophy, Rafalat was empowered with the management of the venture and with the objective of moving out as quickly as possible by empowering local people with a sense of ownership and management.

Site Location and Construction of the First Two Restaurants

In 1988, recognizing that site selection was critical, proposed locations for the first two restaurants were evaluated according to the following ideal features:

1. Size—250–300 square meters
2. One level
3. Frontage—10 meter minimum
4. Corner with return frontage
5. Heavy pedestrian flow
6. Parking capacity for automobiles
7. Proximity to offices, shops, and apartments
8. Proximity to tourist hotels for hard currency

Early-identified sites were rejected and the Soviets pursued tours of low-grade sites. This suggested a lack of will to move the project forward or a genuine ignorance as to the nature of the project. Finally, detailed Pizza Hut location maps were provided and suitable sites for the two proposed Pizza Huts in Moscow would be finalized—one on Gorki Street and the second on Kutuzvosky Prospekt. Preliminary drawings of the restaurants were rendered for both sites and were included in the 1988 Feasibility Study.

Construction began in January 1990. Both restaurants, although conversions of existing buildings, required considerable work. Soviet builders were initially employed but with little performance success. Forced to turn to a West European contractor with multinational experience, the partners gave the $6 million construction contract to Taylor Woodrow, a UK company.

"The quality of work demanded by Pizza Hut necessitated a large proportion of imported materials and labor; only 10% of the building materials and none of the finishing materials were sourced locally. The Soviet partners found it hard to understand why the operation should need to import cement, for instance, but delivery times were as much of an issue as the quality of materials. None of the local suppliers were able to respond quickly to demands or to guarantee delivery dates. Local supplies of equipment were also very unreliable. Taylor Woodrow was unable to ensure that a crane, for instance, would be available on a certain date, and the workforce was obliged to flag down drivers of passing machinery and pay them to lift the heavy loads."

Construction crews consisted of people from six countries: the United Kingdom, Sweden, Italy, Portugal, Poland, and the USSR. The Western crew members assisted the Soviet builders, training them on various building techniques.

After about eight months of building, the two restaurants opened on September 11, 1990. Considerable fanfare and celebration brought extensive free media coverage of the event.

Sourcing

Although Pizza Hut committed early on to "living off the land," this was sometimes quite difficult. For example, the kitchen equipment had to fit in with Pizza Hut's unique production system and was therefore imported, as were the crockery and restaurant furniture. There simply was no Soviet supplier able to make the product to Pizza Hut's specifications.

"We were told how important it was to get local people involved at each step of the way. The phrase 'living off the land' was very much overused in our negotiation strategy, but every time we said it, it conveyed to us an image of where we were going to find local managers and local people to work in our new venture. We were going to try to localize the supplies as much as we could. And we were going to finalize the concept to every extent possible to get it to run in the country. That really shaped our thinking.

"We started focusing on the sole issue of local supplies. I think that if there was one area that frightened us, it was how to get local sourcing to work. Having seen the disastrous state of most Soviet food factories, the poor controls, storage and distribution, we knew that we were going to have to get right into the food production network. Yet we did not want to do the food producer's job.

"We sent out a clear message to suppliers that we would be willing to pay market prices for their goods in rubles, whatever that market price was. We wanted to negotiate with them. We sent signals of encouragement to the supply community at large that Pizza Hut was open for business, paying market prices for goods."

Pizza Hut gained agreement to initially import all food items with no customs duty, although the intent was to source most of the required products locally over time. This would reduce importation costs over five years and increase generation of hard currency. These products would also be marketable as export goods and would generate more hard currency for the USSR.

Using local food supplies as much as possible would put the inconvertible ruble currency earned in the ruble restaurants to good use. Aligning costs and sales in the same currency would also minimize the operation's future margin exposure to exchange rate swings.

Antoniadi's network of local supplier contacts became crucial to the venture's success and also made it difficult to recreate the operation outside of Moscow. Outside of Moscow, local recruits would be needed to establish local supply networks to replicate the Moscow structure.

Some suppliers negotiated long-term contracts to supply Pizza Hut. Vegetables came from cooperatives. Other products, such as flour, were allocated to Pizza Hut on a centralized basis through the state plans. Although a cheese factory had been identified to produce mozzarella to Pizza Hut specifications, by winter the quality of the cheese became unacceptable. All cheese suppliers had to be sourced from the west, along with some of the meat products, proprietary in-house dough and spice blends. Other products, such as the wooden tables and chairs and Turkish cooking oil, were imported.

The Future

Envisioning the future as one with a possible 5,000 units, Rafalat dedicated the success of the venture ". . . to all the visionaries who knew it was possible." Describing the world behind Soviet borders during the mid-1980s, Rafalat said, "It was a world of secrecy, of relatively unknown languages and of cultures that we knew

Exhibit 3
Profit and Loss Statement

	First-Year Economics (Rubles in thousands)			
	Gorki Street		Cafe Typer	
	Rubles	Percent	Rubles	Percent
Gross sales	2,029	100.0	1,747	100.0
Promotion	81	4.0	69	4.0
Cost of sales	730	36.0	629	36.0
Cost of labor	223	11.0	192	11.0
Advertising	101	5.0	87	5.0
Semivariables	183	9.0	157	9.0
Rent	203	10.0	175	10.0
Other fixed	16	0.8	9	0.5
Depreciation	89	4.4	91	4.6
Unit contribution	403	19.8	338	19.4
Start-up	100	4.9	100	5.7
Royalties	102	5.0	87	5.0
Head office	111	5.5	96	5.5
Pretax contribution	90	4.4	55	3.2

very little about." It was ". . . the unpredictable Wild East, to be avoided by all but the most daring. There were, however, individuals, visionaries, who realized that despite the current situation, the region presented huge opportunities for future generations. These opportunities would yield enormous payback, not only in commercial terms, but also in providing bridges between two cultures, bridges which would bring these contrasting cultures and unknown systems closer."

Now, after the prestart negotiations and construction, the task ahead was to develop and implement the major operating systems. Employees had to be recruited and trained. Management and control systems had to be developed, and a new financial system—a hybrid accounting system—had to be developed to reflect doing business in two currencies—hard currency and rubles. **Exhibit 3** provides a projected profit and loss statement for both locations. Rafalat and Antoniadi went to work to put in place systems for employee compensation and rewards, pricing, purchasing, warehousing and distribution, marketing, and tracking of sales performance. They were propelled in their mission by ". . . a powerful vision of a chain of restaurants stretching across the Soviet Union, from Odessa to Vladivostok."

C A S E • *Encyclopaedia Britannica International: Exploring Emerging Market Opportunities*

James W. Camerius, Northern Michigan University*

Laurence Maher, executive vice president of Encyclopaedia Britannica International, leaned back in his chair as another staff meeting concluded in his office at Britannica Centre on Chicago's Michigan Avenue. "Another meeting," he thought, "and still no proposal concerning a marketing strategy for the division in Europe now that the European Economic Community was established, the Berlin Wall had fallen, Communism appeared doomed, and the Soviet Union had disintegrated." The major points of disagreement among the staff were assessing the level of opportunity in these new markets and determining the best marketing strategy to use to enter them.

Thomas Gies, president of the international division of the firm, had asked that another meeting on the same topic be scheduled for next week. Norman Wasz, director of international marketing information, and Polly Sauer, vice president of marketing of the division, were also asked to attend.

Corporate Affairs

Maher had concluded that the firm at the corporate level was in a good position for taking advantage of growth opportunities. He had witnessed a number of changes in the organizational structure, the opening of several new markets, the creation

---

of many new products, and the start of several new business ventures in the company during the last 20 years.

Encyclopaedia Britannica International was a division of Encyclopaedia Britannica, Inc., an American firm which could trace its roots back to the publication of the first edition of the *Encyclopaedia Britannica* in Scotland on June 30, 1768. The company, a privately held organization, had its corporate offices in Britannica Centre at 310 S. Michigan Avenue, Chicago, Illinois.

Encyclopaedia Britannica, Inc., had a wide array of interests in the education field. In addition to the encyclopaedia, which appeared in the 15th edition as *The New Encyclopaedia Britannica,* the firm produced yearbooks, alternate reference works, and learning systems under a variety of names and formats.

Although the firm did not release exact figures, total annual sales were estimated at $650 million. Through wholly owned companies plus agreements with distributors, Britannica did business in more than 100 countries.

The corporate operating departments of Encyclopaedia Britannica, Inc., are shown in Exhibit 1. In addition to the departments of Corporate Finance, Editorial, Public Relations, Corporate Planning and Development, and Human Resources, the division also contained the Department of Asia Product Development. This department coordinated product development and joint ventures for the firm in Japan and China. It also recently had assisted in the development of a Korean Britannica, was planning for expansion in other Asian countries, and was developing a new Italian language encyclopedia.

Encyclopaedia Britannica USA (EBUSA), one of the principal income-producing divisions of the firm, as indicated in Exhibit 2, had the responsibility for sales of Encyclopaedia Britannica products in the United States, Puerto Rico, Guam, Virgin Islands, and the U.S. military. It was established in 1974 as a separate division, consolidating the U.S. field sales organization and the company's support service departments.

Encyclopaedia Britannica products were traditionally sold door-to-door to consumers by a staff of independent contract salespeople. Although direct home sales

---

Exhibit 1　　　　　　　**Encyclopaedia Britannica, Inc. Organizational Chart**

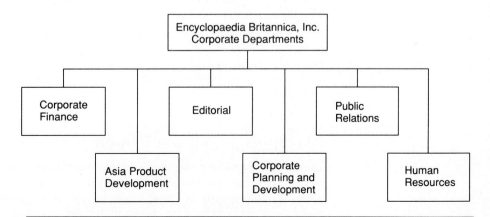

Exhibit 2   Encyclopaedia Britannica, Inc. Organizational Chart

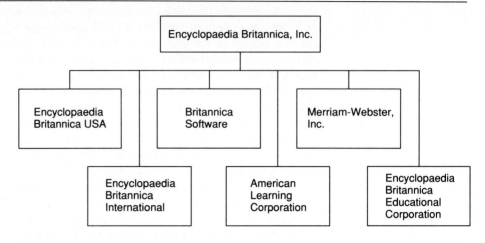

by a highly motivated sales staff still accounted for a majority of sales, in the late 1970s EBUSA expanded its methods of reaching the consumer. It established many more over-the-counter locations at which the product could be sold, including state fairs, shopping malls, theme parks such as Great America, and through large bookstore chains, such as Waldenbooks.

The sales field organization was backed by extensive public relations, national advertising on television and in print, special offers to groups, and direct mail programs which generated inquiries as sales leads. In a third-party program, mailings were made over the name of firms like American Express to reach potential customers at relatively high income levels. Prices in the product line in the United States were established in the Chicago office. Encyclopaedia Britannica, Inc., had approximately 1,800 employees and more than 2,000 independent sales representatives in the United States.

The other principal income-producing divisions of Encyclopaedia Britannica, Inc., were Encyclopaedia Britannica International, which had responsibility for international interests; Merriam-Webster, Inc., which published dictionaries and other reference works; Encyclopaedia Britannica Educational Corporation, which was a major producer and distributor of educational films and multimedia audiovisual materials; American Learning Corporation, which provided programs in individualized learning; and Britannica Software, which specialized in business and financial planning simulation software.

The Spirit of William Benton

Laurence Maher knew that the issues of maintaining control of the organization and planning for expansion had been perceived as problems in the organization for a considerable length of time. Much of the drive, determination, and creative practice of present management was attributed to the entrepreneurial spirit of William Benton who, for 30 years, controlled the firm.

William Benton (1900–1973), a former advertising agency executive, was publisher and chairman of the board of Encyclopaedia Britannica, Inc. from 1943 until his death in 1973.

When the *Encyclopaedia Britannica* was offered as a gift to the University of Chicago by owner, Sears, Roebuck and Company, Benton offered to put up his own money as working capital. The university accepted the gift in 1943 and committed the management and the stock control to Benton, retaining a royalty arrangement providing for editorial assistance from the university.

As publisher and chairman, Benton made the corporate commitment of time, resources, and money to completely control and expand the company. He was responsible for producing the 15th Edition of *Encyclopaedia Britannica.* His longtime friend and colleague, Robert M. Hutchins, observed that "although he was under no pressure to publish a new edition, his own standards led him to conclude that he must do what he could to make *Britannica* better still." He was closely involved in every step of research, planning, design, and initial production of the 15th Edition, while concurrently leading several other distinguished careers, including that of U.S. Senator from Connecticut from 1945 to 1952.

Under Benton's leadership the volume of Britannica's domestic business increased more than fiftyfold. Upon his death he was succeeded as publisher by his wife of 43 years, Helen Hemingway Benton. Robert P. Gwinn, then chairman of Sunbeam Corporation, became board chairman of Britannica in 1973. Under Gwinn's stewardship, Britannica experienced major growth at the international as well as at the domestic level. The William Benton Foundation, a not-for-profit organization, was the primary stockholder.

Marketing in the International Division

The international division, Encyclopaedia Britannica International, Inc., was headquartered at Britannica Centre in Chicago. A small staff, consisting of the division's President, Thomas A. Gies; Executive Vice President, Laurence J. Maher; and Director of International Marketing Information, Norman Wasz, maintained offices there. The division's Vice President of Marketing, Polly Sauer, who traveled extensively on a worldwide basis, also operated out of the Chicago office. An order-handling section, consisting of five people, handled merchandise orders from international subsidiary companies and independent distributors.

The division had primary responsibility for the management of wholly owned companies that sold Encyclopaedia Britannica and other products outside of the United States. These subsidiaries did business in 18 countries: Canada, Japan, Australia, New Zealand, the Philippines, Germany, Belgium, France, the Netherlands, Spain, Switzerland, Austria, South Korea, Italy, England, Scotland, Wales, Northern Ireland, and the Republic of Ireland. Each of these wholly owned companies was considered a profit center and was a complete self-contained unit. Each had its own president, chief financial officer, national sales manager, collection department, and sales force. The products sold in each subsidiary were usually produced in the United States, but in some cases they were produced and manufactured in the local country. There were more than 230 offices staffed by 1,200 administrative employees and 2,000 independent sales representatives in the international division.

The division also had distribution agreements with a number of independent firms in more than 130 countries in the Middle East, Africa, Asia, Europe, and Latin America. An administrative center in Geneva, Switzerland, supervised the distributors in European countries where the firm did not have a subsidiary and in Africa. Asian and Latin American distributors were supervised from division offices in Britannica Centre in Chicago.

The international division was involved in a number of other endeavors such as a joint venture with Encyclopaedia Universalis in France. It also handled distribution of the concise Chinese-language version of the *Encyclopaedia Britannica* in all countries other than the United States and the People's Republic of China.

The product line of the international division consisted of a wide variety of encyclopedia, books, accessory products, yearbooks, dictionaries, and language courses. The *Encyclopaedia Britannica,* published in English in a number of different bindings, was considered the cornerstone of the product mix. The EB international products are listed in Appendix A.

The International Division used a number of methods on the national and local level to obtain sales leads for the direct sales force of subsidiaries. Management identified three types of these activities: (1) advertising, which was conducted on a national level through the various media to encourage response from potential consumers; (2) over-the-counter selling, which took place in high traffic locations like shopping malls, train stations, and amusement parks to take advantage of "walkups"; and (3) "effort business," which involved leads and/or sales that salespeople created on their own without company support programs. The division vice president of marketing spent a considerable amount of her time traveling to plan, implement, and coordinate this part of the marketing program.

Management used a "Source of Order Report" to summarize and review the marketing activities which each subsidiary used to generate sales leads. The use of these tactics changed from country to country depending on trade tradition, custom, legality, interest, and other factors. The report was a complete listing of all of the tools that were used to generate leads for sales representatives. It represented the firm's effort in stimulating demand for the product line. As Maher noted, "In the old days, you went out on the street and knocked on the doors. We don't do that at all. Our salesperson has a name and an address and a place to go when he or she leaves the office." A list of the major items in the report appears in Appendix B.

For most products, prices were established through an annual agreement between the subsidiary president and the Chicago office. Once established in the operating plan for the fiscal year beginning on October 1, prices could not be changed without prior approval from Chicago. The corporate-controlled pricing policy did not permit direct negotiation of the price of the product at the consumer level. Variations in price to the consumer would appear in the individual sales presentation as the sales representative suggested different types and styles of bindings or made special-order deals. The bindings ranged from a high-quality platinum leather binding to a basic red one which was sold primarily to schools.

Appendix A
Encyclopaedia Britannica International Product Line

Encyclopaedia Britannica
The Britannica Book of the Year
The Yearbook of Science and the Future
Medical and Health Annual
The Great Books of the Western World
The Great Ideas of Today
Webster's Third International
    Dictionary
Britannica Discovery Library
The Compton's Encyclopedia
Compton's Precyclopedia
Britannica Pre-Reading Readiness
    Program
Britannica Reading Achievement
    Program
Children's Britannica
Children's Britannica Work Cards
Australian Educational Products
Il Modulo
Anglotutor
Me Diverto Con Le Parole
Encounter English
Encyclopaedia Universalis
Encyclopaedia Universalis Yearbook
Atlas Universalis
Emile Littre Dictionary
Le Grand Atlas De L'Histoire Mondiale
Encyclopaedia Mirador International
The Mirador Atlas

Dicionario Brasileiro
Encyclopaedia Barsa Portuguese
Encyclopedia Barsa Spanish
New English Master Language Program
Gateway to the English Master
New English Master—Junior Course
New English Master—Senior Course
Effective Listening
Modern Business English
Let's Talk About Japan
Japan and I
The Children's Language Package
First Steps in English
Second Steps in English
Third Steps in English
Master Steps in English
The Canadian Encyclopedia
Encyclopedia of Visual Arts
Japanese Young Children's Encyclopedia
BIE-Britannica International
    Encyclopedia
BIE-Britannica Yearbook
Korean Young Children's Encyclopedia
Effective Listening
Deep-Rooted Tree
Korea Trade Books and Tea Company
Interfield Computer Based Language
    Course

The special-offer deal included an extra book or free gift if the customer ordered at that time. Individual subsidiaries were provided considerable latitude in the operations provided they maintained their operating plan and did not make adjustments in prices. A similar program was established in maintaining sales commissions for sales representatives.

The External Environment

Britannica management had identified two basic types of competition in the world market—international and local. International competition came from U.S. firms like World Book, Inc., and Grolier, Inc., which produced the *Encyclopedia Americana.* In the "direct to the consumer market" category, competition was considered

Appendix B
Encyclopaedia Britannica Source of Order Report

Take One Box
  Available Here Sign/Take One
  Counter Display

Untended Displays (large traffic area
  display)
Passouts (cards with sales message)
  Residences and Public Locations
  Retail Locations (bagging)

School Carding (literature handout)
School Lists (parents in area with
  children)

Local Third Party (group discounts)
Referrals (local sales-office created)

Local Direct Mail (mail from sales office
  to customer)
Booklet Drop-off

Telephone Prospecting/Directory
  Special Lists

Inquiries/Call-in/Walk-in
  Direct Contact

Local/Freestanding Draw (free drawing)

SCAP (Small Community Appointment
  Plan)
  Retail Stores (counter)
  Special Functions (counter)
  Shopping Malls/Shopping Centers
  Others
  Free Draw Follow-up

OTC (Selling product over the counter)
  Exhibition/Fairs
  Professional/Trade Shows
  Shopping Malls/Shopping Centers
  Theme Parks/Zoos
  Transportation Centers
  Home Appointment Plan (HAP)
  Others
  Free Draw Follow-up

Other Miscellaneous—Local

National Advertising
National Third Party (home office leads)
Company Direct Mail
Other Miscellaneous—National

---

negligible. In some countries, however, these firms had a fairly sizable presence in the mail order business, selling a range of books including encyclopedia. World Book, Inc., for instance, had scattered success in its operations in many countries such as Australia, Canada, and the United Kingdom.

At the local level, competition was much more intense and varied from country to country. In Australia there was no significant local competition. In England there were a number of local competitors, but Britannica management did not consider the market saturated. In Japan, however, competition intensified because of the nature of the product line and sales force relationships. Britannica Japan, Inc., was but one of many different companies that sold English-language courses in Japan. In addition, at the sales level, loyalties were such that if competition hired away an influential sales manager, the manager typically would take the sales force to the new position. This proved to be extremely frustrating to management in the international division. The firm not only competed with firms that were selling similar products, but it competed for manpower to sell the product. Management had concluded that the situation was true worldwide, and it had become "a more important consideration from a competitive viewpoint than competition for the product."

In some countries, such as Italy, France, and South Korea, local firms produced an encyclopedia in the first language of the country. Also, in Europe many companies produced sets of what were really encyclopedic dictionaries. They were labeled as encyclopedia and accepted by some consumers as substitutes in the marketplace.

A more recent development was the selling of pirated editions of the Chinese-language *Encyclopaedia Britannica*. In Taiwan, for instance, several different companies duplicated the 20-volume Chinese-language version of *Encyclopaedia Britannica*, rebound it, and sold it at a greatly reduced price. A similar situation also occurred with the English-language version. The firm had some court convictions, but the practice continued.

Some companies like Amway, Mary Kay, and Encyclopaedia Britannica found that expansion into foreign markets met with mixed success. The concept of door-to-door selling was not equally accepted in all countries. Moreover, many cultures did not accept the concept of making a profit from selling to a friend, colleague at work, or a neighbor. As a result, alternative ways had to be found by marketing management to reach the consumer on an international level.

A European Opportunity

At the beginning of 1992, the drive for a unified market in Europe had converged with the fall of Communism to make Europe a far bigger and more competitive place to do business. The result, according to *Fortune,* was "a new Europe with big risks and big opportunities." As Executive Vice President of the International Division, Maher had read a number of reports on the topic, had traveled extensively, and had recently discussed the issue with representatives of subsidiaries and other organizations that distributed the firm's product line.

The European Community (EC) provided a new free trade zone through the Single Europe Act (EC-92). The 12 original members were the countries of Belgium, Britain, Denmark, France, Germany, Greece, Ireland, Italy, Luxembourg, The Netherlands, Portugal, and Spain. The European Free Trade Association (EFTA), comprised of the countries of Austria, Finland, Iceland, Norway, Sweden, and Switzerland, was linked with the EC through a free trade agreement. Industry analysis had predicted that this move to a single market in Europe in 1992 would stimulate a wealth of new regional business incentives.

The Republics of the former Soviet Union and the other Eastern European nations of Poland, Hungary, Yugoslavia, Czechoslovakia, Romania, Albania, and Bulgaria were experiencing great political and economic change. The Communist Party was being replaced by democratic institutions in most of these countries. Czechoslovakia, Hungary, and Poland, Eastern Europe's three strongest economies, had agreed to open their markets to EC products within ten years. Albania, Bulgaria, and Romania, the least developed countries of Europe, had trade agreements with the Economic Community. They were expected to develop their home markets first. Yugoslavia had disintegrated in the turmoil of a civil war.

Challenges included a multitude of legal, fiscal, and physical barriers to trade and exchange, as well as linguistic and cultural diversity. Because of the swift and uncontrolled nature of the changes taking place in Eastern Europe, marketing analysts had suggested that firms marketing their products in these countries should carefully monitor events and proceed cautiously. The nations were very different in terms of technology, infrastructure, foreign investment laws, and speed of change. As *Fortune* magazine noted as it described the opportunities and the challenges facing Europe in the decade ahead, "The risks are real, the problems deep."

In 1992 industry experts were suggesting that the largest single market opportunity for U.S. firms would be in the developing nations of Eastern Europe. With the fall of Communism, Central Europe was expected to start growing slowly in 1993, then sprint ahead at up to an 8 percent annual rate toward the end of the decade, according to Scott Vicary, an analyst with the London investment firm of James Calpel. This promising growth was expected to lift the collective GNP of a number of Central European countries, as well as the Economic Community and the European Free Trade Association.

Britannica management had already taken some steps to respond to the development of the European Economic Community. A group had been formed at the division level to study the issues. The presidents of the existing European subsidiaries were brought to corporate headquarters to compare how they did various things. They also discussed what they might be able to do better as a joint effort. Emphasis was placed upon improving the quality of the tasks that were performed, as well as provisions for cost savings. One example of this effort was in the preparation of promotional material. Division management felt it could save money by using common art work and localizing it by putting it in different languages. The cost savings from this effort could be used to hire a better promotion staff and get a better product.

The computer was another area which was perceived as a source of saving and improved effectiveness. One computer was proposed for all of Europe to replace computer operations in Rome, Paris, Madrid, Geneva, and London. The division reasoned that it would have more control and get better service with a centralized staff, more capacity, and faster machines if it could use one computer for all of Europe.

The fear of losing control became a major issue in this setting. "One thing we found out very quickly when we got into this," Maher noted, "everyone was protecting their own turf." Existing subsidiary management was reluctant to give up anything. "They wanted to maintain their own functions," Maher continued. "And, of course, the five subsidiary presidents are afraid we'll end up with one company president in Europe."

The Planning Meeting

Maher and Gies were well aware of how important expansion in the European marketplace was to upper-level management of Encyclopaedia Britannica and to the International Division. For one thing, an increased demand for English-language courses was predicted in the Eastern European countries as people sought ways to learn English. English courses sold by Britannica appeared to be too expensive for the individual consumer in most Eastern European countries.

A second problem concerned how to sell the product at the retail level. "It may be that the home field sales force is not the avenue," Maher said. "Perhaps they'll have to go through bookstores. Perhaps newspaper stores or direct mail. It's not only creating the product, identifying the product need," he noted, "but it's also the distribution method and the restrictions on the amount of disposable income they have." He also suggested Eastern Europe as a source for manpower for a European operations sales force. Sales force expansion and retention had always been primary goals in direct selling activity.

The week had passed quickly. Senior management executives of the International Division assembled again in president Gies's office to consider the question of entry alternatives and market expansion opportunities in Eastern Europe. President Gies opened the meeting with a statement reflecting on one of the goals of the division: ". . . to get quality educational products into the hands of people of all countries." Gies felt that it was absolutely necessary at the meeting to resolve the question of how this goal applied to developing strategies for Europe's new markets.

Maher knew that a detailed analysis of the cultural, social, economic, political, legal, and technological forces of the environment was essential before the company entered a foreign market. He suggested in his initial report that, given its capital constraints, the firm should limit the number of markets it chose to enter. It should only select markets that have (1) low political risks, (2) few restrictions on business, and (3) high purchasing power. He felt that these factors should be considered when analyzing the relevant environments in each of the countries of Eastern Europe to assess market attractiveness.

Four possible Eastern Europe market entry strategies were identified by the executives of the International Division. Each of these possibilities involved an increasing amount of commitment or involvement on the firm's behalf and thus allowed management to have more control over marketing efforts. A fifth view favored consolidation of existing activity.

One viewpoint favored exporting selected products and selling them through an existing subsidiary. The executive supporting this view cited a number of factors favoring this approach. First, experience suggested that this would be a way to get into the market quickly. Second, using an existing subsidiary did not require a great deal of investment or risk-taking since it would use the expertise of established wholly owned companies that already sold *Encyclopaedia Britannica* and other products in Western Europe.

The second viewpoint suggested that an existing firm be given the right to market selected items in the product line for an agreed upon commission or fee. This type of licensing arrangement would be a low-investment form of market entry that would give the organization some form of control since the licensing arrangement could stipulate specific marketing methods. The firm already had contractual agreements with a number of firms worldwide to sell its products.

A third viewpoint called for entering into a joint venture with an existing foreign company. This proposal would also establish a legal presence in the European marketplace and position the firm for European expansion. Existing expertise would be used and market opportunities could be explored quicker. The partner would know the language, understand the culture, and be aware of the needs of the various markets. The executive who supported this approach acknowledged that it might be difficult to find a suitable partner since there was some question whether anyone would have expertise in how to take advantage of what was occurring in Eastern Europe. The operation of such a joint venture, if established, could be supervised from the administrative center in Geneva, Switzerland. It controlled agreements

Encyclopaedia Britannica had with the independent distributors which operated in countries without wholly owned subsidiaries of the firm.

A fourth viewpoint suggested the direct ownership of a new subsidiary which would establish a separate legal presence within a selected country. This approach would not only meet potential regulations, but would establish a presence in countries like Germany to suggest that Encyclopaedia Britannica was a company that cared about different cultures and markets. It would also allow management to have control over service standard levels.

The alternative would require increased investment, the establishment of managerial and operational expertise, and additional time to establish. The risk would therefore be greater.

A fifth proposal voiced by another executive was not to change. The executive believed that the International Division could explore ways in which the existing subsidiaries could consolidate some of the functions to do a better job with the current marketing strategy. Hadn't they brought in the presidents of the European subsidiaries a little over a year ago to consider this very issue? Executive management at that time had concluded that this was an area where there might be a lot of cost savings while still maintaining the autonomy of existing subsidiaries.

The planning meeting adjourned without resolution. Tom Gies asked Laurence Maher to give the "opportunity" issue further consideration. He was to prepare recommendations for another meeting scheduled within the next 30 days.

C A S E • *Acer Computers*

John Wong, Iowa State University
Wu-Ming Hou, Iowa State University
Charles B. Shrader, Iowa State University

1. Early History

Born in 1976 on an investment of US $25,000, Acer has grown from one location and 11 employees into a global concern with 1990 revenues approaching US $1 billion, employing well over 5,000 people at 50 locations in 14 countries around the world.

Acer was founded by Stan Shih, chairman and CEO, who is a homegrown engineer who developed the first penwatch and first Taiwanese calculator before starting Acer in 1976. Through sharing the same vision, Acer's five young founders got together and called themselves the "Gardeners of Microprocessing." Their vision was to promote the development of microprocessing.

After pursing that dream for 15 years, Acer has set a number of achievements. For instance, Acer produced its first personal computer in 1983. The company beat IBM to market with a 32-bit personal computer just three years later, and in 1989, after introducing the fastest PC in the world at that time, Acer shipped its one millionth machine. In addition, the company has won considerable international recognition for its product quality, as well as for design excellence.

From its humble beginning 15 years ago, Acer has become the fourth largest producer of personal computers using the Intel 386 chip in the world, according to InfoCorp, after IBM, Compaq, and NEC. Today, Acer manufacturers a complete range of personal computing products and peripherals, from compact notebook-sized portables to complex multiuser systems and networks.

The Development of Business

In only 15 years, Acer had achieved the position as the leading personal computer maker in its home country, Taiwan, and one of the top ten PC manufacturers in the world. How has Acer achieved such success in such a short time? What kind of investment environment did Acer have? How did government actions influence the computer industry? To answer these questions, it is very important to understand the infrastructure of Acer's host country, Taiwan.

The push into computers was made possible by Taiwan's accumulated experience in consumer electronics and strong supporting industries. For example, the huge computer terminal industry (Taiwan supplies many of the monitors for IBM personal computers) grew out of the television business. A strong parts manufacturing sector allowed a quick entry into personal computers.

Taiwan has traditionally invested heavily in scientific education and in research and laboratories. This results in Taiwan graduating four times as many engineers per capita as the United States. Because the electronics industry is composed of small- and medium-size enterprises, government labs assumed the role of conducting long-term research and transferring technology to the private sector on a cost basis.

In 1980, when exports of labor-intensive goods were still racing ahead, the government opened the Hsinchu Science-based Industrial Park, which planners hope will eventually become Taiwan's Silicon Valley, in a hilly, green area 50 miles southwest of Taipei. The government also offered investors tax holidays, low-interest loans, duty-free imports, and government venture capital with a buy-back option. More than 100 companies have started operations in the Park, one-third of them founded by Taiwanese–Americans and one-third by foreign—mostly U.S.—companies. The value of the Park's production reached $1.7 billion in 1988. The Industrial Park planned to reach the target of $7 billion a year by 1996. Manufacturers in the Park invest 6 percent of sales in R&D, compared with a national average of less than 1 percent in manufacturing.

Another unique characteristic of the economic development in Taiwan is the relative size of manufacturing establishments. In Taiwan, the island's shipments of manufactured goods are dominated by the small- and medium-size manufacturers. The five largest Taiwanese conglomerates account for only 4.2 percent of the island's total shipment. The orientation of small- and medium-size manufacturers is also evident in the personal computer industry. Because the electronics industry is composed of small- and medium-size enterprises, government labs conduct long-term research and transfer technology to the private sector on a cost basis. As an example, the government-run Industrial Technology Research Institute (ITRI) is the electronics key promoter of R&D in the computer industry and high technology electronics field. ITRI develops computer and chip designs, which are then licensed to private companies for production.

Acer's Four Development Stages

Promoting Microcomputing in the Home Country

Founded as Multitech International Corporation (Acer's original name) with 11 employees and a registered capital of $25,000 in 1976, Acer was mainly a trading company, and it designed some products for electronics equipment. Notwithstanding its slow capitalization during its initial start-up, Acer pushed itself in the field of microcomputing. At that time, the microprocessor was a very new field even in the industrialized nations. However, the five insightful cofounders, who averaged 30 years old, knew this field would be a dominant industry in the near future.

From the product life cycle point of view, the microprocessor was in the introduction stage. The environment was quite new to Taiwanese manufacturers. Before entering the microprocessing industry, Taiwanese electronics manufacturing companies had strong original equipment manufacture (OEM) ability. This implies that a lot of skilled engineers have been trained and accumulated relative electronics operation experience that is applicable to the microprocessing industry. Because of the lack of microprocessing knowledge, very few companies were able to enter the market. One of Acer's contributions during its early years was the publishing of a microcomputer monthly magazine, which it called *The Words of Gardeners*. Published in 1978, the magazine was distributed free to those involved in the industry. The purpose of this magazine was that of educating more engineers and cultivating the microcomputing environment. The immensely favorable industry response to the magazine was unanticipated. Circulation jumped from 100 copies to 20,000 copies in two years. It opened the window for young engineers to look into the world of computing. Also, in 1978 Acer set up the Ran Microprocessor Training Center (RMTC), a technical education center which trained more than 3,000 engineers in two years and designed more than 40 microprocessor-related products for many local and foreign companies. In addition, Acer formed a "Microprocessor Club" to provide engineers with the opportunity to exchange information and expertise. Through these efforts, Acer opened the road to the microcomputing industry and trained many engineers. Many of these engineers are now well-known personalities in the industry.

Strengthening the Domestic Market and Developing a Private Brand

The second stage for Acer occurred between 1980 and 1985. In this period, the major tasks of Acer, generally speaking, were to enforce OEM business and to cultivate the self-owned brand product. Because of good design ability and cheaper skilled labor costs in Taiwan, Acer was able to generate stable and large-volume shipments. Through its OEM experience, Acer was capable of moving more rapidly down the learning curve, increasing productivity and thereby reducing unit costs. On the other hand, Acer had been trying to create a new identity and brand-name products. Although its OEM business was still profitable, Acer believed that if it did not create its own brand name, it would not, in the long term, control its own destiny. Therefore, the central strategy of Acer in this stage was to accumulate design and manufacture experience through OEM on the one hand and to proceed to develop a private brand name on the other hand.

The first breakthrough came with the introduction of the Dragon Chinese Language CRT terminal. This terminal won Taiwan's highest production design award in 1980. In the following year, Acer introduced the Micro Processor (MPF-1) which was its first product to hit the U.S. market. The MPF-1 was so successful that it has been deemed a milestone in Acer's march toward the world market.

During the early 1980s the market for computers in Taiwan was still very small, but Acer understood that the market would soon expand. And Acer realized it needed to establish a strong position in the domestic market as early as possible. Therefore, in 1981 Acer released its proprietary Chang-Jei Chinese input system to the Taiwan computer market and made it available free of charge. This Chinese input system not only became a standard in development of Chinese computing, but it also laid a solid foundation for Acer as a bilingual expert. In the same year Acer opened its manufacturing plant in Hsinchu Science-based industrial Park.

The second wave of cultivating the domestic market was the development of the MPF-2 and MPF-3. With these two products, Acer finally brought computing into Taiwanese homes in increasingly large numbers. Besides the MPF-2 and 3, Acer also helped the city government of Kaoshiung, Taiwan, in promoting computer literacy by providing 1,000 personal computers for a large-scale demonstration and training. More than 100,000 people came during the one-week event, resulting in a heightened awareness of computer application and use.

Two years later, in 1984, Acer introduced its first 16-bit computer, the MPF-PC, followed by the Dragon 570, which went on to become the world's mainstream Chinese-language computer. Through technological innovation and cultivation of its domestic market, Acer had become one of the major players in the Taiwanese computer industry.

Entering the Global Market

The third period of development stretched from 1986 to 1989. After years of hard work and continuous innovation, Acer began to orient itself toward the global market. Through the previous two stages of development, Acer had grown to become one of a few companies that led the development of microcomputing and its related peripheral and component industries in its domestic market. But Acer was not satisfied with these accomplishments. In addition, Acer had already taken its first steps toward globalization and, because of its success, globalization soon became a primary objective.

In the fast-growing high-technology industry, the new product with better quality and stronger functions provides a competitive edge for the newcomers. For Acer, the big break came in 1986 when Acer gained worldwide prominence by introducing a 32-bit computer ahead of the world leader, IBM. After the successful development of the 32-bit computer, Acer subsequently introduced its other Acer 1100 families. Since that time Acer has received much recognition for its technological process from the world press. For instance, in 1989 the Acer 1100/16 personal computer was hailed as a "best buy" by *PC World,* a technical computing magazine. The "best buy" award signified that Acer's 32-bit computer was one of the world's best computers and the best choice for users in its class. In 1990 the Acer 1100/33 stood out from among 22 other 32-bit computers of world-renowned brands to capture the "editor's choice" award from *PC Magazine,* another technical computing magazine. That same year, the worthiest achievement to date was the U.S. consumer survey result published by International Data Corporation, one of the world's largest information service companies. The IDC survey showed that Acer, for the first time, led nine other world-renowned computer companies in both product satisfaction and brand loyalty.

By then Acer had clearly set its final goal, which was to globalize its operations in terms of marketing, research and development, manufacturing, and financing. Acer changed its brand name from Multitech to Acer in 1987. A year later Acer also changed its company name from Multitech to Acer. The name change was an attempt to shake off the image of "low-quality" Taiwanese high-technology products. Multitech "lacked the distinctiveness we consider necessary for us to make a real impact on the world market," said Acer CEO Stan Shih. In other words, it sounded as if the company was just another Taiwanese PC clone maker. The Latin meaning of Acer, said Mr. Shih, "is sharp, penetrating, energetic and spirited. These are attributes that we, as a corporation, epitomize."

To finance Acer's globalization effort, Acer solicited funding internationally. An international consortium consisting of Citibank, Chase Manhattan, Sumitomo, and other foreign institutions purchased 13 percent of the company in 1987 at the price of $16 million. Domestically, Acer also listed its firm stock on the Taiwan Stock Exchange at the end of 1988. Acer intended to raise $40 million by floating 10 percent of its equity on the Taiwan Stock Exchange. Even when Taiwan's investors slowed down their present buying frenzy for every sort of Taiwanese share, they still fell over themselves for Acer stock.

In the area of minicomputer technology research and development, during 1987, through an acquisition of Counterpoint Computer, Inc., Acer made much progress. Acer was eager to move into the area of high-end-user manufacturing and through the acquisition of Counterpoint was better able to achieve this goal. Another major effort in research and development was the establishment of a joint venture with Texas Instruments in 1989 to manufacture computer memory chips called DRAMs, a vital part of a computer. The joint venture is set to start manufacturing advanced 4-megabit DRAMs by 1991. The facility is costing its parent companies an estimated $250 million in start-up costs alone, and over the longer haul costs could go as high as $500 million. Acer currently controls 74 percent of the venture, but within five years TI has the option to increase its holdings to 51 percent from 26 percent. All the company's production will initially be sold under TI, although Acer may then purchase up to 50 percent of the plant's output from TI.

The motivation behind the joint venture is both companies' belief that the 4-megabit chip will be the next step in memory technology. In addition, the DRAM shortage crisis of 1988 taught both TI and Acer the necessity of developing sources for DRAMs outside Japan. Because semiconductors, especially memory chips, are controlled by a few suppliers, The TI–Acer DRAM project is important for stabilizing the supply of a key component to Acer and Taiwan's PC industry.

It implies that if the world price for this component is too high, the Taiwan market price can be made more reasonable. At full production, the joint venture is expected to fulfill 20 percent of Taiwan's requirement for the chips.

Despite the uncertainty of the chip market, it is not yet in great demand nor economical for most applications. This results in the cost of using a single 4-megabit chip to be 10 percent higher than four 1-megabit chips for the same function. TI and Acer executives, however, seem to be prepared. "We want to become a major player in 4-megabit DRAMs. We must be there now, or else we will be left out in the future," said David Lim, marketing director for TI's Taipei office. This commitment underlies TI and Acer devoting considerable resources to the joint venture. In the long-term view, both TI and Acer hope that the joint venture will smooth out the DRAM market's volatility due to a limited supply, as well as concentration of production in Japan.

Another exciting Acer product released in 1989 was the 80486-based Acer 1200 machine. This star product's debut at the 1989 Comdex Fall Show in Las Vegas was a resounding success and attracted extensive coverage by the industry media. This, again, proved the wisdom of Acer's commitment to ceaseless efforts in research and development. Acer increased its research and development budget from $15 million to $25.4 million. The increased level of spending reflected management's continued emphasis on new-product development and Acer's commitment to production of leading-edge products to ensure a competitive edge in the 1990s.

To counter skyrocketing office rents and worsening traffic in Taipei, Acer made another major investment by purchasing 124 square miles of land, which entailed a total initial investment of $50 million in 1989. The purchase of an office building and a block of land southwest of Taipei was made to house Acer's growing corporate headquarters. This large block of land, close to Taiwan's second superhighway and the planned superrailway, not only adds considerably to the company's assets, but will accommodate Acer's projected growth in the future. Acer also planned to invest a further $185 million in its new headquarters over the next five years. This real estate investment further illustrates Acer's confidence in its future growth potential.

After becoming a leading PC-maker in Taiwan, Acer realized that much of its success is owed to its dedicated work force and the general favorable background and support provided by the government. Hence, Acer began a program of civic participation and corporate giving. For instance, Acer funded a national table tennis team in 1988. The table tennis team, comprised of 22 elementary and junior high school students, was established September 1, 1988. These players, age 13–17, trained with Acer for four to five years and competed in both national and international competitions. The ultimate goal of the Acer table tennis team is to compete successfully in the 1996 Olympic games.

Following the fast-growing years for personal computer business in the 1970s, the industry began to contract in 1989. Although Acer generated a record of $688.9 million in sales in 1989, an increase of 29.8 percent over 1988, its net earnings shrank from $26.5 million to $5.8 million, down 78 percent from 1988. Poor performance in net earnings was primarily a result of a downturn in the world computer market, losses incurred in U.S. acquisitions, diversified investments, and dwindling profit margins.

The Current Developments

In retrospect, aggressive expansion was propelling Acer from being a Taiwan-based corporation to a global corporation, and from a half-million dollar firm to a multimillion dollar conglomerate. However, after the breakneck growth of the 1970s and early 1980s, the personal computer industry entered into a new and rather competitive situation in the 1990s.

First, since the personal computer became an industry with annual worldwide PC sales reaching $100 billion in 1990, according to International Data Corp., PC makers encountered slow growth in the PC industry since late 1989. With the threats of worldwide recession and the war in the Persian Gulf, PC sales growth had come to a near standstill in the U.S. market. Meanwhile, European PC demand—the main growth engine for many companies—had slowed, too. The global PC sales growth was expected to increase by 18 percent, far less than the 32 percent upswing in 1989. The weak demand resulting from the recession and the over-crowded and mature market dragged down the overall profit margin. With this background, exiting PC-makers have to find niches to survive. Smaller machines, such as laptop PCs, seem to be the wave of the future. Although laptop computers are technically in the same personal computer category, their market performance demonstrates a completely different potential. While ordinary desktop PC growth slowed considerably, these remarkable little machines were posting the fastest growth rates of any type of computer in the world.

Acer similarly encountered the worldwide recession and an increasingly competitive market. To survive, Acer not only has to maintain a leading edge in quality and to innovate products by continuous research and development, it also has to formulate a new strategy to meet the fast-evolving PC market environment. The new strategy envisioned a major diversification undertaken by the company in three directions: software, semiconductor, and network.

Acer executives realized that hardware was rapidly becoming a commodity product. Acer wanted to position the company as a major software supplier, particularly for the Chinese business community which dominated the economic activity of Southeast Asia. Acer's new focus on the Southeast Asian market also underscored the region's continued rapid growth rate, at the time when European and U.S. market growth rate was slowing down. Further, there is renewed interest in running computers in local languages. This played into Acer's strength and past experiences in bilingual systems operations. Acer was already the largest software distributor in Taiwan, acting as the exclusive distributor there for Microsoft Corp. and Ashton-Tate Corp., a leading PC database-maker. The company developed a Chinese version of MS-DOS in cooperation with Microsoft and also introduced a Chinese version of Ashton-Tate's dBase III. Acer expanded its software stable in 1989 by acquiring Princeton Publishing Labs Inc., a New Jersey-based developer of publishing software.

By establishing a joint venture with Texas Instruments, Inc. to manufacture 4-megabit dynamic random access memories (DRAMs) in Taiwan, Acer was assuring itself a supply of these critical components. In the joint venture, TI–Acer scheduled to begin producing 4-megabit DRAMs by the third quarter of 1991. As memory chip prices tended to ride a roller coaster, this venture may prove to be one of

Acer's riskier investments. Acer also concluded agreements with National Semiconductor Corp. whereby the two companies would jointly develop very large-scale integrated (VLSI) chips and National Semiconductor could market chip sets designed by Acer.

To cash in on the trend toward network PCs, Acer had set up a new business unit called Network Computing Business, which would supply integrated network computing solutions. The new unit would report to Leonard Liu, who once was group director of communications and programming at IBM.

In its product portfolio, Acer aggressively expanded product lines in 1990 as part of its drive toward becoming a full-time computer product manufacturer. For instance, Acer introduced the Acer System 25 minicomputer, the Acer 1100LX laptop computer, and the newly released Acer 1200 desktop computer.

On the other hand, Acer formed strategic alliances with other world-leading manufacturers to maintain a leading edge in the computer industry. Early on Acer had established very good relationships and alliances with industry leaders such as Intel, Microsoft, and Auto Desk. These partnerships enabled Acer to acquire new technologies or product specifications on a timely basis, which in turn resulted in shorter product development times and faster product-to-market times. Further development was through a concentrated program of mutually beneficial linkages. This strategy was focused on the win–win basis. In 1990 Acer and Messerschmitt-Bulkow-Blohm (MBB), of the Daimler-Benz Group, signed a joint venture agreement to design, manufacture, and vertically integrate hybrid microelectronic devices. MBB would gain a foothold in Asian markets by way of the resulting joint venture, while Acer would utilize the latest aerospace technology in its industry information businesses. This marked a milestone in Acer's drive to commercialize and adapt aerospace technologies to the computer industry. All the above high value-added, diversified technologies would enable Acer to provide consumers with full-system support, plus better products and services.

International Operations

It's very difficult to self-supply on a small island with few raw resources. As a result, Taiwan has always relied on international trade. International operations are inevitable for any local manufacturing company that wants to keep growing and expand its market territory.

The availability of skilled labor and professional engineering personnel is one of the key reasons many foreign computer companies have chosen to set up manufacturing in Taiwan. The other key reasons are the abundance of high-quality, low-cost electronics suppliers and generous government incentives, which include a five-year tax break. In recent years Taiwan has become an increasingly important source of parts for foreign computer firms, and is second only to Japan.

Taiwan's exports of information processing products, including microcomputers, disk drives, printers, terminals, keyboards, and other peripherals and components, reached $3.7 billion in 1987, roughly 96 percent of the local industry's total output. Of that $3.7 billion figure, 41 percent was purchased by foreign computer companies from local firms on an OEM basis. Another 39 percent was shipped by foreign-owned firms manufacturing in Taiwan.

Most of Taiwanese PC-makers are content to manufacture products that would be sold under foreign brands. Acer's strategy, however, has been unusual. Acer has tried to create its own brand name since its start-up.

Stan Shih, CEO and chairman of Acer, has insisted on this approach. In 1990 46.9 percent of Acer group sales went to the Acer brands. Mr. Shih explained: "You don't control your own destiny, and you don't create enough value if you don't do your own marketing under your own brand name." In addition, he said, "If you do only manufacturing, Malaysia and Thailand can catch up someday. Taiwanese companies need to be even more globalized than American or Japanese companies." He stressed, "Our commitment is to become a global company, not just to make money." Unlike most Taiwanese clone makers which are content to assemble off-the-shelf components, Acer has invested heavily in research and development and market products under its self-owned brand name.

Creating its own brand name turned out to be an arduous task. To achieve that goal, Acer developed specific strategies. First was Acer's long-term investment strategy. This could be demonstrated by its extraordinary emphasis on research and development activities, which have become a deep-rooted tradition in the company. In the early years of the company, when Acer operated as an electronics trading and designing company, Acer spent 70 percent of its revenues on R&D. In 1990 the expenditures of research and development reached $48 million. Acer's R&D expenses represented 4.5 percent to 5.5 percent of its sales of Acer brand products.

Second, Acer has adopted a long-term perspective in its personnel recruitment and hardware investment program. Acer has an executive committee which develops plans for the company for the next two to ten years. The motivation for adopting a long-term perspective in its operation was its intention to generate an adequate lead time for product and market development. Without the huge financial resources of big international firms for R&D and advertising, Acer perceived this as the only viable alternative to build up its competitiveness.

Third, Acer offered its employees equity participation in the company. This type of incentive is very rare in Taiwan. In 1988 70 percent of the company's 4,000 employees were shareholders and 70 percent of its shares were held by its employees. More than 1,000 Acer employees each owned over $30,000 worth of Acer's shares. At that time its employees had become the greatest source of funds for the development of the company. As a result, the interests of the company and those of its employees have become totally integrated. Employee morale and productivity have been very high since this program was initiated.

Internationally, the company defied the standard image of manufacturer in a developing country which relies on low labor costs. On the contrary, Acer had a different way of approaching the global market.

Promoting its own brand name was an important first step in Acer's international business strategy. Besides Mr. Shih's ambition and strong determination, the major purpose of changing the company name was to come up with a more easily recognizable name that could advance Acer's efforts toward globalization. Multitech was awkward to pronounce and had also resulted in legal disputes with some firms using an identical name. Acer spent $35,000 to come up with the new name and the accompanying logo. Acer also launched "Acer New Product Identity" to enhance the Acer brand image worldwide. To achieve global recognition for Acer computers, the company vigorously promoted activities worldwide and actively participated in trade shows around the world.

In the United States, Acer participated in all the key trade shows such as the Comdex Spring and Fall, UniForum, Networld, New York's PC Expo, and the SCO Forum.

In Japan, Acer participated in the AX convention, the Japan Business Show, and the World Design Expo in Nagoya, apart from sponsoring its own Ax Machine Show.

In Europe, Acer attended the CeBIT and SYSTEMS shows, along with a number of smaller shows.

The second prong of Acer's global marketing strategy was its distribution program. Acer's initial international distribution strategy was to penetrate smaller markets, mainly in developing countries where there was less competition. This would allow Acer to gain manufacturing learning experience and expand its market share. In addition, Acer could generate cash and plough the profit back into its international operations. This strategy was highly successful. Acer has become one of the top three PC brands in such markets as Scandinavia, Austria, Southeast Asia, and Chile. In international competition, Mr. Shih tended to liken marketing to a go board (Chinese checkers), in which a player attempts to surround his opponent without himself being surrounded. He explained: "We went from the countryside to the city, from the periphery to the core."

That core, of course, is the U.S. market, which Acer found to be the most competitive in the world and surrounded by more recognizable names. "Even a bankrupt Silicon Valley company had a better image than a Taiwanese company," said Mr. Shih. Although Acer had the technology and could produce top-quality products, Acer lacked a potent sales force and effective distribution network.

Acquisition of high-technology companies became an important step in Acer's drive for corporate improvement and global success. By doing so, Acer could acquire a higher degree of technological competence and marketing channels. The most important of these deals was the purchase of Altos, which was a UNIX-based multiuser system manufacturer and a publicly listed company in the United States. Acer could use the company's existing distribution channels, support staff, and customer base as a launching pad for its entry into the U.S. market. Acer's influence in Europe was also greatly strengthened by the acquisition of Altos Computer Systems which had offices in Germany, the United Kingdom, France, Denmark, and Italy. In all, the Acer–Altos merger resulted in one of the few companies in the world with a complete range of computer systems plus a strong global distribution network. Acer–Altos's full range of products included personal computers, from notebook–sized portables to desktop, bilingual systems, peripherals, Application-specific Integrated Circuits (ASICs), Dynamic Random Access Memory (DRAM) chips, data communication devices, multiuser systems, and computer-related publications. The combined companies have a network of 108 distributors and more than 10,000 retailers spread over 75 countries on 5 continents.

The third component of the marketing strategy was pricing. Acer has been endeavoring to build up its competitiveness in the global market through the production of high-function, high-quality, but medium-priced, product. Although Acer was not a global technology leader, the company tried to be a quick follower of global technological trends. For instance, Acer was the second firm in the world to produce both the 80386 32-bit personal computer and the IBM PS/2 compatible.

In the domestic economy, the new Taiwan dollar has appreciated about 25 percent over two years. Wages in Taiwan had increased between 15 percent and 20 percent annually since 1988, while the inflation rate was running at three times higher than the government's 5 percent target. All of these circumstances had further slimmed the industry's already below-average profit margin. Growing costs had forced the Taiwanese PC-makers to move their manufacturing operations off-shore to neighboring Pacific Rim countries where less expensive labor and land were still available. In 1989 Acer began the construction of its first overseas manufacturing facility in Malaysia. The $20 million plant is scheduled for completion in 1992.

In another significant international marketing development, Acer, along with four local manufacturers and three international financial institutions, formed Fora International Corporation—a global marketing and distribution company dealing in high-tech information products. This new joint venture would enhance Acer's ability to compete in the world market.

The final step is its adoption of a company philosophy which Acer calls "global vision, local view." At the heart of Acer's global investment strategy is its desire to become a truly global citizen. Hand-in-hand with global expansion, Acer followed a policy of being a good corporate citizen, which included the recruitment of local talent, respect for local customs, long-term commitment and contribution to the local community, delegation of authority to local managers, building of a globally consistent corporate image, and the complete integration of global resources. This stems from Acer's belief that any impediment to commerce imposed by national and regional borders could best be transcended via a policy of localization, which has at its heart complete corporate internationalization.

The Organization

From its origins as a trading and publishing company to its present status as a global corporation, Acer inevitably has to keep up with changes in organizational structure in order to meet international competitiveness. As Mr. Shih said: "If you were to ask me what one thing has changed at Acer during the past few years of operation, my answer would be that everything has changed."

Because of its fast growth rate, Acer had to keep up with itself—not only its individual employees, but also the company structure. As Acer entered the global arena, the need for changes to keep up competence became more apparent. The major changes for Acer came in 1989 when Acer underwent two major reorganizations. These restructuring efforts were made in response to global changes in the computer industry, and also to better meet its goal of internationalizing its operation.

The first major change took place in early 1989 when the company was reorganized into business units working independently as profit centers. The business units offered maximum flexibility in operations to meet the needs of global customers. Four business units were established: PCs and bilingual systems; peripheral and ASIC; multiuser and communications systems; and education and publishing. Furthermore, in July Acer merged the network computing, workstation business units, and bilingual system to form the Personal Systems Business Unit. This change put more emphasis on the development of PCs, thereby further strengthening its main product line. In addition, Acer enhanced its networking system.

In April 1989 Dr. Leonard Liu joined Acer as president of Acer Incorporated and chairman and CEO of Acer America Corporation. Dr. Liu had been general manager of the Santa Theresa, California, software and development laboratory for IBM and was a 20-year veteran with "Big Blue." Due to his expertise in the field of management and technology, Dr. Liu would be a valuable asset for Acer in its globalization effort.

That same year, to maintain Acer's competitive edge, Acer hired Alexander Proudfoot, a noted consulting firm, to help set up new systems for material and product management, as well as manufacturing and procurement procedures. The new systems and standardized procedures led to reduced production costs and increased efficiency.

In late 1989 the top management at Acer took a major step to increase efficiency by reducing the number of product models from 5,000 in early 1989 to 700 at the end of the year.

To enhance its global market competitiveness, Acer restructured itself again in 1990. The new structure was categorized into two units: Strategic Business Units (SBUs) and Regional Business Units (RBUs). The Strategic Business Units were further divided into five subunits: Personal/System Computers (includes ASICs); Peripherals; Minicomputers; Home/Office Automation; and Portable Computers. The Regional Business Units included North America, Europe, ALAP (Africa, Latin America, and Asia Pacific), and Taiwan.

The restructuring of Acer with Regional and Strategic Business Units focused on globalized decentralization. In addition, under the banner of "globalizing by localizing," Acer focused on gaining greater operational flexibility and competence. In 1990 Acer increased its international operations from 26 locations to 50.

The Company's Chances and Challenges

Theoretically, mainland China is an ideal place for Taiwan's cash-rich PC-makers to invest. The island is separated by the 100-mile-wide Taiwan Strait from China's Fujian Province. People living on both sides of the strait speak the same language and share the same cultural background. Moreover, the average salary of a PC assembly worker in China is less than one-fifteenth of his Taiwanese counterpart. Additionally, the Chinese government has adopted a number of favorable industrial development policies, including a five-year tax-free grace period to attract investment from Taiwan.

At present Acer is not yet poised to capitalize on these opportunities. This is not just because of the ban imposed by Taiwan's authorities on direct trade with the mainland; there are many ways around that. China does not yet have the spending power to be a large market for personal computers, nor would Acer be able to provide China with the servicing backup on which a computer company's reputation ultimately rests. However, as the market in mainland China grows and matures, Acer is particularly well suited to succeed on the basis of its expertise in Chinese-language computing.

After many years of putting growth before profits, Acer has publicly reversed its strategy. In the first quarter of 1991 Acer reduced its total number of employees worldwide by 400, or approximately 7 percent. This event shocked the high-growth computer market in Taiwan. The change primarily reflects a better rationalization of staff allocation and utilization. On the other hand, Acer expects to realize increased efficiencies from its Malaysian operation. Acer further intends to review all of its manufacturing operations, with the intent of combining existing facilities where feasible, to gain economies of scale and eliminate inefficient operations.

To sum up, after more than ten years of growth and organizational expansion, Acer has adopted a more mature business approach, with an increased management commitment to both profitability and sales growth. To meet its goal as a world-class corporation in the same class as IBM, Hewlett Packard, Compaq, and Apple, Acer needs to forge a new strategy based on research and manufacturing in optimum locations around the world.

The PC Market Worldwide Sales

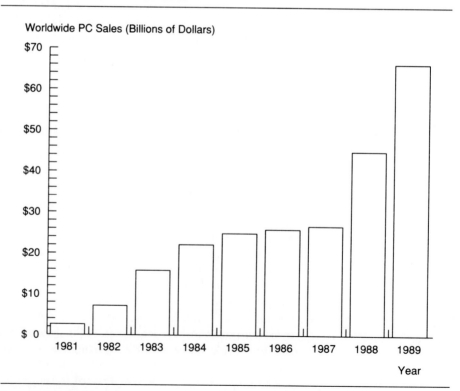

Source: International Data Corp.

Taiwan's Information Products Export Breakdown

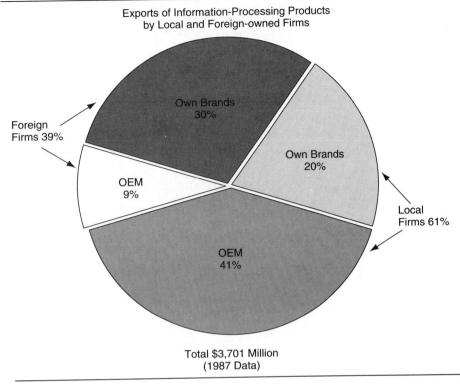

Exports of Information-Processing Products
by Local and Foreign-owned Firms

Own Brands
30%

Foreign
Firms 39%

Own Brands
20%

OEM
9%

Local
Firms 61%

OEM
41%

Total $3,701 Million
(1987 Data)

Source: Taiwan Information Industry Institute.

Total Revenue

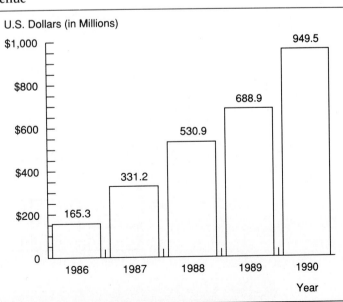

U.S. Dollars (in Millions)

949.5

$1,000

$800

688.9

$600

530.9

$400

331.2

$200

165.3

0

1986   1987   1988   1989   1990

Year

Net Earnings

U.S. Dollars (in Millions)

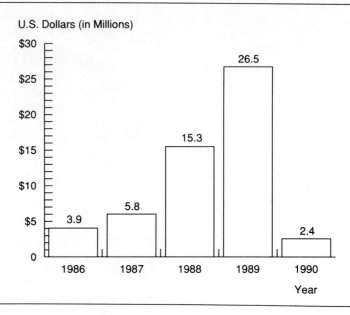

R&D Expenditures

U.S. Dollars (in Millions)

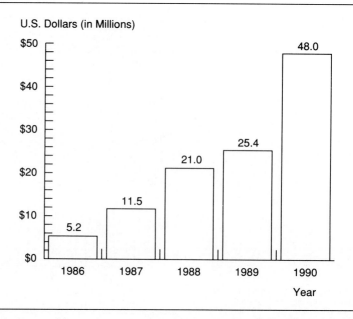

Stockholders' Equity

U.S. Dollars (in Millions)

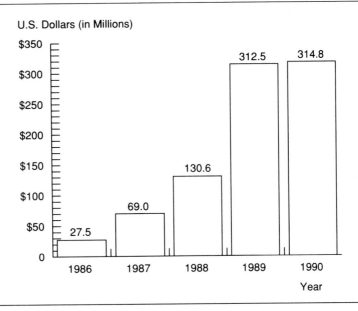

Acer Group Geographical Distribution

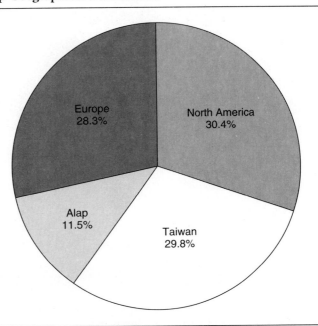

Acer Group Sales by Product

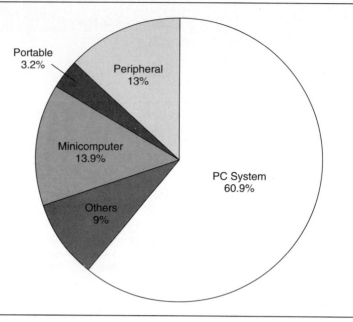

Source: Acer Annual Report, 1990.

Acer Group Sales by Type

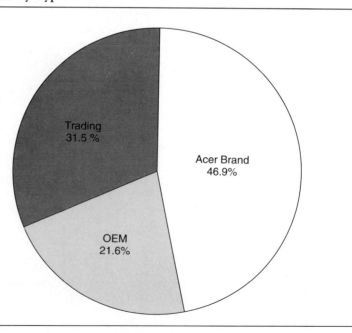

Source: Acer Annual Report, 1990.

Bibliography

Dess, Gregory G., and Peter S. Davis. "Porter's (1980) Generic Strategies As Determinants of Strategic Group Membership and Organizational Performance." *Academy of Management Journal* (September 1984): 467–488.

Dilts, Jeffrey C., and George E. Prough. "Strategic Options for Environmental Management: A Comparative Study of Small versus Large Enterprises." *Journal of Small Business Management* (July 1989): 31–38.

Duncan, R. B. "Characteristics of Organizational Environments and Perceived Environmental Uncertainty." *Administrative Science Quarterly* 17 (1972): 313–327.

Fiorito, Susan S., and Raymond W. LaForge. "A Marketing Strategy Analysis of Small Retailers." *American Journal of Small Business* (Spring 1986): 7–17.

Kotler, Philip. *Marketing Management: Analysis, Planning, Implementation, and Control.* Englewood Cliffs, NJ: Prentice-Hall, 1988.

Namiki, Nobuaki. "Export Strategy for Small Business." *Journal of Small Business Management* (April 1988): 32–37.

Peters, Thomas J., and Robert H. Waterman, Jr. *In Search of Excellence: Lessons from American Best Run Companies.* New York: Harper & Row, 1982.

Porter, Michael E. *Competitive Advantage: Creating and Supporting Superior Performance.* New York: Free Press, 1985.

Porter, Michael E. *Competitive Strategy: Techniques for Analyzing Industries and Competitors.* New York: Free Press, 1980.

Porter, Michael E. "From Competitive Advantage to Corporate Strategy." *Harvard Business Review* (May–June 1987): 43–59.

Rice, George H. "Strategic Decision Making in Small Business." *Journal of General Management* 9 (Autumn 1983): 59–65.

Robinson, Richard B., and John A. Pearce II. "Research Thrusts in Small Firm Strategic Planning." *Academy of Management Review* 9, no. 1 (1984): 128–137.

Robinson, Richard B. "The Importance of 'Outsiders' in Small Firm Strategic Planning." *Academy of Management Journal* 25 (1982): 80–90.

Robinson, Richard B., John A. Pearce II, G. Vozikis, and T. Mescon. "The Relationship between Stage of Development and Small Firm Planning and Performance." *Journal of Small Business Management* 22 (1984): 45–52.

Shrader, Charles B., Charles L. Mulford, and Virginia Blackburn. "Strategic and Operational Planning, Uncertainty, and Performance in Small Firms." *Journal of Small Business Management* 27 (October 1989): 45–60.

Vozikis, G. S., and W. F. Glueck. "Small Business Problems and Stages of Development." *Academy of Management Proceedings* (1980).

"A Well-worn Road to Dominance." *The Economist,* September 17, 1988, 76.

Wright, Peter. "The Strategic Options of Least-Cost, Differentiation, and Niche." *Business Horizons* (March–April 1986): 29–41.

Xiaoge, Xiong. "A Tough Road ahead for Taiwan's PC Makers." *Electronic Business* (January 21, 1991): 73–75.

Young, Lew. "Asian Profiles—Acer." *Datamation* (June 15, 1990): 174.

Name Index

SUBJECT INDEX